Film Musings

A Selected Anthology from Fanfare Magazine

Royal S. Brown

*For Enoch Davis —
with equal doses of
gratitude, respect, and
friendship.*

Royal S. Brown
Huntington, NY
21 July 2008

THE SCARECROW PRESS, INC.
Lanham, Maryland • Toronto • Plymouth, UK
2007

SCARECROW PRESS, INC.

Published in the United States of America
by Scarecrow Press, Inc.
A wholly owned subsidiary of
The Rowman & Littlefield Publishing Group, Inc.
4501 Forbes Boulevard, Suite 200, Lanham, Maryland 20706
www.scarecrowpress.com

Estover Road
Plymouth PL6 7PY
United Kingdom

British Library Cataloguing in Publication Information Available

Library of Congress Cataloging-in-Publication Data

Brown, Royal S.
  Film musings : a selected anthology from *Fanfare* magazine / Royal S. Brown.
    p. cm.
  Includes bibliographical references and index.
  ISBN-13: 978-0-8108-5856-5 (pbk. : alk. paper)
  ISBN-10: 0-8108-5856-8 (pbk. : alk. paper)
  1. Motion pictures. I. Title.

PN1994.B728 2007
791.43'75—dc22   2006023868

~

Contents

~

Introduction

The book that you have in your hands is a *very* selective compilation, representing less than half the original material, of the column "Film Musings" that I wrote every other month for *Fanfare* magazine, starting with the November/December 1983 issue (Volume 7, no. 2) and ending with the July/August 2001 issue (Volume 24, no. 6). The raison d'être of "Film Musings" was to cover recordings, starting on LP and moving to CD, devoted to film music. "Original soundtrack recordings" constitute the bulk of what I covered in "Film Musings," and they constitute an even greater bulk of this book, since I probably applied the editor's scissors most heavily to paragraphs devoted to compilation recordings, whether of film-score excerpts or of pop songs loosely thrown together to represent a particular film that in many instances barely uses most of them. But one of the little changes I have introduced throughout into the writing here, in a move some may find pointless and even self-righteous, is the substitution of the expression "music-track" to replace "soundtrack," since the latter, if presented separately from the film, would offer nothing but a collection of the sounds—gunshots, sirens, breaking glass, whatever—recorded for a particular film and laid in on the . . . sound track. I have also eliminated catalogue numbers and other information, such as names of producers, when indicating the labels for the various recordings. Since this is an anthology of previously published work, I have generally not fudged with the copy, even in instances where, in going back to material written sometimes ages ago, I was less than pleased with the style and/or the content of what I wrote. In instances where I have applied substantial changes I have indicated the new material in square brackets. In several cases I have brought over a film-music review that did not appear in "Film Musings" but was published, for one reason or the other, elsewhere in that particular issue of *Fanfare*. And in one instance of major fudging I actually brought over most of a DVD review I wrote for *The Perfect Vision* to replace my initial comments on *Swann in Love*, since a second viewing of that film on DVD considerably changed my outlook. This anthology may also have a slightly less curmudgeonly tone to it than the column taken as a whole, since I tended to cut more of the negative reviews than the positive ones.

"Film Musings" and, before that, my numerous individual reviews of film-music and classical recordings, first in *High Fidelity* (as of 1970), then in *Fanfare* (as of 1980), began before and ended after the publication of my scholarly study of film music in *Overtones and Undertones: Reading Film Music*, published in 1994 by the University of California Press. From where I sit my writing in "Film Musings" began to improve in its perceptions and maybe even in its style as of the publication of that book. The column started to run to considerably greater length as I probed both the films and their scores in what I considered to be greater and greater depth. And so, for the present anthology, I tended to do less cutting in those later columns than in the earlier ones. Some readers, and even an editor or two at Scarecrow Press, have complained that my job was to review the music and not the films for which it was written. Had I been forced to do that, however, I would have quit reviewing film music recordings (more on that anon) long before 2001, and I would have given up on this anthology. It would of course have been impossible for me to view each and every film attached to the numerous recordings that came across my desk, although I often made efforts far beyond the call of duty to do so. My approach to film-music criticism—and scholarship—has always been that film music generally should not be considered separately from the film for which it was composed. Even "found music" (pre-existing works of classical and/or pop music) needs, if presented on a music-track recording, to be considered in the overall cinematic context. This does not mean that film scores cannot be enjoyed on their own apart from the movie. It does mean, to my mind, that no critical and/or scholarly consideration of film scores can be considered complete without reference to how they relate to the rest of the filmic text. Readers will find that my opinions—and my politics, since movies tend to be a major reflection of the culture that produced them—in many instances are at considerable variance with those of the mainstream press and media. Movies that have been the object of considerable critical praise and much adulation at Academy Awards time—movies such as *Network*, *Life Is Beautiful*, and *Titanic*—have left me enraged at the culture that produced them and dumbfounded at the short-sightedness of those who did not see past their facile surfaces. I make no apologies. As for scores such as the one on which James Horner made a gazillion dollars for *Titanic*, well . . . read ahead. In the face of frequent criticism of both my introducing film criticism into my film-music reviews and of the opinions expressed in that criticism, I was able at one point to take some solace in the following words written by Dean Frey on a Canadian website devoted to the music of Heitor Villa Lobos: "Royal Brown's film music criticism can be enjoyed monthly in *Fanfare* magazine; he also provides the best film criticism since Pauline Kael retired from *The New Yorker*."

As for why I stopped writing "Film Musings" and why, shortly thereafter, I moved away from film-music (and music) criticism, if not scholarship, altogether, the reasons are basically twofold. First of all, writing an 8,000-plus-word column, as it finally became, every two months while holding down a full-time job and, for a time, editing every manuscript that went into *Fanfare*, became an impossible drain on my time, among other things keeping me away from a *heavy* book on film theory on which I have been working for years and which, as of the present moment, I still have not completed. Secondly, I came to realize that there was less and less to look forward to on the film music horizon. Most of the reissues being currently released are by this point for films and scores that hold almost no interest for me as a critic or as a scholar, while most of the new movies coming out since 2001, some of which are nonetheless excellent, offer minimally significant interactions between the filmic text and the score, and, more often than not, minimally interesting music. There is certainly no way that I could have kept an 8000-plus-word column going over the last few years, although I could definitely have whipped up some major enthusiasm for such new scores as John Williams' *Catch Me If You Can* (2002), Howard Shore's incredibly haunting and poignant *Spider* (2002), Niki Reiser's *Nowhere in Africa* (2003), and Philippe Rombi's sometimes *Vertigo*-ish *Swimming Pool* (2003), or reissues, both from the Film Score Monthly Collection, such as Leonard Rosenman's pioneering, atonal score for *The Cobweb* (1955) or what may be John Barry's masterpiece, *Petulia* (1968), released on a CD that features the composer's score for the 1972 *Alice's Adventures in Wonderland*. I also loved the way that Quentin Tarantino, in *Kill Bill, Volume 1* (2003), introduced, among a huge number of film-music references, the main theme, whistled by an exceptionally villainous Daryl Hannah, and a major excerpt from Bernard Herrmann's score for the dreadful *Twisted Nerve* (1968). Beyond that, however, the pickings have been considerably slim, at least as far as my own interests and proclivities are concerned. Let it also be noted that, since I began writing "Film Musings" in 1983, the industry has lost a devastating number of its major composers, including Miklós Rózsa (1907–1995), Alex North (1910–1991), David Raksin (1912–2004), Elmer Bernstein (1922–2004), Henry Mancini (1924–1994), Georges Delerue (1925–1992), Jerry Goldsmith (1929–2004), Stanley Myers (1933–1993), Michael Small (1939–2003), and Michael Kamen (1948–2003).

Grateful acknowledgments are due to many, starting, as I did in *Overtones and Undertones*, with Joel Flegler, publisher and editor of *Fanfare*, who has managed to keep that august journal moving toward the completion of its thirtieth year in the face of massive changes for the worst in the classical-music industry, and who allowed me almost totally free reign, even while occasionally agreeing with my detractors, to write "Film Musings" the way I wanted to. I am also grateful for the continual and enthusiastic support and encouragement I have received from such people as *Film Score Monthly*'s Lukas Kendall, who steered me to Scarecrow Press, John Waxman, the late William Van Wert of Temple University, many of my *Fanfare* colleagues, and a handful of composers, some deceased, some still working, whose names I will not mention lest suspicions arise of conflict of interest, of which, needless to say, there has been absolutely none. Warm thanks are also due to many of the good folks at Scarecrow Press, including Bruce Phillips, Sam Grammer, Jessica McCleary, and Stephen Ryan, the latter getting an additional nod for flexibility and patience. Additional thanks go to Ron Mandelbaum at Photofest. I must also single out master pianist and musician

Jeff Marcus, my fellow film professor Darrell Taylor, composer/teacher Barry Salmon at The New School, composer/teacher/pianist Ronald Sadoff at NYU, and John Waxman. And special thanks to my dear friend and yoga guru, the inimitable Jeff Logan, who keeps the pairs of opposites working together to create structure. A big thank-you is also due to Vic Skolnick and Charlotte Skye at the Cinema Arts Centre in Huntington, New York, who over the years have shown countless offbeat films that I might otherwise have missed. And, of course, I owe a huge debt to various family members not only for their patience and help but also for many wonderful hours of conversation about film and film scores. These include my brother Jeff, my sons Cary and Jason, and my stepchildren, Danielle and Jonathan Panek. They also include Sandra Linsin Comey and Julian Landau. As always, the biggest, most appreciative hug of all goes to my wife Jean . . . infinitely.

~

1983–1984

November/December 1983

[From Southern Cross comes] the Marvin Hamlisch score for Alan Pakula's **Sophie's Choice**, one of the more depressing examples of late of just how much the critical colony and the movie industry are hung up on non-cinema that oozes pseudo-"meaning" from every pore. Not only does *Sophie's Choice* cheapen its subject matter with an approach that ventures perilously near to Woody Allen, and not only does it contain utterly vile acting by the male leads, it also features Meryl Streep in a performance which, were it a piano recital, would be attacked for empty virtuosity by many critics. I was not as bothered as some by the musical intrusions in a film that gets much mileage out of "classical" source music, although if ever a music track should have been turned off, it is during the "Rite on the Brooklyn Bridge" sequence, which Hamlisch's score nastily soups up. But I must say that, like the film, the music leaves me just about stone cold. Whether in the de rigueur love theme or the quasi-Baroque doodlings of "Coney Island Fun," Hamlisch, like a Maurice Jarre, shows a singular lack of harmonic imagination. While this flaw turns me off in non-film composers such as Giuseppe Verdi (could anything be more puerile than the latter's "Queen's Ballet Music" from *Don Carlo?*), I find it anathema in an art that so often depends upon the vertically generated immediacies of harmonic invention. The decidedly non-resonant sound on the *Sophie's Choice* album has a rather harsh edge to it.

January/February 1984

I find myself in possession of a music-track recording (DRG) of the small-ensemble musical score composed for **The Draughtsman's Contract**, Peter Greenaway's sardonic, 17th-century costume drama, by Michael Nyman, whose name is also lent to the performing "band." Like the film, Nyman's inventions are anti-romantic to the nth. Composed in a style that might best be dubbed "Baroque minimalism," the musical cues, as played by the string and wind ensemble, generally feature at least one short phrase—an ostinato, a passacaglia bass line, a chaconne figure—whose repetitions tend to exasperate rather quickly precisely because of the brevity of the figure. Against these figures, the other instruments play various filigrees, many of them quite shrill, in a style that evokes both the Baroque and Modern periods, which wholly suits the film. But while the musical score moves in marvelous, sardonic sync with Greenway's stunningly photographed visions, it becomes grating as hell when listened to apart from the film. Also: I do remember a few cues that feature some singing (by a countertenor?). Why weren't any of these included on the disc? An important document, but not one that is apt to give a great deal of listening pleasure.

Gabriel Yared, who has done the music for Jean-Jacques Beineix's *The Moon in the Gutter*, turns up on a new Varèse Sarabande release as the composer for Peter Del Monte's **Invitation au voyage**. As in *The Moon in the Gutter*, Yared proves to be an absolute master of a kind of moody, musical surrealism. Using a combination of real instruments, human voice (both in vocalizations and some weird, oh-oh punctuations), and synthesized sound, Yared continually comes up with dreamy soundscapes that carry the feeling evoked by such Rota/Fellini scores as *Juliet of the Spirits* and *Casanova* several steps closer to the outer boundaries of inner space. The album also contains one rock number ("Don't Follow Me," composed by Michel Pineda, performed by Nina Scott and Lawlessness, and used as source music in the film) that I found quite palatable. "Assassin," an extended cue by Dominique Guillet, has a calmer but again very attractive pop/rock aura to it. Much of the album is well enough recorded to make it have a kind of demo-disc appeal.

Even further off the wall but in a much less moody and much more sardonic vein is the music-track for **Liquid Sky** (Varèse Sarabande). The movie, which operates on the premise of an outer-space alien that thrives on the chemical produced by the human brain after taking heroin (whence the film's title) and, even more potently, during orgasm, ends up as a slightly passé rehashing of '60s politics and psychedelia, even though visually and narratively it parades as what might be described as punk/sci-fi/feminism. With the exception of a piece of pure punkiana entitled "Me and My Rhythm Box" (sung by Paula E. Sheppard, who plays Adrienne, one of the two female leads in the film, the other, Margaret, being played by the androgynous Anne Carlisle, who in fact also performs as Jimmy, Margaret's male double), the entire score was realized on a Fairlight Computer Musical Instrument to produce sounds thoroughly appropriate to the filmic goings on. These sounds, composed and adapted by Brenda L. Hitchinson, Clive Smith, and Slava Tsukerman, the latter having produced, directed, edited, and co-scripted the film as well, include a wind-up-toy type of piece adapted from Orff's *Trionfo di Afrodite*, a half medieval/half mod adaptation from Marin Marais, and numerous nontonal, minimalist cues that back up a good deal of the picture. One particularly stunning audio-visual combination is for the "Sunset" sequence, which features a spectacular montage of extreme telephoto shots of a sun setting over Manhattan while the music does its own thing with a series of reedy timbres that fall somewhere between the human voice and Indian flutes. Like the movie, which I cannot imagine being shown in more than, say, a half-dozen locales throughout the states, the album for *Liquid Sky* will not be everybody's cup of tea. But, unlike a score such as (ugh!) *Chariots of Fire*, it finds a totally endemic use and idiom for the synthesizer.

Speaking of weird and minimalism, there's Godfrey Reggio's film **Koyaanisqatsi**, for which Philip Glass wrote a score that, with the exception of a few brief moments, runs throughout the entire hour-and-a-half length of the film, whose title is a Hopi word with such meanings as "crazy life," "life out of balance" (the subtitle used for the film), or—I love this one—"a state of life that calls for another way of living." *Koyaanisqatsi* has no characters—indeed, human beings remain conspicuously absent for about the first 15 minutes of the movie—no dialogue (or even voice track), no story per se. Instead, it presents a series of metamorphosing images—cloud patterns shot in time-lapse photography, buildings imploding in slow motion, cars zipping, again with time-lapse speed, along expressways at night, extreme telephoto shots of a passenger jet (I mean, something such as a 1600 millimeter lens must have been used), landscapes, computer-chip grids, etc.—that repeat with much the same hypnotic effect as Glass's music while also, again like the score, leading to subtle metamorphoses (might not Glass be called a "metamorphosist" rather than a minimalist?). In fact, a fair amount of the editing in the first part of *Koyaanisqatsi* is done to the pace of the minimal changes that evolve in the score's many repeated figures. Antilles Records has recorded a little more than half of Glass's score, conducted by Michael Riesman, much of which bears the composer's distinctive stamp, whether in the choral patterns of "Vessels" or the instrumental-ensemble evolutions of "The Grid," which also has choral punctuation. But in the dazzlingly recorded title piece, Glass creates, with a basso profundo (Albert de Ruiter) chanting the film's title and a pipe organ evoking the entire Baroque era, considerably more mood than he usually does. (The closing "Prophecies" has somewhat the same aura, but with chorus instead of bass.) Equally intriguing are the wispy, almost Shostakovian violin filigrees that pop up in the "Pruit Igoe" cue. But for the most part, Glass does not appear to have modified his musical language to fit the cinema's demands; rather, the opposite seems to have taken place, which is one thing that makes *Koyaanisqatsi* such an utterly engrossing experiment. The disc, then, should strongly appeal to fans of this type of music; but it also documents an extremely rare instance of a film score that represents a good 50% of its movie's artistic content.

March/April 1984

Along with *The Draughtsman's Contract* and *Dead Zone*, James Ivory's exquisite **Heat and Dust** ranks as one of only three really decent English-language films I've seen all year. (Foreign films? Try Bergman's *Fanny and Alexander*, Bresson's *L'Argent*, or Alain Tanner's *Dans la ville blanche*.) Based on a novel by Ruth Prawer Jhabvala, who also wrote the screenplay, *Heat and Dust* moves with breathtaking grace between an interracial love affair dating from colonial India and a second interracial love affair involving a contemporary woman (Julie Christie) who is the granddaughter of the first (Susan Fleetwood). As might be expected, the musical score by Richard Rollins, with additional music by Zakir Hussain (Varèse Sarabande), is very much a mixed-bag type of affair. The title theme, for instance, starts off with a sitar/wooden-flute duo and then moves to a bland, salon waltz that sets the mood for the military-aristocracy milieu of the costume-drama sequences. One particularly haunting cue, "Olivia Writes Home," mixes strings with the wooden flute, sitar, and tabla, while another, "Durbar," features that same flute over a rather Philip Glass-ish ostinato. The synthesizer accompaniment figures in "The Dust Storm" bring Glass even more strongly to mind. The album also includes some previously written source music, including some horrendously played national anthems, Schumann's solo piano "Das Abends" (rather heavily played), and some native Indian music. All in all, this album, which has for the most part been very well recorded, is not apt to send people running to their local record stores. The music it offers, however, represents an essential part of *Heart and Dust's* ambience, and, as such, it is of much more than passing interest.

May/June 1984

There definitely seems to be a new film genre looming on the horizon. This genre, which would include films such as *Diva, Invitation au voyage, The Moon in the Gutter,* and *Liquid Sky,* might be dubbed, for lack of a better term, "New New Wave," not in the sense of the so-called "Nouvelle Vague" that produced the likes of Godard, Truffaut, and Chabrol, but in the sense that is often applied to "punk" music. But the "New New Wave" films, while no doubt partially inspired by video-rock visuals, by and large do not revolve around punk-type music. Indeed, much of *Diva* centers on an aria from Catalani's opera *La Wally,* while the film's principal music-track theme (by Vladimir Cosma) has a definite Erik Satie ring to it. *Invitation au voyage* features an incredibly moody, surrealistic, synthesizer score by Gabriel Yared. Having at this point had the chance to see a videotape of *Invitation au voyage,* I can say that the film's spacy, often backlit, agoraphobic visuals combine with the music in an almost unbearably intense manner. Adding to the punk-new-wave aura of all this is the film's androgyny-oriented storyline of a young man [Laurent Malet] who takes over the persona of his rock-star twin sister [Corrine Reynaud, using the name of Nina Scott, a rock vocalist in the film], who has been bizarrely electrocuted while taking a milk bath (I leave it to the readers to imagine the visual image this death inspires).

But perhaps the weirdest of all the "new wave" films is Jean-Jacques (*Diva*) Beineix's second film, **La Lune dans le caniveau** (The Moon in the Gutter), which, like Truffaut's "Nouvelle Vague" classic, *Shoot the Piano Player,* is loosely based on a novel by David Goodis. Starring the omnipresent Gérard Depardieu and Nastassja Kinski, *The Moon in the Gutter* almost totally buries its narrative beneath exaggeratedly stylized photography [by Philippe Rousselot] that in many ways looks like a string of those off-the-wall Chanel TV commercials. Complementing these visuals is another immensely appropriate musical score by Gabriel Yared (DRG), who was born in Lebanon in 1949. For Nastassia Kinski's first entrance, for instance, director Beineix obviously called on Yared to produce a piece of almost stereotypical, "Warsaw Concerto"-type romanticism that becomes the "Loretta" theme which, for all its pseudo Hollywood sheen, turns out to be a very haunting waltz. Elsewhere, Yared, as is his wont, turns to synthesizer, frequently to produce the kind of unrelenting, robot-like, driving rhythms that are also heard in a film such as *Liquid Sky*. A string fugue that accompanies a bizarre, "enchanted" cathedral sequence adds further class to the score, which has been extremely well recorded and which deserves attention as both a document for an offbeat film that bombed and as an eminently listenable work of music in its own right.

At the opposite end of the scale from all this is Michael Curtiz's quintessential piece of swashing and buckling, **The Adventures of Robin Hood**, which, in addition to its splendid acting and sumptuous blending of colors on the screen, is backed by Erich Wolfgang Korngold's second Oscar-winning score. Although excerpts of this have been marvelously reworked and recorded by Charles Gerhardt for the RCA "Classic Film Score" series, Varèse Sarabande now offers a recording of a substantial number of the film's cues, played "straight" and performed by the Utah Symphony Orchestra under the baton of Varujan Kojian. I must say that, having often reveled in the Gerhardt reworkings, I sometimes found it hard to adapt to the original forms of the themes and their true metamorphoses as presented on this album. But there is no question that, for anyone in love with the film and its music, the progression of the cues as heard on this disc is an absolute revelation. Certainly, the score still works gorgeously on a purely musical level: the same types of harmonic/melodic/instrumental elaborations one can admire in the likes of a Mahler or a Richard Strauss abound in Korngold's highly personal style. But what constantly draws the listener into this music—and what made Korngold the consummate film-score composer—is the way the musician thoroughly translates the visceral pulse of the film into his own language, moving at a sometimes dazzling pace through numerous emotional states while always maintaining a characteristic warmth, even during the most ferocious battle scenes.

July/August 1984

As in other punk-new-wave films, one particularly attractive feature about **The Hunger**, which adapts a novel by Whitley (*Wolfen*) Strieber, is its use of music. The film starts off with a punk-rock number ["Bela Lugosi Is Dead," performed by Bauhaus], surprisingly not included on the album, filmed in a classic rock-video style. But by far the bulk of the music, released by Varèse Sarabande, comes either from the archives of the "classical" repertoire or from very modern, synthesizer sounds scored by Michel Rubini and Denny Jaeger. Somewhat as in *Diva*, *The Hunger* deploys an obscure and stunningly beautiful operatic excerpt—the duet "Sous le dôme épais" from Act 1 of Delibes' *Lakme*—in one of its key scenes. Heard first in a piano-solo arrangement supposedly performed by the Catherine Deneuve character in the film, the full, exotic vocal duet returns on the music track to underscore a scene of lesbian lovemaking during which

Catherine Deneuve's immortality is passed on to Susan Sarandon (the link between sexuality and the metaphysics of mortality and immortality also plays a key role in several punk-new-wave films). Elsewhere, the Schubert Trio in E-flat, op. 100, which should be familiar to *Barry Lyndon* fans, appears as source music, with Deneuve, a young, female music student, and David Bowie as the unlikely music-makers. Particularly devastating in the Rubini/Jaeger cues is "The Final Death" (the tautology of this title will be appreciated only by those who have seen *The Hunger*), in which strings combine with synthesizer, often in scream-like configurations, to accompany Deneuve's long, slow-motion fall. It should be noted that the "classical" cues were arranged and supervised by Howard Blake, whose score for *The Duellists* remains an unrecorded film-music gem.

With all the miserable things that can happen to movies, both before and after their general release, it is refreshing to see at least a few efforts being made these days to reverse some of the havoc that has been wrought on films by the Philistines at the financial end. When Luchino Visconti's **The Leopard** (Il Gattopardo) was first released in this country in 1963, it was badly dubbed into English and cut substantially from its initial running time. Recently, however, the film has been re-released in this country, restored to its original length, and presented in its original Italian (yes, even Italian actors in Italian films generally have their voices dubbed in or post-synchronized; but at least we get to hear the language as conceived by Visconti and spoken by actors with considerably more merit than the hacks who generally do this work for Hollywood). The film—a portrait of the dying aristocracy in Sicily in 1861—certainly merits the attention: in a sumptuous but unflamboyant manner, Visconti, much as Ingmar Bergman does in *Fanny and Alexander*, warmly re-creates a small piece of history and its inhabitants while in the process painting some of the strongest characters, in particular the prince played by Burt Lancaster, ever shown on screen. One of the most ingratiating elements of *The Leopard* is its musical score, which Lancaster, in his liner notes for the Varèse Sarabande reissue, quite rightly describes as "lovely" and "graceful." Certainly, *The Leopard* shows Rota at his lyrical and romantic best; the principal theme, for instance, has a swell to it that can become an obsession, particularly for a listener already hooked on the movie. Rota, in fact, even comes out ahead in direct comparison with Giuseppe Verdi who, via his heirs, provided Visconti with an unpublished waltz used during *The Leopard*'s final, ballroom sequence. Even without Rota's own, poignant waltz to make it pale, Verdi's waltz, with its typical oom-pah accompaniment and its flat harmonies, has little to recommend it other than the amateurishness Visconti apparently wanted for the source music. Rota also provides some inspiring, if somewhat Tchaikovskian, battle music. Varèse Sarabande's reissue, it should be noted, contains cues not offered on the 20th Century-Fox recording of *The Leopard* that appeared in 1964.

September/October 1984

Several summers ago, I participated in a seminar, sponsored by the American Film Institute and the Rockefeller Foundation, aimed at showing college professors involved in "film study" what the real world of filmmaking was like. Professionals from all branches of filmmaking—composer Henry Mancini, the late Natalie Wood, cinematographer William Fraker, and director Collin Higgins come immediately to mind—showed up and attempted to bring down to Earth those minds who see anything shaped like a cross in Hitchcock's films as a sign of the late director's Catholicism. The kickoff talk came from Richard St. Johns, an executive producer whose chief role in life is to round up the money needed to put together a given movie. St. Johns immediately scandalized intellectual doters on the "seventh art" by informing us that, in order to determine how seriously he would market a given film, he first showed it to his 12-year-old son for a reaction. Several participants needed to be revived.

In case you think things have changed a great deal in the last five years, look at what happened in the U.S. to **Once Upon a Time in America**, Sergio Leone's long-underway finale for a trilogy that began with *Once Upon a Time in the West* (1968) and *Duck, You Sucker* (1971; in the U.S., the film is sometimes known as *A Fistful of Dynamite*). The version of *Once Upon a Time in America* shot by Leone and shown in most places, including the Cannes Festival, except the U.S. lasts three hours and 40 minutes. Basing their decision on the adolescent mentality that shapes the making of most American films these days, the distributors in this country judged that audiences on these shores were not ready for a film lasting nearly four hours and so have initially released *Once Upon a Time in America* in a version that runs around two and a quarter hours. Having first seen the latter and then, during a recent trip to France, the original, I can report that, if neither version of *Once Upon a Time in America* lives up to the two predecessors, in its three-hour-and-forty-minute version it very nearly does. What has happened to the American *Once Upon a Time?* First of all, it has been re-edited into a literal-minded, chronological film that totally destroys the flashback, opium-dream structure carefully created by Leone, who based part of his work on the autobiography of small-time gangster Harry Grey (né Goldstein) entitled *The Hoods*. Secondly, needless to say, key sequences have entirely disappeared, the most important of which deals with the re-emergence at the end of the film of Deborah (Elizabeth McGovern) who, along with her son (played by the same actor, Rusty Jacobs, who plays the young Max), totally falls victim to the scissors of the American editors. Other parts of *Once Upon a Time in America* have been hit with other forms of artistic modification: a baby-switching scene in the original uses music from Rossini's *La Gazza ladra* and cuts the voice track to produce a silent-film type of comedy. American viewers get to hear the dialogue and no Rossini. Even worse, the American producers have literalized the ending by adding a gunshot to the soundtrack to suggest that Max (James Woods) has committed suicide. The original version remains ambiguous and then concludes with a return to a spaced-out (on opium) Noodles (Robert De Niro).

One thing certainly missing from the American butchering of *Once Upon a Time in America* is the full breadth of the musical score by Ennio Morricone, who also did *Once Upon a Time in the West* and *Duck, You Sucker* (the latter, in my opinion, stands as one of the greatest film scores ever composed). Fortunately, Mercury Records has released

50 solid minutes of Morricone's contributions to *Once Upon a Time in America*. Since the film contains a fair amount of source music, the album producers could have opted to bypass a lot of Morricone's original strains. Instead, most of what can be heard on the album, with the exception of a couple of pastiches and two or three Morricone-arranged appearances of J. M. La Calle's "Amapola," which is associated with the young Deborah, is absolutely vintage Morricone, very often harking back to the level of his masterpiece, *Duck, You Sucker*. As it turns out, in fact, Morricone, according to an interview in the French bi-monthly *Films* (27, 20 May 1984), began working on the music immediately after *Duck, You Sucker*, so that the principal themes had been lying around for eight or nine years waiting for Leone, who had conceived the film as early as 1967, to find a producer. All the melancholy lyricism that dominates *Duck, You Sucker* re-emerges in *Once Upon a Time in America* to haunt the audience all over again, whether in the title theme, the "Poverty" theme with its out-of-tune piano, "Deborah's Theme," which characteristically features a vocalizing soprano, or "Childhood Memories," in which a pan flute played by one of the characters wends its way into the music-track (remember how Morricone incorporates into the score the minimal theme tooted on the harmonica by Charles Bronson in *Once Upon a Time in the West*?). In a particularly devastating bit of music drama, Morricone, toward the end of the score, contrapuntally juxtaposes Deborah's theme with a harpsichord playing "Amapola," which emotionally revives the young Debbie while incarnating the older one. In all this, it is interesting how Morricone almost totally avoids musically suggesting the Jewish ethnicity inherent in the film's setting, an ethnicity that Leone too avoids developing in *Once Upon a Time in America*. Indeed, the way in which Morricone's very broad, very Italian lyricism soars above the ugliness, violence, and ethnic implications (American in *Once Upon a Time in the West*, Mexican and Irish in *Duck, You Sucker*, and Jewish in *Once Upon a Time in America*) of Leone's films represents one of the deep originalities of this extraordinary collaboration.

A while ago, I wrote briefly of Antoine Duhamel's marvelous score for Bertrand Tavernier's *Death Watch* (DJM), which has much in common with the composer's chef d'oeuvre for Godard's *Pierrot le fou* (RCA "Cine Music"). As it turns out, there is a good reason for the similarity. As Duhamel revealed to me recently, director Tavernier was so taken with the *Pierrot le fou* score that he used it as a "scratch track" for *Death Watch* and then insisted that Duhamel compose something along the same lines for the film's final score. As the composer put it, "I was obliged to plagiarize myself."

November/December 1984

In order to see one of 1984's most excitingly original movies, Dutch director Paul Verhoeven's **The 4th Man**, which was nowhere to be found in my local 11-plex theater, I had to make a 45-mile pilgrimage to Manhattan (which, after all, originally belonged to the Dutch). Here is a film which, through the eyes of its novelist hero (who bears the same name, Gerard Reve—as in dream—as the author of the work on which *The 4th Man* is based), explores in as engrossing a way as I've ever seen the spillovers between exterior reality and the sexually and/or religiously inspired creations of the human mind. Along the way, the film also takes on the aspect of a thriller, as the bisexual protagonist seduces (or is seduced by) an androgynous woman whose permanent lover turns out to be the object of the hero's sexual desires. Like a spider, which is one of *The 4th Man*'s principal images, the woman may very well be collecting victims. Adding greatly to the overall atmosphere is composer Loek Dikker's expansive score (Varèse Sarabande), which moves fluidly from cluster-filled suspense sounds to moments of poignantly subdued lyricism, with a moody brass chorale, first heard in the title sequence, serving as a kind of dreamy anchor from another time and space. One is occasionally reminded, in both the music's moments of grandeur and in its more pastoral excursions, of Arthur Honegger, which is all for the better in my book.

CHAPTER TWO

~

1985

January/February

[I began this column with a discussion of the Volker Schlöndorf film, **Un Amour de Swann.** My thoughts on the film itself, if not the music, have changed so radically since my first viewing that, for the first paragraph, I reproduce most of a review I wrote of the DVD of the film for November/December 2004 issue of *The Perfect Vision*. Of all the parts of Marcel Proust's massive, essentially unadaptable, seven-volume novel *A la recherche du temps perdu* (In Search of Lost Time), *Un Amour de Swann* (Swann in Love), the middle section of the first volume, *Du côté de Chez Swann* (Swann's Way), would theoretically be the most adaptable. Here, for the only time in *Recherche*, the narrator leaves the sprawling, first-person re-creation and re-composition of the past that forms the first volume's first part (*Combray*), moves further into the past before he was born, and, in a somewhat simpler third-person style, tells the story of the obsessive love affair of one Charles Swann (Jeremy Irons), an upper-class Jewish man who moves in the most elevated circles of French high society, for a woman named Odette (Ornella Muti), who is essentially a high-class call girl. Yet Schlöndorff, with the help of co-screenwriters Peter Brook, Jean-Claude Carrière, and Marie-Hélène Étienne, has used *Un Amour de Swann* as a pretext for mixing and matching various key themes and characters from across the entire novel, giving a major role, for instance, to the Baron de Charlus (Alain Delon, in an inspired piece of casting), Proust's notorious male homosexual, who shows up on only one page of *Swann in Love* but returns with a vengeance in the subsequent works (Charlus also gets the film's best line—not in the novel—when Swann naively asks him, "Have you slept with Odette?" "Not as far as I know"). With an opening voiceover from Swann, Schlöndorff partially turns *Swann in Love* back into a first-person narrative that brings Swann closer to the novel's narrator. And in a particularly labyrinthine twist, Schlöndorff briefly introduces into the film a "young Jewish man" (Nicolas Baby) who may or may not be Proust's narrator, Marcel. In another expansion into the later volumes, Schlöndorff and his writers depict not only Swann's over-the-top jealousy of Odette but also attribute to him, vis-à-vis Odette, the narrator's later obsession with the possible lesbianism of *his* lover, Albertine. I do not remember particularly liking *Swann in Love* when I saw it during its initial theatrical run. This time around, however, I was blown away by it. In under two hours, the film, even while wreaking havoc with the narrative sequencing, manages to deeply communicate the essence of *Swann in Love* while also evoking important elements and characters from the rest of the seven-volume novel. The production (Jacques Saulnier), set (Philippe Turlure), and costume (Yvonne Sassinot de Nesle) design wonderfully re-create the mostly aristocratic milieu of late-19th-century Paris on which much of *Recherche* focuses, and the acting is uniformly excellent, starting with Delon as the incredibly arrogant and affected Charlus but also including both Irons and Muti, even though both have their lines dubbed (superbly) into French.]

In getting Hans Werner Henze to write the musical score (Milan Records) for *Un Amour de Swann*, Schlöndorff has made [something of a] miscalculation. The music itself—12 Variations for String Sextet and Harp that mobilize other instruments as well, including organ and human voice—is thoroughly haunting, in an expressionistic and occasionally Bartókian way, and Henze fans will not want to be without the disc, especially since it also contains a concert suite of Henze's lugubrious, even more modernistic music for Schlöndorff's *The Lost Honor of Katharina Blum* (1975). But music plays a central, diegetic role in *Un Amour de Swann*, in which a fictitious violin sonata by a fictitious composer (Vintueil) becomes the aesthetic incarnation of Swann's love for Odette. Since Schlöndorff has chosen to use Henze's music diegetically (i.e., it becomes a part of the narrative universe so that the characters can hear it) rather than to turn to one of the composers—most probably Saint-Saëns or Franck—who inspired Proust, he creates an enormous spatio-temporal gap between the milieu and period occupied by the characters and the distinctly modern Henze strains. And it is totally ludicrous that this difficult, non-melodic music should a) become the "national anthem" of Swann and Odette's love and b) be skillfully played at the piano by the character of Odette (Ornella Muti), a high-class call-girl at best. Since Schlöndorff did not choose to have airplanes flying overhead or cars driving by in this turn-of-the-century period piece, one can only presume a penchant for musical anachronism.

One outstanding exception to the generally low quality of music scored for the films of John Ford is the score composed by Alex North for **Cheyenne Autumn** (1964), an impressive and more than slightly absurdist Western that should lay to rest any stereotype that set Ford up as the great purveyor and supporter of an all-American mythology. Why the score has taken so long to surface on disc is anybody's guess. Mine is that North's music is so sophisticated that it scares off potential record producers (not to mention film producers; North has not exactly received a plethora of exciting assignments). Fortunately, the third of Label X's "Soundtrack Collector's Special Edition" releases, a 45-rpm LP-sized disc, has finally filled this lacuna with a good half-hour's worth of music from Ford's 160-minute film. Anyone acquainted with North's score for Stanley Kubrick's *Spartacus* should have no trouble recognizing the composer's particular trademarks—thick textures filled with dissonances that are both contrapuntally and chordally generated; violent, complex rhythmic patterns that frequently, as in the cue entitled "River Crossing," suggest some dark, underlying ritual; unexpected moments of haunting lyricism in which lonely melodies are presented in the barest of textures, such as the English horn and harp combination in "Friend Deborah" (the cue is for a Quaker woman, played by Caroll Baker, who takes the side of the Indians against incredibly stupid government bureaucracy). In the cue for "Dodge City," in which James Stewart plays an off-the-wall Wyatt Earp, North indulges in more than a bit of Ivesian banter by incorporating the "Camptown Races" tune into an otherwise complex musical canvas. Interestingly, as the score rolls on, it, like the film, becomes more subdued and resigned in quality. Throughout the score, furthermore, North incorporates themes that are apparently from genuine Native American sources. Also of note is the use, for *Cheyenne Autumn*, of a pre-film "Overture." Such overtures were put onto the music tracks (with no pictures) of more films than one might imagine, and they have very often been eliminated in re-releases and, of course, TV showings.

March/April

It boggles the mind to watch the way in which the film and popular-music industries are in certain ways coalescing into a single unit whose individual elements defy categorical placement in a single domain or genre. Consider David (*Eraserhead, Elephant Man*) Lynch's stunning adaptation of Frank Herbert's cult sci-fi novel, **Dune**. One of the film's principal heavies is played, in an ingenious piece of casting, by Police rock-star Sting, who has absolutely no connection with music in *Dune*. To further complicate matters, Dune's producers hired the rock group Toto to compose and perform the music-track score (PolyGram LP). Yet the bulk of *Dune's* musical score is composed in a straight, modern-classical style of the type one might expect from anyone of a number of known film composers. Using both a live orchestra and chorus (the Vienna Symphony Orchestra and the Vienna Volksoper Choir) and synthesized sounds, Toto has produced a very dramatic, expansive, primitivistic, and often highly moving score which, while evoking the disparate likes of Shostakovich (11th Symphony), Johann Sebastian Bach, and Ennio Morricone, admirably weaves its way into *Dune's* affective fabric. The frenzied battle sequences, with their distinctive percussion sounds, struck me as particularly effective. Only the disco-ish "Desert Theme," which I seem to recall backed up only the end titles (it has, of course, been made into a single), and "Take My Hand" drag the music down to the unpleasant realities of the current pop/film-music areas wherein dwell the likes of Vangelis and Giorgio Moroder.

A few more words on *Dune*. The film has not been particularly well received. Yet it seems to me that, visually, director Lynch uncannily reproduced that strange amalgam of archaic and futuristic, of dreamlike and real, the story calls for. Lynch also has a peculiar talent for a kind of surreally organic gruesomeness that pervades the film, whether in the very personage of the repulsive Baron Harkonnen (Kenneth McMillan, whose voice is heard briefly on the disc) or in the frequent violence called for in Lynch's own screenplay. The casting is likewise particularly fortunate, with Siân Phillips (who played Claudius' mother in *I, Claudius*) as the Reverend Mother Gaius Helen Mohiam perhaps topping the list of amazingly appropriate embodiments of the novel's characters. Granted, it helps to know the novel so that the viewer can mentally fill in Herbert's narrative complexities, which Lynch of necessity often folds into tight ellipses. And, granted, the film has its moments of pure corn, most of which tie in with the actor chosen to play Paul, Kyle MacLachlan, who is perhaps just a tad too pretty and wholesome to be totally convincing. But, in Lynch's hands, *Dune* possesses a style that both serves its content well and, ultimately, triumphs over it.

May/June

German director Wim Winders' **Paris, Texas** is not the best film I have seen of late. In spite of a simple but beautifully structured screenplay by Sam Shepard, and in spite of cinematographer Robby Muller's breathtaking portraits of various American landscapes, one has the impression that Wenders, who fills *Paris, Texas* with at least three sequences that seem to go on at least 10 minutes too long, is deliberately out to try his audiences' patience. Nothing, however, could be more appropriate to the drawn-out, melancholic longing and the American mythology communicated by *Paris, Texas* than Ry Cooder's mostly guitar-solo score (Warner Bros. LP). As with certain Indian music performed on a sitar or a sarod, there is something almost vocal about the laments Cooder pulls from his instrument, especially in the main theme, with its characteristic portamento. The guitar solo, which by the way has been recorded with stunning presence, gets minimal accompaniment from two other musicians, one playing a strange-looking instrument, the other a prepared piano. The album also features Harry Dean Stanton, who has the film's key role, doing a surprisingly respectable vocal of "Canción Mixteca"; Stanton's voice also dominates Side 2's long voice-track excerpt, in which Stanton gradually reveals his identity to his long-lost wife (Nastassja Kinski), who cannot see him, by telling in the third person the story of their life and times together.

Meanwhile, that granddaddy of modern film scores, Max Steiner's music for the 1933 **King Kong**, has resurfaced on Southern Cross's remastered reissue on LP and CD of the 1976 Entr'acte recording, with the National Philharmonic Orchestra conducted by Fred Steiner. I will immediately say that this *King Kong*, made from orchestrations reconstructed by Christopher Palmer, is one of the most important and exciting film-score recordings ever made. Besides the music itself, Fred Steiner's intense and driving interpretation, the National Philharmonic's impassioned playing, and the absolutely mind-blowing sound, which was good enough on the original disc but warmer and richer on the remastering, greatly add to the overall excellence. And now the CD's astonishing clarity and fullness brings the product about as close to perfection as it can get (my one regret is that only part of Fred Steiner's excellent notes and analysis could be contained in the CD package).

A few words on Steiner's music. Anyone who thinks of Steiner only as a (sometimes wishy-washy) Viennese post-Romantic is due for a jolt when he/she hears this almost unrelentingly primitivistic score whose savagery is relieved only briefly, here and there, by a love waltz or a Broadway overture. For me, the score's showstopper is the "Jungle Dance," a marvelous crescendo, complete with whole-tone scales and quasi-jungle-drum beats, that accompanies the native ritual witnessed by the film director and his crew when they first set foot on "Skull Island." From the cinematic point of view, it is interesting how film audiences are willing to accept the audiovisual illusion of a 45-piece, Western orchestra playing music that a primitive tribe is supposed to be dancing to—shots of drum players and of dancers beating their chests in rhythm to the music fortify the ambiguity between the diegetic and non-diegetic effects of the music on the listener. Steiner's score is also a marvel of motivic organization, with Kong's three-note leitmotiv providing an amazing amount of the subthematic impetus. As the Oscar Levant quotation in the liner notes puts it, "[*King Kong*] should have been advertised as a concert of Steiner's music with accompanying pictures on the screen," which seems all the more appropriate considering that some 75 of the film's 105 minutes are scored (over 18 of the unscored minutes come during the film's exposition at the beginning).

July/August

To my list of best and worst films of 1984 I must add one more to each side. To the worst belongs *Purple Rain*, which I caught up with a month or so ago. The way I see it, the film has nothing to offer cinematically or musically other than a long, loving look-hear at/of Prince, one of the most obnoxious figures our popular culture has yet created. A living oxymoron, Prince exudes a kind of effete machismo that would not be so disturbing if so many people did not take this self-caressing posturing seriously. On the other side, Roland Joffe's **The Killing Fields** deserved to do even better than it did at the Academy Awards. Why, for instance, did Mike ("Tubular Bells") Oldfield's extensive score not even get a nomination? I don't think I have ever seen a film that, particularly during its first half, managed, with a brilliant combination of camera work and editing, to totally involve me in the often brutal realities being depicted. If anything bothered me, it was, during the second half of the film, wondering how in the world Pran's incredible escape could have been true as shown (it is for precisely the type of reaction that this sort of thing evokes in me that I generally avoid films based on "true" happenings).

Certainly, Mike Oldfield deserves a share of the credit for his quite diversified score (Virgin LP, with Mike Oldfield, guitars, synthesizers, and Fairlight Computer; Preston Heyman, oriental percussion; Morris Pert, percussion; Orchestra of the Bavarian State Opera and Tölzer Boys Choir, Eberhard Schoener, cond.). It can be objected that *The Killing Fields* is over-scored—certainly, such cues as "Pran's Theme," with its elegiac high strings, or "Bad News" border on the syrupy and gild the affective lily. And no doubt the series of cues—"The Trek," "The Boy's Burial," and "Pran Sees the

Red Cross"—lay on the Miklós Rózsa a bit heavily. The only thing that really drove me crazy, however, was the John Lennon song (not included on the disc) that backs up Schanberg and Pran's reunion. On the other hand, the kind of thing that Oldfield does best—bizarre ostinato figures, surrealistic percussion effects, a relentless and yet cyclical sense of movement—work to stunning effect for certain cues. I can recall nothing in recent cinema, for instance, quite as devastating as the music/visual amalgam of "The Evacuation." And the Ligeti-ish masses of instrumental and choral space defined in a series of cues beginning with "Worksite" starkly complement the unimaginably grim settings of the Khmer Rouge work camps. The album concludes with an offbeat arrangement by Oldfield for Indian flute and percussion of Francisco Tárrega's famous guitar étude—hearing this piece out of its instrumental context had me bonkers for a week trying to figure out where I knew the music from.

September/October

My favorite recording of the batch that came my way for this column is Southern Cross's CD reissue of Entr'acte's inaugural LP in 1975, Bernard Herrmann's score for Brian De Palma's **Sisters**. I have never understood the preference that has been shown by most people for both De Palma's next Herrmann-scored film, *Obsession*, and the music for that film over the low-budget *Sisters* and its quietly ghoulish score. While both films pay ample tribute to Alfred Hitchcock, *Sisters* is at least close enough to De Palma's early, off-the-wall work to not take itself 100% seriously, while *Obsession* makes the grand error of starring Cliff Robertson and of being totally humorless, the latter a mistake "the master of suspense" made only in his worst films (*Torn Curtain* and *Topaz* come immediately to mind). *Sisters* offers more than its share of "oh no" outrageousness: as one example, the murderous schizo played by Margot Kidder wins the knife she will later kill the film's first victim with on a quiz program entitled "Peeping Tom," where in fact she has met the potential victim. But all this sets off the film's horror and ultimately makes it more scary, just as Bernard Herrmann's "Birthday Cake" theme, for instance, uses a wispy, wistful glockenspiel tune to create one of the cinema's most crushing musical ironies. And while at moments Herrmann does not hesitate to pull out all the stops—the title cue assaults the listeners with a raging full orchestra and two Moog synthesizers—for the most part he relies on the rapier rather than the bludgeon, as opposed to *Obsession*, with its chorus, cathedral organ, and overstated lyricism. Southern Cross's CD, while sacrificing a bit of high end to the LP, has considerably more presence than the latter, so that the full textures of such things as Herrmann's triadic woodwind scoring or his low-string-and-woodwind unisons are revealed with stunning clarity.

Richard Band's score for **Mutant** (Varèse Sarabande, with London's National Philharmonic Orchestra) is a different affair altogether. Although producer Igo Kantor has pulled out, in his brief notes, every cliché in the book in order to justify Band's score as a "throwback to the 'golden era of music,'" much of the score in fact has the kind of post-Bartókian quality that has only sprung up in the last 10 or 20 years in scores by the likes of Jerry Goldsmith, John Corigliano, and James Horner. Nonetheless, there is something mightily refreshing in Band's subtle, orchestral figures, which often go on for some minutes without ever rising above a *piano* dynamic level. I was particularly struck by a strangely Hispanic, piano filigree that continually pops up in an almost concertante fashion. Unlike most film scores that show up on LP or CD these days, *Mutant* stands up well independently from the film, or even if you haven't seen the film. Richard Band deserves to have his star rise.

November/December

"Nicolas Roeg makes movies the way Pablo Picasso painted pictures."—Associated Press review

As I write this, one can currently see in Manhattan two films—the 1983 *Eureka* and the recent **Insignificance**, which won a special prize for technique at the 1985 Cannes Film Festival and to which Zenith Records has devoted a splendid although pretentiously annotated album that includes bits of the film's how-the-hell-is-this-supposed-to-be-taken dialogue. Although based on an absolutely silly premise—the coming together of an actress (à la Marilyn Monroe), a senator (Joseph McCarthy), a professor (Albert Einstein), and a baseball player (Joe DiMaggio) during the course of a single evening—in Roeg's hands what must be a fairly trivial play is expanded, in spite of its limited setting, so that visual symbols of female sexuality and circular temporality—everything from the actress's (Theresa Russell) buttocks and breasts to balloons and at least one piece of breathtaking, circular editing—are set against the conceptualized, male sexuality and linear or super-linear temporality of the Professor (Michael Emil). Paradoxically, just as the Actress has miscarried (and not simply gotten her period, as the *Village Voice* critic asininely suggested), and just as the Professor's theories have led to Hiroshima, the potential coming together of these two sexualities is aborted at the last possible minute (as the screen is at the point of revealing the actress's nipples) by the arrival of the loutish, very un-DiMaggioish Baseball Player (Gary Busey). As *Insignificance*, which is also a wonderful study on the iconography of being, ultimately suggests in its opening sequence, artistic creation may be the only way of bringing sex and time together without the result being death. Although *Insignificance* suffers—less so than *Eureka*, however—from some over-scripting and overacting that are hard to justify on any level, the only thing that is insignificant is the drivel that critics have been saying about it, the worst, perhaps, coming from PBS' "Sneak Previews," whose critics actually treated the film only as a depiction of McCarthy, Monroe, DiMaggio, and Einstein. TV movie critics may very well be the single most harmful force working against the success of intelligent films such as *Insignificance* that dare to present the cinema for what it is—aesthetically manipulable images and sounds—rather than as a replacement for reality. I regularly offer my film students an A+ for the head of Gene Shallit, but nobody has taken me up on it yet.

Anyway, the Zenith music-track album, entitled "The Shape of the Universe: A Souvenir of Music and Dialogue to Remind Us of Nicolas Roeg's *Insignificance*," contains music mostly composed and performed by Stanley Myers (who did a much more extensive score for *Eureka*), whose best efforts are the piece of big-band, slinky jazz entitled "(It's) a Dog of a Night" (especially effective behind the end titles) and "Forever (What the Hell)," an almost overwhelmingly moody piece of slow, *nachtjazz* which, if I remember correctly, even gives the Baseball Player's macho babbling emotional depth at one point (Will Jennings receives co-authorship credit for this cue). Myers and one Hans Zimmer teamed up for several ethereal synthesizer cues, while Theresa Russell à la Marilyn Monroe performs a Myers/Jennings song entitled "Life Goes On." Allusions to the Professor's violin playing and love of Mozart also pop up in a cue or two, most notably Gil Evans' grating and sloppily played (on purpose?) arrangement of the "Jupiter" symphony's second movement. The only unbearable cues are a song entitled "Wild Hearts," performed with a Frank Stallone cum Bruce Springsteen gusto by Roy Orbison, and a disco piece called "B-29 (The Shape of the Universe)" heard beneath a radio broadcast describing the bombing of Hiroshima. The recorded sound is splendid.

And now for something even more completely different: between 1933 and 1936, the pioneering Russian animator Mikhail Tsekhanovsky and Dmitri Shostakovich worked together on a cartoon opera based on Pushkin's satirical poem, "The Tale of the Priest and His Servant, Balda." Unfortunately, the quality-minded Tsekhanovsky refused to use the shortcut of gelatins; this made the project drag on into the ominous mid-'30s in Russia, at which point both Shostakovich and Tsekhanovsky, finding themselves branded as "formalists," abandoned the project; the score, although bearing the opus number of 36, became one of Shostakovich's "unpublished manuscripts." A brief and very catchy suite was recorded several years back on Melodiya/Eurodisc. Now a Melodiya release from the Soviet Union (with Vladimir Pankratov, bass; Sergei Safenin, bass; Elena Unstinova, soprano; Vladimir Matusov, narrator; Chorus and Orchestra of the Maly Opera and Ballet Theatre of Leningrad conducted by Valentin Kozhin) makes available what appears to be a fairly complete version of this cartoon opera. The music is in the classic Shostakovich satirical mode, which is to say that it offers all sorts of set pieces—marches, waltzes, etc.—filled with wrong notes and instrumental grotesqueries highlighted by chamber-like scoring. Unlike Shostakovich's first opera, *The Nose*, however, the music contains few surprises (jolts, yes; surprises, no, at least not for those well acquainted with the composer's oeuvre) other than a few arias where the soloists sound as if they are singing under water (just how this effect is accomplished remains a mystery). One cannot help but wonder, of course, just what kind of depth Tsekhanovsky's apparently brilliant graphics would have added to Shostakovich's occasionally trivial fun-poking. Once again, we must live with the painful realization that a work of art that could have changed the course of a part of Soviet culture has been buried by the political Philistines. By the look of things, this is not likely to change: the Russian-language jacket notes by Shostakovich's official biographer, Sophia Khentova, contain not one mention either of Tsekhanovsky or of the cartoon-opera project, even though the English and French translations do. (Khentova also receives "libretto" credit, which, I suspect, means that she supplied the narration heard occasionally on this disc.) Shostakovich, on the other hand, inches ever closer to having his entire catalog of works represented on recordings.

After the splendid *Body Heat* and *The Big Chill*, director Lawrence Kasdan has returned, in **Silverado**, with the infinitely better of this past summer's two big Westerns, the other being Clint Eastwood's *Pale Rider*. Much of *Silverado*'s success belongs to its screenplay, coauthored by Kasdan and his brother Mark, which creates a heroic quartet out of four totally contrasting characters and then surrounds them with peripheral characters that are even more off-the-wall. The film is likewise helped by the acting and casting. In the latter category, Kasdan somehow even makes the outrageous choice of Monty Pythoner John Cleese as a local sheriff blend in—or skillfully not blend in—with the crazyquilt blend of personae. Interestingly, the expansive, symphonic score by Bruce Broughton (Geffen LP), whose name is unfamiliar to me, is, along with the evil-cattle-baron-versus-innocent-settlers plot, one of the most conventional things about *Silverado*. This is not to badmouth the music, which frequently comes off as a hybrid offspring sired by Aaron Copland and John Williams. The initial, "open spaces" march, which provides a lot of the score's thematic impetus, crackles with an excitement that is generated at least as much by Broughton's conducting and by the beautiful recorded sound, for which Broughton as album producer is also at least partially responsible. Beyond the march, *Silverado*'s various cues provide the requisite amount of suspense, whether in the subtly orchestrated quiet passages or in the big, full-orchestra dissonances. What it lacks is the de rigueur love theme, for the simple reason that *Silverado* has little in the line of a de rigueur love interest. Fans of the big-sound, symphonic film score that takes itself seriously should love this album.

The way I see it, **Cocoon** is perhaps the most dangerous film of the halfway-finished decade. Oh, it starts off innocently enough, with a group of old-folks-home residents finding a fountain of youth in the swimming pool where local aliens store their pods (what else?). But by the time the aliens offer to take the old folks off this planet so that they can become immortal, *Cocoon* becomes the most thinly veiled yet in a series of films (*Close Encounters of the Third Kind, E. T., Starman*, etc.) that are transferring the Christian mythology of salvation to outer space. And so, while sucker critics like Gene Shallit wet their pants over *Cocoon*'s niceness, the movie is subliminally laying down, for millions of viewers, the message that lovable aliens are at hand to wash away our sins and save us from the stress and strife of the here and now, not to mention our mortality. Particularly indicative in *Cocoon* is that the one old man (Jack Gilford) who does not buy into the aliens' offer of eternal life is the film's one obvious Jew. As for *Cocoon*'s final sermon for the "dead," some may see this as ironic; what is really ironic, however, is that the sermon explains the film. Jerry Falwell and company must be licking their chops in glee. I fully expect director Ron Howard's next film to start off with a beautiful, backlit shot of a hydrogen bomb.

James Horner's score for *Cocoon* (Polydor LP), which definitely bears the stamp of Horner's creative profile, is a perfect example of what might be referred to as "back-lit" music: even in its most dramatic moments, it shimmers and glows with an impressionist aura of tremolos, open-fifth motifs, and broad string themes that perfectly suit the film's fundamentalist, fairytale escapism (having now seen *Cocoon* a second time and, on video tape, Ron Howard's previous film *Splash*, which preaches the same message on a schmuckier level, I find myself even more depressed by what the film represents). Horner's music also offers large globs of Tinkerbell-is-dying poignancy, whether in "Rose's Death" or "Return to the Sea." Particularly ear opening is the fox-trot that accompanies the aged heroes' early excursions to the pool-house; but unless I am quite mistaken, this did not make it to the disc, whose only fox trot, the more raucous "The Boys Are Out," is used for a dance-hall sequence, if I remember correctly. Michael Sembello's so-called "hit single," "Gravity," which pollutes the beginning of the album's second side, is the worst piece of synthesizer-pop garbage I think I have ever heard. The out-of-filmic-order arrangement of the cues on this disc is, I feel, a large mistake.

Jerry Fielding: **The Wild Bunch** (Varèse-Sarabande). Lest you be fooled by the warm, nostalgic "Song from *The Wild Bunch*," the instrumental cue that (mistakenly, in my opinion) opens this superb reissue, listen to the ominous, quintessentially Fielding quasi-march in 11/8 that accompanies director Sam Peckinpah's brilliantly serialized sight/sound/music montage in the title sequence, some of the most striking footage in all of cinema. (And lest there be any doubt as to Peckinpah's sympathies, note how his name comes on the screen in a black-and-white frame that freezes William Holden's snarled "Kill' em!") Throughout the film, the late composer's rhythmically offbeat, harmonically acerbic backdrops complement Peckinpah's savage and yet strangely human vision with such sensitivity to the filmic language that one can only regret that this composer/director collaboration did not bear more fruit.

CHAPTER THREE

～

1986

January/February

Richard (*Eye of the Needle*) Marquand's **Jagged Edge** is about as classy a suspense thriller as they're making these days. Granted, *Jagged Edge* has little of the visual flair or the deep, psychological complexity one finds in Hitchcock; and, granted, anyone who understands the musical principle of inversion should have little trouble in figuring out the film's central enigma. But, as in Hitchcock, the real import of *Jagged Edge* lies not in the unraveling but in getting there. And the film features a truly top-notch score by John Barry (Varèse Sarabande LP), a mostly synthesizer affair in the midst of which a non-synthesized (I hope) piano plays a key role, most notably in foregrounding the main theme, aptly described by director Marquand as "one of the sweetest, simplest tunes you will ever hear" (a non-synthesized flute also takes over for the piano from time to time). But a nicely timed blues note gives this "sweet" theme a bit of a kick just when you think it is going to become maybe just a bit syrupy. I listened to this disc about an hour before I went to see the film, and I must say that the predominance of doom and gloom that I took with me into the theater did not quite match the impression left by the film and its music. In spite of their masking by the synthesizer timbres, typical John Barry suspense chords abound in the midst of spacey sostenutos that would not be out of place in a sci-fi film. Nonetheless, the music, when spread out over the entire film, works well, and it has been recorded with very broad, thumpy—and rather hissy—sound.

Nonesuch has released Philip Glass' music for Paul Schrader's **Mishima** (Michael Riesman, cond.), a mosaic biography of the Japanese author that alternates between the present—the author's suicidal, paramilitary last act—the past, and breathtakingly stylized recreations of passages from several of his books. The music is immediately recognizable as Glass—indeed, the opening cue quickly sent my emotions back to what is ultimately a much more interesting Glass score, namely *Koyaanisquatsi*. Strings, including several quartet cues performed by the Kronos Quartet, carry the brunt of *Mishima's* instrumental chores, with the harp also being deployed to great effect. But some rather non-Glassish instruments—electric guitar, snare drum, and timpani—also add to the effect. In fact, the timpani, much more prominent in the music-track mix than on this disc, nicely create the "militaricity" called for in the film while amazingly never departing from the confines of Glass' well defined idiom. If listening to Glass' score on disc begins to grate after a while, this is definitely not the case in the film, where the combination of narrative-within-narrative, set design, and Glass' strange mélange of Western harmonies and Eastern motivic obsessiveness creates a unique aesthetic universe. Incidentally, the synthesizer proved to be useful as a tool rather than as an end in this composer/director collaboration. As Schrader points out in his brief but fascinating note insert, Glass early on provided the director with a synthesizer version of the score, working only from the screenplay. As Schrader writes, "I edited the film to this temp score, altering it as necessary: cutting, expanding and repeating cues. I then played the edited film and score for Philip. He rewrote the music to fit the film's now-precise specifications and recorded it with a full orchestra."

One of the most beautiful film scores ever penned—Franz Waxman's **Hemingway's Adventures of a Young Man**—has now been reissued, this time on a Label X CD. Waxman had the misfortune throughout his prolific career of being assigned to an overwhelming number of mediocre films, a category that certainly suits Martin Ritt's *Hemingway's Adventures*, in spite of the occasional poignancy of the Hemingway narratives, an offbeat appearance by Paul Newman, and a fair amount of picture-postcard photography. That Waxman could produce music of the quality heard in this film is a testimony to the thorough artistic conscience of this neglected musician. It is hard to know where to start in singling out the noteworthy passages from *Hemingway's Adventures*. The opening piccolo/celesta motif, associated with the visual motif of a hawk in flight, remains one of Waxman's most endearing creations, as does the ensuing main theme, a nostalgically autumnal melody that can bring on tears even with no narrative associations. The sweeping love theme for the hero's ill-fated, Italian mistress is only slightly less moving. The score also offers its share of the droll, the weird (a hair-raisingly off-key piano, performed by John Williams, in the "D.T. Blues" cue definitely sets one's teeth to itching), and the exciting, as in "The Major's Rescue," with its breathtaking string chases.

I confess to no small fondness for the Wang Chung score for William Friedkin's grim, ugly, and exhausting **To Live and Die in L.A.** (Geffen LP). Mind you, my younger son threatened me with unspeakable harm if I did not say kind things about this album. And, mind you, I had thought that Wang Chung was a single, oriental musician rather than the *nom de groupe* of two occidental (and very British-sounding) gentlemen, Jack Hues and Nick Feldman. Side 1 of the disc is devoted to four very gutsy vocals, by far the best of which is "Wait," whose surreal instrumental context and explosive vocals (done in unison by the two Wang Chungers) perfectly express the character of Friedkin's snarling film, whose sexism would be offensive were its male characters not all, whether "good guy" or "bad guy," such thorough scoundrels.

Side 2 contains all-instrumental cues, some of which are little more than the simplest of bass lines set to a frenetic rhythmic pace. Once again, however, the very primitiveness of the sounds creates just the right ambience for the movie. More subtle instrumentals also pop up—in "The Red Stare," for instance, a digitally processed piano sounds solo notes against a solo cello and then against various other string groupings. There are even touches of an almost *Liquid Sky*-ish punkism here and there.

March/April

A film I meant to see in the theater but missed is John Boorman's **The Emerald Forest**, which I finally caught up with on videotape. Although Boorman's stunning visuals really need to be seen via a 35-millimeter print in the proper aspect ratio, Embassy's prerecorded cassette does substantial justice to the film. Boorman remains an eloquent spokesperson for the '60s counterculture. Of late, however, his eloquence has tended to be expressed almost totally in visual terms, with such niceties as acting (as witness *Excalibur* and, now, *The Emerald Forest*) going somewhat by the boards. In fact, once you get over being dazzled by *The Emerald Forest*'s cinematography, its music, its immensely sympathetic Amazonian natives (the "Invisible People"), and a surprisingly deep characterization by Boorman's son, Charley, you realize that there's some pretty flimsy material at work. But that's a lot of dazzlement, and no small amount of it comes from the score mostly devised by Brazilian percussionist Junior Homrich, which has been gorgeously recorded by Varèse Sarabande. The score opens with some deeply atmospheric, sostenuto synthesizer sounds complemented by a vocalizing soprano who seems to be the voice of the jungle (Brian Gascoigne co-composed the Main Title and many of the other cues, for which he performs on synthesizer and marimba). But much of the score is made up of a brilliant, multilayered array of diverse percussion sounds (including some produced by the composer pounding on various parts of his own body), native flutes, chants, whispers, pants, etc., sensitively put together by Homrich to add a dimension to the film that can probably only be truly appreciated in a theater with a good sound system.

I missed (or avoided, I forget which) Stuart Gordon's **Re-Animator**, and it has yet to appear on videotape. But Richard Band's score, released by Varèse Sarabande on an album I am informed is selling much better than expected, is too juicy to save for later. In addition to the expected, very dissonant and quite hair-raising horror-suspense sounds that Band has scored both for large symphony orchestra (the Rome Philharmonic performs here) and for synthesizer, the composer has unabashedly raided parts of Bernard Herrmann's score for *Psycho*—not just the violin shrieks, which everybody from Brian De Palma to god-knows-who has snuck onto the horror-film soundtrack, but large sections of the Prelude. Oh, there's a near-disco beat here and there and some shifty modulations to throw Herrmann a bit off center. But whole blocks of the *Psycho* prelude pop up throughout the score with a literalness that puts the little *North by Northwest* pastiche in *Moscow on the Hudson* to shame, and one wonders whether Herrmann's estate is getting any royalties for this. In addition, however, I very much like the ways that Band once in a while carries his Herrmann inspirations into new domains. Further, in the non-Herrmannesque parts of the score, his quieter cues carry quite a bit more than the requisite atmosphere. P.S. Don't look at the back cover if you have a weak stomach.

May/June

A rarity: all five of the nominated scores for the 1986 Oscars—Georges Delerue's *Agnes of God*, Maurice Jarre's *Witness*, Bruce Boughton's *Silverado*, Quincy Jones' *The Color Purple*, and John Barry's *Out of Africa*—represent decent choices, and all have been recorded. My personal choice of these would be the Boughton score, but I had figured until recently that John Barry was probably a shoo-in for *Out of Africa*. But given the exposure Quincy Jones had on the Grammy award show, and given the two-disc album devoted to *The Color Purple*'s music, my bet now goes over to the latter. But more on that in a minute. **Out of Africa** proved to be one of the more pleasant surprises of my recent movie going. To begin with, it is the first Meryl Streep film I have seen in which I was not constantly aware of the actress acting. More importantly, under Sidney Pollack's sensitive direction, this look at part of the life and experiences of Danish writer Isak Dinesen does not just tell a story but creates a warm aura of storytelling. Indeed, one of the most moving moments in the film occurs when John Barry's cue, "Have You Got a Story for Me?" comes in beneath Streep's voice as she begins to spin one of her tales for her male interlocutors. Elsewhere, Barry's efforts, which have been digitally recorded in less than great sound by MCA, struck me as slightly weak for the filmic context. As heard on this disc, the minor-to-major themes, the unison bass figures beneath high string motives, and the rich suspense-chords all manifest the Barry style that we have come to know and love. But the film could have used music with a bit more bite and introspection. The album also contains the traditional African "Siyawe" and part of the second movement of Mozart's Clarinet Concerto (with Jack Brymer, clarinet, and Neville Marriner conducting), which for the film (but not the album) had to be considerably de-hi-fied to sound as if it were coming from an old, windup 78 phonograph.

As for **The Color Purple**, much critical venom has been spewed over the fact that, although *Purple* received a nomination for best picture, Stephen Spielberg was overlooked for best director (the Director's Guild has just partially, and ludicrously, made up for that lapse; but then, Ron Howard was nominated by the Guild for *Cocoon*, so what can you expect?). Well, maybe when Spielberg learns that goo is not synonymous with emotion, he might be able to be taken seriously as a creative artist, although god knows the Academy has never shown a great penchant for basing its choices on artistic quality. But (as one example), when Spielberg repeats ad nauseum the little hand-clapping game between *Purple*'s two sisters, when one presentation of it would have generated ample poignancy, then one can suppose that *The Color Purple*'s (absurd) nomination as best picture had to do with something other than directorial finesse. Moving right along with the Spielberg philosophy that nothing succeeds like excess, Qwest Records has released an album containing two purple-vinyl LPs of close to 80 minutes' worth of the Quincy Jones score, for which close to 200 musicians had to be mobilized, including at least one highly recognizable name, that of Hubert Laws on various flutes (and can that be the vocalist Sue Raney on bass?). If ever there was a mixed-bag affair, this is it. Everything from '20s jazz, gospel music, and native African sounds to a modern romantic background score definitely evoking the '70s and '80s (Georges Delerue, John Williams, and Michael Gore à la *Terms of Endearment* all come variously to mind) make their way into the film's many cues. Probably the most captivating single number in the entire score is the song "Sister," which was nominated for an Oscar and which is solidly belted out by Tata Vega. The sound quality is quite present and full-bodied, save for some crusty old 78 transfers.

Two scores that should have been nominated but weren't are Toru Takemitsu's *Ran* and David Shire's **Return to Oz**. Many months after the latter's release, Sonic Atmospheres (London Symphony Orchestra) has finally released an album devoted to the music for that marvelous fantasy. *Return to Oz* may be one of the most misunderstood films of this generation. While I have nothing but the deepest love for the original *Wizard of Oz* with Judy Garland, Ray Bolger, Bert Lahr, et al., it is totally unfair to measure *Return to Oz*, which tried (and to my mind succeeded) to be something quite different, against it. *Return to Oz* has remained faithful to the surreal iconography of the Frank L. Baum books (several of which supplied the material for *Return*), which are much more complex and frightening than the somewhat smoothed-over images of *Wizard* would lead one to believe. Of course, several critics expressed reservations over just how frightening parts of *Return* are; but these are probably the same people who want to see Warner Bros. cartoons censored for their "violence." Much of David Shire's music has both magic (good and evil) and poignancy. The opening strings, for instance, cannot help but elicit a tear or two. And if Shire briefly lapses into a moment of pure Copland, it suits the Americana mood every bit as well as the film's visual settings. Shire also creates some wonderful creepiness in the synthesized "Dorothy and the Gnome King," while he also gets a lot of thematic mileage from a very catchy "Rag March." Shire's music not only does everything a film score should do for its movie, it also stands up particularly well on recording.

Of course, well before the movies ever had a sound or music track, full scores were being composed for diverse forces including, sometimes, full orchestra, to accompany silent films. Apparently the first major composer to try his hand at such an endeavor was Charles-Camille Saint-Saëns, who, in 1908, scored a Prelude and Five Tableaux for orchestra (including piano and harmonium) to accompany *L'Assassinat du Duc de Guise*, a production of the Film d'Art group, who engaged Académie Française member Henri Lavedan for the screenplay and various members of the Comédie Française troupe to act in and direct it. The music has finally reached LP in the form of a Russian recording of *French Film Music* (Melodiya, C10 20459 009, with the USSR Ministry of Culture Orchestra conducted by Gennady Rozhdestvensky, and with Rozhdestvensky and Victoria Postnikova, piano duet). The Saint-Saëns score, while

not wholly identifiable with the style of the composer's major efforts, is quite fascinating. It starts out somewhere between ballet and what might be termed opera without voice. But toward the end, when the filmic action apparently gets quite dramatic,
the music takes on a quite characteristic film-music quality, with the harmonium
adding an appropriate funereal aura following what I presume is the assassination sequence. The album also contains three all-too-brief selections from the music Arthur
Honegger penned for the Abel Gance Napoléon. Whether in the slightly askew in-
genuousness of the "Children's Dance," the fanfarish pomp of "Napoléon," or the autumnal cyclism of the "Empress's Chaconne," one is made aware of just how barbarous
was Francis Ford Coppola's decision to turn to his daddy rather than to work with the
extant Honegger materials in the recent Napoléon reissue. A quite different Napoléon,
directed in 1954 by Sacha Guitry, is represented here by Jean Françaix's fluffy, occasionally Les-Six-ish music for piano duet, which gets the best recorded sound on the
album. The closing work comes from Darius Milhaud. Entitled Actualités (Newsreel)
and assigned the composer's opus 104, this brief, six-movement suite for chamber orchestra is taken from music the French composer scored for silent newsreels. Much of
it is heady stuff indeed: Milhaud does not flinch at displaying his dissonant, often
polytonal harmonic style and his ear-opening instrumental textures, so that the music here rises to a somewhat unexpected level of sophistication.

  If I read one more write-up on Michael Cimino that damns him because of the
Heaven's Gate disaster, I will begin to offer my film students more than an A+ for the
heads of certain critics. The fact that lots of money was spent on a film that left
many moviegoers and critics cold is no proof that Cimino is history's evilest stalker
of studios. Having seen both the cut version and the restored version of Heaven's
Gate, I am fairly convinced that the film, in spite of or perhaps because of its narrative diffuseness, will come to be considered at least a minor masterpiece. And now
Cimino's **Year of the Dragon** has been jumped on by some as racist, even though it
does not come close to damning the Chinese people as a whole but rather portrays,
within the mythology of countless gangster pictures, the existence of an ethnically
centered gang which, by the way, is pursued in the film by a cop (Mickey Rourke) of
Polish origin who is depicted as a total yahoo. The problems with Year of the Dragon,
which a few critics have touted as marking a new beginning for Cimino, have to do
with the kinds of excesses that, when spread out over the length of a Heaven's Gate
(a much better film, in my opinion), seem much less self-indulgent. David Mansfield's score for Year of the Dragon (Varèse Sarabande) has a little bit of everything,
from all-synthesizer cues, with their de rigueur low unisons, to an all-string cue ("Tai
Tries to Bribe Stan"), with full orchestra prevailing elsewhere. Mansfield happily
avoids the pseudo-oriental clichés one might expect from a score for such a film. Instead, two pieces of hideously sung, Chinese muzak, composed respectively by Yao
Ming and Hwang He, and an intriguing "Main Title" by Lucia Hwong, which uses
some kind of Chinese stringed instrument for the cue's ostinato figure and which I
found to be the most interesting cut on the disc, provide the music track with its required dose of Sinicism.

July/August

One wonders whether Ridley Scott will ever regain the pinnacles he attained in *The Duellists* and *Alien*. *Blade Runner*, while not without visual merit, takes its innocuous narrative too seriously. But *Blade Runner* has masterpiece stature compared to Scott's latest endeavor, **Legend**, the latest in a spate of self-conscious cinematic fairy tales being churned out by the film industry over the past half-dozen years or so. *Legend* first of all makes the mistake of presuming such familiarity with fairytale archetypes on the part of the audience that it simply plunks down its characters and situations and relies on assorted forms of visual and sonic goo to put them across. Unfortunately, it takes more than backlighting ad nauseum and bubble machines to sustain a spineless film on visuals alone. Scott shows more imagination in one of his surrealistic, 30-second Chanel No. 5 commercials than he does in all of *Legend*. About the only thing that redeems the film is a gruesomely evil performance by Tim (*Rocky Horror Picture Show*) Curry as the prince of darkness (or whatever he's supposed to be) who, as J. Hoberman pointed out in a wickedly trenchant *Village Voice* review I wish I had written, actually transforms the virginal heroine into a *Rocky Horror* queen complete with black fingernails and all the trimmings.

Ah, but there is an interesting footnote to all this. *Legend's* producers at Universal, a company never noted for its artistic altruism, despaired over the film's commercial potential and, as producers will do, tried to figure out a way to rework *Legend* into a marketable entity. The only gimmick they could come up with, however, was to replace the score composed by Jerry Goldsmith (and heard, I believe, on European prints of *Legend*) with new music by Tangerine Dream under the presumption, one supposes, that MCA could at least sell more albums that way. As it happens, both scores are available on LP: *Tangerine Dream's* can be heard on an MCA release, while Goldsmith's must be hunted down on an esoteric English import on the Moment label. I would like to be able to scream at MCA's capitalists, stick with the traditionalists, and say that an unspeakable crime was committed when Goldsmith's score was thrown out. But Goldsmith, rarely rising above the material (for which he cannot be blamed), spends most of his time doodling with orchestra, synthesizer, and vocalizing chorus in a lot of near Ravel forest murmurs—this, when he is not setting lyrics to songs that would spell instant death for any diabetic. And his saccharine themes certainly have no more emotional depth than the bubbles and tinsel that help give *Legend* the look of a set for a Mantovani concert. Goldsmith also has the distressing habit of indulging in near-quotations that send the mind and memory wandering off into other musical spaces. One of the principal themes flirts ever so dangerously with (ugh) "The Impossible Dream," while another tune, used principally in a kind of pseudo madrigal, evokes a Poulenc *Mouvement perpétuel* (the one also used in Hitchcock's *Rope*). And there is a chord progression that has me racking my brain (and my record collection) in search of the non-film-music work it comes from.

The Tangerine Dream score, while created wholly by synthesizers, has a more primitive quality to it that probably suits the film better than Goldsmith's (I have seen only the Tangerine Dream version). The otherworldly quality of the processed voices and of various sustained timbres fits decently enough into Scott's fantasy vision, and Tangerine Dream also seems to have its finger much more solidly on the pulse of the film's evil, by far its most interesting quality (the cover artists for both albums would seem to agree with this). On the other hand, I worry greatly over the song "Loved by the Sun," performed by Yes's Jon Anderson, which includes the following lyrics: "Legends can be now and forever, teaching us to love [later 'reach'] for goodness' sake," thus adding rather ominous Sunday-school overtones to Tangerine Dream's gooey, apotheosis harmonies. The album also contains a non–Tangerine Dream song, "Is Your Love Strong Enough?" which likewise has all the impact of a fundamentalist sermon when it appears in the film.

Alan Rudolph continues to be one of the most original voices in American cinema. Unlike Ridley Scott (yes, I know he's British), Rudolph does not simply depend on pretty photography (although this abounds in his films as well) to make his artistic statement—he involves his characters in ambiguous narratives (of which he is the creator) that generally unfurl in urban dreamscapes, whether the fanciful Los Angeles of *Welcome to L.A.* or the otherworldly, non-specific sets (which themselves are mirrored in an architectural model built by the film's principal character) of his most recent film, **Trouble in Mind**, which moves back and forth between artificiality and "reality" in a way that recalls Francis Ford Coppola's much underrated *One From the Heart*, but with a much more interesting narrative structure. With all this in mind, it is not surprising that Rudolph turned to a composer such as Mark Isham for the musical score (Island). True to form, Isham has come up with his patented assortment of sustained, synthesizer unravelings that, here, seem an almost uncanny musical equivalent of Rudolph's nocturnal fantasies. Particularly moving, however, is the way in which Isham weaves various bluesy, acoustic solos—in particular a trumpet (often muted) and saxophone—into the "electronics" he has so skillfully concocted. More disturbing is the presence of Marianne Faithful, who, with a wonderful and, yes, dreamy style but also with a rather grating whiskey baritone, performs the score's several vocals, including the particularly haunting "The Hawk (El Gavilan)," which, although it fits the overall musical profile to a T, was composed by one of the film's stars, Kris Kristofferson. This album is strongly recommended even for those who have not seen the film.

September/October

In the midst of all this year's July 4/Statue of Liberty hype that was so excessive it caused me to flee New York City well before the gooey festivities reached their jingoistic peak, an interesting, Americana memento arrived in the mail. This was Label X's two-disc set of music composed, arranged, and adapted by Joseph Carl Breil for the 1915 New York City premiere of D. W. Griffith's epic, pioneering, and thoroughly racist silent classic, **The Birth of a Nation** (New Zealand Symphony Orchestra, Clyde Allen, cond.). For the spectacle, which included a full orchestra, chorus, and ushers wearing Civil War uniforms, the Pittsburgh-born Breil (1870–1926) followed the standard practice of the day by raiding, for many of the film's "cues," diverse classics, from Bellini's Overture for *Norma* to Wagner's "Ride of the Valkyries," not to mention any number of folk songs, anthems, marches, etc. In addition to all this, however, Breil composed enough original music, which is mainly what this album documents, for conductor Clyde Allen, in his extensive and brilliantly researched liner insert, to offer Breil as "the first American to create an orchestral score for a feature film which mixed so much composition in among the compilation." But Breil was no Saint-Saëns or Shostakovich, both of whom also wrote orchestral scores for silent films, and none of the music here, which ranges in style from Schubert-cum-von Suppe to ersatz Stephen Foster, has much to recommend it beyond its obvious historical value. I personally would have found the album more rewarding had it offered a more accurate picture of the overall score by mixing in more of the compilation cues with the original ones. As I was listening to the end of the album, for instance, one of my son's friends walked in and stood in amazement, wondering what kind of weird album I was auditioning that would jump from "The Ride of the Valkyries" to "Dixie" without batting an eyelash. I mean, this kind of thing is a whole education in and of itself. Nonetheless, it is good to hear just what went into this groundbreaking score, and what prompted one critic of the time to describe the "Love Strain" (later retitled "The Perfect Song" and even later used as the theme for the Amos and Andy radio show) as "one of the most beautiful love themes ever invented" (it isn't). Conductor Allen's 45-piece forces would seem to duplicate, in both size and lack of finesse, the orchestral efforts from that 1915 premiere.

In a totally different vein, the music for one of 1985's two or three truly outstanding films, **Ran**, Akira Kurosawa's Japanese mélange of *King Lear* and *Macbeth*, has finally reached me via a Fantasy release (Hiroyuki Koinuma, Japanese flute; Sapporo Symphony Orchestra, Kiroyuki Iwaki, cond.). Written by one of Japan's best-known "classical" composers, Toru Takemitsu, the *Ran* score is filled with the kind of gloom and open-spacedness that pervade both Kurosawa's directorial vision and Takao Saito's absolutely stunning cinematography. Although the orchestral forces are Western, as are many of the chordal patterns and the John Williams-ish mood-sounds deployed by Takemitsu, the music rises infinitely above the silly westernisms of a score such as the one penned by Takashi Matsuyama for Kurosawa's much earlier *Rashomon*. Not only do the extended passages of solo Japanese flute add a strong aura of authenticity to the *Ran* music, the overall textures as well, even though inspired by the devices of contemporary western music, strongly evoke the visual openness of Japanese prints. But why, one wonders, did Takemitsu suddenly turn to the second movement of Mahler's First Symphony for a moment's inspiration?

Bill Conti's quite lovely and original score for Robert Mandel's **F/X** (Varèse Sarabande) has me more convinced than ever that suspense, crime, and horror films often engender much more interesting music than the likes of *The Right Stuff. F/X* is one of a growing number of films in which the Hollywood industry is turning in toward its own devices—in this case special effects (whence the trade slang "F/X")—to support its flimsy narratives. I haven't seen a film since *The Stunt Man* in which this works quite as well as *F/X*, where the viewer never is fully sure as to whether he/she is watching a mere illusion or an illusion within an illusion. I must confess, though, to a growing weariness over the eternally stupid, nasty, and inept CIA-type heavies that proliferate in films such as this. Conti's score, unlike his efforts for *The Right Stuff* and *North and South*, gets much of its mileage from lightness of touch and genuine creativity. The composer mobilizes both piano and harp, for instance, in order to create a number of musical subtleties (some of them quasi-oriental), including those in a cue entitled "Rollie's Diversion," in which piano and harp provide chordal accompaniment for a theme played on a (second?) harp quasi-guitar. Another cue features nothing but percussion. There are also the requisite calm-after-bloodbath, chase, and suspense pieces, all of them, however, much more effective and affective than the norm, thanks to Conti's deft scoring and his skillful use of diverse ostinato figures. I also much prefer the meatier, non-digital sonics of this album to the sound on *The Right Stuff/North and South*. *F/X* is definitely one of the best scores of the year so far.

Two CD reissues are definite highlights for this column. The first of these, **Sunset Boulevard, The Classic Film Scores of Franz Waxman** (RCA Red Seal), is not exactly a reissue. Not only does it contain the music from the all-Waxman *Sunset Boulevard* album originally issued in RCA's "Classic Film Scores" series, it also includes the Waxman music from the Bette Davis, Humphrey Bogart, and Errol Flynn albums, plus the *Peyton Place* theme from a potpourri disc that originated in England, all of this adding up to almost 70 minutes of music. What characterizes the best Waxman music on this release—and, certainly, many of the composer's major efforts are represented here, including *Prince Valiant, Peyton Place, A Place in the Sun, The Bride of Frankenstein, To Have and to Have Not, Sunset Boulevard, Mr. Skeffington, Objective, Burma!, Rebecca, The Philadelphia Story, Old Acquaintances, The Two Mrs. Carrolls*, and *Taras Bulba*—is a brand of musico-emotional intensity that is certainly seconded by the thoroughly impassioned performances by Charles Gerhardt and the National Philharmonic Orchestra. I have, elsewhere, compared this intensity to that which often pervades the music of Shostakovich. Nowhere is this more evident than in the "chase fugue" from the 1951 *A Place in the Sun*: the music here spookily foreshadows by some six years the string fugue one hears at the end of the second movement of Shostakovich's 1957 11th Symphony, even though it is all but impossible for Shostakovich to have known Waxman's music at the time he composed his 11th. But Waxman was able to apply this intensity to all sorts of idioms, as witness the Gershwinesque yet ominous overture to *Sunset Boulevard* or the absolutely devastating habañera from that same film. Waxman was also a master of moods, particularly the darker-hued and weirder ones, such as in *The Bride of Frankenstein* or *Rebecca*, where electric instruments add their own ghoulishness to Waxman's chromatic themes and harmonies. Even when courting irretrievable corniness, as he does in scores such as *Prince Valiant* and *Taras Bulba*, Waxman shows an élan that carries the listener past the desire to carp too strongly. One might carp a bit more, though, over the eternal predilection of those responsible for the "Classic Film Scores" releases to offer brief excerpts rather than substantial segments of major scores such as *The Bride of*

Frankenstein. On the other hand, the music here reveals so many dazzling facets that one would be loath to part with at least most of them. The recorded sound on the Classic Film Scores albums has always stood as a state-of-the-art prototype of sorts, and this CD transfer simply enhances the clarity and presence of sonics that were hard to beat to begin with, although the added edge of hardness on the CD that slightly cuts into the warmth of the LP sound could certainly serve as ammo for CD detractors. To my ears, the pluses here outweigh the minuses.

The sonics for the original music-track recording of Jerry Goldsmith's **The Blue Max** were always rather shrill and tubby, whether on the initial release or on the Citadel reissue. Varèse Sarabande's CD reissue, however, has been made from the original masters, which, as Len Engel tells it in the program booklet, were discovered in a 20th Century-Fox vault only two years ago. While the basic sound quality remains quite problematic, there is improvement here. There is also some 15 minutes' worth of additional music, some of it not heard in the film, not included on previous releases. Engel, who was responsible for the remixing, has also blended the two-part "Retreat" passacaglia into the stunning, single cue it was intended to be. The score itself is, quite simply, one of the finest, most expansive pieces of film music ever penned. Although broadly symphonic in scope, *The Blue Max* often acts more like a monothematic score, with the soaring violin theme heard at the outset dominating many of the cues. Yet there is so much variety in the way this theme is treated, and so much exciting scoring that does not depend on an established theme, that one often has the impression of a massively developed symphony. Goldsmith's style here presents a strange but effective mélange of American energy and a more English sense of instrumentation and harmony—the Benjamin Britten of *Peter Grimes* comes to mind more than once. Goldsmith also offers a tiny waltz that, in its brief appearance, manages to overwhelm the emotions. All in all, this is music that can be rewardingly listened to without any references to the film.

November/December

Question: Does the following equation—*2001/2010* ≅ *Alien/Aliens*—work? Answer: You betchum. In both cases the originals have a sense of purity to them that is lacking in the cluttered sequels, whether in the proliferation of slabs (*2010*) or of what *Time* magazine referred to as "ughy bugs" (*Aliens*). And if both *2001* and *Alien* generate much of their drama in areas other than acting, both *2010* (which features a particularly hideous performance by John Lithgow) and *Aliens* depend strongly at points on some pretty heavy scenery chewing. Cutely, however, there is also a crossover in this equation as James Horner's "Main Title" music for **Aliens** (Varèse Sarabande; London Symphony Orchestra), whose initial figure in high, unison violins ever so strongly evokes the opening of Shostakovich's 14th Symphony, suddenly moves into the Adagio from Khachaturian's *Gayne* ballet used by Stanley Kubrick in one of the early outer-space sequences in *2001* (the Shostakovich and Khachaturian material also reappears later in the score). The "Main Title" and parts of other cues as well also seem to allude to one of the principal motifs in the Jerry Goldsmith score for the original *Alien* (a rather Sibelian figure in the winds in parallel thirds and fourths over a low unison). And a substantial bit of Mahler pops in towards the end. As for the rest of the music in Horner's score, much of it is sotto voce, creepy-crawly stuff, with wispy figures constantly repeated, whether by the instruments or by an echo effect. In the midst of all this unsettling quiescence, the by-now-familiar fortissimo, high-string clusters suddenly jump out at the listener just as the monsters do. The *Aliens* score also has the requisite amount of action music, some of it rather militaristic in keeping with the World War II-Marines-type characters director James Cameron rather strangely injected into the filmic action. All in all, Horner's music, which has been recorded in rather thin, bodiless sound, struck me, for all of its flourishes and ultra-modernistic outbursts, as a bit old hat. Anyone for a bit of interpretation? In certain ways, the *Alien/Aliens* complex, which works much better than the *2001/2010* pairing, with *2010*'s goody-two-shoes reversal of *2001*'s patterns of good and evil, can be seen as the supreme battle of the sexes, with the woman, who takes over the traditional male hero role in both pictures, wreaking her vengeance on the male species for all of her sufferings, most notably child bearing (the monster in *Alien*, after all, springs from the tummy of a male). By the end of *Aliens*, the traditional family unit is restored, but with the female dominant and having acquired a little girl via heroism rather than via childbirth.

There are scores that one can listen to time and time again and each time get swept away by the sheer beauty of the individual figures. One such score is Bernard Herrmann's apparent personal favorite among the film scores he composed, his music for Joseph L. Mankiewicz's 1947 **The Ghost and Mrs. Muir**, which Varèse Sarabande has just reissued from the Elmer Bernstein Filmmusic Collection on a sumptuous CD conducted by Elmer Bernstein, with sonics that are actually warmer than those on the original LP and that manifest an absolutely stunning clarity and richness of tone. Even in this, perhaps Herrmann's most hauntingly lyrical score, one becomes quickly aware that the composer is not working with the long thematic lines that one might expect from such a score; rather, *The Ghost and Mrs. Muir*, like just about all of Herrmann's film music, is constructed from small cells that are more important as conveyors of harmonically generated affect than as recognizable themes or motifs. Herrmann's ever-varied and subtle instrumental colorations also come to the foreground in this exquisite recording, whether in the harp/string combinations or in the composer's characteristically lugubrious woodwinds. Elmer Bernstein and his forces have done a splendid job in putting together some three-quarters of the film's 42 cues in a soulful performance that captures every bit of the music's—and the film's—romance, mystery, humor, and sadness.

An even more "classic" release from Varèse Sarabande, in mono sound, is the original music track, believe it or not, of Aaron Copland's score for Lewis Milestone's 1949 **The Red Pony**, transferred from 78-rpm disc masters that were made during the 1948 recording session, with the composer conducting, but never intended for release. Little need be written about the quality of Copland's autumnally poignant music, which is known principally through the suite from the score arranged by the composer. Suffice it to say that all of Copland's qualities as a composer come through in this score, which not only musically translates the American spirit in both its most joyous and its saddest manifestations, it also adapts itself fascinatingly to the changing cinematic moods of *The Red Pony*. Only a recording of this nature can reveal just how well Copland accomplished the latter. Invaluable, too, are the parts of the score, such as the bizarre "Moth 'Round a Flame" (could Copland have taken a page from Miklós Rózsa's book, à la *The Lost Weekend*, here?), not heard in the concert suite, that reveal sides of Copland not usually heard. The transfer from 78s has been beautifully handled here, so that the sound, while a far cry from high fidelity, is nonetheless quite listenable. This release stands both as an invaluable document and as a profound musical experience not to be missed.

CHAPTER FOUR

~

1987

January/February

Two of 1986's outstanding films—David Lynch's *Blue Velvet* and David Cronenberg's *The Fly*—and one of its most highly touted—Francis Coppola's *Peggy Sue Got Married*—have generated music-track recordings, all of them from Varèse Sarabande. *Blue Velvet* is merely the most original and most unsettling film of 1986. In the film director Lynch presents a colorized, Southern-middle-class, suspense-film-plotted version of his cult classic, *Eraserhead*. Both films offer something resembling a negative afterimage of a male initiation rite, which in **Blue Velvet** also involves a kind of *Vertigo*-cum-adolescent-curiosity narrative and one of the nastiest heavies (played by Dennis Hopper) ever to snarlingly throw the old "f curse" about the screen. Lynch steadfastly keeps his viewers (and listeners) from "reading" Blue Velvet in any kind of conventional or even coherent way, as witness the wide divergence of critics' descriptions of key elements (the "attack" suffered by the father, the substance snorted by Dennis Hopper through an oxygen mask, the period—'50s or '80s?—in which the film is set, etc.). Every image, sound, and combination of same in *Blue Velvet*, including a "dark" heroine (Isabella Rossellini, daughter of Ingrid Bergman) who is supposed to be a nightclub singer and who can't carry a tune in a bucket, are suspect. And the plasticized humans, fauna, and flora that make up the "family portrait" of the film's denouement hardly inspire cheers for the hero's (Kyle MacLaughlin) triumphal rite de passage.

One of the first things that struck me when I saw *Blue Velvet* for the first time was the title theme by Angelo Badalamente, who, in spite of his very Italian mime, evokes, in the mostly-strings melancholy of the initial music, a rather Slavic or Nordic feeling that is certainly at odds—no doubt deliberately—with *Blue Velvet's* setting. The second cue, "Night Streets," goes even further in evoking Shostakovich, the second movement of whose 15th Symphony comes strongly to mind here. Very much in keeping with the film is the ominous sweetness of the title theme, which also turns up in a later cue in a haunting, serenade-for-strings arrangement. Also worth noting is a cue entitled "Going Down to Lincoln," which starts off with a kind of classical jazz and then moves into a dirge-like fugue, all of which is accompanied by sound effects edited in by Lynch himself. Also to be found on the Varèse Sarabande album (Film Symphony of Prague) is some of the film's source music, including Rossellini's fingernails-on-blackboard rendition of "Blue Velvet" and Roy Orbison's "In Dreams," outrageously pantomimed in the film by a creepily effete Dean Stockwell. On the film's soundtrack, and briefly on the album, one hears some of the bowels-of-the-earth effects that Lynch devised for the *Eraserhead* soundtrack. Lynch also contributed the lyrics to the song "Mysteries of Love" (sung by Julee Cruise), heard as the hero dances with the "light" heroine (Laura Dern), and also heard, without voice, during a visually stunning sequence in which a church at night looms in the background. If "Mysteries of Love" comes across as a bit gooey, the rest of the original cues by Badalamente contain some of the freshest sounds to grace a music track in some time. The album is strongly recommended.

A Brief Interview with Angelo Badalamente

The following is a fairly literal transcription (I couldn't find my tape recorder) of a phone conversation I had with Angelo Badalamente on November 12 after, I swear, I had written the above:

R.S.B.: Can you tell me something about your background and about previous films you have worked on?

A.B.: I did my undergraduate work in music at the Eastman School of Music in Rochester, where I specialized in piano, French horn and composition. Then I got my Masters from the Manhattan School of Music, all the time doing a lot of writing. Then I got involved in the music business, mostly the pop world, writing pop songs and doing a lot of arranging and orchestrating for the music business in general. I also did the film scores for *Law and Disorder* with Ernest Borgnine—it was directed by Ivan Passer—and for a 20th Century-Fox picture, *Gordon's War*. Believe it or not, I've written a full-book, Nashville-flavored musical called *My Kinda Country* that will open out of town and is slated for Broadway in Fall 1987. And now, I'm working on another feature film.

R.S.B.: How did you get involved in *Blue Velvet*?

A.B.: I got a call from the Di Laurentiis office. They wanted me to work with Isabella Rossellini on the vocals we used in the film for her. When I got down there, I met with David Lynch, and he asked me to write, with his lyrics, certain songs for the movie. "Mysteries of Love" was the most important vocal in the film. David wanted a feeling of something like a timeless chant—cosmic and all sorts of things like that. I had to go back to the drawing board several times on that one. Then David Lynch asked me, "Can you write me a main title theme which could be used throughout the film and which would be very classical in nature. Make it a very beautiful, sweeping kind of melody, but Russian in flavor à la Shostakovich, and at the same time make it threatening." I got on a plane going out to visit David on the coast and wrote the title theme—in E minor—during the flight. When I got there, I sat down at the piano, and he really adored it except for one note. I then went to Europe and recorded the score. A very interesting thing happened during the recording session. The first cellist came to me and said, in very broken English, "You know, you are really a combination of Prokofiev and Mascagni." When you're Italian, it's going to show up one way or the other!

R.S.B.: Did you change that note?

A.B.: Oh, yes. I had the opening part of the theme going from minor to major, and David wanted it darker. So I changed what was an F-major chord to an F-minor one and dropped an A-natural to an A-flat in the melody.

Had someone played Howard Shore's music for **The Fly** (Varèse Sarabande; London Philharmonic Orchestra) without revealing the film, I would have sworn it was for an outer-space adventure such as *Alien*, the music for which in fact is evoked at several points in Shore's score. In *The Fly*, director Cronenberg once again shows an uncanny and thoroughly disturbing talent for making audiences feel the invasion of the human body by alien forces that, although transcendent in their way, remain incompatible with human life as we "know" it. The visceral reaction Cronenberg is able to elicit by the simple visualization of the cutting of a large hair on the hero's back has more force than just about anything else in the cinema these days. Shore's music, which avoids the fly-buzz onomatopoeia in Paul Sawtell's score for the 1958 original, somehow seems a bit outsized for the film. Granted, some of the special effects in *The Fly* become quite gruesome, especially in comparison with the more understated, leave-it-mostly-to-the-imagination original. But Shore's very dissonant, full-symphony-orchestra assaults in many instances tend to over-interpret facets of Cronenberg's style that speak well enough for themselves. The music has its striking moments, but none so haunting as the elegiac cue that closes Shore's score for Cronenberg's earlier masterpiece, *Videodrome*.

March/April

Christopher Young's music for **A Nightmare on Elm Street 2: Freddie's Revenge** (Varese Sarabande; Paul Francis Witt, cond.), which I did not see (I finally caught the original *Nightmare* on cable), is, to my ears, a good deal more interesting to listen to than Charles Bernstein's score for the original, which seems to try and rival the film by splattering itself all over the listener. While Young's score contains the expected dissonant outbursts over sustained pedal points, the string glissandos, and the cluster-chords, it remains consistently more subdued and less chaotic than Bernstein's. The

otherworldly opening, for instance, sounds more as if it should have appeared on the
music track for a film such as *Alien*. Young also intersperses enough moments of tonality and solidly defined rhythms into the formless musical blobs and eruptions to re-
lieve the listener, which Bernstein does not do as well. And unless I am crazy, the call
of the humpback whale, which seems to be a popular sound these days, turns up in a
cue entitled "Threatening Angela." Both scores, by the way, have been reissued on a
single Varèse Sarabande CD, which does what more CDs should do by taking advantage of the format's extended recording time. Another Varèse Sarabande CD worth
noting is *The Best of The Twilight Zone, Volume II*, which brings together the Main and
End Titles by Bernard Herrmann; "Back There," by Jerry Goldsmith; "And When the
Sky Was Opened," by Leonard Rosenman; "The Passerby," by Fred Steiner; "The
Lonely" by Bernard Herrmann; and "Two" by Nathan van Cleave, all culled from
Varèse Sarabande's several *Twilight Zone* LPs.

May/June

I did not find myself all that enthusiastic about Ennio Morricone's music for **The Mission** (Virgin; London Voices and Barnet School Choir; Indian Instrumentation by Incantation; London Philharmonic Orchestra), which I would rank as around 7.5 (out
of 10) within the canon of the composer's entire film-score oeuvre (*Duck, You Sucker,
The Sicilian Clan, Once Upon a Time in the West, My Name Is Nobody*, and *1900* would
all get 10's, *The Red Tent* around a 2). What is quite characteristic of Morricone in
The Mission, a Roland Joffe film that lack of interest caused me to postpone seeing until it was too late, is the way in which several totally differing mood elements—a
straightforward dramatic element, abetted by a kind of *1900* lyricism; the religious element, with the de rigueur chanting choir; and the native element, with its equally
de rigueur drum beats—are created and then juxtaposed both independently and in-
terdependently throughout the score. There is also some striking contrapuntal writing, as in both the "Remorse" and "Penance" cues. But it all lacks the affective power
and punch of Morricone's "10" efforts, at least to my ears and emotions. The album,
though, is stunningly well recorded. The jacket, by the way, makes mention of the
fact that the score was not only composed and conducted by Morricone but orchestrated by him as well, which has not been standard practice in a business where composers have guns to their heads just to get the notes on paper, never mind filling in
the instrumentation.

I have not yet managed to watch all of Jim Jarmusch's 1984 **Stranger Than Paradise**, a film some consider to be an "independent" masterpiece, others a colossal
bore. In the little bits I have ever seen, however, I was immediately struck by what
sounds like one of the most original and offbeat film scores I've heard in some time.
Listening to the whole score on a recent Enigma release, I am even more convinced
of the music's excellence and novelty. Here, believe it or not, is a series of cues composed for classical string quartet (Kay Stern and Mary Rowell, violins; Jill Jaffee, viola; and Eugene Moye, cello, a.k.a. the Paradise Quartet) by Lounge Lizard John

Lurie, who also stars in the film and who has created a soundscape that is as remarkable in its sometimes bluesy, sometimes quasi-Eastern atmosphere as it is hypnotic in the almost total stasis of its repeated figures and its drone-like harmonies. This is a score that, furthermore, relates more to the style of the film than to its narrative content and characters, neither of which would inspire this type of music in a conventional film. It is also nice to hear the cues in their totality rather than in the quasi-Godardian snippets that sparsely turn up in the film. Side 2 of this album goes off in a totally different direction with some very free-jazz music scored by Lurie for a Karole Armitrage dance production entitled *The Resurrection of Albert Ayler*. The music, while almost totally devoid of the kind of harmonic patterns one looks for in traditional jazz, has, like *Paradise*, a hypnotic quality to it that, here, combines with a markedly balletic pulse to ensnare the listener's mind and imagination. And close attention to *Resurrection* reveals its more bizarre strains to have nonetheless sprung from the same head that created *Paradise*.

I was delighted to have the CD of Philip Glass' score for **Mishima** turn up (Nonesuch; Michael Riesman, cond.). Certainly, the clarity of the CD sound serves particularly well the spacious textures of Glass' marvelous score, which stands as a milestone of sorts as the first Minimalist score for a narrative feature film (yes, I know about *Koyanisqaatsi*—note the word "narrative" above). In some of the cues, subtle effects with wind chimes, bells, chimes, etc., signal the Japanese setting of the film; in others, quiet tattoos on the timpani evoke the paramilitary march of the Japanese writer Mishima (who also directed a short film in which he played one of the two roles) toward his final act; still others are simply pure, immediately recognizable Philip Glass. Glass aficionados will also have fun seeing what their hero can do with a jazz beat ("Osamu's Theme: Kyoko's House").

July/August

If ever a film score could be used to make an argument in favor of film music as a musical category in and of itself, it is the music co-written and co-performed by Michael Kamen (who is actually the sole composer on six of this album's 10 cues) and Eric Clapton for Richard Donner's **Lethal Weapon** (Warner Bros.), a film that, along with Bob Rafelson's *Black Widow*, just happens to be one of the best of 1987 so far. For this classy suspense film, in which a loner cop played by Mel Gibson (who is the title's "lethal weapon") joins with family-man cop Danny Glover to bring to justice some of the nastiest coke dealers—including a very Aryan-looking Gary Busey, of all people—ever to sneak into frame from behind the camera. Kamen and Clapton have brought together elements of jazz (much of it with fusion overtones) and classical-music styles, with a hint of r&b thrown in. The former has its base in a six-man combo featuring Clapton on guitar, Kamen on keyboards, David Sanborn wailing his heart out on the key saxophone solos, Henry Spinetti doing some wonderfully subtle tattoos on the drums, and Laurence Cottle and Dan Garcia on bass. The classical style, on the other hand, involves the standard symphony orchestra. In some cases, the jazz element predominates, in others it is the fairly modern classical sound that has the upper hand. But in most of the cues, Kamen and Kamen/Clapton have created their own unique "fusion" of the two that quite astonishingly melds the film's "mod" ambience with its thriller narrative. And in listening to this well-recorded album, one cannot help but feel that the music's subtle migrations from mood to mood and style to style have been dictated by rhythms unique to the cinema. Even the fairly standard end-title song, which is performed by Honeymoon Suite and which spells out the psychology of Mel Gibson's character, is not, unlike most, overbearingly out of place.

One does regret the omission, on the Sony Classical CD of **'Round Midnight**, of about half of the film's music. On the other hand, one does marvel at the incredible collection of talent on this recording, including bassist Ron Carter, vibraphonist Bobby Hutcherson, Bobby McFerrin, whose vocalizations sound uncannily as if they were being doubled by a muted trumpet, and, of course, Dexter Gordon, whose often vibrato-less tenor-sax (and on Hancock's "Still time" soprano sax, mislabeled as tenor in the notes) seconds in every way the wonderful persona he creates for the film. And one offers loud bravos to pianist/composer/arranger Herbie Hancock, who wrote some of the film's musical cues and whose piano solos obviously provide much inspiration in the diverse jazz renditions. The style throughout is almost uniquely '50s bop; but it is all done in a way that does not smack in the slightest of pastiche. Indeed, the music for the film's many cabaret cues was recorded live on the film's sets, contrary to standard practice (this is pointed out in the exceedingly intelligent program notes, rare on soundtrack albums, by director Bertrand Tavernier). The various numbers, then, have a particularly fresh quality to their improvisations. There are also several cues, such as "Berengère's Nightmare," that are "pure" film music, with jazz providing the stylistic springboard. My favorite cue on the CD is the haunting arrangement of "Body and Soul," in which Gordon weaves his evocative sax around an achingly poignant chromatic accompaniment from guitarist John McLaughlin.

September/October

Two of the major creative talents working in the U.S. today, playwright David Mamet and filmmaker Brian De Palma, have come together to help shape a movie based on the by now familiar mythology of federal agent Elliot Ness and his battles with Al Capone and the Chicago bootleggers in **The Untouchables**. I happen to be a great fan of both—Mamet's poetization of American slang and his minimalist plots bring him, in works from *The Shawl* to *American Buffalo*, about as close to being an American Harold Pinter as one can get, while Brian De Palma in his best work (*Sisters, Carrie, Dressed to Kill*) has consistently shown an effectively reckless disregard for the stultifying formulae of American filmmaking in movies whose visual brilliance and motivic structures carry them far beyond the derivativeness harped on by many critics. Interestingly, *The Untouchables* has come up as De Palma's most popular film to date with both critics and audiences. This bothers me enormously, since neither the plotting nor the dialogue reveals more than the wispiest trace of David Mamet, while visually, except for an occasional surprising camera angle and one show-stopping, quasi-*Potemkin* sequence in classic De Palma near-silent slow motion, the director has by and large taken refuge behind the Hollywood conventions he has both successfully and unsuccessfully flaunted in the past. But, of course, few critics concern themselves with such things as style, so busy are they oohing and ahing, in perfect sync with the Ronald Reagan mentality (or lack of same), over what a nice moral film *The Untouchables* is. Even the highly touted acting performances by Robert De Niro and Sean Connery left me cold: either De Niro has been playing Al Capone throughout his career without our knowing it or else he simply, once again, quintessentially incarnates himself, while Connery's crusty, Irish Chicago cop comes on just a tad too self-consciously to be convincing. Perversely, I was most impressed by the naturalness of Kevin Costner as Ness, whom most found to be too much the goody-two-shoes.

Composer Ennio Morricone, who also receives credit as orchestrator, conductor, and album producer on the music-track recording (A&M), has written, for *The Untouchables*, one of his tauter and more emotionally probing scores of late, although the album starts off quite unpromisingly with the end-title music, which combines a Benjamin Britten-ish figure with some over-inflated musical heroism (curiously, too, the end-title music is quite shrilly recorded, while the rest of the album, obviously digitally recorded, has much more presence in the sonics). But the main-title theme, with its *Once Upon a Time in the West*-ish harmonica and its *Investigation of a Citizen Above Suspicion* drive, is one of Morricone's most ominously effective inventions. All the other cues benefit, in one way or the other, from the composer's expertise at manipulating suspense (as in "Waiting at the Border," with its out-of-tune piano, its drum outbursts, its obsessive bass, and its acerbic strings), his masterful creation of moods (as in the theme for Al Capone), and, as always, his deep lyricism (as in "Ness and His Family," although a bit heavy here). What is lacking is the multilayered complexity Morricone writes into some of his scores (including *The Mission*), which one finds here only in the "Machine Gun Lullaby" cue, which dominates the quasi-*Potemkin* sequence mentioned above with an electronic celesta repeatedly playing, quasi-music-box, a lullaby tune while low unisons in the strings, bass clusters, etc., gradually and dissonantly crescendo their way into the action, perfectly mirroring the visual/narrative counterpoint of the mother/child innocence versus the gangster viciousness. It's worth the whole film.

Ken Russell is another director who can bowl you over with virtuoso style and then let you down horribly. In Russell's case, however, his sins tend to be in the direction of too much rather than too little style. Known for excess in almost every sense—most particularly, of course, sex and violence—Russell had been on a roll of late with such masterpieces as the 1980 *Altered States* (any film from which Paddy Chayefsky would remove his name has to have something going for it) and the 1985 *Crimes of Passion*, not to mention his erotic and wicked "classical-music video," *Ken Russell's The Planets*, made for BBC TV. But, as much as I was looking forward to it, his most recent effort, **Gothic**, did not hold together for me, at least not on first viewing. Imagine if you will a two-hour-long extension of the prologue to *The Bride of Frankenstein* into every imaginable horror of sex-, drug-, alcohol-, and imagination-induced nightmare and you begin to have an idea of what makes *Gothic* tick as it portrays an hallucinogenic evening in the lives of Lord Byron, Percy Bysshe Shelley, Mary Shelley, and Dr. Polidori. Unfortunately, the film works so hard at its foreplay that by the time it reaches its brilliant climax one no longer cares. But the musical score by Thomas Dolby (Virgin) is one of *Gothic*'s greatest assets. Unlike the very successful scores for *Altered States* (composed in a very modernistic, symphonic idiom by John Corigliano) and *Crimes of Passion* (in which Rick Wakeman raided Dvořák's "New World" Symphony and turned it into a pop-synth score), *Gothic*'s music is the flamboyantly mixed-bag affair that one might more logically expect from a Ken Russell film. Dolby brings in a little bit of everything: horror-film-music pastiches (with some wonderful ghost sopranos vocalizing here and there), Gregorian chant, Baroque styles, modern swishes, glissandos and clusters, quasi-Hindu, etc., while slipping in quotations from Bernard Herrmann (*The Trouble With Harry* and a very recognizable motif from *North by Northwest*), Stravinsky (*The Rite of Spring, The Firebird*), Vaughan Williams, Bartók, et al. There are also quite a (blush) haunting romantic theme for Mary Shelley and a bizarre reworking of "Spinning Wheel," while the album (and, as I recall, the film) concludes with a piece of British rap, if you can imagine such an animal, called "The Devil Is an Englishman," with Timothy Spall, who plays Polidori in the film, doing the vocal. For all its diversity, the score holds together as a whole quite well, thanks in particular to Dolby's expertise in programming the material, most of which is done on synthesizers, electronic and electric instruments, digital processors, and samplers. The Stravinsky snippets, for instance, which Dolby has woven in and out of the score's fabric as motifs, were quite obviously used in a sampled form rather than having made their way to the tape from a direct recording.

Meanwhile, American cinema, in spite of itself, continues to produce new and exciting creative talents. Two of the newest, most exciting, and most creative are the brothers Ethan and Joel Coen, who to date have co-written, produced (Ethan), and directed (Joel) two minor masterpieces, **Blood Simple** and **Raising Arizona**, both of which have scores by Carter Burwell that have just appeared on Varèse Sarabande. *Blood Simple*, which was independently produced, is a weird combination of an utterly scuzzy, southwestern film noir, Hitchcockian suspense, and *Diva*-esque cinematography (done by Barry Sonnenfeld). It is the surreal, dreamy quality of the cinematography that seems to have inspired Burwell, who has come up with one of the most haunting title themes—mostly a simple, six-note piano figure oft-repeated in a Windham Hill kind of way—I have heard in some time. Most of the rest of this fully but hissily recorded score—low growls, suspense percussion, sampled vocalizations—features synthesizer concocted sounds. In total opposition to the grimness of *Blood Simple*, *Raising Arizona* is, quite simply, consistently hilarious. And its humor cuts across all levels of the filmmaking process—the genuinely droll screenplay, the editing (in the mug-shot montage sequence), the camera work (a *Jaws*-like point-of-view tracking shot, complete with *Jaws* music, as one of the baby quints crawls towards danger), and the extra-cinematic references (the *Mad Maxish* character that emerges from the hero's nightmares to take over the action). Burwell's music for *Raising Arizona* does not stand up as well on its own as *Blood Simple*, although the title theme, for banjo, whistler, and Eddie Arnold-type yodeler, has a charm that also fits in with the film's southwestern setting. And a cue entitled "Just Business" offers some impressively modernistic percussion writing. On the whole, though, the mostly synthesizer strains of Burwell's score nicely complement the film's offbeat humor, but only when heard in context.

But if it's style you want, of course, you can generally count on the French. And, certainly, the French director whose creative profile has emerged the most strongly over the last few years is Jean-Jacques (*Diva, The Moon in the Gutter*) Beineix. In his third film, **Betty Blue** (an English-language title that comes nowhere near the French of the original title, *37,2° le matin*), Beineix probes even more deeply than in *Diva* into the dangers inherent in the ever-present tendency of the male to transform the female into an image. And where *Diva* manages to resolve this opposition in a quasi-happy ending, *Betty Blue* turns it into a tragedy that is the most deeply moving of its kind since that of *Vertigo*. Like *The Moon in the Gutter*, *Betty Blue* has found an uncannily appropriate complement to its affective/aesthetic content in the music of Gabriel Yared, which has been recorded on an imported Virgin CD that is worth every effort made to obtain it. It is difficult to describe just how Yared's music manages to translate the morbid romanticism, the intra-artistic narcissism, or the photographic *paradis artificiels* of films such as this (or Peter Del Monte's *Invitation au voyage*) so consummately. Is it the slightly-off-center bluesiness of themes such as "Betty et Zorg"? Is it the moody, minor-mode modulations? Is it the nightmare obsessiveness of cues such as "Des orages pour la nuit," which hides an anguished romanticism beneath its surface? Is it the dreamy expressionism of a quasi-calliope-waltz cue such as "Maudits manèges"? Whatever it is, Yared continues to show that he is to the "New New Wave" cinema what Bernard Herrmann was to Alfred Hitchcock, and this very richly recorded CD stands as a wonderful testament to his talents. One more note: in a manner typical for films of this type, Yared's three principal themes for *Betty Blue* each make their way from the music track into the filmic action, "Betty et Zorg" as a mournful saxophone solo played by an old man at a seaside shanty at sunset, "Des orages . . ." as a very romantic piano solo improbably performed by a young boy in an empty piano showroom, and "Cargo voyage" by Betty and Zorg in the same showroom.

November/December

The Witches of Eastwick (Warner Bros.), directed by Australian George (*Mad Max* et al.) Miller and scored by John Williams, is a top-notch conventional score (but more on *Full Metal Jacket* anon). This, in fact, is the best work I've heard from Williams in some time. With its half-serious, half-romp, always witty overtones, the music falls somewhere between *The Fury* and the frothier *Family Plot*, with the frequent appearance of quasi-hoe-down figures on a solo violin suggesting the firm,

Americana roots of the narrative, very loosely based on a story by John Updike. Williams also nicely integrates some well-conceived synthesizer sounds into the broader canvas created by a large symphony orchestra. And at the moment where a good dose of "Satanicity" is called for, Williams does not hesitate to mobilize all of the tropes—downward glissandos, clusters, multi-*divisi* textures—that have accompanied the devil ever since he showed up in *The Omen*. As for the film, *The Witches of Eastwick* is a work that, thanks to Miller's direction, some wonderfully deep, sharp cinematography heightens the New England settings, and the impressive screen presences of Cher, Susan Sarandon, and Michelle Pfeiffer makes even Jack Nicholson's post-*Shining* mugging swallowable. And the film closes with perhaps the ultimate feminist statement for our age: the reduction of the male devil (Nicholson) to the role of the manipulable image all too often occupied by women in Western art. The *Witches of Eastwick* also contains the most diabolical musical performance—a cello solo by the Susan Sarandon character—since Walter Huston as Mr. Scratch tossed off Bernard Herrmann's four-track variations on "Pop Goes the Weasel" in the 1941 *Devil and Daniel Webster*.

If it's masterpiece cinema you want, you could do much worse than Stanley Kubrick's **Full Metal Jacket**, which will doubtless stand as *the* chef d'oeuvre amidst what is, alas, clearly going to become a spate of films devoted to the war in Vietnam. Even the first half of the film, which at first glance appears to be just another Marine boot-camp movie, is so claustrophobic and, ultimately, so demonic (a Kubrick specialty) that it perfectly sets up the neo-Godardian hell of the second half. Most of the film's score (Warner Bros.) comes from previously existing pop music, much of it fairly gritty stuff, either in the lyrics and/or the down-and-dirty quality of the music and the performances, the quintessential example of which is The Trashmen's "Surfin' Bird." Also included is Nancy Sinatra's growly "These Boots Are Made for Walking," plus Johnny Wright's "Hello Vietnam," The Dixie Cups' "Chapel of Love," Sam the Sham and the Pharaohs' "Wooly Bully," and Chris Kenner's "I Like That," after all of which you get to hear, in what at this point seems like a brutal stroke of musical irony, the Goldman Band's stirring rendition of "The Marine Hymn." It all makes *Platoon* look and sound like *Sesame Street*.

But there is more. Side 2 of the music-track album is taken over by what is billed as "original film music" composed, performed, and programmed by Abigail Mead [the pseudonym for Kubrick's daughter Vivian]. Written in a style that might be dubbed "primitivistic Minimalism," this is some of the darkest, most unsettling music you're apt to hear for some time. Certainly, the most effective and disturbing cue is "Ruins," in which figures that sound eerily like noises one might expect from a construction site at midnight move in and out of a murky soundscape at ominously regular intervals. While Mead's sparsely used compositions are not integrated into *Full Metal Jacket*'s emotional content in a traditional cine-musical way, they reach deeply into the viscera in a manner that is likely to stay with the viewer/listener long past the experiencing of the film. As soon as I heard "Ruins," for instance, I was suddenly transported back into *Full Metal Jacket*'s foreboding and otherworldly settings with a musico-mnemonic jolt that I have yet to come down from. This may not be the "Tara" theme behind Vivian Leigh and Clark Gable, but it is incredibly potent and original stuff that should definitely be considered at Oscar time.

[Of] several CD reissues of material originally released on the various offshoots of Entr'acte [that] have just surfaced, [particularly worth noting is] *Time After Time* (dir. Nicholas Meyer, 1979; Royal Philharmonic Orchestra). This Miklós Rózsa score is the jewel among these CDs. Every theme, chord, rhythmic figure, stretto, and segue echo back to some previous Rózsa masterpiece, whether his film noir endeavors or even some of his more exotic undertakings. Yet several cues in *Time After Time*, a film that supposes Jack the Ripper (David Warner) being chased in a time machine by H. G. Wells (Malcolm McDowell), generate an intensity and excitement that reach a level that even the most action-packed of the composer's early scores do not attain, although some of this may be due to the absolutely thumping sound quality and Rózsa's own magnetic conducting.

~

CHAPTER FIVE

1988

January/February

Jazz pervades Otto Preminger's 1959 *Anatomy of a Murder,* not just on the music track but within just about every area of the film's narrative: the Lee Remick character calls from a noisy jazz club, while the Jimmy Stewart character not only plays jazz piano, he actually gets to sit down and do a few riffs with a character named "Pie-Eye" played by . . . Duke Ellington, who composed the film's first-rate score. Etc. An outfit that calls itself Rykodisc (the Japanese word "ryko" apparently means "sound from a flash of light") has just reissued on CD the old Columbia original music-track recording of Ellington's score, and a magnificent CD it is. The music is mostly in Ellington's classic, big band swing style, with some occasionally ominous scurrying that cinematically darkens things. Just as impressive as the full-ensemble outbursts are the frequent moments of exquisite subtlety where, in a cue such as "Midnight Indigo," for instance, Ellington boils everything down to a string bass, bass clarinet, celesta, and drums. And with its "cast" of featured musicians, including Cat Anderson, Shorty Baker, Harry Carney, Paul Gonsalves, Jimmy Hamilton, John Hodges, Ray Nance, Russell Procope, and Clark Terry, there is just about no way this album could miss. But Rykodisc, just to make sure, has come up with wonderfully clean, present, and full sound that allows you to hear this music about as perfectly as it can be heard.

Although Leonard Maltin, whose opinions I respect, describes Wes Craven's original *Nightmare on Elm Street* as the "standard teen slaughter movie," the series, now in its third episode, has a certain depth generated, it seems to me, by the narrative's dream pretext, which allows for all sorts of weird excesses in the audio-visual realizations of the horror-story twists (forget the acting) that give the *Nightmare* films a legitimate place in the domain of surreal cinema. In this sense, **A Nightmare on Elm Street 3: The Dream Warriors**, in which a bunch of psychologically misfit teens must enter a collective dream to do battle against the malevolent Freddie, who does not fail to exploit each character's weakness, is perhaps the best of the lot in outdoing its own surreality from one sequence to the next (Chuck Russell directed and, with Craven and others, co-scripted). The music for the *Nightmare* films—by Charles Bernstein, Christopher Young, and, for 3, Angelo Badalamenti—has, in its dissonance and raucousness, tended to stress the violent rather than surreal side of these movies. But Badalamenti, who was certainly able to zero in on David Lynch's very different (and much more subtle) dream visions in *Blue Velvet* in one of 1986's best scores, has perhaps caught more of the surreal side of his film than Bernstein or Young did for theirs (Varèse Sarabande). In a score that has apparently "acoustic" sounds but that was entirely recorded using the Synclavier Digital Audio system, leading one to suspect a good deal of "sampling" rather than "live" performances, Badalamenti does not fail to assault the eardrums in the manner of his predecessors. But in certain figures—slashing piano chords alternating with the quasi-*Psycho* slashing string chords, a quasi-string-orchestra cue, a bitonal pastorale with a quasi-*Vertigo* accompaniment, plus the usual expressionistic twistings of waltzes and what have you—the composer shows a certain finesse and lightness of touch that help put all the filmic slicing and dicing in its proper perspective.

March/April

[At the outset of this column, I noted that "Varèse Sarabande's newly recorded version of *The Sea Hawk*" (Carol Wetzel, mezzo-soprano; Utah Symphony Chorus; Utah Symphony Orchestra, Varujan Kojian, cond.) was "so spectacular . . . that *Fanfare* has decided to feature it in a separate review elsewhere in this issue." I am including that review, along with a memorial to George Korngold, to open this column.]

At the risk of incurring the wrath of film scholars, I would say that the closest parallel—and one that works on numerous levels—to the collaboration between director Michael Curtiz and composer Erich Wolfgang Korngold is the one between director Sergei Eisenstein and composer Sergei Prokofiev. Consider only two pairings of films: Curtiz's 1938 *The Adventures of Robin Hood* (co-directed by William Keighley) with Eisenstein's 1938 *Alexander Nevsky*, and Curtiz's 1940 *The Sea Hawk* with Eisenstein's *Ivan the Terrible, Part I* (1943) and *Part II* (1946). Both of the early films deal with folk heroes—Robin Hood more mythic, as is Hollywood's wont, Nevsky more historical, as was the Soviet Union's—and feature lush, extensive scores that have acquired a strong reputation apart from the film (especially in the case of *Nevsky*). The same actors—Errol Flynn for *The Sea Hawk* and Nikolai Cherkasov for *Ivan the Terrible*—returned to play the hero in the next pair of films, neither of which gained quite the reputation of its predecessor and neither of whose scores caught on with the public quite as strongly as the earlier ones. Yet both *The Sea Hawk* and *Ivan the Terrible* brought to a state of near-perfection a unique fusion of music and images—the latter considerably abetted by the cinematographers: Sol Polito (who, with Tony Gaudio, had earlier photographed *Robin Hood*) for *The Sea Hawk*, and Eduard Tisse (with Andrei Moskvin), who had earlier done *Nevsky*, for

Ivan the Terrible—that resulted in a mini-genre that might be called "cine-opera" (as opposed to filmed opera).

A comparison between the climactic duel scenes in *The Adventures of Robin Hood* and *The Sea Hawk* is quite revealing. *Robin Hood* features a classic confrontation between pure good and pure evil incarnated by two major screen presences, Flynn and Basil Rathbone, who force us, as does the somewhat rompish music, to concentrate more on the narrative than on anything else. In *The Sea Hawk*, on the other hand, Flynn squares off against a slightly effete Henry Daniell; but the swordplay, uninterrupted by wisecracks and cutaways, and brilliantly photographed, staged, and edited, attains a rarified aesthetic level that rises above the narrative, a level to which Korngold's savage and enthusiastic music makes no small contribution. But, as Varèse Sarabande's new audio recording reveals, Korngold's contributions merely peak in the duel sequence. *The Sea Hawk* is one of the most elaborately constructed and yet deeply moving film scores ever composed. And in the unique way in which the music coordinates with the filmic action, *The Sea Hawk*, like *Ivan the Terrible*, opened the doors toward possibilities that were never realized—Curtiz and Korngold teamed up on just one more film, the gloomy *The Seak Wolf* in 1941, while Eisenstein died before he was able to do the third part of *Ivan the Terrible*. Nobody, filmmaker or musician, has come along to replace them.

Korngold's score for *The Sea Hawk* contains an incredible 106 minutes' worth of music, which suggests that only a little more than 20 minutes in the film are not scored in one way or the other. From this, producer George Korngold, the composer's son, has culled nearly 45 minutes of highly representative and varied cues, presented sequentially on Varèse Sarabande's new recording. Listening to them, one becomes more aware than ever of the genius and subtlety that went into Korngold's themes, motifs, and instrumental figures, not only so that they perfectly fit the dramatic contexts but so that they ultimately flow with a kind of purely musical logic that is all but impossible to attain in the normal course of film scoring. As Korngold *fils* points out in an interview with Rudy Behlmer printed in the program notes, Korngold *père* used "a highly developed leitmotiv style." But it is a leitmotiv style in the most Wagnerian sense of the term rather than being the usual—and often casual—deployment of motifs in a film score. One of *The Sea Hawk's* principal themes, for instance, is a sweeping, heroic melody, initially played in the strings after the opening fanfares and made all the more interesting by [what sounds like but in fact is not] an extra beat slipped into its mid-section. In one sense, this theme, unattached to any specific character, event, or thing, sums up the heroism and romance of the entire film. Yet in the "Return to the 'Albatross'" cue, for instance, it transforms into a dirge, with opulent harmonies that look forward to late Poulenc, that gloomily evokes heroism manqué. Toward the end, when Captain Thorpe (Flynn), a character based on Sir Francis Drake, is reunited with Doña Maria (Brenda Marshall), this theme returns, in the high strings, to highlight the romantic nature of the situation in a manner guaranteed to jerk tears throughout the audience. Only two characters get their own motifs, Thorpe (a theme derived from the opening fanfare) and Doña Maria, to whom the composer actually assigns two different motifs which at points combine to form a more elaborate theme. The first of these is fashioned from a simple but utterly haunting series of rising, three-note figures that not only combine easily with other motifs, as at the moment when Maria arrives too late to keep Thorpe from departing (we hear her three-note theme followed by the motif for Thorpe's ship, the Albatross), it also forms the backbone of Maria's song (dubbed in the movie by Sally Sweetland and nicely duplicated on this recording by Carol Wetzel); this song, in turn, has been foreshadowed in a sequence where Maria is playing chess with Don Alvarez (Claude Raines). Even when Korngold indulges in a bit of Mickey-Mousing, as in the piccolo figure played bitonally over the initial Albatross music when the monkey comes into frame, it is generally with such subtlety and musical taste that one wishes for some less pejorative designation for this device. And nowhere else does Korngold better show his skill at manipulating instrumental color than in the eerie, almost ghoulish cue for the "Jungle March" that can be heard in part of the sepia-tinted Panama sequence.

I could go on, and no doubt will in an elaborate article some day [actually in my 1994 book, *Overtones and Undertones*]. But this is a recording that speaks eloquently for itself. While nothing, I think, will ever match the verve, élan, and excitement of the excerpts conducted by Charles Gerhardt on two of RCA's "Classic Film Scores" albums (likewise produced by George Korngold), conductor Varujan Kojian and the Utah Symphony beautifully capture the spirit both of Korngold's music and of the film for which it was written. And the orchestra is reproduced in sound which, if not as brilliant as RCA's, has more fullness and depth while also highlighting with superb realism the appearance of various individual instruments, from the tuba to the Chinese temple blocks. Simply put, this recording succeeds perfectly on every level: the music it offers is glorious and stands handsomely on its own. Yet for those who have seen the film, the almost sequential progress of the separate cues, flawlessly assembled by the composer's son, creates such a musical equivalent of the film that one has the impression of reliving the entire movie as one listens to the music.

IN MEMORIAM—GEORGE KORNGOLD

One could revel even more in the glory of the *Sea Hawk* recording were it not that its producer, George Korngold, succumbed to cancer at the age of 58 on 25 November of last year. Born in Vienna on 17 December 1928, and settling in this country for good when the scoring of *The Adventures of Robin Hood* fortuitously brought his father to Hollywood just before the Nazi occupation of Austria in March 1938, Korngold, as an artist and repertoire administrator at RCA, became the producer for the various albums of the "Classic Film Scores" series, a pioneering project that stands out because of the music, both by Korngold's father and by other major film scorers, and because of the stunning sound quality Korngold was able to create. As a freelance producer, Korngold devoted much of his time to recording his father's music, both for films and for the concert hall and opera house. I met with George Korngold on only one or two occasions; but I will always remember the warmth and cheerfulness of this man who attained such perfection in the recording studio. If Erich Wolfgang Korngold left the world a legacy of great music, George Korngold's legacy has become the easy access by thousands of listeners to beautifully executed performances of music which, without him, may very well never have had the chance to soar on its own. Both the man and the artist will be deeply missed.

Like so many films whose producers want them to be fresh in the minds of Academy voters, Bernardo Bertolucci's **The Last Emperor** did not surface until the end of 1987. But it was mightily worth the wait. Based on the true story of Pu Yi, who went from being emperor of China at the age of three to being a simple gardener in the People's Republic of China while passing through stages of both decadence and rehabilitation, *The Last Emperor* dialectically examines, using almost every possible tool, the conflict between fascism and liberalism, just as do such Bertolucci films as *The Conformist* or *Last Tango in Paris*, with the latter film zeroing in on sexual politics (I mean, has the cinema ever portrayed a more monstrous sexual fascist than the one played by Marlon Brando in *Last Tango*?). One constant that binds everything together in *The Last Emperor* (as in *The Conformist*), however, is the sumptuous, stunningly lighted and composed cinematography by Vittorio Storaro. On the other hand, one area in which dialectic manifests itself the most strongly is that of the music, which is the object of one of the initial entries in Virgin Records' new "Movie Music" series. *The Last Emperor* has two principal composers, Ryuichi Sakamoto, a pop musician who founded the Yellow Magic Orchestra and who has a substantial role in the film, and David (Talking Heads) Byrne, an extraordinarily versatile artist who can go from acting quasi-preppy nerds to creating off-the-wall spectacles that amazingly seem to have some continuity with the preppie-nerd persona. Contrary to what one might expect, Sakamoto's contributions have the more Western, classical feeling to them, in spite of the various oriental instruments and musical figures he deploys. Indeed, I find myself wondering whether or not Bertolucci instructed Sakamoto to come up with a sound close to what Georges Delerue created for *The Conformist*. Sakamoto's main theme for *The Last Emperor*, for instance, is a nostalgia waltz; and, further on, he comes up with some moody, string-orchestra cues whose impact grows more from the harmonic than from the thematic structures and which move beyond the more warm, Delerueish romanticism towards the more morbid colorations of an Antoine Duhamel. And in a synthesizer arrangement of the main theme, Sakamoto even seems to be moving in the directions of a Gabriel Yared. It all culminates in a long, final cue (used, I seem to recall, for the end titles) that becomes a wonderful musical apotheosis for the entire film.

Byrne's contributions, on the other hand, are much less involving. I don't know whether Byrne researched what he wrote or whether he was playing by ear, so to speak. But the small-ensemble cues he has produced certainly seem to be imbued with the proper Chinese ethnicity, although this is also the kind of writing one might expect to hear in support of a Brecht play. At any rate, it balances off quite effectively in the film against the emotion and catharsis invited by Sakamoto's music. The album also contains a cue, entitled "'Lunch," composed and performed—on an oriental flute and a string instrument that sounds close to a koto—by one Cong Su; "Red Guard," performed by the Red Guard Accordion Band; Strauss' "Emperor Waltz"; and "The Red Guard Dance." Sakamoto's contributions to *The Last Emperor* should attract even those who haven't seen this politically fair-minded film—although everyone should. The album as a whole, however, will have its strongest meaning for those who have.

Speaking of fascist sexual politics, how about Adrian (*Nine Weeks*) Lyne's **Fatal Attraction**, one of 1987's blockbuster hits? Except for its absurd ending, dictated by preview audiences who were turned off by the original finale wherein the psycho mistress (Glenn Close) kills herself to the tune of *Madama Butterfly* while setting up her family-man lover (Michael Douglas) as her murderer (this ending, I read, may be used for the Japanese release), *Fatal Attraction* is not that offensive a film. Lyne's glossy visual style is everywhere in evidence, the actors create convincing personae, and, it must be said, a good deal of the narrative rings quite true. Unfortunately, however, *Fatal Attraction* has become for Reagan sexual politics what *Cocoon* is for Reagan religion, which is to say a viciously subliminal pitch for salvationism in the latter case and a blatant anti-feminist, pro-family tract in the former. With its current ending, wherein Michael Douglas, with the help of his screen wife, butchers Glenn Close and then ties up all the loose ends with a friendly handshake with the local police, all the catharsis in the film is aimed against the Glenn Close character, as witness the article in *People* magazine that tells of three "true" similar incidents, all of them with a woman as the heavy, or the headline in one of the grocery-store schlock rags that called Glenn Close (not the character, mind you) "the most hated woman in America." Or how about the ad Viking Press is running in the *New York Times* these days: "Quinn has never strayed. But now he is possessed by . . . A WOMAN RUN MAD"? Never mind that, when a man finds himself in the role of the jilted lover [which is the case in the vast majority of instances], his antics often make the Glenn Close character's behavior seem Bo-Peepish in comparison.

At any rate, Maurice Jarre, who composed *Fatal Attraction*'s score (GNP Crescendo), is sort of the perfect composer for the Reagan era: obsessed by the old (musical) formulae that he ineptly applies in times where they cannot possibly work, Jarre somehow continues to manage to convince people that he is the chosen spokesperson for the area he represents, in this case film music. Even when dressing up his score in modern timbres—it takes an "electronic ensemble" of eight musicians to perform *Fatal Attraction*—Jarre does not fail to produce themes, textures, and harmonies that creak with age and sound mushy even through jarring dissonances. Although some of the suspense music has its desired effect in the film, the score's overall sonic profile has a facile, New-Age quality to it that seems rather inappropriate given Jarre's . . . and the film's . . . old-age foundations. This is hardly a CD that you can sit down with and be carried off to your past lives. The bass, however, had my walls buzzing and the pictures on them trembling.

One of the most original movies of 1987, which happens also to contain one of the year's best scores, is **Siesta**, directed in an appropriately New Wave, surreal style by Mary Lambert, who made a name doing Madonna's rock videos. Based on a novel, which I have started reading, by Patrice Chaplin, *Siesta* traces the nightmarish, sexual odyssey of a woman daredevil (Ellen Barkin) as she wanders through Madrid (Barcelona in the book) and other parts of Spain seeking to find out whom she murdered—or was murdered by. The music, performed in part by Miles Davis and composed by long-time Davis associate Marcus Miller (Warner Brothers), acts as a perfect complement to *Siesta*'s disturbing dreamscapes. Although Miller predictably turns to Hispanic figures throughout much of the score, it is the darker side of Spain, as manifested in its Flamenco styles, that colors the entire musical ambience. An incredibly moody and evocative harp figure, which fleshes out with quasi-Flamenco chords a two-note motif that hauntingly makes appearances throughout the score, and which first appears at the end of the first "Lost in Madrid" cue, sums up in its way the sad, otherworldly quality of the entire cine-musical spectacle. Soaring above all this from time to time are the unmistakable timbres and the distinctive soul of Davis' trumpet, which blends in perfectly with the music's ethnic and affective profile. This well-recorded LP stands up particularly well on its own. But mood carryovers from the film cannot help but enhance the overall experience.

Meanwhile, also from the past come two blockbuster CD reissues, both from a most unexpected source, the Musical Heritage Society. As a perfect complement to *The Sea Hawk*, Musical Heritage is offering a CD of the George-Korngold-produced recording, initially released by and as far as I know still available from Varèse Sarabande, of Erich Wolfgang Korngold's Academy-Award-winning score for the Michael Curtiz/ William Keighley *The Adventures of Robin Hood* (Utah Symphony Orchestra, Varujan Kojian, cond.). In comparison with *The Sea Hawk*, *The Adventures of Robin Hood*, Korngold's first venture into swashbuckling romance (a venture, in fact, that he tried to turn down), has more warmth, good nature, and, ultimately, less intensity. Interestingly, too, one is more aware of both the musical and cinematic influences on Korngold here than in *The Sea Hawk*: Gustav Mahler and Richard Strauss leave their mark, as do the very obvious cinematic shifts, which seem to dictate the profile of the score much more often than is the case in *The Sea Hawk*, where just the opposite seems to have taken place. Nonetheless, the music for *The Adventures of Robin Hood* continually casts its glow, excitement, and dazzling colors upon the listener with an infectiousness that endures with or without reference to the film.

The other Musical Heritage reissue is Bernard Herrmann's **Music from Hitchcock Films** (London Philharmonic Orchestra, Bernard Herrmann, cond.). In its original London Phase-4 release from 1969, entitled *Music from the Great Movie Thrillers* because of the bad blood between director and composer, this was the first film-music recording I ever reviewed. Obviously, nothing can match the excitement I felt almost

20 years ago when this LP offered first chances to hear some of the music for *The Trouble With Harry*, *North by Northwest*, *Psycho*, and *Marnie* separated from the films. Only *Vertigo* among the five milestone collaborations represented on this disc had been previously recorded. Since that time, substantial portions of *North by Northwest* and *Psycho* have been recorded, the *Vertigo* original music-track album has been reissued, and a bootleg pressing of the *Marnie* music track—on red vinyl, no less—has surfaced. I have also had the chance to get much of my obsession with the Herrmann/Hitchcock collaboration, the greatest and most significant in the history of the cinema, in my opinion, out of my system in an extensive article entitled "Herrmann, Hitchcock, and the Music of the Irrational," first published in *Cinema Journal* [and reworked in my book *Overtones and Undertones*, if you are interested in following my ideas on this subject about (but not quite) as far as they can be carried]. Yet this reissue still excites the hell out of me. Although Herrmann's pacing of parts of the *Psycho* music is disconcertingly deliberate, particularly when compared to the music-track in the film version, and although the Phase-4 sonics, while ear-openingly realistic, have a dryness to them slightly exacerbated by the CD transfer, the musical qualities of Herrmann's scores come across particularly well here, where the probing light of the Phase-4 sound, rather than showing up flaws, reveals every facet of Herrmann's instrumental and harmonic genius. Herrmann took three of the scores—*Marnie*, *Psycho*, and *The Trouble With Harry*, the latter presented as "A Portrait of 'Hitch'"—and arranged them into suites that have quite a nice flow to them, while we get only three cues from *Vertigo* and merely the title music from *North by Northwest*. This is music that affectively evokes with almost every theme, instrumental figure, and chromatic modulation three of the greatest films ever made—*Vertigo*, *North by Northwest*, and *Psycho*—while also encapsulating two other works that have an important niche in the Hitchcock oeuvre. This is music to get lost in. This is music that makes you want to plunge back into the films and from there back into the music.

May/June

One of the most attractive jobs in the movie world today, it seems to me, would have to be that of "location scout" for one of the literary adaptations by the producer/director team, Ismail Merchant/James Ivory. One suspects that a major reason why the team has been able to make such appealing films on such low budgets is that they have shown such exquisite taste in their photographing of locations and in their editing of this footage into the emotional textures of the sophisticated narratives they have adapted. Certainly, cinematographer Pierre Lhomme's evocation of Edwardian England via his sumptuous photography of the carefully selected locations in the most recent Merchant/Ivory endeavor, **Maurice**, not only sets the stage for the cultural conflicts behind the E. M. Forster homosexual drama adapted by Kit Hesketh-Karvey and Ivory in their screenplay, it also provides a solid anchor for emotions that might otherwise have difficulty finding a place to settle in this difficult story. As usual, director Ivory also gets incredible mileage from his actors, most particularly James

Wilby as Maurice, Hugh Grant as Clive, and an American-accented Ben Kingsley in an offbeat role as a hypnotist.

Composer Richard Robbins, in his various efforts for Merchant/Ivory films such as *The Bostonians* and *A Room With a View*, has often functioned as something of a musical location scout, underplaying his own style in favor of music, original or otherwise, that successfully evokes the period and settings of the movies involved. Certainly, for instance, the musical cue that people associate most readily with Merchant/Ivory's immensely successful *A Room With a View* is the Puccini aria "O Mio babbino caro." If, in his score for Maurice (RCA Red Seal; Harry Rabinowitz, cond.), Robbins does not fail to bring in some music from the outside, most notably arrangements of parts of Tchaikovsky's Sixth Symphony, obviously used as a musical point of reference for frustrated homosexuality, his original contributions heavily outweigh, in *Maurice*, the adaptations. The chordal and instrumental colorations, along with the almost Minimalist harmonic stasis of the score's opening bars, perfectly establish a kind of mysterious haze that orients the listener/viewer's emotions into an atmosphere from which they will rarely be snatched. Robbins also develops two substantial themes, one a more modal tune that attaches itself to Maurice and his sexuality, the other a nostalgia waltz for Clive, Maurice's early love interest, and his wife Anna, whom Clive uses to escape from his homosexuality. Both themes, while solidly developed, have a wistful romanticism to them that subtly suggests the frustrations behind the various protagonists' sexual longings and adventures. Another brief cue, the Scriabinesque "Pendersleigh in Gloom," for solo piano, is one of the most chilling musical recreations of both time and place I have ever heard in a film score. *Maurice* is certainly Robbins' masterpiece to date.

Well, some two years late, along comes one of 1985's best film scores for one of its most offputting movies, **Pee Wee's Big Adventure** (Varèse Sarabande; National Philharmonic Orchestra, John Coleman, cond.). Except for the awful and unfortunately omnipresent persona created by Pee Wee Herman of a 1950s nine-year-old in an "adult" body, this film has a lot to recommend it, including the directorial touches by former animator Tim Burton, and Danny Elfman's music. One wonders whether Elfman and the Pee Wee crew got together and democratically determined the character of the music or whether the utterly captivating Fellini/Rota profile was generated entirely by the composer. Whatever the case, Elfman in many of the cues has the Fellini/Rota "sound" down cold, whether in the major/minor repetitions of a brief motif, the surreal one-steps, or the mercurial mood changes over a Saber Dance beat. Elfman seems to have been inspired chiefly by three Fellini/Rota films: 8½ (mostly), *Fellini's Casanova* (less often), and *Juliet of the Spirits* (briefly). Ultimately, *Pee Wee's Big Adventure* comes across as less poppish and more heavily scored than Rota/Fellini; but the results are mind-blowing. Also included on this CD is Elfman's much less endearing score for **Back to School**. Essentially romp music with a few "serious" set pieces for obvious spoof situations, *Back to School's* fast two-beats, minus the Rota/Fellini spicing, have little character, although I suspect the music works well for the film.

July/August

Well, I had kind of thought that Marcello Mastroianni, who has turned in a plethora of fine performances over the years, might win this year's Best Actor Oscar for his role in **Dark Eyes**, an Italian film directed, with the help of translators, by a Russian (Nikita Mikhalov) and based on an ironic, bittersweet tale by Anton Chekhov. After all, with Bernardo Bertolucci's *The Last Emperor* deservedly sweeping nine of the Academy Awards, Mastroianni might have been expected to ride on his fellow countryman's coattails. But such was not the case. Meanwhile, substantially after the film's release, DRG has brought out a CD of Francis Lai's music for *Dark Eyes* (Christian Gaubert, cond.). I will state straight off that *Dark Eyes*'s main theme, iterated in various lengths several times over the course of the recording, is one of the most haunting pieces of film music to come along in some time. If you like Georges Delerue à la *The Conformist*, you'll love this music, with its poignant, minor-mode romanticism and its breathtaking modulations. Unfortunately, this album, like many "original soundtracks," offers more than its share of source-music filler, ranging from waltzes through mediocrely sung arias to annoying ethnic ditties, so that one impatiently awaits the return of the main theme or Lai's two or three other original cues, which are nowhere nearly as stunning as the main theme. But, oh, that main theme! It's worth the price of the CD. You may be able to get the film out of your soul, but its music will follow you around every corner.

Surfacing considerably after the release of the film is the score composed by Michael Convertino for **Children of a Lesser God**, for which Marlee Matlin won an almost inevitable Academy Award last year (GNP Crescendo; Shirley Walker, cond.). Although the score starts off with a "Main Title" that masses huge numbers of strings to produce a sweetly lyrical cue with an obvious quasi-John Williams modulation, the bulk of this score consists of synthesized and sampled sounds that would certainly not be out of place on any program devoted to "New Age" music. Given the film's story, these spacey sounds seem a particularly ingenious attempt to convey not the reality of the universe within the deaf heroine but rather our emotional conception of it. And if the film's music track attempts to communicate this "unheard music" from the inside out, there is also a point in the film where the hero (William Hurt) attempts to convey to the heroine what the second movement of Bach's D-Minor Concerto for Two Violins, recorded here, sounds like. Only a fairly grating piece of rock, entitled "Boomerang" and sung by Vonciele Faggette, truly intrudes on the atmospheres of this gentle album.

"New Age" is a designation that likewise comes to mind in listening to Vladimir Cosma's score for the by-now classic **Diva**, which has been reissued on CD by Rykodisc (Wilhelmenia Wiggins Fernandez, soprano; London Symphony Orchestra). *Diva*, of course, is the film that brought the aria, "Ebben, ne andrò lontana" from Catalini's opera, *La Wally*, into such prominence that it can even be heard of late in commercials on television. This poignant, Puccini-esque aria is twice sung, quite beautifully, on this recording by Wilhelmenia Wiggins Fernandez, who plays the "diva" of the title; it also appears in a cello/piano arrangement. As for Cosma's original music for the film, a wider variety of cues would be hard to find. The main theme, "Sentimental Walk," has a dreamy, Satie-esque quality to it that beautifully enhances the Impressionistic quality of the film's exceptional cinematography [by Philippe Rousselot]. Elsewhere, Cosma ranges from electronic rock (but with no vocals) to a quasi-Indian, meditational type of music, the latter invoking the universe of the narrative's guru of sorts. All in all, the music does an excellent job of keeping up with the constant shiftings of *Diva*'s kaleidoscopic meanderings, and it is good to have the score on CD, although the sound quality, particularly in the aria, is a bit shrill.

September/October

Had I heard Michael Gibbs' exquisite score for Bill Forsythe's **Housekeeping** (Varèse Sarabande) earlier, I would have certainly moved it to the top of my Academy Award list for 1987, even without seeing the film. Having seen *Housekeeping*, I can say that one of the many strengths of both the film and the score lies in the way it sidesteps the obvious cine-musical device of using '40s and '50s source music in favor of the lovely, pastoral timelessness of Gibbs' score. In the closed-off, three-generational, matriarchal universe created with sublime understatement by Forsythe's direction and Michael Coulter's cinematography—a universe that the American phallocracy does not totally succeed in shattering—Gibbs' chamber-like music, scored mostly for strings, with piano, harp, and occasional woodwinds adding subtle colorations, consistently generates mildly disturbing, deeply nostalgic expanses of affect and mood, mostly through the use of long, dreamy sustained chords and all sorts of haunting, oft-repeated instrumental filigrees. Rather than telling the viewer how and/or when to react, Gibbs' music floats parallel to the film as a kind of alternative means for reaching into the feeling content created by the visuals and the narrative. In brief, this score, one of the most original and moving I have heard in years, offers a marvelously novel complement to a film that imposes its own novelty in the calmest of ways on almost every level of the cinematic language. Not to be missed. (The performances and recorded sound are also exquisite, by the way.)

Godfrey Reggio's **Powaqqatsi** not only stand[s] solidly against the myriad traditions of commercial filmmaking, [it] accomplish[es] its revolt primarily in the area of the cine-musical relationship. *Powaqqatsi* (in Hopi, this title refers to "an entity, a way of life that consumes the life forces of other beings in order to further its own life") continues in the footsteps of his earlier *Koyaanisqatsi* in that it deploys miles of documentary footage exquisitely photographed (by Graham Berry and Leonidas Zourdoumis) and intricately edited (by Iris Cahn and Anton Walpole) with almost no soundtrack to the rhythms and moods of a nonstop score on the music track by Philip Glass (Elektra/Nonesuch; Michael Riesman, cond.). Unlike *Koyaanisqatsi*, however, which concentrated largely on non-peopled land- and cityscapes, *Powaqqatsi*'s shifting frames ultimately involve the human presence. In line with this, Glass' haunting and hypnotic score, a large portion of which is presented on this splendidly recorded CD, waxes more ethnic than one is used to from this composer. This ethnicity, however, remains elusive, only distantly evoking the film's diverse locales through such devices as an obsessively used instrument (a temple bell here, a marimba there) or a Spanish children's chorus singing a lively dance. My first reaction to the score, as I watched the film, was that it did not quite reach the dazzling heights of *Koyaanisqatsi*. Having listened to this CD three times, however—and this music stands up with absolutely no trouble when separated from its film—I find myself totally engrossed—almost obsessed—by Glass' creations. Most captivating, perhaps, are the various versions of an "Anthem," a joyous celebration based around an asymmetrical beat (probably 10/8). And in the final reprise of this cue, Glass does not fail to mobilize the basso-profundo singing of the title word that likewise trademarks the *Koyaanisqatsi* score. But everything in the music, like the film, somehow grabs the soul and carries it forward—and while the Glass sound is unmistakable here, fascinating new territories reveal themselves as well. The stunning recorded sound has a depth to it that is almost liquid.

P.S. Critics and colleagues of mine whose politics come from the left seem to a person to hate both of Godfrey Reggio's films, claiming that, rather than inviting the viewer into a militant posture against the ills depicted—the rape of the land in *Koyaanisqatsi* and the exploitation of humans in *Powaqqatsi*—it offers something of an escapist (into Hopi mythology?) solution. My own point of view is somewhat different. Even though the Hopi titles imply a negative view of what "civilization" has done to our world and its inhabitants, the photography, special effects, editing, and music in both films combine to such a powerful effect that even the worst blights—abandoned buildings and traffic congestion in *Koyaanisqatsi* and methodical exploitation of labor in *Powaqqatsi*—come across as "beautiful." If one concentrates only on the film, the time-lapse photography of traffic moving through urban streets is no less breathtaking than the earlier-presented time-lapse photography of moving clouds. Similarly, and perhaps even more depressingly, Reggio, Glass, and company transform, in an amalgam of telephoto camerawork, high-angle photography, and slow motion, all with Glass' music, a human ant-hill into a marvel of almost pure formal abstraction.

I have tended to like the offbeat films of Alan Rudolph, from the Altmanesque *Welcome to L.A.* through the more surreal *nachtmusik* of *Choose Me* and *Trouble In Mind*, even though I found the obnoxious collection of personae in *Remember My Name* off-putting, and even though I managed to miss the apparently butchered (by the producers) *Made In Heaven*. Rudolph's most recent opus, **The Moderns**, is hard to pin down. While one still finds the strange collection of hermetically sealed characters (at least three of which are played by actors from Rudolph's "stock company," Keith Carradine, Geneviève Bujold, and Geraldine Chaplin) whose artistic and/or sexual obsessions bring them into uncomfortable interactions with other hermetically sealed characters, *The Moderns* opens Rudolph's vision outwards by using a "real" setting—1920s Paris—into which historical personages, including Ernest Hemingway, happen to wander. Rudolph, of course, casts his usual otherworldly magic lantern onto the whole affair. But somehow the claustrophobic close-ups, the cute shifts from black-and-white documentary footage to color footage within the narrative, and his almost constant use of dark lighting never seem to jell with the meanderings of the cynical, mean-spirited story line. But Mark Isham's score for *The Moderns* (Virgin Movie Music) is one of the best things working for the film. Those who might expect Isham's characteristic New-Age sound may have trouble recognizing the composer behind the diverse cues, played by a 10-person ensemble dubbed "L'Orchestre Moderne," heard on this full and richly recorded album. Granted, the dreamier, out-in-space Isham makes a pretty solid appearance in the mostly synthesized cues such as "Les Peintres" and "Je ne veux pas de tes chocolats." But by and large, Isham has managed to take his gift for creating timeless tonescapes and applied this to sounds that definitely evoke the nostalgia of pop music from 1920s France. Along the way, Isham evokes the music of both Satie and Stravinsky (the latter via *L'Histoire du soldat*), perhaps as a musical parallel to the film's historical personages. Particularly ingenious, too, is the way Isham combines, in a final cue, the marimba figure heard in the film's title cue with the song, "Parlez-moi d'amour." The expertise of L'Orchestre Moderne, particularly the solo violin playing of Peter Maunu, definitely contributes to the overall quality of this film score. One also hears a couple of original songs composed and performed by CharlElie Couture, plus a couple of oldies, "Really the Blues" and "Parlez-moi d'amour." The cover art is by Keith Carradine, who plays a caricaturist/art forger in the film.

November/December

Stormy Monday is one of my favorite movies of 1988 so far (as I write, the year has four months to go). Ferociously anti-American, photographed (by Roger Deakins) in a kind of Punk-New-Wave style in an industrial English city [Newcastle], and intricately plotted by writer/director Mike Figgis, this "romantic thriller" is also held together by the magnetic interaction of its performers, including Tommy Lee Jones as the ugly American, Sean Bean as the Hitchcockian hero unwittingly drawn into the arena of suspense, Melanie Griffith as an independent woman trying to free herself from the grips of Jones, and Sting as the eminently likable, mildly sinister owner of a jazz club. Happily for the art of film scoring, the latter locale inspired a rarity in the cinema these days, a jazz score (Virgin Movie Music). And here we have a director—Mike Figgis—who also composed much of the music. I know nothing about Mike Figgis. The album jacket does not even indicate what instrument he plays in his eight-man ensemble. Figgis works here in several styles, most effectively with a kind of soft bop featuring sax, bass, and piano. But he also has come up with some atmospheric, heavily synthesized, jazz-laced suspense cues that create a mood reminiscent here and there of Marcus Miller's haunting music for *Siesta*. The album also contains two wonderful blues cues, including the title song, inimitably written and performed by B. B. King, with some dazzling electric guitar solos. Just to round things out, the "Krakow Jazz Ensemble," a free-jazz group whose presence in the film adds a nice element of humor, also makes a couple of appearances.

I must make note of a French LP released last year, even though it will probably be difficult to find in this country. The title of the album is **Pierre Jansen/Claude Chabrol** (Milan), and it contains music from four films—*Marie-Chantal contre le docteur Kha* (The Blue Panther, 1965); *Le Scandale* (The Champagne Murders, 1967); *Juste avant la nuit* (Just Before Nightfall, 1971); and *Les Noces rouges* (Wedding in Blood, 1977)—in what has been the most prolific, and in many ways the most fertile, composer/director collaboration in the history of the cinema. As the jacket commentary puts it, Jansen's ambition has been to "avoid to the maximum the lowering of musical standards in the filmic discourse," and in an astounding number of his collaborations with Claude Chabrol, who can be considered as a kind of French Hitchcock, he succeeds in this better than most film composers, past and present. At moments one can hear traces of what a Boulez or a Messiaen might have sounded like had either decided to compose for the cinema. At other moments, such as in the haunting score for *Juste avant la nuit*, one of Chabrol's masterpieces, Jansen, with the simplest of motifs in a minor-mode setting that flirts (deliberately) with Stravinsky's *Firebird*, instantly evokes an atmosphere of tragedy that sets the entire tone for Chabrol's devastating portrait of guilt. *Marie-Chantal contre le docteur Kha*, a potboiler and one of Chabrol's weakest films, in spite of the director's brief, hilarious appearance as a poisoned barman, nonetheless has one of Jansen's best scores. Starting with an ominous pizzicato march that briefly turns into a Herrmannesque waltz, *Marie-Chantal* is scored for string orchestra with harp and occasional percussion. *Les Noces rouges*, the weakest in a series of "bourgeois thrillers," has a typical Jansen sound to it, with very transparent orchestral textures highlighted by solo instruments—a clarinet here, a celesta there—evoking moods that move very much in the same orbit as *Vertigo*, but with some occasionally Bergian overtones. And as in Marie-Chantal, the string orchestra, which often simply modulates through series of moody chords (Jansen is most decidedly not a "theme" composer), carries the major load here. *Le Scandale*, a cold and bizarre thriller shot in both an English- and a French-language version, has the most dissonant and violent of the scores represented here. And as in most of his scores, Jansen avoids themes per se and shows a predilection for chamber-like groupings.

Of greater than usual interest is Maurice Jarre's all-synthesizer score for **Julia and Julia** (Varèse Sarabande). I happen to have really liked this film—not as much as *Siesta*, which has a similarly surreal twist to its plot and visuals, or Robert Altman's *Images*, with which *Julia and Julia* shares a certain psychological perspective, or *Invitation au voyage*, an earlier and even more offbeat film by *Julia* director Peter Del Monte (and Gabriel Yared's score for *Invitation* occupies a high spot on my film-music masterpiece list). But so few films exploit the temporal/spatial ambiguities to which the cinematic medium lends itself particularly well that a movie such as *Julia and Julia* that does so already has a head start in my aesthetic sensibilities. Maurice Jarre's otherworldly score for *Julia and Julia* appropriately backs up, most of the time, this drama of a woman (Kathleen Turner) lost between a fantasy world built around her dead husband and a "real" (but in fact equally fantastic) world dominated by her photographer, played by Sting. The score is at its best when moving into areas bordering on Gabriel Yared, at its worst when Jarre tries to play around with themes where, it would seem, he simply cannot avoid being cloying. *Julia and Julia*, by the way, was shot in high-definition video and then transferred to 35-millimeter.

CHAPTER SIX

~

1989

January/February

One of the major releases early on in the existence of the Entr'acte Recording Society was an LP with Franco Collura and the London Philharmonic Orchestra of the late Hugo Friedhofer's score for William Wyler's postwar drama, **The Best Years of Our Lives** (1946), one of the first pieces of film music to attract the attention of a scholarly publication. The initial Entr'acte issue received a fairly negative review from Fred Silber in *Fanfare* 3:1 (November/December 1979), not for the production values, which he found superior, but for the music, described as "old-fashioned and anachronistic" and as "just as banal as the action it is scoring." Well, *The Best Years of Our Lives* has now resurfaced on a Preamble CD, and I must say that I find Silber's evaluation substantially unfair. Lagging behind the avant-garde of his or her profession should never be a sufficient reason to attack a composer's music, although lord knows Shostakovich suffered just this sort of attack at the hands of the *New York Times* Philistines for years. Granted, Friedhofer's very Americana strains for *Best Years* lack the harmonic and rhythmic bite of, say, an Aaron Copland, no flaming radical himself. But the key to Friedhofer's score is its warmth and poignancy, which it provides in such perfect measure for the film that the latter would simply be a different creation without them. Friedhofer's immense sensitivity to the film also shows up in the meticulous way in which he put together the music's motivic structure to flow with the dramatic action. The haunting bridge in the main theme, for instance, reappears in numerous guises throughout the score, even at one point creeping into the bluesy music for "Fred and Peggy," and thus provides a subtle sense of unity that binds together the diverse threads of the film's emotional fabric. And, if I may add a personal note, I can say that, having grown up in the post–World War II era (I was six years old when *Best Years* came out), the music somehow captures for me both the optimism and the hurt of that era in ways that are simply too intangible to write about. Franco Collura and the London Philharmonic Orchestra play this music with wonderful life and conviction, and they are supported by very warm (appropriately enough), full, vibrant sound.

One of the most offbeat and captivating scores of 1988 comes for a movie, Paul Schrader's **Patty Hearst** (Electra/Nonesuch; Michael Riesman, cond.), [for which] actress Natasha Richardson has been highly lauded, even by Patty Hearst herself, for her performance in the title role. From the opening cue, "Mom Dad," in which fragments of the dialogue, spoken by Richardson, are integrated into hypnotic strains played by a small ensemble consisting of keyboards, tabla, percussion, string quartet, and guitar, the listener becomes aware that composer Scott Johnson has extended himself far beyond the normal confines within which most of today's film composers remain, voluntarily or involuntarily. Elements of rock, Indian music, New Age, Minimalism, and atonality blend together here to create an atmosphere quite unlike what one is used to. And quite apart from the obvious cinematic value of all this, Johnson's music speaks quite eloquently for itself without any help from the film. Perhaps I might have suspected that, having turned to Philip Glass for *Mishima*, director Schrader has a rare cine-musical vision.

Another CD reissue from the same folks who did *The Best Years of Our Lives* is Alex North's score for John Ford's next-to-last feature, **Cheyenne Autumn** (Label X), a much more recent release taken, unlike *Best Years*, from the original music tracks. Unlike the LP, the CD also contains extensive notes (by yours truly) on the film and its music. Certainly, *Cheyenne Autumn* is about as anti-stereotypical a Western as one can find, from its sympathetic portrayal of native Americans to its absolutely wicked depiction of Wyatt Earp (James Stewart), and the music fits this profile as well. Instead of the hackneyed, open-fifths set to a solid four-beat that evoke the "Indian" in most Westerns, North composed a broad, poignant, solemn symphonic score filled with modal references to native American themes but extended far beyond the simplism of most cine-musical creations of native Americans. Often jaggedly dissonant, with lots of muted brass and high winds set in the complex textures that readily identify the composer of such scores as *Spartacus* and *Cleopatra*, *Cheyenne Autumn* also has moments of breathtaking simplicity. Listening to the score apart from the film, one can revel in the music itself while at the same time easily becoming immersed in all the complex emotions of the film's narrative. And if the music ends on a note of upbeat catharsis, one ultimately walks away filled with a sense of tragic sadness. *Cheyenne Autumn* is a key score in American film music.

March/April

[Inasmuch as I had seen almost none of the films for the scores I reviewed in this issue, I have cut this entire column.]

May/June

Just for starters, Stephen Frears' **Dangerous Liaisons** absolutely bowled me over. I have always found Laclos's 18th-century epistolary novel *Les Liaisons dangereuses* to be perhaps one of the two or three greatest novels ever written. With infinitely more stylistic finesse and certainly more subtlety than the Marquis de Sade, Laclos, with his intricate games of masks, sexuality, and power, perfectly caught not only the decline of an entire civilization (not unlike what has happened in Reagan America) but also put his finger squarely on the pulse of a major existential dilemma. Surprisingly, I rather liked Christopher Hampton's theatrical adaptation of *Les Liaisons dangereuses* when I saw it on Broadway. But nothing in the play per se can touch Frears' directorial treatment of it. In just one area alone, the director's use of extreme close-ups to communicate the theme of the mask represents a perfect cinematic solution to one of the novel's more complex elements. And his final, visual unmasking of Glenn Close is devastatingly more effective than the deus-ex-machina smallpox devised by Laclos to punish his "heroine" and close off his novel. My only problem in the film is the casting of the too-American John Malkovich as Valmont when Alan Rickman, who played the role in the Broadway premiere, would have been perfect.

And then there is George Fenton's score for *Dangerous Liaisons* (Virgin Movie Music). From the opening waltz, which is both manic and moody, through its more lugubrious, affect-setting passages which, as the film moves ahead, become increasingly pervaded by a three-note motif that rises through the orchestral colors to icily grip the soul, Fenton's music not only complements its film step by step, it invites frequent listenings on its own. Along the way, the composer/arranger/conductor has arranged, adapted, and occasionally even pastiched various bits of Baroque and Classical music, which get quite good performances from smaller orchestral forces and some authentic-sounding harpsichords, a fortepiano (used for a deliciously anachronistic source-music solo), and a "Baroque organ." Indeed, *Dangerous Liaisons* is refreshingly free of any electronic sounds, which allows Fenton's original strains and the Baroque/Classical music to play against each other in a dialectical opposition suggesting both the period in which Laclos's novel is set and the timelessness of its action. And the way some of the older instruments occasionally creep into Fenton's own music brings immediate chills as the listener simultaneously experiences two different time zones.

If it's doom-and-gloom Jerry Goldsmith you want, you could start with the composer's bizarre *Runaway* (Varèse Sarabande) and then turn to his most recent all-synthesizer score, **Criminal Law** (Varèse Sarabande). Can it be that, perhaps out of quiet desperation, Goldsmith is saving his most profound cine-musical utterances these days for the synthesizer, over which he has complete control and where musical difficulties don't demand expensive extra rehearsal time? In this themeless score, much of the impact, affective as well as musical, grows out of layerings of timbres, pedal points, and rhythmic figures (many of them asymmetrical) that waiver between stark simplicity and labyrinthine complexity. All of the 14 cues on this CD, furthermore, are marked by the kind of all-out intensity one used to feel in the composer's orchestral scores but that is largely absent from works such as *Lionheart*. I also found extremely moving the fleeting but very haunting appearances made by a solo, acoustic piano. Further, I found myself wondering whether the ostinato sound (somewhat reminiscent of some sort of Australian pipe) that pops up throughout

Criminal Law is making a deliberate or accidental allusion to Peter Gabriel's brilliant "The Rhythm of the Heat," which is pervaded by a very similar sound.

July/August

In my November/December column, I raved about a French import LP devoted to music by Pierre Jansen for films by the French "master of suspense," Claude Chabrol. Milan has now released a CD of this album, entitled **Pierre Jansen Claude Chabrol Musiques de Films** (André Girard and Andre Jouve, cond.), to which two more scores have been added, *Les Innocents aux mains sales* (Dirty Hands, 1974), and *Le Boucher* (The Butcher, 1969). *Les Innocents aux mains sales*, a film with Rod Steiger and Romy Schneider that I absolutely hated the first time I saw it but turned on to quite strongly when it showed up on cable some years back, has a fairly absurd love-triangle, murder-mystery story that acquires its additional depths from Chabrol's visual flair and from Jansen's music, an obsessive score built around an oft-repeated, very characteristic chord expanded into blocks of string-dominated sound out of which various solos, in particular a trumpet, emerge like phantoms floating over a miasma. *Le Boucher*, one of the director's absolute masterpieces, is also a suspense thriller, but here with cinema verité overtones to it, since the director mobilized an entire French provincial town to provide many of the film's extras and minor roles. At the risk of sounding hyperbolic, I must say that Jansen's score for *Le Boucher* is an absolute milestone of film composing. Not a single theme can be found in this thoroughly but subtly dissonant score, which instead relies on slowly metamorphosing expanses of sonorities that show more inventiveness than in almost any film music I can think of. Indeed, after listening to the diverse electronic sounds being created these days, which have their share of variety but which all, ultimately, are dominated by a veneer of electronic sameness, I marvel all the more at Jansen's creations here. Not that the composer totally shuts off the current: *Le Boucher* has at the very least an electric guitar, electric organ, electric harpsichord, and a vibraphone in its sparse instrumentation. But these are, after all, recognizable as separate instruments rather than as approximations produced by computer chips. But listen to the way that, over gloomy organ rumblings-cum-guitar at the beginning, Jansen produces a totally eerie sound that probably comes from a combination of electric harpsichord and the plucking of piano strings tuned in microtones. Typically for Jansen, too, the score for *Le Boucher* gets incredible sonic mileage out of a small group of instruments: in addition to those already mentioned, one also hears a harp, piano, bells, and chimes, all intricately interlaced in chamber-like textures whose open-spacedness chillingly complements the threadbare purity of Chabrol's provincial tragedy. Since I described the LP as "essential," I'll leave it to the reader's imagination to come up with an adjective for this CD, with its two additions.

Speaking of essential, however, how could any other adjective be applied to the Fontana release of Miles Davis's utterly gripping score for Louis (*Au revoir les enfants*) Malle's first film, **L'Ascenseur pour l'échafaud**, a.k.a. *Lift to the Scaffold*, a.k.a. *Elevator to the Gallows* a.k.a. *Frantic*? Well, try "indispensable" as well. Not only does this

CD, produced by PolyGram Jazz France, offer the original music track as heard on Columbia and Fontana LPs, it also gives listeners for the first time all of the takes done in Paris in 1957 by Davis and four other musicians—Barney Wilen, tenor sax; René Utreger, piano; Pierre Michelot, bass; Kenny Clarke, drums—on the night of 4–5 December as Malle projected loops of the sequences he wanted scored. Thus do we get to hear variants that never made it to the final cut, while we also get a unique insight into how Malle went about scoring his cynical suspense drama about a triangle murder in which the killer gets stuck in an elevator overnight after he has committed the crime while a couple of teenagers go on a spree of their own in the man's car. As the excellent and extensive program notes point out, Malle wanted the music to work as a kind of counterpoint to the visuals rather than "sticking to the images." Thus, cues recorded for one sequence back up another sequence instead, while alternate takes for a particular cue often got recorded into sequences for which they were not intended. Further, all 16 of the original takes can be heard first on this CD without the considerable reverb that was added to accentuate the dramatic impact of the music as heard during the film. These are then followed by the 10 cues, with reverb, of the "original soundtrack." As for the music itself, this is, well, essential Miles. Nothing but the Miles Davis trumpet could wail out with such quiet intensity *L'Ascenseur*'s voice-in-the-night main theme. Nobody but Davis, perhaps, could use the jazz idiom to create such a uniformly ominous atmosphere, even in the fastest passages, where at points either Davis or saxophonist Barney Wilen can be heard in duet with solo drums. This is music that sucks the emotions into its moods with such force that they stay with the listener long after he or she has experienced them. The sound on this CD could not be better. What more can I say?

I found myself quite fascinated and drawn in by a CD devoted to two scores by John Lurie, **Down by Law** and **Variety** (Capitol Intuition). There is an original sound to Lurie's small-ensemble, psychedelic jazz that has nothing to do with trying to manipulate audiences into narrative stereotypes. Instead, Lurie's music has a character of its own that adds an additional artistic dimension to the film that moves parallel to it rather than intruding upon it and coloring all of its theoretically empty emotional spaces. Lurie's music for Jim Jarmusch's *Down by Law*, in which the composer has a major role, is particularly intriguing. A kind of oriental purity informs the music's textures while a nontonal harmonic idiom deforms the score's attempts to establish a true, bluesy profile. One of the cues features a toy piano (and some dialogue), while subtle percussion figures, in a cue entitled "The King of Thailand, the Queen of Stairs," back up plaintive, motivic utterances from the alto sax (played by Lurie). Yet, with a little imagination, one could almost picture this music on the tracks of some sleazy film from the 1950s. The main theme of Betty Gordon's look at the porn film trade in *Variety* is much more conventional, as are several other cues. But Lurie's dissonances and jagged structures do not fail to turn up in other places. The recorded sound here is rich, realistic, and up front. The program notes give no information on these unusual film/music collaborations, but, in exchange, there is actually an excerpt from the *Down by Law* shooting script. Now that's a first. . . .

As of this column, all recordings mentioned are CDs unless otherwise indicated.

September/October

Perhaps, as the 1980s are drawing to a close, I find myself in the same position that numerous film-music fans found themselves in at the end of the 1960s: a golden age seems to have passed, leaving us in a particularly fallow period. Earlier film-music fans regretted the passing of the likes of Alfred Newman, Max Steiner, and Erich Korngold as still-living heroes—Franz Waxman, Bernard Herrmann, et al.—were in their twilight years. For a solid period of time, I was still able to get excited about new directions in film music, although in the 1970s I was severely taken to task by an *American Film* reader for mentioning Bernard Herrmann and Pink Floyd in the same breath. I would still maintain that Pink Floyd's efforts for *More* are just as exciting in their relationship to the film as many of the so-called "classic film scores" are for theirs. Indeed, I would rather listen to the "Crying Song" from *More* than to just about anything penned by Alfred Newman. Of late, however, I am becoming increasingly depressed by what is going on in the fine art of scoring movies. One of the last extremely fertile director/composer collaborations—Claude Chabrol and composer Pierre Jansen—appears to have come to an end as the director's son takes over the musical chores for his father, while a potentially perfect duo—director Jean-Jacques Beineix and composer Gabriel Yared—has been cut short after two common efforts. There seems to be less of an artistic impetus behind Hollywood films than ever before, as marketing research tends to shape more and more of the cinema's collaborative component parts, including the music track. An inordinate number of recordings that come out these days are made up in whole or in large part of recycled pop songs, many of which often have nothing to do with the film. Most LPs and CDs of this nature that come across my desk I do not even bother to listen to any more. Synthesizers have not only cast their aura of timbre sameness over a large number of scores, they have also allowed a kind of hack mentality to take over, since computer chips can transform doodling into almost any sound you want, turning creativity into a reactive rather than a formational process.

With negatives increasingly outweighing the positives in current production, one of the few silver linings lies in the reappearance of substantial goodies from the past, a process that the advent of CDs seems to be speeding up. Thus, by far the most exciting material to pop up for consideration in this issue's column comes from two and three decades back. And the single most exciting release among these newer "classics" is RCA's CD reissue of Ennio Morricone's music for Sergio Leone's quintessential "Spaghetti Western," ***Once Upon a Time in the West***. I personally don't see how there can be any question in anybody's mind that Morricone must be considered as one of the all-time giants of film scoring, not only for the quality and quantity of the scores he has produced by also for the uncanny appropriateness a substantial number of them have for the films for which they were penned. Just for the record, I state one more time the four areas in which the strengths of Morricone's film scores lie, at least for my sensitivities: 1) breathtaking, poignant melodies, in the best Italian bel canto tradition, that never fail to elicit gasps from even casual listeners who wander into my listening area; 2) a neo-Bachian, chorale-like quality to many of Morricone's harmonic progressions; 3) an absolute mastery at contrapuntal juxtaposition of disparate material combined with 4) an absolute mastery at combining instrumental timbres and at mobilizing evocative, new, and/or unexpected ones. To this one might add the composer's total willingness to venture, when need be, into pop, experimental, and/or avant-garde areas. All of these qualities immediately come to the foreground in *Once upon a Time*. The title theme, sometimes carried by Morricone's characteristic vocalizing soprano, has a sweep and grandeur that become the perfect musical equivalent of Leone's vision, which, for all of its cynicism and myth reversals, somehow remains epic in both scope and breadth. Other themes likewise go right to the soul, including the wistful and jocular banjo tune for the character played by Jason Robards, Jr. In a different vein is the eerie harmonica motif—an essential element of the film's narrative, as it turns out—which wanders microtonally between two tones and then becomes transformed into a three-note ostinato over which Morricone weaves yet another haunting theme. An all-percussion cue ("The Transgression"), rather than knocking the listener/spectator out of his/her seat, subtly creates the presence of ominous phantoms on the pseudo-western plains. *Once Upon a Time in the West* may not have the complexity of certain other Morricone western scores, such as *Duck, You Sucker* or even *My Name Is Nobody*, but it more than makes up for this in its gorgeous lyricism and its almost palpable evocations.

Almost as exciting, save that one would like to hear this sweeping score in something other than the slightly tubby and cramped mono sound it was recorded in, is the Varèse Sarabande reissue of Franz Waxman's music for Billy Wilder's **Spirit of St. Louis**, made in 1956 some twelve years before *Once Upon a Time in the West*. In fact, the term "reissue" does not fully describe this CD, since it not only brings together the cues from the original RCA soundtrack recording and from Entr'acte's expanded revival, it adds two additional cues, "St. Christopher" and "Rolling Out," not previously on any release. Of course, those familiar with the score only via the film are due for a surprise, since what is offered here is the music as Waxman recorded it prior to some extensive cuts and rewrites (the latter done by Roy Webb and Ray Heindorf) later imposed by the film's producer, and this is all for the better, since there is not a note that Waxman penned for the film that does not reach the listener on almost every level: the sophistication of the harmonic writing and the instrumentation, via which Waxman was able to evoke every imaginable mood, from surreal loneliness to unabashed heroism; the sharply etched motifs that stir the emotions without overwhelming them; the often jagged rhythms that were one of the composer's trademarks; the witty musical satire; even the subtle organization of the various motifs. There is not a single cliché in this entire score. Even "La Marseillaise" is so well integrated into the musical fabric that it seems perfectly right when it finally appears, which is certainly not the case in the title-theme rewrite done by

Webb and Heindorf. As if this weren't enough, the CD also offers, in its program notes, a specially written tribute to Waxman by director Wilder, a tribute that brought chills to my spine and tears to my eyes.

One of my favorite scores over the last few years was done by David Newman—yes, he's Alfred's son—for Danny DeVito's wonderful *Throw Momma from the Train*. Why this music never made it to a recording, particularly given the popularity of the film, remains a mystery. Anyway, based on this fond memory, I decided to give a listen to Newman's **Heathers**, for newcomer Michael Lehman's film (Varèse Sarabande). An all-synthesizer score, save for a solo harmonica playing a wispy motif that evokes *Once Upon a Time in the West*, *Heathers* has a witty, herky-jerky quality to many of its cues for this offbeat suspense thriller in which a high-school coed rebels against her own clique. I particularly like the way the harmonica motif is woven into the deeper fabric of the cue entitled "Forest Chase." The various Baroque ostinatos also make interesting contributions. But the music has few of the truly clever turns and twists of *Throw Momma from the Train*, or, if it does, they tend to be gobbled up by the electronic sheen. Still, this is an original score for an original movie.

November/December

It is a sign of the panicky marketing mentalities prevalent today that the people who put together **Batman** felt they had to slip into the film, fortunately in minimal, often almost inaudible quantities, several songs by Prince, whose slimy voice, effete/macho posturing, sophomorically suggestive lyrics, and electronically polluted back-ups represent one of the worst things to happen in popular music in decades. I feel fairly certain that nobody was enticed into the theater to see *Batman* by the presence of Prince on the music track. It is also a sign of the times that the first "soundtrack" album to be released for *Batman* contained only Prince's excremental songs (Warner Brothers LP). From what I understand, the album has been selling like hotcakes, which indicates to me that the only reason Prince got into *Batman* was to sell the recordings, not the movie. One wonders how many people appreciated the irony of one of the principal appearances made by Prince's music in *Batman*, which is via a ghetto-blaster that accompanies the arch-villain Joker, deliciously played by Jack Nicholson, as he trashes a museum. By the way, are there readers out there who join me, along with several friends, in always first seeing the Batman logo as two golden teeth hanging over a pair of golden tonsils . . . ?

Fortunately, Danny Elfman's musical score for *Batman*, a major symphonic effort, showed up just in time for consideration in this column (Warner Brothers; Sinfonia of London, Shirley Walker, cond.). First and foremost, Elfman has uncannily captured the darkness, mystery, and decadence of Tim Burton's film, which, as many have noted, solidly evokes Bob Kane's original comic strip and blessedly avoids the campiness of the horrendous TV series (there is also no Robin). In fact, whatever atmosphere and feeling are generated by *Batman* come more from the set design and Elfman's music than from the overall film, which left me curiously cold. In the press

release, Elfman notes the names of Steiner and Herrmann as inspirations, and, I suspect, the latter can be felt in certain areas of moodiness created in the score through
the use of such devices as a very Gothic-sounding organ, sparingly used. But Elfman's
contributions unmistakably belong to the post–*Star Wars* generation of symphonic
film music: busy, intense, and driving, they constantly fill every inch of a theater's audio space with no-respite musical "action" in a way designed for modern sound systems and sensibilities. But the *Batman* music's heroism has more than a twinge of li-
bidinous sadism and gloom attached to it, somewhat as if John Williams had been
asked to do a conflation of *The Fury* and *Star Wars*. Occasionally, though, Elfman relaxes to produce a piece of pure mood, such as in the chilling little cue, "Photos,"
which ultimately modulates into Stephen Foster's "Beautiful Dreamer." Elfman also
leaves an original stamp throughout the score by mobilizing such coloristic devices as
whole-tone scales. And one of Batman's major attributes is the clarity and excitement
of its instrumentation (fellow Oingo Boingo member Steve Bartek did the orchestrations, presumably from Elfman's short score). The Sinfonia of London plays this music with wonderful energy and verve, and it has been sumptuously, albeit quite digitally, recorded.

But, of course, for the big, symphonic film score, nobody—nobody—will ever
match the verve, élan, color, and exquisite emotional and dramatic sensibilities of
the granddaddy of this type of music, Erich Wolfgang Korngold, 10 of whose scores
are represented on a CD reissue of **The Sea Hawk**, the first in RCA's pioneering
"Classic Film Scores" series (RCA Victor; National Philharmonic Orchestra, Charles
Gerhardt, cond.). Simply put, *The Sea Hawk* is one of the best film-music recordings
ever made. The excitedly committed performances are nothing short of spectacular,
the recorded sound about as sumptuous as one will ever hear for orchestral music
(and the CD remastering, done by conductor Gerhardt, maintains or enhances every
one of the LP's qualities, with only a tad of digital harshness here and there). And,
of course, there is Korngold's music, which not only dazzles the ear with its glorious
colors but which creates moods that probe about as deeply as music can probe, affectively at least. Indeed, there is a quality to Korngold's music that touches what Proust
would call *mémoire involontaire* in a way that almost nothing else can: Korngold's
scores do not simply evoke their films, they re-create the emotional ambience of the
entire era that produced them. I want to start reading a seven-volume novel every
time I hear this music. Particularly rewarding on this compact disc is the extension
of *The Sea Hawk*, *Of Human Bondage*, and *Between Two Worlds* into fuller suites
through the inclusion of excerpts recorded on other "Classic Film Scores" LPs. Further, *Between Two Worlds* also contains a kind of rhapsody for piano and orchestra cut
altogether from earlier "Classic Film Scores" releases. Although this segment has little of the longing and tragically hued romanticism of the rest of the score, it is
nonetheless an important part of *Between Two Worlds'* overall musical profile. Other
Korngold excerpts heard here are *The Sea Wolf*, *The Constant Nymph*, *Kings Row*, *Anthony Adverse*, *Deception*, *Devotion*, and *Escape Me Never*. While Korngold fanatics
(and even casual admirers) will want to have the more or less complete scores for

Kings Row (Varèse-Sarabande), *The Adventures of Robin Hood* (Musical Heritage), and *The Sea Hawk* (Varèse-Sarabande) now available on CDs, no conductor has ever breathed life and spirit into the music the way Gerhardt has. *The Sea Hawk* is indispensable.

I started bottoming out on Stephen King as of his novel *The Dead Zone*, David Cronenberg's superb film version of it to the contrary somewhat withstanding, and I have gotten to the point where I don't automatically read every new King effort, or even the mass-market reprints of his old, limited-edition stuff. Of King's recent work, I found the self-reflective *Misery* to be the most harrowing and original. **Pet Sematary**, a novel (about a cemetery that brings those interred there back to life . . . for a price) that supposedly frightened the author himself so much that he did not initially want to release it, left me fairly cold. I would, however, have gone to see the film adaptation of it, since it was directed by Mary Lambert, whose *Siesta* is a masterpiece of sorts. But talk of the literalization of the gore via all the new special effects/make-up technology kept me away. I mean, one thing the novel does have going for it is a certain amount of subtlety. As it turns out, however, the film seconds this subtlety on at least one front, and this is the score by Elliot Goldenthal (Varèse-Sarabande; Zarathustra Boys' Chorus; Orchestra of St. Luke's, Steven Mercurio, cond.). Not unexpectedly in a story in which the first major tragedy is the death of a little boy, the music for *Pet Sematary* makes sparing use of a boys' chorus, not for a main theme (as in the awful *Children of the Corn*) but as a kind of atmospheric backup, often to simple, childlike ostinatos and figures that come across something along the lines of *To Kill a Mockingbird* filtered through Bernard Herrmann. Goldenthal also musically evokes the murk and mist that must surely play a major role in the film's visuals. This he accomplishes through minimally textured instrumental and synthesizer cues in which the volume level rarely rises above a mezzo forte.

CHAPTER SEVEN

~

1990

January/February

If ever there was an anti-stereotypical war-film score, it is Ennio Morricone's for Brian De Palma's devastating masterpiece, **Casualties of War** (Columbia; Trencito de los Andes, Pan Flutes; Orchestra and Chorus of the Unione Musicisti di Roma). No snare drums, no bugle calls, not even a good healthy march here and there. Instead, *Casualties of War* evokes throughout various somber moods, the darkest and most saddening of which is an obsessive, intense, tragic theme, frequently intoned by the horns, that has an overwhelming impact during the crescendo of the cue, "The Death of Oahn." De Palma has been quoted as saying that sorrow was one of the principal emotions he tried to communicate in the film, and the music deeply mirrors this element. From the outset of the action, Pan flutes establish a mournful atmosphere with an overlay of primitivism that has little or nothing to do with any specific ethnicity and a great deal to do with a way of being at odds with the American war machine. And as in all of Morricone's greatest scores, diverse recognizable elements undergo permutations and combinations until they all come together in at least one glorious cue, in this case "Casualties of War," which happens to be the end-title music (there are no opening titles), and which expands into a kind of requiem thanks to the addition of a full chorus. *Casualties of War* is Morricone's second straight score for a De Palma film. The first, *The Untouchables*, was nominated for an Oscar for 1987. At the moment, it should be the hands-down choice for 1989.

But then, the film, director De Palma, his cinematographer, his editor, and at the very least actor Sean Penn should likewise come in for strong consideration at the next Academy Awards. For starters, even in the heavily conventionalized war-film genre, De Palma's gift for pacing and shot mixing allows the spectator's emotions to reach levels of involvement rare in any type of film. And if the tragic heroine of *Casualties of War* has, in De Palma's oeuvre, her closest sister perhaps in Carrie White, it is not because, as Janet Maslin absurdly claimed in a *New York Times* piece, *Casualties of War* is really a horror film but because the director's vision rises above all genre distinctions to evoke, yes, sorrow at the spectacles of the victimization of an innocent at the hands of a patriarchal system that, whether in its religion or its politics, makes no distinction between a penis and a pistol. And if Carrie White is the millions of women belittled by fundamentalist religion hidden in all strata of society, Oahn is all Vietnam, whose ultimately raped innocence is extraordinarily evoked in the cinematography of the Thai landscapes. In this respect, *Casualties of War* differs markedly from *Platoon*, whose sometimes stunning photography is often there as empty prettiness. If there is another film to be evoked by *Casualties of War*, it is *Hiroshima mon amour*. As the nightmare frame De Palma provides for his films suggests, Vietnam for most of us is only a bad dream, occasionally evoked as an ugly image in a movie or as a headline reading "Nixon Resigning" as we take the subway to work.

It stands to reason that John Glen's **Licence to Kill**, the latest James Bond adventure and the second to star Timothy Dalton as 007, has gotten a somewhat lukewarm reception, since it is by far the best Bond flick to show up in years. Besides the fact that Roger Moore has, blissfully, disappeared from the series, Dalton, without comparison to anyone, makes a splendid 007. Unlike Moore and even Sean Connery at times, Dalton is able to project a fine anger that, it strikes me, must come in part from his training as a classical actor on the English stage and that comes close to one of the major characteristics of the arch-loner-spy created by Ian Fleming (I have no idea whether *Licence to Kill* has any relation to the John Gardner novel of the same title; I tried one of the Gardner 007 resuscitations and found it so abysmal that my Bond reading in the future will be limited to "reruns" of the Fleming novels; a major incident in the film does, however, come from the Fleming novel, *Live and Let Die*). But *Licence to Kill* goes much further than Dalton's first 007 outing, *The Living Daylights*, in that the interplay between seriousness and romp is weighted, as it is in all the best Bond films, on the side of the former. No cutesy-poo sled rides on a cello here. Anyway, a new Bond composer has emerged, Michael Kamen, although you'd hardly know this from the way MCA has packaged its CD (National Philharmonic Orchestra), which, alas, looks for all intents and purposes like one of the compilation-pop albums glutting the "original soundtrack" markets these days. As it turns out, the CD has only four pop numbers, including the title song, belted out by Gladys Knight, that opens with a near clone of *Goldfinger*'s opening chords and that ends up as one of the better 007 titles, in spite of the synthesized noise in the backup (nowhere does MCA indicate who composed the music or wrote the lyrics for "Licence to Kill"). Another song, Tim Feehan's "Dirty Love," adds a *Miami Vice* flavor to the goings on (indeed, *Licence to Kill*'s drug-kingpin narrative features, as the heavy, Robert Davi, who has been seen in a similar role on at least one *Miami Vice*). The less said about the other two songs, Ivory's "Wedding Party" and Patti LaBelle's namby-pamby "If You Asked Me To," the better.

As for Michael Kamen, his presence as composer for *Licence to Kill* should come as no great surprise, since Kamen has established a reputation of sorts as a master of action/suspense music. Of course, one of the requisites for writing a 007 score is the incorporation of the "James Bond Theme," credited to Monty Norman, into the music at various points, and Kamen performs his duty with no more or less craft than his predecessors. Where Kamen's music differs substantially from many of the other 007 scores is the emphasis on mood rather than slam-bam pizzazz (although lord knows John Barry has certainly painted engrossing moodscapes as well). In keeping with the narrative's Central American milieu, Kamen makes substantial use of the guitar to evoke the general locale. But rarely does he indulge in the pseudo-ethnic trivialities that tempt most film composers once you put a guitar on their staves. Instead the guitar becomes one of the principal vehicles via which Kamen communicates his dark moods. All in all, *Licence to Kill*, while lacking any truly memorable cues such as the ones that pepper the Barry 007 scores, is quite respectable and functions well in the film.

March/April

Good news: Preamble has reissued on CD (two discs; MGM Studio Orchestra and Chorus) one of the finest Americana film scores ever penned, John Green's **Raintree County**, this from the Entr'acte stereo reissue and not from the original RCA release, neither of which has been around for quite some time. Based on Ross Lockridge, Jr.'s, novel, *Raintree County*, directed in 1957 by veteran Edward Dmytryk, is a kind of *Gone with the Wind*-cum-*Vertigo* epic set in the Civil War but centering around a young man (Montgomery Clift) who is torn between his love for a fair woman (Eva Marie Saint), who represents life and home, and his obsession for a dark woman (Elizabeth Taylor), who is bound up in death and madness. Heretical as it may seem, in many ways, I prefer both *Raintree County* and its score to *Gone With the Wind* and its music. Granted, nothing will ever quite match Steiner's "Tara" theme in its nobility, sweep, and nostalgia. But, although it is of a much softer and subtler variety, the nostalgia John Green managed to build into *Raintree County*'s title theme, heard throughout the film in both instrumental (frequently colored by a harmonica solo) and choral versions (Nat "King" Cole sings it behind the titles, but that version does not show up on the recordings) ultimately reaches more deeply into the soul. And, of course, Green had more psychological complexities to work with than Steiner, and somehow such complexities always seem to produce more enduring and probing musical backing than epics and the characters who revolve around them. The character of Susanna (Taylor) alone generates four separate themes: a "mad theme" dominated by the interval of a minor ninth and often intoned by an anguished sounding alto sax; a second mad theme associated with Susanna's obsession with her dolls (and, interestingly, with her son); a "happy" love theme, one of the score's most endearing melodies; and a more chromatic "melancholy" love theme. The score also offers its fair share of wonderfully vigorous passages, frequently composed in a style described by Green, in his extensive program commentary, as "that modern *western* sound," a rather pentatonic and, to some degree, polytriadic sound that, under the able aegis of certain composers, too well known to require mention, has become the trademark of the open spaces in serious American music of our time. Green also describes how he steadfastly avoided "Dixie" and "Battle Hymn of the Republic," not to mention, for Susanna's madness, the temptation of "vibraphone hazes." History *Raintree County* may not be; but it evokes a beautiful, dark area of the American mythology on both a psychological and a sociological level, and I cannot imagine music that communicates this more consummately, even when separated from the film, than Green's masterpiece.

More good news. After a fair number of mediocre animated features over the last two-plus decades, the Disney Studios have finally come up with something that at least does justice to the Disney name. Not that **The Little Mermaid** can really stand up to the big Disney classics: it still lacks the emotional and mythic depth that, on various strata, helped Disney animated films from *Pinocchio* to *Cinderella* rise to their unmatched heights. And I have to say that the movie's vile tie-in with McDonald's nearly made me boycott it altogether. But *The Little Mermaid* at least shows some of the spontaneity, inventiveness, and charm of its predecessors. And, in fact, a good deal of the film's success lies in its delightfully witty songs, composed by Alan Menken with lyrics by Howard Ashman (Walt Disney Records), who are perhaps best known for their off-Broadway musical, *The Little Shop of Horrors*, and its film adaptation. Variety, coming from all directions, is one of the chief attributes of the Menken/Ashman songs. One wonders whether the Island-accented crab, Sebastian, whose voice is done by Sam Wright (who can be seen as Dizzy Gillespie in *Bird*), inspired Menken and Ashman's catchy, Calypso-flavored tunes, "Under the Sea" and "Kiss the Girl," or whether the character grew out of this novel musical conception. The film's heroine, Ariel (spoken and sung by Jodi Benson), has a voice right out of Broadway, with musical accompaniments, especially in "Part of Your World," to fit. Here, too, the music and lyrics beautifully suggest the mermaid's dilemma as she hesitates over words such as "street" and "feet." As for the villainess, Ursula, a classic, Disney "terrible mother," here with seductive tentacles and a major weight problem, her "Poor Unfortunate Souls" has all the bitchiness of Sondheim's "Here's to the Ladies Who Lunch," all the depth of experience of the old lady's song in Bernstein's *Candide*, and all the self-congratulatory evil of Mephistopheles' cackling aria in Gounod's *Faust*. In a word, the song is a showstopper, infinitely helped out by the booming, snarling, husky voice of Pat Carroll, who, I read, is soon to play Falstaff (say, what?) in *The Merry Wives of Windsor*. One of the few songs that takes a back seat to the visuals is "Les Poissons," a Parisiana trifle song by René Auberjonois as he slices and dices Ariel's colleagues for haute cuisine. The CD also contains a fair amount of pure instrumental backing by Menken, whose cues, some of them incorporating motifs from the songs, are functional but not all that interesting on their own (if you listen carefully, though, you'll hear a quick reference to *Peter Grimes*).

After eight cues of old pop songs, including of course two versions of "Mystery Train" (Elvis Presley's and Junior Parker's), the music-track CD devoted to Jim Jarmusch's **Mystery Train** (RCA Victor) suddenly changes character as composer/actor

John Lurie joins with three other musicians (Marc Ribot on banjo and guitar; Tony Garnier on bass; and Douglas Browne on drums) to create bluesy musical sketches that immediately evoke the film's night moods. Like all great film composers (and I definitely feel he deserves that status, even this briefly into his career), Lurie has a gift for finding instrumental colors and brief figures that somehow directly reach the emotions without the benefit of the usual musical developments. The quasi-oriental way in which he uses the solo banjo at the beginning of the "Mystery Train Suite," for instance, not only relates to two of the film's principal characters, it instantaneously creates two layers of affect that help the viewer get beneath the film's superficia. And the eight-note ostinato heard several times provides a wonderfully wistful accompaniment for some haunting thematic ramblings on the guitar.

It has been difficult for me to work up a great deal of enthusiasm for Kenneth Branagh's film, **Henry V**, which I have not yet seen, given the overwhelming stature of Sir Laurence Olivier's movie version of the same Shakespeare play and its stirring score by Sir William Walton. But the music by Patrick Doyle (EMI), who offers his first feature-film score in *Henry V*, makes one realize just how futile such invidious comparisons can be. The "Opening Title" cue, for instance, starts with a rather primitive motif in the high winds, with only four notes set in an Aeolian mode, and then moves into a haunting theme given a rather tragic hue through the use of close harmonies in the inner voice (a device developed throughout by Doyle with great effectiveness). It took no more than this overture to get me thoroughly involved in a dramatic mood that, I suspect, would only be enhanced but not altered upon seeing Branagh's movie. Throughout the score, Doyle comes up with one captivating musical-dramatic solution after the other, from the nervous "Boar's Head" (I think) theme to the deeply moving dirge for Falstaff. And Doyle does not fail to provide a thrilling musical backdrop for the climactic "Battle of Agincourt": anyone even slightly acquainted with the narrative goings-on should be able to follow the action quite closely with no help from the film. In a couple of the cues, by the way, the Stephen Hill Singers and members of the Renaissance Theatre Company intone a "Non nobis, Domine," with Doyle himself providing the baritone solo. From the sound of the score, I would guess that, where Olivier tried to reproduce the feeling of how a *Henry V* would have been staged in Shakespeare's time (after all, the play really is a screenplay, isn't it . . . ?), Branagh has tried more to communicate Shakespeare's view of history. Doyle's music, at any rate, is breathtaking, and it has been stunningly performed by the City of Birmingham Symphony Orchestra under the baton of Simon Rattle, with exceptionally full and resonant, if slightly digital, sound. Special mention should be made as well of Lawrence Ashmore, who did the orchestrations (which include a tad of synthesizer).

May/June

I must add another score to my best-of-'89 list, this being Elliot Goldenthal's offbeat **Drugstore Cowboy** (NOVUS). Now, the film, directed by Gus Van Sant, offers more original style in any five minutes of footage than can be found in any 50 hours of most films these days. But the whole thing could have turned into a morality tale for the Bush era had not the figure of William Burroughs turned up to put—narratively before the fact but definitely within the fact for when the film was made—the whole "war on drugs" in its true perspective, which is to say a barely concealed excuse to move this country one step more toward the circumvention of the Constitution. Goldenthal's score deploys a combination of synthesizer-generated and acoustic sounds, some of which have the same sort of kinky-frenetic quality to be found in Slava Tsukerman's music for his *Liquid Sky*. But Goldenthal has created a much more varied soundscape than Tsukerman. Many of the synthesized timbres have a resonant, otherworldly quality that strongly suggests the spaced-out universe inhabited by the film's characters (the main role is played by Matt Dillon). One cue ("Monkey Frenzy") features a very freeform, nontonal, tenor-sax improv played by Tom Peterson. Another is a particularly effective/affective nightmare waltz. One of the more intriguing inventions comes, perhaps, in the cue entitled "Heist and Hat," in which sampled sounds of panting become disconcerting percussion figures. I also like the way Goldenthal layers, in certain cues, the timbres he and synth programmer Richard Martinez have created. All in all, *Drugstore Cowboy* represents a successful venture, all too rare, to explore new musical territory in the domain of the film score. My only regret is that it took a film dealing with the drug culture, for which I have no more sympathy than I do for the way our government is trying to eradicate it, to justify such "audacity." Oh yes. The CD also contains six cuts, presented of course at the beginning of the recording, of diverse pop songs.

But, hey, what about Elmer Bernstein's exquisite music for **My Left Foot** (Varèse Sarabande; Cynthia Millar, Ondes Martenot)? Ever since *To Kill a Mockingbird*, Bernstein has proven to be perhaps *the* master, at least among his American colleagues, of what might be called the chamber-film-score, and *My Left Foot* turns out to be one of his crowning achievements within this "genre." "Basically" (as Bernstein puts it) scored for string quartet, woodwinds, piano, harp, and Ondes Martenot, *My Left Foot* immediately communicates an aura of nostalgic intimacy, with the distinctive electronic timbres of the Ondes Martenot adding, at key moments, a sweet but unobtrusive lyricism. In a later cue, however, the instrument also creates a couple of moments of *Spellbound*y eeriness. Indeed, as the music wears on, it becomes sadder and edgier. As Bernstein has described it in the program notes, "Time after time we hear the music turning on itself, struggling with repeated notes, trying to speak, imprisoned within itself, like the brave spirit of Christy Brown imprisoned within a body that had no easy movement and a voice without speech." (Interestingly, some of the more optimistic moments in the score distinctly suggest the composer's famous score for *The Magnificent Seven*.) The CD for *My Left Foot* also contains Bernstein's music for **Da**, a slightly jauntier, definitely more deeply nostalgic score nonetheless quite similar in tone to *My Left Foot*, both in its instrumentation (which includes the Ondes Martenot and more percussion) and in the overall tone (here relating to the way in which a young man, played by Martin Sheen, deals with the death of his father, wonderfully acted by Barnard Hughes).

Ah, but then there's Varèse Sarabande's CD reissue of John Williams' score for John Badham's 1979 **Dracula** (London Symphony Orchestra), one of the best vampire movies ever made and one of the composer's first-rate efforts. *Dracula*, in its instrumentation, its rhythmic figures, and its various harmonic quirks, all in a large, symphonic setting, definitely falls in with the great Williams scores from *Star Wars* to *The Fury*. But, not unexpectedly, *Dracula*, from start to finish, is of a much darker hue than even the music for *The Fury*, Brian De Palma's post-*Carrie* look into telekinetic horror/suspense. It is in particular the main theme that dominates *Dracula*, and a truly gripping theme it is. All the morbidity and decadence of the *Dracula* legend and of Bram Stoker's version of it immediately grip the listener's emotions via Williams' unrelentingly minor-mode melody and never let go. Of course, if you don't happen to care for this particular tune, stay away from this CD, since it dominates just about every cue, even though Williams' mastery at creating cine-musical effect and affect manifests itself constantly.

Three CD reissues from RCA's "Classic Film Scores" series close out this part of the column. The best of these is a recording that departed somewhat from the series' format, with David Raksin conducting the New Philharmonia Orchestra in suites from his scores for **Laura, Forever Amber**, and **The Bad and the Beautiful**. In fact, having regained acquaintance with these Raksin scores via this exceptionally rich CD transfer, I would not hesitate to include this recording in any kind of "best ten" list I would make. If there were (and are) composers out there, primarily functioning as film scorers, who have given the art a bad name, David Raksin should always be cited as a counter example. Just for starters, oh can that man write a melody: not just the kind of foursquare tune turned out by the quart in Hollywood but themes, with their chromatic surprises and their rhythmic twists, of remarkable sophistication. Each of the three scores here, and not just the deservedly famous *Laura*, opens up with a melody that subtly wakes up the mind while immediately carrying the emotions into reaches rarely attained in the cinema. I am convinced that Raksin's half "classical," half jazz(y) score for Vincente Minnelli's *The Bad and the Beautiful*, highlighted by a bluesy sax tune, is one of the principal reasons why the film seems to rise consistently above its soap-opera underpinnings. And there are few works of music, film scores or otherwise, that rise to such a level of pure tragic intensity as the "Plague" episode in the *Forever Amber* music, with its captivating, rhythmically offbeat main theme. It would also be impossible to imagine a score, monothematic as it may be, more perfectly in sync with its film, a story of image and obsession, than *Laura*, the theme for which is heard in several of its moody variations in the brief suite offered here (it would be great fun if some future recording could try to duplicate the primitive but highly effective "piano track" electronic modifications devised by Raksin at one point). This is a theme, in fact, that almost literally "re-creates" the heroine every bit as much as the painting of her within the film—more perhaps. At any rate, Raksin wrote me a letter, following my *High Fidelity* review of this recording's initial release in August 1976, suggesting that another Raksin album might follow. Unfortunately, that has not proven to be the case; but I can only wish, as I did in 1976, that another

Raksin recording of comparable quality will surface same day, perhaps containing suites from such scores as *Carrie* (William Wyler's) and *The Big Combo*, with its wonderful night-jazz strains. Raksin's extensive notes for this CD, by the way, are a strong, added bonus.

I was, many years ago, initially slightly irritated when, not very far into the series, "Classic Film Scores" came up with a **Gone With the Wind** (National Philharmonic Orchestra, Charles Gerhardt, cond.). Given the number of scores that desperately needed recording at the time, I did not entirely see the point of spending so much attention on such well-known music. But the bottom line is that this is about as well played, well recorded, and well arranged a selection from (mostly) Max Steiner's score as we're apt to get. Certainly, all other recordings do not come close to capturing the music's (and the film's) spirit the way this one does. Steiner, unlike Raksin, wrote straightforward, very tonal themes, and he also had a (frequently annoying) knack for finding musical equivalents for the tiniest cinematic details. When he clicked, as it did on both the macro and the micro level in *Gone With the Wind* (and certainly in *King Kong*), he could be mightily impressive. But, as is shown by the "Classic Film Scores for Bette Davis" recording (National Philharmonic Orchestra, Charles Gerhardt, cond.), which, alas, now stands as a memorial tribute to the late actress, Steiner all too often remained on a superficial level—not overwhelmingly so, but depressingly shallow at times. To my ears, there is a blandness (not to mention some occasional soupiness) to many of his scores that, on this CD, becomes all the more apparent in the company of Steiner's betters, Erich Wolfgang Korngold (*The Private Lives of Elizabeth and Essex*) and Franz Waxman (a very dark cue from *Mr. Skeffington*). Only the single cue from Alfred Newman's *All About Eve* puts Steiner in a better light. But the bulk of the (mostly brief) cues on this recording come from Steiner's pen, and Steiner fans, while no doubt clamoring for more substantial representation of the films involved, will want to have it. All three of these RCA CD reissues, by the way, have been encoded for "Dolby Surround" sound, enthusiastically endorsed by composer Raksin.

July/August

The nod for most exciting release in this column's batch of CDs goes to newly recorded excerpts of music from scores by Franz Waxman performed by the Queensland (Australia) Symphony Orchestra under the baton of Richard Mills (Varèse Sarabande). Although the CD starts off unpromisingly with some rather empty "Liberty Fanfares" from *Task Force* and later offers a fairly soupy "Reminiscences for Orchestra" from *Come Back, Little Sheba* that is not particularly to my liking, the bulk of the music is made up of blockbuster Waxman. *Objective, Burma!* not only has its crackling march and numerous passages that take the breath away with their orchestral sweep, it also has moments of pure, nightmarish atmosphere of the type one hears in the "Asleep" cue from *The Spirit of St. Louis*. For *Peyton Place*, although Waxman had the right to indulge in pure schmaltz, he instead produced a beautifully autumnal, hauntingly evocative score, of which this CD offers five excerpts (the original music-track album has also been reissued on CD), that helped Marc Robson's widescreen, sumptuously photographed film rise above its soap-opera underpinnings. Anyway, let's face it, folks: any film and narrative structure that could help pave the way for *Twin Peaks* can't be all bad! And if the piano/orchestra reminiscences from *Come Back, Little Sheba* leave a rather limp impression, the lush, extraordinarily moody Rhapsody for Piano and Orchestra for Alfred Hitchcock's *The Paradine Case* pulls the listener every bit as much into the world of shadows and suspect passions as does the film noir cinematography (by Lee Garmes) of this *Vertigo* forerunner. (Waxman would later reuse the first three notes of *The Paradine Case*'s main theme for the principal motif in *My Cousin Rachel*, whose narrative likewise centers around a possibly treacherous woman.) The chorus and orchestra prelude for *Demetrius and the Gladiators* does not bode well for the rest of the music; but, in fact, the score takes off considerably after the Prelude and constantly absorbs the listener with its anti-stereotypical harmonic colorations and its sometimes quirky instrumental figures. In "Athanael the Trumpeter," an Overture for Trumpet and Orchestra taken from Waxman's score for *The Horn Blows at Midnight* that starts off with a motif later revived in *Peyton Place*, Waxman sparkles and scintillates much the way Korngold does in some of his best work. But the highlight of this CD is the Passacaglia for Orchestra that accompanies the final minutes of the film leading to the murder of Barbara Stanwyck's character in Anatole Litvak's *Sorry, Wrong Number*. By nature obsessive, the passacaglia here creates a ghoulish tension, via Waxman's brilliantly manipulated contrapuntal textures and motivic figures (occasionally evoking *The Bride of Frankenstein*), that help make the suspense of *Sorry, Wrong Number*'s finale almost unbearable. All forces involved—conductor Mills, the Queensland Symphony Orchestra, pianist Piers Lane, trumpeter Geoffrey Spiller, and the Jones and Co. Chorale—provide energetic and committed performances of this sometimes difficult music.

Equally exciting, save that this is not exactly music that you are apt to curl up by the fire with, is the CD reissue of Louis and Bebe Barron's pioneering "Electronic Tonalities" for the 1956 **Forbidden Planet**, directed by Fred MacLeod Wilcox (Small Planet/GNP Crescendo). In these days when just about any hack non-musician with a bankroll can get equipment that will synthesize and/or process an almost infinite variety of sounds, rhythms, and timbres, the Barrons' painstakingly assembled score sounds just as sophisticated now as it did 34 years ago. In fact, it sounds quite unlike anything else that has ever been done in film scoring, past or present, to my knowledge at least. Almost all of the Barrons' bloops, bleeps, gurgles, bubblings, slides, moans, roars, and what have you have absolutely no basis in tonality nor in any timbres one ordinarily deals with. In fact, there is an aura to them that curiously merges the organic and the alien. All this makes the score a perfect complement to this futuristic retelling of Shakespeare's *The Tempest*, all the more so since the viewer/listener has to totally reorient his/her normal cine-musical reactions: rarely, in *Forbidden Planet*, do we have any clear distinction between the Barrons' "tonalities" as a mood-setting music of sorts and what may or may not be diegetic sounds from future

aural possibilities. The letterboxed [DVD] of the film and its stereophonically direc-
tional sound and music tracks is an absolute must. But I for one would not want to be
without this CD: not only does it document a unique moment both in film scoring
and in the relationship between sight and sound, it offers the listener a chance to hear
in a pure state just how brilliant the Barrons were. Louis and Bebe, where have you
been all these years, and where are you now that we need you? (I direct readers interested in further pursuing *Forbidden Planet* lore to Volume 8, nos. 2, 3 [1979] of
Cinefantastique.)

A solo piano begins to play an intro in a fairly traditional style. Then, as if out of
the fog, it turns one of the figures into a subtle ostinato, and the listener is immediately transported into the world of any number of Ennio Morricone masterpieces,
from *Once Upon a Time in the West* to various crime thrillers. Ah, but there's a catch:
one of the major themes (billed as "Love Theme") for Giuseppe Tornatore's **Cinema
Paradiso** (DRG), which won the 1989 Oscar for Best Foreign Film, was composed by
Andrea Morricone, [the composer's son]. And a lovely, warmly nostalgic theme it is.
But the overall "sound" of *Cinema Paradiso*, which follows the life of an Italian projectionist who practices his own censorship on the films he shows, is unmistakably
Ennio Morricone, whether in those wispy, high violins that float atmospherically
above the rest of the music, the warmly inner-voiced harmonies, the taut suspense ostinatos, or the forever creative deployment of instrumental timbres—here including
the guitar and saxophone—in unexpected musical contexts. And in one cue, entitled
"From American Sex Appeal to the First Fellini," Morricone has fun pastiching Andrea Morricone's "Love Theme" through various cine-musical styles including, of
course, Nino Rota, via a chromatic inner line. This is definitely a score to sit and lux-
uriate in, even if you haven't seen the film: it grabs you by the warm fuzzies and rarely
lets go. The playing by the Unione Musicisti di Roma, though, could have been much
better.

How do I hate Steven Soderbergh's **sex, lies, and videotape**? Let me count the
ways. First of all, the movie parades as a liberal's dream, with the beautiful-model type
dropping out of her yuppie/preppie marriage to team up with a man who refuses roots
of any sort. In fact, however, the film merely continues the postmodern glorification
of sex without secretions, with Ms. I-can't-have-an-orgasm riding off into the sunset
with Mr. I-can't-get-it-up. Secondly, while glorifying its sexless couple, the film pokes
merciless fun at its sexual couple and in the process gets in both an ample dose of misogyny (a woman who owns her own sexuality deserves nothing but scorn) and racism
(the sexual sister of Ms. I-can't-have-an-orgasm is a thoroughly obvious Italian/
American type, wonderfully played by Laura San Giacomo). Thirdly, *sex* . . . fails to
follow through on the artistic inventiveness of its opening minutes and instead, no
doubt playing on the popularity of Eric Rohmer with the yuppie/preppie crowd, lapses
into sequences of interminable, boring conversation during which Soderbergh does
not even have the courage to keep his camera still. *Sex* . . . is a dishonest film that
attacks the easy target (the husband's preppiness) while supporting the very sexist/
racist/classist politics that underlie it. In the end, viewers leave *sex* . . . all happy with

themselves for participating in a liberal art film (don't you know, dahling) while in fact they've just witnessed a piece of fascist drek. In the meantime, its musical score, mostly by Cliff Martinez, has been recorded by Virgin Movie Music. I must confess that, unusually for me, I have no memory of the way the music interrelates with the film. As heard on this CD, Martinez's score is mostly New-Age synth stuff, with dreamy figures repeating Minimalistically in the midst of airy, electronic timbre-scapes, occasionally set to the reminiscence of a rock beat. An early cue by Mark Mangini, entitled "Garbage," briefly pits a catchy guitar riff against an equally catchy riff on the banjo. And Martinez's first cue, "Looks Like a Tablecloth," re-creates, with its heavy disco/rap electronic beat, the atmosphere of a subterranean dance club. But the bulk of the score is out in space. Like, oh wow. . . .

I particularly like the music David Shire composed for the shamefully badmouthed **Return to Oz**, reissued on a Bay Cities CD (London Symphony Orchestra). Now, there is nobody in my particular circle of acquaintances—adults and children alike—who doesn't love both the original *Wizard of Oz* and *Return to Oz*, the latter based on one of L. Frank Baum's many sequels to his original *Wizard of Oz* children's novel and re-creating much more closely than the Judy Garland classic the spirit of Baum's rather dark vision. I suspect that, if it is given the chance, this marvelous sequel could become every bit as much a part of the lore of children's/(adult's) films as *The Wizard of Oz*, once the current generation has a chance to depollute itself from the current wave of idiot film critics and their virulent nostalgiaitis. Anyway, I wholeheartedly agree with Bruce Kimmel, in one of the program commentaries (an interview with Shire is also included), that *Return to Oz* is "arguably one of the best scores of the eighties," save that I would omit the adverb "arguably." As of the opening cut, the score captures the story's shimmering magic; by the second cut, it catches the heavy drama, complete with a *Phantom-of-the-Opera* type pipe organ; and from the third cut on, it captures the kinkiness as well with such inventions as an utterly delightful rag march that, by the time Dorothy and her decidedly weird entourage have triumphed over all the evil forces (including Mambi, with her interchangeable heads), creates an aura of warm victory that the viewer cannot help but carry out of the theater. At the other end of the scale, listen to the various grotesqueries deployed by Shire, includ-ing a multi-voiced canon and some unsettling percussion work to evoke the Wheel-ers. And then there is the chilling "Dorothy and the Nome [sic] King," a cue that starts off with an offbeat violin/contrabass duet worthy of Shostakovich and then breaks into a strange, bitonal, quasi-music-box theme played on what sounds like an electronic cimbalom. But Shire also has a wonderful talent for taking a melodic line and giving it just enough little twists to make it head right for the emotions.

September/October

Well, it took a while, but Mercury has finally reissued on CD the original music-track recording of Bernard Herrmann's score for Alfred Hitchcock's 1958 **Vertigo** (Sinfonia of London, Muir Mathieson; cond.). My reactions to this music will come as no surprise to anyone acquainted with my writings on film music. While at this point in my career I am unwilling to make the extravagant claim that *Vertigo* stands as the greatest score ever composed, and for the greatest film ever made—there is just too much greatness out there to pin it all on one score and one movie—it is simply impossible, just for starters, to conceive of a musical vision working more in sync with a cinematic one. By the time Herrmann and Hitchcock reached *Vertigo*, they had already collaborated on three films, so that the composer had been able to internalize some sort of consistent musical profile of the director's art. Indeed, one of the motifs that pops up in the *Vertigo* music comes right out of *The Man Who Knew Too Much*, while the cue for "Carlotta's Portrait" in *Vertigo* is little more than a habañera variation on a cue from *The Man Who Knew Too Much*. Herrmann also managed to come up with a chord, which dominates *Vertigo*'s title cue, whose tonal but non-resolving major/minor structure is a perfect mirror for the ordinary/ extraordinary, life/death, presence/absence mysteries Hitchcock plays around with in many of his films in general and in *Vertigo* most particularly (this same chord will later dominate certain portions of the 1960 *Psycho* score). Rhythmically as well, Herrmann weaves into the musical fabric a hidden waltz that is present in almost every cue but does not find its full waltz potential until the love between the film's hero (James Stewart) and heroine (Kim Novak) is fully realized. The main love theme is likewise esoterically folded into the title music. Herrmann's ear for instrumental color also shapes much of the *Vertigo* sound, with harp and vibraphone contributing to the vertiginous sense of deep resonance while an electronic organ adds a different, gloomier kind of resonance here and there. And as *Vertigo*'s Orphic love story embeds itself more and more deeply into a no-exit spiral, Herrmann's music moves endlessly through more chromatic modulations than ever dreamed of in *Tristan and Isolde*, an opera often evoked in discussions of the *Vertigo* score. When all is said and done, Herrmann appears, in all his Hitchcock collaborations and in *Vertigo* in particular, to have involved himself so deeply in the filmic medium as shaped by Alfred Hitchcock that he was able in a certain way to create something resembling a new art form. *Vertigo* is the sublime accomplishment in that form. As for the recording, the playing by the Sinfonietta of London under the late Muir Mathieson may turn a bit shoddy here and there, but this is *Vertigo* as it is heard on the film's music track, and one can almost discern the dialog at certain moments. The transfer to CD has been handled with particular care, giving the music a more resonant bass and more overall clarity than I have heard on the LP versions. Fortunately, too, Mercury has gone to something that resembles Saul Bass's brilliant title sequence graphics for the cover art rather than reusing the hideous cover of the LP reissue. Ultimately, my only complaint is that *Vertigo* contains some important cues, such as the music for the Sequoia forest sequence, that have never been recorded.

From Varèse Sarabande's ongoing series of CD reissues of MCA original music-track recordings comes **The Fury** (London Symphony Orchestra), an absolute masterpiece from the pen of John Williams. In his score for Brian De Palma's second go-round with the subject of telekinesis, Williams has created music that stands on its own particularly well but that also communicates the entire affective content of the film if you have seen it . . . and to a degree even if you haven't. Williams has been seen as the rescuer and resuscitator of the symphonic movie score, an honor that is not without its pastichy downside. Here, as usual, the composer mobilizes a large orchestra whose individual instrumental timbres are almost always integrated into the broader orchestral fabric. But in *The Fury*, Williams, while working in a solidly minor-mode tonal base, ventures into much more modern sounding, much darker harmonic domains, and much more complex textures, than he usually does, so that the emotions are continually jolted nearer to the level of the collective unconscious than in such more consciously archetype-on-sleeve scores as *Star Wars* and *Superman*. Further, *The Fury* contains one of the supreme musico-visual amalgams of cinema history: around an hour and a quarter into the film, the telekinetic, psychic Gillian (Amy Irving) escapes from the secret, government-run testing center where she is being held against her will. The six-minute musical cue, entitled "Gillian's Escape," begins with some ominous, low figures as Gillian and Hester (Carrie Snodgress) prepare her escape. As Gillian runs out of the building, director De Palma cuts off the voice track and turns to the slow motion he often uses in key sequences, while the music rises to a joyous theme, initially in a bitonal harmonic setting, in the high strings. Additional resonance from various bells adds an eerie note. From this point on, the score slowly becomes darker and darker as Gillian's pursuers close in on her. Action and score reach a pitch of almost unbearable, elegiac intensity as Hester is struck and killed by an automobile in one of De Palma's cruelest manipulations and one of Williams' saddest. Moments later, De Palma and Williams ingeniously create a bit of "Mickey Mousing" that grows totally out of the musical structure as the three shots fired by Gillian's rescuer (Kirk Douglas) coincide with the first three of a series of major triads played in the horns and oboes beneath a high, sustained unison in the violins. The sequence closes with a particularly poignant reprise of the film's dirge-like main theme as Gillian and her rescuer escape. This is music that can elicit tears even without its film; with it, it tears you apart. And the music remains on this elevated level throughout, which the film unfortunately does not. Included on this CD is an original, very *serioso* version of the "Death on the Carousel" cue not heard on the LP and replaced in the film by a synthesized-calliope version of the main theme that speeds and glissandos upward as Gillian's counterpart (Andrew Stevens) telekinetically trashes a carnival ride. *The Fury* CD closes with an Epilogue for Strings, a deeply moving, concert elegy not heard in the film. Those who like *The Fury* will not want to be without its companion piece, *Dracula*, penned a year later, reissued on Varèse Sarabande.

November/December

One of the most frustrating instances of major butchery in the history of the cinema is the studio version of the late Orson Welles' 1941–42 **The Magnificent Ambersons**. As is well known, unfavorable preview reactions to a 131-minute cut terrified studio execs at R.K.O. to such an extent that they not only excised 50 minutes of footage, they reshot and rescored several scenes. While the 88-minute version we now see remains a minor masterpiece, it lacks the ultimate darkness and ingenious structural conception the 131-minute version apparently had. Of, course, along with better than a third of the film disappeared about half of the original score composed by Bernard Herrmann, who, enraged not only by the cuts but by the replacement cues scored by Roy Webb, insisted that his name be removed from the end credits (spoken by Welles behind visuals representing the tools of the various artists' trades. One wonders what was used for Herrmann). Unfortunately, R.K.O. destroyed all the prints and negative trims of the original Ambersons (can it be that not a single copy remains? What happened to the print Welles was working on in Rio de Janeiro?). Happily, the entire original score has been preserved, and it is now available, almost in toto, on a "magnificent" new Preamble CD (Australian Philharmonic Orchestra, Tony Bremner, cond.), the first of a projected 12-CD Bernard Herrmann anthology. Those who know Herrmann's Ambersons music only via the well-known Welles Raises Kane suite will find in the 21 cues recorded here a much darker side to the music (and to the invisible film it was intended to accompany). Oh, Waldteufel's waltz, "Toujours ou jamais," still forms the score's thematic backbone and provides a wonderful jumping-off point for the set of witty variations heard in the Welles Raises Kane suite. The mellow, autumnal Herrmann is also present here, and appropriately so. But beyond the scintillation and nostalgia lies the brooding, angry Herrmann that showed up with more and more consistency in the composer's later work, including his efforts for Alfred Hitchcock and a score such as Sisters, which is foreshadowed several times in the Ambersons score. Generally using chamber-like instrumental groupings, Herrmann frequently deploys the timbral inventions by now familiar to his admirers: low, unison woodwinds (a clarinet doubled by a bass clarinet, for instance), muted brass triads, sostenuto effects from instruments such as the vibraphone, etc. In one cue, a toccata intended for a factory scene, Herrmann limits the instrumentation to all percussion, while what seem like a hundred glockenspiels, along with celesta, chimes, and sleigh bells, give the "Snow Ride" cue a rather obsessive edge. Substantial doses of bitonality in the harmonic language also add to the score's bittersweet flavor, as do the often-complex textures. Ultimately, Ambersons, like all the composer's best scores, relies heavily on the creation of mood and atmosphere through motivic figures, harmonic colorations, and timbre manipulations rather than on extended themes. Conductor Bremner gets well beneath the surface of Herrmann's brooding music, striking a balance between musical effect and affect. Solo instruments fare nicely under Bremner's baton, but the ensemble playing does not always fare as well. I particularly like the recorded sound, which has a depth and liquidity that make me suspect analog recording. Christopher Husted of the Bernard Herrmann Archive not only prepared the score, he wrote the extensive and extremely informative program notes. I personally would have liked a direct comparison with the film's final cut—Husted concentrates solely on the ideal version—but you can't have everything. Meanwhile, unless someone unearths the 131-minute print in a lost attic somewhere, this Preamble CD may remain the best way to experience something like what Welles had in his soul in putting *The Magnificent Ambersons* together. It certainly allows us to experience what the gifted Bernard Herrmann had in his soul.

Well, are you ready for it? From Sire/Warner Bros. come no fewer than three—count 'em, three—CDs devoted to Warren Beatty's *Dick Tracy*, an all time high. I briefly alluded to the first, a Madonna release entitled **Breathless: Music From and Inspired by the Film Dick Tracy** in my last column. Although the CD contains only three songs (composed by Stephen Sondheim) performed by Madonna in the film (plus such hits as "Vogue" and the ridiculous "Hanky Panky"), I would get it just for Sondheim's lilting "Sooner or Later" and Madonna's sultry performance of it. No matter what comes out between now and the end of the year, I cannot imagine anything more deserving of the 1990 "Best Original Song" Oscar. The second release, simply entitled **Dick Tracy**, contains 16 '30s-pastiche songs used in diverse ways in the film and mostly composed by Andy Paley. The instrumental backup comes largely from the White Heat String Orchestra, the vocals from such artists as k. d. lang, Jerry Lee Lewis, Brenda Lee, and Tommy (New Kids on the Block) Page, with his throatily androgynous voice. A campy title song is performed by Ice-T. It's all fairly anodyne stuff, but the style is right, and I applaud the logic of keeping *Dick Tracy*'s music universe self-contained. A piece of advice to Andy Paley: stick to composing and producing and forget the singing.

The third release, **Dick Tracy: Original Score**, contains the original orchestral score composed by Danny Elfman, whose efforts for *Batman* made him the logical choice here. A couple of words about the film: what made *Dick Tracy* work better for me than *Batman* were not 1) Richard Sylbert's wonderfully colorful, comic-book set designs; 2) the uniformly captivating performances and the makeup jobs (Al Pacino and Dustin Hoffman must have had the times of their lives); 3) any great love for the original comic strip. No, what I liked best about *Dick Tracy* is the screenplay by Jim Cash and Jack Epps, Jr., who turn Chester Gould's square-jawed order-freak into a tormented male undergoing a mid-life crisis during the process of which he encounters every possible manifestation of the collective unconscious, including the "child within," who grows quite naturally out of Warren Beatty's very boyish portrayal of the hero, and a complex anima, with Madonna beautifully creating the darker side of the latter. The film even has a solid dose of self-reflectivity, since it is ultimately the male artist, a pianist named "Eighty-Eight Keys" (Mandy Patinkin), who puts Dick Tracy in touch with his dark, female self. Danny Elfman's music for all this comes across as something along the lines of *Star Wars*-meets-*Batman* which, although obviously de rigueur, does not really communicate what the film is all about. Elfman's wit—à la *Beetlejuice*, for instance—shows through in the energy of his scoring and in some of his instrumentation. But his Gershwinesque lyrical theme is simply overshadowed both in quality and affect in the film by the source-music songs performed by Madonna, especially "Sooner or Later."

I have it on good authority that one of the principal outlets for recorded film music is radio programs specializing in "New Age" music. Although I hardly ever listen to the radio, I would not be surprised if even the most conventional scores show up on these programs, since it has always been the job of film music not to provide a sense of closure but rather to leave the emotions open to diverse possibilities. Note how many title sequences—even the most tonal—do not end on anything resembling a cadence but rather stop on a suspended chord that avoids resolution, leaving the sensibilities on the brink and ready to move into the film . . . or wherever. Recently, however, certain composers are producing scores filled with the sweet, non-resolving layers of synthesized (and therefore otherworldly, almost by definition) sostenuto sound that seem to just keep rising up into space and that perfectly define the "New Age" sound. Such a score—and a particularly, um, haunting one it is—is Christopher Young's *Haunted Summer* (Silva Screen), for a film, directed by Ivan Passer, that follows in the footsteps of Ken Russell's *Gothic* by portraying the infamous summer of 1816 spent together by Lord Byron, Percy Bysshe Shelley, Mary Shelley, and Dr. Polidori. From the sound of things (I haven't yet seen *Haunted Summer*), Passer's film bypasses the outrageousness stressed by Russell (no surprise there) in favor of a more opiated atmosphere proper for creating hallucinations—including same rather nasty ones, as the cue entitled "Polidori's Potion" would suggest—and even for transcending same. Composer Young, in his interesting program commentary, notes that "the melodic material in general is very tonal, written in simple closed form homophonic structures, emphasizing four and eight bar melodies," also pointing out that the bulk of the "harmonic vocabulary . . . was inspired by the Lute music of the Renaissance." The overall effect on the listener, however, with all these harmonies and melodies (two or three of them near-quotations that I have yet to pin down) carried into the ethers by various synthesizers and processors, is anything but Renaissance. Sad and relaxing, mystical and airy, optimistic and frightening, *Haunted Summer* is gentle music, "a musical reflection of Mary Shelley's point of view," as Young puts it.

Ryuichi Sakamoto's music for Volker Schlöndorf's brilliant **The Handmaid's Tale** (GNP Crescendo) starts off with some solid, doom-and-gloom evocations on the synthesizer and proceeds into a kind of *ballet mécanique*, all of it quite appropriate for setting the tone for the film's opening. But just as one begins to wonder whether the deep, rather morbidly flavored mood of a score such as *The Last Emperor* will ever show up, along come several cues (difficult to pin down, since the individual titles are bunched together in only two massive groupings) in which the compact chord structures, obsessive motivic fragments, and skillful timbral manipulations that gave *The Last Emperor* much of its atmosphere return to haunt *The Handmaid's Tale*. Indeed, I can think of few film composers who exploit the sound-color potential of synthesizers and sampled sound as skillfully as Sakamoto. And if much of the music here has a dark New Age quality to it, there is also more than a touch of good old-fashioned Expressionism, as witness the bizarre waltz in paired figures of the cue entitled "Travesty." And an exciting ostinato for piano and strings momentarily brings the score into the more conventional action-music domain. The film, one of 1990's best, stands as a devastating re-creation of Margaret Atwood's not-so-science-fictional portrayal of an American society in which the old military-industrial establishment has evolved into a military-religious establishment and in which the subordination of woman has graduated to become the law of the land. And if actresses Natasha Richardson and Elizabeth McGovern excel in the roles of victims, Faye Dunaway and Victoria Tennant are perhaps even better in their incarnations of "right wing women," to use Andrea Dworkin's expression.

Finally, on the coattails of this year's major *succès de scandale*, *The Cook, The Thief, His Wife, and Her Lover*, I have received a CD of music for an earlier [1988] Peter Greenaway film, **Drowning by Numbers** (Venture; The Michael Nyman Band). While still pervaded with Nyman's very recognizable brand of obsessive Minimalism, performed by the composer's quasi-Baroque ensemble, *Drowning by Numbers* is much less bumptious than *The Cook*. Indeed, the music has a much more mellow, even merry tone to it that very much enchanted not only me but several other people who listened to it with me. One cue, "Fish Beach," in which Nyman, with sad, breathtaking lyricism, transforms the bass line of bars 58–61 in the second movement of Mozart's Sinfonia Concertante for Violin, Viola, and Orchestra, also shows up in *The Cook*. It would of course be fun to sit down with the score to Mozart's Sinfonia Concertante and Nyman's score to see just how the composer "resited" (to use his term) the Mozart figures for *Drowning by Numbers*, which sounds nothing like its resitee. Greenaway's film is apparently based on its own set of quasi-Robbe-Grillet permutations and resitings.

~

1991

January/February

[For this issue, I reviewed a new recording of Shostakovich's *complete* score for *The New Babylon* in the classical section of the magazine. Since it is of major importance, I am inserting it here]:

SHOSTAKOVICH: *The New Babylon*: Original Motion Picture Score, op. 18; ***Five Days and Five Nights*:** Suite from the Motion Picture Score, op. 111 (Capriccio, two discs; Berlin Radio Symphony Orchestra, James Judd, cond.). Just when I thought that the growing Shostakovich discography on CDs held no more major joys for me, along comes this new Capriccio set with what has to be considered as the greatest-by-far-score ever composed for a silent film, *The New Babylon*. And we're not just talking about the suite, as restored and wonderfully performed by Gennady Rozhdestvensky on CBS recording. We're talking about the complete music in eight parts that runs nonstop through the 80-plus minutes of Kozintsev and Trauberg's sardonic portrayal of the Paris Commune of 1871, in which the bourgeoisie who shop at the "New Babylon" department store run off and hide at Versailles from the invading Prussians while the workers (the main one a young woman played by Yelena Kuzmina) stay behind and defend Paris. The score, penned by Shostakovich in 1928–29, bursts with the wit and bad-boy audacity characteristic of the composer's post-conservatory works, such as the opera *The Nose* and the *Age of Gold* ballet. *The New Babylon* opens, for instance, with a delightful cancan used by Shostakovich to evoke the tinsel and glitter of the department store at the film's outset. Further into the score, Shostakovich does not fail to use musical collage to evoke the Offenbach cancan. Indeed, Shostakovich, very much in the silent-film tradition, quotes various anthems, such as "La Marseillaise," marches, and folksongs, throughout. But *The New Babylon* is no *Casablanca*, and wherever "La Marseillaise" is, the bourgeoisie cannot be far behind. For the heroic people, Shostakovich saves such folksongs from the French revolution as "Ça ira" and "La Carmagnole," also bringing the orchestral proceedings to a sudden stop with Tchaikovsky's "Old French Song" from *Album for the Young*, as an old man, in one of the film's most poignant episodes, plays an upright piano tossed onto the barricades. Mordant counterpoint also plays a major role in the music. In the fifth part of the score, for instance, a fairly straight version of "La Marseillaise" is suddenly joined in counterpoint by the Offenbach cancan, lest the audience have any doubts about the true interests of the bourgeoisie. Shostakovich's usual array of sharp-edged and occasionally weird instrumental effects likewise abound in this score.

Those who are into pure musical coherency may balk a bit at the long moments of what may seem like filler in this non-suite version of *The New Babylon*. To my ears and sensibilities, however, all the additional music here offers a chance to hear the master at work doing some of the things he did best—and was later to abandon—without the constraint of formal guidelines. Indeed, one can sense here an improvement on some of the full-orchestra experiments Shostakovich played around with sans form in his Second Symphony. And there are pre-echoes of such later works as *Lady Macbeth of Mtsensk* and the Fourth Symphony. On the other hand, the rousing finale of the suite, which includes a contrapuntal juxtaposition of the Shostakovich and Offenbach cancans apparently done by Rozhdestvensky, is nowhere to be found in this complete version, which ends rather abruptly. As if all these musical treasures were not enough, James Judd and the Berlin Symphony Orchestra offer an absolutely stunning performance of the entire score recorded in some of the best sound I have yet heard on CD. I have by now gotten used to shoddy playing and tubby sonics on recordings devoted to famous composers' film music, which those "in the know" obviously have felt worthy of only second-rate efforts. But nothing here is second-rate: Judd and his forces lovingly expose all of Shostakovich's finely honed textures with perfect clarity while at the same time creating a full, orchestral sound that offers no small amount of aural excitement. Judd also imparts both life and energy to the music, which never drags, even during the extended bridges (no small feat, that!).

Five Days and Five Nights, composed in 1960 for a Soviet/East German collaboration, directed by Lev Arnstam, about the Dresden art gallery in the days following the destruction of that city, has almost none of the qualities of *The New Babylon*. Written in a conservative—one is tempted to say cop-out—style that dominates most of Shostakovich's 20-plus film scores after *The New Babylon*, *Five Days and Five Nights* is most notable for its massive quotation from Beethoven's Ninth and a substantial lifting from the composer's own Eleventh Film Score, I mean, Symphony, in the second of the suite's five movements. When all is said and done, I suppose, *Five Days and Five Nights* is one of the more listenable of Shostakovich's post–*New Babylon* scores, and it gets the same loving treatment from Judd and the same limpid sound from Capriccio's engineers as *The New Babylon*.

～

I now pay tribute to one of the cinema's most publicly, if not critically, underrated composers, a composer who, stricken by a heart attack at the age of 57, died much too young, Jerry Fielding. Fielding's music speaks to me on such a deep level that, feeling that I knew the man, I miss him personally, even though I never met him. Bay Cities has reissued on CD the *Four Film Suites by Jerry Fielding* brought out by Citadel two years before the composer's death in 1980. This two-CD set, now entitled **Jerry Fielding Film Music**, is complemented by two additional scores, *The Big Sleep* (1978), one of my all-time favorites, and *The Nightcomers* (1972). As it turns out, five of the six original music tracks represented here resulted from Fielding's extremely important collaboration with British director Michael Winner. Besides *The Big Sleep* and *The Nightcomers*, these CDs offer *Lawman* (1970), *Chato's Land* (1971), and *The Mechanic* (1972). The only other Fielding/Winner collaboration, *Scorpio* (1973), was once available in Elmer Bernstein's Filmmusic Collection. As if the Winner films were not enough, this tribute set also offers substantial cues from what may be Fielding's masterpiece, the subtle and oh-so-haunting *Straw Dogs* for the 1971 chef d'oeuvre by Sam Pekinpah, with whom Fielding likewise had a major collaboration.

What do I like about Fielding's music? To put it as simply as possible, it's the incredible layers of mood, atmosphere, and feelings from the darkest reaches of the collective unconscious, the intensity that the composer was able to infuse into a highly distinctive musical language whose sophistication goes substantially beyond that of even the best most film composers have to offer. Fielding's thematic lines and motifs constantly flirt with atonality, while his harmonies, with their frequent cluster and near-cluster chords, grow out of the Bartók (who is more or less literally quoted in *The Nightcomers*) and post-Bartók school, giving the music an affective depth that would be all but impossible to attain with pure atonality. One thing that always takes my breath away in Fielding is the way dissonances suddenly reach a tentative clearing, with a sustained fourth or fifth in the bass often carrying things over until the next mood. Yet I also love the way the composer's jazz training informs much of his music, not only in more obvious moments such as the melancholy, big-bandish opening of *The Big Sleep*, but also what Jay Alan Quantrill, in his notes for the original album, refers to as "the horn riffs in the Main Title" of *Lawman*. For the latter score, Quantrill also points out that "it is interesting to note how Fielding creates a truly American sound without venturing into the usual Coplandesque mimicry that is characteristic of so much western film scoring." Just the way in which the Main Title's big theme soars in unison violins over Fielding's characteristic close-interval chords is enough to send chills down my spine. Fielding also masterfully displays his various instruments, occasionally coming close to something like Boulez, as in *The Mechanic*'s violently dissonant opening. And then there are the asymmetrical marches and other rhythmic games, such as the near waltzes set in 4/4 time. Favorite moments? Well, the shifting humors of *The Big Sleep*'s Main Title always get to me. But it strikes me that no composer has ever quite so successfully captured the overall profile of an entire film as Fielding did with *Straw Dogs*, which, with its acidic opening chorale and, later on, its quiet, three-note ostinato-theme, just exudes the loneliness and sadness of that ultimately violent film. Least favorite moments: although producer Nick Redman, in his fine program commentary, suggest that "*The Nightcomers*, according to many admirers, may be Fielding's masterpiece," I find this score for Winner's prequel to *The Turn of the Screw* one of the composer's least convincing efforts, with its all too frequent neoclassical-moving-toward-Shostakovich pastiches and its excessively tonal harmonies. Even here, though, there were more than enough signature moments to keep me engrossed. The recorded sound, as originally engineered by Richard Lewzey, has remarkable clarity and depth.

Then there's **Twin Peaks**, the nighttime (in all senses of the word) TV soap opera created by David Lynch and Mark Frost. If there are Trekies, then I suppose I was on the brink of becoming a Peakie, even though none of the non-Lynch-directed episodes had the stylistic clout of the pilot and episode 2. Agent Cooper's nightmare, with its dancing dwarf and its backward-spoken lines recorded frontward and played back backwards to sound foreignly frontward, has already become a how-did-they-get-away-with-that-on-commercial-TV? classic, while the series as a whole is spawning cultural icons all over the place, including, unfortunately, the image of the dead Laura Palmer's face surrounded by its plastic body bag. But by the first season's last episode (written and directed by Frost), I found myself being manipulated past the limits of patience. I mean, the modernist in me can intellectually appreciate the soap opera as perhaps one of the major forms of the "open work," and for a while I was able to revel in how *Twin Peaks* both satirized the genre and pushed it toward new yet logical horizons. But soap opera is soap opera, and the piling up of outrage upon outrage (this season's third episode actually snuck in—gasp—the old "F" curse in the midst of its sick goings on) does not make me enjoy being sucked into an eternal narrative whose very open-endedness invites me to identify it with the "real" world. Further, it is hard to believe that Lynch directed anything other than the opening and closing of this season's initial (two-hour) episode. I got a huge kick watching a decrepit Hank Worden revive his Mose Harper character from *The Searchers* at the outset, and the fairy-girl and her Mendelssohn at the end were a nice touch. But, stylistically, the middle was nothing but talking heads.

Ah, but there's the music (Warner Bros.). Somehow, the mostly synthesizer, mostly Angelo Badalamenti music fits right in with *Twin Peaks'* over-saturated oranges and greens to bathe the goings-on in aura of brooding nostalgia and/or nightmarish anxiety. The main feature of the *Twin Peaks* theme (composed by Badalamenti *and* Lynch) is of course its immediately recognizable accompaniment, whose four-steps-downward progression provides the series' title sequences with a vamp-'til-ready quality that fits in perfectly with the soap-opera open-endedness. "Audrey's Dance" creates a kind of *nacht* swing style that simultaneously captures the good old days the town would like to live in and the queasy angst of the modern period it is stuck with—i.e., "Audrey's Dance" is a perfect musical translation of a major facet of Lynch's vision. The recording also features three Badalamenti (music)/Lynch (lyrics) songs, airily performed by another Lynch regular, Julee Cruise, who always sounds as if she is crooning with two or three of her clones behind several layers of gauze. At least one of these songs, the extraordinarily haunting "Into the Night," also appears in the 50-minute Lynch/Badalamenti TV film, *Industrial Symphony No. 1: The Dream of the Broken Hearted.* But perhaps the real *Twin Peaks* sound can be found in "Laura Palmer's

Theme," an oh-so-dark, minor-mode chordal meditation, in the low-mid-range synthesizer, that suddenly brightens deceptively into a major-mode theme that ends up breaking your heart. Interestingly, this music also becomes the "Love Theme from *Twin Peaks*," and therein lies the crux of the matter. In the good old patriarchal U. S. of A., where video-cassettes of *Henry, Portrait of a Serial Killer* are followed with an advertisement for Henry tee-shirts and posters, and where the body-bag-framed face of a dead woman becomes an icon of popular culture, the ultimate male love is necrophilia. In the end run it doesn't matter whether the dead woman is Laura Palmer or Madeline Ferguson, since every woman in patriarchal cultures worldwide is a potential Madeline Elstir/Judy Barton from Hitchcock's *Vertigo*, sacrificial victims to the male death god. And it doesn't matter who killed Laura Palmer (or Madeleine Ferguson), since most males worldwide are willing to step at a moment's notice into the role of Scottie Ferguson and replace sexual passion with murderous impotence.

Speaking of necrophilia, how about **Presumed Innocent**, from the ever-probing but always distanced camera of Alan J. Pakula? Here is a film in which one of the two principal females is dead from the outset and is only seen in flashbacks, a film in which, just as in *Fatal Attraction*, the dutiful wife restores the sacred family order of Reagan/Bush politics by killing off her husband's lover and getting away with it. Pakula's cool style and narrative structuring make *Presumed Innocent* into less of a monster movie than *Fatal Attraction*, but it is hard to know just how to read it. Whatever the case may be, the music for *Presumed Innocent* by John Williams (Varèse Sarabande) weaves its minor-mode filigrees perfectly into the film's visual and narrative textures. Scored for both acoustic instruments and synthesizers, the score revolves around a wispy, lilting solo-piano theme (probably in a 12/8 meter) that emerges from the solid G-minor tonality like dark figures from a miasma. It also melts away and becomes the base against which a more solid "theme," initially heard in the horns, establishes itself. Although, as Robert Townson notes in his brief program commentary, the film itself is "highly complex," one of the most attractive characteristics of Williams' score for *Presumed Innocent* is its simplicity. Indeed, when he wants, Williams can draw more feelings and atmosphere out of basic, tonal harmonies and modes (solidly minor throughout) than almost any composer I can think of. At its most intense, as toward the end of the "Love Scene" cue, *Presumed Innocent* harks back to the style of such a Williams masterpiece as *The Fury*. In fact, throughout most of *Presumed Innocent* one has the impression that the composer took his musical cues not from the narrative but from the quiet yet unnerving hollows of Pakula's visual style.

A very pleasant surprise comes from New World Records. Entitled **Vladimir Ussachevsky Film Music**, this CD contains a 15-minute, six-part suite the composer did in 1962 for a film version of Sartre's play *No Exit*, and much more substantial excerpts from the score he wrote for Lloyd Williams' experimental *Line of Apogee* in 1967. As anybody with even a passing acquaintance with contemporary music is surely aware, the Chinese-born (of Russian parents) Ussachevsky, who died this past year, was one of the pioneers in this country of electronic music, this at a time (starting with the

'50s) when the creation of electronic timbres and the incorporation of sampled, *concrète* sounds involved infinitely more painstaking processes than now. *No Exit* intriguingly combines various "pure" electronic timbres, the human voice, and various sounds, including what is described as a "pulsing loop of hog sounds," all manipulated, transformed, and developed into a score that not only creates a disturbing sound/music-scape for the surprisingly faithful, white-and-black film adaptation of Sartre's grim play about three characters locked into a (literally) hellish, existential triangle, it also provides rather atmospheric listening on its own, if you happen to feel like aurally tripping for a while. The seven segments, lasting nearly 45 minutes, from the "through-composed" *Line of Apogee*, the music for which I gather runs throughout the entire film (which I have unfortunately not seen), quite fascinatingly create, through a much more varied spectrum of sounds than in *No Exit*, a strong but of course non-literal sense of narrative. Ussachevsky's aural imagination seems to have been working overtime in the mind-blowing variety of incorporated sounds and transformations/manipulations: a fire siren metamorphosing into a woman's voice ultimately broken down into tiny shards; Gregorian chant sounding as if it had been carried by an uneven wind through metal tubes; Ussachevsky himself improvising at a piano that sounds as if it is coming from a distant dream; the hogs again; a sometimes humorous array of electronic bloops, bleeps, and burps; numerous contrapuntal mixes of various timbre fields . . . . These are directions one wishes had been pursued more consistently by the art of the cinema and its music. Meanwhile, not only does this CD stand as an essential film-music document, it also provides the listener with an exciting adventure into a strange universe of sound-generated affect. One not so small point: *No Exit* was not directed by Orson Welles, who did *The Trial* in 1962, as Alice Shields notes in her otherwise probing program commentary, but by one Tad Danielewsky, with Vivica Lindfors doing a particularly good portrayal of the character of Inès.

One of my major film-going disappointments of 1990 was Paul Verhoeven's **Total Recall**. The absolutely brilliant premise from a work by Phillip K. Dick could have led to a film filled with mind-twisting ambiguities. The world it depicts, you see, involves memory modification to such an extent that characters in the narrative totally lose their "reality" bearings, and I would have thought that director Verhoeven was the ideal man to cinematically recreate this postmodern nightmare. Instead, *Total Recall* degenerates quickly into just another Arnold Schwarzenegger movie. Something in it, though, must have mightily inspired Jerry Goldsmith when he composed his score (Varèse Sarabande; National Philharmonic Orchestra), for the music generates about as much drive and excitement as one would imagine possible. Infusing his unmistakable style with its post-Hindemith/Bartók harmonies, into an exceptionally broad orchestral canvas, Goldsmith also spices up the tone colors with judicious use of synthesizer timbres. Even when the music isn't charging ineluctably forward, it more often than not exudes a kind of creepy ominousness that allows one to sit back and imagine how good a film *Total Recall* might have been. In truth, of course, I suppose that the disproportionate number of "action" cues in the score offers a clue as to why the movie does not work. But, oh, do they make for rousing listening. The orchestral playing is first-rate, and the sound . . . .Well, besides the fact that this recording has more than enough sonic thump to carry the listener along with the supercharged music, it also quite stunningly distinguishes between the various orchestral choirs, giving Goldsmith's instrumental textures a life and depth I have never been as fully aware of as on this recording.

March/April

If Adrian Lyne's *Fatal Attraction* in its current form, with its imbecilic ending essentially dictated by acclamation, stands as perhaps the quintessential filmic representation of Ronald Reagan's moribund patriarchalism, the sadly beautiful **Jacob's Ladder**, Lyne's most recent film, may very well become a milestone of anti-patriarchal cinema. You know that *Jacob's Ladder* is going to take off in unusual directions when you discover, early on in the film, that one of its most sympathetic characters is a chiropractor/angel (wonderfully played by Danny Aiello). It takes a little longer to come to grips with the surreal alternative to the American way of death subtly and unsettlingly created in *Jacob's Ladder* by Bruce Joel Rubin's screenplay and director Lyne's absorbing visual style, not to mention a perfectly in-sync acting performance by Tim Robbins. And if you read between the frames of *Jacob's Ladder*, with its ultimate suggestion of mind altering by the U.S. military, you may see just how hypocritical it is for a "war on drugs" to be waged by a country that gives god-like status to the American Medical Association, whose ultimate goal is to cure and/or control everything with drugs (prescription drugs, of course), and god-like powers to the cigarette industry and the National Rifle Association. Just in case you were wondering why the film shows crazed American soldiers killing each other in Vietnam or why an angel would take the form of a chiropractor . . . .

As with *Fatal Attraction*, Maurice Jarre was called on to do the music for *Jacob's Ladder* (Varèse Sarabande). And as with most of the work Jarre is doing these days, *Jacob's Ladder* makes heavy use of various synthesized timbres, very often, in this score, strung together in sostenuto blocks that nicely complement the film's slightly otherworldly goings-on. To these electronically generated sounds Jarre has added vocalizings from the Kitka Eastern European Women's Choir and frequent filigrees played on a shakuhachi (a primitive, Japanese flute) by Kazu Mitsui. It is in particular in some of the shakuhachi passages, where the instrument simply oversaturates the textures with cloying meanderings, that the music began to get on my nerves, which Jarre scores often do. On the other hand, *Jacob's Ladder* also features a rather Delerueish main theme in which a sad, simple, major/minor tune played initially on the solo piano (by Gloria Cheng) ultimately settles into morose chordal accompaniments from synthesized strings. And the way in which Jarre incorporates the distinctive rhythm of a helicopter's rotor into some of the music creates an ambiguity that grimly complements the film's netherworld auras. *Jacob's Ladder* is one of Jarre's better efforts, and it adds a touching layer of affect to the film. This CD concludes, by the way, with perhaps *the* cornball song of all time, Al Jolson's "Sonny Boy." But it works in the film.

If *Total Recall* however turned out to be a lame Arnold Schwarzenegger vehicle, in spite of its exhilarating Jerry Goldsmith score and its Philip K. Dick story, **RoboCop 2**, for which I held little hope, proved to be great fun, particularly since it has something to offend just about everyone. Irvin Kerschner, who directed *RoboCop 2*, has been one of my heroes ever since *A Fine Madness* and, to a lesser extent, *Loving*. But of late he has been given mostly hack assignments, and so it was good to see him get as deeply and as stylishly into *RoboCop's* subtextual bowels as Paul Verhoeven had with *Robo-Cop* before him. Of course, one thing that *RoboCop 2* has going for it is a score by Leonard Rosenman (Varèse Sarabande), whose intense syncopations and brass-laden, Americana sounds keep reminding us, somewhere in the back of our brains, that *Robo-Cop* is nothing, after all, but the latest avatar of the cinematic cowboy. Indeed, if Rosenman's symphonic strains here do not quite generate the excitement of Gold-smith's *Total Recall*, they more than make up for this in the sophistication of the scor-ing, including the four vocalizing sopranos that "make sure that the thoughts and memories of RoboCop were human in character," as the composer puts it, or the com-plex layerings in the instrumental textures, not to mention the originality of the non-tonal harmonic idiom. And, of course, *RoboCop 2's* music does not fail to mobilize those dramatic, rising, open intervals (and the chords they generate) that have be-come a Rosenman trademark. *RoboCop 2*, unlike *Jacob's Ladder*, is a score that works better for me apart from the film in which it sometimes gets buried, although I would have preferred less obviously digital sound. Is it too much to hope that this score will finally bring a "Best Original Score" Oscar this year for Rosenman, one of Hollywood's most creative musical minds, who, upon accepting his second Oscar in a row in 1975 for arranging, had to remind the audience that he also did original work?

Well, you'll pardon my ego, but after I had read Stephen King's **Misery**, I had a per-fect screenplay in mind, a script that would have opened with the graveyard scene wherein the heroine of the novel that *Misery's* captive writer is forced to produce is rescued after having been buried alive. But I never wrote the screenplay, and, alas, it has been committed to film (by no less a writer/director team than William Goldman and Rob Reiner), and, alas, it has none of the self-reflectiveness, little of the daring claustrophobia, and only minuscule jolts of the terror crescendo that helped set *Mis-ery* apart, at least for me, from King's recent work (but then, there's the early stuff; I mean, I'd love to remake *The Shining*, a horrible film based on one of the great gothic novels of all time). Given Goldman and Reiner's willingness to play with the self-reflexivity of *The Princess Bride*, I'm all the more surprised that *Misery* turned out so flat, except that, I suppose, they were probably forced by the producers to play up all the Stephen King cine-clichés, just as Paul Verhoeven had to pander to Arnold Schwarzeneggerism. Even Marc Shaiman's musical score (Bay Cities; Dennis Dreith, cond.) is often deployed in the most hackneyed of ways, with sudden crescendos and outbursts signaling the onset of nasty mood swings by the captress (Kathy Bates) of *Misery's* writer (James Caan), and throbbing action music used to build up suspense.

This takes nothing, however, away from the solidity of Shaiman's efforts here. In his first full-blown film score, Shaiman, who has spent much of his career as an arranger, covers an impressive gamut of musical affect. In the opening cue, for instance, a minimal piano solo perfectly evokes the deep chill that sets the film's tone, while the ensuing slow waltz unobtrusively suggests the doom and gloom to come. Shaiman, as one might expect, proves quite expert at manipulating the various orchestral choirs when the musical goings-on begin to churn. And it has all been recorded with substantial thump.

I take advantage of RCA Victor's CD reissue of **Altered States** (Christopher Keene, cond.) to reiterate [from an early *Fanfare* review] that, to me, Ken Russell had every right to kick Paddy Chayefsky (a.k.a. Sidney Aaron for this movie) off the set of *Altered States*. Chayefsky has single-handedly weighted down, with his bloated, purple dialogue and his dime-store philosophies, more movies, climaxing in the idiotic *Network*, than any screenwriter I can think of. Whatever greatness *Altered States* has comes from director Russell's visual style . . . and its musical score by John Corigliano. One thing that particularly refreshes about *Altered States* is that Corigliano creates amazingly complex layers of timbres working almost entirely with an acoustic symphony orchestra rather than synthesized samplings and recreations. "Amazing" also describes, by the way, conductor Christopher Keene's shaping of this knotty score's many different passages. Essentially, the *Altered States* music communicates in three solidly different styles: a) an immediate, emotion-grabbing, Hollywood simplicity found principally in the love theme; b) a modernistic musical primitivism in which one can detect a certain amount of regularity in the rhythmic language and tonality in the harmonics; c) a basically avant-garde scoring featuring harmonic clusters, often pointillistic instrumentation, and extreme contrasts in the dynamics. Even the latter style, however, generates a kind of Bergian affect that works especially well in this film, which gives a whole new meaning to the term "tripping out." Further, the interaction between the score's three styles creates quite a unique emotional canvas for *Altered States*. The way the love theme ultimately emerges from the musically created chaos in "The Final Transformation," for instance, stands as a supreme instance of cine/musical synching. Corigliano also excels at subtle touches, such as the single low note, obviously from a grand piano, that opens the score and continues to pop in and out of the orchestral miasma. Indeed, it is such effects as this that make me realize just how limited pure synthesizer scoring is. As I've said before, no matter how "ingeniously" electronics can duplicate old timbres and create new ones, there is always an aural overlay of sameness that will never allow such an effect as a single piano note the full excitement and/or mystery it acquires in its "natural" acoustic form. Colleague Walter Simmons, in *his* review of the Corigliano's score [from the same *Fanfare* issue mentioned above], made the excellent point that the cinematic medium actually freed the composer from some of the formal strictures which, in the reviewer's opinion, had led Corigliano into "uncomfortable compromise" in some of his concert works. Detractors of film music, take heed!

You don't have to have a very long memory to recall that Jerry Goldsmith won a well-deserved 1976 Academy Award for his score for Richard Donner's horror thriller, **The Omen**. You may have blocked out of your mind, as I had, the fact that the score's title cue, "Ave Satani," a grim, Stravinsky-cum-Orff incantation that has since inspired numerous horror-film scores, won an absurd nomination for "Best Song." At any rate, Goldsmith's Oscar winner has been reissued on a CD (Varèse Sarabande; National Philharmonic Orchestra, Lionel Newnan, cond.) that should form part of any film-music collection's backbone. From start to finish, Goldsmith's music, orchestrated by Arthur Morton, to whom the composer offers a warm tribute in the program notes, makes the listener's skin crawl, whether via the decidedly nasty-sounding growlings of the mixed chorus or in the eerie and often violently dissonant instrumental effects. To me, the most unsettling of all the cues is "Killer's Storm," in which both the chorus and various instruments moan out downward glissandi that would cast a spectral aura over the sunniest tableau. And in some of the heavier action cues, Goldsmith does not fail to mobilize his characteristic churning brass. The score also has quite a memorable lyrical theme, often heard on the obligatory solo piano, that unfortunately gets arranged as a soupy song entitled "The Piper Dreams," performed by Carol Heather. If you listen carefully, you'll also hear the lyrical theme's opening notes as a motif in the "Ave Satani"—and there's the rub.

May/June

The real tragedy of this year's Best-Original-Score Oscar nominations is that they omitted what to my ears and sensitivities is by far the best score of 1990, Elmer Bernstein's **The Grifters** (Varèse Sarabande), which also may be the best film in a year of exceptionally interesting cinema. Based on the novel by Jim Thompson dealing with the down side of small-time scams, The Grifters might have inspired most directors to raid the vaults for sleazy pop and/or country-western strains. Or perhaps the considerable talents of a Ry Cooder might have been engaged. Instead Grifters director Stephen Frears turned to a classically oriented composer with, once again, spectacular results. Frears certainly got George Fenton's best work to date for Dangerous Liaisons, and he has coaxed yet one more masterpiece out of the ever-reliable Bernstein. Instead of sleaze, Bernstein went first of all for a kind of offbeat, resigned elegance in The Grifters' main theme, a kind of hesitant, Broadway two-step often carried by synthesized timbres that sound something like a cross between a harp and a harpsichord, this over an absolutely haunting accompaniment in a chamber orchestra of mostly brass and winds, with prominent piano as well (to say that I have been obsessed with this theme ever since I heard it in the film and then got the CD would be a gross understatement). Why elegance for a story like this? Well, Frears seems to be successfully establishing in his directorial style a tendency to work against the apparent grain of the story line in many areas of the filmmaking process, including the music, thus forcing the viewer/listener to look beyond the story's surface structures. And so, while

Bernstein's captivating main theme does not seem to belong to the world inhabited by *The Grifters'* three main characters, it always seems to stand just beyond their reach, reflecting their sadness and standing as a fox-trot *triste* to which they could move were they not so preoccupied with their own narrowly defined worlds.

But *The Grifters* is not a monothematic score, even though, remarkably, almost all its material is generated from the main theme, whether its diverse melodic twists or the added-second in the principal chord of its distinctive accompaniment figure. The film's title music (heard second on this CD as "The Racetrack"), with its jarring dissonances and its more intense sweep, sets a tone that one almost forgets until the film's jarring conclusion reminds us that the tragic irony was there all the time. *The Grifters'* score also evokes such diverse Bernstein efforts as *To Kill a Mockingbird*, in its moments of small-world lyricism, and *The Magnificent Seven*, in its jaunty, often triadal humor. I could go on, as I simply do not find a score from 1990 that even approaches *The Grifters* in depth, inventiveness, charm, variety, and, yes, consistency with the composer's personal style. Bernstein describes the film as containing "an odd kind of mordant humor, a touch of reality, and a brooding darkness which imbues the whole with a teasing, elusive quality." His music perfectly seconds these qualities. This extraordinarily well-recorded CD should appeal to even those who have not seen *The Grifters*, which has won four major Oscar nominations: Best Director, Best Actress (Angelica Huston), Best Supporting Actress (Annette Bening), and Best Adapted Screenplay (Donald E. Westlake). May they all win. But again I ask: where the hell was the Music Division?

Readers who are growing leery of my cynicism might want to skip on to the next review (*Awakenings*) without reading what I am about to say concerning **Home Alone** (the movie, not the music, which I rather liked). *Home Alone*, whose plot line, at least in its burglar-trap aspect, brings to mind a vague memory of an Archie comic from the mid to late '40s (can anybody help me out here?), proved to be the hit of this past Christmas season. Yet this seemingly inoffensive comedy about a young boy left to fend for himself when his family inadvertently leaves on a Christmas-vacation trip without him simply reeks of the pro-family-under-God-and-money moral and economic ethics of the Reagan years. Let's start with the house in which the boy is abandoned, an absolute mansion in a lily-white suburb north of Chicago, a house filled not just with immediate family but extended family as well. Then let's take the more obnoxious of the two burglars who threaten the boy's wish fulfillment: as (over)played by Joe Pesci, this burglar brings that unmentionable evil into the tranquil suburb, namely an odor of the heathen big city, in this instance via Pesci's New York City accent and behavior. Let's take the boy's "conversion" of a frightening, old-man neighbor—in a church where Christmas is being celebrated, no less—back into the pro-family mentality (the old man forgives his son for some unspeakable crime). Or, finally, let's take the cathartic return to the fold via the joys provided by the reappearance of an errant mother who never should have left home to begin with. No, folks, this is not just an innocent comedy.

But composer John Williams does his best to make it precisely that in his music (CBS), which works in a similar orbit, albeit less ironically, to that of his delightful *The Witches of Eastwick*. The Main Title has that slightly macabre, scherzando quality—cum Christmas timbres in this instance—that has by now come to be a Williams trademark. But what I also especially like about this score is that it evokes "Christmasicity" without resorting to all the tired old clichés dragged out by Hollywood for almost every yuletide music flick. Oh, sure, Tchaikovsky's *Nutcracker* comes to mind in the cue entitled "Holiday Flight." But Williams' remains the dominant "sound" here, as in most of the other cues. And instead of constantly incorporating existing Christmas songs and carols into his score, Williams has actually composed not one but two original pieces, the bittersweet "Somewhere in My Memory" and a lovely carol entitled "Star of Bethlehem." He also manages to incorporate "The Carol of the Bells" into a brief fugato in the "Setting the Trap" cue. And the composer sneaks in a quick reference to his *Star Wars* score, for what filmic purpose I've managed to forget.

Readers may be expecting me to tear into Penny Marshall's **Awakenings** just as I tore into *Rain Man* a while back, but such will not be the case. Based on the true experiences related in his book by Dr. Oliver Sacks, who has just been furloughed from his position at the Bronx Psychiatric Center, *Awakenings*, as one might expect from a movie with Robin Williams, consistently avoids the kind of pro-patriarchal manipulations that make *Rain Man* such a vicious film. It also avoids the kind of idiot mentality manifested in a recent TV special dealing with Patty Duke, which totally sloughs over the issues of the sexual abuse of which the actress was victim in order to hype the great father/A.M.A. cure-all for manic depression, lithium. *Awakenings* concentrates not on cures but on care, and not on the mechanics of a pathology but on the joy of life that briefly seeps through that pathology (in his communication of same, Robert De Niro has never more richly deserved an Oscar, which I hope he gets for his portrayal of a patient briefly brought out of a 30-year catatonia). Along the way, with its films-within-films and its subtle time layerings, *Awakenings* works in some mind-boggling phenomenology within which we are forced into a paradoxical (only in the patriarchal framework) awareness of how something that never was has always been.

There are those who may find Randy Newman's lightly scored music for *Awakenings* (Reprise) a bit soupy. To be sure, the nostalgia waltz played in such combinations as flute/piano, oboe/harp, etc., is becoming somewhat of a sucker punch in film music, and Newman has already proven quite adept at it in *Avalon*. But somehow (and I liked this music before I saw the film), Newman's strategically placed dissonances and his delayed resolutions make the nostalgia flow overtime in the waltz (entitled "Leonard," the Robert De Niro character). Listening to it, it was as if I was somehow reliving simultaneously some of my own saddest and happiest memories. Besides the waltz, *Awakenings* contains quite a bit of sustained chordal progressions, starting with the theme for Dr. Sayers (Williams), that have a calm, hymn-like quality to them that beautifully counterbalances, sometimes within the same cue, the aching memories of a past that never was, as evoked by the waltz. Indeed, in the end run the score as a whole affectively parallels the interaction between Dr. Sayers and Leonard.

July/August

Bay Cities has followed up on its initial two-CD release of Jerry Fielding Film Music with a second, single-disc volume entitled *Jerry Fielding Film Music 2*. A limited edition "not licensed for public sale" (I hear "Jerry Fielding 1," also a limited edition, is selling quite well), *Jerry Fielding 2* reissues the score for Michael Winner's 1973 *Scorpio* originally available on Elmer Bernstein's Filmmusic Collection, along with suites from *Johnny Got His Gun*, written and directed in 1971 by Dalton Trumbo from his book, and the 1972 TV film *A War of Children*. *Scorpio* has just about everything: a soft, lyrical, Latin-flavored main theme; moments of subtle weirdness, such as the violin duet playing bitonally over an orchestral accompaniment in "Reunion in Washington"; Fielding's wonderfully rich, part-Bartók chords that evoke deep mood wherever they appear; quotations (Johann Strauss, Jr., Sergei Prokofiev) and near-quotations; and the off-center, big-band sound that will create a major part of the atmosphere for Winner's later remake of *The Big Sleep* (1978). Fielding also shows a marvelous touch with timbres, from a solo piano to an electric harpsichord, from massed strings to diverse percussion effects. The savage, 11/8 march of "In the Winder Garden" is yet one more Fielding high point. But then, so is the exhausting, multi-faceted chase-sequence cue entitled "Hide and Seek." The hissily recorded *Johnny Got His Gun* has a much smaller sound to it. But it still reveals much of Fielding's very distinctive profile, whether in the type of dreary, open-spaces chorale that will later turn up in *Straw Dogs* or a nightmare waltz that will be expanded for *The Big Sleep*. A frightening and brutal picture, *Johnny Got His Gun* also has one gruesomely eerie cue in which Fielding electronically manipulated a male chorus to suggest the presence of the departed souls in an envisioned death train. The opening, dissonant, quasi-chorale in the brass followed by yet one more asymmetrical march (in 14/8? 3 + 2 + 9/8?) immediately signals Fielding's presence in *A War of Children*. And throughout the score sustains both affective involvement and musical interest.

Elizabeth and Essex: The Classic Film Scores of Erich Wolfgang Korngold, another reissue from RCA's "Classic Film Scores" series (National Philharmonic Orchestra, Charles Gerhardt, cond.), offers excerpts from *The Private Lives of Elizabeth and Essex*, *The Prince and the Pauper*, *Anthony Adverse*, *The Sea Wolf*, *Deception* (in the form of Korngold's op. 37 Cello Concerto, performed by Francisco Garbarro), *Another Dawn*, and *Of Human Bondage*. Highlights: the wonderful upward sweep that opens the *Elizabeth and Essex* "Overture" (put together from five of the film's principal musical sequences) and the moments of incredible poignancy that follow; the dark, film noir quality of the opening *Sea Wolf* music; the entire *Deception* Cello Concerto, which condenses amazing amounts of high drama and tender lyricism into a brief 12 minutes; the love theme for *Another Dawn*, later used to greater advantage in the composer's Violin Concerto; the recorded sound. Slight drawback: the National Philharmonic Orchestra is not always at the peak of its form in some of the performances here, especially *Elizabeth and Essex*, and I can imagine a better solo rendition than the one given by Francisco Garbarro in the Cello Concerto.

Mark Isham's music for Barbet Schroeder's **Reversal of Fortune** (Milan America), for which Jeremy Irons won the Oscar he deserved for *Dead Ringers*, often ventures beyond Isham's usual synthesized timbres into a mostly string orchestra, although even here I suspect that the orchestral sounds were recorded, sampled, and recycled through Isham's synthesizer. The result is an obsessively moody—and gloomy—score, parts of which, such as the cue entitled "Coma," I could easily imagine backing a film depicting memories of a rain forest (and it would appear that memories are soon all the rain forests will be), what with the eerily evocative percussion effects and the dark soundscapes. Even the cues deploying the sampled orchestra, however, often involve slow, quasi-arhythmic metamorphoses of string chords immersed in synthesizer timbres and resonance, occasionally reminiscent of Howard Shore's extraordinary score for *Videodrome*. Other moments move towards the more romanticized tragedy one finds in Barber's Adagio for Strings, a film-music darling ever since *Platoon*. Not a score to help you out of a blue funk, but definitely a highly effective piece of film composing. Even more effective is Isham's score for Alan Rudolph's stylish and bleak *Mortal Thoughts*, which I hope will get a music-track CD.

RCA Victor has finally reissued **Citizen Kane: The Classic Film Scores of Bernard Herrmann** on CD (National Philharmonic Orchestra, Charles Gerhardt, cond.). The recording begins right off with its showstopper, the breathtaking—nay, exhausting—two-and-a-half-minute "Death Hunt" cue from the score for Nicolas Ray's *On Dangerous Ground*, perhaps the single best performance in the entire "Classic Film Scores" series, which is hardly short on interpretive excellence. But just as welcome—and exciting, in its own way—is the "Concerto Macabre" for piano and orchestra, which plays an integral role in the narrative of John Brahm's 1945 *Hangover Square*. Filled with dark passions and a lugubrious romanticism, but also calling for substantial finger work (which soloist Joachim Achucarro amply supplies here) from the pianist, the "Concerto Macabre" not only provides a perfect vehicle for *Hangover Square*'s deranged pianist (played by Laird Cregar), it also furnishes a devastating musical portrait of the darkened reaches of the character's psychology. Further, this recording offers solid portions of Herrmann's *Citizen Kane* score which, while exquisitely interacting with Orson Welles' masterpiece, does not quite offer the musical interest of the composer's best scores. Included is the aria from the fictitious opera *Salammbo* butchered by Kane's mistress in the film but beautifully performed here by Kiri Te Kanawa, with her sumptuously reedy voice. I remember being less than impressed with Te Kanawa's singing when I reviewed the initial LP released of the recording for *High Fidelity* many moons ago. I can't imagine where my ears were at. But my main problem with this release, then as now, is the total exclusion of any of the Hitchcock/Herrmann collaborations, perhaps the most significant in cinema history. While the excerpts from *Beneath the Twelve Mile Reef* and *White Witch Doctor* are lots of fun, with their musical sound effects and their foreshadowings of later scores, they remain second-rate Herrmann for fourth-rate films. I had initially thought that this lapse simply indicated the imminent release of a quasi-complete *Vertigo* or *North by Northwest* done with the same loving care as to sound and performance as on the

Gerhard-conducted/George Korngold-produced *Gone With the Wind*. Such a project, alas, never materialized, and it is one of the major losses in film-music recordings.

September/October

Like one or two other Jonathan Demme films (*The Last Embrace*, which has a score by Miklós Rózsa, comes immediately to mind), **The Silence of the Lambs** starts off with brilliant splashes of style and then falls into utter conventionality. The initial confrontations between a young FBI trainee (Jody Foster) and an irredeemably murderous—but just as irredeemably brilliant—ex-psychologist named Hannibal Lecter (Anthony Hopkins) are fascinating in their study of character, in their creation of a harrowing cat-and-mouse game, and in the coldness of the settings, rendered all the more terrifying by the photographic style. But Lecter, you see, serves only as a vehicle in the pursuit of another psychopathic serial killer. Once the game is afoot, *The Silence of the Lambs* becomes just another *policier*, with a (female) neophyte relentlessly tracking down a psycho, rather along the lines of Kathryn Bigelow's recent *Blue Steel*, save that *The Silence of the Lambs* gets so carried away with Lecter that it forgets to pay any attention to the new killer, who might just as well be Godzilla. But, in a country in love with its devils, Hannibal Lecter joins the likes of Norman Bates (and his "real life" model, "Eddie" Gein) and Henry the serial killer (don't forget to order your T-shirts) as the latest cine-psycho-culture-hero. And Anthony Hopkins' communication of his character's thoroughly conscienceless narcissism, like so many striking acting performances, has, it seems to me, blinded people to *The Silence of the Lambs'* cinematic and narrative weaknesses. Rather more interesting is Michael (*The Thief, Miami Vice*) Mann's 1986 *Manhunter*, based on an earlier Thomas Harris novel (*Red Dragon*) with Hannibal Lecter, which remains consistent to its high-tech style throughout and which has much better balance.

One reason that I was excited to see *The Silence of the Lambs* was the name of Howard Shore in the score credits (MCA; Munich Symphony). Shore, you may recall, has excelled in setting the lugubrious moods for David Cronenberg films from *Vitleodrome* to *Dead Ringers*. Shore is one of those composers who uses tonality to particularly good advantage. This is not to say that his scores, including *The Silence of the Lambs*, do not have their modernistic side, particularly in the sometimes dissonant, sustained chord structures that slowly metamorphose into gloomy, lonely tonescapes. But Shore creates much of the effect and affect of his *The Silence of the Lambs* score through the unrelenting deployment of the minor mode in elegiac passages carried principally by the strings, generating an atmosphere consistently both sad and ominous. Often built around shifting, non-thematic harmonic progressions, *The Silence of the Lambs* also dramatically integrates several themes into its fabric, one of them starting off disconcertingly like the introduction to the old standard, "Manhattan Serenade." Perhaps the most absorbing—certainly the most morbid—of the cues is a piece of canonic interplay entitled "Lecter in Memphis."

Ennio Morricone's often very dissonant music for John Carpenter's remake of **The Thing**, reissued on Varèse Sarabande, may be one of the composer's least characteristic scores. Oh, some of the string sostenutos tie in with Morricone's music-scape style, and an ostinato figure also pops up here and there for the alert ear. Further, the multi-*divisi*, helter-skelter pizzicatos of "Contamination" recall the locust cue from *Moses the Lawgiver*. Not that *The Thing* is ineffective. Indeed, in its unrelenting bleakness, it works throughout on the same level as Carpenter's gruesome and claustrophobic vision. And the score offers some intriguing musical solutions: I particularly like the offbeat, canonic march of "Bestiality," for instance. *The Thing* is more a score of moods than anything else, and I would be willing to bet that director Carpenter, who has scored most of his own pictures, had a hand in some of the more obsessive of these moods (those cues—"Eternity," "Humanity, Part II," and "Sterilization"—in which the synthesizer forever repeats certain figures).

More or less coincidentally with the appearance in certain theaters of a "restored" **Spartacus** in which Anthony Hopkins looped Sir Laurence Olivier's voice for one non-post-synched sequence, comes a CD reissue (MCA) of the Alex North score. *Spartacus* may be more Kirk Douglas than director Stanley Kubrick, but the music is pure Alex North and stands as one of the great scores in the history of film music. I remember being instantly devastated when I first saw the film by the music behind the title sequence. With its strident dissonances, its brass and percussion instrumentation, and its slashing rhythms, the music immediately stresses the savagery and barbarity of militarism rather than its vainglorious heroism. Even in the midst of the title music, however, North pauses here and there for moments of near tenderness (I refer in particular to the second phase of the march that begins quietly in the basses, tuba, and snare drum). Further on, of course, the score blossoms into some substantial lyricism, most particularly in the "Love Theme," which may start out a bit on the slushy side but which, by the time it is incorporated into the final dirge, should leave no dry eyes. The score is filled with wonderful musico-dramatic touches, such as the militaristic echoes that punctuate the lullaby of "Quiet Interlude." And it is also interesting to see how North shapes what have become identified as "Americana" harmonies and rhythms to the needs of this Roman epic. Beautifully transferred to CD, the sound quality retains the solid thump, but also some of the shrillness, of the Decca original. A must.

November/December

Absolutely the most exciting film-music release for this column is the reissue by Sony Music Special Products on its "Signature" label of John Lewis' score for the Robert Wise **Odds Against Tomorrow** (AK 47487; mono). Released in 1959, Wise's ugly but riveting drama deals with three characters—an older ex-cop (Ed Begley), a black night-club entertainer with a gambling problem (Henry Belafonte), and a white racist (Robert Ryan)—who try to work together to pull off a small-town bank heist. For *Odds Against Tomorrow*, Lewis added to his three colleagues in the Modern Jazz Quartet (Milt Jackson on vibraharp, Percy Heath on bass, and Connie Kay on drums) 20 other instrumentalists, including Bill Evans on piano and Gunther Schuller on

French horn, to create a half-jazz, half-modern-classical sound. Although one might suspect that the use of the "popular," jazz idiom was generated by Belafonte's role in the film, Lewis' music, while occasionally escaping into jivey domains, generally backs up the extremely bleak atmosphere created by the narrative, the wintry locations (in both New York City and upstate New York), and Joseph Brun's black-and-white cinematography. As one example, the main title theme, one of the best in cinema, alternates between a Latin-flavored, big band sound and an extremely moody, smaller-ensemble theme in which the solo piano with harp accompaniment immediately establishes the more intimate, gloomy ambience that dominates the picture. And throughout, wispy, dissonant figures that function much more like cine-musical cues than the music heard in most jazz scores move about like the wind-blown leaves of *Odds Against Tomorrow*'s settings. On occasion, Lewis' ominous, big band growlings tend to overwhelm the picture a bit. But for the most part, *Odds Against Tomorrow* stands as one of the great cine-musical collaborations, and one can only regret that it did not inspire further efforts in this vein.

Well, I lied. Certainly just as exciting as *Odds Against Tomorrow* is Preamble's release of the complete score composed by Bernard Herrmann for Orson Welles' pioneering **Citizen Kane** (Rosamund Illing, soprano; Australian Philharmonic Orchestra, Tony Bremner, cond.). While I am far from agreeing that *Citizen Kane* is "the greatest film of all time," as producer John Lasher puts it in his rather polemical comments "About This Recording," certainly the coming together of various geniuses—director Welles, screenwriter Herman J. Mankiewicz, cinematographer Gregg Toland, and composer Herrmann, not to mention the entire cast—in *Kane* could not have been more fortuitous, with Welles' collages and fusions within the semi-documentary narrative and filmic structures adding a touch of dazzling virtuosity. Certainly, too, the numerous collaborations that Herrmann and Welles had already done for the latter's "Mercury Theater" radio show must have contributed to the total smoothness of the interaction between *Citizen Kane* and its music. Indeed, it strikes me that one of the secrets to understanding what makes Bernard Herrmann's film music unique lies in the radio-score quality of much of his dramatic scoring. Well conditioned before he ever entered the cinema to writing brief cues made up of short musical phrases, Herrmann rarely if ever fell into the heavy-handedness and overscoring one finds in the efforts of even his most talented colleagues. On the other hand, working with the anti-Hollywood-establishment Welles, Herrmann was able, for the "Breakfast Montage" cue in *Citizen Kane*, to put together a complete theme and variations to which the director edited the various scenes of this "montage."

One of the many charms of this score is the wistful, Americana quality Herrmann infuses into many of the cues. But at the heart of the music, just as at the heart of the film, lies a moody, libidinal darkness that latches onto Toland's black-and-white cinematography and colors the visuals with even more somber hues, whether in the doom-and-gloom "Xanadu" Prelude [whose opening motif comes from Rachmaninov's *Isle of the Dead*], with its characteristic low and mid-range woodwind figures, or in the more limpid but utterly haunting oboe (later flute)/harp theme in "Kane Meets

Susan." There is also a magical transition from the darkness into a snow-filled music-scape that evokes an all-too-brief moment of childhood innocence. Most listeners should also be bowled over by the dramatic impact of the aria-without-an-opera Herrmann wrote for one of the film's most memorable sequences. I could go on. Suffice it to say at this point that all forces involved have come up with a brilliant realization of Herrmann's first film score, all the Herrmann-composed cues of which, even those not (or barely) heard in the film, have been included. Not only does Tony Bremner lead the Australian Philharmonic Orchestra in a first-rate performance of the music, to my sensibilities the conductor captures just about every emotional nuance to be found beneath the score's surface. The sound balances Herrmann's timbre tapestries against each other particularly well, and I was knocked out of my seat by the way in which the "Opera Montage," with its electronic manipulations (including the famous record-running-down sound), has been re-created. Soprano Rosamund Illing's performance of the "Salaambo" aria plays no small role in the excitement generated by that particular cue on this CD.

Tim Burton and Danny Elfman are becoming one of the major director/composer collaborations of our era. To the fantasy/reality visions of ex-animator Burton (*Pee Wee's Big Adventure, Batman, Beetlejuice*) Elfman has contributed pop/*serioso* musical amalgams that generally fall on the dark side of Rota/Fellini, although *Pee Wee's Big Adventure* has a number of Rota/Fellini dead-ringer moments. For **Edward Scissorhands** (MCA), Burton's sad, quasi-*Frankenstein* fantasy in which the incomplete creation of a benevolent, mad inventor (played by Vincent Price, of course) walks into a '50s suburb that the Disney-studio artists would not have been ashamed to admit as their design, Elfman has provided as a main theme a kind of dream waltz backed up, to evoke the film's snow motif, by lots of celesta and a vocalizing boys' chorus (performed by the Paulist Choristers of California), rather the kind of thing one would expect for a film like *Home Alone* with a bittersweet ending. But, beyond this poignant theme, *Edward Scissorhands* runs an impressive gamut of musical inventiveness, from full symphony-orchestra outbursts of high drama to lively, two-beat cues that bring the music closer—but not all that much—to pop. The score has been sumptuously recorded. Unfortunately, it concludes with a truly awful song performed by Tom Jones. But the bulk of the music juggles the listener through a unique blend of both the styles and the affect to be found in Elfman's two mentors, Rota and Bernard Herrmann.

In his best scores, Michael Small has always had several things going for him: an advanced harmonic idiom that inconsistently moves in domains reminiscent of Jerry Fielding; an intriguing sense of instrumental coloration; and a gift for saying more with less, as in the chillingly minimal title theme for *Klute*. These qualities definitely work for Small in his score for Michael Karbelnikoff's **Mobsters** (Varèse Sarabande; Artie Kane, cond.). The score mixes a cool, big-band, rather *Pink Pantherish* swing with a fairly contemporary orchestral music that generates the requisite suspense affect. The striking title theme, in fact, manifests very much the kind of wit and mood that I admired so much in Elmer Bernstein's *The Grifters*, but in an idiom reasonably identifiable with Small. The solo-piano/soft-orchestra "Theme for Mara" offers an excellent example of the composer's penchant for understatement. Definitely one of the best scores of 1991.

Sony Music Special Products continues to reissue on CD film music recordings of major importance, expanded with materials not heard on the original LP releases. One of the most attractive of these is Richard Rodney Bennett's **Far From the Madding Crowd**, for John Schlesinger's sumptuous filmic adaptation (photographed by Nicolas Roeg) of the Thomas Hardy novel. Just for starters, *Far From the Madding Crowd* has as its main theme one of those haunting melodies that gnaws away at your feelings long after the film has ended. First heard on the solo flute (played by none other than James Galway), this sad, nostalgia-filled theme later makes appearances on the English horn, which is even more appropriate to the film's mellow, autumnal atmosphere. Overall, *Far From the Madding Crowd* is a lush, romantic work of art painted on broader canvases than one finds in most film-score cues, with a few rare forays into the more modernistic side of Bennett's style (as in "The Storm"). But *Far From the Madding Crowd* also has its more intimate moments in which very modal thematic patterns inspired by the folk music of Hardy's Dorset and Somerset settings weave their way through chamber-like settings. Most of the "new" material here comes from the folksongs amateurishly performed as part of the film's "source" music. Frankly, they intrude unpleasantly into the listening experience. On the other hand, Bennett's formal arrangements of "I Sowed the Seeds of Love" and "Tinker's Song," both performed by the late Trevor Lucas, work particularly well as concert pieces.

CHAPTER NINE

~

1992

January/February

Composer Patrick Doyle's second collaboration with director/actor Kenneth Branagh, **Dead Again** (Varèse Sarabande; William Kraft, cond.), turns out to be every bit as spectacular as—and in at least one way more spectacular than—their first collaboration, *Henry V*. At this early stage in his career, Doyle has already established, within the medium of the symphonic film score, an immediately recognizable style. Working largely, as he did in *Henry V*, within a tonal harmonic base that very often uses minor modes but that also continually surprises the ear with pandiatonic modulations, Doyle, as of the opening "The Headlines" cue, sets a tone of taut and unsettling suspense for Branagh's mystery thriller, in which both the director and actress Emma Thompson play dual roles covering two different time periods set apart by the alternation of black-and-white (for the 1940s past, of course) and color sequences. Particularly effective in this opening cue is the way in which dramatic outbursts are surrounded by quieter passages that create their atmosphere through intriguing colorations, both harmonic and instrumental (the harp and marimba play an important role in the latter area). Woven into this cue as well—and into many of the other cues, sometimes well disguised—is a six-note motif that comes to stand as a kind of *Liebestodt* for both the opera on which the 1940s composer is working and for his tortured, tragic love. Indeed, it is this element of self-reflection, with Doyle's music working both intra- and extra-narratively, that helps raise *Dead Again* and its score a notch above *Henry V*. It all comes to a head in the film's brilliant, climactic sequence, in which the reprise of a dizzying, octave-leap-filled allegro first heard in the "Walk Down Death Row" cue combines with intercuts of the composer conducting in time to the music track to make us realize that all the time we have been watching, in a way, the opera he has been trying to compose. The later introduction, for the only time in the film, of a chanting chorus merely seals this effect, although Derek Jacoby's momentary re-creation of Claudius likewise creates a nice piece of mirroring, in this case intertextual. Although I saw *Dead Again* (twice, in fact) before I heard this sumptuously recorded CD, I have no doubt that the music, under the dynamic baton of William Kraft, will dazzle even those who have not seen the movie. It is by far the best original score of 1991 so far (there are two and a half months to go as I write this).

I haven't heard film music as exquisite as Joanna Bruzdowicz's scores for films by Agnès Varda (Milan; Warsaw Film Orchestra) since Per Nørgaard's (a.k.a. Nørgård) score for the 1987 *Babette's Feast*. Bruzkowicz infuses subtlety and gem-like purity into areas of affect that evoke the deepest of longings, the most profound achings. Quite rightly, the CD opens with an "Evocation" from Varda's most recent work, *Jacquot de Nantes*, a film devoted to her late husband and fellow director, Jacques Demy. I have yet to see *Jacquot*, but if it is as sad as Bruzdowicz's utterly haunting evocation, it must be a wrenching experience. Weaving a solo instrument (a violin, then a piano) in and out of a small string ensemble, the composer bathes with subtle dissonances a melody that, with its sometimes-unexpected intervallic contours, is almost unbearably poignant on its own. The CD returns to eight more cues from *Jacquot* at the end, many of which rework the material from the evocation, including some soft, jazz variations and a solo violin meditation. The end-title reprise of the evocation becomes a "Largo" for soprano saxophone and orchestra. More austere and more bitingly dissonant is the music for *Sans toit ni loi* (Vagabond), Varda's study of a young, homeless woman. Composed for a small group of strings, *Sans toit ni loi* effectively parallels the film's coldness and bitterness while still maintaining a lyrical profile that is quite uniquely Bruzdowicz's. Written for only slightly larger forces, including a solo flute, the score for the 1987 *Kung-fu Master*, while emotionally brighter than either *Jacquot* or *Sans toit ni loi*, is still infused with the simple but probing *tristesse* that marks Bruzdowicz's other scores. *Kung-fu Master*, by the way, stars Jane Birkin and Mathieu Demy (Varda's son, I presume) in a story about an "impossible" love affair between a forty-year-old woman and an adolescent boy. The single cue for the 1987 *Jane B. par Agnès V.* offers a mellow, alto-saxophone solo that beautifully works around some of Bruzdowicz's characteristic intervals. As a bonus (and no doubt as a come-on it doesn't really need), this CD offers Michel Legrand's dramatic ballad "Sans toi" (referred to as "Cri d'amour" in the film), which plays a major role in Varda's 1961 *Cléo de 5 à 7* (Cléo from 5 to 7), certainly one of the high points in the career of one of the world's most original filmmakers. Sung by Corinne Marchand, who plays Cléo, a singer waiting to find out whether she has cancer, "Sans toi" is quintessentially Gallic pop music composed by one of its masters. The program booklet, which gives substantial information on Bruzdowicz and Varda, plus capsule summaries (with stills) of the films, is a model of what this sort of thing should be.

It was with **The Draughtsman's Contract** in 1982 that English director Peter Greenaway made his first big splash in this country, a splash not duplicated—but then in spades—until his recent *The Cook, the Thief, His Wife, and Her Lover*. Profoundly self-reflective and savagely anti-romantic, *The Draughtsman's Contract*, like most (or probably even all) of the director's films, also involves "the rigorous structuring of a central idea carried through to the letter," to use Greenaway's own terms, a structure in which composer Michael Nyman played a role from the outset. Although the initial plan of assigning a different ground bass to each of two sets of six of the draughtsman's architectural drawings proved unfeasible, Nyman was still able to create a score, reissued on a Virgin CD (with The Michael Nyman Band) that offers "a musical parallel with the organizational and temporal restraints that the draughtsman Neville imposes on the Herbert household as he goes about the task of completing the twelve commissioned drawings of the house and grounds" (Nyman). To accomplish this, the composer turned to the music of Henry Purcell (the film is set more or less in the year—1695—of Purcell's death), on whom he has done a fair amount of musicological research. As in other scores in which Nyman has "resited" a composer (the Mozart of the exquisitely anti-patriarchal *Drowning By Numbers* comes immediately to mind), the Purcell of *The Draughtsman's Contract* has been de- and reconstructed into a series of Baroque Minimalist (as I have described Nyman's music in an earlier column) cues that foreground accompaniment figures as "closed harmonic systems." Played by Nyman's 10-piece band, which includes two violins, a double bass, four saxes, a bass guitar, a bass trombone or euphonium, and a piano or a harpsichord, the music is immediately identifiable as Nyman after only a couple of seconds. Performed at a more or less constant loud volume, it is also capable of driving the listener right up the wall in about the same time. Yet there is something strangely captivating about Nyman's music, as there is, for that matter, in Greenaway's films, even while they're sometimes irritating as hell. While this is not a CD I am apt to listen to with any great frequency, it represents an extremely important document of one of the most important, novel, and offbeat composer/director collaborations ever.

March/April

Martin Scorsese is the only director around these days to be able to lay on his film-making with big, thick, sometimes overstated strokes and get away with it. This is certainly the case in his dazzling remake of J. Lee Thompson's gloomy, black-and-white suspense thriller, **Cape Fear**, from 1962. Oh sure, certain moments—Gregory Peck (reprised from the initial version) as an impossibly pompous lawyer, Robert De Niro's movie-monster refusal to die and get it over with at the end—impose their excess with too much of a vengeance. And, granted, Robert Mitchum in the original comes across as a much meaner-spirited, purely nasty individual than Robert De Niro's tattooed philosopher/evangelist who speaks in tongues as he goes down the drink. There are few more chilling moments in the cinema than the one where Mitchum kills the county police officer near the end. But De Niro, of course, embodies the Max Cady for our times, not simply the interloper into the perfect American family but a multiple id figure latching himself onto the psyches of a mother, father, and daughter who show the Ronald Reagan dream for what it was and is, a household in which the term "daddy's little girl" opens a plethora of ugly, subtextual doors. As "daddy's little girl," by the way, Juliette Lewis turns in one of cinema's great performances as Nick Nolte's teenage daughter. The scene in the high-school theater (impossibly located in the bowels of the building) should become a textbook model for acting, set design, script writing, and direction, the latter carried off to skin-crawling perfection by Scorsese's genius.

One of the true heroes in Scorsese's *Cape Fear* is Elmer Bernstein, who, by arranging and adapting original material, has put together one of the best Bernard Herrmann scores in the cinema (MCA). Quite frankly, Herrmann's score for the original film is not, on the whole, one of his best efforts. Filled with suspense-film clichés frequently used in the 1962 *Cape Fear* in insultingly obvious situations, Herrmann's music evokes Harryhausen more often than Hitchcock. BUT: the original *Cape Fear* does have a superbly gloomy title theme featuring a slowly descending figure in the strings and horns that immediately evokes the film's stalking id figure and foreshadows the murky, watery depths of its climax. This is the music that provides the springboard for Bernstein's adaptation, and it gets put to spectacular use almost immediately by Scorsese, not only in the title sequence (designed by Saul Bass, who did *Vertigo*, *North by Northwest*, and *Psycho*, and Elaine Bass) but also in two early scenes, the first showing the tattooed Cady as he is about to leave prison, the second to initially back the Fourth of July parade. The latter in particular is one of Scorsese's masterstrokes, as it transforms the patriotic goings-on into a creepily ghoulish passing-by of specters. The music, furthermore, often imposes itself at such a loud volume that it forces the viewer/listener to take note of it. It also has the effect of enlarging the aura of Cady's presence in the film. Besides the title theme, Bernstein uses some of the other *Cape Fear* music as well, in particular some *Psycho*-esque dronings in the high strings that, in the original, backed part of the sequence where Cady brutalizes a young woman he has picked up at a bar. But Bernstein also went outside of Herrmann's *Cape Fear* for some of the cues, most particularly to the rejected score for *Torn Curtain*, of which Bernstein has in fact made the only recording. The music here, such as the cue for "The Killing," works particularly well within the perspective of Scorsese's more flamboyant but also less literal-minded vision.

Franz Waxman's lush and often morbidly moody score for Hitchcock's 1940 film adaptation of Daphne du Maurier's **Rebecca** has become the latest classic score to be re-recorded by Swiss conductor Adriano and released in the "Marco Polo Film Music Classics" series (with the Czecho-Slovak Radio Symphony Orchestra). It is by far the best. Granted, in listening to the nearly hour-and-a-quarter's worth of music here, one is often solidly aware of the absence of the screen images and dialogue, to which the score, in the grandest David O. Selznick tradition, was often closely synched. It is rather as if one were hearing an opera without the singing or even the vocal lines. But as the cues move forward (fortunately in their order within the film), one's emotions also become solidly enmeshed, even without Hitchcock's movie, in a musical narrative brilliantly manipulated by Waxman. The opening theme, of course, reveals one of the composer's favorite devices: a melody that is chromatic while the harmonies around it remain more romantic, as opposed to the types of themes generated by quasi-Wagnerian chromaticism, which originate in the harmonic foundation itself. This theme not only perfectly sets the affective stage for the film's (and the narrative's) peculiar blend of sentiment and nightmare, it also stands as a kind of musical fetish for the absent Rebecca de Winter, rather in the way David Raksin's famous theme will work for *Laura* some five years later. Following the prologue, however, the score deliberately makes us forget the somber side to the opening: before too long, we not only get a love theme, we also get a charming, secondary melody that suggests the happiness of Maxim de Winter (Laurence Olivier) and his soon-to-be-bride (Joan Fontaine), whose first name neither the book nor the film will ever reveal. Even by the time Maxim and the second Mrs. de Winter marry, this "happy" theme has turned somewhat wistful.

The true turning point in the music, however, occurs as the newlyweds enter Manderlay, the de Winter mansion. As Maxim and his bride unexpectedly encounter the estate's entire staff, captured by Hitchcock in a dramatic long shot, Waxman introduces some rather stately music appropriate to the formality of it all. But the score suddenly casts a pall over the proceedings as music for the sinister Mrs. Danvers (Judith Anderson) drops the mood to a morbid, minor-mode hush that includes a variation on the theme for the ever-absent Rebecca, with whom Mrs. Danvers is thoroughly intertwined. Unfortunately—for filmgoers, not for listeners to this CD—the music heard in the film as Mrs. Danvers enters has a considerably less unsettling effect than the original music heard here, although one of Hitchcock's rare (in this film) stylistic twists somewhat makes up for this as Mrs. Danvers abruptly walks into a close-up from screen left. While some may object that, in restoring Waxman's original intentions, this CD gives a false portrait of the film/music interaction, I could not be more delighted. This transition, as Waxman conceived it, shows both how thoroughly the composer related to the film and Hitchcock's style, and how utterly masterful he was at translating psychological states into music. One might also take note of how cowardly the likes of the David O. Selznicks often were in the face of any musical depth. It is this mood that will dominate much of the remaining score, with its eerie parallel triads, its sparing but disquieting use of the Novachord (a primitive synthesizer of sorts), etc. Even when the love theme and the "happy" music make reappearances, they remind one of the disabused grownup that Maxim must ultimately acknowledge in his child bride. And it all leads to one of the most exciting cine-musical climaxes—Manderlay (and Mrs. Danvers) in flames—in movie history.

I have to say that, on the whole, this CD succeeds in communicating just about everything in *Rebecca* that made it the composer's personal favorite among his scores. But I also have to say that I remain somewhat mystified as to why a conductor with so little sense of musico-dramatic pacing has decided to devote himself to film music. While Waxman infused enough affect into *Rebecca* to make it relatively fail-safe, I found myself frequently waiting for the music to fully liberate itself, as if conductor Adriano's baton were building unnecessary walls here and there. And in one cue, a waltz heard early on in the score, the music bogs down hideously in a miasma of sameness. But *Rebecca* is one of film music's pinnacles. And while one might hope that a future recording will do it the full justice it deserves, this release in many ways represents it well.

For me to say that, with **Hook**, director Stephen Spielberg has hit a new low is a major statement of negativity, since I have never cared much for Spielberg's work since *Duel*. I simply cannot imagine where one would have to look to find more unimaginatively cluttered sets, more leaden directing, more abominable, cliché-ridden scripting, more shoddy photography (some of the shots are dismally overexposed), or more uninvolved acting, all put to the service of an excruciating stretching out—over nearly two-and-one-half hours—of hyperbolic goo. It was, of course, inevitable that Spielberg turn to the Peter Pan story, since no director in history has spent more time not growing up than the maker of *Close Encounters of the Third Kind* and *E.T.* Perhaps if Spielberg were to spend more time aiming at the child within and less time trying to pander to childish adults he would regain the promise he showed (very) early in his career. None of this, however, has kept composer John Williams from coming up with a major piece of symphonic scoring, stunningly recorded by Epic in some of the fullest, richest, most limpid sound I have yet heard on recordings. Oh, the *Hook* music will send your mind running to find out where it has heard a particular turn of musical phrase, harmonic pattern, or instrumental configuration. Williams' score, which sticks to parts of the action like cartoon music, even though much of it was composed before the film was completed, evokes everybody from Wagner to early Stravinsky, from Tchaikovsky to Borodin, from Dukas to Debussy, with stops along the way for some near self-quotations as well. The march of the Ewoks and the overall style of *Home Alone* come especially to mind. One totally incongruous cue—"Banning Back Home"—turns to a sort, semi-electronic jazz/pop that steers quite close to Dave Grusin. But this is all the work of a virtuoso composer and conductor, climaxing in a cue entitled "The Ultimate War" that may be the best cine-musical battle romp since Korngold. And so the unjaded listener can just sit back and revel in the beautifully executed splendor, lyricism, excitement, and, yes, corn of it all, although the recorded score, like the film, does go on too long. One can further revel here in the work of a virtuoso producer (Williams again): this is a CD to take along when you're shopping for a new audio rig.

I had been looking forward to Barry Levinson's **Bugsy**, with Warren Beatty teaming up with Annette (*Valmont*, *The Grifters*) Bening in a portrayal of the life and love(s) of gangster Bugsy (sorry, Benjamin) Siegel. But, essentially, in *Bugsy*, Beatty simply carries his Dick Tracy character over to the other side of the law, leaving one to wonder just how much longer the actor can get away with reprising his little-boy-idealist persona. Incongruous enough for the law-and-order-obsessed Dick Tracy (in a film I nonetheless loved), this persona sticks even more uncomfortably to the skin of one of history's more notorious psycho/outlaws. Meanwhile, Annette Bening, surely one of the strongest female presences on the screen today (or any day), gets to fully strut her stuff only in some occasional repartee generated entirely by James Toback's screenplay. Perhaps had Arthur Penn (in the spirit of *Bonnie and Clyde*) or Beatty himself directed *Bugsy*, the film might have followed through on the promise of its opening half hour. But in spite of some classy silhouette shots, some original editing, a bit of rather forced self-reflection, and some snappy dialogue, Bugsy ultimately bogs down into a bunch of so-what non sequiturs that render even the anti-hero's climactic demise uninvolving, aesthetically or viscerally.

But . . . As of the clarinet figures and morose, droning strings over an ominous, quickly paced walking bass heard behind the opening sequence, the viewer/listener realizes that the score (Epic; Unione Musicisti di Roma) is going to be one of Ennio Morricone's better efforts. Unfortunately, the score as used in Bugsy, usually at quite low levels, contributes little to one's involvement, aesthetic or visceral, in the goings-on. But as heard on this (again) splendidly recorded CD in Epic's "Sountrax" series, Morricone's Bugsy offers a substantial number of musically and emotionally engrossing cues that, throughout, consistently reveal the darker sides of the composer's distinctive profile. To me, two adjectives best characterize Bugsy's overall sound: moody and surreal. Even in the Mahleresque, mid-rangy love theme first heard in the strings in the "For Her, For Him" cue, Morricone floats all sorts of disquieting sounds around the main material, ultimately supplying a kind of bitonal descant in the high strings as the (alto?) flutes take over. Other cues definitely fall in step with some of Morricone's spaghetti western scores, especially Once Upon a Time in the West and Duck, You Sucker, but without the sad warmth supplied by the vocalizing soprano (and, in Duck, You Sucker, the whistler). In another cue, "Bugsy's Arrest," the composer offers yet one more variation on the nightmare march—almost a genre for Morricone—of Investigation of a Citizen Above Suspicion. The CD also includes some remarkably good remasterings of four standards: "Accentuate the Positive" (sung by its composer, Johnny Mercer); "Why Don't You Do Right?" (Peggy Lee); "Candy" (Mercer and Jo Stafford); and "Long Ago and Far Away" (Stafford). But in spite of the sticker on the jewel box that uses these songs as a come-on, most of this CD's hour-plus of music comes from Morricone near the top of his form. It's a shame Bugsy did not take better advantage of it.

May/June

I wanted to like **The Prince of Tides**. I have always admired Barbra Streisand, who stars in and directed the film, for her artistic integrity, even if her work in the cinema moves in an orbit that holds little interest for me. And after Mike Wallace's thorough trashing of Streisand on a recent 60 Minutes, I found myself rooting even harder for The Prince of Tides. But, alas, The Prince of Tides, well directed and acted (and scored) as it may be, mobilizes every cheap-shot plot gimmick and every American cultural bias available in order to hide all but the most superficial sides of the narrative's psychological and sexual abuse issues while painting a horrendously phony picture of the American ethos that comes straight out of the lies of Reaganomics. I mean, the hero (Nick Nolte), an unemployed football coach who nonetheless is able to live on beachfront property, actually brings the son (played by Streisand's son, Jason Gould) of a concert violinist (performed with moustache-twirling villainy by Jeroen Krabbe, a Dutch actor who is getting too many of these kinds of roles) to the glories of American football. And while the character played by Streisand, a psychiatrist (and wife of the concert violinist) living in aristocratic splendor that would do Nancy Reagan proud, runs slipshod over just about all the codes of the profession, ethical and otherwise, the film falls into that good old Hollywood trap of pinpointing the "cause" of a lifetime (actually two or more lifetimes) of dysfunction onto a single trauma—and a trauma that the plot glibly blames on goons from outside the American family rather than looking, at least for more than a couple of seconds, at the true sources from within. A lot of this, of course, comes from Pat Conroy's [nonetheless absorbing and much more complex] novel. But when it's all condensed into two hours of pure, Hollywood mind-fucking, these manipulations become harder to tolerate.

James Newton Howard's score for *The Prince of Tides* (Columbia; Marty Paich, cond.) falls under the category of the sucker-punch score, a term I have used (or should have if didn't), not necessarily pejoratively, to describe the music for such films as *Avalon* and *Awakenings*. Slow-moving, broad, romantic, and either ineffably sad or achingly nostalgic, Howard's score tells the viewer/listener, as of the music's opening measures, exactly where the film will go, emotionally, and even how it will end. Little solo-piano figures immediately evoke childhood; an oboe calls to mind far-off places while all the strings never fail to come in and bathe everything with a warm, sunset glow (the cinematography boasts a lot of sunsets, in fact). Yes, the music generates all the right feelings both with respect to the film and even outside of it. I find myself wanting to call my brother as I sit here writing this column while giving *The Prince of Tides* a second listen to keep my juices flowing. The problem is, of course, the extent to which Hollywood uses this musically generated affect as a smokescreen. I think the extent is obvious. The "soundtrack" CD also includes two vocals by Barbra Streisand not used in the film, the standard "For All We Know" (also offered in an instrumental version with a very unpleasant saxophone solo by Kirk Whalum), and "Places That Belong to You," based on themes from the film score. Streisand opted to avoid interference between her two careers by not appearing as a singer on *The Prince of Tide*'s music track. I think the decision was a mistake, as Streisand's presence as a singer—in the end titles at the very least—would have opened up the film with a tad of self-reflection to stand against its moribund narrative. But then, I would also have used the director/singer's inimitable rendition of "For All We Know" for the Rainbow Room sequence (has Streisand's range actually expanded, for heavens' sakes?).

Has anybody noticed how much the last two Disney animated features behave, at certain points at least, like Broadway musicals? Not that the Disney full-length cartoons, from *Snow White* to *Cinderella* and on, have not relied heavily on songs, many of which have become classics. But in the older films, the songs and music always seemed to grow out of and carry forward the action, as if it were the most natural thing in the world for villains and heroines alike to burst into song. It was all a part of the fairytale ambience. On the other hand, in *The Little Mermaid* and even more so in the Oscar-nominated **Beauty and the Beast** (Walt Disney Records), with music by

Alan Menken and lyrics by the late Howard Ashman, the action simply stops at various points, as it does on the Great White Way, to allow for songs that function more as set pieces than as integral parts of the action and its fantastic underpinnings. Having said that, I will immediately add that the Ashman/Menken songs from *Beauty and the Beast* move one or two steps further along the scale of delight, or at least they did for me, from those for their *Little Mermaid*. Belle's opening song, "Belle," performed with classic Rialto intensity by Paige O'Hara, works particularly well with the classically Disney animated choreography, while the Oscar-nominated title ballad, performed in the film by Angela Lansbury, who provides the voice for an English teakettle called Mrs. Potts, stands pretty close to several of the Disney biggies. I could, however, have done without the instant popification of "Beauty and the Beast" by Celine Dion and Peabo Bryson, whose top-forty rendition of it in the end titles shatters the mood of an otherwise glorious film. Two other songs from *Beauty and the Beast*—"Belle" and "Be Our Guest"—were also nominated. But my favorite of the bunch is "Gaston," an infectious waltz that merrily celebrates all the flaws of the narcissistic Gaston (sung by Richard White), Belle's wooer manqué. If you miss the wit and bite of the Menken/Ashman *The Little Shop of Horrors*, you'll find it all brought back in this cynical masterpiece. Ultimately, even with the Broadway aura mitigating some of the old Disney magic, *Beauty and the Beast* enchanted me almost nonstop. Looking at the all-but-three-dimensional drawings of the beast's castle is like taking a peek into the collective unconscious. And the Disney touch continues to animate the inanimate and the nonhuman with a spirit that poor old human beings can't come close to matching. Indeed, everyone with whom I saw the film, children and adult alike, was sorely disappointed to see the petulant but thoroughly lovable beast finally turn into a mere prince. One final comment: Alan Menken is a great songwriter. He is not, at the moment, a great film scorer, and he no more deserves the "Best Original Score" Academy Award this year than the one he won for his background music for *The Little Mermaid*.

I was looking greatly forward to **Naked Lunch**, as I find David Cronenberg to be one of the few, great auteur directors around at the moment. But I had forgotten how much I disliked the William S. Burroughs novel, which I read many years ago, that inspired the film. Although Burroughs is good for a laugh when he makes an appearance in a film such as *Drugstore Cowboy*, I have never quite understood the esteem in which very serious minds hold the author, whose combination of anus worship, misogyny, and druggie narcissism offers not a single subtextual nicety to provide relief from its crushing, masturbatory superficiality. Cronenberg manages to make his presence felt, particularly in his affinity for organic *grotesquerie*, in *Naked Lunch*, but not enough to save it from its source material. *Naked Lunch* does, however, have two things going for it that are beyond reproach: Peter Weller's post-*RoboCop* incarnation of the main role, a perfect artistic rendering of William S. Burroughs, Cronenberg's denials to the contrary notwithstanding, and the musical score by Cronenberg regular Howard Shore (Milan; Ornette Coleman, alto saxophone; the London Philharmonic Orchestra). One immediately recognizes Shore's trademarks in many of the cues: sustained, dissonant chords, largely in the strings, slowly mutating through various stages of affect while motivic and thematic figures occasionally make their presence felt. In this instance, however, the thematic figures are often supplied by none other than Ornette Coleman, whose inimitable alto-sax sound floats and darts, often bitonally, above Shore's morose soundscapes. As for the title theme, a gloomy orchestral passage that feels rather like an accompaniment, moves along on its own while Ornette's alto sax wails in its own orbit. In one particularly striking cue, Coleman, after a moment of moody interplay with the vibraphone, slips into a microtonal relationship with a solo piano (performed by Shore) playing Thelonius Monk's "Misterioso." Several of the cues are actually composed by Coleman, including the final "Writeman," in which Ornette, bassist Barre Phillips, and drummer Denardo Coleman have a field day playing something that might be described as free, nontonal sax-scat. But even when Coleman is not contributing, Shore continually comes up with his own motifs, such as some very nontonal harp filigrees in the cue entitled "Fadela's Coven," that create all but palpable atmosphere. Several cues also bring in some middle-eastern timbres to complement the locale (Algiers) of the film's second half. The whole thing, which has been recorded with exceptional depth and warmth, gives a simultaneous impression of simplicity and complexity, of harmony and dissonance, of reality and half dream, rather like Burroughs' own disturbing visions, I suppose, but in what to me is an infinitely more palatable form. Not since Jerry Fielding has a composer been able to use such musically sophisticated devices to get into the soul of a movie. *Naked Lunch* is one of the great film scores.

I reacted badly to Phil Joanou's **Final Analysis**, in spite of its solid, suspense-film plotting and its sometimes hyper-imagistic photography, for pretty much the same reasons as for *The Prince of Tides*, but in spades. One more time we have a psychoanalyst (Richard Gere, for heavens' sakes) living in aristocratic splendor treating a client (Uma Thurman) and getting sexually involved with the client's sibling (Kim Basinger). And, once again, we have the theme of sexual abuse, used here, however, as such a totally cynical plot twister that it actually provides, along with a toxic reaction to alcohol, the motivational key that allows the film, in a piece of hair-raising misogyny, to turn its two female leads into monsters. But, like *Naked Lunch*, *Final Analysis* has gotten infinitely classier music, here by George Fenton (Varèse Sarabande), than it deserves. This is the first score in which Fenton, to my sensibilities at least, has fully lived up to the brilliance of his *Dangerous Liaisons*. As of the "Front Title" sequence, triadal, added-note chords establish a rather Herrmannesque tone of tragedy-cum-suspense. But, like his Irish colleague Patrick Doyle, with whom Fenton shares certain orchestral and harmonic mannerisms, Fenton goes beyond Herrmann in the rather larger-scale symphonism of his writing, which manifests itself with particular vigor in the taut, syncopation-filled scoring into which the "Front Titles" quickly crescendo. In the calmer cues, Fenton often generates a kind of Expressionistic angst via subtle inner voices and the usual close harmonies. Certain moments even have a rather Ravelian hue to them, while the cue entitled "The Day Lighthouse" continually suggests the potential of a *Vertigo* turn of events, although only the faintest of love themes ever grows out of it all, which should come as no surprise. By the final cue, including, of course, "The Night Lighthouse," the music whips itself into a frenzy that rarely comes up for breath, helping the viewer of *Final Analysis* to forget or ignore the wholesale manipulations being operated within the narrative. The CD is exceedingly well recorded.

July/August

One of the most gratifying things to occur since I started writing about film music some 22 years ago has been the revival of scores by Erich Wolfgang Korngold. While other film composers may have contributed just as much—and perhaps sometimes more—to the movies they scored, I'm not sure the works of any other cine-musician stand so well on their own so consistently as Korngold's. This is certainly proven in spades by a new Bay Cities release, with Carl Davis conducting the Munich Symphony Orchestra, that offers all but one (a song sung by Nanette Fabray and Olivia de Haviland) of the cues composed by Korngold for Michael Curtiz's masterful adaptation—with the help of Bette Davis—of Maxwell Anderson's play, *Elizabeth the Queen*, retitled **The Private Lives of Elizabeth and Essex** for the film. While lacking some of the action, visual excitement, and musical dazzlement of such other Curtiz/Korngold collaborations as *The Adventures of Robin Hood* and *The Sea Hawk*, *Elizabeth and Essex* makes up for much of this in the deep interaction between the portrayed psychologies of the two main characters (Davis and Errol Flynn) and the musical score, which has the kind of flow and sweep one might find elsewhere only in Wagnerian opera. Just the transition from the opening fanfare, which looks forward to *Kings Row*, into the regal main theme suffices to get chills moving down the spine. Once into the film, the music spends a great deal of time caressing the character of Elizabeth, played by Davis as if she were the reincarnation of Henry VIII's strong-willed daughter. Particularly effective are subtle chromatic figures set in those characteristic, Korngoldian parallel triads. But it is the love theme that absolutely tears your heart out. This is one of those Korngold creations that, just at the point that you think it has nowhere else to go, suddenly soars into a new phase that can literally take your breath away. By the time the theme undergoes its final metamorphosis for the ultimate meeting between Elizabeth and Essex before the latter goes off to the chopping block, one's emotions have all but been drained away. (One wonders whether Flynn was the best choice for the role. He simply comes across as too nice a guy to be willing to offer his head to the axe rather than give up his thirst for power.) But the score has a good deal more to offer as well, including some slightly askew action music that accompanies Essex's ill-fated incursion into Ireland and that looks forward to the Panama episode in *The Sea Hawk*.

In the program notes, conductor Carl Davis describes how he played his videotape of *Elizabeth and Essex* over and over again, even in the hotel room where he was staying during the recording sessions. Well, all that obsession paid off, because his performance captures just about every emotional and dramatic nuance of Korngold's music, from its deepest, saddest lyricism to its subtle ironies. Davis also seems to have inspired the Munich Symphony Orchestra, which performs with both commitment and precision, and with the same involvement in the cine-musical drama. The recorded sound has a good deal of thump and presence, although I'm not sure I wouldn't have liked a bit more reverb. Tony Thomas' notes are quite informative; but they would have been even more attractive had he elaborated at least a bit on the interactions between the music and the drama. Thomas, by the way, gives 146 minutes as *Elizabeth and Essex's* running time, even though the official length given everywhere is 106. Certainly, one hears music on the Bay Cities CD not present on the music tracks. At what point did 40 minutes disappear? Again, it would be nice to know.

For me, Spanish director Pedro Almodóvar keeps getting better and better (at least over the three films of his I've now seen), as does Ryuichi Sakamoto as a film composer. Both talents beautifully interlock in Almodóvar's latest film, **High Heels** (Tacones lejanos), a strange but thoroughly effective mélange of outrageous, cynical humor and ineffably sad, inner-child psychology. Imagine, for instance, a scene in which a young woman, played with wonderful comedic flair and youthful *tristesse* by Victoria Abril, invites her long lost, songstress mother to a nightclub where a femme impersonator is "doing" the mother. Or imagine a plot in which the femme impersonator turns out to be the half-judge, half-police-inspector investigating the murder of the young woman's husband, one of her mother's former lovers. And yet imagine also a deep layer of hurt and unhappiness that runs throughout the film all the way to its achingly moving final shots. Sakatmoto's score (Antilles) adds mightily to the darker hues of *High Heels* with its main theme, a big, Romantic elegy, generally played with great flared-nostril passion by a string orchestra, that picks up where *The Sheltering Sky* left off. If there is a problem, it is that the theme gets repeated so often over the course of the CD's 45 minutes that it might get overbearing for some. But several of the cues in this particular score are not simply reworkings of the main theme but variations that sometimes cleverly hide their source for a while. The second cue, for instance ("Tacones Lejanos"), starts off as a puckish, rather Ravelian evocation for solo piano. The Ravel ambience turns up again in a later cue, "Interrogation," which adds the solo piano to the string orchestra. One cue, "Kisses," borders on Morricone, while two others turn to electronic pop (which, I think, is used for another outrageous scene, in which a group of female prisoners suddenly break into a colorful, revue-type choreography). The CD also offers two non-Sakamoto songs, performed by Luz Casal, that play an essential role. At any rate, Sakamoto's music, even heard on its own, has an immediate affective impact. My only regret is the omission on the CD of the Main Title cue, a moody piece [taken from the Miles Davis album *Sketches of Spain*].

September/October

Varèse Sarabande has just released Thomas Newman's kinky score for Robert Altman's **The Player**. Perhaps the true mystery of *The Player*'s music is just what codes that Altman and Newman got together and found deeply embedded in the film determined the shape of the score, which certainly does not sound like the kind of thing one would expect from a scathing satire of the Hollywood film industry. But Altman has tended to like his music a bit crazy, and crazy—delightfully but also disturbingly so—is precisely what he gets from Newman. What could be described as *The Player*'s main theme appears as the first cue on this CD as "Funeral Shark." It is a whining, languid kind of tune played as a "special effect" on some string instrument or perhaps on some kind of electronic musical saw, all of it very reminiscent of Jack Nitzsche themes for *Cutter's Way* and *One Flew Over the Cuckoo's Nest*. Accompanying this theme, however, is a Steve Reichian assortment of busy effects in the percussion, keyboard, and other instruments, including something that sounds rather like a Great Dane moaning. Even more intriguing, however, is the "Main Title" cue, which mobilizes bells, bass, and bongos to a Latin beat to create an aura of chaos, kookiness, and just plain tuned-outedness. Yet for all his music's athematic qualities, Newman manages to incorporate this material, in various ingenious variations, into much of the score. Occasionally, the score ventures into a kind of free-jazz improvisation, and on more than one occasion we hear more than one layer of music at a time. At one or two points, the tinkling percussion instruments seem to wander into the madness evoked by John Williams' brilliant score for Altman's equally brilliant *Images*. A couple of other pieces creep onto this CD, including a totally weird performance of "Rose's Cafe" sung by Akio Ushikubo. We also get to hear Jack Lemmon—yes, Jack Lemmon; everybody in Hollywood turns up at one point or another in *The Player*—do a brief jazz improv on "Silent Night" at the piano. Needless to say, by the end Newman takes his main theme and transforms it into a perfect piece of full-orchestral, Hollywood overstatement, perfectly in keeping with *The Player*'s devastatingly cynical ending.

Jerry Goldsmith Galore

Coma (Bay Cities). As Bruce Eder points out in his program notes for this reissue, director Michael Crichton, for his 1978 *Coma*, based on the Robin Cook novel, uses the rather original gimmick of keeping the film totally music-free throughout approximately its first half. But once Geneviève Bujold gets on the trail of the hospital plot, involving Richard Widmark and Elizabeth Ashley in particularly nasty roles, to kill off certain surgery patients in order to sell their vital organs at a profit, during which investigation she risks becoming an involuntary donor herself, Jerry Goldsmith comes into the movie with one of his most harrowing and, in certain instances, frightening scores. Making ample use of piano, various piano-generated effects, and strings in ways occasionally recalling Bartók, Goldsmith's music remains aggressively nontonal throughout, although the clarinet and later the high strings announce, in the opening cue, a lugubrious theme that flirts with tonality and continues to lurk around the score's dark corners. Goldsmith also offers a Manciniesque love theme, reprised at the end of the CD in a disco version, followed by an even more trivial disco piece by Don Peake.

Logan's Run (Bay Cities). Although the *Coma* music works to devastating effect in a much better film, Goldsmith's score for the 1976 *Logan's Run*, a story that deserved better than the bland cinematic treatment it got, is a lot more fun to listen to. To begin with, Goldsmith uses, for the first time in his career according to Bruce Eder's notes, various electronic effects, sometimes sustaining them for an entire cue. But these are the bleepings, bubblings, buzzings, and sighings of presynthesizer electronics, and, unlike Eder, I find them refreshingly unsterile, almost organic in quality, much in the way described by Louis and Bebe Baron in talking of their "electronic tonalities" for *Forbidden Planet*. This, as opposed to the timbres of modern synthesizers, which I do find sterile. But *Logan's Run* also contains a number of cues in which the composer deploys in his inimitable way the full symphony orchestra. And, here, the music, both rhythmically and harmonically, generally communicates within more approachable structures, whether in the exciting churnings that have become a Goldsmith trademark or in the sparse, string-unison-against-string-unison evocations of more moody cues. The score also features a particularly imposing, quasi-chorale theme that one suspects was more inspired by *Logan's Run's* set design than by its narrative. Indeed, variety abounds in this score. The exotic dance of "Ice Sculpture," for instance, seems to spring out of a totally different world (as does, for that matter, the sequence in *Logan's Run* it backs). One of Goldsmith's most attractive love themes, if you can call it that, also graces *Logan's Run*. One question: whatever happened to Jenny Agutter?

Hour of the Gun (Intrada). Although best known for the kind of ironic, I'll-never-take-anything-too-seriously role he played in the TV-Western series *Maverick*, James Garner gives us, in the 1967 *Hour of the Gun*, the grimmest, meanest, most single-mindedly vengeful Wyatt Earp ever to appear on the screen. For this bleak drama, directed [as a sequel to his *Gunfight at the O.K. Corral*] by John Sturges, one of the best makers of westerns turned out by Hollywood but a man not known for his sense of humor, Jerry Goldsmith developed almost an entire score out of an elaborate, single theme. First heard in a somewhat fragmented way in the sparse crescendos of the brilliant title sequence, which gets the O.K. Corral gunfight out of the way straight off, this almost hypnotic theme appears in most of the cues, often in orchestral settings filled with unison brass and open fourths and fifths, alternately evoking Copland and/or the Elmer Bernstein of *The Magnificent Seven*, another Sturges western. The theme also appears in a fluffy, quasi-Bachrach arrangement that might just as easily have turned up in a 007 flick and that, fortunately, has nothing to do with *Hour of the Gun*. Most exciting cue: the fandango cum bolero of "Whose Cattle." The sound reproduction on this CD is particularly good, as are the program notes by Intrada head Douglass Fake, who insightfully ties the music into the filmic action.

November/December

As befits a movie in which everything takes place in semidarkness (at best) with a deadly presence lurking mostly out of sight, Elliot Goldenthal's score for **Alien³** (MCA; Jonathan Sheffer, cond.) lets very little light shine into the general gloom of his own low-register musicscapes. A student of John Corigliano, Goldenthal, whose previous movie efforts include *Pet Sematary* and *Drugstore Cowboy*, shows in his music for *Alien³*, particularly the erupting low-brass figures amid churning and whirling strings, parallels to the instrumental and textural preoccupations one can hear in his mentor's score for *Altered States*. Elsewhere, Goldenthal's music scurries (sometimes back and forth from speaker to speaker), snarls, and hides to the rhythms of the film's eponymous villain without ever establishing the kind of style or mood that make Jerry Goldsmith's score for the original *Alien* so effective. The cue entitled "Death Dance," with its ominous rhythmic drive and its musical violence, generates by far the most drama, while throughout the score musical evocations abound that could almost emanate from the action à la the "electronic tonalities" used by Louis and Bebe Barron in *Forbidden Planet*. But in *Alien³*, these grow not just out of electronic (synthesized and sampled in this case) timbres but also from the composer's creative use of the symphony orchestra and various "homemade" instruments (Goldenthal, in fact, receives credit as both composer and orchestrator for this score), such as a piano wire stretched across a room and played with a bass bow. Interestingly, as the *Alien³* music moves along, it tends to metamorphose out of its quasiCorigliano dissonances into a more tonal medium, with Bruckner actually evoked in the final cue. Further, a major musical motif of *Alien³* is an "Agnus Dei" intoned by a boy soprano. Even given the underplayed religious zealotry that is a narrative theme in the movie, and even given the cavernous but hardly cathedralesque settings, the "Agnus Dei" remains somewhat inappropriate as immediate musical backing. But when you consider that the final(?) message in the *Alien* series, like that of the two *Terminator* films, goes beyond the implications of a heroine or hero fighting against unstoppable death force and reaches into the domain of redemptive self-sacrifice, the broader message of the "Agnus Dei" reveals itself fairly transparently.

While Brian De Palma [in the awful *Raising Cain*] continues to use multiple personality as a plot gimmick that thoroughly cheapens one of the most painful—and generally least homicidal—of all psychological disorders, director David Lynch moves both forward and backward in his profoundly disturbing explorations of the darkest roots of the American psychology, roots that very often sprout into the type of multiple-personality disorder shatteringly portrayed, perhaps unwittingly, by Sheryl Lee as Laura Palmer in Lynch's newest film, **Twin Peaks: Fire Walk with Me**, a prequel to the director's notorious TV series. Nobody comes close to Lynch's ability to all but palpably capture, both visually and in the characters he creates, the grandeur of the American landscape and the way it has trickled down into trailer parks, roadside cafes, and wall clocks fashioned out of varnished cross-sections of wood. And very few directors worldwide have the courage to portray the dark side of their cultures in surreal, supernatural visions for which no explanation is offered. For these out-of-time, out-of-space visions *are* the explanation: they place the narrative events in the context not just of a single piece of pseudo-history from which we can walk away but within the perspective of a savage, ugly mythology that will cause these same events, with variations, to continue happening.

In Lynch, whether in *Blue Velvet* or the *Twin Peaks* cosmos, those events are the sexual abuse of women and children—by their parents, by their spouses, by an entire society that would freeze them dead as marketable mother/whore images. Agent Cooper's premonitions are rooted in something much deeper than the personal mythology of his private dreams. And yet one also senses that David Lynch's collective dreams would not have the devastating impact they do if they didn't stem from some form of personal experience. This is certainly suggested, in *Twin Peaks: Fire Walk with Me*, by the recurring image of a masked, Lynch-like little boy, often accompanied by a grandmother figure (this image, in fact, harks back to one of Lynch's earliest films, the 35-minute *The Grandmother* from 1970). Absurdly trashed at Cannes this year, ridiculously dumped sans press screenings in the theaters by its distributors, and idiotically assigned by the *New York Times* for review to its senior old-fart critic, Vincent Canby, who is still applauding himself for liking Buñuel, the excruciatingly sad *Twin Peaks: Fire Walk with Me* is a brilliantly made film that sets its audiences up with a strong dose of the director's offbeat humor and then pulls out the bottom, revealing in its murky but resonant abysses what the "family values" so ardently espoused by the current Washington administration and its fundamentalist backers are really all about.

As he has for all of David Lynch's work as of *Blue Velvet*, Angelo Badalamenti has provided the musical score for *Twin Peaks: Fire Walk with Me* (Warner Bros.). The title theme is a dark piece of profoundly sad blues, with Jim Hynes' muted trumpet wailing softly over a minimal, two-chord, minor-mode progression in the keyboards that ties right in with some of the original *Twin Peaks* music by Badalamenti. I am somewhat reminded here, and even more strongly in the CD's second cue, of David Shire's moody score for *Farewell, My Lovely*. The difference, however, lies in the more pointed and obsessive simplicity of Badalamenti's writing, with its short, repeated figures and its gloomy, electronic drones further lurking in the comers. It is a musical style that somehow moves in perfect sync with Lynch's cinematic vision. Elsewhere, the score does not fail to bring back some of the initial *Twin Peaks*' aching strains, with the main theme appearing in *Fire Walk with Me* to segue, in a way that took my breath away, from the film's prologue, a kind of prequel to the prequel, to the main body of the narrative. Badalamenti's score includes a quasi-rap number, with predictably offbeat lyrics by Lynch himself and with Badalamenti himself growling out the lyrics through some kind of primitive electronics. Lynch also provides lyrics to several other songs, one a bittersweet piece entitled "Questions in a World of Blue" sung by the sugar-voiced Julee Cruise, another Lynch regular of late. In fact, Lynch even composed a couple of the cues and plays "percussion" in another. A collective effort if ever there was one. There are several other cues from this long film that I wish had made it to this CD. The overall score, beyond the title music and the heartbreaking final cue, is not on the same level as the whole of the music for the TV series, but it definitely provides part of the mood and atmosphere that make *Twin Peaks, Fire Walk with Me* the most provocative and profoundly moving film of 1992 so far, although it would appear that most people would rather not deal with the issues it both directly and indirectly raises.

From CAM in Italy comes a series announced as "CAM's Soundtrack Encyclopedia," which includes scores from a remarkable number of French and Italian films, including most of the Fellini/Rota collaborations. Only one of the first 50 CDs has come my way so far, but that one happens to contain one of my favorite scores, **Il Casanova** (Fellini's Casanova), with Carlo Savina conducting. Although the film, which stars Donald Sutherland as the notorious 18th-century sexual athlete, is, to my sensibilities, a tedious, nearly three-hour parade of empty Fellini excesses, the score for some reason is one of the most magical of this amazingly fruitful collaboration. The opening theme alone, a mildly jazzy, surreal waltz played initially on the celesta over an otherworldly accompaniment in the glass harmonica, sets one of the eeriest moods in all of film music. Rota follows this up with another of his greatest inventions, this one a wonderfully herky-jerky waltz, played on some kind of electronic keyboard and a harpsichord, for the "Magic Bird." In the same cue, the music gives way to a classic Fellini/Rota chromatic galop. Another theme that pops up in several cues, the sultry "Canto della Buranella," I'm almost sure turns up in at least one other Fellini/Rota collaboration. A theme also appears that was used in *The Godfather* and that dates way back in Rota's career. As usually happens in Fellini/Rota, this basic material undergoes various metamorphoses, many of them instrumental, before it plays itself out. In its offbeat and almost psychedelic moods, the score comes the closest, perhaps, to the music for one of Fellini's masterpieces, *Juliet of the Spirits*. Unlike the latter film, however, within which Rota explores a number of other spheres of musical affect as well, *Il Casanova* remains pretty much in the domain of the bizarre and grotesque, even when it is quoting from Stravinsky beneath a raucous version of the main theme. This is music that is both obsessive and haunting, and it provides quite a fascinating listening experience more rewarding as a variation on the Fellini/Rota sound than as music to back the great director's disappointing film.

After I first saw David Cronenberg's brilliant *Dead Ringers* in 1988, I eagerly awaited the release of a music-track recording of Howard Shore's limpid and yet ineffably sad score, which from the outset sets a tragic tone from which the film never escapes. Alas, some kind of ugly politics, probably originating in the film studios, kept that from happening, and I have been waiting ever since. Fortunately, this major lapse has finally been redeemed by a Silva Screen CD entitled **Dead Ringers: Symphonic Suites from the Films of David Cronenberg** (London Philharmonic Orchestra [in *Dead Ringers*]), which also includes music for two other Shore/Cronenberg collaborations, *The Brood* (1979) and *Scanners* (1980). More lush and opulent than most Cronenberg/Shore scores—it receives a particularly fine performance in beautifully warm, full sound from the London Philharmonic—*Dead Ringers* nonetheless offers those eerie expanses of sustained string sound in which Shore's characteristic harmonic structures leave evocative and disturbing hollows that musically mirror the frightening voids examined by Cronenberg. The score moves slowly and in the minor mode from cue to cue until, finally, the opening music, forgotten after the title sequence, returns to close the film, its major-mode harmonies making the overall sadness almost unbearable. Particularly rewarding about Shore's *Dead Ringers* music, furthermore, is that it brings other Cronenberg films and their music, *Videodrome* in particular, back into the affective memory, reminding us that *Dead Ringers* is not a single event but part of one of the most original visions in the cinema today.

In startling contrast to the lush symphonism of *Dead Ringers*, *Scanners* opens like something out of a pit orchestra for some kind of oriental spectacle. Little time goes by, however, before various unsettling electronic sounds are joined by a full complement of strings to create that tragic intensity that is one of the earmarks of the Cronenberg/Shore collaboration. Indeed, a decent amount of the *Scanners* music features electronic manipulations that seem to mirror the enhanced mental powers that often run lethally out of control among the film's characters. Particularly effective are the quasi-trumpet calls of the cue entitled "Ephemerol" (the drug that does all that brain enhancing), which somehow evoke both the majesty and the artificiality of those glass and steel palaces that produce products moving contemporary culture further and further past the brinks of its own limitations. Obsessive and often violent, like the film itself, the *Scanners* music is not as easy to listen to as *Dead Ringers*. Yet in certain ways this more primitive side of the composer presents a more multifaceted musical excursion into the director's unsettling universe. As for *The Brood*, one might be tempted to see a *Psycho* tie-in because of the small string orchestra that performs most of the 12 minutes' worth of music here. And, indeed, it must be said that Bernard Herrmann does come to mind at a couple of points. But the score for *The Brood*, which manages to simultaneously evoke both the bleak terror of the film's narrative and the coldness of its Canadian settings, ultimately moves in very different directions from *Psycho*, as does the film. For, while *The Brood* contains many of the trappings of the horror/ suspense film, in the end run it portrays, in its own sick way, a kind of vengeance against the lies and myths of "family values," this in a manner wholly different from but just as devastating as David Lynch. Well, maybe not wholly different. Relentlessly nonthematic and nontonal, Shore's music, while sometimes providing backing for *The Brood*'s violent scenes, tends to set a more general tone of grim ugliness from which there is no escape. For all this, the score offers fascinating listening, although it would be interesting to hear it played by a more professional sounding bunch of string performers. Cronenberg/Shore is one of the unique sounds of modern cinema, and this CD, which has an extensive program commentary by yours truly, represents an essential documenting of it.

CHAPTER TEN

~

1993

January/February

In my last column I reviewed one of my favorite film scores ever, Nino Rota's music for Federico Fellini's *Casanova*, reissued on CD by the Italian company CAM as a part of their series, "CAM's Soundtrack Encyclopedia." Happily, CAM has sent the first 25 releases, handsomely packaged in a plastic case, from this "Encyclopedia," and the next 25 are apparently forthcoming. At the top of the list for the releases I have received so far are most of the remaining scores Rota penned for Fellini films in one of the greatest composer/director collaborations in the history of the cinema. And at the top of that list, for me, is the 1965 **Giulietta degli spiriti** (Juliet of the Spirits; Carlo Savina, cond.). Fellini's first color film, *Juliet of the Spirits* delves perhaps even more deeply into the female psyche, via a character played by the director's wife, Giulietta Masina, than his justifiably celebrated 8½ delves into the male psyche. The story for *Juliet of the Spirits*—a woman facing the reality of her husband's infidelities and of her own sexual repression—could not be more banal. But, of course, Fellini infuses his narrative with a barrage of bizarre, circus-like characters and with colorful (in this case) and sometimes frightening dreams, nightmares, and visions that expand the heroine's personal unconscious into the domain of the collective unconscious (no surprise here, since Fellini was solidly involved in the psychology and metaphysics of C. G. Jung at the time).

Within this perspective, Rota's music parallels Fellini's cinematic visions in an utterly amazing way. The basic materials come from pop music, and no matter how the composer alters them, the 1930s–1940s dance floor is still there, as is the circus arena or the marching band. But alter this material he does, and in ways that are so subtle that one is hard put to define just what it is that gives that surreal cast to the Rota/Fellini score. But it is precisely that surreal aura superimposed over the down-to-earthness of the popular material that carries Rota's music into the same areas of collectivity that the director visits in his narratives. *Juliet of the Spirits* opens, for instance, with a fairly straightforward, fastish foxtrot that immediately acquires a special life through the composer's kaleidoscopically varied instrumentation, with a sax, piano, and bells variously carrying the theme initially presented on an electric organ over bass and drums. A second, much more ingenuous theme, heard first in the electric guitar, represents one of those almost imperceptible shifts via which Rota/Fellini scores transport you beyond the obvious without your being aware of what has happened. Other popular elements abound as well. But in many instances *Juliet of the Spirits*, no doubt because of the "spirits" that haunt the heroine, wears its musical surrealism much more overtly than most Rota/Fellini scores. This is immediately apparent in the second cue, for instance, in which a small women's chorus and a vocalizing soprano bathe the main theme in an aura of kinkiness associated with the character of Susi (Sandra Milo), Giulietta's shadow figure. The combination of a touchingly innocent theme with the disturbing, chromatic chanting of a children's chorus make the cue for "Il Teatrino delle suore" a chilling musical re-creation of what is perhaps the heroine's main trauma. A two-note motif haunts several of the cues like some sort of semi-malicious, winged wraith. And one of the seventh art's most magical cine-musical moments occurs at the end of the film: as a flute solo segues into a warm, non-pop reprise of the main theme, Juliet steps out of the prison of her childhood, as embedded in the house she has shared with her husband, into the tall, green trees of a forest that has become her psychic wholeness. The second part of the main theme then returns to provide the score with an upbeat closing. *Juliet of the Spirits* stands as one of the supreme moments in film scoring. The warmth of the sound reproduction on CAM's CD transfer makes an already indispensable recording even more attractive.

I would be remiss were I not to follow my rave of *Juliet of the Spirits* with more or less equally enthusiastic comments on the preceding Rota/Fellini collaboration, 8½ (Carlo Savina, cond.), since both 8½ and its score have acquired—rightfully so—the stature of classics. Although adamantly self-reflective, the film, Fellini's eighth-and-one-half work as a director, not only examines the midlife crisis of a character who is a film director and is trying to put together his latest work, it offers numerous autobiographical tidbits from Fellini's childhood as well. 8½ remains throughout much more extroverted than the introspective *Juliet of the Spirits*. And exactly the same thing can be said about its music. Rota tampers a good deal less with 8½'s popular tunes, and he introduces a good deal more of them—foxtrots, sambas, two-steps, and the like—than in *Juliet*. Further, Rota, no doubt under the director's guidance, quotes a number of familiar works, including *The Barber of Seville*, *The Nutcracker*, and "The Ride of the Walküre." And, of course, there is the famous near miss with Khachaturian's "Saber Dance" with which the music track romps throughout the film. With all of this, one would think that the score for 8½ does not come near *Juliet of the Spirits*. But. . . . What the 8½ music does have going for it, and in spades, is an utter infectiousness that cannot be found in such abundance in any other Fellini/Rota collaboration, or in many other film/music collaborations, period. Once you hear the opening bars of the circus march that opens 8½, you will never get the music out of your head. But this circus march gives way to a catchy tango that likewise gets under your skin. And by the time several cues have gone by, two or three other themes have likewise charmed their way into your soul, the most uplifting of which is a rising/falling, 10-note theme that somehow seems to sum up all of the film's creative forces. What also characterizes the 8½ music—and one of the stylistic elements that makes it work particularly well with its three-ring-circus narrative—is the constant metamorphoses of the score's many themes, borrowed or otherwise, which also run into each other with such ease that they ultimately seem to form an extended musical composition rather than a series of cues.

I must now direct my attention to yet one other film score, this one American, that must also be considered an essential item in any film-music collection, and that is Elmer Bernstein's **To Kill a Mockingbird** (Mainstream). You all remember *To Kill a Mockingbird*, my favorite excuse to bash the Academy Awards. 1962 was the year Elmer Bernstein's utterly haunting music for Robert Mulligan's film won a deserved Oscar nomination. And 1962 was the year Maurice Jarre's overinflated bombast for *Lawrence of Arabia* took the prize. Oh well. At least *To Kill a Mockingbird* has finally made it to CD, and in a remarkably clear and rich remastering done by Jackie Mills from what do not seem to have been particularly good tapes. Why do I like Bernstein's score so much when I have not bothered to watch the film again since its first run in 1962? Well, to me, even though director Mulligan, screenwriter Horton Foote, and all *Mockingbird*'s actors and actresses, including Oscar-winner Gregory Peck, showed great sensitivity in bringing Harper Lee's wistful novel to the screen, the music tells the story best by bypassing all the narrative gimmicks and getting directly to the emotions. If one were to examine the core of these emotions, I think it would be discovered that they center around both the beauty and the pain tied in with memories of childhood: the beauty and awe of a child's mythic world, with its fears as well as its joys; the ugliness and terror of a world that adults would impose on innocence. And this is what Elmer Bernstein's music communicates.

Mockingbird's title theme, one of the masterpieces of film music, sets up the entire story in a way that neither visual images nor words can come close to: a solo flute leads the way into a small collection of instruments—harp, accordion, clarinet, along with the flute, and then later a solo piano—gathered together very much like the treasures in a child's box of collectibles. A drop in register changes the tone of this pristine and rather unorganized space as a nostalgic, slow waltz, set to a slightly obsessive harmonic accompaniment beneath which the accordion quietly drones, creates an atmosphere that might best be described as remembered summer vacation. The full orchestra then takes over, revealing the theme's full harmonic profile for the first time and carrying the drama forward from childhood. Beyond the title theme, Bernstein's score continues to perfectly set mood, tone, and atmosphere for the film. In fact, the musical cues definitely string together to form a kind of narrative, from the merry Americana of the "Roll the Tire" cue—shades of Bernstein's earlier score for *The Magnificent Seven*—through the angularly modern and more dissonant style that takes over more and more as the world of adults begins to intrude. And there are few more moving cine-musical moments than the return of the main theme in the last cue: the children's mythic monster has been turned into real savior, and the summer has already been transformed into a warm but sad memory. I have had a number of kind things to say about Elmer Bernstein of late, and here is where a lot of that excellence really began to take off. Those who have been turned on by such recent delights as *The Grifters* and *Rambling Rose* will simply discover, in *To Kill a Mockingbird*, that Elmer Bernstein has been doing something right for better than 30 years now. Oh yes. For some strange reason, the 10 cues from *Mockingbird* are followed, on this CD reissue, by six Muzaky arrangements of various film themes I will not even bother to list.

The same year as *To Kill a Mockingbird*, Bernstein came up with another of his best-known efforts, his score for Edward Dmytryk's **Walk on the Wild Side** (Mainstream). Certainly, the combination of Bernstein's growly, gritty, dark, and swingy big-band theme with Saul Bass's graphics of a cat on the prowl creates one of the cinema's most memorable title sequences. While Bernstein comes up with several non-jazz mood cues, which contain moments that here and there parallel *Mockingbird*'s universe, and while the score also offers a fair share of quasi-jazz cues, some of them with improv, it is this main theme, which became a major hit (one of my favorite versions is performed by jazz organist Jimmy Smith), that carries the bulk of the music's emotional weight for the film's seamy, New Orleans–based drama. The *Walk on the Wild Side* CD also offers five themes from other films (three of which are likewise from 1962): John Barry's *The Chase*, with its jaunty, mildly jazzy theme carried mostly by an alto flute; "Cleopatra's Barge" from Alex North's *Cleopatra*, basically a serving of Miklós Rózsa cum Alfred Newman; Bernstein's *A Girl Named Tamiko*, a piece of inflated schmaltz; David Raksin's *Two Weeks in Another Town*, another piece of schmaltz, although not on the same goo scale as *Tamiko*; and the famous *Man with the Golden Arm* (1955), Bernstein's snarly piece of big-band swing that helped establish a short-lived trend toward jazz scores in the movies.

March/April

Were I inclined to give capsule ratings, I would take away half a star from an otherwise perfect, four-star evaluation of Clint Eastwood's **Unforgiven** simply because Eastwood, as an erstwhile, bad-guy gunman who puts on his six-shooters again as the paid avenger of a disfigured prostitute, falls off his horse one too many times. Pratfalls do not a convincing antihero make, and Eastwood's incompetent protagonist never quite descends into the pure negativity one feels he was aiming at. Other than that, however, Eastwood has pulled off, in *Unforgiven*, no small feat in making a revisionist western that in almost no way smacks of the so-called spaghetti westerns that helped make his career starting almost 30 years ago. Eastwood replaces the irony and visual/musical elegance of the Sergio Leone films (*Unforgiven* is dedicated to Leone and Don Siegel) with a grim, humorless vision which, even when it is looking at itself looking at itself via the character of a journalist who tries to create instant copy from

the film's personages, savagely undercuts any hint of glamour in its mythic underpinnings. Thus does Eastwood cast a decidedly long-in-the-tooth Richard Harris as a
would-be legend who gets beaten to a pulp by a sadistic sheriff (Gene Hackman) before his story ever gets off the ground. Thus does the defeated Harris depart in a train
that passes by Eastwood and his cronies, in a shot that takes the breath away, on the
way to their equally unglamorous dirty work.

For *Unforgiven*'s score (Varèse Sarabande), Eastwood turned not only to frequent
collaborator Lennie Niehaus but also to himself. For it is the actor/director who composed the film's main theme, "Claudia's Theme" (for the deceased wife of the Eastwood character, if I remember correctly), a wistful, simple tune often performed by
none other than Laurendo Almeida, whose decidedly lyrical guitar solos provide *Unforgiven* with just about its only trace of musical westernicity. Niehaus' cues, on the
other hand, rely heavily on the strings in a large orchestra out of which dark-hued
harmonies and moody ostinato figures create a mood not unlike what one finds in the
music of Jerry Fielding, for whom Niehaus did orchestrations earlier in his career (like
Fielding, Niehaus found his early musical directions in jazz, although you would never
know it from the *serioso*, classical score heard here). Synthesizer sounds also enter into
some of the cues, particularly the more violent ones.

If you were going to make a movie based on Elizabeth Von Arnim's **Enchanted
April**, about three middle-class and one upper-class Englishwomen who manage to
slip away from London's chill and rain for a month to an idyllic Italian villa, whom
would you choose to compose the score? The only possible choice is Richard Rodney
Bennett. But it seems to me that Bennett, who in fact did pen the sublime music for
director Mike Newell's film version of *Enchanted April*, initially shown on BBC TV,
has outdone himself in this instance. Yes, the British composer has certainly proven
that he is one of a rare breed of film composers these days in his ability to come up
with extended themes, very often pastoral in nature, that encapsulate the affective
essence of a given film, whether *Far from the Madding Crowd* or *Lady Caroline Lamb*.
Not only, however, does the oboe theme for *Enchanted April* turn out to be one of his
most sublime creations (it even gets played by one of the characters during the course
of the film), it is elaborated within hauntingly intimate harmonic and instrumental
settings that do a great deal more to communicate the peaceful beauty of the villa
(the same one that inspired Von Arnim) and its surroundings than the film's cinematography, the only facet of *Enchanted April* that disappointed me (one can only
imagine how the film would have looked in the hands of a James Ivory). When
(rarely) not offering some setting of the main theme, Bennett weaves tapestries of
dreamy mood, with the celesta and Ondes Martenot adding their timbres to those of
the oboe, harp, and a small group of strings, that evoke the kind of musical surrealism
one hears in Rota's *Juliet of the Spirits*.

Most of the music for *Enchanted April* can be heard on a Bay Cities CD (Neil
Richardson, cond.; Royal Opera House Orchestra, Covent Garden, and the New
Philharmonia Orchestra, Marcus Dods, cond.) that also includes portions of the
scores for *Murder on the Orient Express* and *Lady Caroline Lamb*. Certainly, the merry

waltz Bennett wrote as a theme for the eponymous train of *Murder on the Orient Express* is one of the pleasantest surprises in the history of film music. Bernard Herrmann apparently found it quite objectionable that Bennett would compose such an infectious tune for a film dealing with murder, and one can only imagine the doom and gloom Herrmann would have come up with. But, hey, *Murder on the Orient Express* is a piece of fiction that you curl up by the fire with, not a probing into the darkest reaches of the personal and collective unconscious, and the joyous train-waltz just happens to set a perfect tone. Certainly, much darker films than Sidney Lumet's *Murder on the Orient Express* have benefited from anti-type scoring, as witness Carol Reed's *The Third Man*, with its zither score by Anton Karas. The 11-minute cue heard on this CD, in somewhat cramped, hissy sound (the sound for *Enchanted April* is wonderfully full and present), concentrates on the *Orient Express* waltz; but we also get to hear the period-setting foxtrot that serves as the film's title theme and snippets of some classy suspense music that is probably a lot closer to what Herrmann would have wanted. The music for *Lady Caroline Lamb* heard here is the concert piece, "Elegy for Caroline Lamb," arranged by Bennett, with a strong part for solo viola (performed by Peter Mark), from his score for Robert Bolt's almost universally panned examination of the famous British political scandal cum illicit love affair. The centerpiece of the "Elegy," of course, is the big, romantic, and terribly sad main theme, one of Bennett's most memorable, although I'm not sure that the viola is the ideal instrument to carry it. But the music also offers its share of the subtle, dramatic backing, much of it quite moody, that the composer writes every bit as well as his big themes.

An extremely exciting CD re-reissue is Jerry Goldsmith's **Planet of the Apes**, remastered by Intrada from the original session tapes and including for the first time the key cue entitled "The Hunt," which for its first three-and-a-half minutes is a breathtaking, savage toccata filled with bizarre timbres including a ram's horn and a cuika, the latter instrument described by Douglass Fake in his program notes as "a Brazilian drum head device with a rod inserted in the middle of it, producing a startling imitation of the sounds of apes." Now just why this cue, one of the most exciting and musically inventive in the history of film music, was omitted from the original releases is anybody's guess. According to the notes, it was "the single most requested piece of previously unreleased music by Jerry Goldsmith" at Intrada Records, and Fake, who runs the company, is to be congratulated for making it available. But the entire score is a masterpiece from start to finish, and it is presented on this CD in remarkably clear sound whose dramatic stereo separation had a particularly strong impact when listened to on the headphones for my Discman (I also auditioned through my stereo system). In this score, Goldsmith more than meets the difficult challenge of creating a musical primitivism that almost never harks back to the granddaddy of primitivism, Igor Stravinsky. Essentially a themeless score, *Planet of the Apes* is filled with motivic fragments that steadfastly avoid tonality. Surrounding these musical shards are myriad chaotic figures whose prime impact lies in their rhythmic makeup and timbre. Whether in the eerie sighs of a bass slide whistle, in the atmospheric passages for full orchestra (with particularly effective use of the strings), or in countless percussion evocations, *Planet of the Apes* continually generates an atmosphere filled with so much anger and apprehension that the slightly silly film it was written for becomes almost moot.

May/June

Certainly, one of the pleasant surprises of 1992 was the popularity of the independently produced film **The Crying Game**, directed by Neil Jordan, who earlier did *Mona Lisa* and *The Company of Wolves*. Certainly, one of the huge surprises of this year has been the major attention paid to *The Crying Game* by the Academy of Motion Picture Arts and Sciences, an organization not noted for its taste in the offbeat, which *The Crying Game* definitely is, to say the very least. Up for six Oscars—for Picture, Director, Actor, Supporting Actor, Original Screenplay (by Jordan), and Editing—[only one of which—screenplay—it won], *The Crying Game* has gained some of its reputation on a major revelation that occurs about halfway through the picture and that people have been making huge efforts to keep secret. Having seen the film twice, however, I can guarantee that, while the shocker definitely has its jolt value, enjoyment of the film hardly depends on not knowing it is coming. While director Jordan, in various discussions, focuses on the Irish-Republican-Army side of *The Crying Game*, the film in fact deals with numerous forms of colonization, perhaps the most important of which is sexual. Within this perspective, best-supporting-actor-nominated Jaye Davidson pulls off a performance that is so utterly convincing that it cannot help but raise some consciousnesses. And when you get past all that, you can start looking in the direction of Hitchcock's *Vertigo* for even deeper levels of meaning.

Unfortunately, one of the Oscar nominees for *The Crying Game* was not Anne Dudley, whose score (SBK/ERG), initially heard in very brief cues, tends to support the tragic dimension of *The Crying Game*, a film that also has a fair share of bizarre humor. The composer who came immediately to my mind when I first saw the movie and heard its music was the late Georges Delerue, whose string-heavy, mournful progressions of minor-mode chords have carried certain films, such as Godard's *Le Mépris*, into areas of affect they would not have had on their own. Dudley's score similarly carries *The Crying Game* into emotional regions that I think director Jordan, like Godard in *Le Mépris*, had the wisdom to leave almost entirely up to the music to create. Like Delerue, Dudley relies on large masses of strings, with sad colorings from the harp, to carry much of the instrumental weight. And, like Delerue, she relies quite a bit on minor modes that are more important in the droning chords they produce than in the themes they generate. But Dudley goes beyond Delerue in the sharper edges of her harmonic language. Emotionally all but wrenching, furthermore, is the rising figure in the piano and strings that periodically affirms its presence, rather like the dead soldier in *The Crying Game* . . . and in more ways than one. Several very intense cues, including an obsessive march, add immeasurably to the dramatic impact of this score, with its mildly militaristic flavorings. The music-track recording of *The Crying Game* also includes eight songs, most of them heard in the film, including Percy Sledge's wonderful "When a Man Loves a Woman," which backs the opening sequence, and, of course, the rather naïve "The Crying Game," made famous in 1965 by Dave Berry, whose performance appears here. Director Jordan also got Boy George to do a version of it, also heard here, rather coyly claiming that the androgynous singer "had exactly the kind of voice the song needed to bring it to the 90's."

If ever there was a mixed-bag, postmodern western, it is Lawrence Kasdan's 1985 *Silverado*, which does not hesitate to throw Basil Fawlty—sorry, John Cleese—as a sheriff into a fairly conventional story of evil cattle barons against innocent settlers. Somewhat of a throwback to the larger-scale westerns of the 1960s, such as *The Magnificent Seven*, *Silverado* moves a step beyond them in self-consciousness, dumping just about every western archetype possible into its narrative, save a major love interest (which spared composer Bruce Broughton from having to write a love theme). Broughton's opulent, stunningly recorded score, reissued on CD by Intrada, definitely harks back, at least in its rousing main theme, to that quintessential '60s-western score, Elmer Bernstein's *The Magnificent Seven*. Aaron Copland also does not fail to have his say here as well. Filtered through the '70s and into the '80s, however, *Silverado* also sports a bit of John Williams. Beyond all that, Broughton, who certainly does his part to keep *Silverado*'s action flowing, ventures into somewhat more audacious harmonic territory than his predecessors. Major violence erupts, for instance, in the cue entitled "This Oughta Do." Broughton also comes up with some intriguing instrumental colorations, particularly in the score's quieter moments, which are fairly rare. I especially like the way he uses the (twelve-string?) guitar in the moody and quiet cue entitled "To Turley," while the even moodier harp/harpsichord figures over morose strings in "Augie Is Taken" evoke just about anything but the traditional western ambience.

July/August

There are two artists currently working who probably communicate the dark side of American culture more probingly and more unsettlingly than anybody else at the moment. One is filmmaker David Lynch, the other is novelist (and sometimes filmmaker) Stephen King. Of late, King has been even less unveiled in his examining of some of the uglier phenomena brought about by the American patriarchy, such as child abuse (*It*) and sexual abuse (*Gerald's Game*). King has also taken of late to drawing metaphors from the very trade he practices. In his recent novel, **The Dark Half**, King, taking a long, self-reflective look at that part of his soul and/or psyche that is capable of producing one piece of grim fiction after the other, ultimately expands that look into a harrowing vision of the violence underlying much of American society. Of course, almost everything King writes gets turned into a movie, and *The Dark Half* is no exception. From what I understand, George Romero's film based on the novel had been rotting on the shelves at Orion for a couple of years because of that company's bankruptcy. Although I have given up on most Stephen King films, the name of George (*Night of the Living Dead*) Romero, who also wrote the screenplay for and executive produced *The Dark Half*, plus the particular quality of the novel itself, got me into the theater the day after *The Dark Half* opened this past April. I wasn't altogether disappointed. Romero continues to use to great effect the area and environs of Pittsburgh, Pennsylvania, as an Americana synecdoche much in the way King uses parts of Maine. And Romero, with the help of cinematographer Tony Pierce-Roberts, evokes more disquiet with strangely harsh twilight shots than most directors can with buckets of blood. But much of the punch packed by King's novels grows out of the slow—I am almost tempted to say epic—pacing of the various episodes and their buildups, and this is something that even a two-plus-hour film cannot come close to capturing in its need to get quickly from one sequence to the next. The scene, one of the most harrowing in the novel, in which the ex-wife of *The Dark Half*'s writer/hero's agent is murdered ends in the Romero film before the viewer has a good idea of what is going on. I can't even imagine how one would react without having read the novel.

Certainly, however, Romero's *The Dark Half* has one other thing going for it, and that is its atmospheric and generally understated score by Christopher Young (Varèse Sarabande; Munich Symphony Orchestra, Allan Wilson, cond.). Has anybody noticed that Young is one of the most musically sophisticated, original, and versatile composers writing for the movies today? Even when turning out the kind of sad, solo-piano nostalgia-waltz that opens *The Dark Half*'s title sequence, Young, with subtle harmonic and melodic twists, immediately sets his cue apart from the solo-piano emotion-grabbers that have all but become a genre in recent film scores. At the other end of the scale, Young also excels at building up evocative layers of instrumental sound that venture into almost Ligetian territory. Yet those large planes of nontonal musical sound never expand to the point of oppressiveness, as they do in many modernistic scores. Instead, Young consistently decrescendos into quieter areas in the midst of which isolated timbres have their brief, disturbing say before being swallowed back into the sonorous miasma. In between all that, Young also works well within some of the more conventional, minor-mode stratagems of the horror/suspense film. I particularly like the resonant combinations of harp, pianos, and bells in the first cue. About the only thing that even slightly bothered was a somewhat Danny Elfmanesque vocalizing chorus, which struck me as rather out of place both within the score itself and within the context of the film.

When Omega's CD reissue of Ennio Morricone's score for **Sacco and Vanzetti** (Joan Baez, vocals) showed up in my mail, the first music that popped into my head was the song—actually more a refrain than a song—"Here's To You." Performed by Joan Baez, who also wrote its lyrics, "Here's To You" caps Giuliano Montaldo's film with a note of upbeat humanitarianism that nonetheless does not allow us to forget the hate and racism of which the two Italian anarchists were the victims. But for some reason, I had forgotten the absolutely chilling "Ballad of Sacco and Vanzetti" until I began to listen to this CD, an essential item in any film music collection. In this elaborate song, Joan Baez's voice simply soars as her challenging and often bitterly ironic lyrics combine with Ennio Morricone's unique brand of dramatic lyricism in a manner that will almost surely elicit tears of rage and sadness. Morricone has always written well for the female voice, as anyone who has been moved by the vocalizing soprano in many of his scores will attest. But in the three parts of "The Ballad of Sacco and Vanzetti," Morricone outdoes himself as he carries Baez's startlingly rich and expressive voice from areas below the comfortable range of most sopranos to heights that send chills down the spine. Pardon my hyperbole, but the Morricone/Baez collaboration here produces one of the great moments in the history of western music. Nor should one forget the political impact of "The Ballad of Sacco and Vanzetti," which now stands as a rather sad epitaph for a long-vanished period of political idealism. As for *Sacco and Vanzetti*'s instrumental cues, these are vintage Morricone. The opening cue, "Hope for Freedom," offers that blend of bel canto lyricism and Bachian harmonic progressions that form a unique facet of the Italian composer's style, while the more darkly hued cues, with their slashed string chords, their layers of often bizarre timbres, and their unsettling chromatic motif, confirm Morricone as a master of the grim.

The first volume of Bay Cities' limited-edition releases devoted to the film music of the late Jerry Fielding offers eight minutes' worth of music from the score Fielding wrote for Michael Winner's revisionist western from 1972, *Chato's Land*. A newly discovered tape that the composer had prepared for a recording that never materialized (record companies had an unfailing instinct for avoiding quality movie music back then) has allowed the company to bring out a fourth Fielding release, this one entitled **Chato's Land: The Film Music of Jerry Fielding**. Presented in two large blocks that run some 41 minutes, the music for *Chato's Land* immediately identifies itself as Fielding. As in the composer's music for *The Wild Bunch*, quiet drum tattoos underlie much of the scoring, creating a mildly militaristic aura that communicates more than would the standard cowboy/Native American musical clichés about the underpinnings of *Chato's Land*, in which an Apache half-breed played by Charles Bronson is pursued across brutal desert terrain—his land, indeed—by ex-Confederate Jack Palance (who else?) and what Nick Redman in his notes refers to as a posse made up of the "town psychos." One of the fascinating transitions in the musical score occurs about halfway into the first 20-minute segment, when the American militarism implied by the snare-drum tattoos is replaced by percussion figures and harmonic motifs that evoke Chato's Native American origins. It is a perfect musical parallel for the mastery that Chato gains over the posse members as they wander farther into his land. Along with these and many other subtleties I could mention, Fielding offers his usual array of transparently textured tonescapes in which strings and winds in particular move within often nontonal harmonic settings to evoke moods that are all but palpable. A seven-note motif, perhaps intended to suggest the presence of the loner antihero of *Chato's Land*, also floats eerily in and out of the music. Generally communicating from a place of quiet and ominous expectation, Fielding's score also lets loose here and there with outbursts of action music that is all the more intense because its rhythmic patterns and drives are carried forward with a kind of internal continuity generally lacking in film-music cues. Also included on the *Chato's Land* CD is a 15-minute suite of music Fielding composed for a TV western made in 1978 and entitled *Mr. Horn*. More thickly textured, less subtle, more tubbily recorded and, not surprisingly, more reliant on clichés than most of Fielding's scores, *Mr. Horn* nonetheless has its moments where Fielding's individuality speaks through, whether in the expertly manipulated percussion figures or in the music's tendency to constantly suggest the open fifth as its harmonic point of departure. But it is the *Chato's Land* music that makes this CD indispensable.

September/October

Walt Disney Records, no doubt in anticipation of a video issue, has released a CD of just about all the music—songs and "underscore" alike—that appears in **Snow White and the Seven Dwarfs**. No fewer than three composers—Frank Churchill, Leigh Harline, and Paul J. Smith (whose music for *The Living Desert* remains perhaps my favorite Disney instrumental score)—contributed their efforts to the now famous and beloved songs and the background score, with Larry Morey writing all the lyrics. Pieced together from incomplete, nitrate optical tracks, just as they were about to be shipped off to the Library of Congress vaults, and other sources, this *Snow White* offers, in surprisingly good, monaural sound, a more than complete musical profile of the entire movie. What this means is that we get to hear the movie's eight songs linked by considerable amounts of the often melodramatic underscoring, the latter sans dialogue, save a bit of rhythmic declamation done by Snow White, generally to lead into songs. While the underscoring has its captivating moments—the wonderful "Magic Mirror" cue, which just oozes suspense and evil, would be quite comfortable in a film such as *Spellbound*—and while it certainly has a documentary value, it will not in all probability sustain most listeners' interest over the hour-plus length of this CD. It is, on the other hand, utterly chilling to hear Adriana Caselotti's original renditions of Snow White's songs: "One Song," "With A Smile and a Song," "Whistle While You Work," and, of course, "Some Day, My Prince Will Come." One question, though: are Caselotti's very tight vibrato and petite high range entirely natural, or was some fiddling done to get some of those opera-cum-little-girl timbres? The Dwarfs' songs, on the other hand—"Heigh Ho," and particularly "The Silly Song," "Bluddle-Uddle-Um-Dum," and "Music in Your Soup"—don't work quite as well without the visuals. The CD, by the way, offers a longer version of the tiresome "Music in Your Soup" than we hear in the film, and a song, "You're Never Too Old to Be Young," that fortunately never made it to the final cut. The program notes include lyrics for the songs and some commentary on how this recording was pieced together.

One of cinema's more remarkable director/composer collaborations has been the one between "New German Cinema" director Werner Herzog and musician Florian Fricke, who, since 1969, has performed his decidedly non-Western, often New Age/psychedelic compositions with a group he calls "Popol Vuh," named after the Mayan Book of the Dead. Having released several Popol Vuh albums in the past, Milan has now come up with a CD entitled **The Best of Popol Vuh**, which includes three cues from *Fitzcaraldo*, two each from *Cobra Verde* and *Nosferatu the Vampyre*, and one each from *Gasherbrum* and *Aguirre, the Wrath of God*. Although rightly compared in Hubert

Haas' brief program notes to Tangerine Dream, Popol Vuh has quite a unique sound that in most instances is bigger than Tangerine Dream's. Two of the three *Fitzcaraldo* cues, for instance, feature quasi-Eastern-religion chanting from a large chorus (the Choir of the Bavarian State Opera) over instrumental and electronic drones set to a slow, processional beat. Indeed, expanses of vocal sound dominate many of the selections here, from the more Buddhist evocations of *Fitzcaraldo* through the more African strains of *Gasherbrum* to the often high-pitched, non-ethnic sadness of *Aguirre, the Wrath of God*. On the other hand, the all-instrumental (all-electronic, really) cue entitled "A Different World" from *Cobra Verde* reaches even further into expanses of New Age space than most of Tangerine Dream's nonetheless absorbing tonescapes. Yet 1960s guitar riffs often appear in the music of both groups to move the sound a little more back toward a more earthbound center point. Deliciously unsettling from Popol Vuh are the eerie evocations, with wind and percussion, of Gregorian chant that help make *Nosferatu*'s title sequence one of the creepiest in cinema history. Less dark but almost equally unnerving, the other cue from *Nosferatu*, "Oh Hear, Thou Who Darest," offers above its electronic drones some hauntingly archaic figures diversely presented in the piano, winds, and/or sitar. In the history of film scoring, *Nosferatu* occupies a place near the top. I could go on. This CD contains not a single bad cue, and it documents one of film music's truly original styles. Further, you don't have to have seen the Werner Herzog films involved—although I strongly recommend you do—to be transported into this music's netherworlds.

You may remember **Brazil**, Terry Gilliam's Orwellesque parable that only major amounts of protest saved from permanent butchery by the studio. *Brazil*, that rambling, dark vision of the future filled with set design technology out of the 1930s and '40s. Milan has released a CD of Michael Kamen's elaborate score for this 1985 film, the most interesting cues for which engage a large symphony orchestra to create moods from heroic to funereal, with quite a bit of militarism in between, and with styles suggesting composers as diverse as David Shire and John Barry. Given the nature of the film, of course, one is never sure whether to take the moments of high musical drama ironically or straight, and it is to Kamen's eternal credit that he has composed music that can be comfortably listened to within either perspective—or both. Of course, the score contains quite a bit of pastiche music—quasi-TV-commercial background; quasi-pomp-and-circumstance program-opening music; tangos; waltzes, etc., all intimately and intricately related to *Brazil*'s depressing and cluttered screenscape. We also get to hear a few fragments from the film's dialogue. And, of course, the famous song, "Aquarella dos Brasil," makes ongoing appearances, both in a more or less straight version by Geoff Muldaur and even integrated into the fabric of many of Kamen's instrumental cues. Strangely, the name of "Aquarella dos Brasil's" composer, Harry Barrosso, appears only in small print in Milan's program notes. At any rate, the Brazil CD is certainly worth it for such symphonic cues as "The Battle" (again, just how seriously are we to take the heavy musical drama here? Does the fragment from "Aquarella dos Brasil" toward the end sabotage the cue's ominous intensity or reinforce it?).

November/December

Fortunately, Steven Spielberg does not stand for all that is coming out of Hollywood these days, although from the looks of many of the previews I am seeing in the theaters his mentality is trickling down into some pretty low strata. Going solidly against the Spielberg grain, **In the Line of Fire** not only features a particularly intelligent screenplay by Jeff Maguire, it also benefits mightily from the directorial style of Wolfgang (*Das Boot*) Petersen, who shows a particular flair for the taut pacing called for by the action/suspense genre. Petersen also, however, balances *In the Line of Fire*'s diverse narrative facets into a cinematic tableau of much greater complexity than one would have had a right to expect from a film of this nature. Of course, most of the talk about *In the Line of Fire* centers around John Malkovich's performance as a CIA-trained psycho who engages aging Secret Service Agent Clint Eastwood in a cat-and-mouse assassination game. But while Malkovich's acting certainly helps carry his character miles beyond the domain of the cardboard evil one finds in most action/suspense films these days, the ambiguous villain he plays also owes a good deal of his soul to Maguire's dialogue and to the film's editing style, which definitely links Malkovich to Eastwood in ways most unsettling.

Adding to *In the Line of Fire*'s overall class is a substantial musical score by Ennio Morricone (Epic Soundtrax; Unione Musicisti di Roma), who gets to add a few wrinkles to the very recognizable style he has developed for such political thrillers as *Investigation of a Citizen Above Suspicion* and *Sacco and Vanzetti*, not to mention more straightforward crime/suspense movies such as *Città violenta* and *Without Apparent Motive*. This style asserts itself as of the title cue, in which abrupt string chords brutally slash into a rhythmically asymmetrical ostinato in the piano and harpsichord. But a solo trumpet, and later a chorus of trumpets, join in to give the music a mildly Americana aura. Much of the rest of the score alternates between extremely dissonant passages without a distinct rhythmic profile and cues in which Morricone obsessively drives forward various ostinato figures or repeated chords within single-minded rhythmic structures, often march-like in character. In listening to the harmonic violence of some of the cues, in fact, one is tempted to describe the music as post–Alex North. Elsewhere, the composer uses one of his most characteristic sounds—high violins sustaining slowly metamorphosing chords—to create an eerily effective tonal setting for Eastwood's nightmare memories of his failure to save President John F. Kennedy. These same types of chords, however, initially back the score's one lyrical theme, entitled "Lilly and Frank," which creates the mood for the liaison manqué between a much younger, female Secret Service agent played by Rene Russo, in a near-reprise of her part in *Lethal Weapon 3*, and the Eastwood character, who at several points accompanies his wooing with some jazz riffs he plays on the piano. Interestingly, this love theme (of sorts) initially gets presented in halting, staccato chords played by several instruments including, I think, an alto flute, only to be smoothed out later on as the solo (alto?) flute plays it straight.

One of the many facets that I admire in Gabriel Yared's gifts as a composer is his mastery of the many timbres that can be created in the bellies of today's diverse electronic instruments. Most film composers now use synthesizers and the like in at least parts of their scores, and several, such as Yared, employ them almost exclusively. But Yared is one of the few to create a musical style that both seems to grow naturally out of these timbres and to actually inspire new ones. All of this is certainly strongly in evidence in Yared's score for **Map of the Human Heart**, a heartbreaking love saga written and directed by Australian filmmaker Vincent (*The Navigator*) Ward (Philips). The score centers principally around three basic musical ideas. The first of these is a majestic tonescape whose timbres initially evoke the Inuit Eskimo tribe out of which the film's hero emerges. These primitive timbres, which will return to close the film, soon give way to an almost Pucciniesque theme in high parallel chords played by sampled violins that are ultimately replaced by a close approximation of a cathedral organ sounding solemn chords. The second musical idea is a warmer, mid-range theme that marks the beginning of the hero's entrance into the non-Eskimo world. Like the first theme, however, it suggests territory mapped out exterior to the human heart. The third theme, on the other hand, is a simple, two-part song (one with lyrics, the other without) that makes its way into several of the score's purely instrumental cues. As performed (in a girl's voice) by Marie Pelissier, the song features lyrics by Louis Nowra and Philippe Ringenbach that rather improbably focus on the refrain, "O ma métisse" (literally, "Oh, my half-breed"), to reflect the love affair between the film's hero, a half Inuit/half whiteman (Jason Scott Lee), and a half Indian/half French Canadian woman (Anne Parillaud, somewhat miscast, although not as badly as the wholly inappropriate actress chosen to overdub her voice). One of Yared's most haunting inventions, this poignant melody definitely helps the viewer/listener in mapping out the interior reaches of the human heart. In two or three other cues, Yared produces some New Age moods, complete with vocalizing chorus, that in certain instances find particularly appropriate visual expressions, notably a tryst atop London's Royal Albert Hall. Yet the composer also mobilizes what sounds like an entire sampled orchestra along with a sampled children's chorus in the dramatic musical cue that accompanies the eerily lit bombing raid on Dresden. When all is said and done, one simply cannot imagine *Map of the Human Heart* without Yared's incredibly evocative music.

From Cloud Nine Records, apparently a division of Silva Screen, comes a spectacular reissue of Bernard Herrmann's music for the 1961 **Mysterious Island**. While Herrmann's fantasy-film scores have never been among my favorites, as a major fan of the composer's music I could not help but revel in the succession of quintessential Herrmann sounds presented on this CD, the first recording to offer the work in stereo, and a non-literal-minded stereo at that. Missing, unfortunately, is the "Giant Bee" sequence, which was recorded on masters that have disappeared. One thing I particularly like about this recording is the way in which it communicates straight to the viscera the growly buzz of the low winds (the bass clarinet and contrabassoon in particular) that represent one of the many distinctive instrumental colorations in Herrmann's canon. In *Mysterious Island*, Herrmann indulges in fewer of the amateurish repetitions, sequential and otherwise, that one finds in such Charles H. Schneer produced/Ray Harryhausen animated features as *The Seventh Voyage of Sinbad*. Along the way, the composer also takes the time to musically create some of the more subtle and unsettling moods that one finds in his Hitchcock films, even though *Mysterious Island* certainly has its share of crashing brass chords (which Herrmann nonetheless makes harmonically interesting) and obvious musico-dramatic synchronizations. *Mysterious Island* also contains a supreme moment of musical humor when, for the "Phorarhacos" sequence, we hear a reasonable equivalent of a Baroque fugato that starts off in the clarinet and contrabassoon. The recorded sound reveals flaws from aging tapes and a fair amount of hiss (and why is there talking at the end of the "Giant Crab" cue?). But the orchestra has been miked so closely, and the music's volume level is so consistently high, that these are minor drawbacks.

~

1994

January/February

Well, it had to happen eventually. Alex North's "legendary original score" for Stanley Kubrick's **2001: A Space Odyssey**, a source of infinite speculation and frustration for years among film-music aficionados, has finally been issued on a new recording featuring energetic and intense conducting from none other than Jerry Goldsmith, wholly committed and sharp-edged playing from the National Philharmonic Orchestra, and, from Varèse Sarabande, spectacular engineering that gets more depth and breadth out of the considerable brass in the opening half of the score than one would have thought possible in digital sound. As is reasonably well known by now, director Kubrick, some two years into the production of 2001, set composer North up in a Chelsea Embankment apartment surrounded by every possible musical accoutrement so that he could compose the music for the film, guided by some very specific ideas from the director. North composed a dozen cues, including an Entr'acte, for the first half of the film, and was told no music was needed for the second. But when the composer attended the New York premiere of 2001 in April 1968 he discovered that not a note of his score had made it to the music track, which was instead filled with the pre-existing "found" music from the classical repertoire, many of whose cues Kubrick had used on the temp track. Robert Townson, in his half of the extensive program notes that accompany this CD, reports that according to some speculation Kubrick had intended all along to incorporate the cues from his temp track into the final cut and had simply used North as a front to placate the studio bosses, who were insisting on an original score.

Whatever the case may be, North for at least several of the cues was working under the most difficult constraint a creative artist probably ever has to deal with. It is demanding enough for a film composer to come up, in his or her own style, with musical moods to suit a given cinematic situation. But to have to tailor one's idiom around another musical composition laid in on the temp track has to be a composer's worst nightmare. That North was able to produce a "Main Title" cue that duplicates the formal structure and, to a lesser extent, the overall mood of the opening of Richard Strauss's *Also sprach Zarathustra* while maintaining the integrity of his own, very recognizable musical style is nothing short of miraculous. Somewhat less miraculous are the flirtings with the scherzo from Mendelssohn's incidental music for *A Midsummer Night's Dream* for the "Space Station Docking" cue, which Kubrick ultimately backed with Johann Strauss, Jr.'s "Blue Danube" waltz. The heart of the score, at any rate, is its first (pre-outer-space) half, in which the same types of harsh chordal patterns, crackling interplays in the brass and percussion, and often sparse textures that mark North's score for Kubrick's earlier *Spartacus* assert themselves with a vengeance. Indeed, at least one cue, entitled "Eat Meat and the Kill," could probably slip by undetected in one of *Spartacus*' more dramatic scenes. Interestingly, some of this music did in fact make its way to another film, the 1981 *Dragonslayer*. Particularly fascinating in *2001* is the way in which North turns the timpani into a major spokesperson—spectacularly seconded on the CD by the recorded sound—for much of the motivic material. In the second half (save the Entr'acte) of the score, on the other hand, brass and timpani give way to much more understated instrumentation that relies heavily on the woodwinds and on certain "celestial" timbres, including the celesta, various bells, and such ingenious combinations as harp and harpsichord. In one cue ("Moon Rocket Bus"), an eerie, vocalizing mezzo-soprano weaves her way through atmospheric bells and a string-brass accompaniment evocative of Stravinsky. Certainly, many of the moods created by North seem to move very much in the same spheres as Kubrick's hyper-clean visuals and his stripped-down story line.

Which brings us to the main debate, which of course centers around whether or not *2001* would have been a better movie minus the director's temp-track-promoted-to-music track and plus the nearly 40 minutes of music scored by North. Not surprisingly, Varèse Sarabande's program notes bristle throughout with indignation at Kubrick's expense, as if there really is no debate. Kevin Mulhall, in his analysis of the score, even outrageously describes a work by Ligeti as having a "purposeless quality" while North's cue comes off as "more interesting as music." It should not be forgotten that when *2001: A Space Odyssey* opened in 1968 (lacking footage clipped by Kubrick following press screenings) it was not greeted as simply a movie but as an event, and there can be little question at this point that *2001* represents one of the milestones of cinema history. There can also be little question that one of the major reasons for the film's impact was Kubrick's use of the various works of pre-existing classical compositions, from Johann Strauss, Jr. to Gyorgi Ligeti, on the music track. This was not simply another instance of raiding the classics to make up a kind of "cue" score, a tradition in sound cinema that goes back to such films as Edgar Ulmer's 1934 *The Black Cat*. Even Varèse Sarabande's program commentary takes note of *2001*'s non-narrative quality, and Kubrick's ingenious deployment of classical selections seconds that non-narrative quality by allowing the music to stand on its own, as if to suggest an alternate way of communicating the Zen moods created by the visuals, rather than blending it with the threadbare narrative. I am, for instance, no huge fan of Johann Strauss's "Blue Danube" waltz. Yet the cold, aristocratic elegance of the piece, which accompanies both the "Space Station Docking" and the "Trip to the Moon" cues in the final cut, combined with the aura of triviality it has acquired as an overplayed, commercialized commodity, allows the waltz to make an infinitely broader, much less narrative-specific statement on the filmic goings-on than any piece of specifically composed, wholly unknown music could ever do. North's *2001* score, even on a casual listening, comes across as a work of narrative film music, one that fits the older styles of filmmaking that Kubrick successfully broke with. North's music is brilliantly scored, and it extends the composer's reputation as one of film-music's great modernists. It is a shame that North paid the price for Kubrick's need to break new ground. But *2001* is more postmodern than modern, and to my sensibilities—accuse me of heresy if you will—the mishmash of classical selections on the music track is just as essential to the film's overall aura as are its steely cold, sparsely composed visuals and its simultaneously enigmatic and simplistic story line.

As if it were not enough to finally have North's *2001* score, from Silva America comes a complete recording of Franz Waxman's pioneering music for **The Bride of Frankenstein**, which also includes a six-minute suite from the same composer's **The Invisible Ray** (Westminster Philharmonic Orchestra, Kenneth Alwyn, cond.). Portions of the *Bride* score, including the eerie "The Creation" and the wonderfully ghoulish "Dance Macabre," have of course appeared on other recordings, and the cues that remain do not necessarily represent the best parts of the score. Still, Waxman had a wonderful sense of the grotesque, and his ability to manipulate such instruments as an electric organ, harp, piccolo, clarinet, etc. in a cue such as "A Strange Apparition" makes for intriguing listening, even if one is constantly aware of the void left by the absent movie. And although the lilting "Menuetto" from the film's prologue is pure pastiche, it so expertly sets the tone for prologue, in which Mary Shelley (Elsa Lanchester, who will later play the Bride) prepares the stage for the sequel to her famous *Frankenstein*, that one almost doesn't need the movie. Great fun, too, are the ironic quotations Waxman uses from such works as the waltz from Gounod's *Faust* and Mendelssohn's "Spring Song." Further, in listening to the entire score, I do believe I have discovered an underlying key to much of Waxman's music, and that is the Dukas *Sorcerer's Apprentice*, subtle allusions to which seem to my ears to abound in the score without the work ever being quoted directly. It certainly makes sense, aesthetic and otherwise, that the composer would allow himself this little in-joke.

As for the brief suite from *The Invisible Ray*, the music starts off with some marvelously atmospheric strains over a pseudo-African, boom-biddy-boom drumbeat. These give way to a brief appearance of a classic love-waltz followed by a storm sequence in which Liszt's 14th Hungarian Rhapsody plays no small role. The whole thing has even more of a tongue-in-cheek quality to it than *The Bride of Frankenstein*. It should be noted that, since the manuscript for *The Invisible Ray* has disappeared, the music was reconstructed by ear by Steven R. Bernstein from the music track and some scattered acetate discs. The score for *The Bride of Frankenstein* was orchestrated from

Waxman's sketches and/or expanded from Clifford Vaughan's orchestrations by Tony Bremner, who beefed things up here and there—notably the bride's motif in the "Creation" sequence—with some electronics, under the presumption that Waxman would have used an Ondes Martenot or a Theremin had he not been under budget constraints. We also in several instances hear more of the music than was ultimately used in the film. On the CD, the recorded sound is rich and sports quite a bit of reverberation, which struck me as reasonably appropriate. Kenneth Alwyn conducts with a good deal of commitment, but the Westminster Philharmonic Orchestra does not always meet the challenges of his enthusiasm. A major force behind this recording, as well as behind many other recordings and performances of film music, Franz Waxman and otherwise, is the composer's son, John Waxman.

Apart from a few details, such as autumn leaves floating around streets backed by trees in full, green foliage, and atrocious approximations of a Maine accent, Fraser C. Heston's **Needful Things** turned out to be a pleasant surprise, and at the moment it probably ranks fourth or fifth on my list of preferred Stephen King film adaptations after *Carrie, Dead Zone, Stand by Me*, and, perhaps, *The Dark Half.* Rather than going for the cheap thrills and special effects, director Fraser and screenwriter W. D. Richter work hard to capture the spirit of King's mammoth opus, which, while presenting the personage of the devil as the proprietor of a curio shop catering to people's deepest needs, leaves most of the destruction to the characters, whose hurts, frustrations, and darker halves lead them to shop at "Needful Things" in the first place. Contributing greatly to this climate is the wickedly dry performance of Max von Sydow as Leland Gaunt. I haven't seen such wry pain in a villain finding his dirty work made unnecessarily dirtier since James Mason wincingly asks Cary Grant "Games? Must we?" in *North by Northwest.* Also contributing greatly to the overall atmosphere of *Needful Things* is the extensive score by Patrick Doyle (Varèse Sarabande; David Snell, cond.), by far his best work since *Dead Again* (director Heston, in fact, was sensitive to the latter score, as it was *Dead Again* that, as he explains in his program commentary, led him to seek Doyle for *Needful Things*). Of course, the score has its expected tropes: a music-box waltz; the de rigueur satanic chanting of a male chorus; the *dies irae* theme, etc. Doyle also gets Schubert's "Ave Maria" (rather grimly sung by Nicole Tibbels) and Grieg's "In the Hall of the Mountain King" into the act, just for good measure.

But it is what Doyle does with these tropes that makes the *Needful Things* music work so well, both in conjunction with the movie and on its own. First of all, as I've said before, Doyle's music is quite tonal. But he composes best in the minor mode, and almost every note of *Needful Things* is in the minor mode. Secondly, Doyle manipulates the full symphony orchestra with immense skill and dexterity, and in *Needful Things* he often manages to weave in a mixed chorus for good measure. The initial cue ("The Arrival"), for instance, opens with the music-box waltz, but in a dark and ominous version for full orchestra and chorus. This mightily heightens the impact of that theme when further on Doyle reduces the forces playing it to solo harp or solo piano. Still in the opening cue, the music-box waltz gives way to a fast, almost *perpetuum mobile* passage that, with the help of the chorus, builds to a point of intensity that will send chills down your spine. Along the way, Doyle introduces a motif quite reminiscent of the opera theme from *Dead Again*. One wonders whether the composer intended some kind of comment here. In the long cue for the climactic sequence, Doyle flirts several times with the love theme from *Vertigo*. Again one wonders . . . . Many of the cues are closely tailored to the filmic action, but not so much that they do not afford solid listening on their own.

There has been no dearth of recordings devoted to film music by Bernard Herrmann, and in particular Herrmann's collaborations with Alfred Hitchcock. But a new Milan release entitled ***Bernard Herrmann Film Scores, From Citizen Kane to Taxi Driver*** may be the most intriguing of the lot (Claire Henry, mezzo-soprano; Ambrosian Singers; Royal Philharmonic Orchestra, Elmer Bernstein, cond.). While the CD does offer some familiar Herrmann/Hitchcock music from *Vertigo*, *Psycho*, and *North by Northwest*, it also makes available for the first time the weird Prelude for *The Wrong Man*, which alternates back and forth between a Latin-band pastiche and a wispy piece of Herrmanniana, and the "Storm Clouds Cantata" from the second version of *The Man Who Knew Too Much*. I stress that it is the second version, since both of Hitchcock's renderings of *The Man Who Knew Too Much* use that work by the Australian-born Arthur Benjamin, who composed it for the first time around. But in the remake, Herrmann did not simply re-orchestrate the piece, in spite of what Steven C. Smith claims in the program notes. The "Storm Clouds Cantata" as heard in the 1956 *Man Who Knew Too Much* runs substantially longer than the original, thanks to some fleshing out done by Herrmann, particularly in the orchestral introduction, and for good reason. Hitchcock needed more music to back a nearly 10-minute sequence that becomes a tour de force of quasi-silent-film gesturing and editing cum music. And I have to say that it is an utter blast to sit back and listen to the Benjamin/Herrmann cantata without the film. So closely is that music wedded in my sensibilities to the 1956 *Man Who Knew Too Much* that it generates exactly the same emotions, as if a phantom film were floating over my listening room demanding that I bite my nails until Doris Day comes out with that scream. I cannot imagine a performance, other than the one conducted onscreen by Bernard Herrmann in the film, that would better capture the cantata's spirit than the one turned in by mezzo-soprano Claire Henry, the Ambrosian Singers, and conductor Elmer Bernstein with the enthusiastic cooperation of the Royal Philharmonic.

But there's more. The CD also contains excerpts from *Citizen Kane*, including the Finale, which is not quite the recording premiere Milan states it is, since that cue did turn up on the best-forgotten *Citizen Kane* LP done many years ago by Leroy Holmes for United Artists. There is also the "Pop Goes the Weasel" variations, which make several different violin tracks sound like a single instrument in order to turn Mr. Scratch of *The Devil and Daniel Webster* into a true "devil's fiddler" during the brilliantly edited "Barn Dance" sequence; a suite arranged by Christopher Palmer from Herrmann's haunting and unsettling score for Truffaut's *The Bride Wore Black*, which looks backward to *The Trouble With Harry* and *Marnie*, and forwards to *Sisters*; the almost impossibly sad Finale for Truffaut's *Fahrenheit 451*, in which one senses a strong tie-in between the shattered idealism of the Ray Bradbury story and Herrmann's own sensibilities—and note that grim, final chord; and a suite, also arranged by Christopher Palmer, from Herrmann's last effort, his sometimes bluesy, sometimes snarling score for Scorsese's *Taxi Driver*. Milan's multi-miked sound on this CD works particularly well for Herrmann's carefully conceived instrumentations, the timbres of whose inner voices are revealed with particular clarity. Elmer Bernstein offers generally convincing readings of the music, although his *Psycho* cues do not touch the quickly paced tempos used in the film (will anybody ever attempt to duplicate the *Psycho* music as heard in the film? An original music-track is needed). And he milks the *Vertigo* love music almost past the point of no return. Almost. Somehow it works.

This column is dedicated to the memory of Federico Fellini.

March/April

Twentieth Century-Fox "Film Scores" label has just launched its "Classic Series" in spectacular fashion. I start with David Raksin's **Laura**. Although this recording presents the score as a "Laura Suite: Theme and Variations" without separating the cues, it nonetheless allows the listener to appreciate just how rich, original, and varied Raksin's music is in spite of a monothematic obsessiveness that is thoroughly appropriate to the fetishistic psychologies evoked by the 1944 film's narrative and much of its visual structure. Indeed, throughout the movie, the song "Laura" is virtually inescapable, whether coming at the listener from a cocktail-lounge combo, through a phonograph, or hiding in the subtler textures and rhythms of the non-source musical "backing." Raksin, besides composing one of the most haunting melodies ever written, was able to weave this theme in and out of diverse musical situations, showing equal skill as a dance-band arranger and as a thoroughly "classical" composer capable of evoking a wide range of moods, often within remarkably short spaces of time. So thoroughly does the music tie in with the movie that one can almost hear Clifton Webb's narration as the straightforward title theme gives way to a morose, alto(?) flute solo captured between high violins and a sustained bass line, with vibraphone adding yet another layer of resonance. One of the subtlest transformations in the music, in which Raksin produced an eerily dreamy effect through the use of some electro-mechanical manipulations, is unfortunately missing from this recording, since the source materials were too badly damaged to be of use. But the recording is nonetheless invaluable: it reveals one of the greatest practitioners of film scoring at one of his many peaks, and it also features remarkably good sound.

Bernard Herrmann's music for Robert Stevenson's 1943 **Jane Eyre**, which is likewise surprisingly well recorded for the most part, starts off with an intense elegy that, unlike most of Herrmann's film music, has a substantial concert-music flow to it. But by the end of the main-title cue, the music begins to undergo the kinds of rapid, cinematic metamorphoses that will come to characterize the entire score. At the end of the main titles, for instance, a classically Herrmannesque piece of gloom in the low winds and strings, complemented by murky harp figures, gives way to a plaintive oboe motif—a typical Herrmann sound from this period—that finally pulls itself free of the minor mode. The score also identifies itself as 1940s Herrmann, in the cue entitled "Jane's Departure," in a jaunty scherzo that could have come straight out of *Citizen Kane* or *The Magnificent Ambersons*, although the jollity does break down a bit toward the end. Indeed, darkness settles over much of the music here, with occasional touches, such as the piano/snare-drum ostinato that opens the frightening cue entitled "The Fire," revealing other facets of the composer's flair. And an intriguing quotation from Wagner also shows up in the "Mr. Mason" cue. If the score does not assert itself musically as strongly as some of Herrmann's other works, it remains an occasionally violent masterpiece of atmosphere and a definite portender of things to come.

But the real Herrmann showstopper here is the score for Robert Wise's 1951 sci-fi classic, **The Day the Earth Stood Still**. While I have always had a predilection for Herrmann's Hitchcock scores, not only because of the music but also because of the endless possibilities for probing analyses that grow out of the film/music interactions in that towering director/composer collaboration, the Twentieth Century-Fox CD, which classifies as one of the great film-music recordings ever, has brought me to the conclusion that *The Day the Earth Stood Still* stands as one of Herrmann's finest efforts and as one of film music's major achievements. Let's start with the instrumentation, which consists of four Theremins (two high, two low), four pianos, four harps, some 30 winds and brass, percussion (with heavy vibraphone), pipe organ, and a string section reduced to an electric violin and an electric bass. There has never been an electronic instrument quite like the Theremin, whose inventor, Leon Theremin, died late this past year after a long, eventful (to say the least) life. With its pure, throaty timbres, the Theremin produces single tones that eerily evoke both the human and the nonhuman, and I don't think any composer, including Miklós Rózsa in *Spellbound*, has ever captured this characteristic of the instrument with such uncanny effectiveness as did Herrmann in *The Day the Earth Stood Still*. The moaning dialog between soprano and alto Theremin in the "Flashlight" cue, in which a young boy witnesses the alien's return to his spaceship and omnipotent robot, will chill your blood. In other cues, such as "Space Control," the instrument sings in the midst of the rest of the music like an invisible presence that may lurk either inside or outside of the human psyche. And in the cue entitled "Rebirth," Herrmann creates an utterly weird soloist-with-chorus effect with three of the Theremins. But every timbre mobilized by the composer in this score works to perfection: the brass snarl and growl ominously; the timpani rumbles threateningly, frequently in glissandos; the vibraphone waxes ethereal, the church organ outer-space cavernous. Yet one of Herrmann's masterstrokes in the score involves the simple combination of piano and vibraphone, whose Mendelssohnish scherzo ingeniously suggests the hustle and bustle as radar and the radio track the arriving flying saucer at the outset of the film. Simplicity, indeed, is the byword for this score, as it is for the film, with its transparent messages and allegories (no Hitchcockian psycho-labyrinths here). In a word, director Wise and composer Herrmann established the quintessential '50s sci-fi sight and sound almost before that decade got off the ground, and nobody, director or composer, has quite re-attained their level since.

Which may be one reason why director George Lucas and composer John Williams, when they got their **Star Wars** thing going, decided to not even try with the music. I must confess that, as I geared up for the *Star Wars* experience in 1977, I was expecting a score that would at least try and out-Herrmann Herrmann. And so, when I first put my review copy of the original music-track LP on my turntable (this before I saw the film), the Korngold cum Waxman cum Holst cum Prokofiev and god knows who else sound, sans electronics, that Lucas and Williams had chosen as a prototype came as a major shock. What Lucas and Williams had done, in essence, was to strip the sci-fi genre of most of its tropes in order to evoke heroic archetypes on their broadest level (and let's not forget that a significant inspiration for *Star Wars* was Akira Kurosawa's *The Hidden Fortress*). Since that initial shock, I have had great fun playing the Main Title sequence of Korngold's *King's Row* for various lectures and classes I have given: not once have members of the audience or class yet failed to assert with authority that this had to be music for the latest *Superman* or *Star Wars* sequel. On a more sobering note, not once has anybody correctly identified the music, the composer, or the era. For Williams' deployment of the Korngold-heroic mode for *Star Wars* established such a trend in Hollywood that the second-degree scores have all but obliterated the originals from memory. Nonetheless, nobody can deny the immense talent and skill it took on the part of John Williams to come up with a style that, while owing major debts to his predecessors, both in film scores and elsewhere, does not come across as unmitigated pastiche. Indeed, Williams' massive symphonic scoring adds a huge aural component to the overall *Star Wars* spectacle when the films are viewed in a theater equipped with a decent sound system. Further, even at its most derivative, the music for all three films—*Star Wars*, *The Empire Strikes Back*, and *Return of the Jedi*—has such rhythmic and instrumental vitality, and it is performed with such gusto by the London Symphony Orchestra, that it is impossible not to get swept along by it all. In fact, for the last two installments in particular (which might be entitled *Star Wars Meets Sesame Street*), it is probably more emotionally rewarding to just let the music blast through your stereo without visual reference to such puerilities as Yoda and the Ewoks.

Furthermore, the *Star Wars* scores often extend beyond the neo- and post-romantic styles that made their fame. A modernist definitely lurks in certain areas of Williams' creative spirit, and if this side of the composer sometimes latches onto other modernists for inspiration—Stravinsky in "The Desert" from *Star Wars* or Prokofiev in the "Parade of the Ewoks" from *Return of the Jedi*, for instance—it also ventures on occasion into some intriguingly original territory, as in parts of "Land of the Sand People" from *Star Wars* and parts of several of the cues, such as "The Imperial Probe" and the exhausting "Battle in the Snow," from *The Empire Strikes Back*, perhaps the most consistently creative of the three scores. The latter film introduces my favorite theme from the entire series, the deliciously evil march for Darth Vader. Come to think of it, this is one thing lacking in many of the Korngold-scored heroic adventures: do Basil Rathbone in *The Adventures of Robin Hood* and Henry Daniell in *The Sea Hawk* ever get a theme worthy of their wickedness? Williams also shows a solid, Korngoldian talent for turning parts of his themes into leitmotifs skillfully shuffled and multiplied into a variety of musico-dramatic situations. On the negative side of the ledger, Williams has a tendency to write excessively simplistic themes, including the Main Title, which to my sensibilities could stand a few more accidentals. The "Ewok Celebration" in the alternate version heard on the *Return of the Jedi* CD is even more unbearable than the film version, which appears on the mishmash fourth CD in the set.

One thing I have always liked about the arty films put together by producer Ismail Merchant and director James Ivory is the way in which the settings of their films, both exterior and interior, become an integral and important part of the overall cinematic "text." And it was the failure of the filmmakers to fully take advantage of the settings, both interior and exterior, of **Remains of the Day** that ultimately disappointed me. Oh, there is no question that Anthony Hopkins turns in the performance of his career here: I cannot imagine how difficult it must be to show emotion in a character who has devoted his entire life to hiding any feeling. But I have never been particularly fond of films that serve principally as a vehicle for their actors and actresses, and I do not feel that Ivory and Merchant entirely avoided this trap for *Remains of the Day*. One thing that absolutely did not disappoint me, however, was the haunting score penned for the film by Ivory/Merchant regular Richard Robbins (Angel; Harry Rabinowitz, cond.). Robbins, in his Merchant/Ivory scores, has always had an uncanny knack for coming up with musical figures, often repeated quasi-ostinatos, that somehow capture a major piece of a given film's atmosphere, and he does not disappoint in this respect in *Remains of the Day*, which may be his moodiest and most obsessive score to date. In fact, Robbins suggests, in his "Note from the Composer," that the repetition characteristic of musical form in general in a way mirrors the repetitions that form the daily routine of the butler, housekeeper, and servants on whom this film, based on a novel by Kazuo Ishiguor, focuses. This repetition reveals itself in both the score's macro- and micro-structures, with a tight, flowing, exquisitely orchestrated, six-note ostinato that floats right in the middle of the musical textures actually forming the score's backbone. This figure, heard as of the title cue, undergoes various modifications in its configuration and its instrumentation throughout the score. But one is always aware of its presence as it casts its mood over the entire film. Robbins also has a gift for suggesting the existence of full-blown themes with musical fragments that somehow get swallowed up in the harmonic and instrumental atmospheres before they get a chance at melodic coalescence. This, it seems to me, is another principal way in which Robbins' music captures the essence of the Merchant/Ivory dramas, whose characters more often than not find themselves in situations in which they never fully define themselves.

Michael Nyman's music plays a particularly important role in Jane Campion's **The Piano** (Virgin; members of the Munich Philharmonic). *The Piano*, an Australian movie which won the best film award at the most recent Cannes Film Festival, marks yet one more instance where a film that towers over the usual dreck that comes flooding out of Hollywood (bravo to the French for standing up—and winning—against American cinema in the recent trade agreement) has attracted reasonable audiences in this country, and will probably garner a decent number of Oscar nominations. I certainly cannot imagine a more deserving "Best Actress" than Holly Hunter, who, save in a couple of voiceovers, remains mute throughout *The Piano*, in which her character expresses her inner world through a piano that she carts across the globe from Scotland to New Zealand (and how about a supporting-actress nomination for Anna Paquin, amazing, charming, and, in her own way, tragic in her portrayal of the young daughter?). From what I understand, it is in fact Hunter who performs the piano solos in the film, although it is composer Nyman, best known for his collaborations with director/writer Peter Greenaway, who plays them on this CD. Whatever the case may be, Nyman, for *The Piano*, found himself in the difficult position of composing music that represents the impassioned improvisations of a fiercely independent, mid-19th-century woman and that is described in the film as "like a mood that passes through you . . . a sound that creeps into you." Although a colleague of mine whom I greatly respect found Nyman's music anachronistic, I personally feel that the composer seconded Jane Campion's vision with sensitivity well beyond anything one would have dared hope for. First of all, this subtly anti-patriarchal movie, although superficially a costume drama, moves in allegorical spheres that have little to do with chronological time. Secondly, the idiom of Nyman's piano solos, inspired by Scottish folk and popular songs, is not all that far from what a mid-19th-century spirit might have come up with, particularly considering the freedom inherent in folk and popular idioms, as Bela Bartók finally proved once and for all. Nyman's piano solos have a quality to them that is hypnotic, introspective, and ingenuous, precisely the sort of thing a free-spirit living in a self-contained, non-patriarchal universe with her daughter might devise, even if most of the 19th century had not quite reached the kinds of New-Age/Minimalist repetitions that characterize Nyman's writing here.

The high point of Nyman's score is a theme, no doubt Scottish in origin, first heard in a piano/orchestra version in the cue entitled "The Promise" and peaking in a glorious piano solo (all on the white keys) in "The Sacrifice." But Nyman immediately sets the film's tone in the right direction with the dreamy rhapsody of "Big My Secret," which is the first piece we hear from Ada (Hunter) and which becomes what might be called *The Piano*'s love theme. *The Piano* also offers quite a few orchestral cues played mostly by the strings but beefed up in particular with various saxophones—one of the most characteristic timbres of Nyman's style—and alto flute. The opening cue sets a tone of almost Arvo Pärt-ish mysticism, while later music moves in somewhat more characteristically Nymanesque spheres, although we never get anything resembling the sometimes raucous, Baroque Minimalism (as I have described it elsewhere) of the Greenaway scores. One theme, heard in two different cues, actually reminds one of something that Bernard Herrmann might have done had he decided to write in a closed loop.

This column is dedicated to the memory of Carl George Thompson, Jr.

May/June

I always worry, when a film is as solidly devoted to a particular ethnic group as Steven Spielberg's **Schindler's List** is, that its score will be overwhelmed with ethnic and/or pseudo-ethnic musical references. Such, fortunately, is not the case of John Williams' score for *Schindler's List* (MCA). While the music certainly has its share of Semitic overtones—a slow hora here, some mournful clarinet solos (performed by Giora Feidman) there, even some traditional choral pieces—the general tone opted for by Williams throughout most of the score, in which the timbres of the various strings dominate, is one of "gentle simplicity," as Spielberg describes it in his brief program commentary. The score is dominated by a single theme that has the nobility, the grandeur, and, yes, the simplicity needed by the film. But although the theme makes frequent appearances, its reprises strike one more as the ongoing revival of an undying spirit than as leitmotivic repetitions. Adding to the poignancy throughout much of the score are violin solos by none other than Itzhak Perlman, who is accompanied by members of the Boston Symphony Orchestra. Besides adding vibrant timbres to Williams' music, Perlman's solos very much have the effect, as one is watching the movie, of another character speaking his/her voice. In certain cues, Williams also displays his patented flair for cine-musical drama, particularly apparent in "Making the List," in which the music gathers a kind of liberating momentum that tells its story every bit as effectively as the dialogue and the visuals.

What can you say about a movie in which a captive male is for all intents and purposes raped by a woman who offers him the option of screwing her with her artificial arm on or off (he chooses off)? Weird, man. On the basis of four films that he directed—*The Ruling Class, The Changeling, The Krays,* and *"Let Him Have It"*—I consider myself a Peter Medak aficionado. But nothing prepared me—not even Peter O'Toole as Jesus Christ as Jack the Ripper in *The Ruling Class*—for the totally off-the-wall, hyper-noir atmospheres of **Romeo Is Bleeding**. Ostensibly about a bad cop (Gary Oldman) who falls into the web of a femme (Lena Olin) who is so fatale that she makes *Double Indemnity*'s Barbara Stanwyck look like Shirley Temple, *Romeo Is Bleeding* so thoroughly undercuts its narrative with its seedy settings, its distanced visuals, and its half-finished set pieces and tropes that even a sadistic amputation and a live burial leave us curiously uninvolved. In a word, *Romeo Is Bleeding* is a film in which we see everything while we see nothing, and it has to stand as one of the most original and disturbing films of the past few years. Happily, *Romeo Is Bleeding* has gotten from Mark Isham a score that fits it to a T (Verve). Many of the cues are pure jazz, with Isham on trumpet or flugelhorn accompanied by the traditional piano (or vibes), bass, and drums. In listening to them, one often has the impression of improvs done to tunes that are never set forth—and what could be more appropriate to *Romeo Is Bleeding* than that? As the film gets uglier and uglier, Isham and his crew venture out of the more pure bop framework into areas that border on the avant-garde, with various synthesizer timbres often beefing up the proceedings. The cue for "Mona" (Olin) is a masterpiece of moody dissonances, gritty electronic and percussion accompaniment, and bittersweetness in the quasi-harmonica theme that overlays them. Ever mindful of his New Age side, Isham has also created some haunting synthscapes. In the title cue, for instance, the opening, atmospheric electronics lead us to believe that the film noir side of *Romeo Is Bleeding* is going to lead us toward a more *Blade Runner* type of arena. But into these electronics ventures Isham's trumpet, wailing like the soul of Miles Davis lost in some nether land. Bit by bit, the music metamorphoses into the slow, cool, night jazz that is one of its main profiles. But we know that the electronically generated miasmas lurk just beneath the surface. Isham also waxes kinky—of course—here and there, as in the mostly synth cue entitled "Nightmare on Maple Street," which introduces, among other things, a bizarre, quasi-music-box motif that will have its say elsewhere in the score as well. Two previously composed jazz numbers, Abbey Lincoln's "Bird Alone" and A. J. Croce's" I Know Better Now," add their own class to a score that should stand up as one of the best of the decade.

How, one wonders, did the good folks at the Academy of Motion Picture Arts and Sciences manage to choose, in their Oscar nominations for Best Actor, between Anthony Hopkins in James Ivory's *Remains of the Day* and Anthony Hopkins in Richard Attenborough's **Shadowlands**? Perhaps *Remains of the Day* won out because of its near-impossible demands for a wide gamut of emotion from a character whose station in life demands that he show no emotion. But to a certain degree, the stiff-upper-lip demeanor required of the Oxford professor played by Hopkins in *Shadowlands*, the true story of the romance between author C. S. Lewis and American poet Joy Gresham (Debra Winger, who received a Best Actress nomination for her role), does not allow a good deal more room for emotions to expand than the butler played by Hopkins in *Remains of the Day*. In *Shadowlands*, Hopkins' wonderfully subtle performance somehow communicates the entire spectrum of his character's feelings, from his initial reticence through his love to his final, overwhelming grief. I know of no more heartrending scene in any motion picture than the moment where C. S. Lewis and Gresham's son (Joseph Mazzello) finally allow themselves to grieve over their mutual loss.

In his particularly eloquent program note, director Attenborough states that, apart from Hopkins and Winger, composer George Fenton was the "first creative person I sought to involve once I began working with William Nicholson's marvelous script in the closing months of 1992." This early involvement of the composer with the film has paid big dividends, at least to my sensibilities, in Fenton's score for *Shadowlands* (Angel; Choir of Magdalen College, Oxford; London Symphony Orchestra). I can think of few film scores that evoke quite so thoroughly the entire affective character of a particular film as Fenton's music for *Shadowlands*. For the film's opening, for instance, Fenton composed a choral "Veni Sancte Spiritus" that immediately transports the viewer/listener's sensibilities into the "Oxford" mode. Several other cues involving the Choir of Magdalen College likewise set the Oxford tone. But the bulk of the cues relate to the Lewis/Gresham love affair, and the spirit that dominates the calm, autumnal music is one of warmth and sadness. In the cue entitled "The Wardrobe," Fenton uses a haunting piano solo that overlays nostalgia above the warmth and sadness, while in "The Silence," the most recognizably Fentonesque cue in the score, the composer opens with a slow, balletic figure (in 9/8?) in which rich, tragically hued chords in the strings introduce an achingly sad flute solo. But the piano returns later in the same cue, beneath high, sustained violins, to continue the melody in an even more plaintive mode as the strings and harp continue the dance accompaniment. The mood is all but palpable.

One might have thought that the gimmick successfully (in most people's opinions) used by director Godfrey Reggio in *Koyaanisqatsi* and *Powaqqatsi* would have worn thin enough not to bear another shot. In those two films, you may remember, Reggio created tributes to the planet Earth [and its peoples] with what might be called a kind of Minimalist cinema, in which various places and beings are captured in their natural states and then choreographed and aestheticized via highly filtered photography, slow motion, stop-action cinematography, cyclical editing, and, of course, nonstop music by Philip Glass. But after the emphasis on place in *Koyaanisqatsi* and on peoples in *Powaqqatsi*, it was only logical that Reggio turn to animals, and that is precisely what he did in the brief **Anima Mundi**, which covers the entire gamut of fauna from whales to micro-organisms. If what might be termed "early" Glass hit a kind of peak with the sumptuous *Koyaanisqatsi* music, his score for *Anima Mundi* (Elektra Nonesuch; Michael Riesman, cond.) captivated this listener both because of the many familiar Glass devices it contains and because of what I find to be some new and unexpected sounds from the composer. Thus, the cue entitled—what else—"Perpetual Motion" reworks (quite nicely) some of the old Minimalist figures, although it ends in some soul-opening, rather ethereal parallel chords. "Living Waters," which accompanies some breathtaking underwater photography, offers a slow dance within which the strings put together sections of a theme that could almost be described as Herrmannesque. In earlier cues, bitonally juxtaposed figures in the trumpet and later the flute have a rather Shostakovian quality to them. Particularly imaginative, I thought, are the clicking percussion figures and weird vocal utterances that accompany the ballet of paramecia and other wee critters in "The Beginning." The more tribal percussion figures and the surging waves of chords of "The Ark" are particularly effective backing for the larger animals shown in this sequence, while the low rumblings and panting, vocal figures that open "The Garden," along with scurrying flute patterns (can Philip Glass be indulging in a bit of mickey-mousing?), create a particularly eerie sonic aura for the insect world depicted in *Anima Mundi*. The outbursts from a vocalizing chorus over low figures from a church organ that close "The Garden" show Glass at his noblest.

As action films go, **Demolition Man** has more than its share of good moments, although the film needed to be about a half-hour longer in order to make convincing personae out of the post-apocalyptic, underground revolutionaries who are the principal reason why the well-intentioned "Jean Cocteau" has released the all-evil Wesley Snipes from his cryogenic prison in the first place. Beyond all that, *Demolition Man* no doubt gets its greatest mileage out of its numerous jokes about a modern cop (Sylvester Stallone) in a postmodern society where sex is performed with neither physical contact nor bodily secretions and where toilet paper has mysteriously given way to three metal seashells. But one of the best things *Demolition Man* has going for it is the all-but-nonstop action of its electronic and orchestral score by Elliot Goldenthal (Varèse Sarabande; Jonathan Sheffer, cond.). The score opens with a very dramatic, synth/orchestra/chorus "Dies Irae," complete with chimes, that lends its well-known theme to many of the ensuing cues, many of which turn into mini-toccatas that move forward at an exhausting pace. Overtones of Shostakovich, Prokofiev, Prokofiev-via-Danny Elfman, and even Philip Glass turn up here and there. Goldenthal uses electronics quite effectively, particularly when he wants to make witty comments on the goings-on, as in the "Museum Dis Duel" cue or in the synthesizer ostinato that underlies the orchestral upheavals in "Obligatory Car Chase" (I love it!). The score's few quiet moments are also, however, quite effective, particularly the quasi-underwater-gloom created by the harp figures cum sustained strings (and later synth) of the "Guilty As Charged" sequence that dooms poor old Sylvester Stallone to the freeze tank. The Wagnerian etheriality of "Meeting Cocteau" exudes a thoroughly apropos irony. It would have been great fun, however, if the final "Silver Screen Kiss" had contained some hidden musical quotation to second the aura of hyper-nostalgia that surrounds *Demolition Man*'s final scene. All in all, Goldenthal generates so much excitement, tension, and mood that this score holds up particularly well separated from the film.

July/August

Quite rewarding is Howard Shore's music for Jonathan Demme's **Philadelphia** on an Epic Sountrax CD not to be confused with the wildly popular CD compilation of *Philadelphia*'s various pop-music cues. If *Mrs. Doubtfire* [also scored by Shore] versus *Philadelphia* is any indication, Shore finds a good deal more inspiration in the cinema's dark side than in its fluffier visions. For *Philadelphia*'s decidedly dark drama about an AIDS-infected lawyer fighting discrimination, Shore has devised some particularly intriguing harmonic colorations. At several moments in the score, in which, throughout, a solo trumpet plays almost the role of a musical character, a mildly ominous harp ostinato gets bitonally juxtaposed against rather acidic thematic material in the winds, while the strings drone and cluster beneath all this. Strange, closely knit dissonances pop up here and there, as do some thick and disturbing chords in the strings. In some of its more heavily scored moments, the music moves a bit toward Delerue, while at other points a bit of tender optimism breaks through. The music's overall tone, however, becomes more and more somber and depressing as the score moves on. And as if this weren't enough, Maria Callas' very dramatic rendition of the ineffably sad "Ebben? ne andro lontana" from Catalani's *La Wally*, made famous by *Diva*, makes an appearance in the midst of Shore's often droning morbidity. We also get to hear Callas perform "La Mamma morta" from *Andrea Chenier*, while Lucia Popp sings "Non temer amato bene" from *Idomeneo*. All in all, *Philadelphia* turns out to be one of Howard Shore's best and most varied scores. But it is definitely not to be listened to on dark and rainy days.

Whenever people talk of non-film composers getting into the movie-scoring business, one name that inevitably comes up is Aaron Copland who, mostly in the late '30s and '40s, brought his inimitable Americana sounds to a handful of films, most of them based on works by American authors, including Henry James, John Steinbeck, and Thornton Wilder. My favorite of Copland's movie scores is *The Red Pony*, for Lewis Milestone's 1949 adaptation of the John Steinbeck novel about a young boy who finds escape from a disagreeable family in a pony and a sympathetic stable hand played by Robert Mitchum. Poignant, playful, jaunty, and ultimately rather sad, Copland's *Red Pony* music somehow captures the magic of the child's world evoked in the Steinbeck story better than the rest of the movie is able to do. It is this magic that is somewhat lacking on a new recording of *The Red Pony* by Leonard Slatkin and the St. Louis Symphony Orchestra on an RCA Victor Red Seal (or is it BMG Classics?) CD entitled **Copland: Music for Films**. While Slatkin leads the St. Louis Symphony in a lovely and excellently executed performance that has been richly recorded, there is an emotional spirit here that has just not been fully captured. This CD also contains a major showstopper, this being the premiere recording of a reconstruction by Arnold Freed of Copland's music for William Wyler's 1949 *The Heiress*, which includes the title music as originally composed as opposed to the version of "Plaisir d'amour" that the hard-of-hearing Wyler used to replace it in the film's final cut. After a dissonant and somewhat thickly textured Prelude that reveals little of Copland's characteristically open musical spaces, the music for *The Heiress*, of which we get to hear only eight minutes, quickly settles into patterns more familiar to Copland aficionados, whether in the chorale-like passages in the winds that follow the title music or the jauntier pieces of Americana in the ensuing music. Listening to *The Heiress* and to the other scores on this disc, which also offers the *Our Town* suite, *Music for the Movies*, and *Prairie Journal (Music for Radio)*, one realizes just how much mileage Copland was able to get out of his highly distinctive harmonic and rhythmic style without having to resort to the kinds of themes and leitmotifs that dominated Hollywood scores at the time.

This is certainly true of the score for Sam Wood's 1940 film version of Thornton Wilder's *Our Town*. Indeed, if I am always bowled over by the pure musical joy and innocence of *The Red Pony*, I am perhaps even more impressed by how thoroughly and how deeply Copland captured the quiet aches and autumnal nostalgia that pervade Wilder's deceptively simple play about small-town America. And Copland accomplishes this almost entirely with harmonic and instrumental color. Except for the "Grovers Corners" movement from *Our Town*, which I could never tire of listening to, the five movements of *Music for Movies*, which also include selections from the documentary *The City* and from Lewis Milestone's 1939 *Of Mice and Men*, do not quite reach the heights of *The Red Pony* and *Our Town*, although Copland certainly creates an infectious energy in the "Sunday Traffic" and "Threshing Machines" segments. "Prairie Journal," whose music alternates between lively and moody, falls somewhere in between. Again, I find Slatkin's interpretations a tad on the foursquare side.

September/October

In far too many instances these days I have found myself dedicating my column to someone recently deceased, in most cases someone in the film industry but in one case an uncle who played a very important role in my life. Unfortunately, I must now dedicate this column to Henry Mancini, who passed away this past June at the age of 70. As it happens, I knew Henry Mancini personally . . . not very well, but we corresponded and met several times, and, of course, he provided that wonderful interview that appeared in the January/February 1991 *Fanfare* and that is reprinted in my book, *Overtones and Undertones: Reading Film Music*. Mancini was an extremely likable person with a dry sense of humor and a thorough commitment to the fields he worked in. And he is certainly one of the major figures in freeing film music from its enslavement to big-orchestra classical styles. He was capable of composing—and composing well—in just about any style, from the grim, quartertone musicscapes of *The Night Visitor* and *Wait Until Dark* to memorable songs such as "Moon River." But, of course, his trademark was the suave, big band tunes such as the *Pink Panther* theme with bass lines that have more melodic clout than most pop songs. Hank, you were a great composer, arranger, conductor, and human being. You will be missed.

There are film scores that stand beautifully on their own as music while towering above the mediocre (at best) films for which they were written. There are film scores that do not stand up as well on purely musical terms but that considerably enhance an outstanding cinematic creation. And then there are, quite simply, scores that are great music for great films. To the latter category belongs Elmer Bernstein's **The Magnificent Seven**, particularly as heard on a Koch International's splendid new CD with James Sedares conducting the Phoenix Symphony Orchestra. Certainly, no music will ever set the tone of the Wild West as translated by Hollywood quite as excitingly—and quite as quintessentially—as Bernstein's title cue for John Sturges' 1960 reworking of Akira Kurosawa's *The Seven Samurai*. And I'm not just talking about the stirring, major-mode string theme over those rousing, syncopated horn chords. Bernstein sets up this theme with a wonderful, post-Copland scherzando in the strings that serves as a kind of basic, Americana foundation for all the heroism—and anti-heroism—that follows. It's a theme that goes particularly well with the character played by Steve McQueen, although it is not specifically associated with him most of the time. Just as rousing, if not more, however, is the ominous, minor-mode fandango that announces and underscores the presence of *The Magnificent Seven*'s arch villain, Calvera (Eli Wallach), and his gang. This theme, which Bernstein varies in quite creative ways, has both the drive to evoke the relentlessness of Calvera's persecution of the people of a small Mexican village and the Flamenco harmonies to suggest the Hispanic origins of this evildoer and his band of nasties. It also, however, has just enough ties with *The Magnificent Seven*'s heroic theme to imply that the two groups are little more than opposite sides of the same coin. Bernstein's score gets much of its mileage out of the lead-in, the heroic theme, and the fandango. But it offers as well a fair amount of subtle suspense music falling somewhere between Stravinsky and Bartók and, happily, a less-than-expected dose of Mexicana. There is also a nice piece of Flamenco/bullfight music that underscores a trivial scene with Horst Buchholz, who plays a thoroughly annoying character in the film. At any rate, the entire score gets performed with an absolutely infectious spirit by the Phoenix Symphony under the baton of film buff James Sedares, who obviously reveled in every moment of this particular undertaking. Quite close in its pacing and phrasing to the score as it is heard on *The Magnificent Seven*'s music track, the score here has tremendous drive and vitality. Sedares also thoroughly captures the music's humor, its quieter tensions, and its rare tenderness. As for the recorded sound, this Koch International Classics CD comes about as close as any CD I know to reproducing the richness and ambience of the concert hall. This is a recording to take with you when auditioning new equipment. My only, very minor quibble with the project has to do with the reconstruction by Christopher Palmer (and, one presumes, composer Bernstein, who fortunately retained his original sketches) of the score, the original of which, as so often happened, was either lost or destroyed. At the end of Calvera's first appearance, for instance, a percussion figure played on two side-drums—and doubled, I suspect, on the marimba—gets performed on this recording simply as rim shots. A solo guitar prominent in the early phases of Calvera's theme has also either been swallowed up in the recorded sound bit or eliminated. One also wonders whether something a bit less anticlimactic could have been chosen to conclude this CD than the seven-minute Overture for Chorus and Orchestra arranged from Bernstein's score for John Sturges' flat Cinerama spectacle, *The Hallelujah Trail*, from 1965.

Another comment or two: above I assigned the film and the score of *The Magnificent Seven* to equal categories of greatness. Several recent viewings of the film on laserdisc have changed my opinion somewhat. While Sturges' direction, Charles Lang's cinematography, William Roberts' screenplay, the acting, and, of course, Bernstein's score all contribute handily to our involvement in the often rousing action, *The Magnificent Seven* pretty much wastes the roles played by James Coburn, Charles Bronson, Robert Vaughn, and Brad Dexter while cutesying things up with the Horst Buchholz character, who is also given a totally inane love involvement, the only one in the picture. Furthermore, while the film sets up the Steve McQueen and Yul Brynner characters with an act of antiracist heroism, the movie is stereotypical in its treatment of the Mexican heavies and condescending in its portrayal of the Mexican peasants. A scene where Charles Bronson spanks one of the peasant boys for suggesting that his father is a coward stands as one of cinema history's most embarrassing moments. Still, it is difficult not to get swept away by *The Magnificent Seven*'s myth and heroism, and Bernstein's score plays no small role in this sweep, whether heard with the film or isolated on Koch International's—what else?—magnificent CD. Trivia question of the day: how does the movie explain away Yul Brynner's accent?

The reappearance on CD (Carlo Savina and Jacques Mercier, cond.) of Stephen Sondheim's score for Alain Resnais' 1974 **Stavisky** has rekindled my regrets that the composer/lyricist did not divide his time more evenly between Broadway and Hollywood (or other film capitals). I can think of few film scores that create moods quite as palpable and quite as subtle as those of *Stavisky*. With its fast-fox-trot beat and its dance band instrumentation (including sax and banjo), the title cue immediately evokes the 1930s era during which this drama about the notorious French swindler takes place. But Sondheim's close harmonies, his blending of the cue's simple theme into those harmonies, and his unexpected departures into a brief but magical bridge cast an aura of nostalgia over the music that succeeds far better than Resnais' uninspiring mise-en-scène in evoking the layers of memory for which the director, who has not made a good film since *Providence*, has been noted. That magical bridge, associated throughout *Stavisky* with the theme of memory, also becomes the principal generator of musical ambience in several other cues, some of them, such as "Arlette le jour," metamorphosing into more lighthearted moods, some of them moving into more somber territory, such as "Le Bureau la nuit" and "Passé lointain." Further on, it blossoms into a full-orchestral theme of its own (with the main theme subordinated to a reminiscence) in "Arlette la nuit" and, more darkly, "La Maison du père." Waltzes also play a solid role in *Stavisky*'s music. While certain of these are little more than pastiches of salon music, others, such as "La Vie facile" and parts of "Arlette la nuit," recall the irony and Ravelian sophistication of Sondheim's Broadway masterpiece, *A Little Night Music*, composed around the same time. And in the climactic "Le Futur" Sondheim ingeniously transforms his main theme into a near-nightmare waltz. A nostalgia-filled love theme ("Erna") evocative of *Night Music*'s half-lit sets rounds out the music with its sad lyricism. The recorded sound here is reasonably bright and full, but one would wish for more competent instrumental forces in certain cues. A great score for a mediocre film.

It is difficult for me to give an objective evaluation of Bernardo Bertolucci's latest epic, **Little Buddha**, since, for reasons too complex and too personal to go into here, the film hit a particularly deep area of my sensibilities and left me in something like a trance after I had seen it. Were I to try to make a dispassionate judgment about *Little Buddha*, I would say that, after an engrossing opening, the film, in devoting a major block of its considerable running time to a retelling of the story of Buddha, with Keanu Reeves as "Prince" Siddhartha, comes across a bit as a "Buddhism for Beginners." The film also has a certain problem with coherency apparently due to some major cutting. What is one to make, for instance, of the non-character of Evan, who gets some deeply sad funeral music in a part of the score you will not hear when you see the film? Still, in its own way, Bertolucci's expansive and peaceful movie does manage to successfully use a distinctly Western medium to communicate a distinctly non-Western way of dealing with both existence and the cosmos. For me, one of the major reasons for whatever success the film has lies in the acting performance of Ying Ruocheng, who played a sympathetic political indoctrinator in Bertolucci's *The Last Emperor* and who gives an utterly convincing portrayal that is both beautifully warm and deeply spiritual of an old Tibetan monk in *Little Buddha*.

A further plus for *Little Buddha* comes from another *Last Emperor* carryover, composer/actor/sometimes-rock-star Ryuichi Sakamoto, whose multifaceted score can be heard on a Milan CD. As usual, Sakamoto generates major amounts of affect with slowly evolving tonescapes that define themselves infinitely more with unexpected, utterly moving, internal shifts in the chord structures than they do with themes per se. What is billed as *Little Buddha*'s "Main Theme," for instance, is an elegy (mostly) for strings with a grandeur and intensity that tie the music just as strongly into the potential reincarnation, in three different children, of a past spiritual leader as into the ultimate passing of the current one. In its final presentation, complete with vocalizing chorus, the "Main Theme" very simply floods the emotions, or at least it did mine. In a different mode, Sakamoto's minimalist, non-resolving, alterations of the string triads in the "Opening Titles" creates a sense of openness that perfectly sets the tone for the film. A third, rather stately theme, heard in the openings of "Nepalese Caravan" and "Red Dust," beautifully sets the stage for the film's pageantry. And the way in which a woman's voice, chanting in an Indian mode over various Western and non-Western instruments, enters into the "Nepalese Caravan" cue is absolutely magical. Indeed, Sakamoto incorporates various Indian instruments, singing, and musical devices with great success into parts of his score, sometimes more or less "straight," sometimes in more non-Eastern contexts. He also manages to transform the "Dies Irae" chorale into a bittersweet musical experience near the end of the film. The recording further includes some authentic performances of Indian music. From the sound of this CD, Sakamoto has benefited from a substantial body of strings to play his often forte and/or fortissimo themes, and this works very much to the music's benefit.

Varèse Sarabande has now issued Volume Three in its "Legends of Hollywood" series devoted to the music of Franz Waxman (Queensland Symphony Orchestra, Richard Mills, cond.). Lest you think it must be getting close to bottom-of-the-barrel time, a quick listen to this CD will quickly convince you otherwise. Although Waxman did a lot of work for big Hollywood productions such as William Dieterle's 1954 *Elephant Walk* and Victor Saville's *The Silver Chalice* from the same year, both of which are represented on this CD, the composer excelled at finding musical equivalents for the smaller, darker side of life represented in smaller, darker productions. Two such films are Jules Dassin's 1950 *Night and the City* and Don Siegel's 1949 *Night Unto Night*. After a stately opening no doubt intended to suggest the film's London setting, the music for *Night and the City*, heard here in a suite entitled *Nightride for Orchestra*, moves into the kind of crackling, modernistic action music that Waxman composed with particular skill and that we also hear, for instance, in the driving, fugal "Fight for the Cup" music that brings to *The Silver Chalice* a level of artistic sophistication it hardly deserves. *Night and the City* also offers quieter, murkier passages in which Waxman creates a perfect film noir concoction by joining a kind of decadent romanticism to the anxiety-producing dissonances that trademark the composer's best writing. That decadent romanticism gets an even bigger ride in the very somber, often very sad "Dusk: A Setting for Orchestra" arranged from *Night Unto Night*. This is Waxman working, rather unusually, in a domain of almost Herrmannesque musical tragedy, and the results are intensely gripping. Films such as *Night and the City* and *Night Unto Night*, which were directed by major American renegades, represent a side of Waxman's career that needs more exposure.

The noir moods in Waxman's suite from Vincent Sherman's 1944 Mr. *Skeffington* likewise range from murky to intense, while the music for Anthony Mann's 1950 *The Furies* is a good deal more extroverted—and exciting—in spite of the film's heavily psychological overtones. Even for a movie such as *Elephant Walk*, however, Waxman, although producing one of his pop-song big themes, avoids just about all the clichés of the genre. In the process, he comes up with some particularly intriguing instrumental colorings in the music's more somber moments, and his "Elephant Stampede," into which he ingeniously incorporates the title song, is an absolute masterpiece of dramatic underscoring. I could have done without the "Cafe Waltzes" from Peter Godfrey's 1945 *Hotel Berlin*, and the "Montage for Orchestra" of music from the Delmer Daves *Destination Tokyo* (1943) does not strike me as one of the composer's more inspired undertakings. For all its Dresden amens and its biblical-spectacular sobriety, however, *The Silver Chalice* remains one of Waxman's best efforts. Conductor Richard Mills has an absolute gift for capturing the exhilarating drive and, when necessary, the menace of Waxman's more flamboyant scoring, and he fares reasonably well in the quieter mood pieces, although here I would have liked a bit more cohesion. He gets what sounds like thoroughly committed playing from Australia's Queensland Symphony Orchestra, which recorded these works all the way back in 1990.

November/December

What, you may ask, do the recent films **Wyatt Earp** and *Wolf* have in common? Well, to my mind, they represent a healthy tendency that may be emerging in American cinema to go beyond the black/white, good/evil polarities that have until (maybe) now dominated this country's political and narrative mythologies. If the Wyatt Earp played by Kevin Costner in Lawrence Kasdan's epic biography is not the handsome, square-jawed, clean-shaven Goody Two-shoes captivatingly incarnated by Hugh O'Brien in the old TV series, neither is he Jimmy Stewart's dissolute, white-suited gambler/fop who finally recognizes a whore only when she is lying on her back in the bitter revisionism of John Ford's *Cheyenne Autumn*. This is not to say that Costner's single-minded, occasionally self-pitying, often cruel, extraordinarily lucky, and generally not-very-likable Earp is devoid of any heroic stature. But his heroism comes across in Kasdan's *Wyatt Earp* more as a function of the cultural myths within which it operates than as a quasi-religious absolute. In this context, I was even able to swallow Kevin Costner's sleepily ecstatic "Boom!" as he watches fireworks, although it had me screaming during the theatrical trailers. My only problem with this three-hour-plus film is that it needed to be either longer or shorter. Kasdan was apparently devil bent on squeezing in every episode from Earp's life. But either some episodes should have been cut, or else most of them should have been expanded beyond the status of vignettes.

James Newton Howard's big, symphonic score for *Wyatt Earp* (Warner Bros.; Hollywood Recording Musicians Orchestra, Marty Paich, cond.) is fairly predictable. In its textures and some of its chordal colorations, the music comes out of Copland, but minus that composer's finesse at modulating into different harmonic moods. Indeed, Howard more often than not has a fair amount of trouble straying very far from his home tonality once he has established it. This is one of the problems with the nonetheless dramatic, heavily major-mode main theme. I also found quite uninspiring the almost amateurish love theme that first turns up in "The Wedding" and reappears in several other cues. Even the action music, such as the low-pitched march that opens the "O.K. Corral" cue and later accelerates into a kind of sweeping violence, somehow never fully engages the emotions. Of course, maybe all of this is the film score's contribution to the new cine-mythology, which pulls its affective punches somewhat rather than letting the music work you up into too much of a snit against the bad guys or too much of a lather over the action sequences and their often tragic outcomes. But a perverse part of me misses the old way, and, quite frankly, I feel that Howard's *Wyatt Earp* score ties in too strongly to the cine-musical styles of the past to allow one to view it as a liberation of sorts. Interestingly, perhaps the best moments in the score come during the cues in which, with accordion, acoustic guitars, and solo violin, Howard goes after a more authentically ethnic-American sound. Perhaps film composers need at this point to take a longer look at areas such as this.

I had, on the other hand, surprisingly few reservations over Mike Nichols' **Wolf**. I have been leery of Jack Nicholson ever since he and Stanley Kubrick single-handedly destroyed Steven King's gothic masterpiece, *The Shining*. But in *Wolf*, even at the extreme moments of his lupine metamorphoses, Nicholson shows the kind of restraint cum simmering anger that should have made him the ideal choice for the character of Jack Torrance in *The Shining*. In fact, my only problem with Nicholson in *Wolf* came from the fact that his eye popping and scenery chewing in films such as *The Shining* made it difficult to take his understatement as a mild-mannered book-company exec seriously. But overall, Nicholson pulls off what amounts to a virtuoso performance as he modulates from victim through a man/wolf who takes control of things to a wolf/man who makes an agonizing but heroic choice. What I liked most about *Wolf*, however, was the way the film and its screenplay by Jim Harrison and Wesley Strick rewrite one of the most popular mythologies in American cinema. Long the embodiment of the evilness of humankind's dark, animal side, the werewolf is transformed, in *Wolf*, first and foremost into a revolt against the patriarchal culture of rationality and empiricism that needed its werewolf/villains in the first place. Yet *Wolf* does not make the revisionist error of turning the "dark side" into something purely wonderful, as the character deliciously played by James Spader makes perfectly clear. Ultimately, we walk away from *Wolf* accepting the contradiction—which ultimately isn't one—that the dark side and the light side both have their positive and negative elements.

Perhaps the weakest thing about *Wolf* is the way it uses an absolutely remarkable score "composed, orchestrated and conducted" by Ennio Morricone. Just how thoroughly Morricone's score got slighted was driven home to me in spades by the Columbia/Sony Classical recording of the music. I would go to see a film just because Morricone wrote its music, and so it was with numerous expectations that I stepped into my local cinema to see *Wolf* this past summer. Yet, somehow, the music never made a deep impression on me as I watched the film, and the one thing that stuck most with me when I left the theater was a chord progression that harks back to one of Morricone's western collaborations with Sergio Leone. I therefore was not 100 percent expecting the musical glories that came to me from the Columbia/Sony CD. Where to start? Well, the opening cue, "Wolf and Love," offers a masterful reworking of several of Morricone's most recognizable devices—the long, sustained pedal point over which a tragic theme is fragmented by subtle tattoos from the side drums; violins in their extreme high ranges that seem to soar out into space; an eerie figure, played on (I think) an electric harpsichord that I would call a "floating ostinato." Further on in the cue, the fragments jell into a broad, haunting theme that, here and in subsequent cues, comes to sum up the entire mood of *Wolf*. Later, some 40 seconds into the cue entitled "The Dream and the Deer," we hear an extraordinary piece of musical surrealism in the high violins and glockenspiel that sounds like what Erich Wolfgang Korngold might have written had he ever scored a werewolf flick, reminding us of the cinematic traditions that *Wolf* both reinforces and revises. Morricone also, for the film's climactic moments, offers some particularly savage pursuit music. Throughout the score, furthermore, the saxophone and, at one strange moment, the muted trumpet add timbres that evoke hip from a bygone era but that, in *Wolf*, simply fortify the overall aura of unfulfilled yearning. And the aura of finality evoked by the halting string chords at the end of the "Laura and Will" cue sunk me into a mood from which it was difficult to escape. All in all, a stunning score that here and there spookily evokes the '40s and '50s from a composer whose career began to flourish in the revisionist '60s, and who has evolved smoothly over the last years in order to enter the oxymoronic '90s as if he had lived here all the time.

Will we ever see the last attempt to find an appropriate musical score for Abel Gance's silent epic, **Napoleon**? Probably not, and perhaps that is just as well. Contrary to what I had been told, it would appear that only a scant 20 minutes of Arthur Honegger's original score has survived, necessitating a major amount of filling in, which composers such as Carmine Coppola and Carl Davis have, quite unsuccessfully in my opinion, tried to do for the film's recent resuscitation and revival. Now, lo and behold, Honegger student Marius Constant has decided to add to the extant Honegger cues not only certain other works by the composer, such as the Prelude to Shakespeare's *The Tempest* and some of the incidental music for D'Annunzio's *Phaedre*, but also some two hours of his own original music. If the hour's worth of Honegger and Constant on a recent Erato release (Orchestre Philharmonique de Monte Carlo, Marius Constant, cond.) is any indication, the results are just short of spectacular. For the title sequence, for instance, Constant has composed a fanfarish prelude whose stately, polytonal brass chords certainly evoke Honegger (see, for instance, the Fifth Symphony), even though Constant works within a much more ambivalent harmonic context than Honegger usually did. A warm and nostalgic theme later on in the title sequence likewise recalls Honegger, again, however, in a more acerbic harmonic setting. Constant falls into an even stronger Honegger mode, both in chordal richness and in a mid-range string theme, in the cue entitled "L'Armée anglaise," which, along with "L'Assaut," contains some of the most exciting writing in a middle-of-the-road-contemporary idiom I have heard in some time. In "La Terreur," Constant plays around ironically with a French revolutionary song ("Ça ira" or "La Carmagnole," I forget which), giving it first to the solo timpani. Interestingly, none of the extant Honegger score approaches, musically, the modernism one finds both in Honegger's concert music and in Constant's additions. "Violine" flirts brazenly with Mahler, while the "Chaconne de l'impératrice" comes startlingly close to what one might find in a Hollywood film score from the '30s or '40s. And even Honegger cannot resist quoting "La Marseillaise" in one of the cues ("Les Mendiants de la gloire"). On the other hand, Honegger's prelude from his incidental music for *The Tempest*, while sounding in spots quite a bit like silent film music, has quite a musically violent side to it that has been captured exceptionally well by Constant and the Monte Carlo Philharmonic. Whether this same kind of tone appeared in other parts of Honegger's original score we will apparently not know. The performances here are both exhilarating and moving, although some of the brass in the later cues seem a bit out of key with the rest of the orchestra. This instrumentally complex music, with its heavy brass, has also been richly recorded. This is definitely the kind of score that Gance's *Napoleon* deserves.

CHAPTER TWELVE

~

1995

January/February

I would probably have waited for Frank Darabont's **The Shawshank Redemption**, based on Stephen King's short novel *Rita Hayworth and the Shawshank Redemption*, to come out on video had the Epic Soundtrax CD containing Thomas Newman's wonderful score for it not turned up in my mail a couple of days ago. I'm glad I didn't. While I'm not sure that the ending of this longish film quite lives up to the elaborate narrative and character developments that get us there, while it's ambiguous as to whether the film raises our consciousness about or merely perpetuates certain race and class stereotypes, and while I'm coming to the conclusion that no movie will ever be able to capture that aura of skewed Americana into which one plunges as soon as one opens a Stephen King novel, *The Shawshank Redemption* takes the prison-drama genre and adds so many subtle touches to it, starting with that gothic building somewhere in Ohio, I think, that serves as this film's location for the Maine prison of the novel, that the film stands as one of my 1994 favorites. *The Shawshank Redemption* has also been exceptionally well cast, from the supporting roles of the fellow convicts, captain of the guards, and warden, to the two principal roles played by Tim Robbins, as a young banker imprisoned for the murder of his wife and her lover, and the ever reliable Morgan Freeman as the only "guilty" inmate in Shawshank Prison.

Newman's music adds a good deal to *The Shawshank Redemption*. Although the film establishes its initial era by starting off with the Ink Spots' classic "If I Didn't Care," which has happily been included on this CD, the background score quickly establishes its profile, a profile that moves in sync in its own way with the skewed Americana of King's writings. The "Shawshank Prison" cue, for instance, offers a plodding, almost dirge-like, and ultimately quite imposing study in contrary motion played heavily in the strings, a perfect musical equivalent of the cine-prison's architecture. A slightly milder version of this music appears in "Sisters," [a cynical designation for a group of prison homosexual predators]. Yet the musical style has just enough ties with Copland to remind us in just what country this fortress-like citadel is located. The music for the cue entitled "May," which is later reprised in "Workfield," starts off with a great fiddle solo later joined by acoustic guitar to create the more extroverted Americana image that King himself seems to prefer, if not always get, in musical scores. In a totally opposite direction, the very sad, meditational, and nostalgic piano solos that turn up in cues such as "New Fish" and "Brooks Was Here" rather recall the kinds of moods set by cousin Randy Newman for films such as *Avalon* and *Awakenings*. Those same feelings are likewise evoked in the cue entitled "Zihuatanejo," where Newman—oh bliss!—avoids anything remotely resembling the stereotypical Mexicana film score history gives us the right to expect. The kinkier side of Newman that one hears, for instance, in the title cue for *The Player* also shows up here in the offbeat percussion-string-and-electronic figures one hears in "Rock Hammer" and later, although slightly smoothed out, in "Lovely Raquel" (Rita, you see, is only the beginning. Too bad they couldn't have kept King's entire title, since it has deep implications, both textual and subtextual). By and large, we are at a 180-degree remove from the kind of cold violence evoked in Miklós Rózsa's quintessential prison-film music for *Brute Force*. As was the case in *Quiz Show*, director Darabont has not used his musical score as much to create narrative-specific manipulations as to establish an overall mood. And in *The Shawshank Redemption* that mood is mostly one of sadness, resignation, and a nostalgia for free soil. When the musical "redemption" comes, it is set up by a series of wonderfully warm and rich string chords, pieces of the "Shawshank Prison" theme, and snippets of solo piano that finally crescendo into a stately, full orchestra celebration that will send chills into your bone marrow. To round things off, this CD also includes Hank Williams' croakily yodeled "Lovesick Blues" and a hissily recorded aria from *The Marriage of Figaro* conducted by Karl Boehm, both of which, particularly the Mozart, play substantial roles in the narrative.

One wonders whether the appearance of Tim Burton's **Ed Wood** indicates that people are taking movies more seriously or whether they are taking them less seriously than ever before. Probably both. Edward D. Wood, Jr., you may remember, is the director that most serious folks credit with writing and directing the worst film ever made, the 1959 *Plan 9 from Outer Space*, although Leonard Maltin makes a case for Wood's earlier *Glen or Glenda*. Personally, I would rate films such as *Interiors* (Woody Allen), *The Two English Girls* (François Truffaut), *Network* (Sidney Lumet), and such recent Alain Resnais efforts as *La Vie est un roman* or *Mélo* ahead of Wood on my all-time-worst list, since they were made by directors who should have known better. Indeed, there is something perversely refreshing about Ed Wood, since his films naïvely and transparently reveal the kind of crap that Hollywood gets away with every day by being a bit more careful with such niceties as continuity and the structural integrity of sets. At any rate, Johnny Depp, playing Wood in Burton's black-and-white (what else?) film, creates a wholly believable portrait of a sometimes-transvestite filmmaker who was earnest to a fault and who was so caught up with the "broad picture" that he may very well have never shot the same setup twice, even when walls shook or cemetery grass moved with the actors. But it is Martin Landau who, in his moving and of-ten very funny portrayal of Bela Lugosi, whom Wood, um, resurrected at the end of his career, all but runs away with Burton's film. Also watch, however, for a wonderful re-creation of Orson Welles by Vincent D'Onofrio. And Jeffrey Jones is all but per-fect as the Amazing Kreskin.

One of the great things about Howard Shore's score for *Ed Wood* (Hollywood; Lon-don Philharmonic Orchestra) is that, as in the film, you're never quite sure whether you're dealing with parody, pastiche, or the "real" thing. As the coffin closes on the dead actor, for instance, we wonder for a second whether it is Lugosi or Dracula, while Shore's sad and warm music, which culminates in a big statement from a church or-gan, could just as easily be music for the film as for a film within the film. Indeed, Shore allowed himself to be inspired by the deadly serious "sound" of '50s monster/horror/sci-fi flicks, even to the point of incorporating a Theremin into the orchestral palette (he's probably the first film composer to do so in at least two decades). Get-ting a Theremin player was not that easy, however, and Shore had to turn to Steve Martin (not the comedian), who has just finished a documentary on the late Leon Theremin and who recommended a Russian musician named Lydia Kavina. It was only at the last minute that Kavina was able to get a visa to go to London for the recording sessions, which is why Ondes Martenot player Cynthia Millar was kept on call and ultimately contributed her instrument's timbres to one or two of the cues. The throaty tones of the Theremin turn up almost immediately during the very dra-matic pre-title music, over which the "true" story of Ed Wood is introduced as one might present a tale by Edgar Allan Poe. There ensues a wonderful title sequence dur-ing which, in the best post–*Plan* 9 tradition, the camera tracks amidst a bunch of tombstones that announce the actors' and actresses' names. Behind this, Shore's mu-sic throbs with a half-Latin, half-jungle-beat as the Theremin, brass, winds, and per-cussion compete for eerie melodic and chordal fragments that evoke '50s music tracks while at the same time taking a step back from them.

There is also some nice creepy-crawly music for Lugosi, into which Shore intro-duces a cimbalom that reminds us that Lugosi was a Hungarian-born actor and not an avatar of the good count himself. Shore also links brief quotations of the big, minor-mode theme from Tchaikovsky's *Swan Lake* to the Lugosi character as a subtle refer-ence to the music used in the 1931 *Dracula* that launched the actor's career. Another particularly effective musical cue, entitled "Sanitarium," leads us from what could be silent-film music into "straighter" music, including another reminder from *Swan Lake*, that brings us partially back to the reality of Lugosi's morphine and methadone ad-dictions. By the end of the cue, however, we return to some organ-cum-Theremin strains that have the potential for turning what we are watching into an Ed Wood film. Other parts of the score go off into somewhat lighter areas, with some of the cues, such as the hustle-and-bustle music for "Backlot," moving toward pastiche while others play around nicely with the Latin percussion that seems to be a motif of sorts for *Ed Wood's* overall musical profile. Indeed, we also get to hear Perez Prado's "Kuba Mambo" and Korla Pandit's "Nautch Dance" in the film and on this CD, which closes with a fairly straight arrangement of the Main Title music that was apparently used for a music video. (My thanks to Howard Shore, who dedicated this CD to the late Henry Mancini, for talking to me for a few minutes about *Ed Wood*.)

Jane Eyre is one of Bernard Herrmann's most appealing—and least known—film scores. Composed in 1944 for Robert Stevenson's adaptation of the Charlotte Brontë novel, Herrmann's score, taken from the original music tracks, recently resurfaced in the 20th Century-Fox "Classic Series," coupled with *Laura*. Now something closer to the entire score, including music not heard in the film, has turned up in Marco Polo's "Film Music Classics" series, featuring extraordinarily warm and full sound and generally excellent playing from the Slovak Radio Symphony Orchestra, with Adriano conducting. The dark-hued, nearly gothic romanticism of Brontë's novel probably matched Herrmann's soul and spirit more than just about any of the narrative material he worked with throughout his career as a composer, and the musical translation of that spirit in this long score is dominated by a kind of somber wistfulness that Herrmann did not have that many opportunities to develop. Even his later score for *The Ghost and Mrs. Muir* does not venture quite as far into the night as *Jane Eyre*. One does, of course, hear in *Jane Eyre* hints of many things to come from the composer's later work. A theme that appears several times, including the beginning of the cue entitled "Mr. Mason," remarkably foreshadows the "Madeleine" theme in Hitchcock's *Vertigo*. There are also the low, lugubrious figures, often in the winds (the composer had apparently planned on using a double-bass clarinet in the score) and the bittersweet, low-mid-range longings that will become the familiar musical shapes taken by the affect generated somewhere within the composer. On the other hand, one of the score's most haunting cues, "Jane Alone," is an extremely slow waltz with several melodic turns and some acidic harmonic twists that are novel for Herrmann. *Jane Eyre* also has a tragic side, apparent in the title music and a couple of later cues, that is rare in the composer and that at moments almost takes a turn toward Honegger. A brief quotation from Wagner also shows up in two cues. I generally like the way conductor Adriano shapes and voices the moody contours of Herrmann's score which, although romantic in spirit, generates much of its dramatic momentum out of a decidedly non-romantic accumulation of small musical cells, which Adriano makes jell into wholes that are convincing both aesthetically and dramatically. The title music struck me as a bit overdriven, but it is not much different from the way Herrmann conducts it on the 20th Century-Fox release.

March/April

It makes all the sense in the world. Cultures have for many moons been keeping their various demons at bay by taking them out of our dreams and ensnaring them in collectivized mythic narratives or rituals. So there is no wonder that, having escaped the clutches of storytelling since he was "killed" in the 1991 *Freddy's Dead*, good ol' Freddy Krueger should begin haunting the "real" world that initially captured him 10 years ago in a tale called *A Nightmare on Elm Street*. What to do? Why, fictionalize that "real" world—the world inhabited by actress Heather Langenkamp, actor Robert Englund and, of course, writer/director Wes Craven, not to mention a host of other folks involved in the various *Nightmare* movies—so that it in its second-degree turn may capture the forces of evil in a new, rather more imposing version of Freddie Krueger. This is precisely what Wes Craven, returning as director to his creation for the first time since the original *Nightmare*, has done in his dizzyingly meta-cinematic **New Nightmare**, which even includes shots of the devastation wrought by the recent L.A. earthquake. Indeed, not only is *New Nightmare*'s story about the need to create a new "nightmare" to trap Freddie, whose incursions into the dreams of Heather Langenkamp's young son (played by Miko Hughes) are of course dismissed as the imaginings of a child who has seen too many *Nightmare* movies, that "new nightmare" is, naturally, the film the audience is watching as the character named Wes Craven played by Wes Craven writes it and as the various members of the technical crew design its gimmicks and create its eerily infernal sets. And perhaps that is the real solution: a narrative so convoluted, self-reflective, and labyrinthine that it will feed on itself from now until kingdom come, forever trapping Freddie and, needless to say, obviating the need for new, new nightmares.

For the score to *New Nightmare* (Milan; Michael McCuistion, cond.), Craven turned to a composer whose name is unfamiliar to me, J. Peter Robinson, who has played keyboards for Phil Collins and who worked with Craven on the *Nightmare Cafe* TV series. Robinson quite capably takes over where such composers as Charles Bernstein left off, working first of all with a wide variety of synthesized and sampled timbres, most of them moody and/or unsettling. An excellent example of this can be heard in the cue entitled "Wes Craven's Nightmare," in which everything—the low pedal point, the string timbres, the growlings, the bells, the piano, and the voices—is all electronically generated. Like Bernstein, whose original *Nightmare* theme turns up throughout the score, Robinson often turns to the acoustic instruments of a reasonably large orchestra when he needs violent outbursts, with slashed, glissando strings and whooping horns that could really not be duplicated in oscillators, circuitry, and microchips, at least not yet. Interestingly, many of the individual cues, of which there are 33 on this CD, mimic in miniature the film's broader narrative movements. A good example of this is entitled "The Funeral," which starts off with the sad vocalizing of an a cappella chorus (probably sampled), turns chaotic and dissonant as the child is pulled into the grave by Freddie, and then regains a kind of calm that is definitely tainted (a motif recalling the *Spellbound* suspense theme appears frequently in this cue and others). Even the simplest children's theme does not remain exempt from disquieting musical intrusions for very long. Robinson makes particularly effective use of various forms of the human voice (generally sampled), from angry whisperings to choral antics of all sorts, including chanting and some weird glissandos, while the breathy wisps created within his synthesizers also establish a kind of spectral presence. The voices of children playing also act as a sad motif in the film, and it is their chanting that acts as the final attempt to keep Freddie at bay. If I have a criticism of this score, it is that, in supporting the various narrative upheavals, it does not really move in sync with deeper levels of *New Nightmare*'s postmodern mirrorings. While I'm not sure what the music would have to do to attain the same level of self-reflexivity of Craven's ingenious movie, it would be interesting if Robinson had given it a shot.

I haven't yet decided what I think of **Interview with the Vampire**, in which director Neil Jordan, on the heels of *The Crying Game*, returns to a genre that he handled with particular success in his 1984 *The Company of Wolves*. But there is no doubt in my mind that Eliot Goldenthal's music for *Interview* is one of the best symphonic scores to come along in some time (Geffen; Jonathan Sheffer, cond.). The basic sound here might be described as what you would come up with if John Corigliano had let himself be drawn back toward Wagner after having listened to a few Danny Elfman/Tim Burton collaborations. It is a sound that works particularly well for *Interview*, which has some of the hyper-gothic darkness one finds in Burton or Coppola but at the same time investigates some of the deeper and darker psycho-cultural issues that Burton and (of late) Coppola tend to avoid. Thus does Goldenthal not hesitate, in his main theme for *Interview* ("Born to Darkness"), to allude to that grand old trope of horror-film music, the *Dies Irae* chorale. But he does so in a waltz whose sad and somber elegance is a perfect musical translation of the situation of *Interview*'s two vampires, and in particular the one played by Brad Pitt. For, indeed, Ann Rice, in her novel and screenplay, uses the vampire mythology as a lens through which she considers the fundamental situation of the patriarchal male, whose dread of death is so all-consuming that his only fight against it is to become a virtual death machine, sucking life from his victims so that he may enjoy the illusion of immortality. But that death machine hides behind a suave façade of seductiveness, just as the *Dies Irae* of Goldenthal's main theme enfolds itself into a dark, Viennese sumptuousness. That the vampires' victims are principally young, sexual women is perfectly consistent with this fear, since reproduction of the species via women is the visible guarantee of that feared mortality. Thus, it comes as no surprise that a) the Brad Pitt vampire turns a young girl into a vampire-bride who remains an eternal nine or 10 years old; b) there is an implied homosexual relationship between *Interview*'s two vampires, the other played quite wickedly by Tom Cruise.

But I digress. Besides its wonderful main theme Goldenthal's score offers a host of other sounds, including lots of bass clarinet and low, snarling brass. But, again, these musical staples of the horror film, which could easily become hackneyed tropes, instead maintain that sheen and distance that earmarks all of Goldenthal's *Interview* music, from the opening "Libera Me" to the frenzied tarantella, from almost medieval dronings to frightening and frenzied outbursts. Many of these elements come together in the cue (the 15th) entitled "Abduction and Absolution," in which the full orchestra propels the music into a furious whirlwind that quietly abates here and there to allow the piano to state the tarantella theme in its upper registers. A boys' chorus later comes in to close the cue with a return to the opening "Libera Me." Not altogether surprisingly, the end-title music takes the form of one of the great rock songs, Mick Jagger and Keith Richards' "Sympathy for the Devil." Unfortunately, it is not the Rolling Stones who perform it here but rather Guns N' Roses, who work up a good sweat in their own right but never reach the intensity of that classic as heard on the Stones' *Beggar's Banquet* album.

And then there is Stephen King. King, of course, is no stranger to horror fiction. Vampires show up in the early *Salem's Lot*, and I suppose you could say that the hero of *Pet Sematary* plays Dr. Frankenstein to some very special monsters, including a cat. King also introduces various psychic phenomena into many of his sagas, including tele- (*Carrie*) and pyrokinesis (*Firestarter*), while the devil himself likewise pays an occasional visit (*The Stand, Needful Things*). But King's special genius lies in the ways that he indelibly ties the supernatural, when he uses it, into the rock-solid foundations of American culture and its underlying violence, so that the horror in King's novels always seems more natural than super. In what I consider to be one of King's lesser novels, *The Dead Zone*, a man wakes up after a five-year coma to discover that he can see various people's futures merely by touching them. In 1983, director David Cronenberg, making, on the heels of *The Brood, Scanners*, and *Videodrome*, his first excursion into the big-studio system and working for the first time with someone else's story, turned **The Dead Zone** into the one film that is arguably better than the King novel it adapts. Surprisingly, for the filmmaker who blew up heads in *Scanners* and buried a gun in the bowels of *Videodrome*'s hero, the success of *The Dead Zone* lies in the generally nonviolent pathos infused into the narrative by Cronenberg and writer Jeffrey Boam (a screenplay by King himself was rejected as too gory), which allows the hero (wonderfully played by Christopher Walken) to attain the tragic stature one finds in many Cronenberg protagonists, in many of the heroes and heroines of King's novels, but in very few of the characters in cine-adaptations of King.

One thing that King and Cronenberg have in common is that they both grew up in cold climes (King in Maine, Cronenberg in Toronto), and one almost constantly feels—to the bones—that coldness in the film version of *The Dead Zone*. It is a coldness that is likewise captured throughout the extraordinary score for *The Dead Zone*, which, more than 10 years after the film's release, has finally surfaced on an audio recording (Milan; National Philharmonic Orchestra). Composed by Michael Kamen after longtime Cronenberg collaborator (both before and after *The Dead Zone*) Howard Shore was unable to come to agreement with executive producer Dino De Laurentiis, the score creates some of its chilly atmosphere via an intertextual allusion to the frigid landscapes of Finland in the second movement of Sibelius's Second Symphony, which becomes what could be called the score's main theme. But Kamen, who came out of a rock-band arranging career to score *The Dead Zone*, goes substantially beyond that reasonably obvious gimmick. A five-note motif, perhaps generated from the Sibelius, continually turns up in the score to suggest both the tragedy and the melancholy that Kamen, as he suggests in his program commentary, saw in *The Dead Zone*'s protagonist, while obsessive expanses of tonal sameness create a kind of austere music-scape with which the hero's psychology interacts very much as his physical presence interacts with the film's wintry visuals. Interestingly, the score that Richard Einhorn would write some five years later for Arthur Penn's icy thriller, *Dead of Winter*, has some of the same qualities. But where Einhorn's score stays fairly uncomplex and sotto voce throughout most of the film, *The Dead Zone* has moments where the composer considerably lets out the stops, some of them for high drama, some for high violence. Yet moments of quiet sadness also abound, with harp timbres producing particularly stark moods here and there, although they are also used to briefly evoke childhood at one point. The score opens with a strange piece of electronic scoring that sounds quite refreshingly pre-synthesizer. From the sound of this nonetheless reasonably well-recorded CD, a certain amount of degeneration in the original source materials has taken place over the last 10 years.

One of the absolute thrills of my early moviegoing career was the first in a series of science-fiction films produced by George Pal, the 1950 **Destination Moon**. The story is simplicity itself: four astronauts get into a sleek space ship imagined before anyone ever thought of lunar modules, take off for the moon, land there after overshooting it once, explore the moon briefly, and then take off and return on less than enough fuel after divesting the ship of all excess weight, including, most poignantly, a harmonica belonging to one of the astronauts. And I have to say that the musical score by Leith Stevens was one of the things about *Destination Moon* that most impressed my 10-year-old soul at the time. The main theme, first heard in the mid-range winds, strings, and xylophone, is one of those moody, morbid creations that perfectly defines the awestruck psychology of a decade on the brink of civilization's first ventures into outer space, and it weaves its mournful way into several key points in the score, most significantly after the moon landing. Elsewhere, much of Stevens' music has a hard-edged but often moody quality to it that might be defined as falling somewhere between Bernard Herrmann and Alex North, and to my sensibilities that's quite a place to fall. Stevens can, for instance, use brass and winds quite abrasively, as he does for several of the film's more dramatic moments. Yet he can also create passages of strange subtlety, such as the figure heard in the strings, xylophone, and harp just before the takeoff (the sound effects for which we also get to hear), or the offbeat presentation of the main theme in the flute and bassoon over strange violin timbres at the beginning of the moon music. Stevens also offers several other engrossing themes, including, in one of the outer-space cues, an intriguing melody that starts off with seven quickly repeated notes in the flute. Happily, the original music track of *Destination Moon* has been reissued (from an LP released by Omega and then by Varèse Sarabande) on CD by Citadel (Heinz Sandauer, cond.), which presents the music as a five-movement suite, with each movement containing a number of separate cues from the score. The sound, although somewhat pinched and tubby, is generally quite clean and full-ranged, and it is presented in genuine stereo.

May/June

I generally look forward to reviewing recordings of film music by Miklós Rózsa. Even if the score is for a poor film, and even if the music is filled with reasonably predictable genre tropes (fanfares for the royal court and all that), Rózsa almost always manages to mobilize his consummate musicianship to serve his own special brand of cine-affect. The listening experience is thus almost always rewarding, and on many levels. A perfect example of this can be heard in the Prelude for one of Rózsa's best-known scores, the 1952 *Ivanhoe* directed by Richard Thorpe, a splendid new recording of which initiates the new "Excalibur" series at Intrada (Sinfonia of London, Bruce Broughton, cond.). To no one's surprise, the music bursts open with a vigorous processional in which just about all the brass play their pomp-and-circumstance roles to the hilt. But where an Alfred Newman or a Max Steiner would stick heavily to the major mode with no dissonances, Rózsa almost immediately creates a moment of bitonality as the opening B-flat Major chord suspends briefly into the sequential shift to E-flat Major. Further, Rózsa uses the mixolydian mode (which you can get most easily by playing the G-Major scale with an F natural instead of F-sharp) to create a Major/Minor ambiguity that both ennobles and somewhat darkens the music. Other subtle touches abound. The song sung by Ivanhoe (Robert Taylor, whose solemn humorlessness works well for the role) at the opening of the picture, for instance, sneaks its way onto the music track via the low cellos and basses beneath a tremolo string figure, rather as if the music is going to become a passacaglia. Lesser talents would have literalized the theme in the violins or perhaps the mid-range winds.

Of course, Rózsa was working, in *Ivanhoe*, strongly within the Hollywood codes that demanded leitmotivic doubling of the main characters, so that the music must often cut, sometimes in mid-phrase, when the film cuts to a new face. The cue entitled "Squire Wamba," for instance, starts off as a classy fugue. No sooner does the third voice make its statement, however, than a goodbye kiss between Ivanhoe and Lady Rowena (Joan Fontaine) necessitates a shift to the latter's theme (now, I ask you: which is more aesthetically fulfilling, a well-developed fugue or a well developed kiss? Don't answer that question). Then, as Ivanhoe leaves his lady fair's room, a cut to Wamba (Emlyn Williams) outside the door brings on the jocular motif for the jester-soon-to-be-squire. But again, Rózsa's theme for Lady Rowena, first heard in a wistful stretto between the oboe and clarinet, captures one's spirit with such warmth and nostalgia that one can overlook the literal-mindedness of some of its deployments. And if the jaunty motif for Wamba tends to somewhat trivialize that character, it is no doubt in response to his one-dimensional treatment, from which actor Williams does his best to wriggle free, in Aeneas MacKenzie's screenplay. And in more extended cues, such as "Rebecca's Love," Rózsa turns the Hollywood leitmotif system to his advantage in a moving musical dialogue between Ivanhoe's theme and the dark-hued music for the Jewish woman (Elizabeth Taylor) who uses the crafts of a sorceress to save his life. *Ivanhoe* also has one of the most extensive and exhausting battle sequences on film. Setup by a capture scene in which Rózsa's tense musical cue ("Torquilstone Castle") harks back to the film noir period from which he had just emerged, the siege music starts off with a call from Robin Hood's horn (in a major-seventh leap upward, yet!) and quickly steamrolls into some 15 minutes' worth of pure orchestral intensity relieved only briefly here and there by musical cutaways that follow the filmic action. It is breathtakingly exciting music that definitely deserves to be isolated from all the sound effects (the sequence does, however, have remarkably little dialogue).

Bruce Broughton's credentials as one of today's major film composers would not necessarily endow him with the conductor credentials necessary to tackle a score such as this, but he and the Sinfonia of London have done an amazing job with Rózsa's score. Indeed, there is not a moment on this recording, which offers all of *Ivanhoe's* principal musical cues presented in their filmic order (which is essential, to my mind), that does not perfectly capture the spirit of both the music and the dramatic/emotional settings for which it was composed. From the nobility of *Ivanhoe's* main theme to the warmth-bordering-on-passion in the music for the film's two heroines, Broughton expertly integrates the drama with the score's not inconsiderable musical substance. And in the more flamboyant cues, in particular the battle music, Broughton never lets the dynamic sweep overwhelm the complexities of the music's textural and chordal structures. The recorded sound is wonderfully full-bodied, with rich brass and a thumping bass. I would have perhaps preferred a slightly less dry venue than that provided by the Abbey Road Studios, although I must say that this dryness certainly duplicates the ambience of most Hollywood soundstages.

Bleu (Blue). As in virginal and self-sacrificing. As in a woman character who totally effaces both her musical creativity and her selfhood for the two men in her life, her cheating late husband and a son that is not even her own. *Blanc* (White). As in *mariage blanc* (unconsummated marriage). As in a total schlep who takes ugly revenge on the strongly sexual woman who has divorced him because of his impotence. *Rouge* (Red), as in. . . . Well, I have so far missed this third part of Krzysztof Kieslowski's trilogy, *Trois Couleurs* (Three Colors). *Trois Couleurs*. As in red, white, and blue. As in the French flag. But if the final panel of this triptych is anything as pretentious as *Bleu*, as mean-spirited as *Blanc*, and as misogynistic as both films, which I suspect it is, then it will simply add one more work to the list of overrated foreign films that make American audiences think they have seen high art while the best work from abroad continues mostly to languish in obscurity. Of course, *Red* features one of my favorite actors, Jean-Louis Trintignant. . . . Virgin Movie Music has released all three of Zbigniew Preisner's scores on three separate CDs entitled **Bleu** (Silesia Philharmonic Choir; Sinfonia Varsovia, Wojciech Michniewski, cond.); **White** (The String Sextet; The Zbigniew Preisner Light Orchestra, Zbigniew Paleta, cond.); and **Red** (Katowice Symphonic Orchestra, Zdzislaw Szostak, cond.; Sinfonia Varsovia, Wojciech Michniewski, cond.).

Let's start with *Bleu*. To be perfectly fair, I don't think that either director Kieslowski or composer Preisner was going, in the film's original score, for music that was supposed to represent the output of the "great composer." Instead, much of the score revolves around a half-Baroque, half-Polish folk-tune theme that is as elusive as the identity of the composer who may or may not have written it. The score offers numerous versions of this minor-mode tune, including rather mysterious pizzicato strings (rather reminding one of a moment in Shostakovich's score for Grigori Kozintsev's *Hamlet*), chorus (setting a Biblical text), and even wooden flute. More intriguing are the 20-second orchestral fragments that appear in the three "Ellipsis" cues, which work effectively in the film in that they seem to represent possibilities rather than what is to be taken as realities. Other cues on this CD, which has been recorded in thinnish but very reverberant sound, tend more toward the pompous. Essentially, the interaction between the film and its music in *Bleu* suggests provocative possibilities that, in the context of the movie's broader vision, unfortunately remain unrealized.

As for *White*, much of that film takes place in Poland, which, I suppose, explains the more melancholic and folky qualities of the music Preisner penned for this second panel of *Trois Couleurs*. Interestingly, as in *Bleu*, *White*'s initial music appears in very brief snippets, mostly in folk-tunish, rather Semitic fragments heard in solo winds, perhaps to evoke the hero's very solitary voice and the sad song he plays at one point on a comb in the Paris Métro. The music builds on this character for a while, adding a few instruments here and there and at one point turning to the solo piano. As of the middle of the sixth cue ("Home at Last"), however, the score metamorphoses, for reasons that remain a total mystery to me, into a tango that dominates, in diverse variations and in much longer developments, much of the remainder of the film. As the story draws toward its nastily cynical conclusion, viewer/listeners will not have a hard time, as the tango mingles with reprises of the mournful wind tunes, figuring out that the latter relate to the antihero's buffoonish existence in Paris, while the tango somehow resurrects him as he regains his native soil. Better recorded than *Bleu*, *White*'s music is solidly smaller in scope than its predecessor. Reasonably appealing and at some points effectively used, Preisner's score, particularly in its rather tenuous relation to the film, almost seems provocateur.

After the music for *Bleu*, whose style interacts internally with film, and the more offbeat, ethnically flavored music for *White*, the score for *Red* behaves somewhat more like a traditional film score, although my impression is limited to the music alone. A bolero rhythm informs a solid part of the music for *Red*. But by and large this is a quiet and mysterious bolero, often interrupted by moments of sostenuto suspense. As in *White* and to a lesser degree *Bleu*'s main theme, one of the frequent thematic twists in *Red*'s score has a rather Semitic quality to it. But a good deal of the gloomy/moody music suggests that *Red* has a decidedly darker hue to its narrative than its two predecessors, although the finale turns rather soupily optimistic, complete with vocalizing chorus. The well-recorded *Red* CD opens (in Polish) and closes (in French) with a song entitled "Love at First Sight," introduced by an attractively jazzy trumpet/bass duet. And in the middle of score, we hear a haunting, orchestrally accompanied song, composed by Van Den Budenmayer, entitled "Do Not Take Another Man's Wife." Initially vocalized by soprano Elzbieta Towarnicka, the song makes a later appearance with words (in Polish, of course).

July/August

[By this point in the career of *Film Musings* I had begun to take advantage of the freedom allowed me by Editor/Publisher Joel Flegler's to review a reasonable number of films on laserdisc, a medium that at the time had me quite excited. I have religiously cut all of these for inclusion in this anthology, and will continue to do so. But I feel that the following review, which involves a laserdisc issue of Sergei Eisenstein's *Alexander Nevsky* featuring a new recording of Prokofiev's towering score, one of the absolute milestones of film music, laid in on the music track, documents such a major event in film music that I had to include it here. As I edit this book in the waning months of 2005, this laserdisc has yet to be reissued on DVD. The audio CD, referenced below, remains available. Scream for a DVD release.]

I knew the cantata put together by Sergei Prokofiev from his score for Sergei Eisenstein's 1938 *Alexander Nevsky* well before I ever had the chance to see the film. When finally I did get to see Eisenstein's black-and-white masterpiece, I was stunned by a music track so horribly recorded that it often reduces Prokofiev's noble and exciting strains to what sounds like cartoon music played on a child's phonograph. *Alexander Nevsky* is not of course the only sound film to have a poorly recorded music track. But music interplays in such an integral way with Eisenstein's carefully elaborated visual structures, many of which in fact were coordinated to the score, and the music itself is of such a consistently high caliber, that some kind of enhancement of the movie's music was inevitable. Such an enhancement has in fact taken place over the last few years in the form of what might be called "concert screenings" of *Alexander Nevsky*, in which a live symphony orchestra played Prokofiev's original score as the film was projected (these concert screenings were initiated by John Goberman, the man behind the *Live From Lincoln Center* TV series, who also is the Executive Producer of this laserdisc reviewed below). Large-scale, live musical accompaniment started, of course, during the silent era with the original release of films such as Griffith's *The Birth of a Nation* and has continued through recent times for restorations such as *Napoléon* and *The New Babylon*. But for films such as *Nevsky* with a voice and sound track (as minimal as these may often be), the live-orchestra accompaniment poses obvious problems. What was needed, of course, was a version of *Nevsky* with a newly recorded music track.

And so it was that a whoop of joy came from my lips when I realized that the laserdisc package I had just opened contained not a video concert performance of Prokofiev's cantata (I have little use for concerts on laserdisc) but rather a gorgeously restored version of Eisenstein's film with a newly recorded music track conducted by Yuri Temirkanov with the St. Petersburg Philharmonic Orchestra, with Evgenia Gorohovskaya, mezzo-soprano (RCA Victor Red Seal Laser Disc). Since sound was the whole reason this project was undertaken, let me say straight off that the sound quality on this laserdisc (and on the audio CD, RCA Red Seal/BMG Classics) is exactly what one would have hoped for. *Nevsky*, which in its musical style runs somewhat parallel with Prokofiev's *Romeo and Juliet* ballet, is a score that relies heavily on strings and brass (very often low brass), and these two orchestral choirs have been recorded with extraordinary fullness and richness. Indeed, the all-important brass have a warmth and presence that I have rarely heard on recordings. This does of course present a small problem, since the music now not only dwarfs most video pictures, it also differs markedly in quality from the voice and sound tracks. Fortunately, however, Eisenstein by and large treats the scored sections of the movie pretty much like a silent film, with little dialogue and few sound effects intruding upon the film/music interactions. Most of the important dialogue occurs during unscored sequences in the first half of the film.

One does of course wonder just how to react to the film as a whole. On the surface *Nevsky*, not altogether unlike the Warner Bros. *The Sea Hawk* in the United States, comes across as an unabashed piece of pre–World War II propaganda that depicts a "great man" (played by the imposing Nikolai Cherkasov, who would return several years later to play Ivan the Terrible in Eisenstein's last two films) uniting the noble Russians against a band of loathsome Teutonic knights. Indeed, *The Sea Hawk's* Spaniards seem positively benign in comparison with *Nevsky's* Germans, who wear weird helmets and burn babies alive while a grotesque priest and an absolutely Satanic monk go about getting the blessings of their particular deity. But *Alexander Nevsky's* strengths lie not in its fairly trivial good guy(s)/bad guys story but in the sheer poetry of its artistic structure, climaxing in one of the most brilliant filmed cinebattles of all times. There is an exhilarating sense of flow, both in the smaller movement from one exquisitely composed shot to the next (Eisenstein concentrates almost exclusively on in-frame movement [and montage-created movement] while keeping Eduard Tisse's camera totally stationary) and in the more broadly conceived form, to which numerous "rhymes" in both the visuals and the musical score contribute a profound sense of unity. In fact, do not be tempted, as I was, to start right off with side two of this laserdisc, which contains the famous "Battle on the Ice" and its aftermath, the latter rendered particularly mournful by an elegy sung by the mezzo-soprano. Dazzling and extraordinarily moving in their own right, the extended battle and post-battle sequences nonetheless do not acquire their full meaning, musically or cinematically, unless seen and felt in the context of the film as a whole. In this context, even the bizarre helmets that generally cloak the Teutonic knights in an aura of unsettling anonymity acquire their own, dark poetry, although lord knows they are disturbing enough during the "Battle on the Ice" sequence alone.

A few more comments. Although it is difficult to evaluate a performance while following a score together with its film, it strikes me that conductor Yuri Temirkanov has found precisely the right tone for the music by highlighting but not overstressing the score's sometimes heavy drama. Excessive musical theatrics could definitely create a nasty state of overkill when added to the film's highly charged visuals. Temirkanov also gets extraordinary playing from the St. Petersburg Philharmonic, which is truly one of the world's finest orchestras. One might object, in the name of authenticity, that the original music-track performances supervised if apparently not conducted by Prokofiev play an important role in the filmic text taken as a historical whole. One is reminded that the Disney Studios eventually realized the error of their ways and returned to the original Stokowski/Philadelphia Orchestra music tracks for *Fantasia* after having at one point "upgraded" the music track via newly recorded performances of the film's various pieces of classical music. But *Fantasia's* music track was never as badly recorded as *Nevsky's*; and in fact the stereo gimmickry devised by the original Disney crew for *Fantasia* is a good deal more interesting when conjoined with the film than the "genuine" stereo of the rerecording. Further, the forces who recorded *Nevsky's* music track do not play a role in the film. So, hey, I'm willing to sacrifice a bit of "authenticity" to get a *Nevsky* that has to be closer to what Eisenstein and Prokofiev had in mind. I also have no problem with the pretitle title sequence devised by RCA, which includes screen-in-screen portraits of the principal actors and is backed by music from the *Alexander Nevsky* cantata not heard in the film. Purists who want to start with the dreary original title sequence have merely to fast forward to it.

One thing that this year's Academy Awards ceremony revealed, other than that all of the voting members are either tone deaf or on the Disney payroll (or both), is the impressive number of quality foreign films coming from a surprisingly wide variety of countries. Certainly, the only American film among this year's nominees that could even touch the two best-foreign-film nominees I have seen so far, **Before the Rain** and *Strawberry and Chocolate*, is *Pulp Fiction*. *Before the Rain*, a Macedonian film made by first-time director Milcho Manchevski, has in fact been compared, in its nonlinear narrative structure, by *New York Times* critic Janet Maslin to *Pulp Fiction*. But where the violence of the latter's intertwining stories is mitigated by a dry and deadpan humor, the three connected chapters of *Before the Rain* remain crushingly tragic in their depiction of characters moving in and out of the Christian/Moslem enmities that are now tearing apart the country that used to be Yugoslavia. The star-crossed doom that casts its pall over the inhabitants of a small town on the Macedonia/Albania border even extends by association to an event in a London restaurant to which it has no apparent connection. It is precisely the cyclical-circular way in which *Before the Rain*, which quotes from a Shakespeare tragedy in each of its three panels, interweaves characters and situations that at first seem unrelated, that forces us to read the film as something other than a piece of pseudo-history that we can forget once we leave the theater. As a motto read several times in the film's visuals says, "The circle is not round." This low-budget movie from a country that did not even have an independent existence only a few years ago represents filmmaking at its highest level, and the true shame is that American viewers by and large remain so addicted to Hollywood storytelling and the hype that promotes it that films such as *Before the Rain* will not get the screenings they deserve in this country.

Before the Rain's music (London 314 526 407-2) comes from a group that calls itself Anastasia, which is made up of three musicians (Zoran Spasovsky, Slatko Origjanski, and Goran Trajkoski), joined in most of the cues by "special guests" and "additional musicians," who play a combination of electronic and acoustic instruments rather in the manner of Tangerine Dream and Popol Vuh. Unlike the latter two groups, however, Anastasia offers an overall sound that has a decided ethnic flavor to it. Difficult to pinpoint, that flavor seems to my ears to come from a combination of Arab, Indian, and Greek (or more likely Albanian) sources. Thus, a drum that sounds very much like a tabla is often accompanied by an electronically generated drone, over which various voices (a male solo, a female solo, a small group of male voices) both sing and chant in a manner that certainly evokes Mideastern musical styles. Within these cues, characteristic string instruments and rhythms add Hellenic colorations. In one of the rare cues to depart from this distinctive mélange (not surprisingly, this cue backs part of the London chapter), we hear a piano ostinato accompanied by electronic whistlings, with a cello played quite loudly eventually joining in and ultimately settling into a kind of simplified Minimalism, if such a thing is possible. Another London cue features a very moody guitar duet. Except for two cues ("Funeral Theme" and "Death of Alexander"), the music is not particularly action specific. Instead, it establishes a kind of ambivalent, lingering aura that seems to relate more to the film's diverse characters and the places they inhabit than to the tragedies from which they cannot escape. Certainly one of the more effective and unusual scores I have heard in some time, Anastasia's *Before the Rain* benefits from particularly good sound on this London CD.

Well, the other night I went to see the reissue of Sam Pekinpah's 1969 **The Wild Bunch,** the film that brought the spaghetti western back to the United States. Just as in the spaghetti westerns, which Pekinpah's early work helped inspire, *The Wild Bunch* has no good guys, instead offering a hierarchy of murderers ranging from an antiheroic bunch of aging bandits (William Holden, Ernest Borgnine et al.) who have grown weary of their trade to a band of human vultures including Strother Martin and L. Q. Jones, who fight like sibling children as they pull the boots off and gold teeth out of their and other people's victims. Rising only slightly above the level of Martin and Jones is a band of renegade and not very bright Mexicans (a favorite bad-guy stereotype of the spaghetti westerns), while at the other end of things a convict (Robert Ryan) freed by the railroad in order to lead that band of vultures in pursuit of the "wild bunch" becomes the movie's most dignified character. For a long movie, the story is remarkably simple: the aging antiheroes pull off a heist of a local railroad office, getting half the town's population slaughtered in the process, only to find they have been duped. In search of one last big hit that will allow them to retire, the Wild Bunch, in the spirit of moral apathy that dominates the film, contracts with the evil Mexican marauders to rob an army train of its munitions, only to finally attain a weird kind of redemption by massacring most of the Mexican desperados and getting themselves killed in the process.

But of course *The Wild Bunch*'s notoriety rests not on its narrative but on several spectacular sequences that can perhaps best be described with the seemingly oxymoronic expression "poetic violence." Using slow motion, an editing style that almost comes out of early Eisenstein, acrobatic falls, and a good deal of phony blood and gory special effects (lots of exit wounds, for instance), Pekinpah created, for the opening and closing bloodbaths, a purely visual ballet of barbarity that apparently had early audiences running for the bathrooms. The end of the train-robbery sequence also features a spectacular stunt, shown in an extremely long shot, that has an entire posse of cowboys descending into the river on a piece of blown-up bridge. Given the turn taken by today's movies, one wonders just what it is that has caused *The Wild Bunch* to get under the skin of so many people, to the point that it initially received an imbecilic NC-17 rating for its current reissue. Personally, I suspect that it is the story's underlying amorality—American moviegoers, along with the politicians who represent them, live almost exclusively in a hero/villain universe—combined with Pekinpah's cynical portrayal of cine-violence for what it is: an aesthetic spectacle. I do find myself wondering, however, whether Pekinpah spent so much energy filming The Wild Bunch's three or four big sequences that he somewhat lost interest in the material in between them, most of which is filmed in a totally ordinary fashion (the flashbacks, once cut from the film but now restored, are handled in a particularly clumsy fashion). Even what I presume to be the crushing irony of a town of Mexican peasants serenading the "wild bunch" as they ride off to sell rifles to the town's persecutors gets somewhat buried in the aura of male camaraderie that almost makes us want to believe in what we are seeing.

One thing that continually makes The Wild Bunch difficult to "read" is its exceptional musical score by Jerry Fielding, finally released in its original form on a Bay Cities CD. As of the film's extraordinary title sequence, in which the wild bunch rides into town disguised as soldiers while the visuals periodically freeze-frame them in stylized black-and-white stills during which the soundtrack (not the music track) eerily cuts off, we find ourselves looking at both sides of the law, neither of which is a pretty sight, at the same time. Meanwhile, we also see cuts of a group of children torturing a pair of scorpions. Fielding's music, a subtle but dissonant march by a snare-drum tattoo and muted brass, feeds our desire to "read" the characters as soldiers while at the same time undermining that reading through the constant use of a decidedly non-four-square—and therefore antimilitary—11/8 meter. Fielding's score further adds to the ambiguity by starting off with a poignant added-second chord which, rather like the children's faces, forces our emotions toward a direction of tenderness that the carnage we witness on several levels makes us want to avoid. And as the music progresses, Fielding, in a manner unique to his style, turns the parallel thirds that add a mildly Mexican aura to parts of the music into sotto-voce colorings for motivic fragments in haunting instrumental configurations that plunge us into a mood that again seems at odds with what we are seeing. Fielding incorporates an amazing amount of the opening material into the score's subsequent cues while also expanding his horizons here and there, occasionally moving in almost Magnificent Seven directions (as in the train-robbery cues) while at the same time maintaining his characteristic asymmetrical rhythms. Several lyrical moments also turn up in the music, as do several pieces of pure Mexicana, including the song "La Golondrina," which rather ironically concludes the film. The original music-track score for The Wild Bunch was never initially released, as Warner Bros. chose instead to rerecord portions of the music, not surprisingly highlighting the more lyrical cues and the Mexican songs while introducing cuts into cues such as the title music. This new Bay Cities CD atones for that particular sin.

September/October

The first time I reviewed a **North by Northwest** recording on these pages (July/ August 1980), Fanfare devoted a cover to it and Film Musings had not yet been born.

That Starlog/Varèse Sarabande LP featured a new recording of a large portion of Bernard Herrmann's score for the film with Laurie Johnson conducting the London Studio Symphony Orchestra. While partially filling an inexcusable void in the film-music discography, the Johnson recording (reissued on a Varèse Sarabande CD) had several drawbacks, the most serious of which was the unconscionable reprising of the "Main Title" cue to replace the climactic "Mount Rushmore" (properly titled "On the Rocks") cue. Because of that, I wrote that "I will still go to sleep with one eye open looking for a future recording of at least an un-mucked-up *North by Northwest* finale." Well, my 15 years of insomnia have finally paid off with the release in Rhino Movie Music's "Turner Classic Movies" Music series of the complete, and I do mean complete, music tracks for Alfred Hitchcock's 1959 suspense thriller. Although mixed down to mono on release prints of *North by Northwest*, the score, except for its "source" cues, was recorded in stereo, and that is fortunately how it has been issued on this CD, which features exceptionally up-close, very dry sound which, at its best, makes it feel almost as if you are standing in the middle of the orchestra. (The overall sound for *North by Northwest*, musical and otherwise, represents one of the film's strongest technical assets. Listen, for instance, to Cary Grant's half dollar landing on concrete to alert Eva Marie Saint toward the end of the film.) Unfortunately, the 36 years it took before the cans were reopened were not at all kind on *North by Northwest*'s music tracks, and some of the cues, including, alas, "On the Rocks," suffer from significant dropout. All things considered, however, the sound quality is by and large extraordinary.

North by Northwest opens itself to such a rich variety of points of discussion (one of the longest articles ever written on an individual film, Raymond Bellour's "Le Blocage symbolique," is on *North by Northwest*) that it is hard to know just where to start in talking about its music. So I will begin with what is probably a major point of curiosity for readers of this column, namely the non-used music, indicated as "outtakes" in the list of the 50 separate cues found on this CD. The first of these, "The Street," was intended for the first post-title sequence and contains material heard, with various modifications, in several other cues, including the end of "The Auction," "The Police," and "The Airport." On the other hand, the second outtake, "Hotel Lobby," intended for the beginning of the scene in a Chicago hotel following the celebrated cornfield sequence, is an unsettling dialogue of two-note figures for various combinations of clarinets, quite a bit in the manner of that eerie conversation for two Theremins heard when Klatu returns to his spacecraft in Herrmann's score for *The Day the Earth Stood Still*. One wonders, by the way, just where the extra music, similar to "Hotel Lobby" but for full orchestra, tacked on to the end of the "Crash of the Crop-duster" cut on the Laurie Johnson recording came from. Back to the Rhino CD, in other instances we get to hear more of the music—particularly the "source" cues such as "It's a Most Unusual Day"—than turn up in the film. And of course the Rhino CD gives us the chance to hear every bit of the music Herrmann composed including, for instance, the metamorphosis of *North by Northwest*'s love theme into "Madeleine's Theme" from *Vertigo*, which shows up nowhere on the Varèse Sarabande recording.

This occurs first as a trio of clarinets backs the "Farewell" between Thornhill (Cary Grant) and Eve (Eva Marie Saint) at the Chicago railroad station. Herrmann later reprises exactly the same metamorphosis, this time in the full orchestra, when Thornhill, having survived the cornfield attack, appears at Eve's hotel room, a moment that strongly harks back to an unscored scene in *Vertigo*. Even a 20-second gem such as the cue entitled "Flight," heard as Eve drives off and Thornhill is decked by a state trooper, makes this recording invaluable. I also love the fact that the "Overture" ends here on a suspended seventh chord, as it does in the film, rather than unconvincingly cadencing into A Major, as it does on all the other recordings. As for "On the Rocks," the music simply takes one's breath away, not only because of the basic material but also because of the virtuoso manner in which, in this two-and-one-half-minute cue, the composer reworks *North by Northwest*'s fandango "Overture" to kick off the film's climactic sequence. Of course, given the dropouts, I will still sleep, at least from time to time, with one eye open waiting for a rousing, high-fidelity rerecording of this music. But no matter who may tackle *North by Northwest* in the future, he or she is going to have a hard time matching the intensity Herrmann brings to the music as a conductor. Compare, for instance, the somewhat plodding way Laurie Johnson handles certain cues to the composer's taut pacing and phrasing. Indeed, hearing Herrmann's no-nonsense interpretation of his score on this recording makes me wish all the more strongly that someone would bring out the original *Psycho* music tracks. Very simply, Herrmann was never the conductor off the soundstage that he was when leading a studio orchestra in putting together a music track. The sound and balances on this recording, when dropout free, will also be hard to match. Listen for instance to the harp glissandos that punctuate the beginning of the "Crash" cue on the original music track offered here and then try and find them on the Laurie Johnson recording.

Certainly, one of the most original and offbeat directors currently making films on this side of the ocean is Canadian Atom Egoyan. While movies such as *Family Viewing* and *Speaking Parts* have gotten little play in this country, Egoyan's most recent effort, **Exotica**, has been making somewhat successful rounds in the U.S., at least in the art-film circuit. In a style that somewhat recalls the Robbe-Grillet of *La Belle captive*, Egoyan, in *Exotica*, ambiguously moves in and out of the mind of an auditor who may or may not have killed his wife and daughter and who voyeuristically keeps their presence alive by obsessively choosing the same erotic dancer to perform for him (at a reasonably elegant club called Exotica, naturally) night after night and by having the same teenage girl continue to "baby-sit" for his daughter. Into this plot are interwoven the dancer's former lover, with whom she discovered the bodies of the auditor's wife and daughter, and a homosexual aquarium-store owner. The dancer has also had a lesbian relationship with the pregnant (by the ex-boyfriend, of course) woman (played by Egoyan's wife) who owns Exotica. Get the drift? It all moves toward a deliciously ambiguous conclusion in which somehow all of the roles in the film seem to partially merge. As one might expect for a film in which a good deal of the action focuses on exotic/erotic dances, much of the music composed by Mychael Danna for *Exotica* (Varèse Sarabande) takes the form of, well, exotic dances. The most prominent and captivating of these is first heard in the cue entitled "Something Hidden." Over an extremely simple piano accompaniment that would be perfectly at home in a European art film a Near Eastern wind instrument (one suspects Armenian origins) intones a sinuous melody that somehow seems to enfold *Exotica*'s mysteries into its core. Eventually, the theme blossoms into something resembling a Gabriel Yared rhapsody. Many of the remaining cues have this same Near Eastern flavor to them, mitigated somewhat by Danna's substantial use of synthesized timbres to overlay the various native instruments and vocals, often causing the overall ambience to drift toward dreaminess. Synthesized dreaminess, growing out of timbres readily available on instruments such as the Korg X3, solidly dominates the various cues entitled "Field," all of which back surrealistic flashbacks to the search for the missing mother and daughter. And in the last two of the four "Field" cues, the music offers an important interaction with the film by overlaying the "Something Hidden" dance theme, played on various instruments, with the electronic dreamscape music. Danna's music is often as hypnotic and mysterious as the film it accompanies.

November/December

In Memoriam—Miklós Rózsa

Believe it or not, I first became aware of the music of Miklós Rózsa, who died this past July in Hollywood, not via a film score but rather via the ominous, throbbing seventh variation of the composer's early concert work, Theme, Variations, and Finale, from 1933. It is a musical moment that always sends me rushing for the nearest object that can serve as a baton. Ah, but there is a catch to this. That variation always appeared to close a cheap, sci-fi series, which originated in Philadelphia, called *Atom Squad*, which, by the way, opened with a snippet from Stravinsky's *Firebird*. It was from watching that series as a teenager that I fell in love with Rózsa's music. Fortunately, I was also an avid listener to Philadelphia's classical-music station, and it was not long before a program on WFLN revealed both the entirety of Rózsa's op. 13a to me and the name of its composer. Needless to say, I wasted little time procuring the Decca LP of Rózsa conducting the Frankenland State Symphony in his own creations, including the Theme, Variations, and Finale. If memory serves me, I bought the RCA LP of the Heifetz/Hendl recording of Rózsa's Violin Concerto without giving it a test hearing, and I was bowled over. To this day, I remain convinced that this work must be considered as one of the major masterpieces of 20th-century music. Now, I know that I saw *Quo Vadis* and *Julius Caesar* in their first runs, and I must have seen *Ivanhoe* as well. But it was via another blind purchase, this one of the Decca LP with Rózsa conducting music from *The Killers*, *The Naked City*, and *Brute Force*, that I began to associate Rózsa with film music. This LP was followed by *Lust for Life* (Decca again) and *Spellbound* (Warner Bros.), and it was only years later that I was able to catch up with the films for which these sometimes violent, frequently intense, and occasionally lyrical scores were written. Not realizing that the Ray Heindorf interpretation of *Spellbound* was a total reworking of that score, I was bewildered when little of the music from that Warner Bros. release turned up as such on Hitchcock's music track. Where in the world did that "Scherzo" come from? (As it turns out, about a three-measure motif that turns up once in the film [but that dominates the pre-film overture].)

Why was the Hungarian-born Miklós Rózsa one of the giants in writing music for a medium that he did not seem to particularly care for? Different people will give different reasons. For me, there are two principal explanations. First of all, Rózsa's film scores, even at their most action specific, maintain a constant level of musical sophistication, as if the composer always had not just viewing- but listening audiences at least halfway in his mind. Not all film scores can or even should be written this way. But this was Rózsa's shtick, and I cannot think of a single film composer who has been quite his equal in bringing the concert hall to the music track. Indeed, Rózsa was more apt to turn a concert composition, such as his Violin Concerto, into a film score than the usual vice versa. And to his concert compositions Rózsa brought strong—and to my sensibilities devastatingly moving—doses of affect that might facilely be called "cinematic," save that he was doing this before he ever penned a single note for a film. A second reason for Rózsa's importance, and this one definitely reflects my personal biases, is that he was a major factor in bringing both film and film music into its dark, or should I say *noir*, age. While composers such as Franz Waxman and Bernard Herrmann were certainly probing the nether regions in some of their scores, Rózsa virtually created, in the 1940s, a musical "sound" that meant film noir, peaking in Billy Wilder's 1944 masterpiece, *Double Indemnity.* The impact of Rózsa's noir scores grew in part, of course, from the composer's ample use of jarring dissonances and taut, dynamic rhythmic figures. But a major facet of this sound was also his uncanny ability to create themes and motifs whose yearning lyricism touches emotions that we usually turn away from. It was a sound that certain directors, such as Alain Resnais in his brilliant but bizarre and lugubrious *Providence* from 1977, got Rózsa to return to in his final years of film scoring.

Given the importance that Rózsa had in the evolution of my musical sensibilities, it is ironic that I have devoted more space to other film composers than to him, although *Overtones and Undertones* offers an extensive analysis of the *Double Indemnity* score. But Rózsa and Shostakovich were the first two modern composers to get into my blood, and in that sense Rózsa in particular has had a much greater influence on my writing than might be readily apparent. I must also mention the composer's autobiography, *Double Life,* which is one of the most captivating, eloquent, and honest books I have ever read. It was my good fortune to be able to talk to Rózsa once, briefly, on the phone before he had his crippling stroke, and once, in person, after his infirmity, in a long interview at the mini-castle where he resided for much of his life in America. That interview can be found in *Fanfare* 11:6 (July/August 1988) and in *Overtones and Undertones.* Those conversations represented for me a wonderful and, in the case of the in-person interview, a sad link with a world which, with the passing of Miklós Rózsa, has now all but vanished from the present.

If Miklós Rózsa created the quintessential musical sound for those 1940s films depicting the seamier side of contemporary life, he likewise, from *Quo Vadis* in 1951 through *Sodom and Gomorrah* in 1963, pretty much wrote the book on film music for historical epics, and one might wonder how he made the transition so seamlessly. The answer, it seems to me, lies in a certain archaic quality that pervades the composer's work. Good modernist that he was, Rózsa knew that the new in music does not necessarily come from movement forward but instead can simply involve a reinvigoration of the present with the past via such devices as abolishing the leading tone or transparently using open intervals. Even Rózsa's frequent deployment of counterpoint strikes the sensibilities more as a statement against the contemporary, horizontal conception of time and space than as a simple neoclassical device. And so the musical style that paralleled the raw, primitive, inner drives of the noir universe did not have to shift all that much in order to evoke the primal via excursions into the outer history of Western civilization. Perhaps the score that best reveals the overlapping of these two phases of Rózsa's career as a film composer is **Julius Caesar**, for a 1953 cine-adaptation of the Shakespeare play directed by Joseph L. Mankiewicz and starring Marlon Brando as Mark Antony, James Mason as Brutus, and John Gielgud as Cassius. Certainly, the dirge-like passage that follows the choral music in the cue entitled "Black Sentence" could have fit quite comfortably in *Double Indemnity*. At any rate, a new recording of Rózsa's score for *Julius Caesar*, reconstructed by Daniel Robbins and featuring a good deal of music not used in the film and never previously recorded, marks the second release in Intrada's "Excalibur Collection" (Sinfonia of London and Sinfonia Chorus, Bruce Broughton, cond.).

Certainly, *Julius Caesar* owns many of Rózsa's darkest musical moments, and it sets its tone immediately in an initially exciting but ultimately intensely tragic Overture intended to be played in theaters before the start of the film. Significantly, the tragedy communicated by the Overture attaches itself, via a moody theme associated throughout the film with the character, to Brutus, who, as many have noted, is the true focal point of the play. (If any actor has ever given a deeper, more anguished portrayal of Brutus, on film or on stage, than James Mason in the Mankiewicz movie, I don't know who it would be.) Unfortunately, the execs in charge decided to replace Rózsa's Overture with footage, rarely shown since the film's first run, of MGM's Music Department head, John Green, conducting Tchaikovsky's *Capriccio Italien*, of all things. And thus the first taste that viewers of the film get of Rózsa's original score is in the title music, which introduces a much more stately theme associated at the beginning with Julius Caesar (Louis Calhern) and later with Mark Antony. Interestingly, two major cues revolving around the character of Brutus, the unremittingly gloomy "Brutus' Soliloquy," scored mostly for strings, and the brighter but still moody, strings-only "Brutus' Secret," never made it to the film and are heard on this recording for the first time. Particularly ingenious is the way that Rózsa contrapuntally juxtaposes the Caesar/Antony theme with Brutus' theme for the film's final sequence. The brief but terrifically intense "Battle at Philippi" could have come straight from one of the noir films produced by Mark Hellinger and directed by Jules Dassin for which Rózsa wrote some of his most notable music. As conductor Bruce Broughton elicits just about flawless playing from the Sinfonia of London, he captures every bit of the music's intense and somber drama. The recorded sound is full and warm, and it reproduces the all-important brass with particular richness. I would, however, have liked more bite from the strings at just about every level.

Well, joy of joys: two of Ennio Morricone's best—we're talking about crème de la crème from a composer who is no stranger to *crème*—scores have finally surfaced on an easily obtainable American recording. Appearing on a two-CD set entitled **An Ennio Morricone Western Quintet** in the "Classic Italian Soundtracks" series from DRG, these two scores are the 1971 *Giù la testa* (Duck, You Sucker, a.k.a. A Fistful of Dynamite), which forms the middle panel of the late director Sergio Leone's second, and, alas, last, trilogy of films, and the 1973 *Il mio nome è nessuno* (My Name Is No-body), which Leone [executive] produced but was directed by Tonino Valerii. This DRG release also includes scores from three other, much less well-known "spaghetti westerns," *Tepepa* (Blood and Guns, 1969), *Vamos a matar compañeros* (Compañeros!, 1970), and *Occhio alla penna* (Buddy Goes West, 1980). *Duck, You Sucker*, while not exactly a western—the film takes place in revolutionary Mexico and deals mostly with the strange and wonderful relationship that develops between a narcissistic ban-dito named Juan (Rod Steiger) and a nitroglycerin-wielding Irish rebel named Sean (James Coburn) who has had to flee his native land—it definitely has the look and feel of Leone's earlier work, most particularly *The Good, the Bad, and the Ugly*. The character of Juan is so broadly drawn in the screenplay and so grotesquely overacted by a bug-eyed Rod Steiger, whose Hispanically flavored English puts recent Al Pacino accent massacres to shame, that it is a wonder that *Duck, You Sucker* is able to elicit even minimal emotional involvement. (Mind you, I'm not sure that James Coburn's Irish accent is any better. But there's a certain . . . restraint.) Yet, as the relationship between the two "Johns," Juan and Sean, evolves from Laurel and Hardy one-upmanship to Juan's involuntary participation in the revolution, the film becomes downright lyrical and even a bit tragic, and Morricone's score, I feel, plays no small role in drawing the viewer/listener into the action. Certainly, you need go no further than the first cue presented on this set to get carried away by the sweep and haunt-ing beauty of a theme that forms the backbone of one of the most moving cues in the history of film music. Bearing the film's title but in no way serving as the "Main Ti-tle" cue, this theme opens with a whistle motif associated with the Irish revolution-ary and then switches into a soaring melody for vocalizing soprano, electric harpsi-chord, and strings, punctuated here and there with the sung words "Sean, Sean," done first by a falsetto male voice and later by the soprano. Less stirring but reaching even more deeply into feelings of longing and loss is the theme, initially presented in an oboe/English horn unison over acoustic guitar and strings, that first appears in the "Mesa Verde" cue and is developed at greater length in "Mexico and Ireland." Yet a third lyrical theme is initiated by the whistler a couple of minutes into the cue enti-tled "The Dead Sons," and if memory serves me it returns, in the uncut version of *Duck, You Sucker* to sadly close the film. In a totally different vein is the deliciously ironic "March of the Beggars," which starts off as a dialogue between a solo bassoon and a vocal noise dangerously close to a burp and then continues with such instruments as an Indian flute and a tenor(?) mandolin, with quick quotations from "Eine kleine Nachtmusik" thrown in for good measure. I could go on. *Duck, You Sucker* is an incredibly rich and varied score that can even, in the cue entitled "All Jokes Aside," make fun of its own lyricism, with the help of some flatulent electronics. And while the music plays an essential role in the way audiences will "read" *Duck, You Sucker*, the music is probably best experienced on this music-track recording. In the movie, the score, typically for Leone, often gets cut and pasted in a rather fractionalized way. And many of the music's most lyrical movements are slightly wasted on the Irish flashback scenes, which represent the least convincing moments in the film. The recorded sound is quite good and beautifully imaged, with the stereo directionality playing a particularly important role. It does sound as if there was a bit of tape degeneration here and there, and there are some extraneous sounds that made me wonder whether at least part of this transfer was done from an LP. By the way, the original version of *Duck, You Sucker* opens with a shot of Juan peeing on an anthill, a Peckinpah-ish touch lost in the American version, which begins after the act is done.

As if *Duck, You Sucker* weren't enough, *An Ennio Morricone Western Quintet* also offers all 10 of the cues from the original music-track recording for *My Name Is Nobody*, which in certain ways may be the most enjoyable of all the spaghetti westerns. Keep in mind that Leone's two trilogies have a modernist, revisionist, political edge to them, and the writer/director missed few opportunities to alienate (in the Brechtian sense) his audiences. *My Name Is Nobody*, on the other hand, is about as purely postmodern a film as you're apt to get. I mean, in a movie that conspicuously displays a tombstone with Sam Peckinpah's name on it and then calls its horde of ornery varmints the "Wild Bunch," you know you're dealing more with image making than with straight—or even slanted—fiction. Indeed, the film's eponymous hero, played by Terence Hill (the pseudonym of Italian actor Mario Girotti, whose voice is nicely dubbed in the film), desires nothing more than to goad an aging gunfighter named Jack Beauregard (Henry Fonda) into one final, spectacular exploit so that he (Nobody) can use a staged showdown in order to transfer Beauregard's image onto himself. The transition from Beauregard's strategically placed gun at the beginning of the film to Nobody's equally strategic finger in the final freeze frame tells it all. *My Name Is Nobody* also has some wonderful set pieces, including an absurdly comical drinking/shooting match in a bar and a more somber shootout in a house of mirrors, an obvious obeisance to Orson Welles. From the opening cue on this recording, Morricone's score lets the viewer/listener know that nothing and nobody in *My Name Is Nobody* are to be taken all that seriously (but then again, Nobody is to be taken seriously . . .). Nobody's theme is a cheerful, if slightly wistful, tune played on a wooden whistle over accompaniment from a 12-string guitar and bass, with a women's chorus occasionally chirping in with a bit of punctuation, often limited to two notes.

Of course, the score's centerpiece is the theme for the "Wild Bunch" (*Mucchio Selvaggio* in Italian), an exciting allegro heard behind shots, often with a telephoto lens, of "150 pure-bred sons of bitches on horseback" as they ride through the dust. Even here, however, Morricone's tongue is often in his cheek. While the melody whistled over the twelve-string-guitar accompaniment has a strong *serioso* quality to it, the two-note punctuation grunted by a male chorus begins to move the music in a different direction, as does the reprise of the theme on the flutter-tongued whistle. By the time Morricone quotes Wagner's "Ride of the Valkyrie" in rather bloated, brassy, synthesized timbres, one has no idea how to react to the overwhelming presence of this mass of bad guys that Beauregard will have to single-handedly eradicate from the face of the earth, only to be immediately immortalized in a series of quasi-history-book freeze frames. Even when the male chorus helps the theme regain a bit of its solemnity, it is in competition with another chorus that sounds ever so much like bratty children. At two other points in his film, Morricone quotes the ominous ostinato theme developed from the harmonica motif in *Once Upon a Time in the West*. By the end of the film, with the two characters going their separate ways, the music bifurcates. Nobody, now facing his first exploit in Beauregard's boots, or at least in the image of them, gets the sostenuto, sometimes pointillistic suspense music, complete with ticking clock, that backed Beauregard's initial conflict in the barber shop. On the other hand, Beauregard, present mainly via a voice-over letter to Nobody, gets the film's only lyrical music ("Good Luck, Jack"), a typically melancholic Morricone mood piece that starts off with a harmonica theme and then shifts to an even broader melody which, early in the film, gets taken up by the composer's characteristic vocalizing soprano (the indispensable Edda Dell'Orso). For something completely different, try the herky-jerky variation, complete with slide whistle, on Nobody's theme in the "Ballet of the Mirrors." Within the film, there is a wonderful piece of *musique concrète*, no doubt the brainchild of Sergio Leone, made up of the timbres produced by a cow being milked, a horse being brushed, and Beauregard being shaved, all of which sometimes wend their way into Morricone's suspense cues. All in all, there are few films that work quite as deeply and quite as entertainingly on the narrative, cinematic, and musical levels as *My Name Is Nobody*. The score also benefits, on this recording, from excellent sound reproduction and what strikes me as a particularly vigorous performance.

What can one say about the remaining Morricone scores on *Western Quintet*? Well, among other things, that they certainly strengthen the argument that it often takes a great director to get a great score from a great composer. It does not help any, of course, that I know next to nothing about the three other films represented here. And there are certainly some gems scattered among the 33 cues representing these scores. I love the opening cue for *Occhio alla penna* (the title literally translates as "Eye on the Feather," as in a Native American's headdress, I presume), a droll, pseudo-Indian chant punctuated by contrabassoon and grunts, with lyrics that have to be a spoof. Morricone's typically mellow/sad lyricism dominates the next cue, whose chord progressions remind me a bit of Handel. There is also a catchy strut-step piece in which the contrabassoon again plays a major role and in which Morricone gives some nice blues riffs to the solo banjo. A Mexican dirge that harks back to *A Fistful of Dollars* and *The Good, the Bad, and the Ugly* also turns up in two cues. But most of the other music has a fluffy, pop sound to it, which leads me to believe that everybody involved in the film was probably trying too hard to be cute. Probably the best cue in *Tepepa*, which opens and closes with a familiar Mexican tune, is the one entitled "A Meta Strada," a slow, moody series of chord progressions with guitar embellishments. I was also intrigued, in the dirge-like cues entitled "Tradimento Primo" and "Tradimento Secondo," by the bizarre dialogue of guitars (one acoustic, one electric, each one perhaps representing the opposing parties in the "betrayals"), in which Morricone also incongruously gives some Flamenco figures to the electric guitar. *Vamos a Matar Compañeros*, the eight cues of which on this recording include five that were previously unreleased, opens with a jaunty, whistled tune reminiscent of Sean's theme in *Duck, You Sucker*, but in a much more bluesy vein. Particularly attractive is the hymn-like "La Loro Patria," while the ensuing cue, the long "Un Uomo In Agguato," is dominated throughout by a particularly heavy dose of dissonance. But . . . . Well, before I ever saw (in Paris, in its first run) *Duck, You Sucker*, my first Sergio Leone film, I knew the score just about by heart, and it was Morricone's music that got me hooked on Leone. There is little in the three scores above that would have me on a train from Nancy to Paris to catch the film, although, lord knows, I would certainly like to know just what inspired *Occhio alla penne*'s opening war chant. Still, there are a lot of weird, interesting, and stirring moments in these scores, whose presence on *Western Quintet* must certainly be considered as a major bonus, especially for Morricone fans. The recorded sound for just about all the music offered here (over two-and-a-half hours' worth) is very up-front, and I would not be averse to using certain cuts here to demo speakers.

CHAPTER THIRTEEN

~

1996

January/February

Edelton has released a two-CD set (Orchestra della Svizzera Italiana, Mark Andreas and Helmut Imig, cond.) that features the world premiere recording of the music composed by Edmund Meisel for Sergei Eisenstein's silent masterpiece from 1925, **The Battleship Potemkin** (Bronenosets Potyomkin). The second CD offers the score composed shortly after *Potemkin* by Meisel for Arnold Fanck's **The Holy Mountain** (Der Heilige Berg, a.k.a. *Peaks of Destiny*), which gave future director Leni Riefenstahl her entry into the cinema by featuring her as a dancer. While, by the time Eisenstein made *Potemkin*, a fair number of musical scores, such as Joseph Carl Breil's for the virulently racist *The Birth of a Nation* (1915), had been composed to move broadly in sync with specific silent films, and while the very next year Warner Bros. would release *Don Juan* with music (by William Axt and David Mendoza) and sound effects synched via the Vitaphone process, Eisenstein, who rushed to bring out *Potemkin* for the 20th anniversary of the abortive 1905 revolution, of which the film depicts several incidents, initially had to depend on the usual piecemeal improvisations and classical-music borrowings for the movie's premiere, although he had attempted to put out feelers to Prokofiev in Paris to write a "film symphony" for *Potemkin*. But by the spring of 1926 the group responsible for importing Eisenstein's film to Berlin had commissioned a young, Marxist composer named Edmund Meisel, who would die four years later, to do an original score for *Potemkin*. Although Meisel had nothing resembling the close collaboration with Eisenstein that would later be enjoyed by Prokofiev in *Alexander Nevsky* and the two *Ivan the Terrible* films, he was able to consult with the director, who had come to Berlin for *Potemkin*'s German premiere, and the result was music which, according to many critics at the time, greatly enhanced the film's impact, which was already so strong and so revolutionary that *Potemkin* found itself banned in many parts of the world. Just why Meisel's score has lain in obscurity for decades, even to the point that a 1976 Soviet reissue of *Potemkin* raided eight Shostakovich symphonies for the musical backing, is a major mystery. For, as heard on this superbly performed and engineered recording, made all the way back in 1987, Meisel's *Potemkin* turns out to be one of the pinnacles of silent-film music, rivaled in excellence by a score such as Shostakovich's 1929 *The New Babylon*. Meisel's style in his *Potemkin* music might best be described as a strange but effective admixture of post-Wagner and industrial modernism. The score, which constantly shifts direction to move, one supposes, with the cinematic action, is filled with numerous motivic fragments, many of them stridently harmonized and presented in piercing wind/brass instrumentations. Not unexpectedly, dirge and march rhythms dominate many of the cues. But some fairly sophisticated counterpoint also turns up here and there, and the score also offers a reasonable number of more developed themes, many of them taken from folksongs, including the revolutionary funeral march, "The Song of the Survivors," which dominates much of the "People of Odessa" cue. If the tune sounds familiar, that is because it also forms the backbone of the third movement of Shostakovich's 11th Symphony, which is devoted to the same failed revolution as Eisenstein's film. As for the celebrated "Odessa Steps" massacre, which may be the most brilliantly—and devastatingly—edited sequence in cinema history, Meisel's cue features a crushingly loud and dissonant march with a relentless, slow beat hammered out in the brass and timpani. Taking out my video of the 1976 Soviet reissue of *Potemkin*, I turned off the music track (the second movement of Shostakovich's Eleventh Symphony, which certainly generates all sorts of emotions, although its fast pace rather works against Eisenstein's montage) and played Meisel's "Odessa Steps" cue from this CD behind it. The results were quite overwhelming, although the music ran out before the end of the sequence, coming, no doubt coincidentally, to a climax just as the brutal baby-carriage incident begins. The musical counterattack in a percussion-filled cue entitled "Full Speed Ahead" operates on much the same level.

As I have already suggested, both the sound quality—rarely has a full orchestra seemed to fill my listening room so thoroughly and so warmly—and the performance are first-rate. Mark Andreas leads the Orchestra della Svizzera Italiana in an intense, sharp-edged interpretation that shows equally deep insights into both the music and the film. One must be a bit concerned with the authenticity of what is heard here since, for reasons explained by conductor/arranger Andreas in some extensive notes, quite a bit of rearranging and orchestrating needed to be done. It all, however, sounds quite convincing and extremely coherent. What we now need, of course, is a [DVD] reissue of Eisenstein's *The Battleship Potemkin*, preferably projected at the proper speed without the stretch printing used in the Russian reissue, complemented by Meisel's score.

I am somewhat less fond of the music for *The Holy Mountain*, arranged and conducted, in a much less incisive performance (but the sound remains stunningly good), by Helmut Imig. While the score opens with a rather nervous march featuring Meisel's recognizable augmented chordal structures, and while the music soon gets caught up in a slightly dark, romantic swell that certainly foreshadows the kinds of things Hollywood would be doing in its sound films a decade or so later, the cues often seem to move more in parallel with a rather thickly textured Richard Strauss, a style that does not particularly jell with Meisel's antibourgeois aesthetics. And some of the music, such as the fast and swirling "The Great Long Distance Run," which is filled with chromatic sequences, or the obvious storm music for "The Horrible Northern Steep," not only gets bogged down in cornball musical metonymies, it also becomes unbearably repetitive. The score also features a certain number of fairly tiresome pastiches, plus some quotations from Godard (not Jean-Luc) and Chopin. Here and there, however, Meisel does generate some of the same dynamism that dominates his *Potemkin* music. Not surprisingly, this occurs mostly in what titles such as "The Abyss" and "Hallucinations" suggest are the film's more somber episodes. Like Andreas, Imig seems to have taken a fair number of liberties in re-creating Meisel's score. Indeed, Imig's tampering produced one of the score's more interesting moments: the bitonalization of a Chopin nocturne. One wonders, by the way, whether the rest of Fanck's film is as visually interesting as the still that appears on the inner front cover of the program booklet. Interestingly, yet another score for *Potemkin* was composed by Nikolai Kriukov for a 1951 reissue, and I am told, contrary to what Edelton's program notes indicate, that a *Potemkin* score predating Meisel's was written by one Yuri Feier.

Maybe three films in 1995 (as I write in early October) have knocked me out of my socks so far—*The Mystery of Rampo, Smoke,* and, most recently, Bryan Singer's **The Usual Suspects**. Although it has been mentioned in the same breath with Quentin Tarantino's *Pulp Fiction, The Usual Suspects* does not fiddle around with its space/time sequencing in the same, fairly transparent manner as Tarantino's brilliant comedy/suspense thriller. *The Usual Suspects* relies instead on major doses of ambiguity that start in the storytelling and that are mirrored in the film's visual style, which is much more interesting per se than that of *Pulp Fiction.* Every time we think we have explored a character and his/her situation(s) in the film to their logical conclusions, the bottom drops out and we find ourselves wandering in uncharted territory in which we often have to question what we are looking at—a drug dealer/fence who seems to be slightly in drag the second time he appears; an unidentified character, who later turns out to have the incongruous name of Keyser Soze, whom our eyes may have caught in an initial shot but who does not introduce himself into the action until we have doubted his very presence; a bulletin board that seems to be screaming out some message or another; a pile of ropes on board a ship that may or may not hide a secret we desperately seek to learn. . . . One of the great strengths of *The Usual Suspects* is that it generates much of its mind-expanding ambivalence not just on the level of its narrative structure, like *Pulp Fiction,* but also on the more micro level of its montage, and therein lies an interesting story. For one of the extremely rare times in cinema history (Charlie Chaplin comes immediately to mind), the individual who edited a film, in this case John Ottman, also composed its musical score (Milan; Larry Groupé, cond.). I was able to talk to composer/editor Ottman on the phone this past October, and he shared the following information with me:

R.S.B.: Is *The Usual Suspects* Bryan Singer's first film?

J.O.: We did a feature before *The Usual Suspects* called *Public Access*. But we call this our first real feature, since it got distribution. *Public Access* is going to be in selected theaters—probably five theaters nationwide—in late October. It won the Grand Jury Prize at Sundance in 1993.

R.S.B.: Have you scored any other films besides *Public Access* and *The Usual Suspects*?

J.O.: Talk about what's real and what's not! I rescored a classic John Wayne movie called *McLintock!* They were re-releasing the film on video, and apparently Frank DeVol—the original composer—wanted so much money in royalties that it was cost-prohibitive for them to do it. So they hired me—I was doing nothing at that point—and paid me a couple of thousand bucks to write a new score for the film. The funny part of the story is that the original music was married to all the original sound tracks, and they had to redub all the actors' voices with new actors and actresses. John Wayne, Maureen O'Hara, Jerry Van Dyke—it's amazing the job they did. You'd swear it was them. Because the power of association is so strong with the actors, you'd never think they were dubbed. But then another company released *McLintock!* too, and somehow they were able to swing the rights, so basically you can't find the one I did anywhere. I also did an hour-long documentary about autism, plus a slew of student works and industrial films. And that's about it.

R.S.B.: What is your musical background?

J.O.: I played a clarinet for eight years, and I'm a soundtrack fanatic! But I went to film school at U.S.C. When I graduated U.S.C., I was so frustrated with the horrible scores that were in my friends' films that, to give myself training and see whether I could actually do this, I put together this little studio in my house with used pieces of equipment. With the miracle of MIDI technology, I was able to score their films and actually use them as guinea pigs to see whether I could do it. I had a blast. I saw that I could do it, and it mushroomed from there. Classically trained composers really resent people like me who suddenly come along and turn out music this way. But for me it's however you can skin the cat. The MIDI doesn't do it for you. You still have to have the music in your head.

R.S.B.: Although there are hardly any examples of editor/composers, editing and composing seem to me in many ways a perfect marriage. Editing and composing aren't all that different from each other, at least in certain senses.

J.O.: Exactly. As an editor, you have a specific vision of the film. You're a main filmmaker on the film. And the music really completes your vision of the movie. Sometimes, when you give that up to another person, it kind of destroys what you had in mind.

R.S.B.: Did you edit *Public Access* as well?

J.O.: Yes. That's how it all came about. The composing thing was something I dreamed of doing, but I was only scoring short films. But the composer was let go on the movie, because it wasn't working out, and so it was my opportunity to show

Bryan how logical it was. If you think *The Usual Suspects* is a show of music and editing, *Public Access* was built around music and editing. It makes our films different in some way. Bryan knows my style of editing, and he shoots in such a way that he knows what I'm going to do with it. For instance, he shoots a lot of master shots that he knows I'm going to cut up into a lot of smaller shots. One of our concepts is that I'm really banished from the set. On *Public Access*, I actually replaced another editor. They were having trouble putting this one scene together because they were having huge eye-line and geography problems. I came on the film. Having never been there for the shooting, I had no idea what the geography was for the scene. And so I just went ahead and edited the scene, not realizing that I had fixed a huge error. When Bryan came to see the scene, he grabbed me and said, "My God, you did it!" And I said, "Did what?" Then we realized that not having me on the set in a way enables me to see the stuff through the eyes of the audience.

R.S.B.: Who would you say are your influences as far as the music is concerned? I hear some Goldsmith, for instance, in some of the cues.

J.O.: I worship Jerry Goldsmith!

Another note: one of the last captions in *The Usual Suspects'* end titles reads, "Edited on Film," a rather sarcastic message from Ottman, who did the montage on two Steenbeck flatbeds set up in his living room, to all those editors out there today who are putting their films together on video.

Anyway, the music: at the heart of the score lies a moody, rather rhapsodic theme, introduced in a piano solo, that quickly does a strongly cine-musical chromatic dip but rarely strays very far from its initial key of C-sharp Minor. This music, whose two-note accompaniment figure often separates itself from its theme in later cues, thoroughly meshes with the somber atmosphere that pervades both the look and feel of *The Usual Suspects*. Like the title theme, most of the suspense cues, of which there are a decent number, tend to remain fairly confined by a very minor-mode tonal center, except when they are erupting into the kind of cluster/glissando/cymbal-swish violence that is fairly prevalent in the modern suspense thriller. Some of the cues, such as "Payback Time," which churns up a good deal of Goldsmithian drive, are quite dramatic, while others work in subtler domains, with quiet percussion figures and wispy instrumental motifs evoking lurking presences that may or may not be imaginary. The effect the score has on the overall ambience of *The Usual Suspects* is strengthened by an almost total lack of source music in the film. Indeed, the only source music would appear to be the Debussy Prelude, "*Les Sons et les parfums tournent dans l'air du soir*," performed on this recording by Damon Intrabartolo.

Baudelaire once wrote, "In order not to be the martyrized slaves of time, get drunk; never stop getting drunk. On wine, on poetry or on virtue, on Bernard Herrmann, whatever you wish!" O.K., I added Bernard Herrmann. Frankly, I can't think of anything that plunges me into those deliciously dark, anywhere-out-of-this-world (thanks again, Charles Baudelaire) moods quite as quickly and effectively as a good

Bernard Herrmann score. And if tripping out on Benny Herrmann is your thing as well, I have just the CD for you. Entitled **Torn Curtain: The Classic Film Music of Bernard Herrmann**, this Silva America release (City of Prague Philharmonic, Paul Bateman, cond.) features bits and pieces from no fewer than 15 Herrmann scores, one of them never previously recorded, one appearing on CD for the first time, and several appearing with substantially more music than earlier available. Even better, it is definitely the gloomier reaches of the space/time of the unconscious that are musically explored in the bulk of this CD's cues. The recording opens, for instance, with the stately but ominous title music for Hitchcock's 1956 remake of his own *The Man Who Knew Too Much*, which, somewhat abstractly foreshadowing the film's climactic sequence in Royal Albert Hall, backs visuals of a group of "musicians" (actually over-dubbed actors) performing that theme. The music perfectly sets the tone for the drama to come, and its premiere appearance on this CD is most welcome. Just as welcome, however, would have been additional cues from Herrmann's *Man Who Knew Too Much* score, which remarkably sets up the great Herrmann/Hitchcock collaborations—*Vertigo*, *North by Northwest*, and *Psycho*—to come. The first and third of the latter scores, by the way, likewise appear on this release, *Vertigo* in the form of a three-movement suite that has been recorded several times, *Psycho* as a seven-and-one-half-minute suite that, under the baton of Paul Bateman, probably comes the closest, at least until the end, of any of the recorded versions to matching the feel of the music as it appears on *Psycho*'s music track (strangely still never released on recording). Certainly, some of Herrmann's most disturbing and unsettling "music of the irrational" (as I have referred to it elsewhere) outside of Hitchcock appears in J. Lee Thompson's 1962 thriller, *Cape Fear*. This CD offers four musical cues from the film heard in their original guise, rather than the (brilliant) reworking done by Elmer Bernstein for Martin Scorsese's (brilliant) 1992 remake. As composer Bernstein points out in the documentary *Music for the Movies: Bernard Herrmann*, *Cape Fear*'s title theme offers a perfect example of how Herrmann was able to turn the simplest of material—here a four-note, descending motif—into gripping suspense music that immediately exposes the core of the most somber reaches of the soul. It was also Elmer Bernstein who revived Herrmann's rejected score for Hitchcock's *Torn Curtain*, later reusing parts of it in his *Cape Fear* reworking. Although it would be nice to have a CD reissue of Bernstein's recording of the complete music, three welcome cues from Herrmann's *Torn Curtain* do turn up here, including the driving, metallic, and up-heaval-filled title theme and the cue for the murder of Gromek, a sequence that remains unscored in the film (*Music for the Movies: Bernard Herrmann* presents that sequence with Herrmann's unused music, and it quite transforms the scene).

We also get to hear more of the sometimes frenetic, sometimes hauntingly sad music for Nicholas Ray's 1951 *On Dangerous Ground* than is available on Charles Gerhardt's Herrmann anthology in the RCA "Classic Film Scores" series. The cues include the theme for the blind Mary (Ida Lupino), originally scored to include a viola d'amore solo (the soloist, at Herrmann's insistence, actually gets a mention in *On Dangerous Ground*'s title sequence), and played here on a regular viola. The "Night

Piece" for saxophone and orchestra arranged by the late Christopher Palmer from Herrmann's music for Scorsese's *Taxi Driver* features particularly raucous solos from saxophonist Ivan Myslikovjan. Briefly piercing the pall that hangs over most of this recording is the scintillating "Overture" for Herrmann's *Welles Raises Kane* suite, while waltzes from Brian De Palma's awful *Obsession* and from *The Snows of Kiliman-jaro* take the spirit into a netherworld of sadness and nostalgia, as do the two cues from *The Ghost and Mrs. Muir*. As if cognizant of the necessity of bringing their listeners back to planet Earth from their Herrmann trip, the producers of this recording conclude it with a fluffy suite featuring music from four of the Herrmann-scored fantasy films featuring special-effects work by Ray Harryhausen: *The Three Worlds of Gulliver*, *The Seventh Voyage of Sinbad*, *Mysterious Island*, and *Jason and the Argonauts*. My own inclination would be to shut the CD off after the *Torn Curtain* music, which precedes this suite. But then, I'm a Baudelaire man, at least where music is concerned.

Another highlight of my 1995 filmgoing experiences so far was **Il Postino** (The Postman), which, like many films these days, invents a fiction around a true event, in this case the exile of Chilean poet Pablo Neruda (played by French actor Philippe Noiret, the projectionist in *Cinema Paradiso*) on an island off of Italy. The fiction is built around the story of a young Marxist and would-be poet (Massimo Troisi, who died shortly after *Il Postino* was shot) who escapes the life of a fisherman by becoming the temporary postman hired to deliver Neruda's mail. If I don't rank *Il Postino* all the way at the top with my other 1995 favorites, it is because it is ever so slightly dragged down by a kind of touchy-feely cuteness that turns up in a certain strain of contemporary Italian cinema. But, oh, what a music-track (plus) album has been put together by the Weinstein brothers (Harvey and Bob), co-chairs of Miramax Films (Miramax Records/Hollywood Records; Orchestra Sinfonietta di Roma). Inspired by actress Julia Roberts, who had shown up in their offices with six volumes of Neruda poetry upon learning of Miramax's involvement with *Il Postino*, the Weinstein brothers were soon besieged by a league of actors and actresses, all of them Neruda aficionados. The result is a set of 14 readings, most of them accompanied by excerpts from Luis Bacalov's musical score, done by performers who had nothing to do with the film itself: Roberts, Sting, Miranda Richardson, Wesley Snipes, Ralph Fiennes, Ethan Hawke, Rufus Sewell, Glenn Close, Samuel L. Jackson, Andy Garcia, Willem Dafoe, Madonna, and Vincent Perez, with Garcia and Roberts jointly reading "And Now You're Mine (Love Sonnet LXXXI)." Under the supervision of *Il Postino*'s director, Michael Radford, each reader offers what struck me as wonderfully subtle, nuanced interpretations of a wide variety of beautifully translated Neruda poems, many of them celebrations of love and women, with Bacalov's sadly lyrical music heightening their poignancy in many cases. Even without all of this expert help, of course, Neruda's highly visual poetry, with its quasi-musical reprises and its quietly surprising shifts of direction, would speak quite eloquently for itself. But hearing these readings, I felt a sense of completeness, as if Neruda's warmth and humanity were being sent back to the poet via the love this group of actors and actresses has for his poetry.

Bacalov's score is dominated by its main theme, a sweetly lyrical melody often presented on a bandoneon (performed by Hector Ulises Passarella) with a very tight tremolo. The theme undergoes a certain number of mild variations, perhaps the most charming of which first turns up with a full-orchestra, Broadway-tango accompaniment in the "Bicycle" cue. For the postman's lady fair (Beatrice Russo), Bacalov offers a slightly less melodic habañera that is nonetheless very much in the spirit of *Il Postino*'s main theme, as are the other (very rare) departures made by the composer from his basic material. Basically, if you like the main theme, you'll like the musical portion of this CD. And anyway, after you've been swept away by Neruda and the masterful readers who open this CD, it will take a lot more than a half-dozen or so reprises of a slightly simplistic but utterly charming melody to turn you grumpy.

From Citadel comes a three-score recording that [includes two] Elmer Bernstein scores, the impossibly fluffy score for the 1969 **Midas Run** (Rome Cinema Orchestra, Elmer Bernstein, cond.), and the bright and often perky chamber suite for flute, cello, harp, and piano Bernstein composed in 1955 for **House: After 5 Years of Living**, one of a number of short documentaries scored by the composer for American designers Charles and Ray Eames. Also included, however, because they ran out of Elmer Bernstein material, is the late Henry Mancini's relentlessly gloomy, spine-scraping score for Laslo Benedek's 1970 **The Night Visitor**, which ends up being the highlight of the entire release. For those who, forgetting the brooding suspense music for films such as *Charade* or the grating quarter tones that make *Wait Until Dark* even more creepy, see Mancini only as a composer of classy bass lines and sophisticated, *Pink Panther*-type themes, *The Night Visitor* will come as a huge shock. Eschewing his usual big band, Mancini scored *The Night Visitor* for synthesizer and 17 instruments—12 woodwinds (including what sounds like a bass flute), an organ, two pianos, and two harpsichords, with one piano and one harpsichord tuned a quarter tone down from the rest of the ensemble. We also hear a bit of percussion, although this might come from the synthesizer. Tony Thomas accurately states in the program notes that the score "is not broadly thematic but draws its effectiveness from modulations and sustained sounds." I would go one step further and suggest that *The Night Visitor* is wholly athematic. While various winds occasionally take off with extended lines, these in no way become themes in the traditional sense. What we get instead is almost pure mood, with something like a quintessentialized Shostakovich dominating the upper registers while something resembling Bernard Herrmann grumbles in the lower timbres. An obsessive, two-note figure in the low bassoons, piano, and harpsichord occasionally reminds us that here indeed is the composer of *The Pink Panther*. But the quarter-tones turn the motif into something so dark that the panther has thoroughly returned to his native blackness (as Mancini tells it in his autobiography, *Did They Mention the Music?*, one of the pianists on the recording session for the 1967 *Wait Until Dark* actually became somewhat ill from performing some of the quarter-tone cues). *The Night Visitor* is one of film music's most challenging and original productions, and it is a shame that Benedek's drearily uninvolving movie did not prove more worthy of its music.

March/April

Finally! Akira Senju's music for the Japanese film **The Mystery of Rampo**, directed by Kazuyoshi Okuyama, has been domestically released (Discovery; Czech Philharmonic Orchestra, Vaclav Neumann and Mario Klemens, cond.). The movie's main theme (designated on the CD as "Love Theme for Rampo") is a moody rhapsody composed in very much the same vein as some of the scores of Gabriel Yared, whose *Map of the Human Heart* shares a motif with *Rampo*'s rhapsody. But where Yared deploys a good deal of electronics and tends more toward repetition than development, Senju's "Love Theme" is lushly scored for full orchestra and develops its main theme in a somewhat more romantic manner. Indeed, one rather suspects a deliberate attempt to evoke the film music of early Hollywood. There is even a musical bridge, first heard starting at 2:11 in the first cue, that strongly reminds me of some of the less-than-dark moments in 1940s Miklós Rózsa. *Rampo*'s other big theme is a moody, minor-mode, and mildly chromatic waltz that occasionally waxes quite dramatic and that in certain of its versions is interrupted by an incongruously Baroque bridge. First heard behind the main titles, the waltz gets repeated in various guises throughout the film. A third musical block takes the form of a more or less themeless but very moody elegy for string orchestra.

Senju's score sets a perfect tone for the film, in which Okuyama and his co-screenwriters imagine that author Edogawa Rampo (who has been dubbed the Japanese Edgar Allan Poe) meets (ca. 1930) in real life a woman named Shizuko who doubles the heroine of his banned novel, *The Appearance of Osei*, in which a wife allows her husband to suffocate inside a hope chest (ingeniously, a quasi-music-box version of the love theme backs an animated version of the novel that opens the film). In a rather Jungian twist, Rampo turns the woman into a kind of anima figure who gives him inspiration as he writes a sequel to *The Appearance of Osei* in which Shizuko is the heroine. *The Mystery of Rampo* vacillates between Rampo and Shizuko's doomed love affair—Rampo must keep her at a distance in order to write—and a filmic realization of the new novel he is in the process of writing. Along the way, cinematographer Yasushi Sasakibara creates a hyper-real visual style that turns various pieces of Japanese architecture and landscaping into mood pieces that function on the same level as the music. Just about everything in *The Mystery of Rampo*—the screenplay, the directorial style, the photography, and certainly Senju's bigger-than-life romanticism—suggests that feelings can find their true fruition only within the work of art. Unlike most film-music labels, Discovery offers extensive notes to accompany this CD, including a synopsis of the film, some "Director's Notes" from Okuyama, and some "Composer's Notes" by Senju. If I understand correctly, Okuyama released *Rampo* in Japan without music and then decided to add a score for its international release. And what Okuyama apparently requested from Senju, who had previously scored Kazuyoshi's *226*, was not a classic film score made up of action-specific cues but rather a second version of *Rampo* that would express in music what the director expressed in visual images. Certainly, there is no question that in listening to this extraordinary CD, which benefits from a rich and warm sonic ambience and from excellent performances by the Czech Philharmonic, one can pretty much relive *The Mystery of Rampo*, although, interestingly, not a single note of this highly Western score seems to offer the slightest hint of traditional Japanese musical styles. In his notes, director Okuyama writes, "In the annals of film music history, I am certain that the score for *Rampo* will be judged among the finest." Hyperbolic as it may be, I'm not sure this judgment isn't correct. Personally, I would be tempted to apply the same hyperbole to Okuyama's film.

Another film score recording that got under my skin, to the point that listening to it became something of an obsession for a while, is DRG's CD of Ennio Morricone's music for *La tragedia di un uomo ridicolo* (The Tragedy of a Ridiculous Man), one of two scores appearing on a DRG release entitled **A Bernardo Bertolucci Double Feature**. The score is dominated by a rather morose, minor-mode waltz which, in the opening cue and occasionally elsewhere, gets juxtaposed over material that might be said to flirt with "When You Are in Love (It's the Loveliest Night of the Year)." In one cue ("Mungendo Verdi"), Morricone actually creates a triply layered counterpoint by juxtaposing a third theme (of sorts) above the two waltz themes. Over its various appearances, furthermore, the composer colors the waltz with such characteristically (for Morricone) offbeat timbres as a honky-tonk piano, some form of accordion (which, when used, definitely gives the theme a Gallic hue), a mandolin, and a wooden flute. Interestingly, by the time he reaches the final cue, Morricone totally trashes his melancholy theme by giving to it the kind of hideously off-key and inept band that seems to turn up only in Italian movies (including, of course, *The Godfather*). In a somewhat but not altogether different vein is the music associated with the protagonist's wife (Anouk Aimée), a slow, extremely wistful piece initially heard in the upper registers of the piano over slowly shifting chords in the piano and strings, and later picked up by the flute. Two or three other cues suggest the heavy drama underlying the entire film, the most intriguingly Morricone-esque of which features thick, ominous, bitonal chords in the strings and honky-tonk piano, in and out of which float various timbres—a mandolin tremolo, a growl from the contrabassoon, a whine from the accordion—with a high clarinet reminding us vaguely of the opening waltz. And then there is my obsession within the obsession, a kind of punk rock number entitled "Horror Movies" strangely unattributed on this CD but credited in the end titles to a group called Linda and the Dark (now there's an appropriate appellation if ever there was one). Here, a hoarse-voiced young woman, who performs in a kind of rock *sprechstimme* and who sounds as if she's thoroughly certifiable, offers such defiant lyrics as "They say I'm a lunatic because I dress in black/But they'd better watch out or I'll chop them with my ax." Something deliciously morbid and crazy about this song had me going back to it any number of times.

All of which brings me to the ultimate question: what's a nice score like this doing in a film like *The Tragedy of a Ridiculous Man?* *Tragedy*, which was released in 1981, joins the 1973 *Last Tango in Paris* as one of two Bertolucci films I intensely dislike, although for totally different reasons. Somehow, there never seems to be a point to the film's interminable narrative, which features Ugo Tognazzi, performing with the kind of cute confusion that characterizes later Marcello Mastroianni, as an industrialist father who witnesses the kidnapping of his son through the binoculars the latter has given him for his birthday. All sorts of possibilities arise—the rebel son may be an accomplice in his own abduction, as one example—and all sorts of interactions take place between the industrialist and his almost saintly wife. But it all remains completely pointless, and the considerable effect generated by Morricone's music, rather than drawing us into the action, seems to hover around some place outside the film. Even "Horror Movies," which might have infused *Tragedy* with a jolt of the grotesque, is barely heard during a thoroughly dull gathering toward the end of the film. And what, you may ask, is the other Bertolucci film represented on this CD? Only one of the director's masterpieces, the 1971 *Il conformista* (The Conformist), a moody and ultimately tragic setting of Alberto Moravia's novel of an Italian fascist (the always excellent Jean-Louis Trintignant in one of the best performances of his career) sent in the 1930s to Paris to assassinate an anti-Mussolini professor, with whose wife (Dominique Sanda) he falls in love. The music for *Il conformista* was composed by Georges Delerue, who, in the opening cue, which briefly evolves into a rhapsody for piano and orchestra, comes close to duplicating the crushingly sad tone of his score for Godard's *Contempt* (also based on a Moravia novel). A second cue, entitled "Alien," transforms the title music into a waltz (Delerue's favorite mode of musical expression) that gets interrupted by some gloomy chordal figures, set to a dance-step rhythm, that somehow seem to encapsulate *Il conformista*'s overall mood. Two cues later in the score recapture this initial ambience. And that's about it. A cue entitled "Waltz of the Conformist" represents Delerue at his most insipid, while the remaining seven cuts are popular songs and dances from the '30s, all of which are necessary to the film but not particularly something you need to hear on a music-track recording. *Il conformista* appears here in reasonably good monaural sound, *La tragedia di un uomo ridicolo* in much better than average stereo. Didier C. Deutsch's notes offer more information on the movies than on the music, and I'm not sure where he came up with the idea that Delerue scored films by Claude Chabrol.

One thing you can probably count on from a director (David Fincher) who has had experience in music videos is a certain amount of visual flair, both in the camera work and in the editing, generally lacking in most of the movies that come out of Hollywood. One of the first things that struck me as I watched **Se7en**, one of 1995's more successful feature films, was that the entire movie reveals a consistent visual concept as it follows two cops (Brad Pitt and Morgan Freeman) on the trail of a serial killer (Kevin Spacey) who murders his victims in gruesome manners suggested by the seven deadly sins. I mean, *Se7en* outnoirs the films noirs in the way everything seen remains in a kind of blurry (and often rainy) darkness that not only helps set a grim mood but also keeps the viewer worried as to what that darkness will eventually reveal. Further, *Se7en* keeps its viewers in a kind of David Lynchian time warp by showing most of the action in architectural settings that strongly evoke pre-1950s America. Only as the film draws toward its climactic conclusion does it emerge into the light, but that in a nightmarish setting as well, this one filled with high-tension pylons in the middle of nowhere. In its sad denouement, Se7en returns to the darkness, but this time a sharply defined night in which tragedy has replaced mystery. I had forgotten, until composer Howard Shore reminded me of same, that Fincher, in the feature-film department, was previously responsible for Alien³, whose visual profile is just about as strong—and as dark—as Se7en's. What raises Se7en to an even higher level, however, is that its style is not just the empty flash one often finds in music videos but rather is solidly locked into the film's grim narrative. This, in fact, is one of the things that attracted composer Shore to the film. "He's a great visual director," Shore noted in a phone conversation this past December. "He just has a great way with the camera and lighting. And he made it a part of the story and didn't just do it for the effect of it, which you do see in a lot of other films."

Certainly, Howard Shore's score for Se7en comes across as an almost literal musical translation of the darkness that hangs over just about every element of the film. Unfortunately, less than 20 minutes of the hour's worth of music Shore wrote has made it to the so-called "original motion picture soundtrack" (TVT Records). We get to hear a "Portrait of John Doe" (the serial killer), in which low-mid-range thematic fragments emerge within a crescendoing orchestral miasma of gloomy, repeated figures in the low winds and strings. The sound is classic Howard Shore. There is a certain openness in the chordal structures and a rather wistful quality to the thematic material that leads the music, for all its eeriness and morbidity, profoundly into the emotions, which in his/her turn the viewer/listener can project back into Se7en's doom and gloom. "Portrait of John Doe" is followed by a 15-minute "Suite from Se7en," most of which is a themeless progression of thickly textured, often twice-repeated chordal figures in the orchestra, with brief reprises of the "John Doe" material. It is as if Shore had reached into the film and pulled all of its atmosphere into the score. Even on a purely musical level, however, the composer sustains interest by constantly shifting the timbres and chord structures while maintaining an intensity that, toward the end, becomes almost crushing. In the same phone conversation, Shore offered some interesting insights into Se7en and his contributions to the film:

H.S.: There were a couple of special-edition prints made of this movie where they reclaimed the nitrate. It's a process where they take the silver out of the film and then chemically put it back in. The film was so dark, so dimly lit. But on these special prints, it has this kind of glistening quality. It's dark but it's kind of bright at the same time. The green lights up a certain way when the projector hits it.

R.S.B.: How did Fincher come to use you as a composer?

H.S.: I think he had seen a lot of the Cronenberg films, and the Demme pictures as well. Really, it wasn't a hard match to put together, if you think about it. It was a topic that I had sort of covered in a movie a few years ago.

R.S.B.: Except that this score is a lot darker than The Silence of the Lambs. Silence at least has a fairly developed theme, whereas Se7en has all those fragments and motifs.

H.S.: He wanted it like that. We discussed that in a lot of detail. It was different from writing a narrative score, which is what *Silence* is. Jonathan's approach was almost the opposite of his. Jonathan wanted to tell the story, wanted the characters to be as clear as possible to the audience. Jonathan's thrust in *The Silence of the Lambs* was to tell the story of the victim, the woman that Gumb had in the hole. The music is very sad, very tragic in a way. Initially, I tend to approach a movie in that way. I want to tell a story. And I thought the characters in *Se7en* were good. I thought Morgan [Freeman] was a great, sort of tragic character. There was quite a bit more introduction of Morgan's character in the beginning that got edited out. There was more about his retirement. The first scene in the movie shows him in an old farmhouse that he is going to buy outside of town. It's this old, rundown farmhouse, and he takes a piece of wallpaper as a souvenir from it. The wallpaper was a symbol of his retirement, of his just getting out of this hellish city. The little swatch of wallpaper has a story of its own in the movie. It keeps on appearing. When I first saw the film, that was my initial impression. Thinking about the characters and how to work with the characters musically is kind of the type of score that I like to do. And Fincher saw the Mills character [Brad Pitt] as Macbeth—he was doomed. But he kept moving me away from that. He didn't want me to work too much with the characters. He was more interested just in texture and sound. He talked about washes of sound. We talked about Ligeti and that kind of thing. It's a score that is much more abstract than *Silence*, which was more narrative. In the end, I kept on trying to slip it in. Every so often I would kind of slip in things that were thematic and have the score tell the story somewhat. I would do it and sort of wink at him, like "I think this is OK," and he would go with it. I always think that stuff really helps the movie, because it helps the audience. But I did much less of it than I did in a movie like *Silence*.

R.S.B.: There's only 20 minutes' worth of music on the CD. Are we going to get a complete recording on the score?

H.S.: It's just economics, you know. I would have loved to put the score out on its own. It's an hour of music. What happened with the disc had to do with the Trent Reznor song that was used in the beginning of the movie. That was owned by TVT Records. So they managed to get the rights to the soundtrack. They don't do soundtrack albums, they put out song albums. Their inclination was just to put out all these songs and have a little score on it, and I had to fight to get the two tracks. It would have been a really nice score album. It was recorded in Los Angeles with a pretty big orchestra.

R.S.B.: The orchestral sound is really good.

H.S.: It's beautiful. John Kurlander recorded it. I've been working with him since *M. Butterfly*. We've probably done maybe 10 movies together. I've used him pretty exclusively for all the orchestral stuff. He's a staff engineer at Abbey Road. He's the top, head classical recording engineer. He does all the Philadelphia Orchestra recordings, he does the Vienna Philharmonic, all these great classical records. Now he's gotten interested in film music, and he's doing other movies as well. He did *The Scarlet Letter* with John Barry, and he did *Anastasia*, which is an animated thing that Fox is doing. He also has a green card now, so he's been working in Los Angeles. He did this in Los Angeles, and I brought him in to do it. It's a pretty big orchestra. A lot of percussion. There's probably about seven or eight percussionists all the time.

R.S.B.: There's also some electronics.

H.S.: There is quite a bit of electronics, and it's the same technique that I've used for years, where I kind of map out the electronics based on the score. I don't create it beforehand. What I do is that I write the score and program the score into a computer, note by note. I break the counterpoint down into the smallest number of tracks. You might have anywhere from four to six tracks. Any orchestral piece can be condensed into a piano form, or maybe for three or four hands. If you can condense *The Rite of Spring* into a piano score, you can condense everything! So I program those lines individually into the computer, and then I assign sounds to them. They're all abstract sounds. They have no tonal reference to anything. It's a palette of sounds that I've collected for years, and I have them all on an optical disc. I use a big computer, such as a Synclavier, to do it. And so I do the [orchestral] recording, and I videotape the conducting. Then we tap into that with the computer, so that the computer is following the tempos correctly. And then I just add the sounds to the score when I mix. A lot of the recordings I do with Kurlander. I don't remix. It's a lot of live recording. *Se7en* was all recorded live. And then I just added the electronic sounds to give it a lot more depth. It's not doubling any of the orchestra parts. It's doubling certain lines of the orchestra. It depends on how full the score is. If the score has 24 or 30 staves and you have six staves going, the computer is not playing too much. But if you're going 24 staves and you're very filled in, it sort of kicks in all of these abstract sounds. It sort of follows the score in a kind of abstract way. As the music increases in size and intensity, so does the computer part. A lot of times it's very delayed. If, say, you have an E-flat on the downbeat of bar 13, in the electronics you might only feel that three or four beats later. The electronic stuff is not very percussive. They're industrial sounds, environmental sounds . . . very abstract. Things that have been recorded and sampled, with octaves adjusted significantly. For example, you might hear whale sounds two octaves lower than they were recorded. And they're being triggered by the orchestral score and played behind the orchestra. It always sounds like an orchestra playing, but behind it is this other kind of unstable sound to it. It messes with the tonality.

R.S.B.: So it's almost aurally subliminal.

H.S.: Yes. I love it in movies, because so much of the movies work on a subliminal level. I like to work around the edges of it. You know I do. So this kind of helps me with it. It's also a very quick way of doing things. When I mix it, the computer is running all the time, and then it's just a matter of bringing faders up and down.

The thing that's lovely about Kurlander is that he logs everything I do with him into a computer. So every time we start another recording, we're already at the stage where we left off the last time. And so we can just go to the next level of experience.

R.S.B.: So you're always compounding your experience.

H.S.: Exactly. And the orchestra is always done that way too. We've developed a kind of seating arrangement and a miking arrangement for the orchestra that we like, and I tend to write for that. And he sets everything up exactly. I'm also getting used to the different rooms and kind of write to those different rooms. For *Se7en*, the actual record is so much more beautiful than what you hear on the CD, particularly in the Dolby Surround. I don't think the pressing is great, and I don't like the way it is mastered. I just couldn't get into the place that I wanted because of TVT and all that.

Apart from Shore's contributions, the *Se7en* CD features nine selections of source music, from Bach (Orchestral Suite No. 1) to Gravity Kills, that have their own role to play in the movie. Some of these function ironically, such as The Statler Brothers' biblical "In the Beginning," while others, such as Gravity Kills' gritty "Guilty" (this is the TVT property Shore mentions above), could easily have been inspired by *Se7en*. Between these two extremes, we get the Bach—a fairly Romanticized (the way most people like it) performance of the Air on the G String by the Stuttgart Kammerorchester under Karl Münchinger; some great songs by the likes of Marvin Gaye ("Trouble Man"), Gloria Lynne ("Speaking of Happiness"), and Billie Holiday ("I Cover the Waterfront"); and some classy instrumentals by Charlie Parker ("Now's the Time") and Thelonius Monk (his long "Straight, No Chaser"). Only the innocuous "Love Plus One" by Haircut 100 intruded on my enjoyment of the CD.

Mark Isham's music for **The Browning Version** (Milan; Choristers of Reigate St. Mary's Choir School; London Metropolitan Orchestra, Ken Kugler, cond.) had been sitting on my shelf for several months. One reason for this is that I have never liked the Terrence Rattigan play on which Ronald Harwood based the movie's screenplay. Another reason is that I have found most of Albert Finney's performances since *Tom Jones* perfectly awful. But somehow, Mike Figgis does not seem to be capable of making a bad film. A less flamboyant but equally sensitive side of Figgis's sensibilities was revealed to me when I watched *The Browning Version*. Perhaps the major miracle is that Figgis (or perhaps somebody else) actually coaxed a restrained performance out of Albert Finney who, as a private-school teacher described by his students as the "Hitler of the lower fifth" and forced by his own intransigence into an early retirement, invites the audience to read beyond his calm exterior into his tortured inner life, rather in the manner of Anthony Hopkins in *Remains of the Day*. And as in all of his pictures, Figgis has created an intriguing visual "look," mostly centered around the school and its grounds, with the help of cinematographer Jean-François Robin (one wonders whether co-producer Ridley Scott had anything to do with *The Browning Version*'s style). And while I'm not sure that Harwood's updating has helped Rattigan's play any, as a film *The Browning Version* works dramatically on any number of levels. It is certainly impossible not to be devastated by the sadistic remark from the teacher's adulterous wife (Greta Scacchi) that forms the play's core moment.

A good deal of *The Browning Version's* emotional impact must, I think, be attributed to Isham's incredibly sad music. From the dirge-like (there's even a periodic bass-drum beat) opening music, whose lyrical theme in the violins often intersects in poignant, close harmonies with the accompaniment in the lower strings, Isham establishes a tone of pain and longing that really never lets up. Almost all of the score's cues are played at a slow, meditative pace, including the theme for "Taplow," the one student to have a certain rapport with the teacher. Initially presented in the high violins over a characteristic harp figure, this theme turns up throughout the score. Isham ingeniously integrates it, for instance, into the militaristic (but still slow and moody) cue entitled "The Agamemnon," as it is Taplow who gives the teacher the "Browning version" of that Aeschylus tragedy. Here and there Isham adds to his exquisitely subtle orchestral palette the plaintive and poignant boy-soprano timbres of the Choristers of Reigate St. Mary's Choir School. A particularly haunting—and particularly halting—cue entitled "Goodbye" is played mostly by the string orchestra. By the end, both the film and its score shift slightly from pure sadness to a tone of tragic resignation.

If you think about it, there are probably two quintessential Western scores in American film music—that is, if you don't count Aaron Copland's *Billy the Kid*, which should have been a film score (I would love to build a movie around it one of these days). One of those quintessential scores is Elmer Bernstein's *The Magnificent Seven*. The other is Jerome Moross' **The Big Country**, which was rerecorded by Tony Bremner and the Philharmonia Orchestra in 1988 and has just been reissued by Silva America. Composed for William Wyler's sprawling drama, which was released to mixed reviews in 1958, *The Big Country* opens with one of the most rousing title themes in cinema history (and it doesn't hurt any that the title visuals were designed by Saul Bass, who also did the titles for the Moross-scored *The Cardinal*). After a swirling hoedown figure in the violins that instantly establishes the film's Americana underpinnings, Moross introduces a wonderfully expansive theme that owes part of its "Westernicity" to an open-spaced melodic structure that is essentially pentatonic, as conductor Bremner notes in his excellent program commentary. Also adding to the Americana aura that surrounds the theme are the syncopated triads in the accompaniment and the slightly jolting flatted seventh in the accompaniment with which the tune briefly intersects just before the midpoint of its initial phase. Interestingly, from listening to much of Moross' often jaunty music, one would not guess the seriousness of a lot of the action it underscores—or was supposed to underscore, since the music underwent a lot of modifications when it was laid in on *The Big Country's* music track. Although the music takes on a slightly *serioso* cast here and there—what Bremner describes as the "staggering" figure that accompanies the end of an exhausting fight between Gregory Peck and Charlton Heston is a good example, as is the slightly wistful ending of the "Attempted Rape" (of the Jean Simmons character) cue—it is only in the climactic final cues that the darkness underlying the entire film comes to the foreground via some violent chordal figures that accompany the "Duel" and the dissonant funeral march that marks the deaths of the warring patriarchs (Burl Ives and Charles Bickford). As Bremner notes, *The Big Country* is not a leitmotif score. With the exception of a series of dances used as source music for the major's party, little of the music strikes the listener as action specific. It is as if the real inspiration of Moross' score is the "big country" of the Wild West, and that is no doubt the best framework for listening to this splendidly performed and recorded (the digital origins do show, however) reissue.

May/June

Well now, let's see. How to describe Miklós Rózsa's score for Anthony Mann's 1961 epic *El Cid*, which has just been spectacularly rerecorded by James Sedares with the New Zealand Symphony Orchestra for Koch International Classics? The music, with its frequent marches, fanfares, and heavy use of open intervals, does not take long in revealing itself as one of the composer's epic/spectacular scores. Some modal melodic twists and some quasi-Flamenco rhythms and chords also soon let us know that the movie has something to do with Spain. There is also a cue, not heard on this recording, that solidly evokes the Moorish-oriental origins of the film's bad guys, led by a half-veiled Herbert Lom, as they ride to Valencia. But what's this? At several moments, the first of which appear in the composite cue entitled "Courage and Honor," particularly its final three minutes, Rózsa looks back with a vengeance to his noir style, with heavily dissonant chords that often punctuate grim but sweeping melodic lines in jagged rhythmic patterns making it impossible to figure out whether the music is backing a cops-and-robbers chase over a New York City bridge in black and white or a wide-screen, Technicolor battle between 11th-century Spaniards and their bitter enemies. The funny thing is that the gloomy music in this particular cue evokes a situation of honor that is the antithesis of the standard morality of the film noir: the nobleman Rodrigo Diaz (played by an impossibly handsome Charlton Heston) is obliged, because of an insult to his father, to fight and kill the father of his fiancée, Chimene (played by an impossibly beautiful Sophia Loren), who, in order to be worthy of her fiancé, must swear eternal vengeance upon him. I also include as noir those moments when the music comes out from behind the clouds to speak, with muted lyricism, of sadness and resignation. As Martin Scorsese eloquently says of Rózsa in a commentary that opens the program booklet, "His music has the tragic sweep of romanticism." I further single out as a high point in an oeuvre that hardly lacks its peaks the music for the "Wedding Night." Rodrigo, having extracted a promise from King Ferdinand that he may marry Chimene if he returns successfully from a mission, finds himself on the point of consummating his marriage. But the acidically bitonal chords that open the cue immediately tell us that this cannot take place. Still, Rózsa comes up with one of his most haunting love themes. At this point in particular, however, the mournful, Hispanically flavored modalism of the theme and its harmonies combines with the quiet voices of the mid-range strings to communicate the impossibility of that love which, in the film, will be allowed but one moment of human simplicity. Only a composer of Rózsa's genius could have simultaneously captured in such depth both the breadth of the emotions involved and the fatalistic pall that hangs over the life of Rodrigo, the only man in Spain who, as one character puts it, "could humble a king and who would give a leper to drink from his own pouch." The score also is not lacking in the kind of tense action music that only Rózsa could write, and in the music for the climactic "Battle of Valencia," the noir tone returns in more than one instance. For the film's apotheosis, in which a dead Rodrigo grotesquely propped up on his horse leads the Valencians to ultimate victory, Rózsa actually deploys the imposing strains of a solo pipe organ (it is the only example I can think of in the composer's oeuvre, cinematic or otherwise, where this instrument turns up). Heard briefly in the film, the solo organ cue, spectacularly recorded, goes on for over a minute in the version heard on this CD. Conductor James Sedares creates passion, excitement, and sweep in an interpretation that reveals a close understanding of the score's relationship to the movie it was written for while at the same time allowing the listener to just sit back and revel in the sheer power of the music, which receives all but flawless playing from the New Zealand Symphony. The recorded sound, while distinctly digital, has a good deal of breadth, and it captures the timbres of the all-important brass with particular warmth. The program notes by Allen D. Cohen are among the most intelligent and informative I've ever read for a film-music recording. Besides the pre-film Overture, generally cut since El Cid's first run, there is also a certain amount of music heard here that does not turn up in the film.

Hey, this is fun. Get Hannibal Lecter, a.k.a. Anthony Hopkins, to play Richard Milhouse Nixon; hire John Williams to write one of his most somber and moody scores and have a moment of it flirt with the ominous march for arch-villain Darth Vader; and then involve what some would call the directorial talents of Oliver Stone, who brought J.F.K. and the flamboyant Natural Born Killers to the screen and who has never let history get in the way of a nice helping of pseudo-liberal paranoia: no wonder people on both sides of the fence have been screaming foul! As someone whom Nixon drove crazy when he was in office but who can now appreciate the positive things he did accomplish, particularly in the retrospective light of eight disastrous years under Reagan, I found Stone's **Nixon** to be a reasonably well-balanced film. Hopkins creates a remarkably consistent character and has most of the late former president's speech patterns down cold. But, for whatever reasons, I was never able to see him as Nixon. On the other hand, I found Joan Allen utterly amazing as Pat Nixon, but that may be because of the former first lady's relative invisibility vis-à-vis her husband. As for Oliver Stone, I have to say that little irritates me as much as his vacuous use of devices—cuts to black and white, to video, to eight-millimeter; moments of non-continuity editing—which far more profound and talented directors would not be allowed to get away with. Stone is the only filmmaker I know who can take a jump cut and make it look like invisible editing. His use of John Williams' score (Illusion/Hollywood Records) is singularly bizarre. Throughout the film, even during apparently innocuous moments—and there are plenty of these in this three-hour film; I mean, Nixon is just not all that interesting—the musical score lurks quietly in the background, suggesting a kind of hyper-narrative ominousness that strongly undercuts (no surprise there) whatever historical underpinnings Nixon might have. It is the sort of underscoring one might expect behind a scene where, say, Deep Throat leaks state secrets to the Alien bitch-mother in a Bosnian pub at midnight. Once released from the low volume levels of Nixon's music track and heard on its own on Illusion/Hollywood's splendidly recorded CD, however, Williams' score comes into its own, captivating the listener with its rich palette of subtly mixed timbres (no surprise there, either; the composer has shown himself to be a master at this kind of thing from the outset of his career), its consistently murky atmosphere, and its occasional moments of high drama. At only two moments in the 13 cues offered here does the music lighten up—once for a rendition of the "Battle Hymn of the Republic," the other for a nostalgic trumpet solo (performed by Tim Morrison) over a classic cine-Western accompaniment intended to evoke the late president's childhood in southern California. In the opening cue on this CD ("The 1960s: The Turbulent Years"), that same theme appears in a much darker, low mid-range guise following a dirge-like opening filled with thickly textured, inner-voiced chords. One presumes that a nostalgic piano solo that also turns up in this cue was at least partially intended as a metonymy for Nixon, given the president's penchant for impromptu performances on that instrument. Williams also provides some classy suspense music, complete with nervous rhythmic punctuation in the percussion and solo piano, for "The Ellsberg Break-in and Watergate." And, hey, is that Dmitri Shostakovich's "DSCH" motif that pops in here and there? Could the music be suggesting its own political message? The gap between Williams' music here, which comes heavily out of the tropes of the action/suspense film score, and the historical underpinnings of the screen action is so great that one would like to think that Stone is offering his own comment on the postmodern breakdown between history and fiction. John Williams' score stands as one of the best of 1995. Whether it also stands as one of film history's great mismatches or as a brilliant cine-musical comment on the relationship between image (visual and musical) and reality remains open to question. But that's par for the course for Oliver Stone. I should also note that the Nixon recording is an "Enhanced CD," meaning that it is a "hybrid disc" containing standard CD audio tracks as well as an interactive CD ROM section playable on both PC and Macintosh platforms.

From director Michael Mann (Thief, Manhunter, The Last of the Mohicans, and, of course, the whole Miami Vice look), one generally expects the following things on the music track: a) lots of generally quiet, themeless electronics dominated by obsessive rhythmic figures and long drones; b) an occasional crescendo into a kind of celebratory, pop-electronic chant, as in Tangerine Dream's final cue for Thief (in The Last of the Mohicans, this is more than occasional); c) quiet songs, usually performed by a male vocalist in a kind of Jim Morrison voice, slipped in subtly behind the action. It thus comes as something of a surprise that, for his latest opus, **Heat** (Warner Bros.), Mann would turn for at least some of his music to Elliot Goldenthal, best known for his modern-to-avant-garde, large-scale symphonic (with plenty of electronics and other timbres, however) scores for such films as Alien³ and Interview with the Vampire. But as of the title cue, it is apparent that Goldenthal has, with big expanses of sustained string sound, synth timbres, and occasional punctuation from the "Deaf Elk" Guitar Orchestra, fallen in sync with Mann's aesthetics while offering some new wrinkles. Those new wrinkles take the form of added layers of complexity and dissonance that seem very much at home in this three-hour film in which the director examines one of his favorite themes, namely the mirroring that inevitably exists between an obsessed cop (here Al Pacino) and an equally obsessed criminal (Robert De Niro). But if Pacino, in his latest overwrought performance in which we breathlessly await his trademarked outbursts of anger, takes up just about all the screen time on the cops' side, the outlaw side gets divided up among a motley crew that includes, besides De Niro, Val Kilmer, a particularly seedy looking Jon Voight, and even, in a brief appearance, a bearded and crippled Tom Noonan, who plays the serial killer in *Manhunter*. Mann has likewise farmed out his music track to quite a number of different artists. While Goldenthal provides 11 of the 21 cues on this CD, we also get to hear from the likes of Brian Eno, Terje Rypdal, Michael Brook, Einstürzende Neubauten, and, with her New Age drones and chantings, Lisa Gerrard, whose "Là Bas" is heard here in an edited version, along with "Gloradin." And the typical Mann soft, rock vocal comes from Moby in a piece entitled "New Dawn Fades." What is fascinating here is that Mann, for all the disparity, has come up with a remarkable consistency of tone across the 21 cues heard here, with the common denominator being the expansive, droning electronics and the synthesized rhythmic figures. Only in the more purely classical sounds of the Barber-cum-Shostakovich string elegy in "Of Helplessness" and, to a lesser extent, "Of Separation" does Goldenthal set some of the music on a different mood level. Even the Kronos Quartet seems to have been engaged, for the Goldenthal cues, more as a basis for sampling than as a string quartet sound. Only above the low drones at the beginning of "Refinery Surveillance" do we ever hear anything that sounds like a string quartet. This CD is a veritable treasure trove for people who like their listening rooms filled with the spacey sounds of ethers that have somehow turned ominous. Like Mann's film, however, it all takes itself perhaps just a bit too seriously.

July/August

Not only have Robert A. Harris and James C. Katz undertaken a complete restoration of Alfred Hitchcock's **Vertigo**, Varèse Sarabande has brought out an absolutely splendid re-recording of Bernard Herrmann's music for *Vertigo* featuring Joel McNeely and the Royal Scottish National Orchestra, who offer almost twice as much music as one can hear on the original music-track recording currently available on a Mercury CD. In fact, we get a bit of music here and there that does not turn up in the film. The cue entitled "Carlotta's Portrait," for instance, extends close to a minute longer with an additional variation on that theme heard neither in the film nor on the music-track recording. On the other hand, a certain amount of original music that appears in the film (about 12 minutes' worth; my tally of total music from the ASCAP cue sheet, excluding the three source-music cues, comes to 75:30) has been omitted from this recording. In most cases, this amounts to very brief cues or music that brings nothing new to the score. But there are other moments I would like to have heard here: the opening music for the McKittrick Hotel sequence, which combines the habañera rhythm from the just-introduced theme for Carlotta Valdez with droning music that accompanies Scottie Ferguson (Jimmy Stewart) as he follows "Madeleine" (Kim Novak) for the first time in his car; the end of the "By the Fireside" cue and the music that ensues, which ends in a brief hint of the "Love Music," the first time we hear it in the film since the title sequence (the cue sheet erroneously lists as "Love Music" a snippet of "Madeleine's Theme" heard slightly earlier as Stewart sits in his car after the Argosy Bookshop sequence); the cue that precedes Stewart's rediscovery of "Madeleine" in Judy Barton (also Kim Novak) and the cue that accompanies that rediscovery.

But all of that is of little importance. By separating the bulk of Herrmann's score from the film in an excellent performance that has been stunningly recorded, this Varèse Sarabande release reveals, perhaps better than even auditioning the music with the film, just how thoroughly the composer was in touch in his music (if most certainly not in his intellectual pronouncements on the subject) with the deepest levels of the film. From the outset, the score and the visuals make it clear that *Vertigo* is not about a *liebestodt*, in spite of all the comparisons that have been evoked between Herrmann's music and the Wagnerian "love death," but rather a kind of *totenlieb*, a love that is fueled not by the presence of a real woman but rather by the degree to which the woman is kept at a distance through voyeurism and, ultimately, being dead, both figuratively and literally. The waltz, for instance, has always been one of the great cine-musical signifiers of love. And so, early in the film, Herrmann subtly hides the presence of the waltz in the triplet figures of the title music and in the barely perceptible 6/8 meter of the theme for "Madeleine." But the love music does not get transformed into a full-blown waltz until the moment that Madeleine is about to tear herself away from Scottie to rush inside the tower from which she will apparently fall to her death. Thus does the waltz in Herrmann's score become a dance of death. And both the way Herrmann hides the 6/8 meter with "Madeleine's Theme" and the way Hitchcock's camera, the first time it shows "Madeleine," establishes its own gaze turn Herrmann's warm but wistful music not into a direct love theme but rather into a cue that might best be called "Madeleine Seen." Herrmann's music also perfectly captures the multiply-layered complexity of the Madeleine character and what she represents for Scottie: there is the haunting habañera theme for Carlotta Valdez, the long-dead great-grandmother whose spirit supposedly haunts Madeleine; there is the theme discussed above; and there is the love music, which itself has several phases. The musical progression in the "Farewell and Tower" cue stands as one of the keystone moments in all of film scoring. Opening with mysterious variations on the Carlotta Valdez music as Scottie and Madeleine visit San Juan Bautista for the first time, the score shifts to the love theme and then to a dramatic version of Madeleine's theme as

Madeleine, thanks to Scottie's detective work, apparently breaks free of the past. But the death/love waltz then takes over only to be replaced, as Madeleine enters the tower, by a variational reprise of the post-title "Rooftop" music, which announces the same, tragic conclusion. An almost vaporous duet for solo clarinet and high violins ensues as Hitchcock's overhead camera reduces the devastated Scottie to a speck in the eyes of the gods. In the history of film music, perhaps only Erich Wolfgang Korngold showed an equal gift for taking disparate, dramatically inspired musical cells and organizing them into a musically coherent flow.

Cues never offered before on recording also make a most welcome appearance here. The eerie music for the sequence in the sequoia forest, scored mostly for winds and muted brass, with occasional appearances of a dissonant chord from an electric organ, not only transforms the forest into an unsettling, gothic presence, it also provides a strangely tragic backing for Kim Novak's performance, in which she acts the role of a woman acting the role of a woman terrified by her inner demons. And while the "Scottie Tails Madeleine" cues would no doubt never pass muster in the conservatories, they manage for long, dialogue-less moments to sustain an enigmatic mood essential to our involvement in the film. In few of his scores does Herrmann play the strings, brass, and woodwind choirs against each other with such finesse and subtlety, while elsewhere the added timbres of vibraphone, harp, and electric organ create an overlay that might be called the *Vertigo* "sound." Happily, Varèse Sarabande has given Joel McNeely the space to thoroughly plumb both the musical and the emotional depths of the score, and the conductor has obliged with an inspired interpretation that is as fulfilling as a pure listening experience as it is as a musical re-creation of the entire film. His shaping of the pulse and instrumental interplays of the Prelude gives that cue a bit more of a dreamy quality than it has in other recorded performances (which have been numerous). McNeely also has a perfect sense of the subtle chordal and instrumental balances that are essential to the Herrmann sound. But when the moments of high drama come, McNeely captures every bit of the musical sweep that ultimately leads our emotions into that same, crushing void that swallows up *Vertigo*'s main protagonists. The Royal Scottish National Orchestra, while lacking a bit of entrance precision here and there (but nowhere near the scale of shoddy execution elicited by Muir Mathieson from the Sinfonia of London for the original music track), generally responds to McNeely's direction with sumptuous and committed playing. And then there is the sound: I have played parts of this CD for several people, and in every instance I have gotten gasps of admiration for the richness and warmth of the sound reproduction. The brass have a concert-hall depth to them, the woodwinds have incredible presence, the upper strings have that sheen and the lower strings that burr that many recordings, particularly digital ones, tend to kill. This is definitely a CD to take with you when you go shopping for new components for your stereo system. The extensive program notes, a pleasant surprise from Varèse Sarabande, are quite informative. But some of Kevin Mulhall's comments seem particularly off base. He describes the Pierre Boileau/Thomas Narcejac novel *D'entre les morts*, on which *Vertigo* is based, as "a free variation" on the *Tristan and Isolde* myth when the authors, who even have the Scottie character in their book call the Madeleine character "my little Eurydice" after he has fished her out of the water, seem instead to have been greatly inspired by the Orpheus myth. Mulhall also states that "the influence of the book on the script . . . was actually small." In fact, Vertigo follows the Boileau/Narcejac story line quite closely, although screenwriter Samuel Taylor did feel the need to add the character of Midge (Barbara Bel Geddes) to counterbalance Scottie's obsessional behavior with a dose of reality. And why does Mulhall feel that the "Rooftop" sequence that opens the film must be seen as a flashback? No matter. This is one of the great film-music recordings.

Speaking of Pierre Boileau and Thomas Narcejac, this team also wrote the novel Celle qui n'était plus (literally She Who No Longer Was), which French director Henri Georges Clouzot turned into his famous thriller Les Diaboliques. Indeed, it was apparently because of Hitchcock's interest in their earlier novel that Boileau and Narcejac churned out D'entre les morts, which takes the same kind of nasty and morbid plot twist as Celle qui n'était plus. I presume nobody would ever dream of remaking Vertigo, which is about as close to a perfect film as anyone will ever get. But I can imagine a new version taking Les Diaboliques into deeper waters (as it were). Unlike Vertigo, the rather bleak and dreary Les Diaboliques, as well made as it is, remains quite uninvolving once you know its plot twist. Already remade in 1974 as a TV movie, directed by John Badham, entitled Reflections of Murder, Les Diaboliques has now been the object of a theatrical remake directed by Jeremiah Chechik. Unfortunately, Chechik's **Diabolique** takes the story absolutely nowhere, even though, until the end, it follows the Clouzot version almost story cell for story cell. That may be one of the problems. One practically has the impression that director Chechik and screenwriter Don Roos presume a total knowledge on the viewer's part of the Clouzot film, so glibly does this Diabolique move from one narrative block to the next. After showing a minimal amount of interaction between two conspiring women (Sharon Stone and Isabelle Adjani), and between the two women and Adjani's male-pig husband (Chazz Palminteri), the film suddenly moves to an overly drawn-out scene in which the women execute an elaborate murder plot they are never shown concocting. And while the visualization of the story's plot twist could be made into a major jolt even for those who know that twist, Chechik shows such a poor sense of timing in presenting it that it becomes just another step forward in the story line. Never mind that the Chechik/Roos Diabolique shifts the narrative emphasis toward a rather kinky brand of male bashing. Indeed, this gives the character of a woman detective (Kathy Bates) the chance to utter the film's best line (to the neurotically saint-like Adjani): "It's not you. It's men. Testosterone. They should put it in bombs." But it is hard to get all worked up when the bashed (literally and figuratively) male in the film makes the would-be rapist in Thelma and Louise look like a masterpiece of character development. And why does Sharon Stone, who in her first shot has been made to look remarkably like Simone Signoret from the original film, seem to sport a different hairstyle almost every time the camera cuts back to her?

All of this is a shame, since Randy Edelman's subdued and dark-hued score (Edel/Morgan Creek) creates one hell of a mood from the title sequence right on through the entire picture. But the film is so stiff, disjointed, and unmotivated that it simply never gives that mood anything to attach itself to. So, in my opinion, by purchasing this music-track CD, you are getting the best part of *Diabolique*, and you can throw away the film. Mind you, if film music has its share of monothematic scores, Edelman's work here might be said to tend toward the monochord-progression. But as simple as it is, that chord progression, which opens the score and which might best be described as moving from the Georges Delerue of Godard's *Contempt* to the Paul Misraki of the same director's *Alphaville*, generates both a point of departure and a point of return for the considerable musical affect, and I found myself haunted by it. But Edelman does in fact provide a decent amount of additional music for *Diabolique*, none of which, fortunately, seems to have been influenced by the film's heavy-handedness. Between appearances of the chord progression, for instance, Edelman often allows the music to metamorphose into the kind of intense, minor-mode rhapsody with dissonant inner voices one finds in composers such as Sakamoto, Yared, and Senju, but fleshed out in somewhat more purely romantic directions that, in fact, hark back to Delerue without ever falling into the harmonic vapidity of which the latter composer is often guilty. The strings play a major role here, as does the solo piano, which Edelman himself performs. Even in the tauter suspense cues, Edelman often remains low-key, replacing the massive textures and cluster chords heard in so many suspense films with more airy scherzandos, sometimes enhanced by exhilarating, fast drumbeats that heighten the overall tension. The CD closes with a song entitled "In the Arms of Love," performed by Sherry Williams, ironically used to cover up the noises from the murder scene in the film. It might be interesting to see what sort of effect would be obtained if Edelman's score were to be laid in on the music track of the original *Les Diaboliques*, which has absolutely no music other than the melodramatic and rather bizarre title cue by Georges Van Parys, one piece of carnival source-music heard shortly after the murder, and about 15 seconds of end-title music.

Now, if it's dark you want, you need go no further than **Mary Reilly**, a brooding reverse-angle shot, based on Valerie Martin's novel, of Robert Louis Stevenson's *Dr. Jekyll and Mr. Hyde* as seen from the perspective of the good doctor's Irish maid, played in this film with remarkable sobriety by Julia Roberts. *Mary Reilly* brings back from the brilliant *Dangerous Liaisons* a whole host of talents, including director Stephen Frears, screenwriter Christopher Hampton, cinematographer Philippe Rousselot, production designer Stuart Craig, actors John Malkovich and Glenn Close, and George Fenton, who composed the film's hushed and moody score (Sony Classical; London Symphony Orchestra). Certainly, one of the real heroes of *Mary Reilly*, aesthetically at least, is production designer Craig. If *Mary Reilly* has a showstopper, it is that strange architectural space that seems to join a lecture hall to Dr. Jekyll's secret laboratory. With its precarious, chain-supported gangways, this set stunningly re-creates the universe of that lugubrious series of etchings, from 1745, by Giovanni Battista Piranese called *Prisons* (*Le carceri*). But I have to say that I found *Mary Reilly* a much more interesting and involving film as a whole than most people. In his capsule review in *The New Yorker*, Terrence Rafferty notes that *Mary Reilly* "is one of those genre pictures in which subtext has been promoted to text." Agreed. Yet neither Rafferty nor anyone else I have read seems to have understood the gist of that promoted subtext, which I imagine comes in the first place from Valerie Martin's novel. Frears' film, in the way it handles the flashback sequences involving Mary Reilly and her physically/sexually abusive father (one more super-ugly role for Michael Gambon), rather transparently sets up the Jekyll/Hyde character as the emblem of the patriarchal ethos that not only spawns such abuse but that also, tragically, puts women in the situation of loving their abusers. And thus for the first time does Dr. Jekyll become a less sympathetic character than his id-monster double. Indeed, Malkovich's Mr. Hyde comes across very much like the charming if treacherous seducer of *Dangerous Liaisons*. We've come a long way since the toady ghoul played by John Barrymore in the 1920 silent classic.

George Fenton is, to my mind, the film's other aesthetic hero, and his score certainly seconds the reading of *Mary Reilly* I have suggested above. One of the main themes, a solo violin melody probably based on an Irish folk tune and rendered particularly haunting by a rising, chromatic figure in the accompaniment, might best be described as an elegiac lullaby. Yet perhaps even more haunting is the motif for Jekyll/Hyde, a six-note figure with a rocking, minor sixth moving its bottom note down to form a major sixth while the tonic root moves up a half a step, thus creating within a single figure a consonance/dissonance shift that ever so subtly and ever so sadly suggests the two sides of the character. Several other motifs move wistfully in and out of a quiet musical canvas in which Fenton's typical string sonorities, enhanced by a woodwind here, a harp there, create an atmosphere that almost visually hangs over the house of Dr. Jekyll, which we rarely leave throughout the film. Fenton in fact excels throughout the score in creating sonorities, such as the bass flute over string basses heard toward the beginning of the "Mary Meets Hyde" cue, that seem to grow out of Philippe Rousselot's cinematography and the evocative sets. I also particularly like, later in that same cue, the subtly primitive percussion figures and the exotic rhythm that Fenton briefly introduces to suggest the new domain the heroine is entering. At very brief moments, the score acts as if it is going to take off into that kind of romantic/tragic sweep that characterizes Fenton's main theme for *Dangerous Liaisons*. But these moments generally die out before they have much of a chance to assert themselves. Fenton also effectively captures the nightmare frenzy of the "Shopping Trip." Generally, however, the tone remains dark, sad, and subdued, with only one cue, played by a honky-tonk piano to suggest the brothel/pub run by Mrs. Farrady (Glenn Close in a positively grotesque role), working against that overall mood. Even the recorded sound has a kind of cavernous quality to it that seems to move hand in hand with the set design.

September/October

Ostensibly, **Mulholland Falls,** the first American film from New Zealand director Lee Tamahori (*Once Were Warriors*), pays tribute to the Los Angeles noir genre of Raymond Chandler novels (and the like) and the films based on them. We get the late-'40s-early-'50s décor, filtered through haze from the cigarettes that just about everybody smoked, suggesting the twilight and twilit years of the old America. We get the impeccable but somewhat dowdy suits and wide-brim hats. We get the automobiles that are just starting to reveal a more design-conscious Detroit. We get a misty/bluesy score by Dave Grusin (Edel). And of course we get a quartet of hard-boiled L.A. cops (Nick Nolte, Chazz Palminteri, Michael Madsen, and Chris Penn) who are still able to work outside the law and the Constitution as they rid the city with ruthless efficiency of gangsters from New York City and Chicago. *Mulholland Falls* also offers the inevitable femme (Jennifer Connelly, who either makes Jayne Mansfield look like Twiggy or else has benefited from some amazing gown engineering and body-double photography) whose sexuality ends up being fatale to her and to the marriage of the Nolte character and his wife (Melanie Griffith). But director Tamahori casts just enough of a hyper-real aura, partially generated by a film-within-a-film self-reflexivity, over *Mulholland Falls* to keep everything from falling into pastiche. And so, if the original noir narratives and styles partially imply nostalgia for times that were not so noir, *Mulholland Falls* almost palpably creates nostalgia for that nostalgia.

A major factor in the fabric of this multilayered noir on noir is Grusin's music, by far the best work that the composer has done in some time, and one of three outstanding film scores 1996 has produced so far, the other two being *Diabolique* (also on Edel) and *Mary Reilly* (Sony Classical). Although Grusin can be put somewhat in the same category as the late Henry Mancini as a composer of sophisticated jazz sounds modified to fit the affective demands of Hollywood cinema, his music almost always reaches the emotions more indirectly and with a slightly harder edge. Mind you, Grusin can produce wonderful melodies. He proved this as of his first film score, *The Heart Is a Lonely Hunter*, which goes all the way back to 1968, and which has almost nothing to do with jazz. *Mulholland Falls* opens with an utterly haunting theme that has both the bluesiness to call forth the noir atmosphere and the harmonically (and instrumentally) generated moodiness to add the overlay of nostalgia. The closest thing I can think of to this is David Shire's wonderful title theme for the 1975 *Farewell, My Lovely*, the third film version of Chandler's novel of the same title. The main theme for *Mulholland Falls* turns up in various guises throughout the score, most achingly perhaps in the piano/strings version heard in the cue entitled "Just a Girl . . ." But, in a manner recalling one of the best of his earlier scores, the 1975 *Three Days of the Condor*, but perhaps even more subtly, Grusin introduces all sorts of quiet riffs and figures that grow out of jazz rhythms but that are somehow infused with sad, even tragic colors that grippingly attach themselves to the film. At several points in the score, Grusin ingeniously transforms and foregrounds a previously hidden accompaniment figure from the main theme, briefly shifting the balance from its initial dreaminess toward a mood dance that falls somewhere between Broadway ballet and Flamenco. It knocked me out of my seat when I first heard it during a screening of *Mulholland Falls*. Grusin also offers moments of action-specific but generally sotto voce suspense music, some of it militaristic—a major part of the film's narrative ties in with atomic age paranoia. On brief occasions the music flirts with other styles (Delerue and Barry come to mind, along with, would you believe, the Richard Rodney Bennett of *Murder on the Orient Express*' murkier cues). And at the end of the finale (just before the end-credit music), the score reveals some of its Americana roots. The CD, whose warm and resonant sound adds to the music's overall ambience, concludes with the high-voiced Aaron Neville performing a less than pleasing rendition of "Harbor Lights," a piece of source music that shows up early in the film. I've had the *Mulholland Falls* CD for about a month and a half now, and I've already listened to it, in whole or in part, about a dozen times.

Speaking of David Shire: one of the most respected and appreciated scores in film-music circles over the last two decades has been Shire's **The Taking of Pelham One Two Three**, composed in 1974 for director Joseph Sargent's film adaptation of John Godey's wildly popular book. Shire had two different areas of affect to communicate in his music. On the one hand, there is the ugly violence of the storyline: four hoods, headed by a British mercenary soldier between jobs (Robert Shaw), hijack a New York City subway car with its riders and give the city an hour to come up with a million dollars before they start killing off one passenger a minute. On the other hand, there is the whole feeling of working-class New York. As is reasonably well known, the composer's novel (particularly for the cinema) solution to this was to set a half-bop, half big-band jazz style in an atonal harmonic idiom in which for starters the opening theme, and later its retrograde inversion, have tone row written all over them. The resulting music rarely relents in its spine-jarring, harmonic austerity. But with much more standard fare from the rhythm section, including a Latin-flavored accompaniment for the main theme and a non-tonal walking bass in the two cues devoted to the ill-fated subway-system supervisor named Dolowitz (Tom Pedi), the listener may have a hard time deciding whether to snap his or her fingers or to bite the nails on them. Given all this musical sophistication and its multilayered, dramatic ambiguities, it is probably not surprising that, in spite of the film's popularity, no original music-track album was ever released. This situation has finally been remedied, and by none other than Lukas Kendall, publisher, editor, and lord-knows-what-else of *Film Score Monthly*, who has produced the release on a label called Retrograde. Made from the composer's own tapes (the original session tapes apparently no longer exist), this is one of those recordings that has been billed as "licensed for promotional and archival use only" and "not licensed for public sale." Anyway, besides capturing the distinctly opposing faces of the film's drama versus its setting, Shire's score also somewhat mirrors the mildly schizo nature of the film, which, in applying a rather heavy hand in portraying the working-stiff accents and behavior of the transit system employees and cops, continually shifts the film toward the comedic. I mean, you know you're in equivocal territory when one of the supervisors growls, "Screw the goddamn passengers. What the hell do they expect for their lousy thirty-five cents? To live forever?" As mayor of New York, Lee Wallace's Ed Koch clone (before or during the fact, I can't remember) plays the political fool against Tony Roberts' straight man. And if the final freeze-frame on Walter Matthau's bas-set-hound face doesn't cure you of having watched Robert Shaw electrocute himself, nothing will.

The film uses Shire's music quite sparingly, and in one sense this is not difficult to understand, since it is so strong and effective that a little bit of it goes a long way. The initial tone row, for instance, is divided into four equal groups of three pitches each, and the first three notes provide *The Taking of Pelham One Two Three* with a dissonant figure that pretty much encapsulates its entire violent side. The rising third that opens the jazzy accompaniment music also stands alone as a motif of sorts. When the Robert Shaw character first takes over the subway train, militaristic drum tattoos and atonal trumpet calls suggest his character's soldier-of-fortune background, while extremely dissonant, heavy chords in the brass evoke his current behavior (interestingly, the cue ends on a very tonal chord). Cues such as this do not need a good deal of time to make their point. One episode during the film when the music does get a chance to extend itself a bit is during the montage sequence in which the ransom money is being prepared at the bank. Parts of this cue drop down into a kind of quiet suspense jive, while at other points Shire changes the pace a bit with some rather Bartókian chords. Only in the end-title cue, after Matthau has said his last "Gesundheit," which will allow things at the transit police headquarters to return back to their crushingly boring routine, does Shire relax a bit with some moody big-band strains, but even here only after the two tone rows (the retrograde inversion coming first at this point) have had their say. This CD offers the entire score as Shire composed it, including five cues not used in the film, the best of which is the minute-long, walking-bass jam session ("Dolowitz Takes a Look"), which seems like pretty standard fare save that not one second of it hits a tonal base. The recorded sound, some of it in stereo, some in mono, has a good deal of presence and a dry, studio ambience to it that works well for the music. The program notes include an extensive analysis of the score by Doug Adams, who also wrote an excellent article on *Pelham One Two Three* for the April 1996 *Film Score Monthly*, and some comments by Kendall.

November/December

One of the most independent of the independent directors these days is Jim Jarmusch, whose most recent film, **Dead Man**, may be his most offbeat and, for some, off-putting venture yet. If the black-and-white *Dead Man*, for all of its new directions, were not so solidly rooted in the Jarmusch tradition of such films as *Stranger Than Paradise*, *Down by Law*, and *Mystery Train* in particular, one might be tempted to describe it, stylistically, as an amalgam of Spaghetti Western, Jean-Luc Godard, and Robert Altman, with perhaps a bit of late John Ford thrown in for good measure. The film features Johnny Depp in yet one more role as an innocent in over his head. In this case, he plays a Candide-like character named William Blake (of whose poetry he is totally ignorant) who leaves his native Cleveland to become an accountant for a company in the very far West. By the time he fights his way past a sneering clerk (John Hurt) only to be told by the firm's head, a classic, gun-loving wacko played by none other than

Robert Mitchum, that he doesn't have a job, Blake, like Candide, finds himself involuntarily caught up in hideously ugly violence, in this case that of white America, that has absolutely no meaning for him. Forced to kill a jealous husband (Gabriel Byrne) in self-defense and wounded in the process, Blake "spends the rest of the film dying," as Jonathan Rosenbaum puts it in an excellent article/interview appearing in *Cineaste* 22, no. 2. Or, to put it another way, Blake ultimately discovers that the garden he must cultivate is death. The person who prepares Blake's voyage "back to the place where all the spirits came from, and where all the spirits return," as it is put in Jarmusch's wonderful screenplay, is a Native American named Nobody (of course), who quotes the other William Blake and who is continually bemused—and annoyed—by the stupidity of the white man. As played by Gary Farmer, Nobody may now stand as the prototype of the ironic, drolly detached character that is the essence of Jarmusch's vision. Not without resorting to violence himself, Nobody leads William Blake through the wilderness, past a bounty hunter (Lance Henriksen) who kills his two colleagues and eats one of them, and past a group of cowboys that includes Iggy Pop in drag, to his final resting place in a bedecked canoe set adrift on the waters.

What kind of music could possibly be appropriate for a film of this nature, you might well ask. Well, Jarmusch, like most great directors working outside the system, has never been able to force the visual and the musical elements of his pictures into the shape of the narrative and its various events. From the outset of *Dead Man*, for instance, he establishes a hypnotic, visual rhythm through the use of frequent fadeouts whose pacing has nothing to do with the action on the screen. And for the music, Jarmusch sat composer/performer Neil Young down in front of a two-and-a-half-hour rough cut of the film and asked him to improvise a score. The result, much of which can be heard on a Vapor Records CD, is a piece of almost pure mood which, while about as far from action-specific as you can get, weds itself to the feeling of the picture about as thoroughly as any score I can think of. *Dead Man*, for instance, for all of its Old West action and settings, has a decidedly contemporary feel to it. And so the music, although centered mostly on the timbres of an instrument often musically associated with the Old West, the guitar, sends those timbres through the amplifier of an electric guitar well past the point of distortion. For all of the raucous, sonic breakup, however, there is a softness and a tenderness to Young's music, which at times is made up of little more than a minimal, if not Minimalist, single-note, repeated figures. At other times Young sketches out a theme in a slow, laconic drawl not unlike what one might get from a Ry Cooder in similar circumstances. One rather mournful theme in particular seems to dominate the music, and it was quite possibly inspired by a Native American melody. Further, a major element of the rhythms established by Jarmusch at the outset of the film, with its fadeouts and frequent cutaways to moving steam-engine wheels, comes from the throbbings and audio distortion of Young's electric guitar. Here and there, Young deploys a few other timbres, including, I think, those of a harmonium. This recording includes much of Young's music, along with some sound effects and a fair amount of dialogue from the film. Over the music, we also get to hear Johnny Depp reading, quite effectively, from

William Blake, something his character in the film would have never thought to do. Just how much meaning this CD will have for anyone who has not seen the film is uncertain. Having seen *Dead Man*, however, I found that this recording, including Depp's out-of-character readings, in many ways re-created the whole experience for me. Although I generally do not like the intrusion of dialogue in a film-score recording, here I found it welcome, particularly the lines inimitably spoken by Gary Farmer. It was also great to have the dialogue, with brief music, from the extended scene in which Iggy Pop appears. *Dead Man* is definitely one of the great American movies of 1996, and it also shows an amazingly effective alternate route that film music can take.

CHAPTER FOURTEEN

~

1997

January/February

Two things got John Carpenter's *Escape from L.A.*, a sequel to—some would say a remake of—his 1981 *Escape from New York*, off on the right foot, at least for me. The first is the clever computer graphics of the title sequence, which in many instances suggest a kind of degree zero of the very wide-screen, Panavision image the audience is watching. This self-reflexivity carries over into several other points as well. Early on, for instance, a hologram demonstration expands from the old 1.33:1 aspect ratio to Panavision's 2.35:1. Carpenter also makes references to some of his other movies, in particular *Assault on Precinct 13*. And Peter Fonda sacrifices himself to one of the broadest self-parodies you'll find in the cinema. Of course, one can predict five or 10 minutes ahead of time just about everything that will take place in the film's (slightly) futuristic narrative, which involves a super anti-hero-criminal named Snake Plisskin (Kurt Russell, who may look better now than he did 15 years ago) sent in to retrieve, not rescue, the President's daughter in an L.A. that has been separated from the mainland by an earthquake and turned into an isle of exile for any and all who do not toe the line of the radical-right politics that have taken over the US of A. But Carpenter continues to have a flair for this kind of bowels-of-the-darkness violence, and the fact that here, as in his vastly underrated (and very funny) *They Live* from 1988, he confronts, in his own weird way, the fascist conservatism that is trying to take over in this country does not hurt any. I also love the way Carpenter early on sets up the film's (again self-reflexive) ending by having the forces who send Plisskin into L.A. give him an ordinary book (box?) of matches amidst all of the sophisticated weaponry.

The second thing that got *Escape from L.A.* started off right for me was the reprise on the music track, during the title sequence, of the main theme, composed by Carpenter and Alan Howarth, for *Escape from New York*. Carpenter, of course, provided no small amount of emotional and sub-emotional impact for such early films as Assault on Precinct 13 and Halloween by composing his own scores for them. Simple to the nth, these electronically generated scores, built around brief, obsessive figures, with a kind of Mike Oldfield ostinato added to the Halloween music, have a crude and primitive quality to them that moves in perfect sync with the reasonably consistent vision the director has communicated in his films over the last two decades. As Carpenter's success took him into larger-budget filmmaking, he began to bring in other composers either to aid and abet him or in some cases, as with Ennio Morricone for the 1982 The Thing (although there is at least one cue in that score that Carpenter surely composed or improvised), write the entire score. As indicated on the Varèse Sarabande recording, the score for Escape from New York was "composed and performed by John Carpenter in association with Alan Howarth," who is also given credit for "recording, editing, sequencing and synthesizer programming." One suspects, however, that Howarth also had a hand in fleshing out the main theme with some nice, open-fourth harmonies and perhaps even in providing a bridge. One can just hear the conversation: "Come on, John. You've gotta take this somewhere!" To which I would answer, "Not necessarily," since Carpenter, both narratively and musically, tends to work mostly in vertical directions, while Western music, as soon as it acquires any polish, has a strong horizontal component. For the music for Escape from L.A. (Milan), Carpenter turned to Shirley Walker, who worked with him on Memoirs of an Invisible Man and whose work in the film industry has been largely as an orchestrator and a conductor. Besides the title theme, rather unfortunately fleshed out and popped up here from the original version, Carpenter contributed two of his own cues to the score. The first, "Snake's Uniform," is a brief piece for electric bass, electric guitar, harmonica, and (acoustic!) percussion that strongly harks back to Assault on Precinct 13. The second, entitled "Showdown," features the solo harmonica and a hammer dulcimer in a mostly quiet cue that could easily fit, like Russell's Clint Eastwood speech patterns, into a spaghetti Western—more self-reflexivity. Two other cues are apparently a Carpenter/Walker collaboration, while the remaining 11 are pure Walker creations.

In his extremely informative program notes, Daniel Schweiger quotes Shirley Walker as follows: "This sequel was an opportunity to get away from the big orchestral stuff that everybody in town knew I could do. I was able to compose in another style, starting with an homage to John Carpenter. His music is very direct, minimalist and synthy. Using John's approach made me think about what would happen if I didn't play everything. At our first meeting, we talked about how to retain that quality for Escape from L.A. while bringing a symphonic element to the film. Though it's there throughout the score, we wanted the orchestra to become noticeable halfway through the film, and to build exponentially from there." Well, that is precisely the effect that both the film and the Milan CD produce. Early cues, even though more fleshed out, have that "synthy," harmonically obsessive, Johnny-one-motif quality that marks Carpenter's style. Walker also has a flair for funky percussion motifs, which show up in several of the early cues. As the film moves along, the music begins to sound more and more like a traditional movie score, as if the escape from L.A. does not include an escape from Hollywood. Some particularly solemn strains in the final cue reminded me of the opening (and closing) of Elmer Bernstein's wonderful music for *Summer and Smoke*. Elsewhere, Walker's music ranges from quietly jazzy to dissonant big band, with stops along the way at the doors of Shostakovich and Bartók, all of it quite effectively creating moods that work extremely well with the film, in spite or perhaps because of the fact that they do not quite jell with Carpenter's gritty cynicism.

Of course, if you want a well-made Hollywood suspense film that does what well-made Hollywood suspense films do best, namely the total manipulation of your emotions into a good/evil frenzy that leaves no room for any subtleties, you could do worse than **A Time to Kill**, one of several John Grisham thriller novels to be brought to the screen. Set in the modern-day South, A *Time to Kill* opens with the rape and near murder of a black girl by two white rednecks, whom the girl's father wastes little time in gunning down. But the real drama is about how a young, white lawyer (Matthew McConaughey) is going to fight off an especially nasty D.A. (Kevin Spacey, who seems disquietingly comfortable with especially nasty roles) in cahoots with an only slightly less nasty judge (Patrick McGoohan), a resurgent Ku Klux Klan (at the instigation of Kiefer Sutherland, who also excels at especially nasty roles), the black establishment, and the advances of an exceptionally rich and (truly) exceptionally gorgeous law student intent on helping him (Sandra Bullock), so that he can save a) the black man and b) his marriage while in the process c) losing his house, and d) nearly losing the (truly) exceptionally gorgeous law student (to the Klan), e) his client (to the black establishment), f) his dog (a key instrument of well-made-Hollywood-suspense-film manipulation), g) his reputation, and h) his marriage. In classic well-made-Hollywood-suspense-thriller fashion, A *Time to Kill* manages to glue you to the screen while being totally predictable and straining your credibility at almost every step.

Given its character and plot structure, its cast of powerhouse actors and its taut direction by Joel Schumacher, one would have a right to wonder just how much more drama could be brought to A *Time to Kill* by a musical score, and as I watched the film I was consciously aware that the music was doing little or nothing to get me more involved in the drama. I was also aware, however, that the score by Elliot Goldenthal (Atlantic Classics; Jonathan Sheffer, cond.) was of a good deal more than passing interest musically. As usual for a Goldenthal score, there are frequent passages with absolutely no tonal center and lots of big dissonances at various volume levels. At one particularly effective moment, Goldenthal ominously slips a quiet but massive string cluster, beefed up here and there by snarling brass, in behind a gospel song performed by The Jones Sisters. Goldenthal also gives A *Time to Kill* its own instrumental profile. In the opening cue, a hammer dulcimer (which sounds like a less throaty cimbalom) and a pennywhistle establish an almost Irish-countryside ambience that nervous string figures and an occasional drumbeat almost immediately shatter. The composer also brings in a harmonica (A *Time to Kill* takes place in the South, remember), very often in growly spurts that undercut the down-home lyricism stereotypically associated with that instrument. In the quickly paced music that follows the gospel-song episode, the harmonica becomes one of many instruments to make brief intrusions, sometimes limited to a single note, into the orchestral miasma. In an early cue, Goldenthal similarly disfigures the timbres of a saxophone, only to bring out, a few cues later, the instrument's full lyrical potential in one of the variations on a haunting, very tonal pavane-lament that provides *A Time to Kill* with most of its musical affect. Even in situations that almost always call for underscoring, such as the abduction of the Sandra Bullock character, the composer comes up with novel solutions to old film/music problems, in this case a solo violin that does a kind of grotesque dance around a four-note ostinato figure once the music has turned atonal after an initially violent upheaval in which the harmonica has played its usual unconventional role. Elliot Goldenthal is probably one of the most gifted musicians working in the film-music business today, and I'm not sure that anybody has yet figured out how to take full advantage of those gifts.

In his very brief program comment for the music-track recording of Ry Cooder's music for **Last Man Standing** (Verve), director Walter Hill writes, "He's done nine scores for me—I think this is one of the best." OK. So why, one wonders, did Hill originally turn to Elmer Bernstein for a score that was eventually thrown out? Because of Bernstein's association, via *The Magnificent Seven*, with the revisionist American Western, which *Last Man Standing* purports in part to be? What, one also wonders, did a reputable director such as Hill have in mind by doing such a mindless, humorless remake with Bruce Willis of Akira Kurosawa's *Yojimbo*, which has already benefited from a dynamite redoing in Sergio Leone's *A Fistful of Dollars*? Why, furthermore, does Hill emphasize *Yojimbo* over *A Fistful of Dollars* in his pronouncements on the film, since the desolate, western setting of *Last Man Standing*, which features a lone killer coming into town and selling his considerable talents to both sides in a blood feud (here between the Italian and the Irish mafias), definitely evokes the Leone film, as do a fair number of details, such as the trashing of Willis' car à la Eastwood's mule at the beginning of the film. And did Hill really think people would get heavily involved in a film whose principal action involves Bruce Willis bursting into rooms like a gangbuster with two guns a'blazing? I do, however, have to agree with Hill on the quality of Ry Cooder's score, which is by far the best thing about *Last Man Standing*. I feel a little bit like the Billy Crystal character in *Throw Mama from the Train* looking for just the right word, here to describe the Cooder sound, only to have Danny DeVito's mother (the late Anne Ramsey) come up with "sultry." Yes. Sultry. That's it. Much of the music in this long score has that typical Cooder lazy and somewhat ominous sultry quality to it, particularly in cues such as the one entitled "We're Quits," built around a slow dialogue between a very resonant electric bass (for which there is probably a specific name) and an acoustic guitar. And I love the way the composer often brings his characteristic portamentos into the low bass. Cooder also makes extremely effective use of the slightly spacey sounds of synthesized strings in sustained chords into which wander all sorts of brief but evocative timbres. Indeed, as if to further complicate the ethnic overtones of *Last Man Standing*, Cooder, in addition to his usual guitars, keyboards, electric bass, percussion, and synth, mobilizes such exotic instruments as a bamboo flute, a "Soenap Flute" (whatever that is), various Indian percussion instruments, and a zarb. In the cue entitled "Felina," the two flutes join in an extraordinarily haunting duet with the zarb (I presume) and other instruments adding an atmosphere that is all but palpable. In another cue ("Lucy's Ear"), Cooder does a great slow blues on a steel (I think) guitar while various electronic timbres wail quietly but ominously in the background. Baritone sax and vibraphone play a dreamy blues duet in "Bathtub." I also particularly like the totally nontonal droning of various sounds, electronic and acoustic (including vibraphone), of "Felina Drives." We even get a dramatic cathedral organ (or a good synth equivalent of same) and a (sampled?) vocalizing soprano in one cue ("Drive to Slim's"). Given all of *Last Man Standing*'s empty bullet cartridges clinking onto corpse-strewn floors, one would expect a fair amount of action music from Cooder's score, but this does not turn out to be the case. Here and there the composer tautens things up with some low ostinato, and/or fast percussion tattoos and/or raucous electronic effects. At points in "Find Him," things get positively chaotic for brief moments. In between this and the more, um, sultry material is the pop/jazz mood Cooder establishes in the Main and End Titles. But the overall atmosphere remains low key as the music moves from one configuration of timbres to the next. In many ways, this is an amazing score that reveals sides of Cooder that have not shown up anywhere near this extent in his previous efforts.

A compilation of newly recorded orchestral suites from one of the classic film scorers is the Volume 4 of **Legends of Hollywood: Franz Waxman** (Varèse Sarabande; Queensland Symphony Orchestra, Richard Mills, cond.). The scores represented here include *Untamed*, *On Borrowed Time*, *My Geisha*, *The Devil Doll*, *My Cousin Rachel*, *The Story of Ruth*, *Dark City*, and *A Christmas Carol*. Waxman, although no slouch as a melodist, never, unlike, say, a Victor Young, let his often memorable themes run away with everything. Even, for instance, in the fullest presentation of the big theme from *My Geisha*, which became a popular tune under the title "You Are Sympathy to Me," there is always something interesting and unconventional going on either in the orchestrations or in the harmonic structures . . . or both. I also like the way Waxman, in the same score, subtly integrates the occasional oriental sounds into the score's overall fabric rather than letting them dominate the music, as many Hollywood composers would have. The main theme for the 1952 *My Cousin Rachel* is particularly fascinating in that it recalls not so much Waxman's music for another Daphne du Maurier novel, *Rebecca*, which director Henry Koster had in mind when he went to make *My Cousin Rachel*, but rather the composer's score for Hitchcock's *The Paradine Case*, which deals with a similar subject, namely a mysterious woman (here Olivia de Havilland) who may or may not have killed her husband. Particularly welcome, too, is the music from William Dieterle's 1950 film noir *Dark City*. The drive generated by the opening three minutes of the "Finale" is as dynamic and electric as you'll hear from this type of score. But I also like the quiet, bluesy mood Waxman was able to create for the suite's middle movement, "Stroll in the Dark," which very subtly alludes to a Loesser/Styne song, "I Don't Want to Walk Without You" associated with the Lizbeth

Scott character in the film. *The Story of Ruth*, directed in 1960 by Henry Koster and heard here in a three-part suite, is one of Waxman's most tense and dramatic scores. The score for *A Christmas Carol*—the 1938 version with Reginald Owen as Scrooge— is a wonderfully varied compilation in which the composer wittily integrates every-thing from Christmas carols to Handel's famous Sarabande into the musical canvas, concluding with a full-blown "Hark the Herald Angels Sing" that will send chills down your spine. *Untamed* has a good deal of dash and excitement, while *On Bor-rowed Time* is jauntily charming. I could, however, have done without the suite of characterless waltzes from the 1936 *The Devil Doll*. Richard Mills conducts this music with wonderful verve and sensitivity to the music's dramatic implications, and the recorded sound is particularly warm and rich.

March/April

In an interview I did with him a few years ago, composer David Raksin, reflecting on the difficulties he had coming up with the title theme for *Laura*, said, "As I'm sure you know, I can write tunes faster than most people can inhale and exhale." What mod-esty may have kept him from adding is that he can also write *memorable* tunes, per-haps not at quite the same speed but certainly with greater frequency than most mu-sicians, film scorers or otherwise. And certainly one of the most memorable of those tunes is the frequently recurring "siren song" created for the 1952 **The Bad and the Beautiful**, the complete, original music tracks for which have now been released in Rhino's admirable "Movie Music" series (monaural). Produced by John Houseman, directed by Vincente Minnelli, and featuring a large cast of major stars, including Lana Turner, Kirk Douglas, Walter Pidgeon, and Dick Powell, not to mention Barry Sullivan, Gloria Grahame (who won a Best Supporting Actress Oscar for her por-trayal of Powell's southern-belle wife), Gilbert Roland, Leo G. Carroll, and Vanessa Brown, *The Bad and the Beautiful* is, if such a thing is possible, a piece of loving self-flagellation that examines the ugly side of the motion-picture business by focusing on a single-minded, ambitious producer (Douglas) who a) cans his director/partner and best friend (Sullivan) as soon as he gets the chance to make a non-B movie; b) feigns love in order to get an alcoholic actress (Turner) off the bottle and back into her role; and c) sets up, with tragic results, the southern belle with an actor (Roland) in order to get her out of the hair of her husband/writer (Powell) so that he can finish his screenplay.

All this is pretty ugly stuff, and even though the narrative mildly counterbalances it with a mildly optimistic final shot and, throughout, with some weak protestations from a studio boss (Pidgeon) as to how the producer, for all his manipulations, in fact got each of his three victims started on a major career, one wonders just how *The Bad and the Beautiful* would come across without Raksin's score. The music is dominated, although to a lesser extent than *Laura* is with its main theme, by an utterly haunting blues melody, usually carried either by the high strings or an alto saxophone, that is the "siren song" requested by Producer Houseman. Characteristically for Raksin, the theme has an elusive, rhythmic asymmetricality to it, in this case created by the division of its two phases into a group of 10 bars followed by a group of nine (in contrast, the bridge, heard less often, has the standard two groups of eight bars each). And although it was dubbed a "siren song," the theme has a decidedly instrumental cast to it—it is hard to imagine anybody even considering putting words to it as Johnny Mercer did for "Laura." But, in fact, Dorey Previn did just that. More to the point, perhaps, is the fact that this theme does not attach itself to any particular character or situation: we are about as far from a leitmotif score here as it is possible to get. Instead, the siren song weaves its way in and out of *The Bad and the Beautiful's* action, coloring it with hues of sadness and resignation while at moments suggesting a possible optimism. Once in a while, a timbre change carries the melody into darker corners, as when a muted trombone accompanies the moment when the actress just gives up (in the cue entitled "Lonely Girl"). Raksin also ingeniously hides pieces of the theme in unlikely spots, such as the dirge initially heard during the funeral of the producer's father and later reprised at the moment of the betrayal of the director. (If memorable themes are a Raksin forte, so are highly charged moments of tragedy, such as in the "Plague" sequence in *Forever Amber* or the march to Golgotha in *The Redeemer*. The two dirges here are only a notch or so below this in intensity.) But by and large Raksin's haunting theme and its various metamorphoses are there to activate our emotions in all of their ambiguous glory rather than to manipulate them by pointing in certain action-specific directions.

While Raksin himself has conducted a 16-minute suite from *The Bad and the Beautiful* on a sumptuously recorded RCA Victor CD, it is wonderful to have the entire score available, even in the often less-than-ideal monaural sound on the Rhino release, which was taken from a sometimes defective quarter-inch dub of the original, stereo music tracks, which, as has happened with depressing frequency, somehow got destroyed. We get to hear a fair amount of scherzo-like, very Americana cues that accompany transitions and moments of Hollywood hustle and bustle. Some of these come across as polyrhythmic. We get to hear some in-joke musical satire, whether the cowboys-and-Indians fragment that accompanies a take from one of the producer's "B" films or a piece of modal solemnity that accompanies the shooting of a "Phrygian Wedding." Rhino also offers a fair number of outtakes, the most poignant of which is the ineffably sad music that accompanies a set of scenes, cut from the film, in which the producer works, with feigned romantic nudgings, at getting the actress back on track. The composer himself must have had major respect for the unused music, since it turns up in the suite recorded by RCA. Totally intriguing in a different vein is the brief cue entitled "The Dark," in which sustained, low, dissonant, piano chords captured after the initial attack create a slightly tongue-in-cheek ambience as the producer and his best-friend director hash out, in an almost darkened projection room, how they will put together their "B" horror picture. Almost as invaluable as the music are the 15 pages of program commentary by Raksin himself, who gets thanked after his notes for his "unadulterated goodness, unending generosity, and unyielding wit," all of which can be felt in both his verbal and his musical notes. This is a model of how film-music recordings should be presented. One final comment: the Motion Picture Academy should get off its collective derriere and offer David Raksin a lifetime achievement award. Besides the fact that such a tribute is richly deserved and long overdue, Raksin, at the age of 84, remains a vivacious raconteur, and his presence at the Oscar ceremonies would considerably enliven that crushingly boring event. It is time for Hollywood to stop waiting until its after-the-fact awardees have to be unembalmed to receive their just due.

A couple of days before this past Thanksgiving, I gave David Raksin a call at his home in California to get some clarification on a few things about *The Bad and the Beautiful* not mentioned in his voluminous program notes. Here is some of that conversation:

R.S.B.: How did you get involved in *The Bad and the Beautiful*? Was it through John Houseman?

D.R.: I think what happened is that Benny Herrmann wanted to do the picture. I don't know whether Houseman was with him on this or not—it's just possible he was not, since John was pretty astute about things. How Benny would have been on the picture I don't know. In any case, MGM would not have it. So apparently, Benny, or so he or somebody said, recommended me to Houseman. Well, Houseman knew me for years, and that's how I got on the picture.

R.S.B.: Your main theme is pretty sophisticated. How did it go over?

D.R.: I was trying to figure out how the hell you reduce the theme to 10 fingers, which isn't easy, because it's a complicated piece. But I realized that I was going to have to sell it in some way, which is not my forte, to John [Houseman] and [Director] Vincente [Minnelli]. So I said to John Green [head of MGM's music department], "Look. I can't play this well enough. Why don't you let me make a demo." And he said, "Sure." So I went on the stage and recorded a version of it, which I orchestrated myself. And then I took the acetate and went over to Vincente's place. John was there as well as a couple of other people. So I played it for them. Blank stares. That usually means "the end." Well, the other two people piped up and said, "Wow! What a fabulous tune. Do you mind if he plays it again?" I played it again, and they said, "One more time!" And by the end of that Vincente and John decided they liked it. Those two people were [Betty] Comden and [Adolph] Green. They were there to visit Vincente, and fortunately their sophistication saved the day.

R.S.B.: How did you structure the music? It certainly isn't a leitmotif score.

D.R.: Actually, there are three different sets. There's one for the first third, which is with the director. The theme itself is used only in the middle [dealing with the actress]. But the whole final part has material that is all based on it, like that scherzo: it's all based on the theme. The last part, the one with Dick Powell, has a different theme. In this case, the picture is about Jonathan [Kirk Douglas] and this so-called charisma that he has. And so the job of the music is, as John said, a siren song to persuade you in a way that words cannot do.

R.S.B.: Did you have as much trouble writing this theme as you did writing *Laura?*

D.R.: I didn't have a lot of trouble writing *Laura.* I just wrote a lot of themes, and I didn't think any of them were good enough.

R.S.B.: O.K.! Did you have to write as many themes to come up with this one?

D.R.: I don't know exactly whether I wrote other music. I may or may not have. Strangely enough, I never thought of that. But when I actually got around to it, bam! there was the tune. I don't elaborate my tunes, and I don't add phony chords to them or things like that. People think I do, but I don't. I'm that way by nature.

R.S.B.: I can't imagine this theme with lyrics. Do they work?

D.R.: They're really not bad. As a matter of fact, Mike Feinstein has recorded it in a wonderful arrangement.

R.S.B.: What about those piano chords that you use in the cue called "The Dark"? Did you just record them after the attack, or did you modify them in other ways?

D.R.: I've done that many times. I started doing that at Universal years ago, and then I did it at Fox in some of the grue and horror pictures, and then I did it in *Laura* in the apartment scene, except that these don't have the vibrato I used in *Laura.* I recorded them after the attack and then cut them in so that they were on two adjoining tracks so that they would overlap ever so slightly.

R.S.B.: You're writing your autobiography now, aren't you?

D.R.: Yes. Also, the people who publish *Sheet Music* have just published a book of my songs and other themes.

Speaking of Bernard Herrmann. . . . In fact, it seems as if I'm speaking even more of Bernard Herrmann than ever before, and that's saying something. If there is a composer who is more "in" these days, film or otherwise, I don't know who it would be. Students tell me that the music for *Vertigo* seems to be showing up at least twice a day on one of New York's classical-music stations, and there has been a veritable deluge of new Herrmann recordings over the past year or so. [One of the most recent] is from Varèse Sarabande (VSD-5759; Muir Mathieson, cond.; Robert Townson, prod.) and offers the original music tracks of Herrmann's score for *Vertigo.* "What's this?" you ask. "Didn't Varèse Sarabande just bring out a gorgeous new recording of most of the score with Joel McNeely conducting the Royal Scottish National Orchestra? And isn't the original music-track recording still available from Mercury?" The answer to both questions is yes. But there are two catches. The first is that this new music-track release is a byproduct of the restoration of *Vertigo* done by Robert A. Harris and James C. Katz. This restoration ended up in a 70-millimeter, VistaVision print that, as I write, is still showing in theaters around the country, including New York City's mammoth Ziegfeld Theater, where I saw it this past Halloween. Among the elements that were cleaned up by Harris and Katz were the music and sound tracks, resulting in a stereo presentation of both the sound and music that had many people beaming, while others complained that *Vertigo's* aural components now overbalanced the picture as a whole. The latter was not my impression. While I don't claim to have a solid memory of the quality of the print that I saw when the film was first released in the summer of 1958 (but I'm quite sure it did not have stereo sound), my impression in watching *Vertigo* on the Ziegfeld's huge screen was that this experience was not all that different from the one filmgoers used to have in the days when theaters were not multiplexed down to the size of a large living room, and when projectionists did not spend their time playing video games while the film ran through the system from a single, giant reel. The image at the Ziegfeld was so sharp and so large that it had me constantly looking past the main action to see what details Hitchcock and his crew put into the backgrounds. The stereo sound was a bit disconcerting at first, since I had only heard the picture in mono to that point. But there was nothing jolting or flamboyant about it. And while I did notice certain sounds for the first time—Madeleine's body thumping on the roof of San Juan Bautista's chapel, for instance—other sounds, such as the clanking in the rooftop sequence when the bad guy comes up the fire escape, are not even as loud as they appear on the MCA laserdisc currently available or on a 16-millimeter print I have seen. On one or two dialogue-less occasions Herrmann's musical score did rather overwhelm everything else. But on the whole the Harris/Katz restoration works beautifully, precisely because one walks away with the feeling that this is the way *Vertigo* was meant to be seen and heard.

The second catch is that Varèse Sarabande's new music-track release contains almost twice the amount of music as the original Mercury release. This would have been even more exciting had the McNeely recording not already filled in most of the gaps, but considerable advantages still remain. One of these is that the extended, droning cues, mostly for clarinets and strings, that accompany James Stewart as he follows Kim Novak in his car, are heard here in their original, slowish tempos, whereas McNeely speeds them up a bit, which I found slightly disconcerting. Missing from this recording are the cues entitled "The Graveyard" and "Tombstone," the music tracks of which were too badly damaged to be used (Harris and Katz were fortunately able to unearth a music-and-effects reel in Spain for the restoration). But McNeely offers a wholly satisfactory version of them. This new release, on the other hand, does contain three cues that do not appear on the McNeely CD: 1) "Mission Organ," a brief snippet in which the electric organ that adds eerie timbres to parts of the score presents itself as pipe organ doing some Bachish modulations; 2) very moving variations on earlier material, including the love theme and the Carlotta Valdez music, in "The Past"; 3) more variations on the love theme and a piece of Mickey-Mousing that follows Stewart's rising gaze to Novak's hotel room in "The Girl." Still missing is the cue entitled "The Hotel," which starts off with an imposing variation on the Carlotta Valdez music in the low strings. The recorded sound on this new, original music-track recording of *Vertigo* is similar to what one hears on the abbreviated Mercury release, save that some of the cues are in mono, due to a change of the recording venue from London, where the musicians staged a sympathy strike, to studios in Vienna, which were apparently either not inclined and/or not equipped to record in stereo. That sound is fairly dry and up-close, and a few, brief moments of music not offered by Mercury definitely reveal substantial tape deterioration. Note for instance how the dry sound highlights the extremely *détaché* flute playing in the title music, whereas that instrument is barely audible on the McNeely recording.

As anyone involved in film music is aware, Howard Shore, surely one of the busiest of movie composers these days, has spent much of his career working in some of the cinema's darkest corners, in spite of the occasional *Mrs. Doubtfires*. Those dark corners include almost all of the work of David Cronenberg, from such early masterpieces of the grotesque and bizarre as *Scanners* and *Videodrome* all the way through to the director's most recent film, *Crash*. Shore's music also pulls viewers and listeners irretrievably into the depths of gloom in such pictures as *The Silence of the Lambs* and even more frighteningly in *Se7en*. Within that perspective, King Richard III of England as portrayed by William Shakespeare seems the perfect candidate for Shore's music. Indeed, Shakespeare's broadly painted themes in *Richard III*, described by Shore in a conversation I had with him this past July as "death, betrayal, killing, seething, anger, love," are the stuff that operas are made of. But there is a catch. **Looking for Richard**, which Al Pacino, as director, writer, and actor, put together over the last four years, is not simply a film version of Shakespeare's *The Tragedy of King Richard the Third*. Part documentary, part *Richard III*, with Pacino (brilliantly) playing the title role, the film spends a good deal of time cutting back and forth between the play itself and discussions of both Shakespeare in general and Richard III in particular both with people off the street as well as with actors, Shakespeare experts, and various contributors to the making of *Looking for Richard*, including co-producer Michael Hadge. As composer Shore describes this multifaceted experience, "It's the relationship of Pacino to himself and also as Richard. You see him as a bunch of different people in the movie. He's the director, and he's the writer, and he's Al Pacino in the movie with his baseball hat on [backward], and he's Richard as a street person—a contemporary Richard—and he's a fully costumed, Elizabethan Richard. And he's talking about it all. You're getting a lot of levels of information about this particular play and how he approached it." To this I would add that Pacino's multi-tiered, half-documentary/half-Shakespeare-play approach is communicated on yet another level by some of the most original editing to ever turn up in an American studio film. Boiled down from some 80 hours of footage, *Looking for Richard* cuts without warning not only between the various Pacinos but also from various facets of the documentary to parts of play, some of which get repeated in and out of costume, thereby undercutting the normal senses of causality and continuity that have been the sine qua non of American montage since the days of Griffith.

As for the music (Angel; London Voices; London Philharmonic Orchestra), Shore feels that the documentary side of *Looking for Richard* freed him from the usual conventions of action-specific film scoring, since it allowed him to concentrate on the play itself: "In a sense, I felt as if I was writing my version of *Richard III*, which could then be applied to the film. That's different for me. It's interesting how the music relates to the movie, because it's not really written as a movie score. It's almost like a parallel to it, with its own sort of form." In the *Suite for Richard* heard on this recording, that form also parallels to an extent the structure of *Looking for Richard*. Just as

Pacino's film is made up in part of blocks during each one of which a particular character or situation is examined from all sorts of angles, each of the seven movements of this suite concentrates on a character such as Margaret, Clarence, and Lady Anne, or on an event such as Richard's death. Shore spent a good deal of time doing research for his score, going all the way back to Gregorian chant but also listening to such works as Bedřich Smetana's symphonic poem, *Richard III*, from 1858, and Sir William Walton's celebrated score for Sir Laurence Olivier's 1955 film based on the play. If Walton's music, with its trumpet fanfares and frequently heroic themes, might be said to represent a vision of Shakespeare's England, Shore's perhaps reflects more a medieval darkness that seems to hang over the play, whose action is based on historical events from the 15th century (Richard III, the last Plantagenet king, ruled from 1452–1485). Shore's goal was to make the music "feel very contemporary, somewhat medieval, and not too movie-scorish." One of the ways in which the composer created that sound was through the extensive use of unisons, often heard in long, somber bass lines that then go back to open fourths and fifths while avoiding the classically tonal interval of the third. Interestingly, Shore, who of late has been taking stock of his extremely fertile career in film scoring, realized that this "medieval" color has much in common with the style that he has generally been using all along. And he notes, "That was one of the things that helped me get along so well with Ornette [Coleman] when we did [Cronenberg's] *Naked Lunch*. He loves to play with that kind of material. It's much easier to play with that than if I was writing using a lot of thirds, nines, or flat thirteens. . . . A lot of the basic harmony that I work with is always built up in fourths and fifths, and layered fourths and fifths on top of each other. It's very open in that sense."

Shore's other basic concept for his *Richard III* music was the use of a mixed chorus. This created the problem of what texts to use. The composer's novel solution was to take advantage of Shakespeare's own language, but translated into Latin. The translations were done by the composer's wife, writer Elizabeth Cotnoir, who also added phrases of her own that she made into poems. Combined with the dark sounds generated by the orchestra, the slow chanting of the mixed chorus often creates an almost overwhelming sense of doom that is even further enhanced by the use of a church organ (the one in the All Saints Church in Tooting, England). Opening on a heavily brooding tone, the score gathers a momentum that climaxes in the sixth movement ("Ghosts"), which then gives way to a dirge-like finale ("Henry, Earl of Richmond") that not only sends Richard off to his horseless demise but that closes the music—and the film—on a note of high tragedy. And if you listen carefully at one or two moments, you can almost hear the main theme for *The Silence of the Lambs* beginning to take shape, perhaps inviting us to "look" for *Richard III*, or at least Shakespeare's version of him, among our favorite serial killers. Missing from the *Suite for Richard*, on the other hand, are some more lighthearted, often dance-like cues in a rather Elizabethan mode that Pacino requested for certain moments in the film.

[I close this section with a review of two recordings of Shostakovich's music for **Alone**, which appeared elsewhere in the March-April *Fanfare*]:

SHOSTAKOVICH: *Alone*, op. 26. Walter Mnatsakanov conducting the Minsk Chamber Choir; Byelorussian Radio and TV Symphony Orchestra. RUSSIAN DISC.

SHOSTAKOVICH: *Alone*, op. 26. Michail Jurowski conducting; Svetlana Katchur, soprano; Vladimir Kazatchouk, tenor; Members of the Berlin Radio Chorus; Berlin Radio Symphony Orchestra. CAPRICCIO.

Now here's a surprise: not one but two new recordings of Dmitri Shostakovich's second film score, *Odna* (Alone), which, like his pioneering music for the silent *The New Babylon*, was composed for the directorial team of Grigori Kozintsev and Leonid Trauberg. Actually, the feminine ending of the Russian word *odna* would invite the translation of "A Woman Alone," which would certainly suit the film's subject matter which, as described by Jay Leyda in his indispensable book, *Kino*, deals with "a young graduate from a Leningrad teacher's training school [who] is assigned to the wilds of the Altai with nearly fatal results for her." Made in 1930–31, *Alone* falls into that peculiar niche in film history between the end of the silent era and the beginning of the sound era. In fact, Kozintsev and Trauberg both planned and shot *Alone* as a silent film, and it was only after the shooting was completed in this form that the directors turned to the new technology and added sound effects, music, and even bits and pieces of dialogue (Alfred Hitchcock's 1929 *Blackmail* was done in very much the same way, save that the "Master of Suspense" was able to reshoot some of the scenes in order to add dialogue).

The extensiveness of Shostakovich's music for *Alone* would suggest that, in the manner of a silent film, it underscores much if not all of the movie. But this is not the wildly satirical, often very contrapuntally sophisticated music one finds in *The New Babylon* (also available on Capriccio), which is arguably the greatest score ever composed for a silent film. Indeed, *Alone* starts off rather unpromisingly with a march (it sounds more like a polka to me) in the type of near-Offenbach style that drags down Shostakovich's last two ballets and much of his film music. And it does not take long for a tenor, in the next cue, to burst into the music doing what tenors do best: blustering, in this case about what a great life it will be (presumably down on the old collective farm). But in light of much of the ensuing music, one starts to suspect satirical intentions in this opening material. As of the third cue, Shostakovich begins to steer the music in much darker directions. That third cue, for instance, opens as a slow, elegiac piece for strings (and later winds) somewhat in the mood of the First Piano Concerto's second movement but also looking forward to some of the later symphonies. And at the end, a solo soprano and then a women's chorus enter in a poignant aria (of sorts) imploring the heroine, played by *The New Babylon*'s Yelena Kuzmina, to "stay" (in Leningrad, if I read things correctly). The score also abounds in lonely woodwind recitatives, the first of which is a long piece for solo bassoon, and further on solo clarinet, over harp and strings that probably evoke the bleakness of the Altai surroundings. The end of the cue breaks down into a rather grotesque, pointillistic banter between (I think) a bassoon and a contrabassoon. Another recitative, this one for oboe, turns up in a Largo cue (number 11 on both CDs) in which Shostakovich audaciously sustains the same dissonant chord beneath the entire solo.

A very gloomy set of slow chord progressions from a church organ, followed by a mournful oboe solo, backs a scene showing the heroine alone in her cabin. In a singularly bizarre cue for what action one can only imagine, a muted trombone does a series of long, moaning, downward glissandi over a slow processional in the low strings and bassoon. Another particularly unsettling cue introduces the eerie timbres of the Ondes Martenot in the midst of some warbling wind figures while on occasion the trombone provides a startlingly long downward glissando. In a totally different vein, one finds, in a cue intended to evoke the presence of an organ grinder, one of the most moving pieces in all of Shostakovich's oeuvre, a sad waltz for a small group of woodwinds. There is a poignancy here that oddly looks forward to some of the film scores of Nino Rota. I could go on. One finds numerous echoes of earlier works, such as *The New Babylon* and *The Nose*, as well as pre-echoes of things to come, including *Lady Macbeth of Mtsensk* and the Fourth Symphony. And *Alone* is not lacking in the kind of instrumental impertinence—a bassoon and contrabassoon playing off a piccolo and an E-flat clarinet, for instance—that dominates much of the composer's early music. In many ways, *Alone* becomes a kind of extended mood piece. But it is also one of the most varied and consistently gripping of any of Shostakovich's works, and it is not to be missed.

To my knowledge, this is the first time this amount of music from *Alone* has shown up anywhere. A Melodiya LP from 1983 features a 17-minute suite of the music arranged by Gennady Rozhdestvensky, who has been responsible for numerous resuscitations of the composer's early works, and this may have made it to a CD that never came my way. But as far as I know, that is it. On the basis of the performances and the recorded sound, it is hard to know which of these two CDs to recommend. Russian Disc offers somewhat more present sound, while Capriccio's engineers have opted for a warmer but somewhat backed-off ambience. Conductor Walter Mnatsakanov starts the work off in a more relaxed vein and then picks up the pace as the music progresses, whereas Michail Jurowski moves in just the opposite direction. On the whole, I think I prefer (marginally) Mnatsakanov, although the Byelorussian Radio and TV Symphony Orchestra's playing is not always up to that of the Berlin Radio Symphony Orchestra. But there is a solid reason to prefer the Capriccio release, and that is that it features two cues, the one with the Ondes Martenot and an extended piece in which the soprano sings, unaccompanied, a very mournful aria that alternates with the tenor's continued attempts to push the good life; that do not show up on the Russian Disc CD.

May/June

There is a telling moment near the middle of **Lost Highway**, David Lynch's first movie since the absurdly reviled *Twin Peaks: Fire Walk With Me* from 1992. Arrested and condemned to death for the murder, which he may or may not have committed, of his wife Renee (Patricia Arquette), Fred Madison (Bill Pullman) transforms—or perhaps morphs, although you don't see it happen—in his prison cell into a young garage mechanic named Pete Dayton (Balthazar Getty). Released from prison and back to work at the garage (the owner is played by none other than Richard Pryor), Pete is picked up by an apparent hood named "Mr. Eddy" (Robert Loggia) in his Mercedes so that he, Pete, can listen to a quirk in the motor. As they are driving along a country road, they are tailgated and then passed by another motorist. Infuriated, Mr. Eddy, a first cousin to *Blue Velvet*'s Frank Booth, as incarnated by Dennis Hopper in the role he was born to play, runs down the other car and, with his two hired guns at his side, beats the shit out of the driver while screaming out motor-vehicle-guide homilies on the dangers of tailgating. This is classic Lynch, exposing the nightmarish underbelly of American culture and turning it slightly loopy by the discrepancy between the textbook-like words and the violence with which they are delivered and enforced. The substance of the nightmare itself forms a constant theme in Lynch's cinema, starting as far back as his bizarre short film from 1970 entitled *The Grandmother*. It is the nightmare of a male-dominated culture so hung up on control that its members lash out brutally against any possibility of the tailgating/anal rape that would put them in the category not of women but of the way in which they see women as objects to be dominated. In this sense, pornography becomes perhaps the principal, imaged support of that culture. And, after the father/daughter incest/murder of *Twin Peaks: Fire Walk With Me*, the nightmare of *Lost Highway* settles squarely into pornography. But the way in which Lynch does this in *Lost Highway*, which proves that a great artist can retain his creative identity while striking out into new territory, is via the either murky or hyper-real images of a surrealistic, circular/cyclical, dreamlike narrative structure perhaps best described in some p.r. material as a "moebius strip." This is no good-guy/bad-guy movie in which the conquering of a porno monster makes us forget that the real purveyors of sleaze, including, in *Lost Highway*, Mr. Eddy and another character (everything in the film happens in twos), drive the kinds of cars, wear the kinds of clothes, and live in the kinds of houses offered by our culture as the rewards for gaining the most control. Just as a moebius strip becomes twice as wide when you cut it in half, *Lost Highway* ends back on the outside of the inside where it started, with no offered explanations to make the nightmare go away once we wake up . . . or leave the movie theater.

If you look carefully in the end titles of many David Lynch films, you will see that the director also credits himself with the film's "sound design." And, indeed, the sound in Lynch's films does not include just the music track, dialogue, and various ambient noises. Lynch also mobilizes numerous pieces of in-between audio that complement the nightmarish fadeouts, whiteouts, and losses of focus while joining with the composed score to form a kind of otherworldly *musique concrète*. But in the music (and sound) for *Lost Highway* (Nothing/Interscope), Lynch has expanded his horizons by turning not just to his usual (as of *Blue Velvet*) composer, Angelo Badalamenti, but also, under the guidance of producer/composer/performer Trent Reznor, to a bunch of pretty funky, hard-edged rockers, starting with Reznor's own group, Nine Inch Nails. Ordinarily, on compilation albums such as this one, many of the assembled songs receive only minimal exposure—at best—in the film. Such is not the case with the over

70 minutes of music heard on this CD, almost all of which, if memory serves me, plays an integral role in the complex scheme of source and non-source music that forms a major part of *Lost Highway*'s sound design. Mind you, there are some familiar Badalamenti strains here, particularly in the poignant synth drones of "Haunting & Heartbreaking" and "Fred's World." And in "Fats Revisited," Badalamenti does the kind of off-center resiting of a familiar American style that gives his *Twin Peaks* music much of its disquieting flavor, save that here the composer goes to a big-band sound rather than a small combo. But Badalamenti also composed the cue that turns into the grating piece of free jazz Fred performs on the tenor sax near the beginning of the film. And in "Police," the composer moves into some pretty eerie territory. I also recall from the film a cue composed in the somewhat Slavic style Lynch asked for in *Blue Velvet*; but that cue does not seem to have made it to the music-track CD. Also supplying some of the non-source music is Barry Adamson, whose theme for Mr. Eddy echoes with references to Henry Mancini, possibly as a reminiscence of the *Peter Gunn*–era TV role of T.H.E. Cat played by Robert Loggia. Just about all of the rock cues, many composed originally for *Lost Highway*, are dark and soft, as on a Michael Mann music track; low and weird, in the manner of the Bauhaus number that opens Tony Scott's *The Hunger*; or gritty and funky, as in I don't know what. In the latter category certainly belong the two cues by gutter-voiced German artist Rammstein, as do the two cues supplied by a group known as Marilyn Manson. Nine Inch Nails' "The Perfect Drug" bridges the latter two categories (NIN's Trent Reznor also created some spacey electronic sounds for the cue entitled "Videodrones: Questions"), while The Smashing Pumpkins' "Eye" pretty much falls under the "dark and soft" rubric, as does David Bowie's "I'm Deranged" (with a nod toward the funky), which opens and closes the film's moebius strip. Oh yes: in the middle of all this we also get Antonio Carlos Jobim's charming but by now muzaky "Insensatez," possibly to evoke the era of Pete Dayton's mildly hippie parents (the father is played by Gary Busey). That brief snippets from the voice track, both over the music and between cues, fit right in will give you an indication of just how of-a-piece Lynch's artistic vision really is. Listen to this CD from start to finish and you will have a pretty good idea of the course your moods and fears are asked to run as *Lost Highway* waltzes, as a kind of decidedly spacey version of *La Ronde*, within its two-sided undimensionality.

Substantial excerpts from three of Miklós Rózsa's best—and darkest—scores are the object of a new recording by James Sedares and the New Zealand Symphony Orchestra (Koch International). Produced within a two-year period, these films include two directed by Billy Wilder—**Double Indemnity** (1944) and **The Lost Weekend** (1945)—and one by Robert Siodmak—**The Killers** (1946). The first and the last are both bona fide films noirs that present two of the most fatales of that sub-genre's femmes, Barbara Stanwyck and Ava Gardner. Yet, interestingly, the most consistently murky of the scores here is the one for *Lost Weekend*, not a film noir at all but rather a mildly moralistic but harrowing black-and-white portrait of an alcoholic (Ray Milland, in an Oscar-winning performance) who comes close to destroying himself and everyone he loves. Although Rózsa's music has those brief moments, typical of the composer, when the sun appears feebly through the storm clouds, including a warm but sad theme for the love between the alcoholic and the woman who has stood by him, the score by and large creates on ongoing tapestry of tension from which there seems to be no relief. The backbones of this tapestry come from the dirge-like title music and from what amounts to the film's main theme: on the heels of using that throaty, electronic instrument, the Theremin, to create a timbre aura for the apparent paranoid schizophrenia of *Spellbound*'s hero, Rózsa, in *The Lost Weekend*, returned to that instrument for a chromatic melody, not all that far from *Spellbound*'s suspense theme, that seems to embody rather than symbolize everything that is both terrifying and overwhelming about the hero's addiction, which at the time the American liquor industry did its best to keep from depiction on the silver screen. Indeed, one of the strengths of the *Lost Weekend* score is that it, like most of Rózsa's work for the cinema, has more of a metonymical than metaphorical presence in the film, which allows it to work against and flow with the text in ways that are more contrapuntal than illustrative. This is perhaps most evident in the cue that accompanies the alcoholic's DTs. While some might object to the quick, upward glissando in the violin's high registers as being an overly literal musical depiction of the mouse hallucinated into existence by the alcoholic, the cue as a whole reproduces so strongly, and in its own language, a descent into madness and fear that the filmic action becomes almost superfluous. And thus can one forgive Rózsa his little (and very effective) onomatopoeia.

I have written and lectured so often and at such length about Rózsa's perfect score for that perfect film noir, *Double Indemnity*, that I find myself a little overwhelmed trying to come up with a few sentences about it here. Every section of the score stands not only as an engrossing musical experience, as the recording of substantial excerpts from it here certain bears out, but also as an interlocking piece of the ongoing dramatic text, to whose deepest reaches only the music allows us complete access. We have the funereal theme introduced in the title music, which suggests both the aura of death that hangs over the film and, particularly via a visual tie-in, a kind of Oedipal crippling that forms part of *Double Indemnity*'s subtext. There is a wonderfully subtle, quietly mysterious theme/motif that shuttles us back and forth between present and past, and, Orphically, between the living and the dead. And there is a love theme that never quite gets off the ground, and for good reason. More sparsely scored than either *The Lost Weekend* or *Double Indemnity*, both from Paramount, *The Killers*, from Universal, features a more explosively dramatic score built around a four-note motif that later turned up so literally in Walter Schumann's famous *Dragnet* theme that Rózsa was able to sue successfully and receive royalties every time the motif was used. In fact, I find Rózsa's score, while wonderful to listen to, much too heavy for the first part of the film, just about the only part to retain the simplicity of the Hemingway Nick Adams story that serves as the film's point of departure. After that, however, the music works exceedingly well. *The Killers* contains, for instance, a haunting mood piece, a nocturne heard during a prison scene as Burt Lancaster's cellmate tells him about the stars. But the real musical showstopper occurs in the film's penultimate scene: following the piecing together of the events, presented in a series of disconnected flashbacks, leading up to Lancaster's rubout at the beginning of the film, an insurance investigator (Edmund O'Brien) sets up a trap in a nightclub for the hoods (William Conrad and Charles McGraw) who killed Lancaster. As the hoods begin to make their move, a solo piano that has been playing innocuous cocktail-lounge music segues without warning into a boogie-woogie pattern that stays ominously stuck in the same minor-mode key. As the action, which includes some balletic camera work, intensifies, Rózsa bitonally juxtaposes the orchestral score—principally the four-note motif—over the solo piano. I can think of few examples where film and music complement each other so consummately.

Fortunately, this cue has been included in the *Killers* suite offered here, and it comes across quite convincingly. Indeed, most of the music, which pretty much offers the essence of each score, is played by Sedares and the New Zealand Symphony Orchestra with deep involvement in both the musical and dramatic elements of the score. The one major exception to this is the excessively slow tempo chosen for the title dirge to *Double Indemnity*. While, as I have suggested elsewhere, the major attention now being paid by symphony orchestras to movie scores is going to force film-music fans to rethink their passion as interpretable "classical" music, at least in concert performances, Sedares' plodding beat for *Double Indemnity*'s opening cues does not work musically, and it certainly would not jell with the film. Other than that, however, I found the performances both moving and, in the appropriate spots, exciting to listen to.

Two of my favorite French film composers, Gabriel Yared (well, Yared was born in Lebanon; but he has done most of his work for French films) and Antoine Duhamel, are currently making a rare appearance on domestic CDs, Yared for **The English Patient** (Fantasy; Academy of St. Martin in the Fields, Harry Rabinowitz, cond.) and Duhamel for **Ridicule** (London; La Grande Écurie et la Chambre du Roy, Jean-Claude Malgoire, cond.). For the life of me, I cannot fathom the huge success, including a passel of Academy Award nominations, of *The English Patient*, written and directed by Anthony Minghella. Set during World War II, the film spends much of its time in the company of a thoroughly dislikable, dying, badly burned patient (Ralph Fiennes cum tons of makeup) being cared for in the ruins of an Italian mansion by a nurse (Juliette Binoche, in yet one more performance combining the mother and the whore into one neat little package) who has an inexplicable crush on him. The rest of the film is created mostly from flashbacks as Fiennes tells the dreary story of his ultimately tragic love affair with a married woman (Kristin Scott Thomas). Into all of this walks a vaporous individual (Willem Dafoe, sans fingers) who reveals that the Fiennes character is in all probability a fascist. I suppose that what has turned most audiences on in *The English Patient* is the double love story; but just what appeal these characters might have in this languorously paced film to make one care that they are in love remains miles beyond me. For this narrative, one might expect Yared to have come up with one of the broadly rhapsodic themes in which he specializes (as in, for instance, another star-crossed-love story, albeit a much better one, *Map of the Human Heart*). And, indeed, several of the cues in Yared's complete score do have that quality to them. Unfortunately, what might be called the principal rhapsodic theme has a distressing resemblance, in its opening few measures, to the waltz from *Carousel*, and I found it hard to get that out of my mind, even though the music is attractive enough in its own right. At another point, Yared flirts dangerously with a moment in the second movement of Schubert's "Unfinished" Symphony. But after several listenings, a good deal of Yared's score has begun to grow on me, in particular a haunting theme, best heard in its solo-piano versions, written out in the manner of, and sounding very much like, a Bach Prelude, but with poignant turns of phrase that get under your skin in a hurry. This particular cue seems to grow naturally out of Bach's Goldberg Variations, the opening of which is played by the Juliette Binoche character at a piano found in the ruins of the monastery (Julie Steinberg plays it on the CD). Another point of departure for the score is a Hungarian love song, performed unaccompanied by Marta Sebestyén, which relates to the Hungarian origins of the Fiennes character, although the desert settings in parts of the film would make you swear the music is Arabian. The CD also offers some period source music from the likes of Fred Astaire, Benny Goodman, and Ella Fitzgerald.

As for director Patrice Leconte's *Ridicule*, this 18th-century costume drama, nominated for a 1996 Oscar in the Best Foreign Film category, deals with the tribulations of a provincial nobleman (Charles Berling) who arrives at the French court seeking help from the king in alleviating the problem of the brackish waters on his domain that are causing his serfs and their children to die of fever. In order to get anywhere near anybody who is somebody, he must learn, rather like a Candide entering *Dangerous Liaisons*, the wicked art of witty conversation up to and including the insult adroitly thrust like the point of an unbated foil. If all of this seems like shallow substance indeed for an entire film, keep in mind that the nobleman must also a) bed down one of his fellow aristocrats (Fanny Ardent) while b) simultaneously wooing, more or less, the daughter (Judith Godrèche) of the doctor (marvelously played by Jean Rochefort) who has saved his life and become his mentor in the game of *ridicule*. Also keep in mind that c) the daughter, who spends much of her time working on (and in) a homemade diving suit, is not only beautiful but bright, and not about to put up with the kind of *merde* that everyone else takes as the normal course of events in the upper crust. And, climaxing this engrossing if Gallically dispassionate series of jeux d'esprit is an absolutely devastating moment when the sharpest of the tongues falls from the heavens into the pits of hell with one enthusiastically misplaced sentence. As one might expect, composer Duhamel, in his score, has attempted to capture the spirit of the music of the film's period, and he is very much helped in his efforts by the style and timbres of Jean-Claude Malgoire's La Grande Écurie et la Chambre du Roy, founded more than 30 years ago, and billed as "the first French ensemble dedicated to the performance of early and Baroque music on authentic instruments." But while some of the cues amount to little more than pastiche, many of them feature bitonal dissonances and occasional wrong notes that skew the music towards more modern times just as surely as does Leconte's incisive direction. And while the overall style definitely calls forth the lingering spirits of composers such as

Jean-Baptiste Lully, Duhamel moves as far afield as Brahms in some of the styles evoked by his music, as in the halting, drawn-out cue for "A Tedious Supper." Still, those who, like me, are looking for the moody, harmonically generated lyricism, which definitely has its roots in a certain Baroque style, of such Duhamel scores as *Pierrot le fou*, *La Mort en direct*, or even *Weekend* (it is to the music for this savage Jean-Luc Godard film that *Ridicule* is perhaps closest in spirit) are apt to find this score somewhat frustrating, with one major exception. The cue that opens this CD and then, in an expanded version, closes it went straight to an area of my sensibilities that is totally capable of obsessing for hours on a single musical phrase, and I have on several occasions found myself shuttling back and forth between the last and first cues just to keep this particular sound in my ears. In this march-like but fast, vigorous, and *serioso* piece, played with captivating verve by Malgoire and his ensemble, Duhamel brilliantly introduces just enough musical modernism into the late-Baroque style to keep the listener's spirit dancing with equal gusto in the 18th and 20th centuries. These two cues are worth the price of the CD. Trust me.

July/August

Time was when the (anti)heroes and, on much rarer occasions, (anti)heroines of David Cronenberg's films were always impelled by some kind of hubris to use the inventions and advances of modern civilization, whether psychotherapy (*The Brood*), gynecology (*Dead Ringers*), science (*Scanners* and *The Fly*), or communications technology (*Videodrome*), to push the human mind and body past the limitations imposed upon them by the gods, whatever the latter may or may not be. It is out of these hyper-Newtonian odysseys and their inevitably tragic conclusions that the intriguing and highly disturbing narratives of Cronenberg's films would always take shape. More recently, however, Cronenberg's protagonists, whether the William S. Burroughs heroin addict of *Naked Lunch* or the diplomat obsessed with a Peking Opera diva passing himself off as a woman in *M. Butterfly*, have jumped off the deep end before the stories even start, leaving the films trapped in a kind of theme-and-variations vortex with no real place to go. Nowhere is this more true than in Cronenberg's latest movie, **Crash**, which might have been endless had the writer/director/producer not exhausted the combinatory possibilities offered by five characters (two male, three female), sex (much of it anal, from the look of things), and car wrecks. Seriously, *Crash*, based on a J. G. Ballard novel, does little more than move in a steady progression from one steely, cold tableau of characters—male/female, female/female, male/male—having sex before, during, and/or after car crashes, with an occasional stop for re-creations of famous accidents—James Dean's, Jayne Mansfield's—that serve as something like hyper-imaged paradigms for the film. In this ballet of mechanistic necrophilia, all the characters seem resigned from the start to the total submersion of the human life force, including its long-vanished manifestation in sexuality, within the all-consuming death presence of steel, glass, and speed. In *Crash*, scars and various prosthetic devices literally replace sexual organs. We are miles away here from the hero of Cronenberg's *The*

Dead Zone, who, like the main character of *Crash*, is transformed by a car crash at the beginning of the film but who, unlike his *Crash* counterpart, spends the rest of the film trying to maintain—or perhaps regain—this humanness after the accident has given him second sight. If there is a redeeming factor to *Crash*, it is that in certain ways its narrativeless fugue of eroticized surrender to machines represents a logical phase in David Cronenberg's career. I shudder to think where he might go from here. But on the basis of *Crash* and Steven Spielberg's awful *Empire of the Sun* I certainly have no desire to go out and read a J. G. Ballard novel.

Ah. There is another redeeming factor in *Crash*, and that is the musical score by Cronenberg regular Howard Shore (Milan). What is immediately striking about Shore's music, at least for those who have followed his career, is that *Crash* sounds like a Cronenberg score. It has, for example, a kind of moody, harmonic obsessiveness that ties in perfectly with the Cronenberg universe. In this instance, that obsessiveness centers around a four-note figure that continually suggests a tritone-to-open-fourth resolution standing as the score's tonal essence. Because of that four-note sparseness, both the horizontal and vertical structures have on occasion an almost oriental quality that harks back in particular to *Scanners*. What gives *Crash* a particularly unique aura, however, are the interplays between several distinctive choirs of timbres created by six electric guitars, three harps, three woodwinds, percussion, and electronics. If, for instance, the raucous timbres of the electric guitars certainly suggest, as of *Crash*'s impressive title sequence, the mechanistic side of the filmic action, the sometimes imperceptible takeover of the guitar theme by the harps humanizes the music somewhat, as does the appearance of a solo flute and, later, a solo clarinet over a very gloomy accompaniment from the harp and guitar in the cue entitled "Mirror Image," perhaps the most Eastern music in the entire score. In "A Benevolent Psychopathology," the string orchestra has its say as its expands the original harmonic base into a kind of elegy that reaches both the transcendence and the tragedy that conclude *Videodrome*, perhaps Cronenberg's masterpiece to date. Here and there more ethereal sounds briefly move the music into another sphere, and on one occasion everything breaks down into an electric miasma. There is also a mystery and coldness to the music mildly reminiscent of Richard Einhorn's score for Arthur Penn's brilliant *Dead of Winter*. But by and large the music, like the film, makes only subtle shifts away from its initial focal point.

I suppose that, if someone were to hold a gun to my head and force me to give my 1996 best-original-score Oscar to a single composer, it would still be to Dave Grusin for *Mulholland Falls*. But it would be an agonizing decision, given the presence of Howard Shore's *Looking for Richard* and, now, John Williams' **Sleepers** (Philips). Based on Lorenzo Carcaterra's novel, *Sleepers*, both as a book and as a movie, has been the object of a certain amount of controversy, most of it centered around the author's claim that the events it depicts are based on fact. While I have no problem accepting the story of brutal physical and sexual abuse of boys by guards at the juvenile detention center where they are incarcerated, I must admit that the film's final third strained my credibility: mobilizing all of the social elements, criminal and otherwise, of the Hell's Kitchen milieu where they were brought up, two of the detention-center survivors—one an assistant district attorney (Brad Pitt), the other an aspiring journalist named Lorenzo Carcaterra, a.k.a. "Shakes" (Jason Patric)—conspire to make sure that their two other friends are acquitted for the murder of the most heinous of the guards (Kevin Bacon). But that is somewhat beside the point. The fact is that Barry Levinson as both writer and director has put together a haunting vision of Carcaterra's book that constantly shifts perspective in order to give the story a kind of tragic nobility. At moments, dialogue becomes all but inaudible as Levinson allows camerawork and editing (there is a surprising, for a Hollywood film, amount of creative montage in *Sleepers*) to communicate on their own terms. More often than not, Levinson also keeps the camera at a discreet distance from the various acts of violence, whether the spousal abuse suggested in the opening sequences or the ugly events at the detention center. I also very much like the way certain small details both foreshadow and reprise various of the narrative themes. Special mention should also be made of Michael Ballhaus' cinematography and of the uniformly fine cast which, in addition to the actors mentioned above, also includes Robert De Niro, Dustin Hoffman, Bruno Kirby, Minnie Driver, and the ageless Vittorio Gassman.

One of the most creative elements of director Levinson's style in *Sleepers* is the way in which he uses Williams' score. At certain moments, we barely hear the music, which becomes as subliminal as the darkened corners it evokes. At other moments, as in the scene where the Jason Patric character and a young woman (Driver) are trying to convince the priest (De Niro) they have known since childhood to bear false witness, the music rises above the dialogue as if to suggest, as in a Greek tragedy, that mere words no longer suffice for what needs to be communicated. As for the music itself, I find myself almost at a loss for words to describe just how powerful Williams' generally quiet and understated score is, both for what it adds to the movie and on its own. The music's general tone is unremittingly somber—indeed, when director Levinson wants lighter moods, he inevitably turns to pop music from the film's various eras, which begin in 1966 and end in the '80s. But that somberness takes on a number of faces. The main-title music, for instance, opens with a mournful horn solo soon joined in a bittersweet, chamber-like counterpoint by a solo flute. Quiet, sustained chords from the strings take the music into a territory inhabited perhaps by only one other film composer, Jerry Fielding. A Fieldingesque sense of loneliness and emotional desolation will return at several points in the score, sometimes in more fleshed-out figures in the brass. In the title cue, just as you wonder where the music could possibly go, Williams switches to a warmer, midrange chord that announces the continued development of the opening theme. Beneath this, however, the distinctive timbres of an electric bass now ambiguously suggest other paths—jazz, perhaps, or rock, maybe—that the background score will never follow. The title cue concludes with another mood, this one created by synthesizer timbres over which Williams establishes a three-, perhaps four-note motif that will return often in the film, frequently over an eleven-note ostinato that shows up throughout the score, usually in the more dramatic moments. Devastatingly effective as well is the way in which

Williams transfers this musical mood to a boys' chorus in the cue entitled "Saying the Rosary," whose music builds up in some of the score's most complex textures and timbre mixes (including chimes) as Shakes flashes back to a particularly brutal scene at the reformatory. I also very much like the grim, somewhat Morricone-esque fast march that accompanies the black-and-white montage sequence of "The Football Game." At most points, however, the music, like the camera, keeps its distance from the brutality, underlining its ominousness with quiet sostenutos and clusters into which other timbres, such as a synthesized bongo drum, make unsettling appearances. The Philips CD is overproduced: even with the bass on my preamp set at flat, the electric bass rattled the glass on the various framed pictures and movie posters in my studio, and there was a noticeable hum, also apparent when I played the CD on my Discman. The sound also strongly reveals its digital origins. But all of this detracts little from the overwhelming impression that Williams' music leaves on the listener.

Given his relatively small output as film composers go, Erich Wolfgang Korngold has fared reasonably well on recordings. Still, one has to ask why attention to a score as good as *Another Dawn* has been limited until now to a six-minute excerpt (gorgeously performed, to be sure) from Charles Gerhardt on RCA's *Elizabeth and Essex* release. A partial answer comes from the program notes by Tony Thomas that accompany **Erich Wolfgang Korngold: Another Dawn; Escape Me Never** (Marco Polo; Moscow Symphony Orchestra, William T. Stromberg, cond.), who is particularly dour in his comments on the films themselves, and arranger John W. Morgan. *Another Dawn* (1937), which I have never seen and which is not available on video, is described by Thomas as "a mild and improbable soap opera . . . set in a remote British Army outpost in the Sahara Desert." Starring Kay Francis "on the downside of a long career" and Errol Flynn, *Another Dawn* was pared down by its producers to a mere 73 minutes, in the process of which a substantial amount of Korngold's original music was left on the cutting-room floor. Working from "the original conductor books and timing notes on the original music sessions," Morgan and his crew "were able to reassemble the music and include virtually all the major cues in the score," including music for a not-as-happy original ending (Flynn doesn't get the woman) that was replaced by a happier ending (Flynn does get the woman) that called for much less music. We owe a major debt to Morgan as well as to William Stromberg, the Moscow Symphony Orchestra, and Marco Polo for this alternately crispy and lushly performed rendition of Korngold's score, which further benefits from sumptuous recorded sound. Rarely have the composer's exquisite instrumental textures been presented with such clarity and yet such warmth. As many readers are probably aware, it is from *Another Dawn* that Korngold drew the heartrending opening melody, which for whatever reason always tears me apart emotionally, for his Violin Concerto. But that theme is far from standing as *Another Dawn*'s only lyrical attraction. At least two other fully developed melodies get substantial play in the score. One is a mellow, midrange piece that may very well have been in the back of Max Steiner's head when he wrote his famous pop tune for *A Summer Place*. The other has a much more deeply rooted poignancy to it. *Another Dawn* also features a very chromatic, almost bumptious waltz, a very Mahlersque march, and no small amount of scintillating action music—did ever a cricket match get more exciting musical accompaniment?—that strongly sets up such scores as *The Adventures of Robin Hood* and *The Sea Hawk*. And in "The Battlefield," we find Korngold in an unusually dissonant mood. As for *Escape Me Never* (1947), the composer's last score for Warner Bros., what we have here is a completion, running under eight minutes, by Morgan, using cues from elsewhere on the music track, of a ballet cut short during the film. The style is unmistakably Korngold, although here and there with a bit more Richard Strauss than I would have cared for. But neither its melodies nor its drive rise to the level of *Another Dawn*. And, frankly, I find that Korngold's music has its greatest impact when given more space to develop—Korngold and Prokofiev were perhaps the only composers ever to imagine film scores as a single, structural entity, and to have nearly an hour's worth of the score from *Another Dawn* is a major gift to (film-)music lovers.

If you are of my generation—not decrepit but old enough to remember when people said "excuse me" when they bumped into you—watching MTV's animated series *Beavis and Butt-Head*, which I have never been able to do for more than five-minute stretches, can be a kind of mind-flushing experience. I mean, these two sub-dropout types, whose most significant activities generally involve bodily parts and secretions I was brought up to believe probably did not exist, make Bart Simpson look like Miss Manners and Albert Einstein rolled into a neat little package. So, in spite of a certain amount of slack-jawed amusement I may have watching behavior that would have doomed me to an early demise, I do not have any intention of sitting through the feature-length and (gasp!) uncensored **Beavis and Butt-Head Do America**, directed and co-written by Mike Judge, who created the series, and I was certainly in no hurry to listen to Milan's music-track CD (London Metropolitan Orchestra, Allan Wilson, cond.), for which, if you can imagine, I was asked at the last minute to contribute program notes. I declined. Imagine my surprise, then, when, upon putting the CD into my car stereo, out came a whopping, big-time symphonic score by John Frizzell that demands to be taken seriously. Too seriously, of course. As of the opening, creepy-thing-crawling-around-in-the-dark pizzicatos followed by a *molto serioso* moment of brass-heavy, temple-of-doom dramatics, you realize that Judge and composer Frizzell have conspired to make *BAB-HDA* feel like a heavy-duty action-adventure picture, and I suspect that this probably adds mightily to the film's humor. Certainly, Frizzell does not miss too many tricks of the trade as he goes, mostly at a loud volume, through most of the musical tropes for the genre. The funny thing is, though, that this is pretty sophisticated music, as befits a man who came out of both the USC and the Manhattan Schools of Music. It certainly goes trillions of miles beyond the rock-video music that interrupts the duo's little TV dramas and upon which they offer diverse sucky comments. Frizzell has had the good taste, if such a word can be used within a hundred-mile proximity of the cartoon duo, to play it straight most of the time, with the results that a good deal of his score would fit comfortably into a live-action film with heroes and heroines who no doubt never touch themselves "there," who never leave track marks in their underwear, and who politely blow their snot into handkerchiefs. Along the way, Frizzell does a wicked send-up or two on very obvious styles, such as the daytime-quiz-show pizzicato scherzo of "Beavis the Sperm" (see what I mean?). We also get about a half a minute of gorgeously performed Gregorian chant, entitled "Judgorian Chant," with sumptuous, cathedralesque resonance. My guess is, however, that the words, which I could not understand, could not be translated onto these pages. For whatever reasons, the score, on the CD if not in the film, ends up leaving the classical strains for a raucous cha-cha. In the brief program notes, Frizzell is quoted as expressing the wish "that his score will help open the ears of Beavis and Butt-Head's teenage fans to orchestral film music." In the words of John Wayne's Ethan Edwards, "That'll be the day."

September/October

If I had to pick out a single adjective to describe Philip Glass' score for **The Secret Agent** (Nonesuch; English Chamber Orchestra, Harry Rabinowitz, cond.; Michael Riesman, cond.), it would be "haunting," a word unfortunately substantially overused by music critics. OK. Let's try "exquisite." "Sublime." Whatever. I can't remember the last time a film score got so substantially under my skin via the recording rather than the film (the last one via the film was *The Mystery of Rampo*). In fact, I have been so taken with Glass' music that part of me does not want to alter my perception of it by seeing the film. And so, contrary to my usual practice, I will comment first on the score, then, somewhat against my better judgment, watch the film via the Fox Home Video laserdisc, and then comment on the film/music interactions. Where to start? Well, the first cue opens with a Bachish cello solo, vibrantly performed by Fred Sherry, that is soon joined by a moody and quite beautiful English-horn solo (played by Henry Schuman), whose timbres will show up in much of the music. And therein lies the classic Philip Glass core: two musical ideas, the one more or less Baroque, the other a theme with a certain basic cine-affect, that invite forward-moving development and instead become repeated within a nearly closed loop with variants. If one regrets the vanishing of certain motifs in classically developed music that carries them off in time, Philip Glass' motifs seem perhaps even more poignant because they rarely have the chance to move forward in time. *The Secret Agent* abounds in such figures. One of them seems ready to take off in Tchaikovskian directions, another evokes the darker reaches of a more Sibelian vision. Yet both stay frozen in a kind of eternal present. And in manners wholly characteristic of his style, Glass often foregrounds fragments that, in normally developed music, would form part of an introduction or an accompaniment. But where these types of motifs often tend to be fairly self-assertive in other Glass works, here they frequently appear in much more wistfully subtle contexts. A perfect example of this is the cue entitled "The First Meridian," in which repeated, two-note figures in the high strings (and other instruments) alternate with a kind of spacey, rising figure in the solo harp. None of this description, of course, really suffices to communicate what is going on in the music. For reasons of sentence structure, for instance, I failed to describe the longer two-note figure that rises beneath the repeated two-note figures of "The First Meridian" to asymmetrically group the notes in a 3/5 pattern. And how can I capture in words the all but palpable dark spirit created by the mildly polytonal string chords that alternate with brief chime strokes in certain cues? Mind you, I'm predisposed to liking Philip Glass' music, since I have never heard a work by him, film score or otherwise, that hasn't moved me, often on several levels simultaneously. But I don't think any Glass work has ever reached so deeply into my soul as *The Secret Agent*.

Which is a good deal more than I can say about the movie. Based on Joseph Conrad's novel (inspired by a true incident), and written and directed by Christopher Hampton (best known for his play and screenplay based on the Laclos *Dangerous Liaisons*), *The Secret Agent* is a costume drama that tells the unremittingly bleak story of the tragic intersection, in 1880s London, of the lives of an apparent anarchist who sells himself to the highest bidder (Bob Hoskins, who also executive produced); his wife (Patricia Arquette); her retarded brother (Christian Dale), who is her only raison d'être; a lowlife revolutionary (Gerard Depardieu); and a nihilist bomb-maker known as the "Professor" in the novel (Robin Williams, in yet one more uncredited role). While the film is well acted (I even liked Depardieu; maybe he's better when he doesn't speak his native French), icily photographed (by Denis Lenoir), and directed and scripted to create an inexorable sense of doom, *The Secret Agent* does not have a single character who made me care what happens to anybody, so that all I was able to do was sit back and marvel at how ingeniously the Conrad novel sets everything and everybody up in a fatalistic trap. This is one of those movies in which almost the entire soul is provided by the music. The trouble is, at least in my perception of things, that Glass' wonderful score never really attaches itself to the action. I now understand the mournful tone that dominates almost all the cues; but that tone, which is quite human in Glass' score, failed to create within me any sympathy for the film's cold parade of inimical characters. And I was intrigued to note that the motif I identified above as Tchaikovskian is in fact associated in the film with the Russian embassy and with yet one more odious human being, a French-speaking Russian who actually sets the final tragedy in motion. The "First Meridian" cue, my co-favorite in the score, along with the title music, is associated not so much with the bomb plot as it is with the locus that is targeted, which is the Greenwich Observatory. It is also interesting to see how Glass' music lends itself particularly well to the sometimes sudden music-track cuts made in the film within cues that play themselves out more fully on the CD. In fact, the low electronic drone with high vocalizing woman's chorus that introduces the cue entitled "Winnie?" (which eventually becomes a reprise-variant of the opening music) is separated from the rest of the cue and used in a fairly classic suspense-film manner for a climactic scene. All in all, *The Secret Agent* is a well made but extraordinarily grim film that even Philip Glass' exceptionally moving score fails to humanize.

November/December

The arrival of a new Varèse Sarabande recording offering every single note of Bernard Herrmann's **Psycho** (Royal Scottish National Orchestra, Joel McNeely, cond.) has inspired by following random observations on both the film and the music:

1. It seems to be generally presumed that the character of Norman Bates is directly modeled, via the Robert Bloch novel, on the real-life, Wisconsin farmer named Ed Gein. Gein, however, was not a serial killer, and the one or two murders he is known to have committed were not of attractive young women but of older women who resembled his mother. Gein went much more enthusiastically about his other passion, which was robbing graves of older women's bodies. And Gein's skills with a hunting knife were applied not in the taxidermical preparation of the cadavers he acquired but in removing the skin and various body parts from them, which he would wear during certain rituals performed by the light of the moon. I doubt, however, that anybody would dare to make a movie about the real Ed Gein, as it would reveal too much of what really goes on in the collective unconscious of patriarchal culture. Instead, our various cultural productions tend to eternally return to the Edgar Allan Poe aesthetics of the death of the beautiful woman (and where would Hollywood be without that image?). If *Psycho* escapes at least partially from some of these psycho-cultural/aesthetic traps, it is because Hitchcock here, as in most of his films, ultimately forces his viewers to travel miles beyond their misogynistic, thriller veneer, and in this particular instance in particular the Bernard Herrmann score hugely contributes to that journey.

2. One thing I especially noticed in listening to the entire *Psycho* score from beginning to end was how the music begins to move into a grim and bleak musicscape that seems among other things to mirror the gray wasteland of Norman Bates' mind once that "psycho" character comes into the picture via Anthony Perkins' brilliant incarnation, whether in early cues such as "The Madhouse" or "The Swamp" (the latter lifted almost note for note from Herrmann's 1933 Sinfonietta for Strings which, like almost the entire *Psycho* score, has the instruments muted throughout) or in a later cue such as "The First Floor." One suspects that, consciously or unconsciously, Herrmann structured the score as a whole to set up the audiences with more of a suspense-thriller type of music, only to leave them dangling over the void once Marion Crane (Janet Leigh) has veered off the main highway. This of course is exactly what Hitchcock's film does, save that the director shocks us into the void with the first murder scene, where Herrmann begins to create the void's unsettling expanses almost as soon as we meet Norman Bates. Early on, a number of Herrmann's cues, all based around the title music, have a frenetic rhythmic drive to them appropriate to the thriller genre, while at other moments the composer even creates a kind of sad, subdued lyricism, most particularly in the cues "Marion" and "Marion and Sam." Of course, like so many of Herrmann's "themes," the music in these cues, which in a way seem to celebrate Marion's love and mourn her forthcoming death simultaneously, is put together out of motivic fragments (here three-note figures) stretched out almost to the breaking point by harmonic sequencing. But if the sequence, in which the

same figures are repeated within the same harmonic context at different pitch levels, can be and often is turned into a trite device for musical melodrama, nobody has ever used it within cinematic situations as masterfully as Herrmann. Herrmann may, as David Raksin has often put it, have worshipped at the church of "Our Lady of the Perpetual Sequence." But the patron saint and resident muse of that church certainly knew, more often than not, a lot about music drama and how to subtly draw it out with sequencing that owes more to Wagner than to Liszt. As *Psycho* moves on, Herrmann's music loses almost all of its rhythmic definition as it frequently settles into long passages of droning unisons and non-resolving, tonally ambiguous (at best), sostenuto chords.

3. One of the advantages of the kind of long collaboration that Herrmann enjoyed with Hitchcock is that it led to a kind of understanding of certain thematic elements in the director's oeuvre that Herrmann was able to translate into music. Thus, as I have often noted, does a characteristic minor/major seventh chord suggested as of Herrmann's first Hitchcock score, *The Trouble With Harry*, become the harmonic keystone of the *Psycho* music. In *Psycho*, one can also hear a strong similarity between the droning music in "The Peephole," which starts shortly before Norman begins to spy on Marion as she undresses for that fateful shower, and the strains that accompany Jimmy Stewart as he plays the "private eye" by tailing Kim Novak in his car. In this way, Herrmann musically links together, across *Vertigo* and *Psycho*, that key Hitchcockian theme of voyeurism. Interestingly, the film creates an ingenious and seamless segue from the "Peephole" cue, which ends on a long shot of Norman sitting at his kitchen table, to the ensuing "The Bathroom," in which we hear a figure associated from the outset with Marion but here ominously—and ingeniously—set to the characteristic rhythmic figure of "The Peephole." On the recording, these are presented as two distinct cues, with "The Peephole" ending on a reasonably logical minor chord cut from the film.

4. How has it happened that the original music tracks for *Psycho*, one of the most influential, important, and essential-to-the-movie film scores ever penned, have never shown up on recording?

As far as I am concerned, Joel McNeely and Varèse Sarabande have come up with what is certainly the most listenable version of *Psycho* ever recorded. McNeely has modeled his pacing of much, if not all, of the music on what we hear on the film's music track, capturing particularly well the intensity of the more dynamic cues, such as the title music and its various resurfacings (interestingly, I got the title music on the CD and on the MCA laser disc of the film to play totally in sync for over a minute, until finally the film version pulled ahead a little bit, probably due to the music editor's scissors). McNeely and his forces also bring off Herrmann's shrieking violins about as well as could be imagined, although I don't think that this music to slice-and-dice your victims by will ever really work all that well separated from the film. The quieter, more drawn-out passages, of which there are many, are particularly effective in the way McNeely and his forces cause them to reveal the textures Herrmann was able to create within the limited palette of the various string timbres, and some of the credit here must also go to the way Varèse Sarabande has combined a warm, rich resonance with close miking to produce a particularly vibrant recorded sound. McNeely performs the full cues here as they appear in the original score, rather than with the occasional edits used in the film, so that bits of extra music are heard here and there, along with an entire, previously unrecorded cue, entitled "The Cleanup," which brings back in a more frenetic and drawn-out form musical figures originally heard in "The Water." This cue was composed for a sequence ultimately edited out of the movie. And then, at the end, in the cue for the climactic "Discovery" scene, Herrmann, for the music preceding the swirling violin figures that end the cue, again raided his Sinfonietta for strings (its final bars). This was replaced in the film by a reprise of the shrieking violins as Norman appears dressed as Ma Bates. In a sense, of course, Herrmann was right to use new music, since the shrieking violins are really murder music, whereas death is (just barely) averted in this scene. But Hitchcock obviously knew a musical showstopper when he heard one, and he or someone else rightly figured that something much more decisive was called for here. I personally would have recorded the "Discovery" cue as it is heard in the film (the absence of that final reprise of those shrieking violins leaves something of a hole in one's emotional experience) and then included Herrmann's original intentions at the end of the CD. But that is a minor quibble for a recording that is outstanding in almost every area.

Unlike *Psycho*, Robert Mulligan's 1962 **To Kill a Mockingbird** (Varèse Sarabande; Royal Scottish National Orchestra, Elmer Bernstein, cond.), adapted by Horton Foote from Harper Lee's popular novel, is a decent, what-you-see-is-what-you-get picture that offers little in the way of depth. Indeed, to my sensibilities, it is Elmer Bernstein's haunting, poignant, and very Americana score that carries one's spirit beyond the transparent messages of the film into areas that cannot be explained away, or even expressed in words or story plots. Interestingly, when assigned to do the film, composer Bernstein agonized for six weeks over where to take the music until, as he puts it in the program notes for this CD, "I realized . . . that its real function was to deal in the magic of a child's world. That was the whole key of that score, and it accounts for the use of the high registers of the piano and bells and harps, things which I associated with child magic in a definitely American ambiance." That decision to musically plunge (mostly) into the magic of childhood via a simple and ingenuous music scored mostly in chamber-like textures was absolutely right for the film, but it certainly went against the big-is-better tendency that has tended to dominate American cinema. The same year that Bernstein scored *Mockingbird* (his music was nominated for an Oscar), Maurice Jarre's pompous and inflated *Lawrence of Arabia* took the best-original-score Academy Award.

No matter. The time when Jarre was overscoring everything in sight has come and gone, while Elmer Bernstein continues to evolve as a film composer. Further, it might be suggested that *To Kill a Mockingbird* stands as the prototype for the kind of music that one hears constantly these days behind the action of what might be called the neo-nostalgia picture. The deep heart of Bernstein's music is established as of the Main Titles, in which an unaccompanied theme in the higher registers of the solo piano creates a halting, achingly evocative waltz. Harp, accordion, solo clarinet, and a few other instruments intermittently join in as the theme is partially developed (the harmonic accompaniment remains a near drone), only to finally blossom into a full-blown, but hardly oppressive, melody first presented by the solo flute and then given to the orchestra's full string section. The score reprises this music in various forms throughout, and by the time it returns in the End Titles, there is usually not a dry eye left in the theater or viewing room. Bernstein also marvelously captures, to the same waltz rhythm but with new music, the fascination and fear the children feel toward their seemingly weird neighbor, Boo Radley (Robert Duvall, in his first film). What is especially admirable about the music in the cues that revolve around Boo, in particular "Creepy Caper" and "Peek-A-Boo," is that Bernstein does not yield to the temptation of manipulating audience reactions by making the music too sinister, and in this way he musically sets up the film's emotionally overwhelming climax in which Boo is revealed to be the hero who has saved the film's two children by killing the real villain. In the cue "The Treasure," Bernstein, using an even more halting waltz figure, comes quite close to re-creating a theme expressing the madness of Alma's mother in *Summer and Smoke*, composed a year earlier and, like *Mockingbird*, definitely one of the composer's finest moments. Americana syncopations and other characteristic figures turn up in certain of the film's other musical situations, some of them fairly ominous. Even in the moments of highest drama, however, as in parts of "The Treasure," "Lynch Mob," and "Assault in the Shadows," Bernstein never overstates his case, even sometimes allowing the solo piano (in the lower registers, of course) to suggest what lesser composers would have mobilized an entire orchestra to put across, although when he needs to Bernstein can draw on the brass and percussion as well as, and usually with more finesse than, anybody in the business.

One thing I particularly like about this recording of *To Kill a Mockingbird* (the original tracks, in mediocre sound and a less convincing performance, can be heard on a Mainstream CD, while Bernstein's unfindable LP rerecording with the Royal Philharmonic Orchestra on his own record club label is never apt to resurface on CD) is the soul and feeling Bernstein imparts to it as a conductor. Interpretation of a given film score tends to remain a secondary issue for original music-track recordings, all the more so since at least some of the music's affective depth grows out of its interaction with the cinematic text. Interpretation acquires a much greater significance when the score is re-created in a new performance. In this rendition, Bernstein the conductor probes a little more deeply beneath the music's surfaces than on the original music tracks. There is a give-and-take to the performance of many of the cues, particularly the more subtle ones, that definitely heightened my involvement in the music and its various layers of dramatic meaning. The whole thing comes across, perhaps, as a bit bigger than it was intended to be for the film, a phenomenon due no doubt in great part to the superior orchestral forces, along with the warm and resonant sound. But for most, and certainly for me, this will enhance the score's listenability without reference to the film. To my ears and sensibilities, Bernstein has very much struck a perfect balance between the original music-track sound and a more symphonic presentation of the music. And a major tip of the hat to Varèse Sarabande here for offering all of the cues as they were written, and in their filmic sequential order, rather than compressing and compacting everything into a suite. This and the *Psycho* CD represent the way film-music re-recordings should be done. Varèse's *Mockingbird* CD also offers about 10 minutes more music than presented on the Mainstream reissue of the original soundtrack recording, and it contains an additional cue ("Remember Mama"), very much based on the title music, that does not appear on Bernstein's "Filmmusic Collection" LP.

While thinking about what I would say about Jerry Goldsmith's music for the 1966 *Patton*, coupled with five cues from *Tora! Tora! Tora!* on a fourth release in Varèse Sarabande's "Film Classics" series (Royal Scottish National Orchestra, Jerry Goldsmith, cond.), which stars George C. Scott in an Oscar-winning performance as the crusty (to say the least) general, and which is directed by Franklin Schaffner, with whom Goldsmith often collaborated (Schaffner's 1968 *Planet of the Apes* contains one of Goldsmith's best efforts as a composer), the musical figure that popped most often into my mind was the triplet motif, usually heard in paired trumpets and repeated in a fading echo effect, that occurs throughout the score. Looking for a way to describe the impression this motif always leaves on me, the expression "military specters from the past" kept coming to mind. Then I read in the program notes for the new Varèse Sarabande CD that, indeed, Goldsmith had intended this particular motif to represent Patton's belief in reincarnation, something I am fairly sure I didn't know before. So, obviously, Goldsmith hit his musico-dramatic mark, at least as far as one viewer/listener is concerned. (I would also note that Goldsmith is particularly adept at this sort of thing, as witness the haunting flute figure that gives much of the *Alien* music its character.) Now, there is no question that one thing that gives the triplet motif its spectral quality in the original score is the use of the echo effect, and at least one person I have talked to—a very respected colleague in the field—felt that Goldsmith's attempts to re-create that effect acoustically for this recording destroy the phantom-like aura sought by the composer. I pretty much disagree. Again, we are faced with the problem of what happens to film scores once they begin to come around for the second and third time. Even though this recording apparently presents all of *Patton*'s musical cues (plus one not used) in their filmic order, it is still a quasi-concert performance, and while it is not unknown for even live concerts to include electronic effects, I personally find that Goldsmith, through the judicious use of decrescendos and offstage instruments, has effectively translated the echo effect for this symphonic performance. If I dwell excessively on this brief figure, it is because it plays a major role throughout Goldsmith's brief (very brief for a film that runs close to three hours) score, which is remarkably subdued for what some would consider to be war-film music, except, of course, that *Patton* is, in the end run, basically a character study, and one that offers no facile solutions. As portrayed in the film, General Patton will be loved by the hawks and loathed by the doves. The film, and certainly actor Scott, seem to constantly attempt to validate both sets of feelings. In his score, Goldsmith gets quite a lot of mileage out of quiet figures (many of which seem to grow out of the triplet motif) that move in and out of the orchestral musicscape without seeming to have a place to go or a place to land. At moments, *Patton* has an atmosphere not un-reminiscent of Respighi's *Pines* and *Fountains of Rome*, while at other moments the music falls rather interestingly into a territory somewhere between Copland and Britten. Of course, *Patton* also offers a by now familiar march, perhaps most effective when reduced to its piccolo/snare-drum instrumentation. But has ever a composer written a cornier fragment of music than the inappropriately syncopated bridge that, to my sensibilities, momentarily strips the march of all its dignity (and irony)? Goldsmith does pull out all the stops once or twice, most notably in the cue entitled "German Advance," in which the music rises in intensity and contrapuntal complexity to a peak worthy of Shostakovich.

Perhaps even more intriguing, and certainly more exciting, is Goldsmith's score for Richard Fleischer's 1970 *Tora! Tora! Tora!*, which I had never heard before (for good reason, since I've never seen the film, and since the music has apparently never been recorded). Goldsmith was faced with the chore of creating music that would represent both the Japanese and the American sides in the events leading up to (and including) the attack on Pearl Harbor. Among the ways in which he accomplishes this is by creating a theme based on the Japanese *In* scale and initially presented on the koto (followed by the serpent, of all instruments). But this theme is eventually given, in very dramatic fashion, to a full, Western symphony orchestra, with a battery of low trombones offering a very dramatic statement of it. In subsequent cues, we get some of Goldsmith's patented action music in which the churning intensity simply never lets up, even while the composer constantly shifts the musical timbres, sometimes suggesting the Orient with such instruments as the high flute, sometimes deploying more classically Western timbres in the strings and brass, and at yet other times creating offbeat sounds, such as what I think is a prepared piano used as a percussion instrument, that seem to belong to both camps and neither at the same time. In the quiet and often mysterious cue entitled "Imperial Palace," Goldsmith jarringly presents one of the themes in two oboes tuned a quartertone apart. All in all, *Tora! Tora! Tora!* contains some of Goldsmith's most stirring and original music, and I'm surprised it has not been given more attention until now. At any rate, it receives a vividly dynamic performance from Goldsmith and the Royal National Scottish Orchestra. The brass are in particularly good form here, as they are in *Patton*, and the entire orchestra seems to have risen to the challenge of what sounds like quite difficult music. Interestingly, the less complicated *Patton* receives a somewhat less polished performance, with the strings offering some pretty lax playing in the "Funeral" cue. The sound is rich and vibrant, with just a touch of digital edginess more apparent in *Patton* than in *Tora! Tora! Tora!*

It's one of the oldest story lines around: the local sheriff (sometimes with a physical disability) sits around, occasionally making a minor arrest but in general allowing the local big shots to run the town any way they want. Suddenly, some incident causes the sheriff to find his conscience and, risking not only his position but his very life, he puts the hurts on all them varmints who have made him into a laughingstock. And there, in a nutshell, you have the story of **Cop Land** (Milan; London Philharmonic Orchestra), written and directed by James Mangold, except that here the town is modern-day "Garrison," New Jersey; the bad guys are an enclave of New York City cops, all from the same precinct, living just across the George Washington Bridge under the watchful eye of the mob guy (Harvey Keitel) who has helped them get their nice, suburban homes in exchange for certain, drug-related favors; and the sheriff, who is deaf in one ear, is none other than Sylvester Stallone with an added 30 pounds. That change of image will probably get Sly an Oscar nomination, which is bizarre considering that he works so hard to shed his superhero image (you know, Rambo et al.) that he positively sleepwalks through the entire film. Gary Cooper would come across as Jim Carrey in comparison. If you can note anything in Stallone's monochrome acting that suggests a change of heart once he decides to go after the bad guys, you're a better person than I. But the real problem with *Cop Land* lies in the total invisibility of its various motivating forces. I mean, I have never seen a film in which the viewer has to accept on such total faith the various nasty things the characters do to each other. Harvey Keitel is a villain because, well, he is Harvey Keitel, and maybe because he has a New York accent. But there is not an ounce of background to get one involved in caring, positively or negatively, about Keitel's behavior, and the same thing can be said about almost every character and every piece of action in the film, from the early scene on the George Washington Bridge to the unbelievably perfunctory denouement. Even Robert De Niro gets thrown away as an internal-affairs cop who gets a gratuitous voice-over narration to open and close the film. Mind you, I'm all for effects without obvious causes; but then at least have the courage to turn the filmmaking processes in an experimental direction. Trouble is, *Cop Land*, which comes out of Miramax and includes some kind of production involvement from the Sundance Institute, looks as if at least some of those involved intended it to be considered as an "independent film." Pretty soon, every film that doesn't have 10,000 explosions, 40 dinosaurs, a body count of several hundred, and overpaid actors and actresses staying totally in type will be sneaked in the back door as independent films so that the studios can maintain their big-spender image. Who's kidding whom?

On the heels of *Crash* this is the second Howard Shore effort in a row that, in terms of aesthetic quality, outdistances its film by several hundred miles. The general tone of the *Cop Land* score is very much in the same vein as Shore's grim and lugubrious music for a much better film, David Fincher's *Se7en*. Indeed, in the spirit of *Se7en*, the overall photographic feel of *Cop Land* is dark but dark with nowhere near the narrative tie-ins or the technical expertise one finds in *Se7en*. Indeed, I find myself wondering whether the composer didn't have to turn back to *Se7en* for his inspiration, so bleak and tragic is much of his music for a film whose bleakness and tragic depth seem desired rather than created. I will go out on a limb and state that Howard Shore is without a doubt the most effective musical evoker of the dark side of things, the irrational if you will, since Bernard Herrmann. The miracle here is that Shore, unlike most of his colleagues when they aspire in similar directions, pulls this off without sounding the slightest bit like Herrmann. *Cop Land* contains a perfect example of how he manages to do this: what might be considered *Cop Land*'s principal motif, which is harmonic rather than thematic in nature, is a sometimes two-, sometimes three-chord progression presented in a kind of dirge-like moan. The first chord has, on the top, an F-Minor triad whose root-position character is partially denied by the use of the third (A-flat) in the bass line. This chord metamorphoses, on the top, into a distant 6/4 chord in A Minor, with the 6/4 character of this top chord partially denied by the use of the tonic note (A) in the bass line, which has moved up a half a step. When the third chord is used, the bass line moves up another half step to B-flat, while the top turns into a suspended, very Shoresque chord formed from C, B-flat, and F. Ambiguities abound: tonic versus 6/3, 6/4 versus tonic, chromatic versus diatonic, even pandiatonic versus diatonic. The voice leading is ingenious, and yet all the voices do is continue to lead . . . into a suspended chord, into the darkness, into nowhere. Who knows? I am not suggesting that these sounds are brand new to Shore's music, any more than Bernard Herrmann's distinctive harmonic language, particularly in his Hitchcock films, was without precedents and parallels. What I am suggesting is that Shore, like Herrmann, has found a unique way to isolate harmonic sounds familiar to Western listeners from their normal developmental contexts and, by stripping them from these contexts, to create intense moments of cine-affect by exploiting their vertically suggested ambiguities. *Cop Land* is, however, a more varied score than *Se7en*: Shore creates some extremely dramatic moments out of figures, sometimes frenetic, sometimes processional, in the drums and brass, all of it typically enhanced by the electronic layering that has become pretty much a constant in the composer's work. At other points, an almost pure electronic miasma emerges. Different chord progressions, particularly in the brass, likewise contribute to the music's dark, even morbid moods. Amazingly, Shore also wrote an original bagpipe cue for a funeral sequence to replace the eternal "Amazing Grace," and the bagpipe timbres show up periodically in the score. At one point—and I even noticed this while watching the film, for whatever reason—a single beat from the chime seems to permanently seal the music, if not the film, into a no-exit aura.

On **Bernard Herrmann Conducts Great British Film Music** (London; National Philharmonic Orchestra) London continues to reissue the important Phase-4 recordings of film music, both his own and by other composers, recorded by Bernard Herrmann near the end of his life. The real find on this particular CD is the suite of music composed and arranged by Constant Lambert for the 1948 *Anna Karenina*, directed by Frenchman Julien Duvivier and co-scripted by a major French playwright, Jean Anouilh. The "Forlane" movement is one of the most haunting single pieces of film music I know. Other scores include excerpts from Bax's *Oliver Twist*, Arthur Benjamin's *An Ideal Husband*, Vaughan Williams's *The 49th Parallel*, Walton's *Escape Me Never*, and Bliss' *Things to Come*. Added to this CD from the *Great Shakespeare Films LP* is the Prelude from Walton's music—a perfect score, if ever there was one—for Olivier's *Richard III*. Performances are often ponderous (Herrmann should have stuck to composing and had someone ghost conduct for him), the playing less than stellar. But much of this music is available nowhere else (to my knowledge), and it needs to be heard.

CHAPTER FIFTEEN

~

1998

January/February

It is amazing just how durable the film noir is. One might have thought that, once the darkness, cynicism, and pessimism of the '40s had given way to the seemingly brighter moods of the '50s, noir films would have died a painless death. Yet the genre, or whatever you want to call it, continues to spawn an amazing number of classy films, many of them with outstanding musical scores. Just picking one each from the last three decades, you have Roman Polanski's 1974 *Chinatown* (music: Jerry Goldsmith); Lawrence Kasdan's 1981 *Body Heat* (music: John Barry); and from 1996 Lee Tamahori's *Mulholland Falls* (music: Dave Grusin). Two other great, recent noir scores that pop arbitrarily into my mind are David Shire's for Dick Richards' 1975 remake of *Farewell, My Lovely*, and Jerry Fielding's for Michael Winner's 1978 remake (much more faithful to the Chandler novel) of *The Big Sleep*. And, of course, how could one ignore Miklós Rózsa's music for Carl Reiner's 1982 noir spoof *Dead Men Don't Wear Plaid?* And now, toward the end of 1997, we get one more noir that deserves to stand with the best of them all, neo- or otherwise, Curtis Hanson's **L.A. Confidential**, based on the novel by James Elroy. Like *Mulholland Falls*, L.A. Confidential takes place in 1950s Los Angeles, and, like its predecessor, *L.A. Confidential* has a narrative that alludes to efforts made by the City of Angels police force to purify the whole area of mob influence. But the deepest drama takes place on the level of several individual police officers who wade more and more deeply toward the ugly center of a swamp of an interlocking web of sordid crimes and intrigues that it will take more than one viewing of the film to sort out. That, of course, is as it should be, at least for film noir. Not only does the very labyrinthine quality of the narrative stand as a kind of structural metonymy for the film's essential darkness, it forces the viewer to plunge into deeper textual levels than those to which more straight-line narratives allow easy access. But L.A. Confidential's screenplay (by director Hanson and Brian Heigeland), while leading the viewer down multiple, interlocking paths toward the abyss, also manages to ingeniously move the story forward via the strong characters it creates, in particular an officer (Kevin Spacey) who on the side serves as the police advisor for a TV cop show (ironically) called *Badge of Honor* (the film makes no effort to hide allusions to *Dragnet*); another officer (New Zealand–born Russell Crowe), who alternates between saving damsels in distress and beating the shit out of the criminals he and his colleagues arrest; and a bright, young cop (Australian actor Guy Pearce) whose arrow is not so straight as to prevent him from rising quickly in the L.A. police hierarchy. Piled on top of all of this is a postmodern self-referentiality that defines itself on both sides of the law: on the one hand there is a hood (David Strathairn) who specializes in making available prostitutes who look like Hollywood stars, which leads to a wonderfully comic moment in this otherwise grim piece of filmmaking; and on the other hand there are the ongoing scenes showing the making of an episode for *Badge of Honor* (be sure you don't leave the theater or turn off your VCR before the end titles are over). In between, meanwhile, is a columnist (Danny DeVito) for a sleazy crime magazine who is actually responsible for setting up some of the busts made by various members of the department.

Interestingly, the music for many of the best of the new (or neo-) films noirs has modeled itself not on the dissonant and steely symphonism of scores such as Rózsa's *Double Indemnity* but rather on the more big-band, bluesy, if still sinister, tone of scores such as David Raksin's *Laura* or *The Big Combo* (*Farewell, My Lovely, Body Heat,* and *Mulholland Falls* come immediately to mind). Jerry Goldsmith's score for *L.A. Confidential*—what there is of it—falls somewhere in between. The blues sound does not turn up until the Russell Crowe character's liaison with one of Strathairn's whores, a Veronica Lake look-alike beautifully played by Kim Basinger, while other cues tend more toward orchestral noir minus some of Rózsa's bite, with the most involving music being a dynamic cue in a 7/8 meter that turns up toward the end of the film. Unfortunately, and insultingly, the first "original soundtrack" CD for *L.A. Confidential* (Restless) to be released offers less than three minutes' worth of the Goldsmith score, which is all the more ridiculous since, unless my impression is wrong, there is more than enough room on the disc for at least most of what Goldsmith wrote. We get the 20-second theme for *Badge of Honor*, a brassy bit of big-band blaring followed by a moment of walking bass to open the CD, and a double cue to close it. The latter starts off with the rather sad blues theme played, predictably, on the solo trumpet with some orchestral accompaniment, followed by the taut 7/8 music, which builds on the blues theme while the accompaniment offers closely knit chords in the kind of Kurt-Weill-cum-Broadway pattern reminiscent of parts of Elmer Bernstein's score for *The Grifters* and Dave Grusin's for *Mulholland Falls*. The absolutely dynamite sound makes one regret even more the absence of more of the Goldsmith cues. I mean, couldn't we have at least had the complete end-title music? Between these two cues one finds the usual source music, in this case mostly pretty good stuff. I am reminded, for instance, of just what an expressive, rich voice Dean Martin had ("The Christmas Blues" and "Powder Your Face With Sunshine"). We also get two top-flight instrumentals from the Gerry

Mulligan Quartet, one with Chet Baker ("Makin' Whoopee"), the other without (Mulligan's slightly bitonal rendition of "The Lady Is a Tramp"). I am also a sucker for the dreamy, late-night foxtrots that no group performed quite like Jackie Gleason's orchestra, with its lonely trumpet solos ("But Not for Me"). On the other hand, Kay Starr's "Wheel of Fortune" and Joni James' "How Important Can It Be" stand, to my sensibilities at least, as a reminder of how aesthetically, morally, and politically void the '50s were, more often than not. And an A+ to the anonymous writer of the program notes who, for the first time, as far as I know, on a compilation album, ties all of the source-music cues into the filmic action. [Happily, Varèse Sarabande eventually released a CD devoted to the Goldsmith score.]

After a dark, probing score for a dark but thoroughly unprobing film in *Cop Land*, Howard Shore has come up with another dark and perhaps even more intriguing score for a film that has a good deal more substance to it, David Fincher's **The Game** (London). Not surprisingly, there are moments in Shore's music that strongly recall his last effort for Fincher, the grim and lugubrious *Se7en*, in particular the slow moanings, often repeated in pairs, of mid-range, open-interval chords. But much of Shore's music for *The Game* would seem, to my ears, to define a new phase in the evolution of the composer's cine-musical style. It all starts off with a very tonal, Satie-esque slow waltz in the solo piano to accompany what appear to be eight-millimeter home movies of the hero (Michael Douglas) as a young child (if I remember carefully, the movie offers the piano music in very low-fi sound, although it acquires rich sonics for this CD). But a continuation of the home movies into a scene showing the suicide of the boy's father reminds us, subliminally at least, that we are being manipulated by a narrative, even if it is a narrative within a narrative. And Shore's cue, via a segue with a snippet of "Happy Birthday," crescendos into a sad, even tragic-sounding piece for full orchestra. It is once again the birthday of the Michael Douglas character, a financier divorcé who lives a hermit's existence in a huge mansion with a fulltime housekeeper living in a modest house off to the side. For a present, his apparently somewhat derelict brother (Sean Penn) offers him the fully paid services of an outfit called Consumer Recreation Services, which offers to shake up his rather rigid existence by creating "events" in his life in such a way that he will never know whether they are "real" or part of "the game," an interesting but slightly stale premise reminiscent of Borges' story "The Lottery in Babylon."

Once the game is afoot, Shore's music takes off in an unexpected direction: the solo piano from the beginning rises to the instrument's high registers to play continuous, rhythmically even, single-note filigrees whose non-systematically atonal character makes them reminiscent of similar figures in Jerry Fielding's *The Mechanic*. Beneath the piano's serpentine wanderings, Shore, frequently throughout the score, creates a second musical layer out of very low unisons moving in more tonal directions in the strings. The juxtaposition of the piano's fuzzy atonality with the strings' fuzzy tonality produces a kind of weird bi(a)tonality that seems particularly appropriate to the picture. One suspects in fact that the lonely meanderings of the solo piano stand as something of a musical metonymy for the Michael Douglas character, whose child personality from the home movies seems doomed to merge, via what may or may not be a game and via the more sophisticated visuals of the 35-millimeter film, with the adult persona of the suicidal father. Much of the music, then, has this kind of bi-planar character to it. But Shore at times fleshes out the orchestral textures, even while the piano continues its lonely trek; and if you listen carefully, which is one of the advantages of having a music-track CD such as this, you can hear additional layers of sound that are something of the composer's stock in trade. In the cue (the sixth on this CD) entitled "Congratulations on choosing C.R.S.," for instance, we can hear, in between the spaces of the intersecting piano and low strings, a repeated figure (probably electronically generated) that sounds like some sort of ghostly machine chugging away in the background. It's eerie as hell. If I have a criticism, it would be that the whole thing—musically, narratively, cinematically—comes across as perhaps just a bit too doom-and-gloomy, which probably has to do more with Fincher's vision, which has been pretty consistent across *Alien³*, *Se7en*, and *The Game*, than Shore's. There are ludic implications, perhaps most strongly suggested by the solitary dance of Shore's piano, to the entire story that don't really come forth in the narrative until the end, which rather quickly turns the whole thing from a postmodern nightmare into a picaresque adventure. Shore's music for *The Game* stands in my book as one of the year's most original and engrossing scores. The recorded sound has been particularly well realized, with the bass tones giving the plaster on your walls pause for thought. Oh yes: the CD ends with The Jefferson Airplane's "White Rabbit," with Grace Slick slinkily intoning such deliciously '60s lyrics as "One pill makes you larger, and one pill makes you small / And the ones that Mother gives you don't do anything at all." I love it.

Varèse Sarabande has come up with a CD offering, for the first time as far as I know, of Jerry Goldsmith's music for **The Mephisto Waltz** coupled with a 22-minute suite for the 1972 **The Other**. It is an indispensable recording. Directed in 1971 by Paul Wendkos, *The Mephisto Waltz* is a supernatural thriller about a music journalist (gee, what kind of species is that?), played by Alan Alda, who falls under the spell of a dying concert pianist (Curt Jurgens) who, in order to continue with his concert career and his incestuous relationship with his daughter (Barbara Parkins) after his death, satanically transfers his entire being onto the journalist, a pianist manqué even after four years at Juilliard. The increasingly terrified outsider in *The Mephisto Waltz*, as in Roman Polansky's *Rosemary's Baby*, filmed three years earlier, is the wife of the possessed man, played here by Jacqueline Bisset, one of the most stunningly beautiful women—probably too beautiful for the role she has to play in this film—ever to appear on a movie screen (and anywhere else, for that matter). It is also Bisset's acting, with its characteristic mixture of irony and intelligence, that gives this reasonably well-made chiller much of its substance (this was an era when directors of photography were using Vaseline on their lenses for the murkier scenes). Given the film's title, it comes as no surprise that a certain portion of the music in Goldsmith's score, and almost all the solo piano music within the narrative, comes from Liszt's well-known orchestral work, later transcribed for solo piano, of the same title. Nor is one startled to hear, in various guises, the frequent appearances of the *Dies Irae* theme. But over and above all that, *The Mephisto Waltz* turns out to be one of Goldsmith's most gripping and inventive scores. The music features an unusual array of modernistic devices, and not just the cluster chords and the chaotic glissandos that were beginning to wind their ways into film scores at this time. *The Mephisto Waltz* has musical moments that may very well be aleatory, and if they're not, they certainly feel aleatory. And Goldsmith also adds to the music's unsettling quality by throwing in various extraneous sounds, some of them electronic, including a very disturbing man's voice. The composer also shows amazing creativity in the ways in which he integrates the Liszt work into the score: sometimes we get just the piece's characteristic solo-violin figure, which interestingly sounds quite at home within the milieu of Goldsmith's 20th-century modernism. At other points, Goldsmith blends the distinctive, churning figure in the low strings of Liszt's *Mephisto Waltz* with his own, none-too-shabby rhythmic drive. The final, Liszt/Goldsmith crescendo is one of film music's finest moments. This CD, which opens with the 20th Century-Fox fanfare, seems to offer just about all of the film's non-source music over its 11 cues. Missing is the source music, in particular the solo-piano version of Liszt's *Mephisto Waltz* heard throughout the film and performed by Goldsmith's teacher Jakob Gimpel who, to be honest, does not quite make a case for the performance as coming from the "world's greatest pianist," whether in Jurgens' skin or Alda's. The recorded sound is excellent, with very well defined stereo directionality.

Where *The Mephisto Waltz* flaunts its evil and pounds away at the nerves as of the brilliant musical/visual amalgam of its title sequence (designed by Phill Norman), *The Other*, directed by Robert Mulligan and based on a novel by Thomas Tryon, who also wrote the screenplay, creeps into the soul much more subtly, and it may, in the long run, be a better film. Set in rural Connecticut around 1935 (a headline seen early on about the Lindbergh kidnapping helps set up the film's climax), *The Other* focuses on what appear to be twin boys up to the kinds of antics that boys that age will forever be up to, particularly if they have the whole, wide outdoors to do them in. But as the film progresses, we begin to become aware that the two boys, even though actually played by twins (Chris and Martin Udvarnoky), are never seen together in the same frame, and it will soon turn out that one of the twins was killed in an accident. And as various catastrophes begin to pile up within the twins' orbit, we also become aware that the live twin is feeding off his dead sibling's apparently malefic powers (although it is never 100% clear just which twin has the dark[er] side), which have been inadvertently released by the magic innocently taught to the living twin by his well-meaning Russian grandmother (the marvelous Uta Hagen) following the death of his brother. But all of the evil takes place so quietly and generally so far out of sight that its presence ultimately has a much more disturbing effect on us than any of the bad vibes generated by *The Mephisto Waltz*. In his music, Goldsmith, quite rightly, chose to musically complement the film's visual nostalgia while also setting a trap for the viewers at many points by creating figures more suggestive of innocence than evil. The title theme, for instance, opens with a sweet piccolo (I think) solo over repeated harp arpeggios that is soon taken over by the strings in a moment of supreme, Gold-smithian lyricism. And there is one very Americana musical romp that does not be-gin to give a clue as to the film's darker side. But, for instance, cymbal and gong rolls beneath the music's initial strains suggest that all is not as rosy-cheeked and apple pie as it appears. And as the score progresses, other musical tropes characteristic of the genre begin to turn up, including a bitonal merry-go-round waltz that leads to a brief but violent climax. In the ensuing music, a high unison string theme suggests a cer-tain sweetness, a sweetness that is, however, offset, in a twin kind of way, by the mildly bitonal accompaniment in the harp and the rest of the orchestra. About halfway through the suite offered here, we hear a particularly chilling duet between quiet chimes and a solo flute later joined by such instruments as an electric harpsi-chord and later the high violins. Unfortunately, about half of Goldsmith's original score never made it to the film, and included in the suite offered by Varèse Sarabande is some of the unused music. *The Other* is neither as well recorded nor as well per-formed as the score for *The Mephisto Waltz*, and a couple of moments are marred by some minimal wow.

One of the clues that **Gattaca** was not going to be your completely standard Hol-lywood picture was that in my movie-theater area (Long Island), it was not showing at many of the standard cinemas that pick up most of the biggies. Another clue was that it received a lot of less-than-enthusiastic reviews from the critics around the country, a sure sign that a particular movie is almost bound to fall somewhere outside of the ordinary. Yet a third "indication" is that *Gattaca* has a score by Michael Nyman (Virgin/Jersey) who, until he did the somewhat mainstream *The Piano*, was probably best known for his collaborations with offbeat (to say the least) British director Peter Greenaway. Well, *Gattaca* may not be for all tastes, particularly those tastes accus-tomed to body counts in the hundreds, explosions all over the place, special effects galore, zero character development, more stunt people than actors, narratives clut-tered up with zillions of plot fragments thrown in to try to make a pointless story look meaningful, and a thorough undercutting of any possibility of emotional involve-ment. Indeed, where the latter point is concerned, I suspect there are those who would criticize *Gattaca* for being sentimental. So be it. It certainly brought tears to both my wife's and my eyes at more than one point, particularly at the end. Indeed, *Gattaca*'s strong affective impact may be one of its most important messages. While what the surface of this (slightly) futuristic tale written and directed by Andrew Nicoll (the first feature for this New Zealand–born filmmaker) communicates—that it's what is inside a human being that counts, not what's outside—may strike some as simplistic, its story of an imperfect human specimen (Ethan Hawke) trying to pene-trate quasi-racist barriers created by and for a new generation of genetically engi-neered human beings strikes frighteningly close to home, a home for which Holly-wood's plasticized actors and glitzy products are the role model par excellence. And so even the fact that the makers of *Gattaca* managed to turn out a film that cuts through contemporary culture's death-obsessed sterility with the simplest of means— outstanding acting, subtle production design (by Jan Roelfs) that is just the other side of here, an outstanding score, and a strong screenplay that has no problem appealing to the viewer's inner self—is significant in and of itself. And as my brother pointed out to me (all the way from Denver), another element of *Gattaca's* humanness and simplicity can be found in the fact that what forces the Ethan Hawke character into counterfeiting his genetic material from blood, urine, and various other samples taken from a genetically perfect Englishman (Jude Law, in one of the year's great performances; the screenplay in fact was modified to justify his accent) who has been crippled in a suicide attempt are barriers that have been erected not by a police state but by a supposedly democratic society.

There is absolutely no question that one of the prime contributing factors offered by *Gattaca* in allowing the viewer/listener the kind of access to his/her inner world that most films cut off is the score by Michael Nyman. This may sound strange when one considers that the relationship between many of the composer's Greenaway scores and their films is often more strongly based in mathematics than in the emotions. Yet Nyman, even more solidly here than in *The Piano*, has managed to carry over many of the most immediately recognizable characteristics of his style into a much warmer setting where they nonetheless seem totally at home. Instead of the more raucous timbres, with lots of saxophone, produced by the Michael Nyman Band, Nyman here sets much of his music in the warmer reaches of the string orchestra. The film's main-title theme, entitled "The Morrow," ultimately expands into something closely resembling a well-developed melody. Yet it is made up of somewhat static, two-measure cells whose (here) mildly obsessive presence imparts that unique Minimalist quality characteristic of much of Nyman's writing. Sad and somewhat languorous, this theme will reappear, with sometimes significant variations, throughout the film. Perhaps the supreme moment of affect, however, comes from the second cue, "God's Hands," which, via a slow, haunting lullaby, leads us from the present into a flashback showing background on the Ethan Hawke character (this music, too, makes additional appearances in the film). Elsewhere we find many other characteristic Nyman devices, including four-measure figures that get Minimalistically repeated with slight variations, and a fast type of four-beat romp that comes as close to raucous as this score ever gets. At other moments, however, the composer ventures into new territory as he piles up string timbres to produce some pretty heavy cluster effects. And in one cue ("Only a Matter of Time"), Nyman juxtaposes in a very Shostakovian way two thematic lines in the high, unison violins playing in a register about an octave higher than Shostakovich ever got. There is also a horn theme that would fit comfortably in many of the nostalgia films that continue to come out of Hollywood. In the midst of all this, we also get to hear an "Impromptu for 12 Fingers," basically Schubert's well-known Impromptu in G-flat with some extra embellishments that are supposed to be playable only by the 12-fingered pianist who performs the piece in the film (in fact, however, the arrangement sounds like what it is: Schubert's basic music with some added figures easily played by another set of hands but utterly impossible even for someone with a dozen digits). By the end, Nyman uses the entire string orchestra and a few other instruments to carry his flowing blocks of thematic fragments to a pitch of intensity that is both tragic and triumphant. Ultimately, it is music that with both sorrow and optimism denies the denial of death. *Gattaca* offers one of the most meaningful marriages of music and film to come along in some time, and Virgin deserves eternal gratitude for making what appears to be the entire score available on this richly recorded CD.

Speaking of father/daughter incest (see *The Mephisto Waltz* above), the second release on Lukas Kendall's Retrograde label offers John Barry's long-sought-after music for **Deadfall**, available ages ago on a 20th Century-Fox LP. *Deadfall*, written and directed by British filmmaker Bryan Forbes, with whom Barry was collaborating for the sixth and last time, is a classic example of a story (in this case taken from a novel by Desmond Cory) that is much too complex to be squeezed into a two-hour film. I have just re-watched a video of the movie, and I'll be damned if I can figure out half of what is going on. What, for instance, is actress Nanette Newman doing in the film other than providing a beautiful face and a totally empty persona? And who is the guy she is bedding down at the end of the film? And why does he have the diamond that a very young Michael Caine wants to rob? Described in Leonard Maltin's *Movie and Video Guide* as "overdirected," *Deadfall* in fact has little going for it beyond the perversity of part of its plot and some classy style from director Forbes. No doubt leery, after films such as the 1954 *Rififi* and the 1964 *Topkapi*, of offering one more choreographed jewel heist, Forbes obviously decided to try something different and apply the choreography to a montage cross-cutting between a concert hall and the jewel heist, with the concert-hall music backing it continuously. The results are spectacular. Even before the concert, Forbes, with an ironic grin on his face one suspects, cuts between the timpanist tuning up (with lots of glissandos) and the beginning of the heist, which takes place at a palatial mansion. Once the work, a 15-minute Romance for Guitar and Orchestra written especially by Barry for this film, begins, Forbes mixes the shots so vertiginously that we are never quite sure of where we are. At one point, for instance, Caine's grappling hook falls many feet to the stone courtyard below. We expect a worried reaction shot of either Caine and/or his accomplice (Eric Portman), an older man who has offered him both a cut of the take and his young wife/daughter (Giovanna Ralli) in trade for his skills; instead, Forbes cuts to a close-up on the head of guitarist Renata Tarrago. We also get to see shots of (a very young) Barry himself conducting the orchestra, while all the time we listen to the conductor/composer's Romance. Throughout the film, Forbes, although not as spectacularly as in the heist/concert sequence, continually finds ways of drawing the viewer into the film's visual structures. The director has a particular knack for attracting the eyes toward characters apparently hidden in the background.

Although the Romance for Guitar and Orchestra is probably the major raison d'être for this CD, I have to say that for me the greater interest lies more in the interactions between the music and the film than in the Romance as a pure concert work. In the opening theme, heard in the unison violins over simple strummed chords from the guitar, Barry introduces what strikes me as a very awkward modulation, which is not surprising considering that the composer has spent much of his career sustaining harmonic moods (the same minor-mode triad with an added second, the most characteristic sound in many of the composer's scores, carries through the entire "Laser Beam" cue in *Goldfinger*, for instance) rather than developing his harmonies out over an extended composition. Mind you, the Romance is nonetheless an attractive and moody work that occasionally erupts à la Rodrigo into some climactic, quasi-Flamenco chords. As for the rest of the music, *Deadfall* may be one of the least action-specific scores Barry ever penned. Most of the cues back either moments of transitions or scenes that call for little dramatic enhancement, and the result is that much of the music simply stays in the background and creates ambience, something Barry is particularly skilled at doing. But the best moment of "instrumental backing" in the film involves, after a rather Shostakovian introduction in the low unison strings, a reprise of a section from the Romance as Forbes cuts back and forth between extreme close-ups of the father telling his wife/daughter the truth about who she is (this cue is not included on the recording). Perhaps one reason this is so moving, apart from the narrative action, is that, in spite of the film's Spanish setting, the guitar is conspicuously absent from all of the musical cues save this one and, of course, the Romance. But there is one other major element of *Deadfall's* music, and that is a classic, minor-mode John Barry song, "My Love Has Two Faces," alternately belted out or moaned with throaty sultriness by Shirley Bassey, who, of course, did Barry's *Thunderball* title theme. Interestingly, "My Love Has Two Faces" is closer to "From Russia with Love," composed by Leslie Bricusse, than it is to *Thunderball*. There is even a turn of phrase that will lead you right into *From Russia with Love* if you're not careful. As I said, it's a good song. But when you consider that one of the two faces of the woman's love is that of her homosexual father/husband (as the Maltin guide quips, "And you think you have problems?"), then the song's lyrics, including such goodies as "The first kiss you gave me / Woke a sleeping dream / And I began to scheme / How we would never part . . . ," seem sick and perverse at best. The theme from the song turns up throughout the score, and it is also presented on this CD (but not on the original LP) in a version, not heard in the film, sung by an unidentified "male vocalist" whose range is barely two or three notes below Bassey's. An unbearable piece of pop schlock entitled "Statue Dance," heard as the vapid Nanette Newman dances around a bust, should have been left off the CD. All in all, this reissue restores an important link in Barry's recorded oeuvre, and it has been beautifully remastered with warm, full sound. The extensive program notes, by director Forbes, Jon Burlingame, and Kendall, are also a definite plus. Still, if I had to choose my essential Barry to resuscitate, it would be *Petulia*. And while we're at it, let's bring out a good video of Richard Lester's rather lugubrious masterpiece. A CD of the score and a DVD of the film are available.

March/April

"Without the music I would have no interest in filmmaking."—Mike Figgis

Ever since the 1988 *Stormy Monday* Mike Figgis has become one of my favorite film directors. Of Polish origins (as I understand) but born in Carlisle, England, Figgis spent his early life in Nairobi, Kenya, only to settle with his family at the age of eight back in England, in Newcastle, where in fact *Stormy Monday* is set. One characteristic of many of Figgis' films is a kind of extremely sharp, hyper-composed, hyper-colored, hyper-real visual style, reminiscent of a director such as Jean-Jacques Beineix. High-art elitists might argue that this style has its origins more in music videos and commercials than it does in the pure art of filmmaking, to which I would respond that much of the most interesting work that is being done with photography and montage these days shows up in commercials and music videos. Figgis is also one of the rare persons working in commercial film who doesn't feel the need to immediately, or in some cases ever, answer some of the questions that might be elicited by his sometimes labyrinthine narratives or even by his often enigmatic visuals. This is particularly true of the first three of Figgis' films—*Stormy Monday, Internal Affairs*, and particularly *Liebestraum* (I seem to be one of only a handful of people on the face of the planet to find *Liebestraum* one of the truly brilliant films of the last 10 years)—all of which have thriller elements (I have not seen Figgis' first film, *The Home*, which I do not think has been released outside of England). But even his most recent movie, **One Night Stand**, which in certain ways might be considered a light comedy or perhaps even what Stanley Cavell has called a "comedy of remarriage," offers many more of such instances of ambiguity than one might suspect. There is, for instance, an eerie moment in the film when, in a darkened hospital room, we see a long shot of an older man standing at the foot of the bed of a young man (Robert Downey, Jr.) who is dying of AIDS. The man quickly disappears, and it is only later that we learn that this was in fact the AIDS victim's father. And in *One Night Stand*, as in most of the director's films, the hero, in this case a director of commercials (ahem) played by Wesley Snipes, is both something of an outsider and a loner who experiences the world differently from the way most other people experience it. This starts as early as *Stormy Monday* with the drifter played by Sean Bean; continues through *Liebestraum* with the character of an architect (Kevin Anderson) drawn into a web of sexual intrigue and possible incest in which the barriers between present and past break down; and peaks in *Mr. Jones* (Richard Gere as a manic depressive), *The Browning Version* (Albert Finney as a misfit boarding-school teacher), and *Leaving Las Vegas* (Nicholas Cage as a suicidal alcoholic). In *One Night Stand*, although the Wesley Snipes character is married and has his "one night stand" with another woman (Nastassja Kinski), it is also implied that in his earlier life he has had a liaison with the dying homosexual, so that by the end of the film Figgis is able to set up a shot in such a way that we are never quite sure how the story will resolve itself between the two pairs of couples, which in this film could in fact include the possibility (not realized, of course; this is, after all, a Hollywood film) of Snipes leaving with his lover's husband (Kyle MacLachlan, who is also the gay character's brother). I also very much like the ways in which Figgis works, in *One Night Stand*, against racial stereotypes, whether in the casting of African-American actor Snipes in the lead role or Chinese-American actress Ming-Na Wen as Snipes' oversexed and reasonably aggressive wife.

But there is another side to the Figgis story, and that, of course, is that he was trained as a musician and has therefore worked on the scores, both as composer and as jazz trumpeter, for several of his films. In fact, music often plays an important role in the Figgis narrative. *Stormy Monday*, for instance, centers around a jazz club (with Sting playing the proprietor) while also giving the director/composer's own group (The People Band) the chance to appear as the "Krakow Jazz Ensemble." The Franz Liszt work of the same title wends its way in and out of both the convoluted plot and the visuals of *Liebestraum*, while in *Mr. Jones*, Richard Gere, who in fact is a pianist, is given the chance to do one of his improvs in a piano store. A key sequence in *One Night Stand* takes place at a concert given by the renowned Juilliard Quartet, whose members were miked live as they played on an elevated platform that permitted cinematographer Delcan Quinn (also the Director of Photography for *Leaving Las Vegas*) to shoot them from all sorts of strange and wonderful angles. Later on, Figgis brings back the Cavatina movement of Beethoven's op. 130 on the music track at a particularly poignant moment. But as I watched *One Night Stand*, I also began to suspect that the music had in fact to be Figgis' most elaborate score to date, a suspicion that was confirmed in the director/composer's program notes, which I wish I could quote in their entirety, for the original music-track recording (Verve). As Figgis notes, "This was the first time I have ever had enough of a budget to use an orchestra and a choir. Listening to ninety musicians playing things that I had only heard on keyboards was rather like an 'out of body' experience." Mind you, the music for *One Night Stand* still offers a fair amount of the soft jazz one hears in other Figgis scores. The title cue, which continues on into the picture as Snipes walks through the streets of New York telling his story to Quinn's highly mobile camera, creates a mood not unlike that of Miles Davis' *In a Silent Way*, particularly when Figgis' trumpet quietly joins in over the electric keyboard, electric guitar, and subtle tattoos from the traps. A dreamier version of the same mood backs the long cue entitled "I'd Like You to Stay," whose title pretty much explains what is going on (Figgis likes to break up his mistily photographed lovemaking with frequent fadeouts). Figgis also creates some slow mood-blues in such cues as the love theme ("Max and Karen" in its longer version, "Karen and Max" in the shorter one) and "A Question for Charles?" But throughout Figgis also creates some solidly non jazzy sounds, often using the string orchestra, sometimes with vocalizing chorus, sometimes with a solo woman's voice, to create sustained expanses of almost pure affect, most of it sad, some of it almost tragic, as in the cue entitled "Life Is an Orange," which comes across like the beginning of a requiem. Two cues, "Angels #2" and "Angels #3," provide an almost mystical musical backdrop for the very vaguely—and very beautifully—photographed ballet (or whatever it is) that the gay man appears to be staging. In a cue entitled "The Mugging," Figgis shifts from his mournful, moody strings to a frenetic jazz lick (including, briefly, a vocalizing woman's voice) as Snipes and Kinski are attacked by a man and a woman as they walk through a New York City parking lot. The CD also includes jazz organist Jimmy Smith's classic "The Organ Grinder's Swing," Nina Simone's version of "Exactly Like You," Jacques Loussier's jazz meditation on Bach's Air on the G String, and, of course, the Juilliard String Quartet performing, with a deliberately slow tempo as per Figgis' intentions, the movement from Beethoven's op. 130, which, of course, needs to be heard in toto. Another jazzy cue very much in tune with the entire score, with some nice playing on the vibes and a stronger bit of vocalizing from the woman's voice, is credited to one Arlen Figgis. I find this to be one of the most important music-track CDs of the year. The music may not be devastatingly original, but it works so well with the film and, in fact, plays such an integral role in it that *One Night Stand* would indeed be unthinkable without it. But this particular score also stands up quite well on its own, as do, naturally, the various pieces of source music.

But perhaps the best film of-the-year so far—and it is the last day of 1997 as I write—is ***The Sweet Hereafter***, directed by Canadian filmmaker Atom Egoyan and based on the novel by Russell Banks, who is a very hot product at the moment. The film, in fact, has already won the Grand Prix at the Cannes Film Festival. The story line is simplicity itself: A lawyer (Ian Holm) arrives in a small town in British Columbia, where he tries to persuade the parents of children who died or were injured in a school-bus accident to bring a lawsuit against anyone who could possibly be found negligent in the affair. The film's subtly dramatic moments grow out of the sometimes-conflicting reactions of the townspeople to the lawyer's proposals, out of the townspeople's reactions to each other within the situation, and out of the lawyer's relationship with his heroin-addicted daughter. But what makes *The Sweet Hereafter* a great work of narrative art is, as is more often than not the case, not just the quality of its storyline but the manner in which it is told. First and foremost, Egoyan, unlike most of those working within the Hollywood system, is not afraid of ambiguity. The film is solidly more than half over, for instance, before its opening, generating image—an overhead shot of a young man and an obviously nursing mother sleeping on a mattress on the floor with a very young girl lying between them—fully opens itself to understanding—rational understanding, that is, since the image instantly communicates on much deeper levels. And throughout the film, Egoyan juxtaposes a sizable number of narrative events whose logic within the chronological time of the narrative universe never becomes fully clear. It is also difficult to find high enough praise for the way in which Egoyan has allowed Paul Sarossy's wide-screen Panavision cinematography to create the bleak, lonely, but ultimately beautiful exteriors as one of the strongest presences in the film. Sarossy, in discussing the Panavision cinematography, has been quoted as saying, "It opens up a whole new dimension compositionally: It's just sort of instantly beautiful to look at, no matter how mundane the subject that the camera is pointed at." Sarossy also goes on to say that "Atom wanted to find the landscape in the characters' faces, and the format is quite ideal for that. The terrain of the face fits in the context of the greater geography." And when it comes to re-creating the accident itself, Egoyan and Sarossy's camera instinctively and discretely moves backward, creating an image that is infinitely more disturbing than all the closeups and the shots of accident victims desperately trying to escape that would surely have filled many moments of a Hollywood version of the same incident. The film also has certain David-Lynch-ish touches of the banal grotesque, whether the disturbing presence of a stroke victim in certain sequences or the unexplainable mask used by a stenographer toward the end of the film (the device, which

I thought was for breathing, is, I am informed by my lawyer brother, actually part of a dictating device to cover up the sound; you learn something every day). There is also something of a Zen element in both Egoyan and Lynch, although in the former this tends to be more visually generated, whereas Lynch actually incorporates it into his narratives.

It would be difficult to imagine music playing a more integral part in a film than the score composed by Egoyan regular Mychael Danna for *The Sweet Hereafter* (Virgin Music Canada; Sarah Polley, vocals). Danna establishes the principal theme and mood for the film as of the title sequence, behind which we hear, inexplicably for the moment, what sounds like a slow processional from the late-medieval period. As it turns out, the cue, appropriately entitled "Procession," is performed by the Toronto Consort, which here includes a lute, recorders, sackbut, shawm, two vielles, and percussion. The haunting, modal main theme, originally presented in the lutes and then on a silver flute (just so the medieval flavor does not become an absolute) is later taken up by the Persian ney (a rather nasal wind instrument) as the music moves into a dramatic swell. As with everything else in *The Sweet Hereafter*, it takes a while before this non-narrative element of the film merges, at least to a degree, with one of its narrative elements, in this case the reading, by the film's teenage heroine, from an illustrated book of "The Pied Piper of Hamelin" to a twin brother and sister who will die in the accident, while the babysitter will emerge from it as a paraplegic. Added to the Banks story by Egoyan, the "Pied Piper" story works in the film not as a metaphor but rather as an expansion of the story into the domain of the archetypal and archaic. And so before we are even introduced to "The Pied Piper," Danna's music stands as a metonymical expression of that story and as a musical creation of that archetypal/archaic dimension (p.r. material for the CD states that Danna was going after "a timeless, fable-like quality"; but I feel it's much more than that). The medieval quality dominates many of the cues, sometimes with reprises of the main theme, sometimes going off in more extroverted directions, whether the fast dance that turns up in "It's Important That We Talk," sometimes boiling down to a sad hush, as in the lute/vielle duet that opens "It Was a Wonderful Time in Our Lives." Later in that same cue, we hear an absolutely captivating lute solo over a quiet figure in the drums; eventually, the main theme returns in a flute/recorder duet. Danna also, however, creates, via a sparse use of electronics, some more otherworldly effects, as in the dreamy dance for piano and flutes over a quiet synthesizer drone in a highly reverberant acoustic that closes "It Was a Wonderful Time. . . ." Overblown flutes within the same acoustic setting create the musical backdrop for "Thin Ice." On one or two occasions, one also notes an almost Near Eastern quality to the music, perhaps reminiscent of the director's (and the composer's?) Armenian origins.

But there is another entire dimension to the score for *The Sweet Hereafter*, and that is a set of songs that fall somewhere between country/western and folk, and that are performed by a septet that includes vocals by actress Sarah Polley, who in fact is first seen in the film performing with that group outdoors at a county fair of some sort. The title song, with lyrics from the Robert Browning poem, was composed by Danna and

Polley, while Danna wrote the music and Polley the lyrics for "Dog Track Drizzle" and "Boy." Polley also performs two other songs, both arranged by Danna, Jane Siberry's mutedly sad "One More Colour," and The Tragically Hip's "Courage." Perhaps the most important element of all of these songs is the sweet, immature quality of Polley's voice, which, whenever it appears on the music track, reminds us that the character she plays in the film is an adolescent girl, not the sexual woman her father has incestuously turned her into. This in turn relates to the film's ambiguous generating image, the orally told story that grows out of it, and, finally, the film's second, tragic father/daughter relationship. When all is said and done, all of the diverse elements of the filmmaking art blend together with such exquisite subtlety and perfection in *The Sweet Hereafter* that it does an injustice to the work of Egoyan, Sarossy, Polley, and all others concerned to try and separate them.

Another novel I have not read, nor in this instance am I apt to, since this is not the kind of popular fiction I enjoy, is John Grisham's *The Rainmaker*, which has been turned into a movie called, no doubt because the author has blockbuster clout (this is the Grisham's sixth film adaptation), **John Grisham's The Rainmaker**, which I had no intention of seeing until a) I remembered that it was directed by the venerable Francis Ford Coppola, and b) I listened to the score by the venerable Elmer Bernstein (Hollywood). I mean, how can you not want to see a film when its music brings together elements of some of the best scores—in particular *Walk on the Wild Side, To Kill a Mockingbird,* and *The Grifters*; there is even a bit of *The Magnificent Seven* in the cue entitled "Goodbye Dot"—by one of Hollywood's best composers? The title cue, appropriately enough entitled "Sharks" for this typical Grisham lawyer saga, opens with a dissonant chord in the winds that suggests anything but the mood to follow, in which a jivey Hammond B3 electric-organ solo played by Mike Lang leads into a big-band swing number with a 6/8 lilt to it totally in the mode of *Walk on the Wild Side*. One wonders, in fact, whether Bernstein's use of the Hammond organ throughout the score might have been inspired by Jimmy Smith's famous version of the *Walk on the Wild Side* theme. But the music quickly changes tone again as Bernstein boils things down into small combos—organ over a piano ostinato in octaves, a bluesy theme in the, would you believe, Ondes Martenot over bass and drums—that have the more acidic quality of a score such as *The Grifters*. Throughout the 12 cues recorded here, there is scarcely a mood, instrumental configuration, or rhythmic figure that Bernstein does not stop and examine at least briefly (in fact, the score rarely settles into a single style for more than 20 or 30 seconds). The music for "The Fight," in which the film's fresh-out-of-law-school hero (Matt Damon) encounters, pretty much in the dark, the abusive husband of a woman (Claire Danes) he has met at a hospital where he has been ambulance chasing, becomes the kind of pulsating half-jazz, half-classical angular ballet that dominated the musical scene, both in films and on Broadway, during the 1950s, although a very dissonant solo violin shakes up that style a bit. The cue entitled "Who Is Jackie Lemancyzk?" (an examiner for a sleazy insurance company the young lawyer is trying to track down) eventually moves to an almost corny string ostinato over which the Hammond organ and (I think) the Ondes Martenot create something that could almost be an *Ed Wood* pastiche à la the Howard Shore music for the Tim Burton film. We get several lyrical themes (the young lawyer, of course, ultimately winds up with the abused woman), one of which is heard in the solo guitar and strings at the beginning of the cue entitled "The Trial Ends." Toward the end of the "Donny" cue, Bernstein gives us a jaunty, walking-through-small-town-America theme set to an 11/8 meter, the whole thing lasting a bit over 30 seconds. And in "Shenanigans," in which the young lawyer and his corporate-hotshot adversary (Jon Voight) accompany an almost clown-like judge (Dean Stockwell) into his chambers, Bernstein turns to a herky-jerky dance with almost pointillistic instrumentation and bad-boy dissonances very reminiscent of the mechanical-bird cue in Nino Rota's score for Fellini's *Casanova*. I could go on. The whole CD, although not spectacularly recorded, offers a spectacular, constantly varied listening experience. I guess the question I would have to ask, however, is what is all that rich, clever, and varied music doing in this film? In trying to create an integrated image of the film and its score, my mind keeps breaking that image down into two wholly separate works of art, the music eminently listenable, the film, while corny and manipulative, reasonably engrossing, thanks mostly, I suspect, to Coppola's skill in using his actors, who in this film also include an almost unrecognizable Mickey Rourke as a thoroughly crooked lawyer and—here's that word again—the venerable Teresa Wright as the old woman who gives the young lawyer a place to live. Just why Coppola and/or his producers decided that this tale of ambulance chasing, corporate rape, spousal abuse, and whatever else, most of it set in a small Mississippi town (keep in mind that Grisham himself got a law degree from the University of Mississippi), needed such a sophisticated score is anybody's guess. As much as I am a fan of traditional film music, I would have used only source music in this particular film. But that's no doubt one good reason why I'm sitting here at my word processor writing this column rather than making films . . . or scoring them.

Varèse Sarabande's new release of Jerry Goldsmith's **Planet of the Apes** is at least the third CD avatar (the last one in my collection is on the Intrada label) of Goldsmith's hugely original music for the first in a series of movies that part of me wants to find subtextually fascinating while the other part finds them quintessentially silly. As the second release in the second wave of "Fox Classics" now taken over by Varèse Sarabande, this version of the music for director Franklin J. Schaffner's 1968 sci-fi hit will probably remain the definitive one, at least until a new format takes over from CDs. It includes almost 20 minutes' worth of cues, or parts of cues, previously unreleased, and it features exceptionally clear and well-defined sound that will give you no qualms about sending your earlier recordings off to your local secondhand CD store. What makes *Planet of the Apes* one of the most appreciated and respected scores in the history of film music? Well, for starters there is the amazing battery of original timbres that Goldsmith came up with, some of them, including those produced by stainless-steel mixing bowls, taken right out of his kitchen. The score also mobilizes ram's horn, friction drum, and the particularly eerie sounds of a bass slide-whistle. Other offbeat effects are obtained by such devices as scraping a triangle beater across a gong or air blown through the inverted mouthpieces of the brass instruments with echo and reverberation. The oddly vocal gruntings of the Brazilian cuika bring some of the ape sounds into the music track, most notably in the "Intruders" cue, heard here for the first time on recording. Goldsmith also makes extensive use of the piano as both a coloristic presence and a percussion instrument. But one of the amazing elements of the score is the manner in which Goldsmith integrates these "instruments" into the overall fabric of a large symphony orchestra beefed up with just about all the percussion instruments available. Another element of amazement is that, for this big-budget film aimed at large audiences, Goldsmith was able to get away with music, heard prominently throughout the film, that not only offers nothing even resembling a lyrical theme but that, in fact, deliberately and methodically steers clear of tonality throughout almost all of its cues (16 on this CD). While the basic musical language comes, as it often does in Goldsmith, via Bartók—there is even a pretty direct quotation in "The Clothes Snatchers"—the composer continually explores devices, such as huge cluster-chords, that would be considered pretty avant-garde in concert music. Of course, no film composer has ever been able to create quite the kind of extended yet musically logical frenzy that one hears in Goldsmith's action cues. Listening to "The Hunt" can leave you exhausted. Yet Goldsmith also offers numerous moments of almost pure, low-key mood, as in the interplay between such instruments as vibraphone, chimes, and claves in the "Trial" cue. As if all this weren't enough, the CD concludes with a 16-minute, previously unrecorded Suite from the 1971 *Escape from the Planet of the Apes*. Although the music heard in this suite has a certain common base with the original score, along with even more overt Bartókisms, it also introduces at various moments a mild pop sound carried principally by an electric guitar and electric bass.

My partiality to the scores composed by Bernard Herrmann for the films of Alfred Hitchcock is certainly no secret. But in a recent review of a CD-reissue of one of Herrmann's Phase-4 recordings of his film scores, I noted that his music for the 1959 cine-adaptation of Jules Verne's **Journey to the Center of the Earth** must be considered one of his supreme accomplishments. And so now we have, as Varèse Sarabande's first release in the second wave of classics from the 20th Century-Fox vaults, the original music tracks, recorded in very present, very unreverberant, and very clearly defined stereo, composed by Herrmann for a corny film made irretrievably awful by the acting of Pat Boone (and who ever said that Boone could sing?). Scored almost entirely for winds, brass, and percussion, along with a cathedral organ and four electronic ones, *Journey to the Center of the Earth* contains a whole battery of familiar Herrmann sounds, including frequent appearances of those gloomy, unresolving, parallel triads, played both straight but also often broken up into small (usually two-note) motifs, in the low clarinets, muted brass, and/or solo vibraphone. Indeed, some of the music would be just as comfortable in a Hitchcock film. The opening of "The Canyon," for instance, is right out of *North by Northwest*. But then there is also the amazing Prelude, which, with descending series of chords announced by the cathedral organ and taken up by a large number of brass instruments, leads us straight to the center of the Earth long before the film ever gets us there. If you use a little imagination, it is not hard to hear Herrmann's cramped modulations of the small musical cells played by brass, harp, and bells in "Mushroom Forest" as a prelude to Minimalism. And, of course, lest we forget, Herrmann also offers that archaic instrument, the serpent, as an aural metonymy for one of the many monsters (in this case a giant chameleon) that pop up during the voyage to the Earth's core. Described by David Raksin as sounding like "a donkey with emotional problems," the serpent creates a wheezy, colorless blat to which the adjective "flatulent" would seem to best apply. The CD also offers, mistakenly in my opinion, several songs, two not heard in the film's final cut, rendered almost colorless by Pat Boone's bland baritone (I also seem to recall a student song, not offered here, that gives Boone the chance to use the expression "ki yi" at one or two points that make his unmemorable dialogue even more unmemorable; but it has been many years since I've seen the film). The perfunctory quality of Steven C. Smith's brief program note for *Journey* is fairly insulting. Smith also, in my opinion, makes the biographer's mistake of relying almost wholly on the composer's own description of his music, which stresses the film's "malevolent color" and "terror." To my sensibilities, the most effective parts of the music suggest both magic (in its purest chthonic sense) and awe. Where all of the various monster and disaster music amounts to skillful but hackneyed cine-musical overkill, with the timbres of the serpent bordering on the comical, the eerie, floating chords in the electric organ and vibraphone of "Atlantis" transport the soul across eons of vast silence so effectively that one can forget all of the papier-mâché and glitter of the film's chintzy sets.

May/June

With all of the hoopla that has been built up over director James Cameron's **Titanic**, has anybody stopped to look at the crushing absurdity of spending $200,000,000 on a film that uses up at least 75% of its time on a love story that trashes the rich—you know, the kinds of people who occupied the first-class quarters aboard the Titanic? Of course, mitigating this irony is the fact that throughout most of its three-plus-hour running time, *Titanic* looks (and sounds; but we'll get to that in a moment) as if it cost maybe $200,000 to make. I mean, why reconstruct a 9/10-scale model of the ill-fated ocean liner if your apparent main interest is filling the screen with talking heads (in this case mostly Kate Winslet and Leonardo DiCaprio)? Even as the ship is going down, the best thing Cameron as screenwriter could come up with is Winslet and Di-Caprio screaming "Rose!" and "Jack!" at each other several hundred thousand times. Then again, I suppose this is preferable to the over-the-top manner in which Cameron has painted those awful rich people. As Winslet's American aristocrat (is that an oxymoron?) fiancé, Billy Zane might as well come on scene twirling a handle-bar mustache and accompanied by those stormy moments from the *Poet and Peasant Overture* that served silent melodramas so well (but save a few hisses as well for David Warner as Zane's evil valet). And with people uttering nary a gasp as they are hit by rushing water that is only a couple of degrees above freezing (one can survive for about four minutes in such water, I am told), I am reminded of a truly horrible film from the Disney Studios called *The Black Hole*, in which various crew members walk through a mostly destroyed spaceship without benefit of anything to compensate for the total lack of oxygen and air pressure. Further, *Titanic* gives one practically no sense of what it feels like to be on an ocean liner (having crossed the Atlantic on ships four times—not in first class, mind you—I can attest to this to some degree), nor does it create more than the most totally perfunctory presence of the various passengers. Even the venerable Kathy Bates gets maybe two or three minutes of screen time—maximum—as the "unsinkable" Molly Brown. Cameron also manages to devalue underwater footage of the recently discovered Titanic wreck by weaving it around poorly scripted plotting and dumb acting, although it was fun to see 88-year-old screen veteran Gloria Stuart play the current-day Winslet character. But 101 years old she absolutely ain't (I will, however, root for her at the Oscars). And Stuart's final gesture in the film may represent the most hypocritical moment the Hollywood film industry has come up with to date, and that's saying something.

Contributing to the cheapening of what could and should have been a great film (hey, give me 200 mil and let me take a shot at it) is the totally blah and lackluster musical score by James Horner (Sony). Perhaps Horner thought he was still working on *Braveheart*, since *Titanic's* mildly ethnic opening theme, which dominates the film right on through to its final "Hymn to the Sea," is played by the same Uilleann pipes (electronically beefed up here and there) heard in *Braveheart*. Once the bland-bland-bland, major-mode music moves into the orchestra, Horner's idea of coloration is to add some breathy vocalizing from a singer who goes by the name of En . . . , sorry, Sissel. The rippling, 6/8 Impressionism followed by the seafaring nobility of "Distant Memories" has become such a film-music cliché that just about anybody but Horner would have been ashamed to use it. To suggest the hustle and bustle of the Southampton port, the composer could come up with nothing better than some limp syncopations trivialized even further by sampled, vocalizing chorus. The Uilleann pipes and Sissel take turns with the theme for Rose, initially heard above a fairly standard keyboard-synth setting that might be dubbed "throaty celesta." As melodies go, I suppose this one isn't so bad—or it wouldn't be if one didn't constantly have the feeling that the music is trying to manipulate you into feeling just how genuine and tragic Kate and Jack's love is. Eventually, of course, Rose's theme gets turned into a tune, "My Heart Will Go On," sung by tiny-voiced Celine Dion. One has to imagine Horner and Will Jennings, who wrote the lyrics, watching a past Oscar ceremony as they put "My Heart Will Go On" together, and I will be dumbfounded if this doesn't get the Best Original Song award. Once disaster strikes, of course, Horner does not fail to provide some pounding action music, not one note of it something you haven't heard in hundreds of other film scores. Sony's recorded sound is thumpy, bassy, and a bit mushy. Of course, my opinion here represents a decided minority, even for the gawdawful music. Indeed, the really depressing news here is that the *Titanic* CD looks as if it is going to become the all-time moneymaker, if it hasn't already, for "original soundtrack" CDs. And there is practically no question that *Titanic* will gobble up just about every Oscar in sight this year, maybe even setting a record (you heard it here first). That thought is so discouraging that I think I'll probably skip watching the ceremonies this year . . . and go to a good movie.

July/August

If ever there has been a more misleading trailer for a film than the one for Gillian Armstrong's **Oscar and Lucinda**, I can't imagine what it would be. I swear, after seeing the trailer (we used to call them "previews"), I thought that the film was about a 19th-century man and woman who somehow meet and spend the rest of their lives gambling on a riverboat. Or something like that. As it turns out, however, the film, based on Peter Carey's 1988 novel, deals with a pair of misfits, one an English minister (Ralph Fiennes) whose partially unwilling attachment to his father and his father's strict religious views never allows him to quite get in touch with the real world, the other an Australian heiress (Cate Blanchett) whose strength of character and soul keeps her at the outskirts of patriarchal culture. The gambling to which both are addicted is nothing more (and nothing less) than the emblem of the marginalization of both characters, Oscar with respects to existence itself, Lucinda with respects to society. Oscar's inability to get the spirit to join with the flesh, try as he might, ultimately finds its expression in the symbol, brilliant in the novel and perhaps even more brilliant in its physical presence in the film, of a glass cathedral that he ultimately transports, piece by piece, from Sydney to a godforsaken outpost hundreds of miles away. For *Oscar and Lucinda*, Thomas Newman, who earlier provided the wonderful, oft-quoted music for Armstrong's *Little Women*, has come up with one of his best scores (Sony). This is no small tribute, since for my money this youngest son of Alfred Newman has over his 14-year career, from *The Player* through *The Shawshank Redemption* and *Little Women* right on to his most recent scores, come up with some of the most distinctive and effective film music to be produced by the current generation (or any generation, for that matter). Right from the outset in the Main Title ("Prince Rupert's Drop"), with its mixed bell sonorities, its hauntingly archaic harmonies (open fifths are a frequent feature of Newman's cues), and its rhythmically persistent theme, the music defines itself as pure Thomas Newman. It also, however, sets a perfect tone for the film. The opening bell timbres, which carry over into the register and textures of the solo piano's presentation of the main theme, aurally suggest the glass cathedral to come much later. Indeed, there is a transparence to Newman's writing that throughout serves as a kind of musical metonymy for the film's central metaphor. But adjectives that one might apply to the main theme—jaunty, obsessive, offbeat—likewise easily describe the two main characters. And I can't help but wonder whether the theme's rhythmic profile was inspired by part of a line from Carey's novel read by Fiennes (from the Random House AudioBook) on the final cue offered on the Sony CD: "But what would one intend?" she asked. "What would one intend . . . ?"

Still in the Main Title, the music suddenly shifts to a choral passage (performed by the Paulist Boy Choristers of California), making the visual of the father's small, wooden church being transported down a marshy river (foreshadowing the later transporting of the miniature glass cathedral) almost superfluous. Interestingly, Newman's music is subtly marked by the composer's American roots. The cue entitled "Six Rivers to Cross" definitely has a hoe-down quality to it, while the poignant theme first presented in the solo flute in the slow, sad waltz of "Throwing Lots" (with Newman's characteristic bell sonorities still in the background) mildly harks back to the theme created by Max Steiner for the native-American woman called "Look" in John Ford's *The Searchers*. But the modal turns and twists taken by Newman's themes and motifs can also easily suggest the roots of the American roots, as they do in *Oscar and Lucinda*. I also very much like the way Newman horizontally unfolds his open-interval harmonies at such moments as the rapid, unison violin figures that open "Dutch Hazards." Another particularly memorable cine-musical moment occurs during the scene when the Australians accompanying the transportation of the glass cathedral open fire, with the casual arrogance of the white, Anglo-Saxon male, on a band of black aborigines. Newman's music, rather than indulging in the usual doom-and-gloom clichés, weighs on the soul through the rhythmic and timbral heaviness of halting figures coming from the low strings that accompany portentous, mostly unison notes that are held in the horns. Yet the music is just a step or two away from what could almost become a dance-like romp if it were given the chance, and in this instance it takes the subtle balance established between Newman's resited music and Anderson's non-manipulative direction to bring out the full horror of the scene. I could go on. In this score, Newman runs the gamut from high drama through merriment to some very subdued *misterioso* evocations. I also particularly like the way the composer uses the human voice, including a boy soprano, as another instrument in his non-traditional orchestral palette. The music-track recording also contains a couple of non-Newman choral pieces, one Bruckner's *Os Justi*, the other Samuel Wesley's hymn "Blessed Be the God and Father," the words for which seem particularly appropriate to the filmic action.

Alan Rudolph's probing and, ultimately, deeply moving **Afterglow** features an exquisite score by frequent collaborator Mark Isham (Columbia). And, in fact, the trailers for *Afterglow* were just about as misleading as those for *Oscar and Lucinda*: you have the impression that the film is about little more than some fairly hip wife-swapping, with Nick Nolte going after the much younger Lara Flynn Boyle, setting up his wife (Julie Christie) to make a move on Boyle's decidedly disinterested husband (Jonny Lee Miller). But once the film gets its foundation built—and *Afterglow* starts out as one of those movies you're not sure you're not going to walk out on, so painfully self-conscious is the mating dance done by the neurotic and sexually frustrated Boyle around the world-weary Nolte—it erects a complex superstructure of failed relationships, parental as well as spousal, that reaches its apex in a heartbreaking letting-go by Julie Christie, who solidly deserved the Best-Actress Oscar nomination she received for this role. Throughout his 25-plus-year career, Rudolph has almost never used music in traditional ways, which comes as no great surprise from the man who was Robert Altman's assistant director on the 1975 *Nashville* (Altman, whose Lion's

Gate Films was behind many earlier Rudolph efforts, produced *Afterglow*). Indeed, Rudolph's early masterpiece, *Welcome to L. A.*, can be seen as a kind of intimate variation (all of Rudolph's films have an element of intimacy that he certainly did not inherit from his mentor Altman) on *Nashville*, while for his next film, the 1978 *Remember My Name*, the director got blues singer Alberta Hunter to compose and perform the songs that wander in and out of the film's narrative. Indeed, even when the music in a Rudolph film is not identified as coming from a particular "source," one often has the impression that it just as easily as not could be. This is certainly the case for the 10 cues of mostly soft bebop composed by Isham for *Afterglow*. I have to confess that I was so engrossed in the film (once it got off the ground) when I saw it in the theater that I really didn't take major note of just how the music was used, although my memory is that most of it is non-source "backing." In his brief program note, director Rudolph states that "this music was recorded live." Does that mean that, as did Miles Davis and company for Louis Malle's *L'Ascenseur pour l'échafaud* (*Frantic*), Isham and his musicians created the music as they watched scenes from the film? Or does it mean that this music was being played off-camera during the shooting of at least some of the scenes?

Whatever the case, I would think that the Columbia CD of *Afterglow* will appeal at least if not more to jazz lovers as it will to film-music buffs. Purists may object to the lack, within the various cues, of the classic improvised breaks, although improvisation almost certainly plays some kind of role in just about every cue. But I cannot imagine how anyone would not be moved both by the haunting music and by the incredibly soulful performances by Isham (on both trumpet and flumpet, the latter an instrument—half trumpet, half flugelhorn, invented by David Monette and described in Isham's newsletter at www.isham.com as one of the "new trumpets you have seen that look like rocket ships," that are "beautiful," and that "play very well"), Charles Lloyd (saxophone), Gary Burton (vibes), Sid Page (violin), Geri Allen (piano), Billy Higgins (drums), and Jeff Littleton (bass). At no time throughout the score does the septet play as an ensemble. Instead, Isham works out the music through various instrumental combinations, some of them classic, some of them spine-chillingly unexpected. Isham's solo trumpet (or, more likely, flumpet) starts off the sad, opening ballade ("After the Glow Has Gone") pretty much as a standard jazz quartet, with the sax later taking over. On the other hand, the second cue ("Yeses, Noes, and In-Between") begins as a slow, sad trio among sax, bass, and piano, with the latter playing a simple but poignant accompaniment figure. And then, quietly, the violin makes an appearance, and suddenly the music takes on several added degrees of that unspoken intimacy so essential to Rudolph's cinema. (I'm not normally a huge fan of jazz violin; but Isham has taken such skillful advantage of the instrument's middle ranges, and Sid Page's playing jells so thoroughly with the rest of the ensemble, that it's difficult not to become a convert here.) Gary Burton's vibes do not enter until the fourth cue ("Hope and Charity"); but when they do, Burton plays the quiet and subtle filigrees with such finesse that one partly wishes he had been given a larger role in the music. In the sixth cue ("Yeses and Noes"), which almost unnoticeably brings back the accompaniment figure from the second cue, flumpet, vibes, and bass offer an exquisitely dreamy trio. As should be apparent, the music's general tone is quiet and inner-directed. But in one cue, not surprisingly entitled "Frenzy" sax, piano, bass, and drum take off in fairly raucous (for this score, at least), almost free-jazz directions. After this moment of near chaos, however, the music returns, in its final two cues, to introspection and melancholy. A moment that almost takes the breath away occurs in the ninth cue ("Afterglow"), when the flumpet unexpectedly joins the violin an octave lower as it soars upward with a bittersweet motif established by both the violin and saxophone at the cue's opening. The solo violin then reprises this music in the hushed passion of the brief final cue. Enough said. The recorded sound is perfect, the playing beyond superb for a score that perfectly captures the spirit of Alan Rudolph's film while mirroring in various ways its complex interrelationships. The music also stands gloriously on its own.

If someone were to ask me to make a list of the 10 best film-score recordings, one of them would certainly be the Entr'acte LP brought out in 1976 of Max Steiner's score for the original **King Kong** directed in 1933 by Merian C. Cooper and Ernest Schoedsack. That recording, which has resurfaced several times on CD on various Entr'acte avatars (Label X, Southern Cross, etc.), features composer Fred Steiner (no relation) conducting the National Philharmonic Orchestra in a wonderfully dynamic, well-played performance with spectacular recorded sound that can hold its own with just about anything you will hear today. Now Marco Polo has brought out a new CD of Steiner's classic score with William J. Stromberg conducting the Moscow Symphony Orchestra in a reconstruction done by John Morgan. And so, you may ask, is this new recording necessary? Yes and no. No, because the recorded sound lacks the brightness, depth, and balance one finds on the Steiner version. No, because the Moscow Symphony Orchestra does not play as well as the National Philharmonic, at least not here. And no, because Stromberg's interpretation of the music, while serviceable, seems more literal-minded than Steiner's, which has punch and spirit to spare. Yes, on the other hand, because King Kong is one of the great film scores of all time, and it can therefore certainly withstand multiple ways of looking at it. As is well known by now, Steiner was able to get an unusually large orchestra for the time, although certainly not as large as he would ideally have needed, as John Morgan points out in his program note. It is in fact little short of miraculous that Steiner was able to even conceive of a symphonic score of this scope at a point when sound recording for the cinema was barely out of the stone age and when many of the studio execs were still looking to cut and paste classical borrowings to use on the by now more extensive music tracks. Not unexpectedly, Steiner more often than not mobilizes his instrumental forces to produce driving, fortissimo passages of a kind of naïve but nonetheless effective musical primitivism that definitely established a standard that Hollywood still looks back to (if Stravinsky is a factor here, it is more the Stravinsky of *The Firebird* than *The Rite of Spring*). Yet Steiner was also capable of some wonderful moments of musical understatement. The fog generated by the winds, harp, and strings in "A Boat in the Fog," for instance, is all but palpable. And I have always loved the almost ghoulish tritone figure Steiner uses as the backbone of the march that accompanies the crew members once they take off after Kong. Another major strength of the score is the unity that Steiner gives it by generating an incredible amount of the musical material—even the love theme—out of the three-note motif for Kong that opens the score.

All of which brings me to my final "yes." The Fred Steiner *King Kong*, originally made for LP, offers under 50 minutes' worth of the music, which means that some judicious choices had to be made. Certainly, the essence of the score is there. But it is definitely fun to have the complete music—plus some—for the film, although I am surprised it does not run longer than 70-plus minutes, since it feels to me that, after the 10 to 15 minutes of expository action that opens this 104-minute (with cuts restored) film, the music almost never stops. Perhaps the part of this CD where the listener becomes the most aware of what was missing from the earlier recording is in the cues that back the tracking of Kong on Skull Island, almost a half hour of pure Steiner tone painting, much of it so driven that you will find yourself exhausted after listening to it. There is also some additional music for a scene when the cook's pet monkey escapes, and for some footage preceding the elevated-train sequence for action ultimately cut from the film. I guarantee you that you will not have to follow the cue titles to know when the "Little Monkey Escapes" music—Steiner's largest debt to *The Firebird*—begins. Further, in preparing the score from the original audio components, the surviving full scores, and Steiner's original annotated sketches ("which," Morgan points out, "contain every note he composed for the film"), John Morgan, who in fact was involved in the Entr'acte project, did not attempt to literally reproduce what is heard in the movie but rather what he imagines the composer would have wanted under ideal circumstances. Or, as Morgan puts it, "This recording is not a recreation of the 1933 music tracks, but a musical performance of the complete score as Steiner's original sketches dictated. When we noted differences in the soundtrack as compared to the original sketches (whether added or subtracted bars, repeated phrases, or instrumentation additions or deletions), we first tried to determine why these changes were made. If we felt they were primarily made for technical reasons (avoiding a sound-effect conflict, re-editing the film, etc.) we deferred to Steiner's original conception[s] and implemented them." For my money, this approach makes this CD an all the more valuable contribution to recorded film music. Of course, if you have seen and heard *King Kong* as many times as I have, there are little moments that will jolt you even as they give you a broader knowledge of what the composer originally intended. Besides the considerable material by Morgan, the 35-page program booklet contains Steiner tributes from such diverse people as visual-effects artist Ray Harryhausen, author Ray Bradbury, musician Louise Klos Steiner Elian (the composer's wife), and BYU Film Music Archives curator James D'Arc. Ray Faiola, Director of Audience Services for CBS Television, provides "cue notes," while conductor Stromberg also gets his say at the end. Poster art, pages from the sketches and the score, and various photographs are also included.

Back to the '60s via Ryko

Rykodisc, a company with an apparently huge commitment to film music, has begun a series of "original soundtrack recordings" which, although dubbed as the "Rykodisc/MGM Soundtrack Series," features music from a bunch of films released by United Artists (and often originally recorded on that company's record label). While the releases offer film music from the '60s through the '80s, three of the four CDs that form the batch I have so far received mark a particularly significant turn—positive for some, anathema for others—in the history of movie scoring, a turn that took place during the '60s. Although jazz and even some pop music, including rock 'n roll in the 1955 *Blackboard Jungle*, had begun to make inroads into film scoring, classical music, most of it symphonic, pretty much remained the standard as the '60s got underway. But with the arrival on the scene of such composers as Henry Mancini in the U.S., John Barry (originally) in England, and Michel Legrand and Francis Lai in France, all of whom proved capable of working in the more traditional veins as well, the film industry almost overnight came up with a new musical sound that involved not only a fairly easy-to-listen-to fusion of jazz and popular styles (with just a tad of classical thrown in for good measure) but that also demanded at least one marketable pop tune for almost every film. Soon, it seemed as if every film out of Hollywood had to have a song in it somewhere, and, in fact, I remember reading a review, probably in the *New York Times*, of an early Jacqueline Bisset film called *The Grasshopper* (1970) that complained of precisely that phenomenon. Film-music purists of course saw this new tendency as just about single-handedly destroying the post-romantic to modernistic paths so carefully and lovingly laid down by the Max Steiners, the Miklós Rózsas, the Bernard Herrmanns, the Franz Waxmans, et al. And, indeed, there is no question that Universal's love affair with the new sound brought the spectacularly successful Herrmann/Hitchcock collaboration to a screeching halt. Still, there is no question that in fact the old way of scoring was simply not appropriate for many of the suaver, hipper films of the '60s. What would the James Bond flicks be without their (usually John Barry) title songs (and where would all those misogynistic voyeurs have gone without the Main Title visuals)? And, frankly, if you have to stop cold the action of a movie such as *Butch Cassidy and the Sundance Kid* to get a song such as the Burt Bacharach/Hal David "Raindrops Keep Fallin' on My Head," then I'm all for it. Hollywood's mistake, as always, lay not in coming up with new directions but rather in trying to cash in on them with each and every film (I can't wait to see how they're going to make *Titanic II: The Disaster Strikes Again*; perhaps they'll raise the wreck from the bottom of the sea and refurbish it so that, oh, Jerry Seinfeld and Helen Hunt can find a way to make the mightiest of ocean liners sink again). Alfred Hitchcock needed something deeper than Francis Lai; Norman Jewison didn't. Anyway, I should note that each of these Ryko CDs includes brief CD ROM material from the movies with snippets of dialogue occasionally interspersed between the musical cues. Here's the first batch:

    1. Michel Legrand: ***The Thomas Crown Affair***. Michel Legrand's score for Norman Jewison's frothy 1968 thriller about a cat-and-mouse game between a master

thief (Steve McQueen) and an insurance-company investigator (Faye Dunaway) opens with one of the best songs from the cinema '60s, "The Windmills of Your Mind," sung, in a manner of speaking (or perhaps spoken, in a manner of singing), by Noel Harrison (Remember him? No? How about *The Girl from U.N.C.L.E.*? Still no? Rex's son? Ah. . . .). Although the lyrics by Marilyn and Alan Bergman come across a bit as Revlon psychedelic, the song has a beautiful flow to it strengthened by Legrand's characteristic motivic and instrumental figurations, some of which smack faintly of Bach. Later on the recording offers an instrumental version with the theme carried mostly by a solo harpsichord. As if this weren't enough, Legrand offers a quieter second song, a ballade entitled "His Eyes, Her Eyes," for which I think he also wrote the lyrics, and which in one cue he sings with his usual élan in heavily accented English. And a second melody in that same song, which also turns up by itself in other cues, is perhaps even more striking than the opening theme, which serves as a motif throughout the score. As for the instrumental "backing," much of it is in a clever jazz style, sometimes funky, sometimes cool, of which Legrand is an absolute master. At one point, the composer joins in on a fast cue with some scat singing. I also love the dreaminess of the cue entitled "A Man's Castle," with its echo effects in the flute and its moody sustained chords. Of course, Legrand can wander on occasion dangerously close to Montovani and/or the Tijuana Brass. But that is all part of the '60s shtick, and, on the whole, *The Thomas Crown Affair* is absolutely one of the best scores of its kind. And as a vocalist, Legrand is irrepressible.

2. John Barry: ***The Knack . . . and How to Get It***. If you counted the number of great comedy directors in the cinema, you would have trouble getting past the 10 fingers on your hand. Richard Lester was a great comedy director, whether in the Keystone Kops-cum-nihilism style of the two Beatles films (*A Hard Day's Night* and *Help!*), the zany bedroom antics of *The Knack*, or the half slapstick, half heavy-drama of what may be the best film version(s) ever of *The Three Musketeers* (cut into two films, the second of which became *The Four Musketeers*). Lester also had a darker side, as witness the underrated *Petulia*, which to boot contains what I consider to be John Barry's finest score. *The Knack . . . and How to Get It* features Rita Tushingham in her usual role as a slightly naïve, slightly kooky, overly sensitive young woman who in this case wanders into the lives of two men, one who has "the knack" (to attract woman), the other of whom is out to get it. John Barry's score is dominated by a single theme, a wonderfully jaunty, half-major, half-minor jazz waltz that would have made Hank Mancini proud. It turns up in just about all the cues. Barry gives the theme variety by moving it in and out of various jazz riffs, many of them involving an electric organ à la Jimmy Smith (Alan Haven in this case). One of the only two cues ("Blues and Out") that totally escape from the main theme is a slow, big-band blues featuring some classy organ work from Haven. Interestingly, the opening bars of the "Main Theme" cue briefly suggest the possibility of one of those James Bond sequences in which a larger space capsule devours a smaller one. Then, all of a sudden, the title theme bounces into play, and all is well. Unfortunately, there is also an uncredited male vocal of the main theme built around the most hair-raisingly sexist lyrics one can imagine (of course, the

film itself would hardly qualify for a feminist award). But then, that was the '60s as well: for Hollywood as well as in most of the rest of life sexual liberation meant greater availability—and greater exposure of their various body parts—of women for the benefit of men. If you like the main theme, get this CD. You'll certainly hear enough of it.

3. Burt Bacharach: ***After the Fox***. This score has one thing going for it, and that is the bouncy and absolutely delightful title song, with lyrics by Hal David that feature a post-Beatles group called The Hollies in a series of positively silly dialogues with Peter Sellers ("Who is The Fox?," "I am The Fox." "Who are you?" "I am me:" "Who is me?" "Me is a thief.") Be warned, however, that the song is completely addictive, and after you go through the house singing "Who is the fox?" "I am The Fox" for the 10th or 20th time, you are apt to be murdered by a family member. After that, the score descends rapidly into pure fluff. Bacharach, unlike such colleagues as Legrand and Mancini, had few gifts for composing dramatic "backing," and just about all the other cues for *After the Fox* are either some kind of pastiche, ethnic or otherwise, or pieces of watered-down pop music that either sound like a song accompaniment begging for a tune or a lyric, or a feeble attempt to satirize suspense music. I might add that the video clip from *After the Fox* presented on the CD-ROM portion of this recording squelched whatever desire I might have had to see the film.

September/October

This column is dedicated to the memory of my father, Joseph Lee Brown, 11/6/05–6/20/98.

There are certain films—the late Samuel Fuller's *The Naked Kiss* and the Coen brothers' *Barton Fink* come immediately to mind—that are so subversive that one cannot help but wonder how they ever got through Hollywood's notoriously conservative and self-serving studio system. At this point, although I really need to see the film again, **Bulworth**, produced, directed, and co-written (with Jeremy Pikser) by Warren Beatty, not only joins that select group, it may take grand prize as the wickedest slam yet taken at American politics, ethics, and, ultimately, culture. Don't let the theatrical trailers mislead you. *Bulworth*'s previews make it look as if the film offers little more than the portrait of a senator (Beatty) who, wearying of the Washington game, all of a sudden decides to drop such platitudes as "As we enter the next millennium . . ." of DC-speak and reveal what every politician (and probably everybody else) knows but lacks the courage to put into words. Early in the film, Senator Bulworth does in fact find these words, first as he addresses a group of African Americans in a church, second as he mingles in a Beverly Hills mansion with wealthy Jews from the Hollywood establishment. Along the way, *Bulworth* hits a few other major targets as well, most particularly the news media, whose members would never risk their multimillion-dollar jobs to ask a single truly pointed question of a politician. Satirical? Yes. Funny? Often. But groundbreaking? Not as such. What carries *Bulworth* into new territory is that Beatty the director chose not just to make a political film, but to make a film politically, to paraphrase French filmmaker Jean-Luc Godard. And the means via which Beatty accomplishes this are by and large musical. You see, although he initially insults the black congregation to hell and back, Senator Bulworth ultimately merges with the African American community to such an extent that he begins to deliver most of his decidedly radical political ideas via the chosen music of a large portion of that community, rap and hip-hop. *Bulworth* has been criticized as being, for all its off-the-left-end politics, condescending to African Americans. I would mildly agree with that assessment in at least two areas: a) Senator Bulworth ends up with a girlfriend, played by Halle Berry, who is absolutely stunning, who is 40 years younger than he is, and who just barely looks black, which is totally characteristic of American films, in which black males are allowed to markedly display physical characteristics of their racial origins but in which most black women, particularly the ones in leading roles, could just about pass as dark-skinned whites. This facet of *Bulworth* is at least as condescending to women as it is to African Americans; b) a black drug dealer (Don Cheadle) who uses barely adolescent boys to distribute his wares and do his dirty work is miraculously converted by Bulworth's rhythm-rhyme rhetoric into a community leader. As hoaky as this narrative twist is, however, it is altogether possible that Beatty may be suggesting a broader point here, which is that the possibility for change at least exists on the left. . . .

What Beatty has understood in *Bulworth* is what no other maker of mainstream political films such as Costa-Gavras has understood, and that is that it is all but pointless to attack a political philosophy with its own modes of discourse, which in the West involve a) a use of a very rational form of verbal language and, b) in its narrative arts such as (usually) the cinema a very rationalized plot structure. This is something that, on the heels of World War I, the Dadaists and, more importantly, the Surrealists immediately grasped (Surrealism, in fact, envisaged itself as much more of a political movement than an artistic one, and it is no accident that most of the Surrealists embraced communism). And so, while there is something mildly ridiculous (which, I suspect, is part of the point) about a white man in his sixties running around dressed up like a ghetto denizen and spouting radical political ideas to the rhymes and rhythms of rap and hip-hop, the viewer of *Bulworth* quickly comes to understand or at least *feel* the "logic" not only of the fictional senator's using the most visible victims of narcissistic capitalism as his power base but also of the way he uses the strongly antirational music of those victims to pillory the purveyors of greed as they make themselves unattackable by hiding behind moral platitudes, religion, and an Ozzie-and-Harriet vision of family values (those who watched A & E's recent documentary on the Nelsons will by now have realized what a fiction that is). Imagine trying to remember what was said during a lecture delivered exclusively in, say, the spondee of Edgar Allan Poe's "The Raven." Getting into that mode of discourse would take a massive reprogramming of one's brain cells, which, of course, is the whole point. Now, Interscope has released a CD offering a selection of the actual rap and hip-hop numbers that pop up as source music throughout *Bulworth*, not including, from what I could gather by looking at a copy in a record store, Beatty's inimitable (fortunately!) contributions. After several tries, I was unable to get Interscope to send me a review copy, which is perhaps just as well, since rap and hip-hop are miles away from my particular areas of expertise. But therein lies another story. *Bulworth* offers another whole set of musical cues contained in a very characteristic score composed by none other than Ennio Morricone and released on CD by RCA. And, here, one suspects either some major flimflamming by Beatty and/or yet one more (much more heavily) disguised political message. As Senator Bulworth begins to enter his period of breakdown, during which he will not sleep for several days, he sets up another way out of the one-way street he has entered by hiring a hit man to kill him while taking care, of course, to heavily insure his life via a kickback from an insurance company lobbyist. And so, throughout much of the movie, we keep seeing shots of what may or may not be the actual gunman, accompanied almost every time by Morricone suspense music (heard mostly in the second of the two "suites" on the CD) written very much in the style of some of the composer's earliest thrillers, such as the very political *Investigation of a Citizen Above Suspicion* from 1970. The suite starts off with classic Morricone kinky/kinetic suspense strains as a plucked mandolin and tuned drums create a march accompaniment that can best be described as strobe-like over which high winds, piano, and what sounds like a very pinched trombone make fragmentary contributions. A middle section sinks much more deeply into chaos as amassed strings trilling in cluster or near-cluster chords rise slowly in pitch while various instruments create highly fractionalized punctuation. The suite then returns to a more civilized version of the opening music, this time in slashed string chords and harpsichord, a Morricone trope if ever there was one.

The way in which the suspense music creeps into the film every time we think we see the killer is such an over-the-top, manipulative, Hollywood film/music stereotype that one quickly tries to come up with an answer for what Beatty is trying to do. My answer is twofold: a) The actor/director used this as a gimmick to help sell the film both to the studio—20th Century-Fox in this case—and to the public; b) perhaps unconsciously, Beatty may have been using this element of the film as a comment on the normal modes of cinematic discourse, in this case via one of its classic narrative genres, the suspense film. And even here, Beatty goes further: by the end of the film, subplot (or parallel plot) becomes subtext (or parallel text) as Bulworth, emerging in senatorial duds from his "nervous breakdown" after a long sleep but apparently still ready to pursue the course he has begun, is shot down, not by the hired gun but (apparently) by the insurance-company lobbyist. Cinematographer Vittorio Storaro's shot of the empty spaces in the night air where the assassin had just stood is perhaps one of the most devastating comments ever on the politics of greed and righteousness wherein even political assassins get sucked up into the emptiness built into the rhetoric of the highly entrenched establishment to engulf any attempt to get a foothold in reality . . . any reality. But there's more still. The first suite of Morricone's score is built upon the varied alteration of two opposing cues. The first cue is a purebred piece of Morricone sad nostalgia that constantly borders on the elegiac, with low, unison strings supporting a mellow theme, in parallel thirds in the midrange strings. One in fact keeps waiting for the voice of Morricone regular Edda Dell'Orso to break out with one of her classic vocalises; instead, the composer shifts to a minor-mode cue, with tremolo strings suggesting something more ominous while, instead of Dell'Orso, vocalist Amii Stewart belts out a vocalise (in later variations a few words creep in) in a black, gospel style. It is only after Morricone has set up this alternative that, upon returning to the more bittersweet opening music, he allows the theme to soar with Dell'Orso's unmistakable voice. The appearance of this quintessential Morricone sound is so inevitable and so beautifully timed that it brought a tear to my eye. I must confess that, when I saw *Bulworth*, the dialectics set up in Morricone's first suite totally escaped my notice. Perhaps, ultimately, they are best communicated in the suite heard on the RCA recording. Whether these dialectics become more apparent in subsequent viewings remains to be seen. The bottom line in all this is that *Bulworth* stands as one of the films of the decade, and in many ways it makes some of the most original, creative, and, ultimately, political uses of various kinds of music ever to show up on a commercial film. Even the unconvinced, however, should have no trouble relating to Morricone's gorgeous, intriguing, and disturbing music-as-usual.

Well, what would "Film Musings" be without coverage of some major, new Bernard Herrmann recording(s)? For this column we have three, one a new release, one an invaluable, new presentation (not really a reissue) of a key score, and one a (very old) original music-track issue. The new release is Varèse Sarabande's all-but-complete recording, with Joel McNeely conducting the National Philharmonic Orchestra, of the composer's unused score for Alfred Hitchcock's close-to-terrible **Torn Curtain** from 1966. As is well known by now, Hitchcock, after hitting the absolute peak of his career with *Vertigo* (1958), *North by Northwest* (1959), and *Psycho* (1960), moved from Paramount to Universal, which for all intents and purposes tried to push one of the cinema's two or three greatest creative geniuses into the mainstream. Part of Universal's way of selling the Hitchcock product was to try and persuade the director to discard Herrmann, his composer of standing since *The Trouble With Harry* in 1955. Hitchcock stood his ground with the studio; but he did ask his composer to lighten things up a bit, also insisting on no musical cue for a scene in which an East German secret-police agent is killed by Paul Newman and an actress looking very much like Liv Ullman, who, ironically, force the agent's head into a gas oven. Herrmann, a thoroughly irascible man hardly noted for his flexibility, went right ahead and did what he wanted, perhaps out of perversion but more likely armed with the knowledge that, in *Psycho*, he had been able to bring Hitchcock, who had wanted no music for the shower scene, around to his way of thinking. Given the success of the composer's earlier work with Hitchcock, one can hardly blame him for feeling that he would be able to convert the director by the sheer force of his music alone. But Hitchcock, perhaps aware in some part of his being that he had made a really crappy picture, was in no mood to compromise: when he walked into the recording session and found himself listening to the playback of a snarling, growling, intensely driving main theme played by a wind-heavy orchestra with no violins or violas, and when he learned that Herrmann had gone ahead and scored the murder scene, he immediately walked out. Later, after a heated phone conversation with the composer, Hitchcock removed Herrmann from the project, and thus came to an end perhaps the greatest composer-director collaboration in the history of the cinema.

Perhaps Hitchcock should have hung around for some of the other music. For, a good deal of the score, heard nearly in toto on this CD (only a 21-second and a 16-second cue missed the final cut), is made up of quite placid cues—gloomy music to be sure, but music that kind of runs the gamut of all the various sotto voce suspense sounds that turn up in the Herrmann/Hitchcock collaborations. One frequently re-curring motif, a slow, four-note figure—often G-E-flat-F-G-in parallel minor triads—appears in whole or in part in both *Vertigo* and *North by Northwest*. There is also some very tender music—perhaps not the gushy love theme Hitchcock wanted but tender nonetheless—in the cue entitled "The Hill" that directly quotes from the theme for Madeleine in *Vertigo*. Herrmann's music might have slightly improved this incredibly phony scene, in which Newman, against a backdrop better suited to *The Wizard of Oz*, confesses all to his mistress (Julie Andrews; the scene would have been perhaps a bit more convincing if the screenwriters had left the female character as the wife rather than being oh-so-mod and making her a lover), but nothing could really save it. Con-clusions? I love the frenetic pulse and the unleashed anger of the title cue, even though the theme itself, musically speaking, is one of Herrmann's most naïve. The music for the killing of Gromek, the secret police agent, likewise drives straight to the gut (so much so, in fact, that Elmer Bernstein added it, for a climactic scene, to his arrangement of Herrmann's score for *Cape Fear* for the Martin Scorsese remake), and, as it happens, it works quite effectively with the action, as can be seen in the 1994 documentary *Music for the Movies: Bernard Herrmann*, available in VHS and on laserdisc from Sony. Herrmann's novel instrumentation—16 horns, 12 flutes (includ-ing piccolo, alto, and bass), nine trombones, two tubas, two sets of timpani, eight cel-los, and eight basses—also frequently makes the music feel like a fusion of the com-poser's Hitchcock work with his fantasy-film efforts from the same period. On the whole, however, one suspects that Herrmann was no more inspired by Hitchcock's film than were audiences, critics, and scholars, and one cannot really include *Torn Curtain*, for all of its stirring and/or intriguing moments, in the pantheon of the great Herrmann/Hitchcock efforts.

Finally, as a part of the "Fox Classics" series it has taken over, Varèse Sarabande of-fers what looks like a complete recording of the original music tracks, conducted by Bernard Herrmann, of the music he composed for Joseph L. Mankiewicz's 1947 **The Ghost and Mrs. Muir**. Interestingly, here, at almost the opposite end of his film-scor-ing career from *Taxi Driver*, Herrmann shows exactly the same proclivity for taking a simple, four-note motif (in this case four steps down from the top of the scale, not the "Jeepers Creepers" figure) and extending it into what sounds like a developed theme that acquires most of its lyricism from the harmonic and instrumental colors that sur-round it. In the case of *The Ghost and Mrs. Muir*, the theme is, bar none, one of the composer's loveliest. We hear it as of the title sequence: after a dramatic introduction in which a sweet, falling figure in the high violins and winds answers a rising swell from the depths of the orchestra—all this, no doubt, a musical metonymy for the sea, which is just about omnipresent in the picture—Herrmann allows his four-note motif to slowly evolve into a theme made all the more haunting by subtle presences in the instrumentation, in particular a solo harp. On the basis of this opening, one would be led to suspect that *The Ghost and Mrs. Muir* would continue as a large-sounding, symphonic score, and, indeed, Herrmann called for a 67-player orchestra, including an electronic instrument that is probably an Ondes Martenot. But, in fact, I would say that the majority of the cues are scored for markedly reduced forces, sometimes no more than a handful of winds. In the cue entitled "Bedtime," Herrmann boils one statement of a charming, quasi-sea-shanty theme (a tune in two simple measures, the first 5/4, the second 4/4) down to a solo clarinet and vibraphone over a drone accompaniment in two other winds, a sound that strongly recalls the composer's radio work. Even the main theme rarely returns to the full orchestra throughout much of the film: in the cue entitled "Poetry," for instance, Herrmann offers it in an instrumentation that sounds like little more than a string quartet (plus the inevitable harp). It all works perfectly. *The Ghost and Mrs. Muir* is a kind of *Vertigo* in reverse in which a young widow (Gene Tierney) finds, over the course of her life in a seaside cottage haunted by the spirit of its previous owner (Rex Harrison), that her one, true love is with "someone dead," to use the expression from *Vertigo*. Unlike the Hitchcock film, however, *The Ghost and Mrs. Muir* keeps its passions mostly beneath the calm and resigned surfaces of its two main characters—only the sea itself seems to be allowed to express any turmoil, and that itself is undone by the descending figure that concludes the opening music. (The very ending of the "Late Sea" cue could easily be transplanted into the church scene in *Vertigo* without most people noticing the difference.) Ultimately, one walks away from the film, or even just from its beautiful score, which in many ways contains its essence, filled with feelings of a kind of dreamlike mystery and, throughout, a nostalgic sadness that surely must have been one of the major components of the composer's own soul. This recording, put together from the original master tapes in 1994 by the invaluable Nick Redman, is an essential document both because it offers the score as it was originally recorded for the film and because it features the composer's highly moving interpretation of his own music. Although one notes some occasional distortion, particularly when the (rarely) amassed violins gather for a strong statement of the main theme, the often small forces involved come across with a great deal of warmth and clarity in the recorded sound (but why the fadeout on the final chord?). And, for reasons that Redman once explained to me but that I have forgotten, there is a very real stereo effect here.

Even though I have taught **Carrie** (1976) over each of the last two years (and will again this coming fall), I had somewhat forgotten, until Ryko finally reissued the haunting and disturbing musical score on CD as a part of its massive set of releases taken mostly from the old United Artists catalogue, just what an excellent piece of film scoring Pino Donaggio came up with for erratic director Brian De Palma's brilliant screen adaptation of Stephen King's early novel. Having already engaged the talents of Bernard Herrmann for the much underrated *Sisters* and the much overrated *Obsession*, De Palma had every intention of turning again to Herrmann as he began preproduction work on *Carrie*. The composer's death brought an end to the brief Herrmann/De Palma collaboration, and so the director turned to Italian composer Donaggio, who had produced a stunningly successful score for Nicolas Roeg's equally stunning adaptation, in *Don't Look Now* (1973), of Daphne du Maurier's study, set in Venice, in suspense and the paranormal. The choice seems almost too obvious, since *Carrie*, in a very different way, is likewise a study in suspense and the paranormal, the latter manifested via the telekinesis deployed by the film's Cinderella/Ugly Duckling heroine (Sissy Spacek) initially in self-protective and, ultimately, massively destructive (even more so in the novel than in the film) ways. Interestingly, Donaggio's solution for the initial musical mood for *Carrie*, which was marketed, of course, very much as a horror/suspense film, is quite similar to what he came up with for *Don't Look Now*. Where the latter opens with a simple, childlike melody played haltingly on a solo piano (the way a child would) that is finally deployed in a crushingly tragic version for full orchestra in the film's concluding sequence, *Carrie*'s initial theme, rather than suggesting all of the story's many sinister elements, is a bittersweet melody that poignantly captures both the irretrievable loss of the heroine's childhood and her utterly sad, failed attempt to enter adulthood. And in its own strange way, it also captures the edenic innocence rather paradoxically suggested by De Palma in the steam-filled, slow-motion sequence filled with nude, adolescent girls romping in a locker room, seen behind the main titles. Of course, Donaggio does not fail to get the nervous juices flowing with certain cues: the composer's ominously slow and even figures in strings and brass combine with De Palma's slow-motion (again) pacing to create almost unbearable suspense in the scene leading up to the inevitable prom catastrophe, while his brutal cutting short, with a wild, repeated outburst in the strings and chimes, of a sad reprise of the title music in the final sequence stands as a perfect musical equivalent of one of the cinema's most terrifying moments (depressingly, perhaps, almost none of my students these days have any knowledge of what's coming, and the scene never fails to send at least one of them running hysterically for the exit). De Palma also had his composer briefly allude to *Psycho*'s famous shrieking strings at several key moments where *Carrie* applies her telekinesis, and Donaggio further quotes briefly from a tense moment in his *Don't Look Now* score at one point. None of this is heard on the present recording. But for two scenes in which he could have brought out much heavier cannons—the moment when Carrie, having been sent home from school after she has gotten her first period, goes downstairs to face her religious-fanatic mother (Piper Laurie); and the climactic scene in which Carrie's mother stabs her in the back at the top of those same stairs—Donaggio chooses instead to create an achingly sad, repeated figure carried mostly by the piano and bells. Chorale-like music suggests, almost ironically, the imposing presence of the interior of Carrie's house, in which De Palma disconcertingly evokes a rather Catholic iconography to complement the mother's obviously fundamentalist Protestant religious beliefs. Along the way, we also get two popular songs, composed by Donaggio, with a mild country-western flavor to them (the second, "Born to Have It All," is an arrangement of the main theme). Both of them, sung by Katie Irving, work during the prom sequence at making the audience believe, against all evidence, that this fairy-tale will have a happy ending. I could go on. Suffice it to say that I can think of few more effective interactions between music and film. Ryko's most welcome CD reissue offers the same cues heard on the original United Artists LP, along with very brief excerpts of dialogue (the first of which is backed by some sustained-string music not otherwise available on recording), strangely presented out of narrative order, and a reprise of the entire main theme which, after the final sequence, originally just gets faded out on both the original recording and in the film's end titles. Ryko also offers a CD-ROM presentation of the film's theatrical trailer.

November/December

For many, including me, one of the most pleasant movie-going surprises of the summer of '98 was **The Truman Show**. In fact, of course, there is not a whole lot to be surprised about if you look at some of the talent involved in the film, including screenwriter Andrew Nicoll, a New Zealand native who wrote and directed the wonderful *Gattaca*, and Australian director Peter Weir, whose films, from *The Last Wave* through *Picnic at Hanging Rock*, *The Year of Living Dangerously*, *Witness*, and *Fearless* have always explored the darker layers of life and the myths, sometimes of transcendence, attached to those somber places. And if one thinks about it, Jim Carrey, who carries from film to film his persona of manic innocence, often expressed through a smile as broad as the L.A. Freeway, was the perfect choice to play the role of Truman Burbank, who, from the moment he was born and for the next 30 years, has lived on the gigantic, geodesic soundstage of a soap opera of which he is the only unwitting star. The drama of *The Truman Show* lies in the main character's gradual discovery that he is trapped in a mammoth staging of the capitalist mythology, which, via product logos and the mini-dramas of advertising, promises an earthly paradise via the glories of consumption. The chief medium via which this carrot-on-stick pseudo-religion and its iconography are promulgated is, of course, television, and in that sense *The Truman Show* stands as a brutally cynical laying bare of the absurdities of capitalism's promise of an earthly paradise. Watching Carrey as he begins to become aware of the trap he is in, as his smile starts to ever-so-slightly sag, I was reminded of a wonderful routine by mime Marcel Marceau in which he puts on a mask with an insipid smile and then grows more and more terrified as he realizes he cannot remove it. Truman, finally, begins to move past the mask, and one thing that is particularly intriguing about the film is that the various stages in this hero's journey closely reflect the three pillars of enlightenment, an interpretation that comes to me via my cousin Tom Thompson, a hypno-therapist who has pulled off the minor miracle of successfully establishing a yoga center in a small North Carolina town. Initially, we have "great doubt," which begins in the film when a woman named Sylvia (Natascha McElhone) from his (staged) past tells Truman that his entire life is an illusion, at which point

Truman begins to question a "reality" that is not as it seems and to realize that things are not what they appear to be. In this sense, Sylvia becomes something like a guru for Truman. Then there is "great faith," the recognition that there is something deeper than the life he is living, that there is something beyond these appearances. And, finally, there is "great determination," in which Truman meets his fears (of water, of death) and becomes free (from the TV show . . . maybe) by leaving the polluted Eden of capitalist promises and walking out of it all through a door in the midst of a huge, quasi-Magritte sky.

Musically, there are several particularly marvelous moments in *The Truman Show*: for starters, as the emergingly enlightened hero begins to wander frenetically through the town in search of chinks—bogus elevator banks and things like that—in the illusion's armor, the music track begins to offer what I initially thought was a cue from Philip Glass' score for *Koyaanisqatsi* but which in fact turns out to be the cue entitled "Anthem—Part 2" from the composer's music for the *Koyannisqatsi* sequel, *Powaqqatsi*. For me, something mightily exhilarating arose from the combination of the narrative events surrounding Truman's initial stages of escape from illusion, and in particular here the illusion of chronological time, and Philip Glass' particular brand of Minimalism, which definitely tends through quasi-mantra repetitions of simple musical cells to break down the inexorable sense of forward movement in time that grows out of the harmonic and rhythmic languages of more traditional Western music. In retrospect, however, I realized that I had been at least partially caught up in the trap of facile association. Because, of course, what we are watching is in fact not just a movie but a movie showing a television program as it is happening. Behind all of this sits the character of the appropriately named Christof (Ed Harris), the inscrutably benign (Harris is perfect in the role), godlike creator/producer/director of *The Truman Show* who often has to choose music on the fly to accompany moments, such as Truman's initial stages of discovery, that fall outside his and/or the show's total control. And so, at this moment when we are all ready to fall into the normal cinematic trap of letting the music tell us how to experience a particularly dramatic turn of events, we come to realize that in fact this is music chosen by a TV producer to shore up our prepackaged concepts of how this event should sound and feel musically. This is no longer enlightenment but what Roland Barthes would call "enlightenmenticity." And even if we tell ourselves, "Ah, yes, but Peter Weir really chose this music," it comes down to the same thing doesn't it? Or it would if Weir were not constantly reminding us of how film/music manipulation really works.

There is for instance a wonderful scene inside the huge TV studio out of which *The Truman Show* originates. Truman is sleeping (as millions watch around the world), and as Christof carries on a conversation in the foreground, in the very distant background we see Glass himself, sitting at a piano and playing one of his original cues for the film, a quiet but rhythmically offbeat (3 + 3 + 2) quasi-berceuse entitled—what else?— "Truman Sleeps." And so, while Philip Glass' musical style offers us something unique by taking Western harmonies and rhythms and "minimalizing" them to such an extent that they seem to communicate a more "Eastern" sense of time, the Western media have co-opted this music (commercials have been doing this for years: out of women's liberation we get "You've come a long way, baby") in order to provide a cheap short-cut to the East without the potatoes ever having to leave the couch. This is precisely why the Philip Glass score is so totally wrong for *Kundun* and why it is so totally right for *The Truman Show*, which, in addition to several other original Glass cues, also mobilizes some of Glass' music from *Anima Mundi*—the quirkily scurrying and primitivistic "The Beginning" and the slow, massive, dreamy, quasi-*Gymnopédie* strings, winds, and organ of "Living Waters," both devastatingly appropriate to the film—and the delicate but obsessive "Opening" for *Mishima*.

But there's more. For the more "contemporary sound needed for some of the cues, Weir turned to German-born Australian composer Burkhard Dallwitz, whose credits in fact include quite a bit of TV work. And so, the first three cues, all quite brief, heard on Milan's exceptionally well-recorded CD of music from the film all relate to the established events of the TV show and feature the electronically generated timbres that are now an ingrained feature of both TV and film music. Low, synthesized drones segue into excited but still quiet string figures as "Trutalk" builds up (complete with voiceover narration) into a come-on intro for the show. "It's a Life" features sampled, vocalizing women's voices over an electronic drone and some fairly soupy solo-piano strains, while "Acquaphobia" offers, along with the standard low drones and occasional percussion figures, sampled water sounds along with a constant swish that reminds us that even the air in Truman's home town is a palpably controlled presence. The next cue, "Dreaming of Fiji," however, ties in not only with the character of Sylvia and the place where Truman supposes her to be living but also with his deep-seated impulse to escape, and it is here that, not unexpectedly, we get the first Philip Glass cue, a typical Glass modulation loop in the strings and harp. And so it goes. As Truman's (real) desire to transcend is co-opted by *The Truman Show* and transformed into an intriguing new "plot" twist, Dallwitz's music intensifies, with lots of percussion from a synthesized rhythm section and, in the cue entitled "Drive," some frenzied electric guitar. When Truman gets to meet Sylvia, we get some exaggeratedly soupy romantic strains. And as we watch Truman set sail, we get sucked in by broad music of hope from Dallwitz, only to realize, as the music turns ominous, that both the hope and the potential disaster are part of a manipulated narrative that steadfastly blocks our every attempt to move from the outside in. And there's more still.

Fairly early on in the film, Truman flashes back to his teenage date with Sylvia, and during part of this sequence Weir offers, rather than Dallwitz or Glass, the crushingly moving, almost dreamy "Romance" second movement from Chopin's First Piano Concerto as performed by Artur Rubinstein with Stanislaw Skrowaczewski conducting at a rather high volume level on a well remastered cue on this CD. And thus does the director add a third stratum of musical meaning to the pot, that of nostalgia for a time when movement within chronological time, rather than being fought off by the religion of Paradiseism or denied by New-Agey re-readings of time generated within the religion of Paradiseism, was allowed to generate its own meaning, an emotional reaction, expressed it seems to me in much of Chopin's music, to the tragedy of impermanence, including the deepest feelings of love carried away by time. But, of course, we are hearing, and feeling, Weir's—and/or Christof's—co-opting of that particular stratum as well. No matter how many exits from the illusion may seem to exist, we always walk into another illusion. Lest we forget, the very title *The Truman Show* refers both to the TV program and to the movie we have just watched. As Weir writes in a Pirandello-esque comment in the program notes, "Sometimes the music is Christof's choice, sometimes it's mine!" And so, when Truman walks out the door at the end, we have a wonderfully cathartic, and satisfyingly dramatic, illusion of the escape from the illusion. But the movie does not and cannot offer us transcendence. But by forcing us, via its *mise-en-abyme* (an untranslatable French expression implying infinite mirroring) plot structure and its multiplied musical reflections of same, into an awareness of the trap that we as moviegoers and film watchers are caught in every bit as much as Truman is. *The Truman Show* at least provides ground for a first possible step.

Two other points. I was in Melbourne, Australia, a little over a month ago, and in that city's newspaper *The Age* on August 1 appeared an article by David Thomson entitled "Film noir to film deadpan." In this article, the author, writing about *The Truman Show*, makes the following extremely perceptive points: "All the movie textbooks say that extensive shadow or low-key lighting is oppressive, foreboding, angst-ridden, and so on. That's how you get the look of film noir, of horror movies, and of everything from *In a Lonely Place* to *A Touch of Evil*, pictures whose titles and dark imagery make you want to reach for Prozac. There's an opposing principle—that high-key photography, the absence of contrast, and the radiance of light everywhere make us feel happy and bouncy. That's the way musicals were lit, as well as a lot of romantic comedies and decades of TV sitcoms, from *Lucy* to *Seinfeld*. Yet the aura of bright light is increasingly one of the most sinister things appearing on screen. It's the light that pours over produce at the supermarket, that supplies the sheen of desirability in advertising. It has become the epitome of fakery, as opposed to illumination." Keep that in mind the next time you watch *The Truman* Show . . . or *Seinfeld*. Secondly, *The Truman Show* runs 24 hours a day and is exclusively focused on Truman's life (even the commercials are manipulated into the narrative, as happens all the time in "real" movies and TV these days), during which one has to suppose that there are occasions when he has sex with the bouncy, blonde wife (Laura Linney) the program has set him up to marry. Yet neither Weir's nor Christof's *The Truman Show* even allude to this, as far as I remember. It figures. Sex became necessary only after Adam and Eve were kicked out of paradise. . . .

Knowing that I would be reviewing John Williams' music for the latest Steven Spielberg epic, **Saving Private Ryan**, I went to the show (with wife and stepchildren) with my ears on extra-high alert. And I was immediately struck by how quiet, sad, even nostalgic most if not all of the music was. Only a muted snare-drum/bass-drum motif that turns up in many of the cues gives you at least the traditional kind of hint that this film has anything to do with the military, never mind, at the outset at least, one of the bloodiest battles—Normandy—in the annals of war. No marches, no huge instrumental outbursts. As the film progressed, I began to become aware that the music was beginning to get on my nerves. I didn't quite understand why, other than the fact that it just didn't seem to belong with the film. And so I approached listening to the music-track CD on Dreamworks with no great amount of enthusiasm. And then a funny thing happened. As I listened to Williams' elegantly understated music apart from the film, I realized that this score has nothing to do with the razzle-dazzle heroics or even the sometimes-overwhelming tragedy of the classic war film. The best description I can come up with for Williams' *Saving Private Ryan* is that it is music about resignation and the memory of deep, irreplaceable loss only vaguely tied in to the military by those drum rolls and by a certain sense of the nobility that we tend to attach to our war heroes. At many points, Williams boils the music down to a simple duet— trumpets or horns, occasionally a pair of woodwinds—in which the two instruments move in and out of dissonant intervals. At other times, we get warmer, quasi-chorale passages from the full brass. The strings and brass early on offer a theme filled with, yes, sadness and resignation, that turns up throughout most of the score, frequently played by the low and midrange brass. And in the end-title music entitled "Hymn to the Fallen," also used to open the CD, Williams offers a hint of that musical icon of American heroism, Copland's *Fanfare for the Common Man*. Even in the cue for "The Last Battle," the score maintains a soft, hymn-like profile that turns away from the battle itself to remember its dead soldiers. Only occasionally does the composer provide us music that attempts to communicate the uncommunicatable about the actual presence of (the) war itself. Towards the middle of the cue entitled "Defense Preparations," we get a sudden turn into the minor mode (in its typically unstereotypical fashion, most of the music is written in the major mode) and something that almost resembles a march. But it only hints at what is to come rather than quasi-illustrating it. As one might suspect, Williams as both composer and conductor gets for his score the kind of playing that most film composers can only dream of, thanks to a full-bodied and wholly committed performance from the Boston Symphony Orchestra (the Tanglewood Festival Chorus vocalizes briefly in the "Hymn to the Fallen"), recorded in Boston's Symphony Hall.

And then I understood the reaction I had while I was watching the movie. In a sense, Williams' music for *Saving Private Ryan* represents the movie the way it could have been, but largely was not, made. Rather than the music not working for the movie, it was the movie that unfortunately proved to be out of sync with the music. Spielberg could, like Williams, have chosen to go against type by finding an original approach to the anti-war movie, something perhaps along the lines of the final sequence of *Schindler's List*. Instead, he chose to go the traditional route by framing the picture in a horribly acted, badly photographed scene from the "present" that flashes back to the battle of Normandy and then to a partly true mission to remove a certain Private Ryan from combat duty so that his mother won't have to face the death of a fourth son. The rest of *Saving Private Ryan* is pretty much a traditional war movie—a relatively decent one, but a Hollywood war movie nonetheless. To be sure, the much-heralded Normandy battle sequence, done without music, may be the most brutal depiction of a near-suicidal battle scene ever filmed. But it is still all special effects, sound editing, prosthetics, hand-held cameras, rapid cutting, and various gimmicks (lenses with the coating scraped off; things like that), and it is very obvious from the beginning that the film's very visible star, Tom Hanks, will be the one to get to the German bunkers. And, of course, the film will focus on the Hanks character all the way through to "The Last Battle." The war films of Samuel Fuller, most particularly perhaps his last one, *The Big Red One* (1980), plunge much more deeply into the very situation of war with infinitely fewer special effects, much less noise, and minimal, if not Minimalist, editing. And at those moments when Spielberg tries to get arty, as in an interminable scene with the soldiers spending the night in a church, the film falls totally flat. Interestingly, in his brief program note for the Dreamworks CD, director Spielberg confirms my impression that, of his 16 collaborations with composer Williams, *Saving Private Ryan* "probably contains the least amount of score"; he also implies that the tone of the music, as I have described it above, came from his composer's creative imagination. In this instance, it would be intriguing to see what the composer would have come up with had he directed the film.

CHAPTER SIXTEEN

~

1999

January/February

Apt Pupil was directed by Bryan Singer, whose offbeat and convoluted *The Usual Suspects* turned out to be one of the best crime thrillers in many years. But where *The Usual Suspects* tends to stay on a subterranean level as it creates an almost supernatural figure of practically infinite power, *Apt Pupil*, based on a novella by Stephen King, looks at the will to power right out in the open, in a manner wholly in keeping with King's vision. Here, a straight-A high-school senior (Brad Renfro), having recognized a notorious Nazi war criminal (brilliantly played by Ian McKellen) on a bus, shows up at the former Nazi's secluded house and blackmails the concentration-camp torturer into giving him a description of the Holocaust that is much closer to the reality of the situation than the material taught to him in class. One thing the film certainly seems to suggest is that we have become so saturated with images of horror that we are acquiring an almost unquenchable thirst for the "real thing." But in the process the student brings a monster back to life, mostly in ways that are all the more unsettling for seeming like such a normal part of a power struggle between two individuals. Also in the process, the student turns into the perfect "apt pupil," by the end comfortably and coolly, as he prepares to reach out for the American dream, bullying his guidance counselor into a submissive pulp with the threat of a brutal half-lie, half-truth [the ending of King's story is even more chilling]. Even in this all-American setting, however, director Singer, not surprisingly, tends to keep his camera in and around the darkness of the Nazi's slightly eerie house while also, at least for these scenes, maintaining a somewhat labyrinthine editing style. While Singer's off-putting visuals do contribute to creep-out factor, one somewhat misses a solid sense of the high-school and family milieus, as these are, after all, the principal locus of the irony that is an essential element of Stephen King's vision. It is this sense of milieu that, among other things, helps make Brian De Palma's *Carrie* one of the best King adaptations ever. Still, as a depiction of the power of evil and the evil of power lurking beneath the homey surfaces of Stephen King's America, *Apt Pupil* casts its disquieting spell quite effectively.

As was the case with *The Usual Suspects*, the musical score (RCA; Larry Groupé, cond.) as well as the editing for *Apt Pupil* were done by the same artist, John Ottman. Ottman's score has something of that same aura of big, symphonic, minor-mode tragedy that one hears in a score such as John Williams' *The Fury*. Ottman, however, often ventures off into some snarling dissonances that occasionally erupt in wild clusters and glissandos in the best late-modernist fashion. In other cues, Ottman is content to maintain a more understated profile. I particularly like the way he slips in some very quiet, bitonal chime figures beneath the gloomy strings of "The Speech," as one example. In the "Main Titles" and "End Titles" cues, Ottman mobilizes a solo clarinet and a solo violin to give a mildly Semitic flavor to music that ultimately erupts into a heavy waltz. Quite effective as well is the occasional use of a vocalizing chorus, particularly in the quiet glissandos of the cue entitled "Cat Bake," which, if I understand correctly, was actually composed by conductor Larry Groupé. And there is something decidedly unsettling about the shouts of a demonstrating crowd choreographed into a heavily accented section of the very late cue entitled "Apt Pupil." I have two main problems with the score. The first is the main theme itself, which turns up throughout the score. As was the case with Gabriel Yared's main theme for *The English Patient*, the opening of this melody flirts just a little too closely with a fairly well-known song, in this case the one sung by Bette Davis in *What Ever Happened to Baby Jane?*, for me to be entirely comfortable with it. Besides this, however, director Singer has allowed Ottman to lay on the doom and gloom just a bit too heavily. For my sensibilities, the film would have done better with a very small amount of very simple music. At the very least, given the obvious parallels created throughout the story, there should have been some kind of American pop song to counterbalance the decadent strains of "Das ist Berlin," which makes an ironic appearance at several points in *Apt Pupil* and is included on the music-track CD.

And then there's **Dark City**, not the 1950 noir film with Charlton Heston but a sci-fi thriller directed, storied, co-written, and co-produced in 1997 by Egyptian-born (in 1965) Alex Proyas, best known as the director of *The Crow*, which starred the late Brandon Lee as the comic-strip avenging angel. The multitalented Proyas might have written the score as well, since he is also a composer, but those chores were given over to Trevor Jones. Like *The Crow* as well as movies such as the first *Batman* and *Dick Tracy* before it, *Dark City* definitely has that nightmarish, surreal look, thanks in part to the production design by Patrick Tatopoulos (with George Liddle), of the old hero/action comic books. And with its mixing of era artifacts, *Dark City* falls on a visual continuum somewhere between *Brazil* and *Blade Runner*. In *Dark City*, however, we get to see an entire city periodically morph into new versions of itself, thanks to computerized effects that must have represented a substantial percentage of the film's budget. And therein lies the principal tale. From my point of view, and I will frankly admit that the mythic perspective interests me more than just about any other element of the cinema (I am, in fact, writing a book on the subject), *Dark City* stages nothing less than the struggle for emergence on the part of modern, phallic-individual-oriented patriarchal culture out of the more collectively oriented pre-patriarchal cultures. The latter are represented in *Dark City* by a civilization of generally tall, white-faced aliens in long coats and bowler hats with a dislike of (Apollonian) sunlight but also of water (hey, nobody said the symbolism was going to be consistent). Endowed with collective rather than individual memories, the aliens have also, à la *Forbidden Planet*, made a machine that allows them to "tune," i.e., alter the material world via purely mental forces, whence, among other things, the morphing buildings. Having discovered that they are dying out, the civilization seeks to uncover the secret of that great, patriarchal oxymoron—eternal life—by running a group of captured earthlings removed to an ersatz city out in space somewhere (a more somber version of *The Truman Show* in this sense) through a series of "experiments" whereby, each night (or day) at 12:00, their memories (thank you, Philip K. Dick)—and therefore their entire sense of being—and physical environments are reconfigured, this, paradoxically, in order to glean what it is that gives the earthlings' culture its single-minded (literally and figuratively) sense of continuity.

It is out of this novel concept that *Dark City* generates its most engrossing visual effects, character involvements, and plot twists, since the breakdown of that continuity of physical space, chronological time, and causality imposed on modern culture by Newtonian physics (among other things) is infinitely more cinematically interesting than the eternal attempts of Hollywood to impose its linear narratives on all facets of the movie-making process. Indeed, one of my principal criticisms of *Dark City* would be that it could have spent a lot less time on computerized effects and a lot more on the simple yet profound daily metamorphoses undergone by the dark city's unwitting inhabitants. Still, *Dark City* leaves one staggered with a sense of the evolution from a) a pre-patriarchal period of "darkness" dominated by a cyclical-circular sense of time that grew out of a collective relationship to the material world; b) the patriarchal period, with its absolute sense of linear time and its obsession with conquering death; c) a post- and/or hyperpatriarchal period in which the phenomenological/ontological sense of cyclical-circular-nonlinear time and discontinuous space has its locus in the human mind. Unfortunately, the plot of *Dark City* revolves around a classic, patriarchal hero played by Rufus Sewell, who comes very close to attaining the level of woodenness of Stephen Lack in David Cronenberg's *Scanners*, with which *Dark City* also has more than one point in common. This "hero" joins his colleagues in films as far-ranging as *Invasion of the Body Snatchers* (and its two remakes) and *12:01*, both its short and feature-length versions, as a character who somehow manages to fall outside of the mass ignorance and is therefore able to fight against the imposed situation. That *Dark City*'s hero is able to win the battle, complete with sunshine, sea, and, of course, the woman (the ever wonderful Jennifer Connelly), turns the film a bit preachy for my taste.

The musical score for *Dark City* (TVT Soundtrax) gives you just about exactly what you would expect from composer Trevor Jones, which is to say a dark, melodically single-minded, sometimes heavily textured, almost exclusively minor-mode, drone-dominated set of cues scored for symphony orchestra and such a vast array of synthesized, electronic, and sampled sounds that one often has no idea where the electronics stop and the acoustics start, an ambiguity that, of course, perfectly suits the film's postmodern card-shufflings. A case in point is the fairly haunting love theme for Sewell and Connelly (who have been implanted with an infidelity scenario by the aliens), which is played by an instrument, probably an ewi (as in electronic wind instrument), whose timbres fall somewhere between a flute and an Ondes Martenot, although the latter definitely wins out in a later version. A good deal of the score flirts with the "Mars" movement from Holst's *The Planets*, and Jones at one point does not fail to come up with a near-literal quotation of that 5/4 figure that John Williams turned into a sci-fi/action trope as of *Star Wars*. I also hear a bit of Patrick Doyle in some of Jones' harmonic and rhythmic configurations. A very low-voiced (sampled?) male chorus beefs up some of the drone figures and seems to actually create the presence of the aliens in the music. As was the case for *Apt Pupil*, I think that *Dark City* would have fared even better had its musical score not been quite so bent on ramming "action film" into the viewer/listener's sensibilities. There is a wonderful moment, for instance, when the hero takes note of a weird-looking accordion in the back seat of a car (a 1951 or '52 Ford?) driven by a police officer (William Hurt, who gives the film a good deal of its class) who has arrested him. The officer notes that it was given to him by his mother but that he can't remember where or when—for good reason, since the memory has been implanted and the object willed or morphed into existence. And at this same moment we hear accordion timbres travel to the musical score (the cue is entitled "Memories of Shell Beach," which throughout effectively generates a quiet sense of nostalgia). Had both the film and the score worked more consistently on this kind of level, we might very well have had a masterpiece on our hands. As it is, *Dark City* definitely deserves your attention—the whole package, however, rather than the "original soundtrack" CD, which also includes six songs that range from the badly sung and unbelievably innocuous (Anita Kelsey's "Sway," mouthed by Connelly, who is supposed to be a night-club singer, at least in one of her avatars; Kelsey's only slightly better "The Night Has a Thousand Eyes"; Echo & The Bunnymen's "Just a Touch Away") to the downright horrible (The Course of Empire's "The Information"). On the other hand, Hughes Hall's "Sleep Now," which actually gives the film one of its important lines, could easily have been part of the original score.

The very existence of a complete, previously unrecorded Herrmann/Hitchcock score—in this case **The Trouble with Harry** (Varèse Sarabande; Royal Scottish National Orchestra, Joel McNeely, cond.) would be cause enough for rejoicing. Yes, a decent representation of the music for Herrmann's first Hitchcock collaboration was arranged and recorded by the composer as a *Portrait of Hitch*. But the music, as it weaves its way through the score's 40 brief cues, has such charm, wistfulness, and wit, with a few doses of understated Herrmann/Hitchcock suspense thrown in, that I'm amazed that an "original soundtrack" recording was never released or that someone didn't get around to recording the entire score before this. Released in 1955, *The Trouble with Harry* was perhaps Alfred Hitchcock's only true black comedy, at least as a film, as opposed to TV, director. Yet the movie, starring Shirley MacLaine (her first screen role), John Forsythe, Edmund Gwenn, Mildred Natwick, Mildred Dunnock, a pre-Beaver Jerry Mathers, and, lest we forget, that actor with the great first name, the late Royal Dano, is built around the classic Hitchcock theme: the intrusion of the extraordinary into the ordinary. In this case, the extraordinary is the body of MacLaine's ex- (and late) husband, whose disposal and non-disposal cause a small ripple in the lives of a tiny New England community. The ordinary is Hitchcock's most loving treatment of small-town Americana since Santa Rosa, California, in the 1943 *Shadow of a Doubt*. In this case, Hitchcock went to Vermont and, with cinematographer Robert Burks, captured that state's gorgeous fall foliage. *The Trouble with Harry* also has a subtle element of self-reflexivity, since the John Forsythe character is a painter whose portrait of the cadaver creates one of the plot twists (the film also has one of Hitchcock's cleverest cameo appearances). Herrmann's score sets a trap of sorts for the viewer-listeners, since it suggests at least the possibility of a suspense film, particularly when it hammers out five times an augmented chord that, with one more added note, will become the minor-major seventh that will set the tone for *Vertigo* and *Psycho*. But the clouds quickly dissipate, giving way to a jocular theme in the bassoon that lets the audience know that *The Trouble with Harry* will be more comedy than black. After perfectly setting the stage, Herrmann continues to move in sync with Hitchcock. His nostalgic, modal string evocations in several cues capture the autumnal moods every bit as lovingly as, if in more subdued hues than, Burks' cinematography. His love music for Forsythe and MacLaine looks forward to *Vertigo* ("Madeleine's Theme" in particular) minus that film's angst. His bright and chirpy music for the absentminded, bookworm doctor is so corny that it becomes endearing. The cue for "The Burial" has a bit of the *North by Northwest* flavor to come. And Herrmann shows his utter genius, [developed from his radio days], for capturing a particular mood with a single brush stroke in the eerie solo-harp and solo-clarinet figures first heard in "The Closet." In spite of the score's generally genial tone, conductor Joel McNeely sets a good, taut pace for the music from the very outset, constantly maintaining a perfectly balanced tension in which Herrmann's highly delineated instrumental timbres get their full definition. One or two cues, such as the doctor's theme, are perhaps a bit overly hard-driven, but in no way enough to detract from the overall effect. The recorded sound is both clear and resonant, although it could stand perhaps a bit more depth.

I have seen so many movies, listened to so many scores during them, and reviewed so many "original soundtrack" recordings that I'm lucky if I remember from one month to the next what I have felt, thought, or written. But in the case of Peter Sellers' fourth outing as the deadpan, bumbling Inspector Clouseau in **The Pink Panther Strikes Again** (Ryko), directed with his usual comic flair by Blake Edwards, I have a very distinct memory, even though the film was released in 1976, of falling in love with an absolutely delightful Henry Mancini theme that turned up in the film. When

I got the LP to review (for *High Fidelity*), I discovered that this had been dubbed "The Inspector Clouseau Theme," and it later turned up, as Andy Dursin notes in his excellent program commentary, "in at least one of the subsequent films." A kind of melancholy, slow polka with a slightly Slavic flavor to it (perhaps in reference to the Russian spy played by Lesley-Anne Down), Mancini's haunting, utterly catchy tune suggests perhaps more than anything a kind of sad-circus-clown tradition out of which the Clouseau character may have at least partially grown. The theme gets perhaps its best timbres from the electronics of the initial version, whereas the acoustic solos of the reprise weight it down just a bit. Clouseau's foil is, of course, the utterly hip panther who gets his name from the diamond that is the object of everybody's envy in the initial *Pink Panther* film. A sumptuously recorded version of Mancini's very hip big-band theme for the eponymous feline opens this CD, although it gets frequently interrupted with snippets of everything from the *Funeral March of a Marionette* to *The Sound of Music* to accompany the animated antics of the Pink Panther and a cartoon Clouseau in a movie theater during the extended title sequence. For *The Pink Panther Strikes Again*, the late and very lamented Mancini also came up with one of his best dance-band love themes. Entitled "Come to Me," the song is better heard in its lush instrumental versions (cum heavy strings) than as intoned by the hammy Tom Jones, who, in his vocal, is later upstaged by a quavery-voiced Jacques Clouseau himself. Another song, "Until You Love Me," hideously (on purpose) sung in a high voice by Michael Robbins, also gets a very smooth instrumental version, trademarked by the composer's unmistakable style. Unmistakable, too, are the cool alto and bass flutes and the suave added-second chords (and the like) that remind us even during such "suspense" cues such as "Along Came Omar" that jazz minds are behind this whole thing. Of course, the "original soundtrack album" wasn't, since Mancini just about always rerecorded his film scores for the commercial market. But this CD also includes six cues, in rather tubby mono sound (as opposed to the opulent, non-digital stereo of the first 12), from the original music track. A CD-ROM section, which ran much more smoothly on my computer than those on the earlier Ryko CDs, offers the film's original trailer, and in wide screen. Essential Mancini.

Ask yourself what would be the one plot gimmick for a fantasy and/or sci-fi film that even Hollywood would not stoop to using, and your answer would have to be, "Well, you see, they take this team of scientists, shrink them down to sub-gnat size, and then send them in a minuscule submarine into the body of an important scientist to remove a brain tumor from the inside." Nah. Yet that is exactly the story of Richard Fleischer's 1966 film, **Fantastic Voyage**, which ended up getting a lot of critical acclaim and winning no small amount of popularity at the box office. Go figure. Even more incongruous is that the film features a score (Film Score Monthly) composed by one of movie music's most musically sophisticated and more often than not uncompromising composers, Leonard Rosenman. Rosenman in fact seems to have compromised very little for *Fantastic Voyage*, producing a score that in many instances uses its modernisms not as a way to add jolts and volts to suspenseful or violent scenes—few of the unusually long cues in fact sound action-specific—but rather in a musically organic way that organizes both harmony and timbre in manners that border on serialism. It is probably stretching the point to call the music "atonal," as the composer does in his extremely informative preface to the program notes, at least without explaining in what sense this is meant, since, unlike Rosenman's pioneering score for *The Cobweb*, the music does not appear to be organized around a tone row but rather generated from a very sci-fi-sounding four-note motif that gets repeated in very un-Schoenbergian ways in every cue. But the fact remains that the music not only has no real tonal center, it in fact deliberately mobilizes harmonic structures that solidly deny the very possibility of such a center. And the arrangement of these structures into constantly shifting timbral groupings, some of which shimmer and scintillate in quite Boulezian manners, further alienates the music from anything normally associated with Hollywood film music. In a different vein, I love the way Rosenman concludes the score with his signature "pyramid" of rising, dissonant intervals.

One might wonder how a score of such refinement and complexity found its way past the studio watchdogs into *Fantastic Voyage*. At least part of the answer would seem to lie in the fact that not one note of Rosenman's score begins on the music track until the "fantastic voyage" has begun, a decision that appears to have been the composer's. Consequently, one might speculate that the primary function of Rosenman's music is to create a soundscape every bit as alien to what we know as what we might experience as mites traveling along the veins and arteries toward the brain. Interestingly, in order to avoid "soundtrack" music in the title sequence, somebody involved put together a clever electronic/*musique concrète* cue using typewriters, sonar bleeps, a heartbeat, and various electronic sounds. The fairly unresonant sound on this CD creates a spectacular sense of sonic space, very realistically defining the individual timbres while at the same time capturing the full breadth of Rosenman's multifaceted timbral palette. I thought I detected a moment of very slight wow at a couple of points, but this is only a minimal distraction. *Fantastic Voyage*, never previously available in any form, has been completely remixed in stereo from the original 35mm magnetic film elements. It is part of a part of a new series of limited-edition (the pressing is limited to 3,000 copies) music-track recordings called "Silver Age Classics" available only through Lukas Kendall's invaluable Film Score Monthly, [which, as I write, continues to release at least one new score every month]. At any rate, as this absolutely invaluable release of *Fantastic Voyage* makes devastatingly clear, Leonard Rosenman remains perhaps one of the most wasted musical talents to have set foot in the Hollywood establishment. One can only fantasize on what might have happened had the composer received assignments worthy of his considerable talents.

Unless you miraculously found a way to get your hands on the "Soundtrack Collector's Special Edition" of the original music track for **Body Heat** released by "Label X" on an LP-size 45-rpm recording, or unless you were God and managed to get hold of the CD reissue, you have had a major hole in your film-music collection since Lawrence Kasdan's reworking in 1981 of the classic film noir *Double Indemnity* in *Body Heat*. Starring John Hurt as a barely competent lawyer (is that a tautology?), Kathleen Turner, in her first screen role, as the *femme très fatale*, and Ted Danson as a double-

iced-tea-swilling DA, *Body Heat*, even though it flaunts one of the major noir traditions by setting its story in sunny (and hot) Florida, somehow manages to create the
dark moods and inextricable webs of intrigue necessary for noir, not to mention the
conscienceless characters. Of course, this being an '80s film, everything goes quite a bit
further over the top: Hurt's character seems particularly helpless, Danson's DA has
none of the moral underpinnings of his Edward G. Robinson counterpart in *Double Indemnity*, and Kathleen Turner's seething sexuality—and the film's graphic treatment of
it—could not even have been dreamed of in the first wave of noirs. And like Jerry
Goldsmith's *Chinatown* in 1974 and David Shire's *Farewell, My Lovely* in 1975, John
Barry's score for *Body Heat* (Varèse Sarabande) helped redefine the musical sound of
noir, interestingly by centering the music around a big, bluesy theme derived from jazz
styles that viewers of the first-wave noirs could have easily related to, whereas many of
those earlier films used jaggedly dissonant symphonic scores in a "classical music" style.
Initially presented in a soulfully wailing sax solo over chordal figures, first offered in
bell-like synthesizer timbres that rock gently back and forth between F Minor and
C-sharp Minor, Barry's *Body Heat* theme is, quite simply, one of the moodiest and most
gripping tunes ever composed for the screen. It returns, in various guises, frequently
and essentially throughout the film, identifying itself as much by its obsessive, minor-
mode, added-note harmonies as by its haunting melodic configuration, keeping the
viewer/listener forever floating in the warm, murky waters of hidden drives, sexual as
well as murderous, tortuously rising to the surface. But there is other music as well: the
melody first heard in the high registers of the sax in the cue "I'm Weak" attaches itself
to (and leads naturally into) the colorations of the main theme while also moving off
in more wistful directions; the broadly defined, minor-mode string theme of "I'm Burning Up" manages to simultaneously suggest the romantic and the tragic; the partly major-mode ballad that opens "Chapeau Gratis" before it returns to the "I'm Burning Up"
theme sounds like an instrumental version of an unheard vocal; and Barry even throws
in some of his classic action-suspense sounds in "I'm Frightened," which momentarily
gives way to a few solo-organ bars, an ingenious musical equivalent of a clown (in
many ways himself) the Hurt character sees driving by in a car. Joel McNeely and the
London Symphony beautifully capture the moods and obsessiveness of Barry's score,
which has been sumptuously recorded and which features solos from Andy Mackintosh
(alto sax), David Hartley (piano), Mo Foster (Fender Bass), Eric Crees (trombone),
and Neil Percy (drums), who individually or in combinations join together to expertly
create the small-combo sound that sooner or later flows into Barry's big-strings symphonism. In comparing this version to the original music track, I would say that Mc-
Neely and his forces create a slightly drier, slightly more *détaché* sound than one hears
from Barry and his orchestra in the film version. But this in no way is a drawback.

March/April

When serious discussion on film begins, one of the topics that often comes up of late is
what is referred to as "sound design," which refers to patterns, textual and/or subtextual,

in the use of sound that transcend and/or transgress, one way or the other, the usual pseudo-mimetic demands of commercial filmmaking. It now strikes me, after seeing and hearing Pakistan-born director Shekhar Kapur's *Elizabeth*, with its wonderful score by David Hirschfelder (London; New London Consort, Philip Pickett, cond.), that we should mobilize the term "music design" to indicate a pattern not just in the kind of music and where it's used but in the way it evolves, or doesn't evolve, with the picture. One such pattern that comes immediately to mind is the deliberate nonuse of Jerry Goldsmith's music throughout just about the entire first half of the 1978 *Coma*. As developed in Kapur's film and its screenplay by Michael Hirst, *Elizabeth* presents three solidly delineated phases in the career of England's Queen Elizabeth I (Cate Blanchett): the Protestant Elizabeth's insecure life and loves under the realm of her predecessor, the very Catholic, very "bloody" Queen Mary (Kathy Burke); the incipient moments of Elizabeth's reign during which she reestablishes the Church of England and fights off, with the help of her trusted counselor Sir Francis Walsingham (the ever marvelous— and very ominous in this instance—Geoffrey Rush), various threats to her life and throne, the main threat coming from the Pope himself, played by the incredible John Gielgud; and, at the very end, Elizabeth's final determination to play her role to the hilt and become the "virgin queen," thereby establishing the foundations of modern England.

Although the entire film, as photographed by Remi Adefarasin, is unusually dark visually, the first third, which opens with three "heretics" being burned at the stake, suggests other forms of darkness as well, doom-and-gloom carryovers from the Middle Ages and, the film suggests, Catholicism. Musically, composer Hirschfelder evokes this visual, narrative, and historical darkness in a very *serioso*, modernist symphonic style, complete with mixed chorus, that moves between Holst, Vaughan Williams, and Bartók. Out of the low, male-voice (later joined by women) chanting beneath ominous, very minor-mode motivic figures in the orchestra, the Overture to *Elizabeth* quickly crescendos into a chorus-and-orchestra climax of chilling intensity, later tailing off into almost avant-garde clusters and glissandos in the chorus and percussion. The score continues this tone unchallenged throughout the first third of the picture; even the music for the romance between Elizabeth and Robert Dudley (Joseph Fiennes) may be the gloomiest "Love Theme" in the history of the cinema. The cue for Walsingham, which opens, harmonically and instrumentally at least, with reminiscences of Holst's "Neptune," maintains an unbearably mournful tension as it rises to an almost Bergian peak of unresolved, unrelieved tenebrousness. Once Elizabeth ascends to the throne, on the other hand, the music moves back and forth between Hirschfelder's dark symphonism and late-Renaissance styles, some of it pastiches by Hirschfelder, some of it by composers such as William Byrd, to suggest the coming of the light. A dance-like quality tends to dominate the cues in this part of the "music design." And then, once the final transformation has taken place, Kapur and/or Hirschfelder ingeniously introduce the slow, noble, and stately "Nimrod" variation, beefed up here and there, probably unnecessarily, with a vocalizing soprano, from Elgar's *Enigma Variations*. And thus is modern England born onto the music track. But the Introitus from Mozart's Requiem also gets into the act here. It's all manipulative as hell, and it works like a charm, or at least it did for me. While Hirschfelder does little that is unexpected in the music; while he doesn't shy away from some overused film/music tropes, such as the buildup via a rhythmic ostinato in the strings in "Conspiracy"; and while he flirts just a little too closely with Holst from time to time, he instantaneously engages the emotions, via thoroughly appropriate harmonic devices and strikingly mobilized tone colors (note the high strings and harp in the "Love Theme," for instance), with a skill worthy of Ennio Morricone. I don't know how much, if at all, Hirschfelder contributed to *Elizabeth*'s music design. But whoever was responsible for it has produced one of the most memorable interactions between film and music in recent memory. As for Cate Blanchett's Elizabeth, all I have to say is that I found her girlish fidgeting as the pre-queen Elizabeth singularly inappropriate. That type of visible nervousness would have been drummed out of the spirit of anyone born into royalty by the age of, oh, two days.

Rarely have theatrical trailers turned me off on a movie more than the ones for **Stepmom**, which I vowed I would never see, muttering to myself that soap opera seems to be the chosen mode of expression for the "family values" crowd. But then I listened to the score composed and conducted by John Williams and recorded by Sony, for which company Williams seems to have become one of the house composers (and conductors). The music moved me fairly deeply, as many of Williams' scores have these days, and so I figured I would go ahead and see the film just so I could bad-mouth it with authority in this column and elsewhere. Well, that might have worked for the new *Psycho*, but *Stepmom* turns out to be a much more complicated affair. The first clue comes as of the titles, in which you note that the film's two stars, Susan Sarandon and Julia Roberts, are also two of its three executive producers (i.e., they rounded up the money to get it made). Rarely, in fact, has a film "belonged" to its actresses to the degree that *Stepmom* belongs to Sarandon and Roberts, who play the roles of an older, divorcée with two children, and the much younger, new woman in the life of the ex-husband (Ed Harris, who tries gamely throughout to establish a presence vis-à-vis the two women). Many of the film's conflicts revolve, not unexpectedly, around Roberts' problems with the two children and, of course, with their mother, who also soon discovers she has terminal cancer. These are, of course, real-life situations that, when jammed all together into a two-hour movie, can come across as terribly hokey and manipulative; and the speed with which everything passes by can make a TV serial look well developed in comparison. One also has to raise an eyebrow in suspicion at implied political agendas that throw the primary responsibility for parenting onto women, which is not only sexist, of course, but also insulting to the ability of males to be deeply, meaningfully involved in child raising. But, somehow, *Stepmom* manages to at least partially communicate motherhood not mainly as a submission to the patriarchal order but as a profound woman's strength with roots reaching deeply into the pre-patriarchal past, thanks largely to the performances of Roberts and Sarandon, and to the story by Gigi Levangie, who also, with a host of other writers, did the often wonderful screenplay. In this sense, the gradual acceptance of Roberts into the ex-wife's world takes on the aura of an initiatory process within the world of women, although it is also somewhat tinged with overtones of symbolic incest within a youth-obsessed, male-dominated culture that does not even question the pairing up of the Harrison Fords with the Anne Heches or, moving up a notch, the Susan Sarandons with the Paul Newmans. The film, miraculously sidestepping pseudo-spiritual explanations involving such things as heaven and angels, also deals with the issue of children and death in about as real and heart-wrenching a way as I've ever seen. Not an easy read, any way you cut it.

The first reaction that I had to John Williams' score for *Stepmom*, with its bell-like sonorities floating in a heavily resonant acoustic ambience that probably owes as much to electronics as to the recording venue, was the childlike poignancy he captures from the very outset. Again I say, it's manipulative as hell, but it works. And when Williams moves into the score's main theme, one senses an almost deliberate allusion to the "Beauty and the Beast" waltz from Ravel's *Ma mère l'oye*, although there is also more than a hint of Satie's Third *Gymnopédie*, in spite of the lush orchestrations. In a way, of course, this fairytale aura supports what may be *Stepmom's* most pernicious subtextual element, namely the strongly upper-class milieu in which everything takes place. The ex-wife lives in an old, utterly gorgeous, three-story house overlooking the Hudson River somewhere in Westchester County, while the father shares a stunning, two-story loft apartment somewhere in lower Manhattan with his soon-to-be new wife. One of the film's early conflicts revolves around the fact that Roberts has forgotten that the 12-year-old girl's horseback-riding lessons take place on Mondays, not Tuesdays, every fourth week (or something like that). (But, later in the film, a horseback ride with the mother and daughter in the middle of a snowy night is guaranteed not to leave any dry eyes in the theater.) But, hey, fairytales have classically been the carriers not just of the "wisdom" of the contemporary culture but of the vestigial magic lying beneath its surface (as I said, *Stepmom* is a hard read). Another major element of Williams' *Stepmom* score is several cues in which guitar solos, played with apparent total involvement by Christopher Parkening (whose humming is picked up by the close miking), carry much of the music's considerable lyrical weight. Williams has also, from the beginning of his career, proven quite adept at writing lighthearted music, which he provides at just the right moments in the *Stepmom* score, whether in the quasi-scherzo, very Americana cue entitled "The Soccer Game," or in the more animated-cartoon type of pseudo-suspense for "Ben's Antics." But in the end run it is that sad, sometimes almost elegiac waltz that stays with you. Somehow, it works as a kind of musical archetype for all of the sadnesses, major and minor, of childhood, not to mention the many losses of adulthood, and it is quite capable of bringing back the tears that came out during the movie.

I have on at least two occasions waxed very enthusiastic about David Raksin's music for **Forever Amber**, a costume drama directed in 1947 by Otto Preminger and starring Linda Darnell, Cornell Wilde, and George Sanders. My enthusiasm was based on a then new recording of a suite of the music conducted by the composer for RCA's "Classic Film Scores" series. Now, Varèse Sarabande has made available much more substantial portions of the score arranged by the composer into a substantial, four-movement suite from the more than 100 individual cues (110 minutes' worth) of the original music tracks conducted by Alfred Newman, remixed in 1994 by the invaluable Nick Redman from the original optical film elements. Based on what Jon Burlingame describes in the program booklet as "Kathleen Winsor's notoriously racy 1944 novel of an ambitious farm girl who slept her way to the throne room in 17th-century England," the film's costume-drama status did not keep Raksin from applying his considerable musical sophistication to the score. Even Amber's theme, while charming and ingenuous, is filled with meter shifts that in their own way let you know that the composer at least (as was the case for *Laura*) did not find the heroine all that easy to read. And, as I've stated elsewhere, Raksin's music for the story's darker moments—those involving sickness, death, and the plague—have a tragic intensity rare in any dramatic music, film-score or otherwise, although this element comes across more strongly on the composer's recording of the suite than on this "original motion-picture soundtrack," in which this music is broken up over a number of different cues. One thing made even more apparent on this original-soundtrack recording than on the newer version, on the other hand, is the ingenious way in which the composer organized much of the material around what Burlingame describes as "a single musical device, a ground bass around which Raksin builds various melodies and harmonies." This device becomes apparent even in such an early cue as "The Chase." Further, Raksin also has an ingenious way, at certain points, of building up layers of harmonic textures that somehow translate into very action-specific moods as well. The score also contains some pastiche music for the court scenes. All in all, the sound on this CD, although shrill at points, and very imbued with that old studio dryness, is quite acceptable, and one hears a directionality that Nick Redman, in an early set of notes, once explained away but that I *still* don't understand.

May/June

The name of composer Carter Burwell is most often associated with the seven films, all of which he scored, done by Joel and Ethan Coen, from the initial *Blood Simple* through *Fargo* right on up to *The Big Lebowski*. Burwell in fact gave a very eloquent presentation on his music for the Coen brothers' films, and an equally eloquent question-and-answer session, at the "Cine-Sonic" conference in Melbourne, Australia, this past summer (a book of the various presentations, including Burwell's [and an article by yours truly on "Sound Music in the Films of Alain Robbe-Grillet," was published in 1999]). But Burwell has been getting a lot of work from other filmmakers as well, and we hear the composer at his best in the poignant, touching, and ultimately tragic (musically and dramatically) **Gods and Monsters** (RCA), which stars Ian McKellen as the veteran, English-born, homosexual film director James Whale in the last days of his life (in 1957). Tonally based and slightly Minimalist in the way it constantly, but often rhapsodically, reexamines a limited number of harmonic progressions, Burwell's score from the outset establishes a somber and very self-contained mood that evokes both the passion and the impossibility of what the film presents as the aging director's fixation on his beautiful young gardener (Brendan Fraser), who likewise faces a no-exit situation vis-à-vis a man whose art entrances him but whose sexuality infuriates and terrifies him. Another element of the film that the music captures, in spite of its generally slowly unfurling patterns, is a nostalgia for a lost past, for a possible lover killed in the First World War, a nostalgia brought to the point of near-hysteria by a stroke that has left Whale physically intact but subject to random resurfacings of smells, sounds, and visions from his past (Proust would have been ecstatic). Using a small group of strings, four woodwinds, harp, piano, and a tad of percussion, Burwell starts off the score, in a cue entitled "Arise Clay," with an utterly haunting series of expansive chordal metamorphoses, mostly in the minor mode but with mild dissonances leading along paths that never quite resolve. But the theme that perhaps best suggests the Whale character—his uncontrolled visits into the past, his mostly unused artistic spirit, his physically unrequited love—is a slow, poignant waltz that again never quite resolves and that is first heard in the cue entitled "Dripping" (a reference to an olfactory memory of the congealed meat-fat eaten in the director's dirt-poor English family during his childhood). And at the outset of "Love in the Trenches," one has the momentary impression that Burwell is going to head in directions Mahlerian (one thinks of Luciano Visconti's use of that composer's music in his 1971 *Death in Venice*). All in all, a gripping, sometimes achingly moving score, conducted and produced by Burwell for this CD. RCA's program commentary offers a brief note of gratitude to Burwell from the producers of *Gods and Monsters*, and a more extended essay from director Bill Condon, who, for instance, perceptively describes the music's slow waltz as "almost a dirge for a European culture that was destroyed by World War I."

A Civil Action, an alternately—and sometimes simultaneously—touching, atmospheric, scathingly ironic, and humorous film directed by Steven Zaillian, is based on a nonfiction book by Jonathan Harr that tells the story of a New York City (I think) lawyer named Jan Schlittman (played with a marvelous mixture of laid-backness and involvement by John Travolta) who, initially in spite of himself, gets himself and his small firm involved in a lawsuit against some large corporations for polluting the water in Woburn, Massachusetts, where an inordinate number of children have died of leukemia, apparently as a result. A typical, Grisham-esque story of hero legal beagles taking on the big guys, right? Well, not exactly. *A Civil Action*, like the true story it is based on, has a number of unexpected twists, not the least of which is the downfall of an entire law firm because of Schlittman's hubris in taking on a company (the Grace Corporation) that out-mans him at every position, in particular that of the opposing attorney, Jerome Facher. The latter role is played by Robert Duvall, whose outrageously deceptive aura of noninvolvement is fortified by such props as an ancient briefcase held together with Scotch tape and a white (yes, white!) tennis ball that he tosses against a wall in the middle of deadly important (for the other guy) phone conversations. The highpoint in *A Civil Action*'s humor and irony comes during a sequence that cuts back and forth from a law-school class on cynical courtroom tactics

("Never ask a witness a question that you don't know the answer to," or words to that effect, as one example) taught by Facher, and the actual courtroom drama in which, of course, Schlittman plunges right ahead and asks a question to which a witness gives a devastatingly unexpected answer.

Now, given this subject matter, name a composer to whom, based on most of the films he has scored, you would mostly likely never turn. Does Danny Elfman come to mind? Well, he might, but he has turned in an amazingly evocative score for *A Civil Action*, available on a beautifully recorded (with a very creative use of directionality) Hollywood Records CD (Artie Kane and Daniel Carlin Jr., cond.). My first reaction upon hearing the score was, "Good grief! Danny Elfman has morphed into Thomas Newman." And, indeed, the opening cue on the CD, entitled "Walkin'," with its kinky, bell-like timbres and open intervals set to an evenly paced, moderato four-beat, has more than one moment in common with Newman's wonderful title theme for Robert Altman's 1992 *The Player*. But a more careful listening (my third) revealed a slightly heavier beat that is definitely in Elfman territory, as are the brief choral groanings that punctuate the music as well. Still, the score as a whole has a definite Newman aura to it. But there's a good reason for this. Newman foremost, but several of his colleagues as well (now including Elfman), has found a subtle musical style based not around memorable themes but around atmospheric, oft-repeated harmonic and/or instrumental figures that evoke an America that maybe was or might have been but that now can be experienced mainly through the lenses of Hollywood's movie cameras, to which this musical style is indelibly wedded. A particularly haunting case in point in *A Civil Action* occurs in the cue entitled "The River." Although I have seen the film only once, as soon as I experienced the coldness of Elfman's almost icy filigrees, I knew it was for the moment when Schlittman/Travolta, standing on a bridge and later along the shores of a cold-river winterscape in rural Massachusetts, comes to the decision to take on the case (I hope I'm right!). And, in fact, the music here, for all its bleakness, maintains that overlay of nostalgia that makes the viewer/listener realize that it is the land as much as the people that makes the lawyer change his mind. Or at least that's what the riveting amalgam of Elfman's music and Conrad L. Hall's cinematography made me feel. This particular musical style, especially in Elfman's hands, is also perhaps only one or two steps away from some of the ethereal strains of Arvo Pärt's recent music, and there are moments when I definitely had the sense that Elfman was about to tread that ground. Elfman also mobilizes the chorus in several cues to vocalize what sounds like a folk tune. Yet another of *A Civil Action*'s supreme moments comes during the recounting by a father of the death of his son as he and his wife were driving him to the doctor's office. Here, any music would have been superfluous, and Elfman and all others involved are to be congratulated for having avoided the temptation, which lesser talents would have given into all too readily, to underscore the scene. And, the next time you see *A Civil Action*, remember this motto that popped into my head during a pretrial sequence early in the film: Never thank a shark for not biting you.

As my late father used to say, when in a poker game you don't play the cards, you play the other players. He ought to have known: the first of several transcontinental, summer-vacation car trips we took from Las Cruces, New Mexico, to my grandparents' cottage on Canandaigua Lake in New York were in a '39 or '40 Chevy coupe he won during the war in a poker game from a well-known character actor in the movies. Or so the story goes. I bring this up because we seem to be moving, in the cinema, away from the old image of the poker player as either a disreputable (if sometimes lovable) card sharp or as someone chosen by God and country (such as Mr. 007) to get the right card at the right time. If the aura of disreputability has not entirely vanished, recent movies are nonetheless telling us more and more about the fine art of winning at poker as a kind of athletic contest in which superhuman concentration is just as important as it is for a baseball pitcher. Even living with dear old Dad, I never knew what a "tell" was (a characteristic gesture that "tells" what is going through another player's mind at a crucial moment) until such pictures as the 1994 *Maverick* or, now, **Rounders**, directed by John Dahl, best known for a couple of slick post-noir films, *Red Rock West* (1992) and the wicked *The Last Seduction* (1994). *Rounders*, in fact, is a near-textbook study of a young gambler (Matt Damon) whose gifts for the game are those of a natural-born athlete but whose friendship with another young gambler (the up-and-coming Edward Norton) of the opposite, do-anything-(including cheating)- to-win-immediately school, causes him a reasonable amount of misery.

I remember thinking to myself, as I was watching *Rounders*, how much I liked the musical score by Christopher Young (Varèse Sarabande), a series of mostly jazz cues that by and large stay quietly in the background and complement the action with a layer of musical atmosphere. But if anything Young's 21 cues for a 10-piece jazz combo, with occasional contributions mostly from the strings of a larger orchestra, work even better when separated from the film. Several of the cues stand on their own as fairly well-developed pieces, some of which even include mini-breaks for various instruments, including vibes, electric organ, sax, flute, and keyboard. Other cues have a more raucous blues-cum-rock beat catch to them. But even when Young does little else but establish pure mood, as in such cues as "The Catch" (with its 3+3+2 beat), "Ode to Johnny Chan," "Tapioca" (a particularly brooding, slow, minor-mode meditation mostly for vibes, soprano sax, bass, and drums that moves close to those icy cold reaches of John Lewis' *Odds Against Tomorrow*), or "Finger Up Your Spine," Young creates such haunting figures and such instantly gripping affect that you don't want to even think about turning your attention elsewhere. In fact, one reason why it is sometimes so difficult to write about film music is that its best composers just seem to have an instinct, as soon as they know they're scoring a movie, for finding harmonic and instrumental figures, whether written in a jazz or a classical style, that instantly reach the emotions, hold them, and don't let them go. And that particular essence of film music remains elusively hard to define. Indeed, *Rounders* leaves its jazz base on occasion to offer a series of very quiet, very slow cues, mostly for keyboard and strings, that evoke an aura of aching sadness in a mode that perhaps can only be defined as "film music." And after several listenings to the score, one becomes aware of a certain thematic unity that binds the 21 cues together. The slow intro to the main-title cue, for instance, introduces a keyboard motif that later shows up in the non-jazz cues, while the softly swinging, 6/8 jazz-waltz that follows presents a theme later picked up, again by a non-jazz cue, in a very slow 6/8. All in all, I really cannot find enough superlatives for this music: Christopher Young, for my money, belongs to the elite of current film-music composers, and I can only wish that his name would show up more often in major films.

Well, my goodness. I can't remember the last time I heard a film score offer anything resembling the sophisticated "Agitato dolorosa," a severe and violent piece scored for string quartet in a probably atonal harmonic idiom, that opens Elliot Goldenthal's music for Neil (*The Crying Game*, *The Butcher Boy*) Jordan's predictably unpopular but unjustifiably vilified **In Dreams** (Varèse Sarabande; London Metropolitan Orchestra, Jonathan Sheffer, cond.). Given the nature of the movie, however, the music, which ends up covering quite a varied parcel of different territories, comes as somewhat less of a surprise. Billed pretty much as a horror-suspense film about a woman (Annette Bening) with psychic and telepathic powers whose dreams tune her in on the mind of a serial killer (Robert Downey, Jr.) of young girls, a killer who will soon victimize her own daughter, *In Dreams* likewise refuses to settle down comfortably as a one-dimensional text. It all starts with the creepy images of an entire town submerged, to make way for a dam, beneath a lake from which the serial killer, bound to a bed by abusive parents, will emerge (Goldenthal's switch from string quartet to eerie electronic soundscapes lets you know exactly where you are). On the broadest level, one can read the film as the broadly tragic depiction of the situation of women and children in patriarchal culture. This is a tragedy that both director Jordan and composer Goldenthal refuse to romanticize, Jordan by never relenting in his depiction of the thorough trap in which the Bening character and her daughter, and other mothers and other daughters, find themselves, Goldenthal by composing cues that rarely afford the audience the escape via catharsis that has classically been one of the prime functions of Hollywood film music. Yes, one cannot help getting caught up on several occasions in the brutal pathos of the situations in Jordan's film, and, yes, Goldenthal on occasion takes a deep breath and creates music that aches with the deepest possible sadness, most particularly in a quiet, slightly wispy cue for solo piano that appears in two cues relating to Claire's dreams. And the score climaxes in a massive "Elegy Ostinato" that grows out of a mood evoked, with traces of Bernard Herrmann and John Barry, at several other points in the score, most notably "Rebecca's Abduction." But the quasi-atonal string-quartet music will return in a second cue, this one with some grating outbursts on the sax (played by Bruce Williamson), while several other cues create a raucous wall of angry sound to which no fewer than five appropriately named "deaf elk" guitars contribute their electronically distorted twangs. Even the final song, "Dream Baby," with music by Goldenthal and lyrics by Jordan, hardly provides the uplift that would normally schmaltz up an ending in which the dead mother joins her dead daughter: is this Heaven, or is it a statement of how patriarchal culture wants to view its women and children, namely as distantly idealized and decidedly dead images? Jordan and Goldenthal rather lead you to the latter conclusion. I also find quite indicative Jordan's use of the song title "In Dreams" to replace the title of the Bari (*Dead Ringers*) Wood novel *Dolls Eyes* on which the film is based. In fact, the appearance in Jordan's film of Roy Orbison's hyper-corny pop classic (spectacularly well mastered on this recording) forces a brutally cynical overlay on many of the song's lyrics: Who *is* that "candy-colored clown" who "tiptoes to my room every night," and what is he really doing while he's whispering "Go to sleep, everything is all right"? And the refrain "In dreams I walk with you / In dreams I talk with you" perfectly describes a major element of the film's narrative. Of course, David Lynch got there first by using this song, best imagined accompanying whiskey-soaked denizens of roadside, smoke-filled bars conjuring up visions of little angels to be abused, in a sequence from *Blue Velvet* that may offer one of the most crushing re-readings ever of a pop-culture icon. In *In Dreams* Jordan also uses the Andrews Sisters' "Don't Sit Under the Apple Tree," also heard on this CD, to somewhat similar effect. Not a pretty sight or sound. If you need to live a lie, then by all means go and see the dreadful *Life Is Beautiful*. If you want something closer to the truth of what really goes on in patriarchal culture, try *In Dreams*.

Using time-lapse photography to compress chronological time and considerably speed up visual events—"clouds chasing clouds across a New Mexican desert, the mass dynamiting of a failed housing project in St. Louis, hives of people swarming in and out of Grand Central Station, hectic traffic swapping lanes on the Los Angeles freeways"—Godfrey Reggio, in the 1983 **Koyaanisqatsi**, created an 87-minute montage-ballet with no plot, characters, or dialogue, choreographed to a haunting score by Philip Glass, whose immediately recognizable style of continually repeated, slowly metamorphosing musical figures borrowed from the four tonal corners of classical music move in perfect sync with Reggio's time-out-of-joint visuals. Long as unavailable as the film it accompanies, Glass' music has finally turned up on CD (Nonesuch; Albert de Ruiter, bass; Western Wind Vocal Ensemble; Members of the Philip Glass Ensemble, Michael Riesman, cond.), not as the "original soundtrack" once available on an Antilles LP but in a newly recorded version that considerably expands most of the cues while featuring several musicians from the original, such as Glass regular Michael Riesman as conductor and keyboardist (including the organ), and bass Albert de Ruiter, whose repeated vocalization of the film's title word on a low D wonderfully and, dare I say, mystically establishes the dark, primal tone out of which the entire film and the entire score emerge. (It might be noted that the instrumental configurations have slightly changed from those of the music-track recording. There are more strings and fewer winds, for example.) As Glass pointed out in conversation with Tim Page reprinted in the latter's excellent program notes, which also supply the description of the film quoted above, "This is music that might conceivably have been written at any period in history. . . . And yet it's new, don't you think?" Absolutely. Glass' brief figures, whether from the darkest depths of the instrumental ensemble or the brightest highs, are not so much developed as subjected to a process of osmosis, with the transitional membrane being all of musical history. In listening to them one can have such temporally unsettling impressions as experiencing Beethoven filtered through Mussorgsky, as is the case with a unison figure in the strings (sans violins) in the cue—a movement really—entitled "Pruit Igoe." I am also entranced by the way Glass moves into the timbres of an a cappella chorus his patented, lilting triplet figures that alternate back and forth in groups of two and multiples thereof. If there is a criticism to be made, it is that the music is so utterly captivating, the images so mesmerizing, and the combination of the two so exhilarating that the critique of modern culture implied by the film's title, a Hopi word meaning variously "crazy life," "life in turmoil," "life disintegrating," "life out of balance," and/or "a state of life that calls for another way of living," does not wholly correspond with the viewer/listener's impression of the film. Indeed, a film-studies colleague of mine at Queens College, film scholar Jonathan Buchsbaum, who has had a visceral dislike of *Koyaanisqatsi* from the moment it opened, has described it to me as "a Luddite paean to a pre-lapsarian Navajo cosmology." I have much more positive feelings toward the film, and I'm willing to live with its contradictions.

July/August

I had a pretty good idea that I was going to hate **Life Is Beautiful** (La vita è bella), written and directed by Italian comic Roberto Benigni, who also stars, before I ever saw the picture. But nothing, whether the numerous clips I had seen from the film or the several articles I had read about it or, for that matter, the numerous and totally undeserved Oscar nominations it garnered—it won for Best Foreign Film, Best Actor, and Best Original Dramatic Score (by Nicola Piovani)—prepared me for just how really unbearable it is. Let's start with the obvious, which of course revolves around the question of how one can make a slapstick comedy whose last half is set in Auschwitz at the end of World War II. As one *Life Is Beautiful* admirer, shocked at how much I loathed the film, pointed out to me, Holocaust survivors very often used storytelling and humor as a way to get through the horrors from day to day. True, and it would not be difficult to imagine a very touching film that would focus on the various ploys used by the concentration-camp victims in the almost impossible task of keeping their spirits from total meltdown. Franz Waxman's recently released cantata *The Song of Terezin* is a moving testament to the beauty that can paradoxically grow out of the most nightmarish situations. But for the above argument to work, *Life Is Beautiful* would have had to evoke, if such is even possible in images, something of the black side of things that necessitated the humor in the first place, and such is emphatically not the case. For starters, the film's set design for Auschwitz, with its clean walls and arches and its pools of colored light in the background, evokes nothing more terrifying than a slightly surreal backdrop for a play. Even a massive pile of naked cadavers stumbled upon by the Benigni character (in the mist, of course) comes across as a painting to be placidly studied in the quiet halls of a museum. Almost totally absent is the sense of anything resembling the humanity imprisoned in the camp. And, indeed, in one of the film's most tasteless scenes, the Benigni character, named Guido, proves to be so hyper-narcissistically involved in his own private morality of family values that he "translates" a German soldier's very serious orders to Guido's fellow inmates into a continuation of the game he has been playing with his little boy to shelter him from the grimness of the situation he is in. Never mind that lack of knowledge of the orders would quickly lead Guido's barracks mates to a swift death or much worse. For Guido, nothing matters but his wife and child; for Benigni, who cannot be absent from more than three or four shots during the entire picture, nothing matters beyond the decidedly stale comic shtick he manically works at maintaining throughout the film. He even tries to make comic the slave labor (yes, I've heard that Benigni's father did forced labor during the war; so what?) of carrying impossibly heavy anvils in impossible heat to be melted down to supply the Nazi war machine with more weapons to help them in their quest for racial purity, except that these two brief scenes don't even work as comedy. And to make matters utterly worse, when the liberation does come, Guido's little boy sees the American tank that rescues him as nothing more than a prize in the la-la-land game obsessively created by his father, a prize that leads him to ultimate reunification with his aristocratic mother. No wonder Americans, who are showing an increasingly huge propensity for being sucked in by empty images that keep them away from any awareness that would lead to real political action, have gone gaga over *Life Is Beautiful*. One can imagine that the film will be a huge video hit as nuclear families isolated in their suburban, burglar-alarmed houses watch it on big-screen TVs in surround sound before getting in their SUVs and taking off for a weekend ski-trip. . . .

But *Life Is Beautiful* not only repulses in its Holocaust-as-*Sesame-Street* politics, it totally fails in every department of the filmmaking process. The entire first half of the film is given over to a series of feeble gags barely warmed over from the likes of Keaton, Chaplin, and Fields, gags held together by only the slightest of narrative threads (Guido's love for the aristocratic woman he eventually marries). Almost all the characters introduced into the film beyond Guido, his *principessa*, and his little boy stay around only long enough to be useful for the particular routine at the time before vanishing without comment or explanation. One character (played by Horst Buchholz) who does return in the second half of the film does so in such a totally predictable way that the impact of his inhumanity gets mitigated to the point of nothingness. How anyone could ever have thought of comparing Benigni with Chaplin is beyond me. Benigni's only contribution to the physical art of comedy is wearing a face that generally makes him look like a jackass, while the huge bulk of his comedy is verbal, and comes from badly written (the Italian is not much better than the English translations), almost always unfunny lines delivered in a near-scream from start to finish of the film. Unlike Chaplin's little tramp, Benigni's Guido remains crushingly one-dimensional throughout: one never has a sense not only of his Jewishness but also of whatever sensibilities might have pushed him into running a bookstore. And the child actor who plays the little boy self-consciously walks through the film like a refugee from a Bill Keane "painting." Once in a while, in the Italy-based first half of the film, Benigni, in what always appears to be an afterthought, creates bland little scenes depicting Italian anti-Semitism. To make sure we know that this is serious stuff, the director-writer-star had his composer write creepy-scary music used in a laughably hackneyed way more appropriate to Kato and Inspector Clouseau than to the mentality, to use much too polite a word, of fascist thugs.

As for Piovani's music (Virgin), the score, like the film itself, comes across as something pretty close to monothematic, that mono theme in the music being a bitter-sweet, tango-like, Rota/Fellini-type tune that is catchy enough in its own right but that, even in the minor variations it undergoes, wears very thin very fast. A second, oft-repeated cue, heard first on the CD but introduced much later in the film, is a quasi-lullaby with (acoustic) guitar accompaniment that basically becomes the love theme. Apart from that, the CD recording offers us a bit of the creepy-crawly-nasty music, several period pastiches, one of which is particularly unlistenable, and the famous "Barcarolle" aria (sung by Monserrat Caballé and Shirley Verret) from Offenbach's *Tales of Hoffman*, which, like just about everything else, plays a role that is crushingly superficial in spite of all of Benigni's efforts to give it portentous meaning by attaching it to Guido's love for Nora. And so, Roberto Benigni, while images appear in the paper and on TV every day of masses of Kosovar refugees forced from their homes—those who haven't been raped, tortured, and killed, that is—by yet one more nation of people filled with ethnic hatred fueled by a racist dictator, don't tell me that life is beautiful. It may have its moments, but those moments surely do not come from the sights and sounds of a self-serving, manic comedian falling flat as he unsuccessfully tries to fill the shoes of the greats who preceded him while exploiting one of history's greatest tragedies for a bit of extra mileage. And I do hope you carry those two Oscars to your mantelpiece more convincingly than you did those anvils in *La vita è bella*. In case readers should think that the above simply represents the rantings of one of *Fanfare*'s resident curmudgeons, I invite them to read my colleague Stuart Liebman's scathing review of *Life Is Beautiful* in *Cineaste* 24:2–3.

OK, folks, this is going to be complicated, so bear with me. First of all, let me say that you will have to look hard to find more achingly poignant, intensely beautiful music, film score or otherwise, than what turns up in much of John Corigliano's score, mostly for solo violin and string orchestra, for **The Red Violin** (Sony; Joshua Bell, violin; Philharmonia Orchestra, Esa Pekka Salonen, cond.). Much but by no means all of that poignancy, that aching, intense beauty is generated in the often heard "Anna's Theme," which initially establishes itself haltingly in the solo violin's midrange but ultimately blossoms into a broad, soaring theme defined as much by the utterly haunting melody itself as by the very consistent, chromatic harmonic structure beneath it (which is probably one reason Corigliano was able to generate out of the score a Chaconne for Violin and Orchestra that I will discuss anon). The musical work that is probably closest in spirit to Corigliano is possibly the opening, brooding Nocturne of Shostakovich's First Violin Concerto, save that where the Shostakovich exudes perhaps 75% darkness and death and 25% a sense of loss, the Corigliano seems to communicate the presence of both in more or less equal measure. Even at its most elegiac, as in the "Death of Kaspar" (a child prodigy) or in the cues for the departure of the composer's wife, which at one point get boiled down to a hushed string quartet, the music never plunges wholly into the blackness. But while Anna's Theme towers over much of the music, and, even when it doesn't, subtly informs motifs and harmonies in other cues, Corigliano's score, which moves incredibly in sync with the film, touches so many times and places that it would be impossible to fully describe them all here. Suffice it to say, first of all, that the film's narrative, which follows the peregrinations of a violin from its creation in Cremona to the present day, naturally creates the need for a certain amount of source music, most of it composed by Corigliano—a Vivaldi-esque concerto for violin and string orchestra played by a consort of orphaned boys at a monastery; an Étude cum metronome worked up by an orphaned prodigy (performed by Austrian prodigy Kristoph Koncz) to a dizzyingly fast tempo; music played by a series of Gypsies (the last a woman) who have recovered the violin from the grave of the child prodigy; a virtuoso solo piece performed in concert by a 19th-century English violinist named Pope (Jason Flemyng); even the music that Pope composes on the spot, as it were, while making love, first (in a cue entitled "Coitus Musicalis") with his wife (Greta Scacchi), then with another woman, a scene in which the wife discovers the betrayal not with her eyes but with her ears. Miraculously, there is something of Corigliano in just about all of these cues. Further, one becomes aware, in listening to the score, that the composer, rather than imitating the music of each period and place shown in the movie, has managed instead to simultaneously infuse into his score the styles of just about all the periods involved—Baroque, Romantic, Modern (I don't hear much Classical). Speaking of modern, I love the moment at the opening of The Red Violin where, following a moody and mournful theme-motif, the camera tracks through the numerous instruments hanging in the violin maker's shop: here Corigliano's music creates a quiet cacophony of clustered violin timbres, with both music and visuals suggesting a kind of primordial scattering of elements that will begin to shape themselves into the musical and narrative universes. The score will later refind this modernism in the final episode in Montreal. On the other hand, as the violin makes its "Journey to China," Corigliano comes up with quiet, mysterious, and gripping music that perhaps falls somewhere between Berg and Mahler. Equally remarkable is the solo-violin theme, a virtual juggling act of tonal and atonal devices, for the modern-day violin expert Morritz (played by the somewhat improbably cast Samuel L. Jackson, who at one point seems to recover his character from Pulp Fiction as he dresses down a hotel clerk).

And now for the complexities. In many ways, The Red Violin can be considered as an ultimate artistic realization of an aesthetic articulated by Edgar Allan Poe but that goes all the way back to the myth of Orpheus and no doubt beyond: "[T]he death of a beautiful woman is, unquestionably, the most poetical topic in the world—and equally is it beyond doubt that the lips best suited for such a topic are those of a bereaved lover" ("The Philosophy of Composition"). It is in fact amazing how many narratives, both cinematic and otherwise, are generated by the image of the death of a beautiful woman (try Dirty Harry for starters, or, for a profound meditation on the subject, Twin Peaks and Twin Peaks: Fire Walk With Me). But the central metaphor of The Red Violin all but literalizes the poetics of absence whereby such a death becomes the core inspiration of a work of art, and the work of art the "lips" of the bereaved lover: shortly after the beginning of the film, the (beautiful) wife (Irene Grazioli) of a Cremona violinmaker (Carlo Cecchi) dies in childbirth. This particular Orpheus—the violinmaker—brings back this particular Eurydice by taking her blood, adding it to varnish, and then, using a brush made from her hair, painting his greatest achievement as an artisan with that blood-reddened varnish. The beautiful red violin, then, immediately replaces, as an objet d'art in its own right, the dead woman. Even more disembodied, however, since music is one of the most nonrepresentational of the arts, is the music that the red violin will eventually make, and that, of course, is where John Corigliano comes in. The film was not built around Corigliano's music, which seems almost impossible when one confronts the final product. According to the composer in an interview conducted by Robert Carl and published in *Fanfare 22:5*, director/co-writer François Girard, who also did the acclaimed *Thirty-Two Short Films about Glenn Gould*, had wanted to use nothing but pre-existing ("found") music for *The Red Violin*, which would have given the film much more historical feel. Out of Corigliano's amazingly unified score, on the other hand, grows sense of the mythic, of the perpetuation of the death-of-the-beautiful-woman aesthetics across the centuries: throughout we have the sense of a modern composer drawing floods of (post)Romantic angst out of a Baroque musical figure (the chaconne). This is not the sometimes ultramodern John Corigliano heard in many of his concert works as well as in the film score (his first) for Ken Russell's *Altered States*, a movie that certainly goes against the grain of much Western narrative. This is John Corigliano putting himself in the soul and skin of the Orphic artist and creating a fairly conservative but nonetheless stunningly beautiful musical metonymy of the original artistic text moving in parallel to the film itself. In fact, Corigliano creates at the very outset a metonymy within the metonymy by giving Anna's Theme initially to a solo vocalization by a woman's voice (Rebecca Starr), then bringing in the solo in unison with it, and finally having the solo violin replace the voice, which indicatively does not return until the End Titles, by which point, of course, this cinematic embodiment of the Orphic aesthetic, this particular time-transcendent presentation of the myth, has died its own, narrative death.

So, where do I stand in all of this? To be honest, I'm not 100% sure. There is no question that Corigliano's score, if not perhaps Girard's film, joins a large body of works of art that I love generated by the Orphic aesthetic, whether other works of music, the poetry of Stéphane Mallarmé, or, of course, Hitchcock's *Vertigo* (and its score), and that's just for starters. There is also no question that *The Red Violin* is in fact a meditation on, rather than just a realization of, not just the death-of-the-beautiful-woman aesthetic but the equally pernicious blaming of the woman for giving us mortal life: many of the male characters touched in the film by the red violin come to a bad end. And perhaps the most ironic examination of this aesthetic comes from its final extension into the world of capital, which further distances the instrument and its music from their point of departure in the physical world. And while director Girard does not venture into the modernistic as much as his composer, he does in fact remind us of the narrative's mythic underpinnings by unexpectedly cutting back and forth throughout the film between the narrative's various episodes, most significantly the reading of the wife's tarot cards, which in many ways microcosmically defines the narrative's entire structure. The bottom line is that the music, whatever aesthetic it embodies, is utterly gorgeous, and it is played with exquisite intensity by violinist Joshua Bell, who seems to thoroughly identify with the score's deep affect while perfectly negotiating, when necessary, its sometimes fiendish virtuoso demands. And one suspects that no one short of Esa-Pekka Salonen and nothing short of the Philharmonia Orchestra could have so perfectly matched Bell intensity for intensity, virtuosity for virtuosity. It is difficult to imagine that any score this year will come close to touching Corigliano's *The Red Violin* for the 1999 Best Original Score Oscar, although the members of the Academy's Music Division manage to make fools of themselves year in (including this March) and year out. As for the concert work entitled "The Red Violin": Chaconne for Violin and Orchestra developed from the score and included on this CD, I find it a mistake. *The Red Violin* was conceived as a film score, and none of its cues lasts over four minutes. The linking together of the musical material from some of these cues via various devices of concert-hall composing strikes me as artificial, arbitrary, and, ultimately, not terribly convincing. Further, the music, rather than being expanded by the addition of other instrumental timbres in the Chaconne, actually loses the bite and lyrical depth given it by the string orchestra. The Chaconne is by no means an insignificant work of music, but it pales next to the film score that inspired it.

[David Cronenberg's] *eXistenZ* starts off in an old wooden church wherein a celebrity computer-game-designer named Allegra Geller (Jennifer Jason Leigh) is about to demonstrate to a control group (which could just as easily be a group-therapy session) her latest marvel, a virtual-reality game called "eXistenZ" accessed via a decidedly organic-looking (no surprise there; this is David Cronenberg, remember) module whose joy-stick (of sorts) looks like an enlarged nipple. In a way, *eXistenZ* seems to take over where the 1983 *Videodrome*, the last Cronenberg film to feature an original screenplay by the director, leaves off, with a kind of crazed revolutionary assassinating (or here attempting to assassinate) a representative of the evils of virtual reality. Allegra escapes with a handsome member of the control group named Ted Pikul, played by Jude Law, who here replaces the sharp-edged contours of his English accent (as heard, for instance, in *Gattaca*) with something resembling a Canadian accent. Needless to say, Allegra and Ted pass the time away by entering her game, which necessitates the creation of an anus like (shades of *Naked Lunch*) "port" in the small of Ted's back into which a very umbilical line to the game module is plugged. Most of the action with this "game" takes place in places such as a rural gas station and a dreary ski slope sans snow (interestingly, the whole film was shot within a 60-mile perimeter of Toronto). The characters are light years away from their counterparts in *The Matrix*: Jennifer Jason Leigh could play Mother Teresa and still come across as hysterical and neurotic, while Jude Law acts out his part with all the enthusiasm of a golly-gee-whiz American (OK, Canadian) kid playing his first game of cowboys and Indians. The closest he comes to an arsenal is—are you ready for this?—a gristle-gun fashioned from the remnants of a Chinese meal. It fires human teeth for bullets. This is all pure, old-fashioned Cronenberg, the Cronenberg from before *Naked Lunch, M. Butterfly,* and *Crash* (the latter a film that becomes brilliant only after you have seen it at least for a second time), the Cronenberg whose heroes and heroines constantly seek to transcend the limitations of the physical world only to find themselves overwhelmed (and often fascinated in spite of themselves) by the squishiest, gooiest, grossest, most slurpy and organic physicality that the world has to offer. What carries *eXistenZ* into something of a new arena is its dimension of Möbius-strip self-reflexivity, within which the "villains" that Allegra and Ted fight against are both those who would steal the secrets of her game and those who would abolish virtual reality altogether. Within this context, the surprise ending basically isn't.

eXistenZ represents the ninth collaboration between Cronenberg and his fellow Canadian, composer Howard Shore (RCA Victor). One reason why this important collaboration has worked so well, it seems to me, is that while Cronenberg is busy plunging often unsympathetic characters into archetypal battles of the mind versus the flesh, Shore provides a brooding layer of affect that applies not to the characters, whom Cronenberg generally disengages from the kinds of emotional involvements that generate traditional underscoring, but to the ultimately tragic nature of the struggle itself. Thus, while a composer such as John Corigliano in *The Red Violin* creates, through an expanded use of the anticipations and resolutions of tonal harmony, an emotional canvas that strongly mirrors the psychological tensions and releases of the individual psychology and the personal unconscious, Shore, through the use of such devices as drones, open intervals, and short figures that repeat obsessively rather than resolving, reaches into the much more archaic territories of the collective unconscious. Rarely is the music in any of the 20 cues for *eXistenZ* very far away from a sustained, very low D, over which Shore adds a low-midrange figure based around three notes, the D and A of which create a characteristic open fourth while a G-sharp just momentarily ungrounds the music. Over these two superimposed layers often appears a third, a slow theme that initially rises evenly in the high violins, which later split into parallel sixths. This type of layering, which is quite characteristic of much of Shore's music, has the additional effect of de-emphasizing the narrative's horizontal movement, out of which the more conventional human emotions grow, while catching the viewer/listener's imagination in a much more vertical flow, if such is the word, that seems to move outside of chronological time. Further, while string timbres (and no doubt a fair amount of electronics) pervade much of the *eXistenZ* music, Shore makes very effective, if limited, use of such instruments as the solo piano, harp, and, yes, Theremin, that primitive but unmatchably rich-voiced electronic instrument whose very presence in the music seems a comment on the organicized sci-fi that is David Cronenberg's own, special creation. The music has been recorded with particular richness, and performed with particular intensity under Shore's direction.

Can it be that the world is never going to get enough of Hitchcock's **Vertigo** and its Bernard Herrmann score? On the heels of the film restoration completed two years ago, the stunning videos of that restoration, and the appearance on two Varèse Sarabande releases of most of the cues from the original music tracks as well as a re-recording (again of most of the cues) by Joel McNeely and the Royal Scottish National Orchestra now comes *Feature Film*, both a piece of installation art and a 75-minute film put together by Scottish artist Douglas Gordon. To make a long story very short, Gordon went to Paris in 1998 and, in the studios of Radio France, filmed (in super-16) conductor James Conlon leading the Paris Opera Orchestra in a performance of the Bernard Herrmann score—and we're talking about every note of the original music, even such minuscule cues as the vertigo attack that closes the opening scene in Midge's apartment or the 10-second reprise (for harp and celesta only) of the title music as Judy Barton is in the beauty parlor. The footage shot by Gordon shows only the body of the conductor, and mostly the head and hands, in action. In the installation version Gordon's film exactly reproduces the time of the Hitchcock film, with Conlon in frame during the musical cues while, when dialogue and sound effects subliminally take over during the unscored time slots, the camera tracks through a concert hall. The film version (blown up to 35-millimeter) shows only the musical sequences. But there's more. A sumptuous program booklet featuring stills from the film, insert essays by Raymond Bellour (on Gordon's work) and yours truly (on the score), and a CD (which times at 74:35) of the Conlon/Paris Opera Orchestra performance of Herrmann's music has been co-published by Artangel Afterlives, Book Works, and Galerie du jour-agnès b. Besides the fact that Conlon's is the only recording of all of Herrmann's score (including a few notes that didn't make the film), the performance and the sumptuous recorded sound on the CD definitely make this book worth tracking down. While those familiar with the film and recordings of the music may find themselves jolted by the very fast pacing of the title music, it rather works, and I find particularly effective the soft attacks via which Conlon brings in the motifs (generally in the brass) beneath Herrmann's spiraling arpeggios. Conlon and the Paris Opera Orchestra create throughout a very rich sound that fully captures the high drama of cues such as "The Rooftop," "The Tower" (spectacular!), and "The Nightmare" as well as the surreal dreaminess of "Scottie Tails Madeleine" or "Carlotta's Portrait" (this CD, by the way, has no separate cues whatever). Conlon also captures perhaps better than any conductor I've heard the moments of deep and tragic sadness. American bookstores can order *Feature Film: A Book by Douglas Gordon*, which retails at $45, through D.A.P., 155 Sixth Avenue, New York, NY 10013; phone: (212) 627-1999; fax: (212) 627 9484. The ISBN number (1 870699 23 8) should be included. Individuals may order it directly from Artangel, 36 St. John's Lane, London, ECIM 4BJ; phone: 44 171 336 6801; fax: 44 171 336 6802; e-mail: artangel@easynet.co.ukwww.innercity.demon.co.uk. The price is £ 24.95, plus £ 6 postage and handling. (My deep thanks to Gerrie van Noord at Artangel for her help with this information.)

September/October

From where I sit, the whole *Star Wars* phenomenon stands right up there with New Coke as one of the brilliant marketing ploys of all time. Slightly change the sacred formula—and the name—of America's icon soft drink and you create a massive wave of nostalgia that gives an incredible shot in the arm to the sales of (old) Coke. Of course, it was probably all a fortuitous accident (yeah, right), and maybe it was just as fortuitously accidental that George Lucas started off his *Star Wars* series in 1977 with the fourth episode (*A New Hope*), thus creating, when he released **Star Wars, Episode 1: The Phantom Menace**, another wave of nostalgia that had the children of those who flocked to the theaters 22 years ago queuing up for weeks in advance to be the first to see this fourth/first installment, which Lucas, after passing on episodes 5 and 6, has again directed, in a manner of speaking. Composer John Williams, in fact, in his brief comments in the program booklet for the original music-track recording (Sony; London Voices; New London Children's Choir; London Symphony Orchestra), notes that, during the first intermission for the recording session of *The Phantom Menace*, "several of the younger players approached me and explained that, as children, they had seen and heard *Star Wars*, and immediately resolved to study music with the goal of playing with the London Symphony." Certainly, the world's orchestras can always use more quality players. But was Episode 1 worth waiting for? Was it worth all the hype that had theaters in my area staying open all night with continuous showings? Well, whenever I try and pin anyone down about what he or she liked about *The Phantom Menace*, the conversation inevitably turns to the subject of "special effects." Not much story, horrible acting, characters who would make fingernails screeching across a blackboard seem like blessed relief (more on that in a moment), but great special effects. The question that immediately arises, of course, is why not just stick to computerized video games and save beaucoup bucks. Even *The Phantom Menace*'s apparent arch-villain, Darth Maul, is basically a special effect, a grotesque, hooded figure with a face that looks like a death mask turned inside out. No character development (even the earlier episodes had some), just a bad guy who looks like the end of the world.

OK. Did I have fun watching the film? Did I get caught up in the action? Well, yes and no. Yes, because there is something mightily infectious about the *Star Wars* mythology and all of its good guy/bad guy heroics (Lucas apparently likes to think of the movie as a silent film complete with music; maybe that's why all the actors in the series seem to have forgotten everything they ever knew about speaking lines). Also, *The Phantom Menace* affords the intellectual pleasure of inviting you to figure out who is going to become who in the already filmed episodes 4, 5, and 6. Take a look at the name of the actor (Ian McDiarmid) who plays Senator Palpatine, check it against the cast of characters in *Return of the Jedi*, and you've figured out a piece of *Star Wars* history. John Williams, in a wonderfully subtle musical clue that incorporates a piece of the final phrase of Darth Vader's theme into the theme for the towheaded kid named Anakin Skywalker (Jake Lloyd), subtly jolts our unconscious with a forward memory of who Anakin will grow up to be. I also have to say that some pretty stupid things have been written about *The Phantom Menace*. Some guy on the Web actually criticized director/writer Lucas for his "anachronistic" concept of economics, noting that the whole kickoff point of *The Phantom Menace*'s plot has much in common with 18th-century mercantilism rather than with modern economics. Duh. That's one of the bases of the whole postmodern shtick of the *Star Wars* movies: they're sci-fi films taking place not in the future but in a distant past with governments and commerce routes that deliberately suggest the political and economic systems from long ago. But, even sitting back, taking a deep breath, and trying to let myself go with the flow, I found myself ready to commit murder as of the introduction, early in the film, alas, of a character named Jar Jar Binks, a half-fish, half-human (if you're in a charitable mood) creature from a kingdom of underwater beings whose leader can find nothing more frightening to do than roar as he shakes his blubbery, salivating lips back and forth. Now, as of the initial *Star Wars* I had a problem with the droid named C-3PO, whose prissy complaining effectively watered down several of the film's heaviest action scenes for me. And by the time we got to the Ewoks in *Return of the Jedi*, I had already pretty much given up on the whole series. But, compared to Jar Jar (did Lucas's grandchildren come up with these names?), C-3PO comes across like Zorro, while the Ewoks measure up to nothing less than Attila's hordes of Huns. The only reason I can think of for deflating much of *The Phantom Menace*'s drama with a whining, sniveling, bumbling, and, yes, stupid creature whose nearest equivalent is the Joe Pesci character idiotically welded into the *Lethal Weapon* series is that the film's producers felt they needed to give those good folks who waited outside theaters for weeks to get into the first *Phantom Menace* screenings someone to identify with. And we still have to put up with C-3PO who, being a droid, doesn't have to worry about such things as aging and mortality (for which we should be somewhat grateful, I suppose, since it—aging, real or imagined—spares us the presences of Carrie Fisher, Mark Hamill, and Harrison Ford in *The Phantom Menace*). And don't get me started on Yoda. . . .

Meanwhile, John Williams valiantly continues to supply action, suspense, mood, and lyrical, even tragic music that adds to the postmodern aura of the *Star Wars* series by evoking not the sci-fi films we have come to know and love but rather Hollywood's swashbuckling adventure dramas—*The Adventures of Robin Hood*, *The Sea Hawk*, for example—from the '30s and early '40s, with their opulent symphonic scores by the likes of Erich Wolfgang Korngold and Franz Waxman. As in those old adventure dramas, Williams' score gives the impression, even though there are in fact breaks, of a nonstop, flowing, musical backdrop that captures the viscera as of the film's opening second (audiences of *The Phantom Menace* have been known to cheer wildly when those familiar opening fanfares get the film cranked up) all the way through to its final logo. Williams, as always, proves particularly adept—he's maybe the best in the business—at mobilizing the full orchestral forces for whirling and swirling accompaniment to the fastest-moving action sequences. And the very dark march Williams scored for the "Droid Invasion" cue, ominously introduced by mostly quiet tattoos from a variety of percussion instruments, confirms in my mind that somebody must have been thinking back to *Spartacus* for this climactic sequence. Williams also provides the Jar Jar character with an unmeritedly witty march-scherzo that offers a hint of Prokofiev. The only new lyrical theme *The Phantom Menace* provides is the one for Anakin Skywalker, and here Williams, with his ambivalent, major/minor melody that flirts with Darth Vader motifs, tells us a good deal more about who Anakin is than either Lucas' characterization or young Jake Lloyd's acting. Of course, the noble but slightly lonely theme for "the force" also returns from the earlier films, but only briefly at a couple of points, and if you listen carefully you'll hear a fuller version of the Darth Vader march at one or two points. Williams also deploys both a mixed and a children's chorus in varied ways throughout the score, sometimes seeming to call forth cosmic mysteries, at others using low, male-voice chanting to suggest the death-shrouded evil of Darth Maul, and finally reducing everything to almost inaudible whisperings as Jedi knight Qui-Gon Jinn (Liam Neeson, who depressingly manages to come across as something like a Harrison Ford with a British accent) moves into another state of being. Much less effective is a rather innocuous ostinato figure, heard as of the score's second cue, that generates an equally uninteresting theme. All in all, every note of the score exudes *Star Wars*, and that, of course, is exactly what was wanted. But from where I sit, Williams will never lose his skill, but he does seem to have somewhat misplaced the spark. Sony's sound reproduction is both full and rich with only a hint of digital shrillness here and there, and particularly effective definition of solo instruments. But you can bet your model Titanics that this will not be Sony's one and only release of *Phantom Menace* music. Stay tuned.

Now, I would be the last to say that there's not a place for what people like to call the "good, old-fashioned entertainment" that *The Phantom Menace* purports to be, although I suppose I could think of better ways to spend the megabucks that were poured into the picture (maybe donations to the scholarship fund of a good acting school?). But what I find truly galling is how the public will rush to fill the theaters to see rotten prints (you wouldn't believe the number of black flecks that filled the screen when I saw *The Phantom Menace*, only two weeks after it opened) of hyped-up pieces of pseudo profound fluff while at the same time letting themselves be frightened away from a truly exceptional film such as **Beloved** that goes beneath the surface and stays there without offering any simplistic explanations (may the force be with you indeed). *Beloved*, directed by the gifted Jonathan Demme and based on Toni Morrison's Pulitzer Prize–winning novel, takes a long (the film runs 171 minutes), dark look at the situation of an African-American woman named Sethe (Oprah Winfrey, in the performance of a lifetime) in Cincinnati during the period of slavery, not from the sugar-coated, white-man's perspective that Steven Spielberg overlays on *The Color Purple* but, if I may put it this way, from within a cultural perspective that generally remains foreign to the Hollywood perspective and the critics who write about it. From the outset, *Beloved* fills the screen with a magical but frightening presence that is never rationalized away, even after that presence is incarnated in the form of the strange and childlike adolescent named Beloved (Thandie Newton). As Beloved's presence becomes more and more disturbing, even, to a degree, demonic, the film forces the viewer to continually consider all of the possibilities of her presence, both good and evil, both innocent and corrupted, without offering an easy way out via facile moralizing, inflated heroics, or cheap plot manipulations. On all levels, whether in the visuals, the characterizations, the tortured unfolding of the story line from Morrison's novel, and the many other elements that went into the creation of this extraordinary film, *Beloved* communicates a sense of the human that runs all the more deeply because it leaves its mysteries where it belongs: as mystery. But *Beloved* also makes us feel, perhaps more strongly and more inescapably than any other narrative film I can think of, the trans-generational suffering passed down across the years from the first slaves to the most contemporary African American.

Another one of those levels on which *Beloved* communicates so deeply is the musical score by Rachel Portman (epic/Sony Music Soundtrax). In listening to the several Portman scores that have come my way over the past several years, I have one impression that remains fairly constant, and that is of a kind of overall unity that provides all, or almost all, of the individual cues with the sense of a single thread running throughout the music. In a bad mood, one could rail against some of Portman's scores as being facilely monothematic, although those monothemes are always quite lovely. But no such temptation exists here. First of all, Portman creates an even more primordial impression of unity here by using a single drone from which the very slow, simple musical material intoned by the human voice (both solo and in chorus) and various instruments departs and to which return it returns, either through implication or in fact. This very much complements the feeling one gets from the entire film, in which one constantly intuits a beginning out of which all of the action grows and back to which it continually points. Whether that beginning is Africa itself, the arrival in America of the slaves, or Sethe's tortured act out of which the very presence of Beloved emerges remains ambiguous. And that leads me back to another element of the score that I found both thoroughly captivating and quite ingenious, although I suspect it wasn't consciously mapped out. The score opens with a cue, entitled "Headstone" (the visual of which provides a solid clue for where the film is heading), in which a solo, low-alto voice (Oumou Sngare) dreamily intones a haunting chant in what is probably an African language. Yes, one certainly feels this (in retrospect, at least) as a disembodied voice suggesting the presence that is and is not Beloved. And when, near the end, in "Beloved Is Gone," a solo wooden flute plays a theme that is different but based on the same musical mode in a higher register, we can say, "Ah, now that Beloved has been exorcised, the human presence created by the voice passes to a musical instrument." But that would be too facile. And so, later on in that cue, the chorus, then the solo voice, and then the solo clarinet take up the music, as if to create Beloved as a constant presence/non-presence. This brings us to Portman's deployment of the small number of instruments that appear in her score. There are sounds—the solo woman's voice, the wooden flute, some percussion and wind instruments, an apparent African language—that certainly evoke Africa as the starting point. There is some choral vocalizing in particular that suggests the music created by the slaves on the plantations where they toiled. Portman also offers a handful of modern, Western instruments—a clarinet and a harp in particular—whose presence generates yet a third dimension. And then, just for good measure, Portman also throws a cimbalom into the instrumental mix of a couple of cues, suggesting an Eastern European timbre that may relate to the composer's own ethnicity, which, if it does, would be her way of adding her own presence to the film's multiple levels of time and space. And I particularly love the cue entitled "Cincinnati Streets," in which Portman mobilizes just about all of the instruments from the *Beloved* palette, including the cimbalom, in droning, mournful music that never abandons the tone of the score as a whole. All in all, I cannot imagine a film score complementing a film in a more thoroughly consummate way than Portman's music does for *Beloved*, which has also been recorded with exceptional presence, atmosphere, and clarity.

Somewhat to the same degree that *The Red Violin* has visualized, narrativized, and musicalized the Edgar Allan Poe aesthetics built around the death of a beautiful woman, Bernardo Bertolucci's most recent film (it dates from 1998), **Besieged**, has visualized, narrativized, and, to a much lesser degree than *The Red Violin*, musicalized the Freudian metaphor of woman being the dark continent. *Besieged* tells the story of a woman named Shandurai (Thandie Newton again) from an unidentified African country (the African scenes were, I think, shot in Kenya) whose husband has been arrested and made a political prisoner. Having escaped to an unidentified Italian city (shot, I believe, in Rome), Shandurai works to complete her degree in medicine while earning her rent by housecleaning for a homely pianist/composer, an English(?) bachelor named Jason Kinsky (David Thewlis), who occupies the opulent apartment above her room. Needless to say, Kinsky falls hopelessly in love with Shandurai, who refuses his advances, which leads him to selflessly (yeah, right) sell off all of his possessions, including, finally, his grand piano, to get the money to pay for her husband's release. In a twist worthy (sort of) of O. Henry, Shandurai falls in love with Kinsky, which finally gives Bertolucci the excuse to show her bare breasts—just at the moment her husband arrives in the Italian city. While not as hopelessly, virulently, old-fart sexist as Bertolucci's previous film, the horrendous *Stealing Beauty*, *Besieged* still continues the Bertolucci mythology that goes all the way back to the 1973 *Last Tango in Paris*, wherein a white male (Marlon Brando in *Tango*) attempts to compensate for the total void in his soul by obsessing on a beautiful, sensual young woman (Maria Schneider in *Tango*) to the point of co-opting, or attempting to at least, her entire being. In *Besieged* the co-opting extends not just to the beautiful, sensual young woman but to her very ethnicity, and this begins right away via the casting of Thandie Newton, who, unless I'm missing something, is much too light-skinned to be a native African. Her very presence on the screen, then, combined with her supposed identity as a native African suggests a black woman whose body has been colonized by the whites. But besides working its way through the narrative, the co-opting/colonization also takes place, rather ingeniously I must say, on the level of the music, almost all of which, in *Besieged*, plays an active role within the film.

Kinsky, you see, is initially seen and heard playing such works as Mozart's Fantasy in D Minor and the E-flat-Minor Prelude from Bach's *Well-tempered Clavier*, Book I, works that do not exactly say anything to Shandurai. Following, however, a visit to an African church, where he begins arrangements to free Shandurai's husband and where he hears a local choir perform a traditional work called *Mambote Na Nje*, Kinsky returns to his apartment and composes a conservative-modern—and quite thrilling, for

Western sensibilities—Ostinato (more of a toccata to my ears) in an idiom falling somewhere between Ravel and Albéniz but built, in its fast episodes, on an asymmetrical rhythmic pattern that breaks down as 2+2+3+2+3. It isn't African, it isn't primitive, but it somehow moves Kinsky slightly closer to his obsession while allowing him to remain comfortably ensconced in the aesthetics of the European aristocracy, which his apartment certainly evokes. Counterbalancing Kinsky's music, according to composer Alessio Vlad (who has also done scores for such films as the recent *Jane Eyre* and *Tea with Mussolini*) in his program notes, "is the carefree and youthful sound of African pop," which in *Besieged* takes the form of two numbers, more Latin than African to my ears, composed and performed by Papa Wemba, along with single numbers by Salif Keita, Ali Farka Toure (with Ry Cooder), and Pépé Kallé/Empire Bakuba. Falling outside of these two domains (in the space between the keys, as it were) in *Besieged*'s narrative are two wonderful, genuinely African (I presume, since, indicatively, Vlad says nothing about them in his notes) songs composed and wonderfully performed within the film by J. C. Ojwang, who accompanies himself on a small, lyre-like instrument while keeping the beat with percussion pieces attached to his ankle. Ojwang's non-narrativized presence, his voice, which ranges from near mumbling to something best described as a chanted shout, with some sobbings also turning up in the second song ("Nyumbani"), and his music are hands down the principal contribution to whatever artistic or social depth *Besieged* may have. And, precisely because Ojwang stands outside of the film's narrative, his presence and the Africa evoked by his music inspire some striking, quasi still shots, including single, bare trees filled with children, from cinematographer Fabio Cianchetti. (I also have to say that *Besieged* has more than its share of imaginative, lyrical editing, a rarity in almost all films these days.) At any rate, if you want to have all of the music described above, it is available on a Milan CD. The pianist who performs Vlad's Ostinato, which, with Ojwang's songs, is worth the price of the CD, is Stefano Arnaldi, who also performs the classical pieces, including a pretty blah rendition of Scriabin's well-known D-sharp-Minor Etude. Besides the Ostinato, Vlad also composed a wistful, more lyrical work, entitled Arpeggio, taken from the slow sections of the Ostinato, and both pieces have been arranged by Arnaldi in a final "Titoli di Coda" (End Titles).

Finally, I return to John Williams for his music, in its initial CD appearance, for what may be one of the most perverse American films ever released through the studio system, Arthur Penn's almost universally reviled **The Missouri Breaks** from 1976 (Ryko). True to form (Penn is the director of *Bonnie and Clyde*, don't forget), Penn, in *The Missouri Breaks*, makes a hero of an outlaw, in this case a scruffy, Wild West horse thief played by Jack Nicholson (you can tell where Penn stands when Williams, in his music, accompanies a train robbery with a jaunty, banjo-heavy hoedown). In the manner of many classic Westerns, this film makes you hate the big landowners right from the start, in this case via the particularly gruesome hanging of one of Nicholson's cohorts. But what sets *The Missouri Breaks* apart not only from the classic Western but even from Penn's other films is its main good-guy (because he's not a horse thief)/bad-guy (because he's an out-and-out psycho), a hired gun brought in by the landowners to get them ornery horse thieves. Given the name of Robert E. Lee Clayton, the character is played by Marlon Brando in one of the most outrageous performances ever recorded on film. Sporting a mane of dyed-blond hair and a thick Irish accent, and having mastery of any number of exotic and grisly ways of killing people, Clayton even appears at one point, with no obvious narrative justification, dressed up as a sweet little old lady from the prairie. I could go on, as I happen to find *The Missouri Breaks* one of the most vastly underrated films of the last couple of decades; suffice it to say that it is a film that definitely deserves a second chance.

At any rate, in *The Missouri Breaks* John Williams strays about as far from the heroic symphonism of *Star Wars* et al. as he ever got, and, on the basis of this score and others, such as *Images*, one rather wishes he had pursued this direction a bit more often. Scored mostly for a small ensemble of instruments, many of which evoke the Wild West, including harmonica, fiddle, banjo, guitar, and steel guitar, the music also offers some more offbeat timbres, including electric harpsichords and bass harmonica, while also mobilizing other electric or electronic instruments, including a prominent electric bass and an electric keyboard. The Main Title is both eerie and understatedly chilling: in the midst of a widely separated dialogue between a slow, three-note, unison-ostinato on the electric bass and dissonant strums on the guitar, the harmonica intones, more as a series of motifs than as a theme, what amounts to the film's ominous main theme. The music crescendos once into a full-ensemble, bluesy piece, with drum accompaniment, that has roots in both pop and jazz, only to die back down to its original tone, making clear what directions the film is going to take. Still, the score is not lacking in folksy tunes and rhythms, and it also features quite a haunting love theme, a dreamy, slow-moving melody that seems a natural for the harmonica, on which it is frequently heard. But when it comes to psycho music, Williams is right there with the kinky sounds of his electric harpsichords, which offer a grotesque gavotte in "Bizarre Wake," and which bitonally float in a very unsettling manner over drone accompaniments, including one generated by the bass harmonica in "Confrontation," for those sequences in which Clayton is up to no good. The climactic "The Chase" features a particularly effective, at times almost pointillistic, shuffling of timbres, including timpani, cluster chords at the high end of the piano, something that sounds like the plucking of a loosened guitar string, electric harpsichord, wind machine, and an array of other percussion instruments. Particularly well recorded and remastered on this CD, the *Missouri Breaks* score is apparently a rerecording, although nothing is mentioned about this in Jeff Bond's good but too-brief program notes. Why do I say this? Because the Ryko CD also offers three "bonus tracks," listed as "film versions," apparently taken from the original music track. The version of the love theme entitled "Jane and Logan" that concludes the bonus tracks features that electric keyboard, whose sound is largely absent from what I am presuming is the rerecording. *Missouri Breaks* shows another side of the multi-gifted John Williams that needs to be much better known.

November/December

American film-director Stanley Kubrick, who died unexpectedly at age 70 this past March, and to whom this column is dedicated, fortunately completed one last film, **Eyes Wide Shut** (which he also scripted and co-produced), before his demise, and it has turned out to be one of his most controversial works (well, its surface topic is sex, so what did you expect?). In the midst of all that has been written, most of it blather, the one thing that has been pretty much ignored is the ways in which *Eyes Wide Shut* fits into Kubrick's oeuvre as a whole. Kubrick, like several American colleagues who came into prominence in the '60s and '70s, such as Arthur Penn, Robert Altman, and Brian De Palma, pretty much made a career of going against the grain of the American ethos and/or of the material he worked with. And if Kubrick was able to take an essentially subtle, essentially cool novel such as Stephen King's *The Shining* and send it over the top in a variety of ways, most flagrantly with Jack Nicholson's absurd performance, the director's real specialty was the colding—not cooling, but colding—down of hot material such as Anthony Burgess's novel *A Clockwork Orange*. But perhaps in none of Kubrick's films has this tendency shown up with such a perverse vengeance as in *Eyes Wide Shut*, which the director aged in his mental refrigerator for at least three years. Take one small casting detail for starters: the highly emotive, if not downright hysterical on occasion, Harvey Keitel and Jennifer Jason Leigh apparently originally played roles later taken over by the infinitely more placid Sidney Pollack and Marie Richardson. But then, since we're talking about casting, how about the ice-cold, if not downright plastic on occasion, appearance of husband-and-wife Tom Cruise and Nicole Kidman as the hugely wealthy married couple on whose sexual fantasies the film focuses? Well, actually, it's the wife who has sexual fantasies, which she makes the major mistake of communicating to her husband. He, in the adolescent fashion that characterizes the sexuality of most American males, promptly goes about tracking down his fantasies in real life, only to arrive at a (literally) dead end each step of the way. (In its practically nonstop depiction of women's bare chests, starting right off with Kidman's, and by having Kidman sit on the toilet right off, again in plain view, Kubrick visually evokes the two principal obsessions of that adolescent sexuality, breasts and bathrooms.) The film's central sequence finds Cruise in a Long Island mansion and right smack in the middle of a masked-ball orgy (censored, via computerized imaging, to get the film an R rating) that seems to have Black Mass overtones but that is about as satanic and disturbing as a masturbation party at an upscale frat house.

But that, dear readers, is the whole point. *Eyes Wide Shut* is not about sex but about the patriarchal male's displacement of his sexuality onto or into such things as impossible wealth, voyeurism, game playing, aesthetics, and, ultimately, death. Kubrick consciously or unconsciously reinforces this by making the film a virtual (in all senses of the word) orgy of visual pleasure for the viewer. As one example, Steadycams turn the hallways of opulent New York City apartments into labyrinths bathed in burnt-amber lighting. And not only do none of Cruise's forays into playboy darkness end up in sexual consummation, to the point that a great alternate title for the film would be *Coitus Interruptus*, all of them end up in some kind of death, actual or implied, or violence, actual or implied. Ultimately, whether Kubrick intended it or not, *Eyes Wide Shut* offers an extraordinarily bland view of sex but an extraordinarily scathing presentation of the sexual psychology—should I say pathology?—that characterizes the patriarchal ethos.

Now, as I've suggested before, one of the ways in which Kubrick has more often than not colded down his films is by the replacement of the classic original dramatic score with selections made up from "found music," whether Ludwig van and company à la Moog in *A Clockwork Orange*, the wide gamut of styles and moods from Johann and Richard Strauss to Gyorgy Ligeti in *2001*, or the rich glories of Handel and Schubert, among others, in *Barry Lyndon*. Certainly, one of the principal functions of the action-specific cues in scores composed originally for a particular movie is to engage the emotions, to literally create affect, and as swiftly as possible. The very fact of coming from concert works having their own existence outside of the film makes the music in Kubrick's movies impose itself on the viewer/listener, who, to a greater extent than with the original film score, is forced to separate the music—and its affect—from the action in quite a different, more distanced way. Interestingly, *Eyes Wide Shut* starts off in an almost total emotional void by using, to back the title sequence, a thoroughly blah waltz from Shostakovich's *Jazz Suite No.2*, which turns up as the second selection on the music-track CD (Warner Sunset/Reprise). Many of the other cues are jazz standards or oldies—"When I Fall in Love" by the Victor Silvester Orchestra; "I Got It Bad (And That Ain't Good)" from the Oscar Peterson Trio; "If I Had You" performed by Roy Gerson and a small combo; "Strangers in the Night," played by the Peter Hughes Orchestra; and a wistful piano solo by Brad Mehldau, later joined by bass and drums, of "Blame It On My Youth"—most or all of it heard as source music either for the film's opulent party sequences or for the jazz-club scenes (indicatively, it is a jazz pianist, played by actor/director/composer/producer/writer Todd Field, who serves as the conduit between Cruise and the orgy). And as non-source music (I think), Chris Isaak's growly rock number "Baby Did a Bad Bad Thing" provides a particularly ironic commentary on the action. But the real musical showstopper of *Eyes Wide Shut*—and it stands right up there (or almost), in my opinion, with Richard Strauss's *Also sprach Zarathustra* in *2001*—is a strange solo-piano piece entitled *Musica Ricercata, II*, by Gyorgy Ligeti. Essentially a chromatic fantasy on two notes (a third comes in later) hammered out on single keys in the middle of the piano and then quietly echoed in a unison played at the instrument's opposite ends, *Musica Ricercata* initially appears with no obvious rhyme or reason around the middle of the orgy sequence and then obsessively returns with no obvious rhyme or reason throughout the rest of the film. What is particularly eerie is that the Ligeti fragments announce themselves at the kind of volume level that makes you look around the screen to see who is playing the piano (the pianist, in fact, is Dominic Harlan, not that you ever see him or his instrument). Yet it soon becomes obvious that there is no "source" for these timbres, and one begins to feel their presence as something like the manifestation of the invisibility of the Cruise character's subverted and displaced libido. Ultimately, however, Kubrick never provides any real interpretive out, and this particular instance of film/music interaction stands as one of the true moments of genius in the director's output.

Apart from all that, the director did in fact use a small amount of original music in *Eyes Wide Shut*, for which he turned to young composer Jocelyn Pook. The first of Pook's four cues backs Kidman's sexual fantasy, interspersed at various points in black-and-white footage, about a young naval officer seen briefly at a hotel. Scored for solo violin, cello, and viola, and what sounds like a string orchestra but may be a synthesizer, since the notes indicate Pook as the performer (although there is also a conductor), the "Naval Officer" cue falls in a moody area somewhere between Ernest Bloch and Arvo Pärt that might be described as dreamlike, save that it slowly crescendos to the type of high volume level that Kubrick favors. The second cue, "The Dream," moves in similar territory, but with the addition of some organ-like timbres. The "Masked Ball" slips into the filmic narrative, with quasi-string drones (and some solo work, probably acoustic or at least sampled) backing a truly weird, low-male-voice chanting that may be in a foreign language, may be in a made-up language, or could even be, à la David Lynch, a segment sung backward and played back backward (it turns out, I just find out, that the chanting comes from highly religious Hindu scripture, and that it has been excised from versions of the film sent to Europe and South Africa). A high voice later joins in. I remember this ritualistic music being accompanied by the jazz pianist (Field) at a keyboard in the film, and that may very well be the case, since keyboards do amazing things these days. Pook's final cue ("Migrations"), on the other hand, starts off hinting at the Ligeti and then moves into a piece of quasi-oriental atmosphere with some sort of plucked timbre playing a kind of ostinato against which a tabla and an electric bass provide an obsessive rhythmic accompaniment. Over this we hear more chanting, this with an obvious Indian or Near Eastern flavor. I have no memory of where this shows up in *Eyes Wide Shut*. All in all, Pook's music has both atmosphere and originality, and I will be interested to hear what she can do when given more material to sink her teeth into. As for the CD as a whole, which has been quite well produced, it will appeal primarily to fans of the film, to those fascinated by the use of music within it, and/or to those who might simply want a nice sampling of "standards" setting off a lot of weird sounds.

CHAPTER SEVENTEEN

~

2000

January/February

Perhaps one of the major signs of just how good a movie **The Sixth Sense** is can be found in its warmly sad, quietly nostalgic, generally understated score by James Newton Howard (Varèse Sarabande; Pete Anthony, cond.). The trend these days in horror/suspense/ghost-story films, of which the recent remake of *The Haunting* is a prime example, is overkill, particularly in over-the-top special effects and musical scores that try even harder than the plot gimmicks to jolt you out of your seat, stadium or otherwise. Of course, *The Sixth Sense* is not exactly horror, suspense, or ghost story. Rather, it is very simply a film about death: not only how we deal with the event itself but also how the vestiges left behind can be reframed in space, time, and images that take on a considerably different shape from the physical space and linear time within which Western culture tends to define life and deny death. Note: if you have not seen *The Sixth Sense* and do not want to have the film's final revelation unfolded to your eyes, skip to ["March/April"]. There is no way I can write intelligently about the film, or its music for that matter—and if you buy the CD without having seen the film, don't read the title for the last cue—without talking about this revelation and others. I have to say, however, that I saw *The Sixth Sense* a second time, and found it even better. Written and directed by M. Night Shyamalan, who was born in Madras, India, in 1970 but raised in suburban Philadelphia, *The Sixth Sense*, which was shot in Philadelphia, tells the story of a child psychologist (played with incredible warmth and sensitivity by the much maligned Bruce Willis) who, shot at the beginning of the film by a client on whom the therapy had not taken, seems to spend the rest of the film redeeming that failure by helping another young boy (Haley Joel Osment) deal with his "gift" of seeing dead people. As it finally turns out, however, one of those dead people is Willis himself. In this wonderful closed-loop relationship, Willis, by finally convincing the boy to listen to what the dead people want to tell him, finds his own release from the no-man's-land between life and death in which he finds himself throughout much of the film.

But from where I sit *The Sixth Sense* suggests at least two additional dimensions that further reveal some kind of non-Western spiritual processes at work (according to the mini biography on the Web's IMDb, Shyamalan was sent to a Catholic school, where in fact he actually shot his previous feature, *Wide Awake*, but was raised in a "different religion"; my guess is Hinduism). First of all, for reasons much too involved to elaborate here, my reading is that the emaciated, probably adolescent, possibly already dead young man who shoots Willis and then himself at the beginning of the film is also the boy helped out by Willis in the rest of the film, which further closes the loop in their relationship: not only does Willis find his release in being seen and heard by the boy, the boy/adolescent/boy finds his release in being seen and heard by Willis. Several arguments work against this reading, including the seemingly specific time frame given by the film for the action that follows the shooting. But it is in the nature of narratives defined by nonlinear, circular, and/or cyclical time to defy explanation in terms of a verbal rationalism that can only be elaborated in linear terms. Perhaps the only valid way, for instance, to tell of a dream, Sigmund Freud to the contrary notwithstanding, would be to make a movie of it, since the very process of filmmaking allows for the creation of visual paradigms that can be explained only in their own terms. Which brings me to my second point: throughout *The Sixth Sense*, images—photographic, audio, video, reflections—play a significant role. In the initial sequence, Willis's face pointedly reflects from the glass in the frame of a testimonial to him. The boy's mother (another warm and sensitive portrayal, this one from Toni Collette) looks at various photographs of him on the wall, in each of which can be found a wisp of light suggesting perhaps either his own death and/or that of the invisible presences around him; either way, after looking at these pictures, the mother experiences the same sensation of coldness experienced by Willis's wife (Olivia Williams) shortly before the initial violence (one of the reasons for my interpretation). Willis, listening to a tape of the violent client, hears another voice in the background saying, in Spanish, that he doesn't want to die. And, most significantly, the dead girl named Kyra (Mischa Barton) to whom the boy finally listens reveals her own murder through a video she shot while she was alive. If you think of it, when we look at an image we are seeing a ghost of sorts: the image brings into the present the physical likeness of someone who is no more. Even if that person is still alive, the version of that person in the time and space of the image is a thing of the past, never to return as (fully) alive. Thus do the labyrinthine loops of *The Sixth Sense* expand to embrace the audience, which is looking at (dead) images of dead people looking at dead people looking at. . . . This way of looking at death is such a relief from the bogey-man theatrics of most horror/suspense/ghost-story films that *The Sixth Sense* would be a breath of fresh air if it were half as good as it is.

Howard's music, sparsely used in the film, opens with a theme—more a harmonic/rhythmic motif really—in the solo piano (probably a synthesizer) and harp that immediately generates an aura of sadness and nostalgia thoroughly appropriate to *The Sixth Sense* but also a familiar trope of sorts in film scores from Elmer Bernstein's *To Kill a Mockingbird* on. There's a twist, however: this opening motif, soon joined by two flutes and then expanded into strings and chorus (the latter probably sampled), is set to an asymmetrical meter that could be notated as 6/8 + 7/8. If the off-centeredness of the meter already suggests something beyond the obvious nostalgia/sadness mode, the fact that the beats add up to 13 offers an even more obvious link between music and narrative. Quiet chord progressions in other cues mildly suggest a chorale (one of the film's significant settings is a church) without ever quite getting there. The first cue that backs the boy's decision to "Help the Ghosts" ingeniously alternates between quiet figures—tremolo strings, a harp glissando, mild cluster chords—suggesting the boy's dread, and a deeply melancholic waltz figure in the piano suggesting the other side of that fear. This same pattern continues even more dramatically—and even more movingly—in the climactic confrontation with "Kyra's Ghost," which near its end brings in a particularly chilling near-whisper from the vocalizing chorus. "Kyra's Tape," in a surprising—and, again, chilling—musical shift, mobilizes a vocalizing (in mildly dissonant chords) male chorus with a particularly deep voice underlying it: as high strings, a solo trumpet, and a chime join in, we sense the inevitability, the helplessness, the heartbreak as if it were all happening in the present. And that final revelation! After similar musical patterns that chill and break the heart in turn, the music moves to a solemn, full-orchestra, minor-mode climax that finally settles back into that solo piano and a series of hushed, chordal utterances from various orchestral choirs. This is music that could bring tears to the eyes without any reference to an outside narrative. Having that reference and listening to this haunting score, you may want afterward to walk on the beach or in the nearest woods and open your soul to the elements.

March/April

If there has ever been a movie that proved that the worth of a work of art lies more in how it's made than what it's about, it's **American Beauty**, brought to the screen by writer Alan Ball and first-time (amazingly), British-born (in 1965) director Sam Mendes. The story is classic, with variations, of course: a middle-aged, upper-middle-class man (Kevin Spacey) living in the 'burbs with a frigid (for him), anal-retentive wife (Annette Bening) and a rebellious teenage daughter (Thora Birch) tells his supervisor to take his job and shove it, and then embarks on a strange journey of self-liberation that has him flipping burgers and coming within an inch of seducing his daughter's best friend (Mena Suvari). But Ball's screenplay is so scathing, Kevin Spacey's delivery of Ball's dialogue so searingly caustic, and director Mendes' mildly surreal handling of the material and the actors so off-center that neither the word "comedy" nor even "satire" comes close to describing this film, which, after you've laughed your head off and gasped in disbelief at the utter cynicism of some of Spacey's lines, leaves you positively devastated. Just for starters, *American Beauty* pulls off the difficult task of telling where it is going right from the start while leaving you wondering how and even where the film is going to end. Of course, it being a contemporary film, *American Beauty* does not spare the details of just how Spacey satisfies his sexual needs; and when he is caught in the act by his wife, Spacey delivers, in one of the many highpoints of his acting career, an hysterically funny yet somehow, given the situation, corrosively tragic litany of just about all the euphemisms for masturbation in the English language. It being a contemporary film, *American Beauty* also self-reflectively replays major snippets of its action via Hi-8 video footage shot by the anarchically entrepreneurial teenage son (Wes Bentley) of Spacey's ex-Marine-colonel neighbor (Chris Cooper, with Spacey one of the best actors on the screen today). Yet, in the midst of all this mordant intensity, *American Beauty* has one moment of supreme tenderness that will stay with you long after you've stopped oohing and ahing at the brutal sarcasm. I won't reveal the details of the scene; suffice it to say that it involves a moment between Spacey and actress Suvari, the latter revealing, in this moment, just how deeply she has played her role of the high-school slut throughout the film.

If I had directed (alas!) *American Beauty*, my immediate, no-brainer first-choice for the musical score would have been Thomas Newman, not just because of the obvious satirical edge he imparted to a film such as Robert Altman's 1992 *The Player* but even in his more serious work, whether *The Shawshank Redemption* (1994), *Oscar and Lucinda* (1997), or *The Horse Whisperer* (1998), in which offbeat combinations of timbres and kinky rhythmic patterns are never very far from even the most lyrical moments. Happily, Newman did in fact compose the perfectly in-sync score for *American Beauty*, for which Dreamworks has released two CDs, the first offering two Newman cues and 10 songs heard (probably) within the film, the second, which I will now proceed to review, featuring (all?) 19 cues from Newman's score. The key instrument in many of *American Beauty*'s musical cues is the marimba (or an electronically sampled equivalent thereof), which dominates the opening cue ("Dead Already") with a catchy, oft-repeated figure in thirds later joined by an electric bass in such a way as to distantly evoke a blues accompaniment. Other instruments, such as the tabla and other sonorous percussion instruments, an occasional slide whistle, and some electronics join in to help create a busy filigree of sound, wholly typical of the composer. That sound is even more pronounced in later cues such as "Lunch with the King," which is bright and frisky, but just hypnotic enough in its repetitions as to unsettle the emotions ever so slightly. Also characteristic of Newman are wonderful moments in which the musical phrases halt over a sustained note (frequently in the bass) just long enough to make you think they're going to die out, only to revive and continue on their mildly frenetic journey. Yet early on Newman also introduces, in the high registers of the piano, one of those touching nostalgia themes that he also writes so well, a sad, lullaby theme that, like Spacey's opening voiceover, sets a tone of sad resignation that counterbalances the acerbity of the surface narrative. And when this theme reappears much later in "Angela Undress," we can have no doubt at all as to the trap both Spacey and his daughter's friend have created for themselves. Nor, upon hearing the music in the final (pre-end-title) cue open up into a near ballad—a ballad accompaniment, really—can we have any doubt at all as to how to emotionally "read" the end of *American*

Beauty. Immediately identifiable as Thomas Newman as of the first notes of its first appearance in the picture, the music for *American Beauty,* while creating its own very strong profile, also alternately complements, comments upon, interprets, and even on occasion contradicts what we are experiencing in the picture with a profound thoroughness that reveals the work of a consummate musical dramatist.

Listening, before I had seen the film, to Ennio Morricone's score for **The Legend of 1900** (Sony; Accademia Musicale Italiana), labeled as "A Fable by Giuseppe Tornatore," best known as the director of *Cinema Paradiso,* was something like watching a theatrical trailer that totally misrepresents the film it promotes. This is through absolutely no fault of Morricone, who in fact, for reasons I will explain presently, may be the only composer on the face of the planet who could have produced what is ultimately the film's main theme. No, the fault in the first instance belongs to Sony, which crams several versions of this theme into the CD's first few cuts when in fact the theme's very existence forms the core mystery around which *The Legend of 1900* fashions its surprisingly convoluted (given the simplicity of its basic premise) narrative. Heard very early in the film only as a snippet of solo-trumpet source-music that reproduces a piano theme disastrously played back on an almost destroyed 78-rpm master in the possession of a music-store owner, the theme does not return until the near-completion of the film's long flashback, where it is improvised by a magical pianist (Tim Roth) as he catches sight of a stunning young woman (Melanie Thierry) as she passes by a window on the ocean liner where he was born (in 1900) and that he will never leave. The music is supposed to translate what is perhaps the one moment of pure beauty in the life of a supremely lonely individual, and it is supposed to have an immediately devastating effect on the emotions of those few people who hear it. Imagine, then, having to compose such a theme as a complete outsider, so to speak. Many movies have asked similar tasks of their composers—Krzysztof Kieslowski's awful *Blue* from 1993, with its colossally blah score by Zbigniew Preiser, comes immediately to mind—and none have come close to getting what Ennio Morricone has provided for *La leggenda del pianista sul'oceano,* as it is known in Italian: a theme of such striking, heartbreaking beauty that one is convinced it could only have come from the soul and fingers of the movie's sad little boy who translated most of his life, and ultimately his love/death, through the piano. Of course, to those who have become acquainted with the Morricone's frequent flights of sublime lyricism over a career that has produced close to 400 film scores this will come as no surprise. Indeed, this past semester a woman in a graduate film-music course I was teaching noted that a professor of hers had once stated that an entire tradition had come to an end with Puccini. After being introduced for the first time to excerpts of *Once Upon a Time in the West,* and hearing its score, she remarked, "Now I know that's not true." Amen. (I would also note that the quasi-Debussy chords of "Nocturne with No Moon" are likewise, although on a much smaller scale, a wholly convincing musical representation of a musical representation.)

On the other hand, even if all of the cues were presented in narrative sequence on Sony's "original motion picture soundtrack" CD, one would still have a hard time figuring this music out without having seen *The Legend of 1900*. Who would have guessed, for instance, that the insistent F/F-sharp discord, which sounds like a repeated mistake in the simple, four-note motif of the cue entitled "The Crisis" (and later "Second Crisis"), absurdly placed near the beginning by Sony, is in fact the childlike translation of the pianist's return to loneliness once the young woman has disappeared? My initial guess, based on my knowledge of the film's basic premise, was that it represented the pianist's revenge for an out-of-tune instrument. Or who would have thought Jelly Roll Morton's "The Crave," dazzlingly performed here by Amedeo Tommasi (who also contributed some of the film's original ragtime), was not just a piece of shipboard source music but instead one unit of a contest between Morton (played by Clarence Williams III) and the pianist known as 1900? (One wonders why 1900's victorious piece of furious chromatic improvisation did not make it to the music-track CD.) One also has to have seen the film to understand that the abrupt intrusion of wild ragtime into placid dance-band numbers in the cues misleadingly titled "1900's Madness" in fact represent flights of fancy more or less accepted by those on board. And although Morricone and Tommasi's "Study for Three Hands" gives us a clue to the fairy-tale impossibility of many of the pianist's performances, this facet of the story comes across even more strongly in the film, particularly at those moments when Tornatore double-exposes an extra set of hands at the keyboard. But the score is also peppered with moments of full-orchestra Morricone that will surely please the composer's fans, whether in the rather atypical but sumptuously rich and moody orchestral blues of "A Goodbye to Friends," in the much more characteristic swell of noble and tragic lyricism from the midrange strings in the brief "Before the End," or the dreamy and slightly acidic layers of sound in "I Can and Then." The end titles conclude with a vocal version of the main theme with lyrics by former Pink Floyd member Roger Waters, who also breathily sings them. This is not quite as bad as it sounds, although the initial electronic accompaniment is ghastly. The recorded sound is sumptuous.

Speaking of morally ambiguous, there are few crime writers who have delved more deeply into that area than the late, Texas-born Patricia Highsmith (1921–95), who once wrote that "art has nothing to do with morality, convention or moralizing." A solid number (well over a dozen) of Highsmith's short stories and novels have been adapted as films, most notably, of course, the very first, in Hitchcock's *Strangers on a Train*, which, paradoxically for the "Master of Suspense," considerably undarkens Highsmith's psychological thriller about traded murders and guilt. Another well-received Highsmith film is the more recent (1977) *The American Friend*, adapted for the screen from *Ripley's Game* by German director Wim Wenders. Now an outstanding adaptation of Highsmith's **The Talented Mr. Ripley**, the first in a series of open-ended novels devoted to that character, has turned up from British director Anthony Minghella, whose Oscar-winning *The English Patient* from 1996 drove me crazy (in the negative sense; no cynical comments, please). Perhaps what works best in the film is the unsettling way in which we are very quickly suckered into identifying with Ripley, partly because of the character himself, partly because we see him as a poor, struggling artist trying to find a niche among the very rich, and partly because of actor Matt Damon's portrayal of him. We go on to slowly discover that this "self" we latch onto has no self other than the identities he appropriates both from others and even from his surroundings. Indeed, Ripley the fictional human being is as existentially two-dimensional as words printed on a page or images on a movie screen. Minghella has received criticism in some quarters for the casting of Damon, whose almost aw-shucks boyishness and whose previous roles as pretty much of an all-American kid (even if he has major psychological hangups, or even if he runs into some problems gambling—hey, that's all part of the game these days) would seem to work against the role of the extremely, yes, talented, not to mention homicidal, manipulator he turns out to be in *The Talented Mr. Ripley*. At least one critic has even suggested that the harder-edged Jude Law, who plays the spoiled rich kid whose identity Ripley partially appropriates, would have been the better choice for Ripley, and Damon for Jude Law's character. But I would suggest that those critics probably have gotten their absolutist ideas of what good and evil look like from watching too many bouts of WWF "wrestling." Highsmith is anything but absolutist (ambiguity, anyone?), and Minghella has seconded her vision with a piece of casting that is right up there with Hitchcock's use of Robert Walker in *Strangers on a Train*, who was pretty much limited to apple-cheeked roles in his previous films. Damon is by far the best of the on-screen Ripleys—better than the much too beautiful (but nonetheless two-dimensional) Alain Delon in René Clément's 1960 *Plein Soleil* (Purple Noon), which adapts the same novel, and better than the much-too-creepy Dennis Hopper in Wenders' *The American Friend*. I should also note that Highsmith's particular vision of blurred, even multiple, identity, which Minghella likewise has not shrunk away from, extends as well to gender roles. Indeed, early on (in 1953) Highsmith, under the pseudonym of Claire Morgan, wrote a lesbian love story entitled *The Price of Salt*, and her final novel, *Small G: A Summer Idyll* (1995), deals with the intersections in a bar in Zurich (where the author spent her final years) of characters of varying sexual persuasions.

Interestingly, except for the ending, the area where Minghella is the most unfaithful, literally at least, to Highsmith's novel is music. Indeed, almost from the outset, in which the film shows Ripley accompanying a woman vocalist in an art song, one becomes aware of the huge role music will play in the film. Not only is Ripley a classical pianist (which he isn't in the novel), the Jude Law character (Dickie Greenleaf) pursues his passion as an idle rich artist living the high life in Italy not as a painter, as in the novel, but as a jazz saxophonist. In a lengthy and highly intelligent commentary, an unfortunate rarity in film-music recordings, that appears in the program booklet for Sony Classical's music-track CD for *The Talented Mr. Ripley* (Harry Rabinowitz, cond.), the director explains his decision as follows: "Music is at the heart of the film *The Talented Mr. Ripley*. In adapting Patricia Highsmith's marvelous and profoundly disturbing novel from the fifties, it struck me that sound would more pungently and dynamically evoke the period in a film than the motif of painting Highsmith uses in her book. Jazz, with its mantra of freedom and improvisation, carries the burden of expression for the existential urges of Americans leaving home to redefine themselves in Europe." But Minghella also uses this very premise to create one of the film's major ironies: "But as the story unfolds it becomes apparent that, just as in music, where truly great extemporizing begins with Bach and Mozart, it is Ripley, the so-called square, who is the more genuine improviser." The result of all this is that the music track is filled with jazz, some of it "found" ("Ko-Ko" by Charlie Parker, "Nature Boy" by Miles Davis, "The Champ" by Dizzy Gillespie), some of it new performances, extremely well recorded, of standards by the "International Quintet" of British trumpeter Guy Barker, with Law and Damon adding their vocals in one cue, and Damon doing a breathy (which is how you sing when you haven't been trained) solo of "My Funny Valentine" in another.

But that's not all. For *The Talented Mr. Ripley* Minghella returns to Lebanese-born composer Gabriel Yared, who won a Best Original Score Oscar for *The English Patient*. Now, Yared would remain one of my heroes if he had never composed for anything beyond two films by Jean-Jacques Beineix, *The Moon in the Gutter* and *Betty Blue*, and, even more significantly, for Peter Del Monte's shadowy, morbid, and, yes, ambiguous (and utterly extraordinary) *Invitation au voyage*. I also love much of his *Map of the Human Heart*. In these early scores Yared, through very simple means, created all-but-palpable masses of intensely dark mood whose outer limits extend both into the surreal and into crepuscular rhapsody. Yared's scores have become somewhat less interesting as he has moved into more commercial ventures. But in his music for *The Talented Mr. Ripley* Yared, who according to Minghella was (unusually) "closely involved with the film since the earliest drafts of the screenplay," has regained something of his old form. His eight contributions (about 25 minutes' worth) to the Sony music-track CD start off rather unpromisingly with "Italia," which, in spite of an intriguing initial accompaniment from at least two harps, has a rather travelogue-ish tone to it that is no doubt deliberate. But in the next cue, the haunting, line-against-line "Lullaby for Cain" (probably the song performed, in a more "classical" manner, at the film's outset but presented here in its end-title version as sung with rivetingly quiet intensity by the airy-voiced Sinead O'Connor), Yared's music begins to move into those soul-enveloping expanses of gray so frequently haunted by his creative spirit. It does so even more strongly in the ensuing cue, "Crazy Tom," which over an obsessive, motoric accompaniment in the low and midrange strings that opens and closes the cue, introduces a slightly askew, slightly exotic theme in the oboe that leads the amassed instrumental forces into several highly dramatic crescendos, all of it quite close to the *nachtmusik* rhapsodies of Yared's earlier days. Ingeniously, in the cue entitled "Mischief," a vibe solo representing Ripley's jazz-self plays over a rather unsettling accompaniment that includes a downward vocalization from a female voice and that seems to represent the void beneath Ripley's role. The theme from "Crazy Tom" returns in the broader, more sustained, more fully orchestrated cue entitled "Ripley," while the lullaby makes a dreamy, unsung, quasi-music-box appearance in the cue enticingly entitled "Proust," which also flirts with the "Crazy Tom"/"Ripley" music. "Promise," with its soprano-sax solo that occasionally clashes bitonally with the opulent accompaniment mostly in the strings, moves into an area of almost pure sadness

with a tinge of acidity, and it pretty much stays there in the elegiac, occasionally almost Mozartean "Syncopes," which ends with a searing version of the lullaby in the
strings and which closes Yared's contributions to *The Talented Mr. Ripley*'s music on
this CD. As Minghella has noted, "The character of Ripley is a deliberately opaque
one, and his inner being, its dislocations and yearnings, needed teasing out. Ripley often doesn't know or understand what he's feeling and yet his perspective is the one
through which every moment of the film is refracted. Gabriel's task was, in part, to
imagine he was listening to the troubled music of Ripley's heart and to make it heard."
Put another way, Yared had to do for Ripley, but in a much more indirect way, what
Morricone did for 1900 (the character). That he accomplished it in such a thoroughly
moving fashion is a major proof of the genius of one of film-music's lesser-heard
voices. The recorded sound, except in the overly digital engineering of the excerpt
from Vivaldi's Stabat Mater recorded specially for this film, is warm, rich, and full.

May/June

"I suppose he's all right, but give me somebody a little more normal."—Mina Se-
ward re. Count Dracula

OK, folks, are you ready for this? At some point back in 1998 somebody at Universal
decided that it would be a neat idea to add a musical score to the all but music-less
1931 version of *Dracula* directed by Tod Browning. There's a certain logic if not historical correctness to that, since one can be reasonably sure that it was technology
and not aesthetics that kept movies from early in the sound era from being heavily
scored (Leonard Maltin, in the capsule review appearing in his *Movie and Video Guide*
of the James Whale *Frankenstein*, also from 1931, suggests that the film "cries for a
music score"). But here's the kicker: either that same person or somebody else also decided that it would be a doubly neat idea to have Philip Glass write that musical
score. "Philip Glass?" you ask. "Isn't he the guy who keeps repeating the same musical fragments over and over again in such a way that it defeats our usual sense of musical time?" Yup, same guy. "But wouldn't that work against the narrative flow that's
particularly essential to a horror film such as *Dracula*?" Yup, it sure would. "Well, does
it?" Yup, it sure does. "Then why in the world did they do it?" Beats the hell out of
me, and, oh surprise of surprises, there's not a word in the cover insert of the Nonesuch recording of this "score" performed by the Kronos Quartet to explain whatever
rationale there was. I do seem to recall that initially the Kronos Quartet performed
Glass' music live to screenings of the film, and it may be that this whole thing was intended as nothing more (and nothing less) than a piece of postmodern performance
art destined to live and die with its moment. But, thanks to the popularity and amazing versatility of DVDs, Universal, as a part of its "Classic Monster Collection," released last September, at the same time as Nonesuch's CD, a DVD on which you can
watch a) the original version of *Dracula* with its *Swan Lake* title music and its moment
of the *Die Meistersinger* Overture during an opera scene—period; b) the same film but

with Glass' music running pretty much nonstop (*Swan Lake* vanishes, but *Die Meistersinger* stays, since it is a part of the narrative); and, c) the Spanish-language *Dracula* shot on the same sets after the English-language crew was done but with an entirely different cast and a different director (George Melford, with Enrique Tovar Avalos), who brought a much greater visual flair and, over its much longer running time (104' as opposed to the 75' for the English-language version), a more relaxed coherence to the film. Unfortunately, the "Conde Dracula" (Carlos Villarias) was no Bela Lugosi. The DVD also offers a documentary in which you can see more film historians than you've ever witnessed in your life, along with such figures as studio boss Carl Laemmle's niece, who had a small role at the beginning of the film (the woman in glasses), and Bela Lugosi's son.

I would suspect that you have to divide the experience of watching the Glass-scored *Dracula* into two categories. The first includes classical-music listeners who are familiar with the composer's music; the second comprises people who have never heard a note of the composer's music except, perhaps, subliminally in *The Truman Show*. There may be a third category of viewer/listeners who know Glass only through such offbeat films as *Koyaanisqatsi*, *The Thin Blue Line*, or *Mishima* (of course, there are also slightly more mainstream films such as *The Secret Agent*, one of Glass' best film scores, and *Kundun*, one of his worst). At any rate, I can speak only as a member of the first category, and, from that vantage point, I have to say that watching the 1931 *Dracula* with the Kronos Quartet sawing away at Glass' typical figures in the background (but in warm, full, and vibrant sound totally uncharacteristic of the film's era; it's quite a sonic jolt when *Die Meistersinger* squeaks its way onto the music track) felt very much like watching a movie and attending a concert at the same time. Even though the music runs almost nonstop, in no way does it create the impression of a silent-film score, since the latter almost always at least attempts to be action- and mood-specific. Only rarely, on the other hand, does Glass' music coordinate with the filmic action, and that only in the form of a sudden cut to a louder episode whose dramatic impact immediately gets dissipated by the repetitions. The one moment that I found even mildly effective from a dramatic standpoint occurs early in the film when Renfield enters the good count's castle. Here, there is something about Glass' start-stop figures and his use of tremolos that evokes the dark, creepy grandeur of the place. The music for "The Storm" starts off and ends as turbulently as anything in Glass' oeuvre, but it pretty much gets drowned out, if you'll pardon the expression, by all the noise going on. And the stridently (and surprisingly, for Glass) dissonant, but very wispy, figures in the ensuing cue ("Horrible Tragedy") likewise have their principal impact heard apart from the film. In the end run it can't even be said that Glass' music does nothing for the film, since it doesn't seem to be playing in the same place or time. Ultimately, it's thoroughly irrelevant. Which brings us to the next question: "Yes, but how does it stand on its own?" Answer: well enough, if you like Glass (and he certainly covers much of his familiar territory over the score's 26 mostly very brief cues), and if you're not looking for any startling new directions from him. And there are always those moments, such as a little three-note figure in the violin in "Lucy's

Bitten" (reprised as a kind of leitmotif in "Women in White"), that generate an instant of affect that is so evanescent that you want to run off after it. And you constantly have the impression that a second or two from Beethoven here, or Grieg there, or whoever, has leaped out of a stray score and wandered into a time loop. That's Glass, and it's mesmerizing, if you're into that kind of thing. But laid down on *Dracula*'s music track all it does is compete for your attention, and that's just not fair. I would, however, love to be able to turn off the Philip Glass part of my brain to see what it would feel like to watch the Glass-scored *Dracula* without instantly recognizing that wholly characteristic concert-music style. I should also add that the Kronos Quartet performs this score in a manner that seems fully committed to the music, and they attain quite a peak of intensity in the closing bars.

Postmodern? Did I use the term "postmodern"? You haven't witnessed postmodern until you've seen **Titus**, a film adaptation of Shakespeare's early play *Titus Andronicus* directed by Julie Taymor, who had done the art design for and directed a stage version of the play, and who before *Titus* was director and art designer for the Broadway-musical version of the Disney film *The Lion King*. *Titus Andronicus*, of course, is about the purest revenge tragedy Shakespeare ever wrote, with roots extending back into the darkest recesses of Greek tragedy, with the eponymous Roman general (Anthony Hopkins) finally feeding the flesh of her sons to Tamora (Jessica Lange), whose sons, in their act of revenge for the execution of their brother by Titus, had raped and mutilated his daughter Lavinia (Laura Fraser). Significantly, Taymor, who has an amazing sense of what might be called visual syntax, uses the Roman Coliseum not only as a constant point of departure and return of the action but also as a locus via which to mirror the audience. In an NEA interview, she explained her decision in the following terms: "The coliseum becomes 'the bookends,' the first theater of cruelty where audiences sat there and watched the spectacle of violence as pure enjoyment." But into this and other settings pours the most motley and sometimes even phantasmagoric assortment of costumes, architecture, and settings you will ever see on a single screen, starting with ancient Rome (and even a bit of Greece) and passing through fascist Italy on the way to the programmed violence of video games. We also get to see (a lot of) Jessica Lange in a gold bustier that would make Madonna blush. And can some of those facial gestures by Hopkins reminiscent of the good Hannibal Lecter be accidental, given the culinary predilections of both characters? Yet, in the midst of and in contrast to all of this, quite an admirable lot of actors and actresses deliver the Bard's dialog as if to the manner born, so that, somehow, one leaves the theater with the sense of having witnessed a Shakespeare play. Even here, however, Taymor introduces a child character who circulates throughout the film and whose final gesture in the film is so visually and narratively moving that it thoroughly mitigates the revenge element of the text, as does Harry J. Lennix's strangely sympathetic portrayal of Tamora's Moorish lover, Aaron, who, as written in the play, foreshadows Iago in his scheming and purely evil cruelty. And is it Hopkins' portrayal or the character himself that makes me see this Titus as an early incarnation of Lear? It's not so much that there's no place to hang your hat here as that you can collect a lot of hats and then hang them comfortably or uncomfortably just about any place you want. Now, that's postmodern.

Another strong element of Taymor's directorial style is the balletic quality she imparts to some of the onscreen action. And here in part is where Elliot Goldenthal's sometimes quite amazing score comes in (Sony; London Metropolitan Orchestra; English Chamber Choir; The Mask Orchestra; The Pickled Heads Band; Steven Mercurio, Jonathan Sheffer, cond.). For starters, you'll have to look far and wide to find a more dramatic combination of music and visuals than in *Titus'* opening (or close to) sequence, in which Goldenthal's "Victorius Titus" accompanies Taymor's sharp-edged and, ultimately, pretty frightening choreography of the returning troops. Indeed, from the look of the movements and the sound of Goldenthal's music, with its imposing choral chanting (in Latin) and its slowly paced but hugely imposing wind-and-percussion figures, one hardly has the impression that this is a victory parade; you'd have to look back to Alex North's title music and Saul Bass' title design for Stanley Kubrick's 1960 *Spartacus* to find such an immediately grim evocation of the horrors of militarism. Similarly, the bleak momentum of "Coronation" may imply some pomp and circumstance, but definitely of a usurpative nature. Throughout the score, Goldenthal offers no small amount of quickly propulsive and exciting but ominous music, some of it in what might be described as a post-Shostakovich vein (as in "Arrows of the Gods"), that mobilizes the full forces of the symphony orchestra with breathtaking effectiveness (and both the performances and the recorded sound in these cues are of demonstration quality). But for just about every hard-driven, *marcato* cue Goldenthal offers more understated looks back into the darkness. A big, descending, four-note motif in the violins, for instance, lets us know at several points in this score where very little gets repeated that we are indeed watching a tragedy, no matter how grotesque at points. Very low chanting from a male chorus creates a funereal aura at several moments, while a cue such as "Tamora's Pastorale," with its morose, rippling figures in the winds, may suggest a green plain, but one that is abandoned and shrouded in fog. There is also an appropriately labeled, strings-only cue entitled "Adagio" whose mournful lugubriousness sinks us more deeply into despair than Barber's aching sadness.

Given, however, the postmodern amalgams of Taymor's style, it would have been somewhat misguided to limit the musical backing to something close to the classic, if highly modernistic, symphonic film score, and neither Taymor nor Goldenthal opted for this. Goldenthal's most blatant departures from style and implied era occur in several cues of big-band (the Pickled Heads ensemble, I presume) music—swing here, a boogie-woogie there, a stomp that nonetheless, in its minor-mode relentlessness and its raucousness, manages to maintain the overall ominous tone while suggesting the 1930s and '40s, and, by implication, the fascism that grew up in that period. The cue entitled "Titus' Vow" wanders at one point between a satirical march à la Prokofiev and a much more ghoulish march/polka reminiscent of Danny Elfman. One cue, "Philimelagram," seems to start off in *Das Rheingold* and end in *Parsifal.* The extended "Pickled Heads" (wherein the heads of his two sons are brought back to Titus in fluid-filled jars), a piece of almost pure musical surrealism, if such a thing is possible, starts off with distorted allusions to hip-hop; moves into a raucous episode filled with electronics, some Near Eastern figures, and a suggested rock beat that at one point moves from left to right across the speakers; evokes the '60s with an electric organ and, ultimately, something along the lines of a TV-detective-series theme à la *Peter Gunn*; offers some quasi-calliope spiced up with sporadic synthesized noises; and ends up with a distorted polka out of the worst nightmares of Nino Rota and Danny Elfman. We also get a cue taken from Goldenthal's score for A *Time to Kill*, which in fact provided Titus with two of its musical motifs. The CD concludes with an Italian song entitled "Vivere" (To Live), heard at two or three points in the film, that was probably recorded in the '30s or '40s. Conclusion: Elliot Goldenthal's *Titus* is nothing less than a virtuoso score. While it occasionally falls short of pure musical satisfaction, and while, like the film, it manages to create a certain emotional distance between the work of art and its spectators, *Titus* offers such an ongoing, brilliant array of mostly symphonic creativity that I am stunned that it did not receive a "Best Original Score" nomination for this year's Oscars. This is, at any rate, a CD to take with you when you go out to buy new sound equipment.

Americana of a very unusual sort—narratively, filmically, musically—pervades **The Green Mile**, written and directed by Frank Darabont, who also wrote and directed *The Shawshank Redemption* in 1994. This is Stephen King's dark, scary, even supernatural US of A. Yet, in spite of the fact that the narratives of both of these Stephen King adaptations take place mostly in prison and involve wrongly incarcerated men, these are gentler tales in which, interestingly enough, it is the good that gets blown somewhat out of proportion—particularly in *The Green Mile*—rather than the bad. Imagine the following situation: death row in a Southern (*The Green Mile* was shot mostly in Tennessee) prison in the 1930s (the walk to the electric-chair chamber is called "the green mile"); a patient and understanding captain of the death-row guards as played by Tom Hanks, which should tell you something right there; two other guards of almost equal equanimity, including one (beautifully played by David Morse) nicknamed Brutal (he isn't); a Native American and a Cajun inmate (Graham Greene and Michael Jeter) who sadly but stoically await their ugly fate; a compassionate warden (the omnipresent James Cromwell) with a terminally ill wife (Patricia Clarkson); a new inmate named John Coffey (Michael Clarke Duncan), a gargantuan black man accused of raping and murdering two young girls but whose hands, which are the size of waffle irons, have the power to heal; and, of course, a mouse who circulates among the condemned. Wait a minute: are we in a Disney film or what? Well, of course, evil does enter the picture in the form of a sadistic guard with connections (Doug Hutchison) and a fourth inmate, this one an irredeemably nasty dude nicknamed Wild Bill (Sam Rockwell); and as the film winds along its leisurely way (it runs over three hours) we ultimately come to see what Stephen King shows us best, namely the ugly underbelly of the American ethos. Yet in *The Green Mile* this is filtered through such wonderful humanness on the part of the good guards (and warden) and the good inmates, and through such all-encompassing goodness on the part of the huge black man, that we (finally) leave the film sad but uplifted, rather than whipped, exhausted, and relieved, as is usually the case after one has read a King novel or witnessed a film made therefrom.

As for Thomas Newman's extensive score for *The Green Mile* (Warner Sunset), this too is not your classic cine-Americana sound. Yet, as director Darabont writes about Newman in his program commentary, "As a composer, there is none better for conveying a sense of wonder, adding a touch of irony, giving a hint of mischief." Darabont also notes that "His is a light touch indeed, nimbly avoiding at all turns the obvious or heavy-handed." There is, in fact, something distinctly but non-cinematically American about Newman's particular brand of irony and mischief, which often seem to have their origins in the pure fun of just sitting (around the campfire, perhaps) and making music that often flirts in various ways with the blues. Newman in fact loves to play with timbres that either come from or suggest folk instruments, and one finds listed among the extra instruments for *The Green Mile* such oddities as a bowed traveling guitar (say what?), a Vietnamese banjo, a laud, a jaw harp (the same thing, I presume, as Jew's harp), struck metal, tonut (eh?), and bowed dulcimer alongside such Newman staples as the bass marimba and the piano (electric or otherwise). That lightness of touch not only denies the European-concert-hall origins of much of film music, it also manifests itself in the constant playful percussion figurations that show up in the majority of Newman's film-music cues. Darabont also notes, however, that "nobody infuses emotion into a scene better than Tom." All of these elements—including the emotion—come together in the score's first instrumental cue (the CD opens with a snippet from a chain-gang song, "Old Alabama"), entitled "Monstrous Big": over a drone we hear a nimble rhythmic figure created by the bass marimba and electric bass punctuated by some electronic sounds and a couple of instruments plucked in a bluesy manner (the piano later joins in in kind). In the midst of this, however, the strings enter with rich, lazy, rather dark and moody midrange chords that immediately establish the almost palpable yet undefinable presence of affect that draws you immediately into the film. Then, some 45 seconds into the cue, unison violins soar upward, hinting at a whole universe of tragedy but cutting short before carrying you totally into it.

I would need to reference the film before guaranteeing the accuracy of my analysis of the ensuing cue, entitled "The Two Dead Girls." But if this cue does in fact come early in the film—and I am presuming that it backs the sequence showing the discovery of John Coffey holding the two murdered girls—then the music tells us something that we suspect all along but that is not positively revealed until much later in the narrative. I won't reveal what it is; suffice it to say, however, that the same high, tinkling piano figures that follow the calming of the opening electronic miasma turn up at a similar moment in "Coffey's Hands" (the first healing that we see), and represent the shimmering ashes of evil that Coffey breathes out once his laying on of hands has been successful. It would take me several more paragraphs to describe all of Newman's music—32 of the 37 cues offered on the Warner Sunset CD. I single out two. The first is the wonderfully droll, start-stop music for the mouse, played by low, pizzicato strings and (bass?) marimba, which, if I am not mistaken (and the title of a later cue would seem to confirm this), is based on a dance step called the turkey trot. At the opposite end of the scale is the extended (for good reason) upheaval of "The Bad Death of Eduard Delacroix," with wild percussion crashing all over the place and brass snarling out with a violence rare in Newman's oeuvre. The CD also offers, in addition to "Old Alabama," several other pieces of source music, the most significant being the song "Cheek to Cheek," sung by Fred Astaire from the music track of *Top Hat*. If movies, or at least one of their huge early stars (Rita Hayworth), represent the exit-point of *The Shawshank Redemption*, they represent the entry-point into the flashback that is *The Green Mile*. I should also add a note about the stunning sound quality of this CD, which, if you have access to a magnifying glass when looking at the back cover, you will discover is in fact an HDCD. I needed no little red HDCD light on my player to be swept away by the manner in which the resonant bass sounds of "Monstrous Big" filled my listening room, to marvel at the exceedingly sharp definition of the musical space between my speakers, or to melt in the glow of the warm timbres of the string chords. Even in the fortissimo mayhem of "The Bad Death . . . ," the sound remains remarkably clean and well defined. I'm not set up to do an A/B test, so I can't say how much of this is just the engineering itself, the HD element, and/or my player. I can say that it sounded quite spectacular on my Discman, but that a lot of it was a bit too much for my car stereo.

I didn't rush out to see **Angela's Ashes**, Frank McCourt's enormously popular memoir of his childhood, which, while extremely well written, ultimately left me exasperated at its almost unrelenting and unvaried descriptions of the abject poverty in which he and his siblings grew up in Ireland, thanks largely to a lovable, story-telling, but alcoholic and therefore by-and-large unemployable father. I note, however, that people I respect enormously, including my Irish daughter-in-law, Niamh, have loved the memoir. I also am no huge fan of Alan Parker, who directed the film adaptation. But John Williams has received an Oscar nomination for his score for *Angela's Ashes* (Sony), and, much more important, it took no more than the opening few measures of the opening solo-piano ostinato-motif to draw me completely into what turns out to be some of the most haunting film music I have ever heard. So I am left with no choice but to rave about it here, with the understanding that I have read the book but not seen the movie. First of all, it strikes me that John Williams has reached a second peak in his career as a film composer, as I swear I have heard nothing but one masterpiece after the other from him of late. Second, Williams deserves huge credit here for resisting the temptation to fill his score with the standard clichés of Irish and, where Hollywood has more often than not been concerned, pseudo-Irish music, although I suspect he has subtly mobilized a certain number of ethnic elements. Instead, Williams has returned somewhat to the heavily minor-mode gloom one finds in such scores as *The Fury* (1978) and *Dracula* (1979), but with the intensity of those scores toned down to the point that rage and terror have been transformed into sadness and a sense of deep, deep loneliness and longing. The style here reaches as far back as the late romanticism of, say, Grieg, moves through a more post-romantic sound closer to, say, Elgar, but ultimately ends up as pure John Williams.

Part of that softening of tone may be due to the fact that the music is scored mostly for string orchestra, beefed up here and there only by a solo flute, solo clarinet, solo oboe, horns, and harp, plus, of course, the piano, although it sometimes feels as if Williams generates more passion out of a string orchestra than many composers attain with every instrument in the book. But whether played by the full forces or by one of the solo instruments, the score's two principal themes go straight to the soul. The first, more tied perhaps into that loneliness, opens with a wistful repeated figure that soon accompanies a G-Minor (initially) theme knocked just slightly off its purely tonal course by a momentary half-step shift downward. The second theme, also initially presented on the solo piano, is more defined by its chordal structures, and seems both more oriented (I'm guessing) toward the adult world and more tragic, particularly when the full string orchestra picks it up. These two themes, which move between various instruments (the solo oboe, played by John Ellis, is particularly striking) and groupings, dominate a good deal of the music, although a cello solo that seems to think of going atonal here, or a harp solo there, briefly move the music into new territory. At one point, when the father has gone off to England, where wartime work is plentiful, the music, which becomes somewhat nondescript, largely abandons the original themes for two cues, the second of which ("Delivering Telegrams") is a scherzo for string orchestra, with lots of pizzicato and just a hint of the second theme. There is also a moment with quiet, sustained high strings and celesta, when I knew we were dealing with a celestial event before I even looked at the cue's title ("Watching the Eclipse"), while the big, final (pre-end-title) cue, "Back to America," is as pure a piece of triumph-mitigated-by-preceding-unhappiness as you're apt to find in the canons of film music. In addition to all this, the CD offers two source-music cues, "The Dispy Doodle," performed by Nat Gonella and His Georgians, and Billie Holiday's version of "Pennies from Heaven." I also note that a number of the cues here open with narration, spoken by Andrew Bennett, taken from the book. While I usually object to this sort of thing, Bennett, Irish brogue and all, reads the texts in such an understated yet deeply moving way that I actually found that it contributed to my overall enjoyment of the recording.

July/August

[All of the reviews were cut from this column.]

September/October

Many of the films directed (and often co-produced, scored or co-scored, and written) by British director Mike Figgis fall into that area defined by film scholar Laura Mulvey as "liminal," movies of betwixt and between that slip in somewhere between the norms of commercial cinema and the anti-norms of experimental film. Even such early thrillers as *Stormy Monday* (1988) and *Internal Affairs* (1990) reveal both a striking, sometimes hyper-real visual style as well as ingenious manipulations of characters within complex and often ambiguous narrative structures. And few filmmakers working out of the studio have dared remain so vertiginously in the dream state as Figgis did in his 1991 *Liebestraum*, which I consider to be one of the masterpieces of the last decade (the 114-minute version, please!). And despite its fairly straightforward story about an alcoholic on a path of self-annihilation, the 1995 *Leaving Las Vegas*, which received four Oscar nominations (and one award), was shot with super-16mm cameras and film, which allowed the director much more flexibility in moving about Las Vegas than he would have had with the standard 35mm equipment ("We didn't have to get a permit from the city or rope off the streets," Figgis noted. "We just jumped out of the car, set up the camera and started shooting"). *One Night Stand* (1997) creates chains of characters whose paths intersect in unexpected ways, while in *The Loss of Sexual Innocence* (1999) Figgis goes one step further and creates not only chains of characters but chains of interlaced narratives going all the way back to Adam and Eve. In this context Figgis' seemingly out-of-nowhere **Time Code** (also spelled *Timecode*), which simultaneously projects four interconnected films shot on location in West Hollywood in continuous, precisely synched, 93-minute segments on Sony DSR-1 digital videocams (one of which was manned by Figgis himself), comes perhaps as something less of a surprise. *Time Code*, which opened this past April, has been released in only a handful of theaters, which is all the more unfortunate, since the film will work on video only on the largest of home-theater screens.

Still, it is no small wonder that Figgis was able to get any kind of commercial release for a film such as *Time Code*, even though its "experimental" qualities would be considered fairly benign on the anti-norm side of the ledger. The real miracle, however, lies on the norm side, for *Time Code* works brilliantly as narrative cinema, or at least it did for me. While there is no question that it takes a certain amount of acclimatization to the basic device of a quadruply split screen for the viewer to begin to keep track of the film's separate narrative threads, the viewer can in fact begin to sort things out rather quickly, thanks in part to Figgis' astute manipulations of the sound and voice tracks (with the help of sound mixer Robert Janiger), which lead us via our ears to focus our eyes to a greater or lesser extent on what is perhaps the most important of the four interlocked narratives at any given moment. *Time Code* has perhaps two principal narrative blocks: starting at the one end we have the stalking and bugging of a beautiful aspiring actress (the stunning Mexican actress Salma Hayek) by her wealthy lesbian lover (Jeanne Tripplehorn). At the other end we have a major piece of self-reflection as Figgis takes us into a film studio called Red Mullet Films (the same name as the production company for *Time Code*, of course) where the various execs are trying to come up with a movie. The principal exec (Stellan Skarsgård), who seems to be crumbling into pieces, is having an affair with Hayek, while his wife (Saffron Burrows) initially talks to her therapist (Glenne Headly) in an all but inaudible conversation from the upper-right quadrant. Many other characters move in and out of the action, including a masseur (Julian Sands) who pounces on the various studio execs as soon as they have a free shoulder, and an independent filmmaker (Mia Maestro) who toward the end of *Time Code* offers a very cogent apologia for the entire movie. But in spite of a certain coherence between the various narrative threads *Time Code* remains a strongly aleatory experience—doubly aleatory when you consider that Figgis, who shot 60 x 4 takes of this highly mapped-out but also largely improvised film, has promised alternate versions, [one of which can be found on the DVD of *Time Code*].

Still, toward the middle of *Time Code* Figgis suddenly jolts all of the viewer's disparately wandering feelings into a single direction by a particularly ingenious manipulation on the music track (which is not split into four, acting instead something like an aural coating over all four visual panels): leaving the soft-jazz/pop-oriented score that dominates much of the film (more on that momentarily), the director unexpectedly moves to the second movement (Adagietto) of the Mahler Symphony No. 5. Now, the Adagietto from the Mahler Fifth could bring tears to one's eyes if it were played behind a Three Stooges comedy. Coming as it does around midpoint into *Time Code*'s multi-split narrative(s), it grabs the viewer by the viscera and focuses the affect of the remainder of the film, over which the Adagietto hangs like a pall, more single-mindedly toward the unsettling conclusion. Most of the rest of the score, which is available on a Milan CD, typifies the musical sound for the films in which Figgis has had a hand in the composing. Even though Figgis' musical background comes mostly via rock bands and music videos, the Figgis cine-music sound largely defines itself as jazz. The original cues for *Time Code* were co-composed by Figgis and keyboardist Anthony Marinelli, who has an impressive number of film and TV credits, and who also worked on *Internal Affairs* and *Leaving Las Vegas*. The key word here is "moody," whether in the more spacey sounds of the "Main Title," with its extended, very resonant sax solo (I'm tempted to write "cadenza") wandering above dark chords from what I presume are synth or sampled strings; in the equally spacey "Abstract Blues," with two (sampled?) women's voices doing slow vocalises over similar chords; or in the more funky but largely minor-mode night-jazz of "Disco Void" (with a great muted trumpet), "Sunset Strip," or "Red Reggae" (again with muted trumpet).

We also get both vocal (performed by Skin . . . that's what it says) and instrumental versions of a very sultry song, with a great minor-major shift in the refrain, called "Comfort of Strangers," which, although composed by Figgis and Marinelli, apparently has had a life apart from *Time Code*. Another sultry song is "Single," written by Ben Watt and Tracey Thorn, and performed by Everything But the Girl (again, that's what it says). Arlen Figgis, who I presume is related to the director (program notes, please?), gets credit, along with Richard Johnson, for the cue entitled "Future Strings," which slips fragments of a string quartet somewhat à la Shostakovich into an electronic soundscape that eventually moves over to a jazz/pop beat. All in all, Figgis, even when he uses other people's music, manages to maintain throughout the score pretty much of a unified mood that gives us a distant sense of the darker side of the characters we see on the screen—sorry, screens—while also perhaps communicating their essential aloneness. Then, out of nowhere, the Mahler Fifth Adagietto plunges us into the furthest reaches of that darkness and that loneliness. The performance offered here, from a Naxos recording conducted by Antoni Wit with the Polish National Radio Symphony Orchestra, does not plumb the depths of this music to the degree that, say, a Leonard Bernstein does, but I suspect that is precisely what Figgis wanted in order to avoid overkill. This is, at any rate, a CD that holds up quite well on its own. But I leave the final words to Figgis himself (from the "Preliminary Production Notes" in Time Code's press kit, which also includes a great T-shirt): "Music is the one thing that binds all of the four images together. It's a very important part of *Time Code*, the real rhythm to which the story is set. The film itself, after all, is almost a musical piece."

Now turning high up on the rungs of commercial cinema but returning way back into the past, I close with a newly recorded version, with Frederic Talgorn conducting the Royal Scottish National Orchestra, of Franz Waxman's wonderful score for the 1957 **Peyton Place** (Varèse Sarabande), a film that, as Robert Townson puts it in the program booklet, "succeeds beyond its potential," although one might argue that the Grace Metalious novel on which the film is based realizes a potential for which few have given it credit. Set in a fictitious New England town with many scandal-provoking ties to the real world, *Peyton Place* mostly takes place just prior to the American entry into World War II, and involves everything from budding teenage romance to rampant classism to incestuous rape, suicide, and murder. Soap opera? You bet, but brought off supremely thanks to the coming together of a strong vision from director Mark Robson; an excellent screenplay by John Michael Hayes from Metalious' basic material; a uniformly strong cast including Lana Turner, Lee Philips, Lloyd Nolan, Arthur Kennedy, Diane Varsi, Russ Tamblyn, Terry Moore, Hope Lange, and even David Nelson; evocative and atmospheric cinematography (in CinemaScope), often shot on location, by William Mellor; and, of course, Waxman's complex and probing score. It is, I must admit, the kind of thing that big-studio, high-budget cinema does best. Indeed, only this kind of filmmaking could complement its characters and narrative situations with such a solid sense of place, via the photography, and with such affective depth, not just with respect to the characters and the story but even with respect to the rural, small-town-Americana locations.

Waxman's score is particularly intriguing in this sense. On the one hand, the composer, who includes two New England folk tunes among his themes, has definitely created a leitmotif score, with most of the major characters, save the drunken and sadistic Lucas Cross (Kennedy), associated with a particular theme, and often with a particular combination of timbres. On the other hand, at least four themes or motifs seem to float freely throughout the film, sometimes suggesting a character, sometimes a situation, sometimes a mood, sometimes the entire setting. These include: a) the opening motif, with its distinctive chimes doubling the melody; b) the big, dramatic, main-title theme, more often than not associated, in much softer, aching variants, with Selma Cross (Lange) as the film moves forward; c) a jaunty, scherzo-like theme; and, of course, d) the theme from *Peyton Place*, a big, violin-laden tune that soon struck out on its own to become a popular song as well as the theme for the TV series based on the movie (and the novel). While the latter theme in particular often seems to attach itself to the film's young heroine (and narrator), Allison MacKenzie (Varsi), at many points it perhaps suggests the potential, realized and unrealized, for love that is one of the story's principal, multi-developed facets. Although the music frequently communicates both longing and sadness, on only two occasions does the music turn dark, in both instances in situations involving Selena Cross and her abusive stepfather. On a purely musical level I very much like the way Waxman takes timbres associated with one theme and on one or two occasions uses them for another. Particularly effective, too, is the way he takes Constance MacKenzie's (Turner) rather Scottish-flavored theme and plays it canonically in solo flute and solo cello as she seems to dialogue with her depressed daughter but in fact is essentially talking for herself. And Waxman is the only composer I can think of to have fully realized the lyric potential of the piccolo, not only here but also in his haunting score for the mediocre *Hemingway's Adventures of a Young Man.*

The "original soundtrack recording" of *Peyton Place* was originally brought out on LP by RCA Victor, and later reissued on an Entr'acte recording featuring extensive liner notes by yours truly. This newly recorded Varèse Sarabande release not only brings *Peyton Place* to CD for the first time (as far as I know; one never knows what goodies have sneaked out from the various and elusive metamorphoses Entr'acte has undergone), it also offers four cues—"After the Dance," "Summer Montage," "Leaving for New York," and "End Credits"—not included on the original recording, thus giving us just about all of the film's music. Conductor Frederic Talgorn interprets the music in a manner very in tune with the drama and quite similar to what we hear on the music track. He gets particularly incisive playing from the all-important strings, and quite decent all-around performances from the rest of the Royal Scottish National Orchestra, which has been captured in very rich sound that lacks perhaps just a tad of depth.

November/December

Can it be that James Horner is getting typecast as the official composer for maritime-disaster movies? After *Titanic,* now comes **The Perfect Storm**, directed by Wolfgang Petersen (best known in this country for *Das Boot,* speaking of maritime disasters), and based on Sebastian Junger's book documenting the events surrounding three meteorological events that disastrously come together to create a storm so violent that, among other things, its 120-mph winds and its 100-foot waves gobbled up a fishing boat from Gloucester, Massachusetts. That fishing boat and its crew, headed by Captain Billy Tyne (George Clooney, who, in spite of his perfect set of white teeth and impossible good looks, is reasonably convincing in his portrayal of a weathered salt and skillful boatman), become the principal focus of *The Perfect Storm,* although the film also cuts fairly often to a daring (do I hear foolhardy?) rescue of three people on a private yacht by the Coast Guard and Air National Guard. *The Perfect Storm* being a Hollywood narrative film, the screenplay, by William D. Wittliff, obviously needed to pad the story with diverse relationships in order to make us "care" about the characters on Tyne's fishing boat. Although transparent as hell, and giving us very little feel about what life in a fishing town is really like (up to and including the almost total lack of anything resembling a convincing Gloucester accent; Clooney doesn't even try, which is perhaps all to the better), all these preliminary human relationships set up effectively enough the main event, which is the storm itself, whose massive waves and ferocious winds have been devastatingly re-created (I can only presume that it must have felt like this) by digitized special effects. Although the film, wisely perhaps, ignores the horrors of drowning spelled out in detail in Junger's book, one leaves the theater exhausted and, yes, more than a bit sad.

But then, on the other hand, there's James Horner's overbearing score for *The Perfect Storm* (Sony). First and foremost, the extended storm scenes absolutely do not need music—not a note. The various "natural" sounds, starting with the wind, reproduced on the soundtrack are an essential part of the storm, and they need to be experienced every bit as directly as the overwhelming visuals. *Any* dramatic musical "backing" at all would amount to overkill. But Horner's bloated orchestral strains add insult to injury in their lack of anything resembling developmental sophistication, in their sheer loudness (Horner reminds me of the typical ugly American in a foreign country who thinks that if he screams loudly enough in English he'll be heard and appreciated), and in the utter amateurishness of the harmonic language. To make matters worse, Horner creates, as what I presume to be the principal "storm theme" (or maybe it's supposed to be "heroism within a storm"), a six-note motif that offers no musical interest to begin with but that gets repeated so often with such little variation that I was ready to run screaming from the theater. Trust me, folks, I was willing to give Horner a chance. And so, when the music opened with a quiet horn theme over a solo guitar that generates a nice dose of mellow nostalgia, I began to think that maybe the composer had begun to change his ways. But then—IT HAPPENED! A little more than a minute into the opening cue there's James Horner, adding one more episode to a distinguished history of lifting other composers' music, in this case a figure, in the same key, instrumentation, and harmonies, that appears in Copland's *Appalachian Spring* ballet, and it turns up throughout the *Perfect Storm* score as one of its principal motifs. I mean, I can see wanting to evoke some instant Americana by turning to the music of one of this country's greatest evokers of things American. If I had the chance I'd make a *Billy the Kid* movie based entirely around Copland's ballet on that subject. But, somehow, Horner needs to let his listeners know that this is the direction he is taking, rather than snatching one of Copland's loveliest inspirations and incorporating it as his own while giving no credit anywhere—not in the main titles, not even in the mass of names that always appear in the end titles these days. This, however, is only one of the many sins committed against the art of music in *The Perfect Storm*, and if there were such a thing as nominations for "worst original score," Horner's efforts would be right there at the top of my list. Frankly, I find it appalling that he has become something of the official house film-composer for Sony Classical. Oh yes: The End Titles are backed by a song, entitled "Yours Forever," by Horner, with lyrics by John Mellencamp, who also hoarsely sings it, and George Green. Guess whose *Appalachian Spring* figure gets incorporated right into the guitar intro. Guess what overbearing six-note motif also gets incorporated into the song. Guess who's going to run screaming to turn off his stereo . . . .

Looking over the filmography of Roman Polanski, I find that it is difficult to come up with an overall assessment of his checkered career as a film director. I would say that Polanski showed his best promise in the horror/suspense genre with the 1968 *Rosemary's Baby*. But then, going down the list, which includes a number of films made early on in Poland that few have ever seen, one cannot discount such films as *Knife in the Water* (1962), *Repulsion* (1965), *Macbeth* (1971, perhaps most notable for its casting of the sadly underused Jon Finch in the title role), *The Tenant* (1976, with Polanski himself playing a role right out of Kafka), *Tess* (1979, a widescreen Thomas Hardy adaptation that feels like Polanski only in its obsession with a beautiful, young woman), and *Death and the Maiden* (1994). And while I find myself in that vast minority of film buffs in not turning on to the 1974 *Chinatown*, the importance of that film cannot be denied. But there are also some outright disasters, starting with the remarkably unfunny *The Fearless Vampire Killers* in 1974. So, what to make of Polanski's latest effort, **The Ninth Gate**, an adaptation of *El Club Dumas* by Spanish novelist Arturo Pérez-Reverte. To be honest, I'm not sure. On the surface the narrative comes across as a deadly serious tale of attempts and counter attempts to invoke the powers of Satan by piecing together a coded message from nine engravings contained in three separate copies of a 16th-century book whose author was burned at the stake. The middleman in all of this is an unscrupulous rare book dealer named Dean Corso, played by Johnny Depp, an actor with a reputation for picking and choosing his roles. For all the implied doom and gloom, however, I found it all but impossible to get involved in, or even take seriously, any of the film's major events, even those in which some of the more gruesome scenes in the engravings are brought to life. One reason for this may be the performance of Depp, who, as is his wont these days, shows such a humorless lack of involvement in anything or anyone that I just didn't give the slightest tinker's dam what happens to him. Another reason is that Polanski, as is often his wont, not only keeps his distance throughout most of the film but also, as the ending nears, actually turns things in a lugubriously farcical direction, first with a black Mass, led by Lena Olin, that would fit comfortably, until it crumbles into shreds, into *Eyes Wide Shut*, then with the attempt to acquire Satan's powers by the character who comes closest of any in the film to being an archvillain (Frank Langella), who ends up barbecuing himself in the process. But what might be perceived as Polanski's weaknesses also add up, from another perspective, to strengths. The basic story of *The Ninth Gate* is in fact pretty trashy, and by inviting the viewer to concentrate on nonnarrative details, such as the way he shows the eyes of an important female character (Emmanuelle Seigner) early on in the film, the almost imperceptible floating of this same character into the action of several scenes, or the appearance that both exteriors and interiors take on in Darius Khondji's often-filtered color cinematography, Polanski turns the film into something other than your oft-told story of Satanism.

This applies right through to the ending, where Polanski, rather than spelling things out (although it's pretty obvious), coaxes, via a stunning and very artificial long shot, the viewer's imagination to pass on its own through that ninth gate. (The "User Comment" that appears at the end of the nonetheless indispensable Internet Movie Database's entry for *The Ninth Gate* actually considers as "negative" the fact "that the ending left something to the imagination." Go figure.)

The musical score by Wojciech Kilar for *The Ninth Gate* (Silva America; City of Prague Philharmonic and Chorus, Stepan Konicek, cond.) fits perfectly into this discussion. A veteran composer, born in Poland in 1932, with close to 150 scores to his credit, including Polanski's *Death and the Maiden*, Kilar, in his music for *The Ninth Gate*, not only had the nerve to try his hand at the creepy-crawly-morbid genre, he actually managed to bring it off, for reasons that, once again, I'm not sure I can explain. The strings-only main-title music, which backs a surreal piece of computer animation that makes the camera appear to zoom through a series of doors and gates (nine, I presume), starts off with some very low rumblings in the strings, and then moves into a very slow, very minor-mode theme that might best be described as a *valse morbide*, somewhat in the vein of Ron Goodwin's gloomy waltz-theme for Hitchcock's 1972 *Frenzy*, but heavier and just enough this side of stereotypical to be intriguing if not altogether moving, just like the film. In a different, although still minor-mode (almost every bar in the score is in the minor mode) and somewhat expected vein, the theme for Corso turns out to be an acidic but jaunty, slightly jazzy near-polka initially heard in two very different versions: the first plucks out the theme in midrange strings and harpsichord over a heavy one-two beat in the low strings, with a very loud trumpet supplying a fragmented theme; the second builds it up to a trio of bassoons playing in parallel chords, with the beat reduced to what sounds like a single double bass and solo piano, and a solo clarinet supplying the theme. It never occurred to me, as I watched the film, that those involved intended to associate this theme with the character of Corso; rather, I heard it more as a kind of transition music. But, as *The Ninth Gate* moves (slowly) forward, "Corso" gets quite a bit of play, most impressively in a bolero that makes up the "Plane to Spain" cue. And, if you listen closely, you'll hear a modification of this theme in the de rigueur low-male-chorus chanting in the black-Mass sequence ("Chateau Saint Martin"), which may give you something of a clue as to where the film is heading.

Yet another "theme" is the eerie music for Liana (Lena Olin), one of Corso's rivals in his quest. Here Kilar moves into instrumental upper registers as an obsessive four-note motif recalling the *Spellbound* suspense motif resonantly repeats over and over again and then undergoes slight metamorphoses, all of them maintaining the even, four-note structure, and all of them oft-repeated. Polanski's reduction of this music's volume to a very low level during the first meeting between Corso and Liana is typical of a facet of the director's style that keeps you forever craning your neck to see more or, in this case, straining your ears to hear more. In a number of the cues Kilar adds a vocalizing soprano (Sumi Jo) to the timbres, most notably in the "Vocalise" that opens and closes the music-track CD and that serves as the end-title music in the film. I have to say that the music here, in spite of the naïveté of some of the writing (such as the alternating minor/major chord figures at the opening), constantly sent chills down my spine in a manner very much à la Morricone, up to and including the doubling of parts of the soprano line in very high, unison violins. I should also note that, even though it's my job to listen to music in many of the films I see, I often get so caught up in the action that some of it escapes my notice. Such was not the case in *The Ninth Gate*. Every musical cue, some of which turn up at rather over-obvious points, somehow imposes its presence without seeming all that necessary to the action it backs; and if it puts your emotions in gear it is not so much vis-à-vis the action but rather because of the innate language of the musical style itself. As much, then, as I had major reservations about the film, and as much as I would not perhaps want to admit that I liked the music as much as I did, I have to say that I let myself get moved close to the point of obsession by Kilar's score. Again, go figure. I watched *The Ninth Gate*, by the way, on an Artisan Entertainment DVD, which looked and sounded stunning. In fact, so rich and clearly defined was the music track on the film, both in sound quality and in its directionality, that I worried that the CD would not live up to the DVD in this respect. I needn't have worried, as Silva America's CD is of demonstration-disc quality: the sound is as full, the various instruments as sharply defined, as any I have heard, and the CD definitely duplicates the very broad-range directionality of the DVD. Although the program booklet offers no notes, it does present the nine engravings that appear in the much-sought-after books of *The Ninth Gate's* narrative. Nothing is said about them, but I'm presuming they were created for the film, particularly since the nude maiden astride a seven-headed dragon in the last one has a strong resemblance to actress Seigner.

There's an old routine by satirist Stan Freberg called "St George and the Dragonet," a takeoff on the radio (and later TV) show *Dragnet* and its all too predictable formulas. When Sergeant Joe Friday, a.k.a. St. George, finally arrests the dragon, he nails him on the charge of devouring maidens out of season. The dragon screams at the top of his lungs something to the effect of "You'll never pin that charge on me, copper!" "We're also booking you on an 805 [or whatever number]," replies Friday/St. George calmly. The dragon screams even more loudly: "An 805! WHAT'S AN 805?!" "Overacting." Well, they should have booked the entire cast of **Beneath the Planet of the Apes** on an 805 (or whatever). Or maybe they should have booked screenwriter Paul Dehn for excessively ludicrous dialogue. I mean, even behind their ape masks such otherwise respectable actors as Maurice Evans, Kim Hunter, and James Gregory deliver their lines with such exaggerated pompousness that you could swear they're mugging at the camera. James Franciscus, as one of the only two human beings you see for much of the picture, simply seems incapable of taking his lines seriously, and whatever efforts he makes are not helped much by such obvious editing that you are always waiting for that cut to make his lines extra significant. Linda Harrison, whose only function in the film is to provide a satisfying object for the gaze (and, I have to say, she does that quite admirably), doesn't even speak a word; yet every time the film cuts to a reaction shot from her (that's all she does: react) she has exactly the same wide-eyed expression of fear and bewilderment. And, lest we forget, there's that master scenery chewer, Charlton Heston, who, although absent from most of the film, makes up for all the lost time with a vengeance when, in the film's final sequences, he turns in a faux-tragic performance that would make even the hammiest of Lears seem understated. The less said about the mutants—former humans living in the remnants of New York City and worshipping an alpha/omega (doomsday) atom bomb in the remains of St. Patrick's Cathedral—the better. All of which is a shame, since, moving forward—quite logically, I have to say—from the original concept by French novelist Pierre Boulle (who also wrote *The Bridge on the River Kwai*), this 1970 sequel to the wildly successful *Planet of the Apes* had the potential to become one of the wickedest comments ever on modern culture's obsession with death as salvation from both materiality and animality.

Beneath the Planet of the Apes also proves to be an unfortunately flimsy vehicle for one of the boldest film scores ever penned for a mainstream Hollywood film, this after a stunningly and, yes, boldly original score from Jerry Goldsmith for the 1968 first installment. Not surprisingly, then, *Beneath's* score—stridently nontonal (not serial) and for the most part arrhythmic—comes from the pen of Leonard Rosenman, who had already broken Hollywood ground in such equally unworthy vehicles as the 1955 *The Cobweb* and the 1966 *Fantastic Voyage* (but you should not miss the stunning film/music collaboration of the 1960 *The Savage Eye*, in which Rosenman's very modernistic chamber score provides a running, quite acidic commentary on this black-and-white movie that began as a documentary of life in and around L.A. and ended up as a part moralistic, part brutally ironic, part movingly real narrative film). Also not surprisingly, Rosenman's original score never made it to recording at the time, instead appearing in a highly reworked, somewhat less jarring, half-hour rerecording on an LP that, woe of woes, insultingly features substantial bits of dialogue from the film. That situation has finally been remedied by Film Score Monthly in its "Silver Age Classics" series, which features Rosenman's entire original score, along with the rerecording on Amos Records brought out around the time of the film's release, and a couple of "bonus tracks." Rosenman's music is so relentlessly dissonant and depends so heavily on sharply contrasting fragments batted back and forth between the instrumental choirs at various pitch levels (also sharply contrasting) that it would be difficult to describe what is going on musically without becoming overly technical. Unlike Goldsmith, who deployed a vast battery of exotic percussion instruments, including aluminum mixing bowls, in his music for *Planet of the Apes*, Rosenman uses mostly the conventional instruments of the standard symphony orchestra, minus strings except for harp and piano (and, just perhaps, some double basses), unless my ears or the recorded sound very much deceive me (and in spite of the information given in the program notes). Rosenman did add strings to the rerecording, no doubt to restore some warmth to the timbres for the average listener.

On the original music track, Rosenman constantly creates musical shards that build up to extremely dissonant chords and then fall apart again into scattered timbres, with woodwinds, brass (often muted), and a large battery of percussion instruments (including vibraphone, bells, timpani, side drums, and a host of others) vying for the extremely dislocated musical space. Also unlike Goldsmith, whose characteristic motor rhythms dominate many of the *Planet of the Apes* cues, Rosenman generally avoids staying in a regular meter for more than several measures at a time, save in several action sequences, most notably the near-toccata in "Narrow Escape" (and even here the meter does not remain constant), the much more violent music that concludes "Second Escape," and the fast, grim march of "Off to War." Once in a while Rosenman relaxes into moody chordal patterns that border on the tonal. And at quite a number of points throughout the score the composer slips in that musical "pyramid" of quickly rising open intervals that he definitely uses as a signature in just about all of his work for the cinema. For the most part, however, even the quietest moments in the music have that distinctively atonal quality to them; just how systematic this is, and just how thoroughly Rosenman has interrelated the various cues, would require substantial study of both the written music and the film. But I suspect a level of sophistication here that goes solidly beyond the impression provided by one or two listenings or one or two viewings (if you can stand to sit through the film more than once). The sound quality on FSM's CD is decent enough, and well defined stereophonically, although it would be nice to hear an audiophile recording of Rosenman's painstakingly crafted score. All in all, a musical effort so stunningly forward-looking that one can only sit back in amazement that it ever got past the studio bosses' desks, and one can also only muse longingly at what might have happened had Rosenman ever teamed up consistently with a filmmaker with even half the vision of a Hitchcock or a Claude Chabrol (Chabrol's early collaborator, Pierre Jansen, often worked in much the same territory, although in a less assertive way, as Rosenman).

CHAPTER EIGHTEEN

~

2001

January/February

Once in a while I manage to miss the theatrical engagement of an important film I know I should see, and I have to wait for the film to turn up on video. Then the film shows up on video—in this case a gorgeous DVD from New Line Home Video that includes a whole second DVD of supplemental material—and I'm so busy that it takes me a month or so to get to watching it. Sometimes the film turns out to have been well worth the wait. Sometimes the score does as well. Such was the case, to a degree, with Roman Polanski's *The Ninth Gate* (both the music and the film). Such is even more the case with director/writer Paul Thomas (P. T.) Anderson's **Magnolia**, which features original songs by Aimee Mann, who won an Oscar nomination for one of them, and an original score by Jon Brion (Reprise; Thomas Pasatieri, cond.), who should have won an Oscar nomination. But I'll get back to that in a moment. I'm not sure how one should follow the trajectory from Anderson's 1996 *Hard Eight* (a.k.a. *Sydney*), a fairly simple, average-length psychological thriller, through his 1997 *Boogie Nights*, a more flamboyant, quite a bit longer and more complex, and rather unreadable take on the 1970s porno industry, up to *Magnolia*, a very long (it runs three hours and eight minutes), very complex interweaving of related and unrelated narrative threads and the very diverse characters involved in them that, even more than *Boogie Nights*, all but defies categorization. Indeed, if I had to come up with a box within which *Magnolia* could uncomfortably be squeezed, I would simply use the name of director Robert Altman, for it is Altman who pretty much owns the patent on the multi-character/multi-story film in which a quasi contrapuntal elaboration of character and situation becomes infinitely more the point than any particular narrative situation devised by the director and his writers.

But *Magnolia* moves on other planes as well. Where Altman generally maintains something of an ironic, even, at times, existential, detachment from his characters and his narratives that I have always liked, Anderson doesn't flinch at depicting the angst caused by the Mamet-like traps his characters have either created for themselves or had created for them, nor does he pull back from the occasional flood of affect unleashed when his characters—some, not all—confront their traps head on. Anderson also has something of a Peter Greenaway tendency to throw in elements implying some type of coded meaning that the film seems to invite us to crack without giving much help. These dements can appear either trivial, such as the frequent appearance of the number 82, or cataclysmic, such as the film's much-talked-about climactic event, the details of which I will not reveal in deference to those who have not seen the film (not that it would make that much difference). In the end run, however, Anderson's mobile network of interwoven characters and narrative situations takes on a rhythm and depth that make Magnolia, quite rewardingly, unlike any other film I've ever seen. Thus, to pick an arbitrary starting point, a wildly successful self-help pitch-man (Tom Cruise) with an evangelical misogyny is called to meet his dying father (Jason Robards, Jr.) who had abandoned him as an adolescent and whose youngish and hysterical second wife (Julianne Moore) crosses the path of a black kid from the ghetto whose path has earlier crossed with that of a sensitive, rather philosophical police officer (Anderson regular John C. Reilly) whose path has also crossed with that of a particularly hysterical woman (Melora Walters) with a serious coke addiction and a serious aversion to her abusive father (Philip Baker Hall, another Anderson regular) who is the MC of a quiz program that pits adults against kids, in particular a young genius (Jeremy Blackman) who has to deal with his abusive father (Michael Bowen), and that is on the TV screen at a bar where a former Quiz Kid (William H. Macy) is trying to hustle money from a pompous, gray-haired man played by Altman regular Henry Gibson . . . . Even when some paths don't cross, the characters and situations also interact thematically and across time, expanding to all but infinite proportions the question of coincidence posed at the outset by the film's narrator [Ricky Jay, who also has a small role in the film]. The similarities between two separate sexual encounters by two separate couples seen near the film's opening also shed some light, miles in advance, on one of Magnolia's major enigmas.

With complexities this far-reaching, one would certainly not expect Magnolia to have enclosed its music within the conventional movie-score confines. The music generally associated with Magnolia can be found on another Reprise CD that features not just the eight original songs, all of which are soulful and reach quite deep, composed by Aimee Mann for the film but several other pop numbers as well, including Mann's performance, which I found stunning, although other critics haven't, of Harry Nilsson's "One," which opens the film. But, not surprisingly, there is a whole other side to the music, a string-heavy, extraordinarily moody instrumental score penned by Jon Brion, a singer/songwriter, session artist, and composer who also produced some of the songs on the Mann CD and did some of her arrangements. Even here, however, one of the main points, besides the excellence of Brion's score, lies in the way director Anderson has incorporated the score into the film. Magnolia opens, as I mentioned, with Mann's rendition of "One." And, behind the opening, black-and-white setup, one also hears some brief "odd pieces of musical business," as the end-titles put it, put together by Brion and colleague Fiona Apple, including a barely recognizable snippet from a waltz theme that will turn up much later in the film. After that, *Magnolia* remains devoid of anything resembling a background score for almost 40 minutes. Then, emerging seemingly out of the blue behind a segue from John C. Reilly leaving the ghetto to a shot showing Jeremy Blackman poring through dozens of different books in a library, we hear, in a cue entitled "A Little Library Music," a very drawn-out, very mournful, very minor-mode passage played mostly in the midrange and low midrange strings, supplemented by a few wind timbres. This gives way to a cue ("Going to a Show") that seems more inspired by the onscreen movement, highlighted by long, fast tracking shots in a TV studio-turned-labyrinth, than by the narrative action. Again in the minor mode, the cue might best be described as an Allegretto and as jaunty, save that it mitigates only slightly the aura of gloom that hangs over "A Little Library Music" as it moves obsessively forward above an evenly paced, near-ostinato figure in the bass in which bassoon timbres play a key role. The ensuing "Showtime" picks up immediately where "Going to a Show" leaves off, taking the Allegretto theme through all sorts of phases, from a reduction to a small group of winds to a full, tutti assertion of it. Brief departures back into the pure mournfulness of the "Library" music break up the otherwise almost balletic movement of this cue, which runs for over 10 minutes on the CD. But that doesn't tell the whole story, because, in the film, once Brion's score starts, it becomes almost another character in the film, continuing almost nonstop for nearly a half hour behind wildly differing scenes, including a painfully uncomfortable interview of the Tom Cruise character by a black woman journalist, with only a few interruptions necessitated by source music. At one particularly virtuoso moment the sound from the TV show and the Allegretto theme form a rather bizarre counterpoint that indiscriminately creates a continuous aural flow behind several different scenes with many different characters. It all comes to an end, appropriately enough, when the quiz-show moderator announces "End of Round 1." Turning to *Magnolia*'s "other" score, there is one point, late in the film, when a number of the various characters in their separate scenes join in with the unseen Mann in singing the lyrics to her song "Wise Up." All in all *Magnolia* offers some of the most original interweavings of sound, music, visuals, and narrative action I have ever witnessed in a commercial film.

But that's not all. Brion's music moves in other directions as well, including into high, elegiac, quasi-*Parsifal* strings in two different cues that back the "breakdowns" of various characters. In the second of these two cues, the long (11 minutes on the CD) "Stanley/Frank/Linda's Breakdown," the music eventually migrates back to the Allegretto theme, this time, however, set, forever in the minor mode, to the pace of a lugubrious, slow waltz that, at its most dramatic moments, evokes a bit of Prokofiev. And into the last of the slow, mournful cues ("Chance of Rain") Brion introduces a mildly dissonant, three-note motif that will eventually return, as the "Magnolia" theme, in the sad, slow, wistful end-title music. But for Magnolia's pre-end-title epilogue, which is entitled "So Now Then'" both as a title card in the film and in the score, Brion comes up with a surprising change of pace in more folk-like music, complete with non-vibrating vibes and steel (I think) guitar, that, if not entirely happy, at least suggests that, following the film's various apocalypses, life can now move forward. I suspect that one of director Anderson's primary goals was to get Brion to extend to near infinity the kind of deep, penetrating mood created at numerous points in numerous film scores, but only ephemerally. Bernard Herrmann, of course, was a master at mood extension. But Brion has ingeniously managed to out-Herrmann Herrmann in this area without even coming close to mimicking, quoting, or pastiche. And, here, I can't resist quoting Anderson in his program note for the CD: "The process for creating the score for this movie was, I'm told, unique. Jon and I would watch a monitor and I would move my hands as an indication of the mood required. Jon would sit at the keyboard and let his eyes dart from the monitor to my body language and let his hands play. Essentially, Jon would play to what my hands were trying to say musically. He would watch my face grimace and he would play that. Any face that you can make, Jon can translate musically." The sound on this Reprise CD is amazingly full-bodied, resonant, and rich: just about as good as I can imagine it getting. Oh yes: the music-track CD also offers a very brief, very catchy, big-band intro, in the manner of the *Tonight* show theme under Johnny Carson, for the quiz program.

If you are at all involved in non-mainstream films the name of Copenhagen-born (in 1956) Lars von Trier will be familiar to you, not just as the director of such films as *Europa* (1991, a.k.a. *Zentropa*), *Breaking the Waves* (1996), and *The Idiots* (1998), but also as the cofounder, with fellow Danish filmmaker Thomas Vinterberg, of a cinema movement known as Dogma, a.k.a. Dogme 95, which has as its point of departure the view that such '60s movements as the French New Wave did not really liberate the cinema at all but rather, with their auteurist orientation and heavy reliance on the standard filmmaking processes, further contributed to the bourgeoisification of an already heavily bourgeois art form. Believe it or not, Dogma not only has a Manifesto (which can be accessed on the Web at www.dogme95.dk) but also—are you ready for this?—a "Vow of Chastity" that spells out a series of rules that, if followed, would help lead to the democratization of the cinema—and allow the filmmaker(s) a listing on the ranks of Dogma movies. These rules include such stipulations as the necessity of location shooting, of sound and music miked live rather than laid in after the shoot by Foley artists and the like, of hand-held cameras, of color photography, etc., up to and including a proviso that "The director must not be credited," which is interesting, considering the fact that the 16 movies listed as Dogma films all include a director credit. All wisecracking aside, however, Dogma represents an important and in many ways fruitful reaction against the stultifying effect that all those mega-budget, purely formulaic Hollywood productions have had upon the art of the film. And there is also no question that huge advancements in technology, such as the Digicam (used by Mike Figgis in making *Time Code*), have allowed some to escape from beneath the crushing weight of the commercial film industry. With all that in mind, it is interesting that what is probably von Trier's most widely seen and perhaps most controversial film to date, **Dancer in the Dark,** breaks just about every one of

Dogma's tenets: although it takes place near Seattle, Washington, it was filmed mostly in Sweden and Denmark, as von Trier refuses to fly; it is shot, or at least printed, in a widescreen (2.35:1) aspect ratio rather than the so-called Academy ratio insisted upon by Dogma's "Vow of Chastity"; it features two violent deaths; etc. On the other hand, there is enough hand-held camera movement to have sent my wife running from the theater with a violent headache after only 10 minutes.

Almost everything written about *Dancer in the Dark*, a melodrama/tragedy straight out of silent film (save that it is also a musical), starts the same way: it is a movie that will provoke violent reactions both for and against. Yet many reviewers have maintained a position squarely on top of the fence, both loving the movie and hating themselves for loving it. My position, with one exception that I will discuss anon, is by and large positive. I may hate myself for letting my emotions get swept away by the film's unabashedly manipulative plot device: a sweetly innocent Czech immigrant named Selma, played by Icelandic songstress/composer Björk, works in a factory in rural Washington state in 1964. Due to a congenital illness she is rapidly going blind; but, in spite of her handicap, she works at two menial jobs to put money away for an operation on her rebellious teenage son (Vladan Kostic), who likewise suffers from the unspecified disease, before it is too late. Selma is surrounded by people who, for the most part, want nothing but the best for her, most particularly an enigmatic factory coworker played by Catherine Deneuve in one of her most understatedly moving portrayals. All to no avail: as Hamlet says, "It is not, nor it cannot come to good," and indeed it doesn't (although not entirely), but not before your emotions have been torn asunder 20 ways to Sunday. I may also hate myself for letting myself be swayed by the blatantly black-and-white politics of von Trier, who also wrote the screenplay, and whose attacks on the American way of life are as heavily weighted and thoroughly manipulative as the melodramatic narrative. Yet there is also more than a shred of truth in the film's depiction of a legal system that works against the poor on every level, and one need look no further than the state of Texas for a least a partial validation of von Trier's politics. Whatever: the bottom line is that *Dancer in the Dark* sucked my viscera straight into the film, thanks not only to von Trier's direction and scripting but also to a once-in-a-lifetime performance by Björk. According to those who were there, including Deneuve, Björk did not simply play Selma, she was Selma, so totally immersing herself in the role that she was left in a state of total exhaustion, a state exacerbated by bitter struggles with director von Trier over the music she composed for *Dancer in the Dark*, which ended up winning the Palme d'Or for Best Film and, for Björk, the Best Actress award at this year's Cannes Film Festival, much to the displeasure of many.

And it is Björk's music, of which I have been a major fan ever since I listened to "Venus as a Boy," that adds another entire dimension to the film. As it turns out, Selma's major escape from the utter dreariness of her life comes via fantasies built around Hollywood musicals. We first see her rehearsing, in a reasonably inept fashion, the role of Maria for a local production of *The Sound of Music*. But Selma's greatest successes come, of course, not in real life but in song-and-dance routines spontaneously created in her mind in the most unlikely situations—work centered around metal-stamping machines at the factory; walking home across the railroad bridge accompanied both by a lovable but dim-witted would-be boyfriend (Peter Stormare) and by a passing train; a courtroom scene; and, most crushingly, in the song entitled "107 Steps" . . . well, I won't reveal the particular context for that song. According to von Trier, these numbers were simultaneously shot with 100 separate Digicams, a figure that most writers, including me, have a hard time swallowing. There is no question, however, that the musical numbers, choreographed by Vincent Paterson (*Evita*, *The Birdcage*), have a much more colorful, much more heavily edited look to them than the rest of the film. Even here, however, these song-and-dance routines, performed mostly by actors and actresses who are neither singers nor dancers, have a no-doubt desired amateurish quality to them that certainly contributes to reading the film as an anti-musical, as does Selma's line that "Nothing dreadful ever happens in a musical," since in fact several dreadful things do occur in *Dancer in the Dark*. And in "107 Steps" von Trier takes his anti-musical so far into the blackness that there is no way you could figure it would work. Somehow it does. Far from amateurish, however, is the quality of Björk's songs and her performance of them, most which can be heard on a CD entitled, very much in line with the little-girl persona Björk often projects, *Selmasongs* (Elektra; Vincent Mendoza, cond.). The Elektra CD does not make it clear whether the songs (and Overture) are taken from the original music tracks or were rerecorded. My guess is the latter since, for instance, the male voice in "I've Seen It All" is attributed to Thom Yorke, who, in fact, sings much more solidly on key than I remember Peter Stormare performing it in the film.

No matter. The songs as heard on the Elektra CD immediately communicate the moods and atmosphere of *Dancer in the Dark*, and they instantly identify themselves as Björk, first and foremost by her extraordinary voice, which can go from silence to an extreme high note, perfectly on pitch, without taking a running start. Many opera singers could not do as well. Björk's characteristic start-stop phrases, and the often hypnotic instrumental accompaniments (orchestrated and sometimes arranged by Vincent Mendoza), into which bell-like figures are frequently introduced, likewise could come from nobody else. The sound is unique, whether in the sometimes strange, whole-tone phrases of "Ovalda," which opens with a rhythmed chorus of factory sounds (talk about Techno!), in the more romantic duet of "I've Seen It All," with its hints of train rhythms, or the more heroic motifs of "New World." Strangely missing from this recording is the musical number that takes place in the courtroom, paradoxically the most polished of the film's routines, among other reasons because it also includes Joel Grey as a former star of Czech musicals whom Selma has (tragically) claimed as her father. For *Dancer in the Dark* Björk also composed an instrumental Overture accompanied, on American prints of the film at the insistence of the distributor (New Line), by an overlapping series of abstract paintings by Pers Kirkeby. Based on the main theme of "New World," and arranged and orchestrated by Mendoza, the Overture comes just a tad too close to James Horner for my taste, although it certainly creates a mood.

To return for a moment to the film itself, the reservation I mentioned above has been succinctly expressed by Jonathan Rosenbaum in a review that appeared in *The Chicago Reader*: "The movie's not so much about [Selma's] modesty and compliance—the stupid grin with which she greets virtually every misfortune—as it is about von Trier's appreciation of her passive suffering (not quite the same thing as respect or understanding), which ultimately becomes an exaltation of his own feeling rather than hers." The movie, not only in the character of Selma but also in the character of a neighbor's wife whose greed sets the whole tragedy in motion, also flirts much too closely with the saint/whore dialectic that is one of the principal ways in which the very (male) establishment von Trier seems to oppose strips women of their identity. For all of this, and for all of the film's stylistic incongruities—or, as the journalistic cliché will always have it, perhaps because of them—*Dancer in the Dark* leaves the world of contemporary commercial cinema through the front door and sneaks back in through the back door via the no-longer-well-trodden paths of silent-film melodrama, and in the process has somehow allowed many viewers, including me, access to that creaky roller coaster of affect that only a battle of good versus evil from the good ol' days can provide.

A movie that initially looked as if it was going to take off more than it did this past summer was **The Cell**, a first-time feature from music-video director Tarsem Singh and writer Mark Protosevich. Starring Jennifer Lopez, Vince Vaughn, Vincent D'Onofrio, Marianne Jean-Baptiste, and a team of over 40 visual-effects artists of different sorts, *The Cell* presents itself as a serial-killer film, with the title referring to an automated, glass-enclosed "cell" that, upon a remote cue, fills with water until it drowns its abducted victim (a woman, of course) while her agony is recorded by video cameras. The film's facile plot device revolves around how to rescue the latest victim from the hidden site before the water starts, given the fact that the killer (D'Onofrio, the classic serial-killer mesomorph with stringy blond hair) has fallen into a coma just before his arrest. And it's here that *The Cell* takes off into some pretty fascinating territory—not in the narrative, but visually and musically. The Jennifer Lopez character, you see, is a young social worker with a particular aptitude for wending her way through the labyrinths created by a sophisticated device that allows her to enter the mind—mindscape would be a better word—of one of her patients, a young boy (Colton James) who has been in a coma and whom she calls Mister E (as in mystery?). Thus, the opening sequence takes place in the spectacular vista of the boy's mindscape of frozen waves of immense sand dunes rendered otherworldly by various colored filters, and surreal by the isolated presence of such objects as a horse frozen in motion or the wreck of a boat. It will come as no surprise to those accustomed to this kind of story that Lopez's services are engaged by an FBI agent (Vaughn), who gets her to enter the mind(scape) of the comatose serial killer, a considerably more disturbing and dangerous place than the young boy's. It is a phantasmagorically colored netherworld filled with imposing sets (a massive staircase built into an equally massive wall), grotesque tableaux that suggest the killer's obsession with turning his victims' bodies into possessable dolls, and one of the eeriest and coldest images of stylized violence (think sectioned horse) I have ever seen on film. While the plotline creeps into these sequences—Lopez does some pretty impressive inner-child work while she wanders through the past and present corners of the killer's mindscape—and while all does not come off without some major, rather gruesome hitches and some nail-biting suspense (if it did, of course, we wouldn't have a film), my initial impression, after watching a theatrical screening of *The Cell*, was that the serial-killer narrative was little more than a flimsy excuse to create a context for allowing the immensely fertile visual imaginations at work here to have a field day in four major sequences with almost no dialogue. A second viewing (on a widescreen VHS dub from New Line, which distributes the film), however, has somewhat altered that view, as the serial-killer narrative and the mindscape excursions intermesh so thoroughly that one comes to sense a quasi-musical development of *The Cell*'s visual and narrative themes—suspended bodies, immersion in water, horses, etc.

A major element in *The Cell*'s overall effect (and affect) is the musical score by Howard Shore (New Line; Bachir Attar and The Master Musicians of Jajouka; London Philharmonic Orchestra), whose soundscapes sometimes startle, sometimes take the breath away (occasionally both at the same time) in often complex masses of sound that move on planes parallel to, if not always in sync with, the film's stunning mindscapes. One of the first things that strikes the listener in the cue ("The Cell") that accompanies the film's opening sequence is the distinctive timbres, rhythms, and harmonies of Middle Eastern music as provided by The Master Musicians of Jajouka, two of whose compositions, "El Medahey" and "Memories of My Father," also blend in with the sometimes strident, sometimes quietly ominous strains of Shore's original music. Described by Shore in his brief program note as "a special caste, living in the foothills of the Rif mountains of Morocco . . . , [who] are the spiritualists and . . . bear the mark of the conjurer," The Master Musicians were introduced to the composer by jazzman Ornette Coleman's "Midnight Sunrise." I find this particularly significant, since Shore to an extent does with The Master Musicians in *The Cell* what he does with Ornette Coleman's playing in his score for David Cronenberg's 1991 *Naked Lunch*, which is to say that, throughout the score, he often weaves his own music around The Master Musicians' performances, bringing in a low-brass motif here, underlying it with an electronic drone there, etc. In other cues where Shore's often ultramodern, Western-classical style predominates, the composer nonetheless introduces some of The Master Musicians' native instruments, particularly the percussion, into the proceedings. Now, even though one can find the slightest of narrative justifications for this music in the film's sand-dune mindscape (and at one point dreamscape), by and large there is no more narrative tie-in between the Moroccan music and the film than there is in Mychael Danna's score for 8MM. One senses in Shore, as in Danna, a willingness to allow his creative spirit to speak with the voices of non-Western idioms used as a musical language in and of themselves rather than to create narrative-based associations (when you think about it, not a single Korngold-scored film takes place in 19th-century Vienna).

One could of course propose that the "exotic" country suggested by the Moroccan strains in the score for *The Cell* is none other than that of the mind, and, in fact, this works up to a point, but not entirely in this film where there is nothing cut and dried about crossing over from the outside to the inside—and vice versa. Even the rhythmic clapping heard in parts of the non-mindscape, climactic cue entitled "The Drowning" suggests some sort of frenzied, non-Western dance of death. Elsewhere Shore has produced one of his most complex and modernistic scores. Massive upheavals of string sound and snarling brass on occasion not inappropriately recall moments in John Corigliano's music for Ken Russell's 1980 *Altered States*. At other points the score hushes down to that mournful alternation of chords that typifies a certain latitude on the map of Shore's own mindscape. Driving motor-rhythms generated out of heavy drumbeats create moments of heavy drama in several of the cues, including "The Drowning." Fine Line's music-track recording also allows us to hear details of the score that get swallowed up in the often-formidable sound effects that accompany them in the film. In the "Tide Pool" cue, for instance, Shore inserts, on a whiny electronic instrument that remains all but inaudible in the film, that silly staple "Mairzy Doats," which the killer has been singing in his bathtub just prior to falling into a coma. All in all, the 19 cues from the original score heard on this CD form, just as the film's disparate threads do, an interwoven whole in which any attempt to establish one-for-one, unidimensional relationships to the filmic action is really beside the point. Indeed, don't look for the titles of the various cues, some of which appear in a different order from in the film, to be of much help. *The Cell* marks a major step in the musical evolution of a composer who has never been willing to rest on his not inconsiderable laurels.

The prospect of seeing **The Way of the Gun** had me reasonably excited, as it was written and directed by Christopher McQuarrie, who came up with (and won an Oscar for) the brilliant screenplay for director Bryan Singer's *The Usual Suspects*, which I consider one of the best new-noir thrillers in years. Well, one of the elements I most liked about *The Usual Suspects* was its subtlety. *The Way of the Gun* opens with a general brawl accompanied by an extremely loud rock song on the music track, although it also features an unexpectedly droll car chase in which slow, not fast, speed and alleyways provide the getaway. *The Usual Suspects* ingeniously piles enigma upon enigma; *The Way of the Gun* has its questions that remain unanswered after one viewing, but they tend to stay surface deep rather than tied in to the very substance of the film. But, like *The Usual Suspects*, *The Way of the Gun* gets a lot of mileage out of juxtaposing disparate blocks of characters out of whose often-accidental crossings of paths the narrative conflicts grow and multiply almost ad infinitum. French Freudian/philosopher/analyst Jacques Lacan, with his "signifying chains," would have had a field day with McQuarrie's plotlines. Many critics have evoked the names of Quentin Tarantino and the Coen brothers in writing about *The Way of the Gun*. But perhaps the major figure that casts his shadow upon the overall feel of *The Way of the Gun* is the late Italian director Sergio Leone. As in Leone's "spaghetti Westerns," the early two or three in particular, the question in *The Way of the Gun*, which is set in New and old Mexico, is not who are the good guys and who are the bad guys. No. It's who are the lowest of the low on a pecking order made up of nothing (with perhaps one or two dubious exceptions) but scoundrels, to put it politely.

But *The Way of the Gun*'s petty hoods (Ryan Phillippe and Benicio Del Toro), who go by Butch Cassidy and the Sundance Kid's surnames, Parker and Longbaugh, end up making the Clint Eastwood roles in the early Leone films look like Roy Rogers, and therein, perhaps, lies my chief problem with this nonetheless well-made film. Phillippe and Del Toro initially come across as a couple of wisecracking, fatalistic losers who have simply made crime—the way of the gun—their chosen profession. But as the film moves into its main story line, which has the pair kidnapping a very pregnant surrogate mother (Juliette Lewis), these same characters who have at least partially engaged our anti-establishment, Butch-and-Sundance sympathies turn out to be conscienceless thugs who would emotionlessly torture their own mothers to get what they wanted. The fact that this double read, rather ingeniously maintained throughout the film, is characteristic of McQuarrie's style doesn't help much, and, by the time the film reaches its long, climactic shootout in a Mexican bordello, one begins to wonder whether there's much more involved here than a particularly ugly brand of violence. Another major element in McQuarrie's double read, by the way, comes by way of an "adjudicator," sent after Butch 'n Sundance for fairly unclear reasons by the wealthy mobster who is paying Juliette Lewis for her baby, played by James Caan as a likewise fatalistic, somewhat more philosophical enforcer whose stiff-necked movements are apparently the result of an old gun wound. And if *The Way of the Gun* had maintained throughout the level of crushing irony contained in its last line, spoken by a character who maybe has two or three other lines in the entire film, it might have moved one or two steps closer to being a class act.

Ah, but there is another element in *The Way of the Gun* that had me pretty much bowled over throughout the film, and that is its score by Joe Kraemer, about whom I know absolutely nothing, other than that he's probably Seattle-based (Milan; performed by SeattleMusic). In his relatively extensive and most welcome program note, composer Kraemer drolly opens by listing the four rules he and director/writer McQuarrie set up at the outset: a) no guitar; b) no songs; c) no big orchestra; d) minimal spotting of music. After a particularly long period of gestation and frustration, however, composer and director ended up breaking all four of those rules, although not quite, perhaps, to the extent that Kraemer suggests. Yes, he ended up scoring for a full orchestra with some minimal electronics. But he really doesn't mobilize all of his forces as an ensemble until the rather slick bringing-together of the music's five or six principal elements in the first third of the end-title music. Elsewhere, Kraemer quite effectively sustains a good deal of interest in the score's minimal basic materials—not a real theme in sight, but a handful of haunting motifs, all of them minor-mode, and most of them no more than five or six notes long—by modifying in a reduced-instrument context the timbres involved in the numerous permutations and combinations of the basic materials. (Unlike many composers who get hung up not just in the minor mode but in the same key throughout the score, Kraemer tends to vary the key from cue to cue, which may have a basically subliminal effect when you watch the film but which definitely enhances the pure listening experience.) And, yes, there are songs, but only three (not heard on the Milan CD), plus Kraemer's own, sometimes neo-Spike Jones "How to Make a Margarita," offered at the end of the Milan CD and heard, in the film, as convenience-store music. But, yes, the guitar certainly is a prominent instrument in the score, right from the outset, where a quickly strummed, dissonant chord enters into a long, antiphonal dialog with a loud, slightly over-the-top figure from the timpani, an absolutely perfect way to set the mood for *The Way of the Gun*. Castanets also play a prominent role here and there, biting even more strongly into the composer and director's initial desire not to be too "on-the-nose" with the neo-Western thing. And, yes, the director ended up spotting quite a lot of music into various moments of the film—over an hour's worth. But from where I sit, that definitely works to *The Way of the Gun*'s advantage while also further contributing to that double read. The Milan CD, by the way, is in the HDCD mode, and it sounded spectacular on my minor venues (car stereo, computer CD-player with some pretty nice Boston speakers), just a bit over-recorded but still mightily expansive on my stereo system, whose CD-player (a Classé 1.5) has the HDCD chip.

OK, I'll admit it: I'm ecstatic to have Varèse Sarabande's new recording, with Joel McNeely conducting the Royal Scottish National Orchestra, of Bernard Herrmann's score for Alfred Hitchcock's 1964 **Marnie**. Even at one's most cynical, it is difficult to explain how it has come to be that, of the seven (discounting whatever Herrmann's contributions were to the electronic soundscape of *The Birds* and his discarded score for *Torn Curtain*) Hitchcock/Herrmann collaborations, only one—*Vertigo*—saw an "original soundtrack" recording released around the time the film came out, and only one other—*North by Northwest*—has legally seen the light of day, and that only recently, since the film's release. I say "legally" because, some time after *Marnie* hit the theaters, a pirate label that called itself Sound/Stage Recordings brought out a bootleg LP of the original music tracks (which the label dubbed a "symphonic poem") printed, in honor of the filmic symbol of the eponymous heroine's apparent psychosis, on transparent red vinyl. If I am not mistaken, the availability of that same recording on a pirate CD has soured the sources that could bring the original tracks out legally on so doing. So it is particularly good to have a CD of what appears to be all the cues, some of them lasting under a minute, that Herrmann composed for Hitchcock's underrated psychological mystery. I am also grateful to the CD for having gotten my mental juices flowing full tilt on a Hitchcock/Herrmann collaboration that I have tended to neglect in the past. In some ways, Herrmann's work for *Marnie* is quite different from his other work, both for Hitchcock and for other directors. For starters, what can be considered as *Marnie*'s main theme is actually a pretty extended (for Herrmann) melody rather than a series of sequenced modulations of a four-note phrase. One reason for this is undoubtedly the pressure that Universal was putting on Hitchcock to get his composer to come up with more marketable scores. I have another suggestion, to which I'll return in a moment.

But, listening to the main-title cue and the various manifestations of its several segments throughout the score, I became aware of something much more significant going on. Like the 1945 *Spellbound*, *Marnie* has as one of its central themes a psycho-analytical cliché, in this instance that the thievery of a kleptomaniac (Marnie, played by Tippi Hedren in a performance that has never gotten the credit it deserves) is actually the stealing of love that the individual in question never received as a child (in this case from her mother, stunningly played by Louise Latham). Hitchcock in fact offers, in *Marnie*, a deconstruction of that cliché. This is immediately apparent in the way the director and his various screenwriters, ending with Jay Presson Allen, a woman, changed the substance of the final revelation in the original novel, a first-person narrative written by a male author, Winston Graham, from a woman's point of view. In the Hitchcock film, unlike in the novel, Marnie's trauma goes back to a direct instance of child abuse by a man (played by Bruce Dern in the flashback), and her subsequent adult career as a thief involves not, psychologically speaking, stealing love but rather, politically speaking, reclaiming her identity as a woman from the male establishment, as represented first and foremost, as in *Psycho*, by money. Significantly, Herrmann's title music has three distinct phases. What serves as an introduction, a chaotic upheaval of strings, brass, and winds with at least three separable motifs, becomes the music that signals those moments in the film when Marnie gets too close to her repressed memories, triggered by the color red. The sweeping, romantic music that follows could easily be seen as the theme for Marnie herself. I would suggest, however, that the Marnie suggested by this theme is the one that the male gaze, including that of the camera itself, attempts to possess. The first time the theme appears in the film proper, for instance, is when a faceless brunette emerges from the water of a hair rinse reincarnated as the classic Hitchcock blonde. On the other hand, the third phase of the title music offers a brief, sequentially repeated motif set to a gallop rhythm, which seems to represent both Marnie's inner self and her projection of same onto a huge horse named Florio. Although this motif rarely asserts itself in the film until the climactic foxhunt sequence, at which point her "id," triggered both by the color red and by the sight of hounds tearing a fox to shreds, runs out of control, it actually appears in a quiet, subtle, and haunting variant, with the final two notes initially metamorphosing in timbre from strings to flute, in the film's first underscored narrative sequence, which shows Marnie, from the back and as a very dark brunette, before her transformation into a Hitchcock blonde. The purse she is carrying has such an obviously vaginal shape that Hitchcock must have gone to great lengths to track it down. It is this same purse that is blatantly foregrounded in the film's opening shot, an all-but-silent sequence showing Marnie (brunette, from the back) walking down an eerily abandoned train platform suggestive of surreal vistas located somewhere between de Chirico and Hopper.

If this were a scholarly article I would go on at great length. Suffice it to say that, just as Hitchcock's *Marnie* departs somewhat from what was normally expected from the "Master of Suspense" while remaining perhaps one of the most quintessentially Hitchcockian of all the director's films, Herrmann's score becomes much more of a character study than one is used to from the composer, even while the music could not be more Herrmannesque. The score also offers other musical material besides the three phases mentioned above, most notably what would pass for a love theme if one could define as love the sexual blackmail of a woman by a man (Sean Connery) who goes so far as to rape Marnie, who is guilty of that terrible sin defined by the Freudians as frigidity, during their honeymoon voyage. If there is one Hitchcock/Herrmann score that Marnie on occasion recalls, it is not the expected *Vertigo* but rather *Psycho*, at those moments when Herrmann reduces the orchestral forces to mostly strings playing in lugubrious, two-chord alternations, as in "Red Flowers." "The Safe," which introduces a pizzicato chord repeated in a pattern familiar from *Psycho*, comes even closer. As for the Varèse Sarabande recording, it is, for the most part, satisfactory, without attaining either the sonic or interpretive excellence of McNeely's earlier *Vertigo* recording for the same label. McNeely tends to be just a tad hard-driven and breathless, particularly in the music's more lyrical moments, and the recorded sound is on the shrill side and overbalanced to the left. But these are minor flaws compared to the luxury of being able to follow the glorious strains of Herrmann's musical narrative from start to finish.

A recording that has me almost as ecstatic is a CD, "produced for the promotional purposes of the composer," from a company called Airstrip One that offers the original music track by British-born (in 1938) Howard Blake for Ridley Scott's first feature, **The Duellists**, and also includes the same composer's music for **The Riddle of the Sands** (National Philharmonic Orchestra; John McCarthy Singers [in *Riddle*]). I have over the years expressed on more than one occasion the regret that this exceptional music, one of the most haunting romantic scores ever composed, never made it to recording, and now, 23 years after the film's release, we have it, although not in the most accessible of ways. Blake's score for *The Duellists* gets a lot of mileage out of its main theme, often heard in a solo flute or oboe over a string orchestra. But what a main theme it is! Composed in a solid B-flat Minor, Blake's very long-breathed melody moves relentlessly and gloomily forward in the minor mode, occasionally making unexpected turns that will take your breath away. But this theme also owes much of its character to the extraordinarily rich harmonies and the instrumental textures, mostly from a string orchestra, that contain and define them. Although the theme is played straight in various guises, most spectacularly in the string-orchestra-only end title music, it enters in less recognizable forms at other moments, whether in pizzicato fragments in the basses in such cues as "I Renounce Love" and the brief "Cellar Duel," missing from the film's final cut, or in a source-music piano waltz for "Mme. de Lionne's Salon." And what sounds at two or three points like a new, even more morose, dirge-like theme could actually be chordal accompaniment for the main theme.

On one or two occasions the score becomes more modernistic, with at one point some reasonably understated cluster chords in the strings. And in two longer cues, "Russian Winter" and "Final Duel in the Woods," Blake creates something resembling a musical narrative. There are also several period pastiches, including a fairly bright, dance-like cue heard several times, and a fife-and-drum piece. The remarkable thing about all this is that Blake has composed a score in an almost thoroughly conservative romantic style, yet has somehow managed to sound wholly original. Also remarkable is the way the music weds itself from the outset to Scott's film, taken from a Joseph Conrad story ("The Duel") based on true events. Set in Napoleonic France, the narrative follows one soldier's (Harvey Keitel) obsessive, relentless, 20-year quest for satisfaction in a duel from another soldier (Keith Carradine) who he feels has slighted his honor. Almost on equal footing with these two characters are the film's many landscapes and settings, stunningly, often surreally captured by director of photography Frank Tidy, with director Scott as his camera operator. One of the cinema's supreme comings together of image and music takes place at film's end, as Blake's solo oboe, offering a variant of the main theme, plays behind a shot of Keitel standing atop a hill as the sun breaks through a mass of overhanging storm clouds. *The Riddle of the Sands*, directed in 1979 by Tony Maylam, and based on Erskine Childers' well-known 1903 spy novel about a German plot to invade the east coast of England, features an equally conservative score by Blake (although with a few more excursions into modernism), but one that lacks the spine-chilling theme that hangs over *The Duellists* like a cloud of sad inevitability. Interestingly, the apparent (I've never seen *The Riddle of the Sands*) title theme is a minor-mode song with a decidedly Dvořákian flavor sung in descant and in German by a small women's chorus. This song provides motifs for several of the cues, including the dramatic march of "Carruthers Reboards the Train." Much of *The Riddle of the Sands* was shot at sea and in and around Frisian Island locations, and portions of the score suggest its maritime setting, most particularly the rather Holstian "Into the Fog." The villainous Germans, on the other hand, get more strident, more complex music. All in all an interesting score, but not close to the level of *The Duellists*.

March/April

I had a rough idea of the main story line of **Unbreakable** before I saw the film, directed by M. Night Shyamalan, who, like *Magnolia* director Paul Thomas Anderson, will turn all of 31 this year (Anderson, in fact, already has). Still, once I began to watch *Unbreakable* I found myself slightly mystified at the written captions, appearing at the film's outset, detailing statistics on comic-book consumption in this country. It did not take long before the film set forth the relationship between comic books (action comics in particular) and one of its main characters, a black man named Elijah Price (Samuel L. Jackson) who, born with a disorder that made his bones extremely breakable, has become the very successful proprietor of a Philadelphia art gallery specializing in original plates and what have you from the action comics. But, as in the director's previous film, the highly successful *The Sixth Sense*, the full meaning of *Unbreakable*'s principal theme does not fully reveal itself until close to the ending. I will not spoil that ending for those of you who haven't yet seen the film but plan on doing so. I would simply suggest that here, even more strongly than in *The Sixth Sense*, I get the distinct impression of an artist looking in on the particular mythologies of

American culture as something of an outsider. Raised in the wealthy burbs of Philadelphia by physician parents, who actually returned to their native Pondicherry so that Manoj Nelliyattu Shyamalan, as he was originally named, could be born there, the director, in *Unbreakable*, subtly implies that action comics are the true history of American culture, not in any literal sense (indeed, a lack of literalism is one of the trademarks of Shyamalan's films) but rather in the way the ongoing battles of an absolute good versus an absolute evil reflect a major obsession of the Puritan mentality that is currently undergoing a major resurgence in this country.

And so into this picture must come a hero who is "unbreakable," and that unlikely individual, in the film, is a balding security guard named David Dunn (Bruce Willis), who mopes his way through life until, following his miraculous survival of a train wreck in which everyone else was killed, he is approached by Price who, with major support from Dunn's son (Spencer Treat Clark, one more wonderful performance by a young actor), tries to "out" the superhero Dunn may be keeping under his gloomy wraps. Shyamalan, consciously or unconsciously, has hit the mythology dead on: Dunn's superhero status grows from the apparent indestructibility of his body, whereas the film's force of evil resides in an individual who is mostly mind, and quite visibly of a woman born, whereas the Dunn character seems to be an autochthonous entity unto himself. If all this seems to have a major potential for garishness, that potential has been largely undercut by Shyamalan's quiet, understated cinematic style, which disturbs the viewer more with unusual camera angles (the obsessive, between-the-seats pan shots on the train at the film's opening, for instance) than with in-your-face special effects, and which, as in *Wide Awake* and *The Sixth Sense*, gets a good deal of mileage out of the Philadelphia locales the director knows and obviously loves. Of course, with its subject matter *Unbreakable* has flamboyant moments that carry the film into territories only suggested in *The Sixth Sense*. Even here, however, Shyamalan avoids the action-film clichés: the trashed car from which the woman is rescued does not explode and burst into flames the second she is pulled clear; the evildoer vanquished by Dunn in his moment of apotheosis does not pop back up from the dead to wreak further havoc on audiences' nerves (and patience). And look carefully at the picture in the newspaper treatment of Dunn's heroic exploit, for therein lies the key to much of the film.

Given *Unbreakable*'s subject matter, one would also expect more flamboyance from the musical score than in the ineffably sad and largely quiescent music for *The Sixth Sense*, and, to an extent—but only to an extent—that is what James Newton Howard, brought back by Shyamalan after his exquisite score for *The Sixth Sense*, has provided (Hollywood; Pete Anthony, cond.; Metro Voices, Nick Ingram, cond.; London Oratory School Schola Boys). The score's very dark, very minor-mode theme/motif, which starts off in the strings and features haunting chromatic shifts in the inner voices, has a somewhat bigger feel to it than the main theme for *The Sixth Sense*. Indeed, the tragedy that Howard so heartbreakingly communicates in *The Sixth Sense* seems to extend into broader territory, which is thoroughly appropriate for the more depersonalized mythology of *Unbreakable*. And a major crescendo soon leads the opening theme/motif into a heavy, pop beat that could be rock, or could be suggesting the rhythms of a railroad train. My initial interpretation, after I saw the film, was that the rock beat deliberately tied into the film's superhero mythology. But, after listening to the music-track CD, I'm not so sure that's the case, particularly since Howard rarely returns to it. Instead, I was struck by how insistently Howard maintains the music's almost overwhelmingly mournful tone, cue after cue, supplementing it at one point with a wispy waltz in the high registers of a super-resonant (electronic?) piano, adding, at another point, a pensive trumpet solo that seems associated with the Willis character. For instance, in the scene where Dunn, as his thoroughly convinced son watches, pumps enough iron to build a steam locomotive, Howard, rather than providing quasi-*Rocky* (a quite different Philadelphia film!) fanfares, keeps the tone hushed and almost morbid, as if to suggest that the very need for an unbreakable hero is a quiet tragedy in and of itself. Even in the major musical upheaval that underscores Dunn's one physical confrontation with evil in the film, Howard manages to keep that sad, nostalgia-laden solo-piano figure moving about in the upper registers. It is only within this type of context that, when Howard, in the cue entitled "Goodnight," creates a more straightforward elegy in the solo cello, strings, and harp, it comes as something of a relief!

Back in 1965, some 11 years before George Lukas took very similar material and turned it into Joseph Campbell for eighth-graders in the first *Star Wars* film, a sci-fi writer named Frank Herbert (1920–86) produced **Dune**, the first (and best) of a series of novels following the fortunes of a royal family with the name of Atreides (the name comes from the Atreus of Greek mythology, whose lineage includes Agamemnon, Electra, and Orestes). The novel is postmodern in the best sense of the word, and in many ways. First and foremost it plunges us into the kind of empire battles out of which modern patriarchal culture emerged, so that we often have the impression of reading either history or historical fiction (the true postmodernist would argue that there's no difference, but I'll let that alone). But since these battles take place, in *Dune*, in the future, and across galaxies rather than between countries or feudalities, with the sumptuous castles and antique trimmings set against the usual space ships, laser gimmicks, and what have you, *Dune* becomes that perfect, unresolvable, postmodern oxymoron, a historical-sci-fi novel. Herbert plays the same games with the novel's underlying, and often very deep, mythologies, with the most obvious, unresolved antimony lying in the very patriarchal rise to full messianic status by the novel's young hero, Paul Atreides, versus a mystical spirituality based on the all-embracing existence of a cosmic force that needs far more than a cuddly Muppet to keep its fires burning. That task instead belonging to a grim and determined sisterhood called the Bene Gesserit that includes Paul's mother (who went against the order by having a male child) and an imposing mother superior with the unlikely name of Gaius Helen Mohiam (Herbert's often off-the-wall names—Duncan Idaho also comes immediately to mind—merit a study in themselves). Add to this a desert planet (Arrakis, a.k.a. Dune) with a nomad people living underground in rubber suits that recycle every body fluid, and sandworms the size of the Empire State Building, and it is difficult to understand why the movie-going public had to wait through three—count 'em—*Star Wars* episodes before Herbert's novel finally hit the silver screen.

Not that people didn't try. Arthur P. Jacobs, who produced the *Planet of the Apes* films, originally had a nine-year option on *Dune*, but died a year after he acquired it. Chilean director (*El Topo*) Alejandro Jodorowski then acquired the rights and was all set to do a very surreal version with set design by Salvador Dali and other graphic work by artists such as H. R. Giger, whose haunting, semi-organic artwork for *Alien* stays in the mind like an unforgotten nightmare. But that project ran out of money, and the rights were acquired by Italian producer Dino De Laurentiis, who in 1984, the year *Dune* was released, opened the DEG Studios in Wilmington, North Carolina. After going through several screenplays, including an initial one by novelist Herbert, and after losing Ridley Scott as director, De Laurentiis ended up with what must have seemed at the time like an extremely unlikely choice for director, David Lynch, whose reputation began to grow with his hyper-grotesque *Eraserhead* (1977), and who went somewhat more mainstream with the 1980 *The Elephant Man* (De Laurentiis' daughter, Raffaella, actually produced *Dune*). Lynch, who ended up writing his own screenplay, and whose cinematic art frequently involves the depiction, implied or direct, of a kind of squishy organicism lying beneath the illusory solidity of the orders created by modern culture, brought his own very visual and very aural brand of the postmodern to Herbert's historical futurism, and, somehow, the two visions jelled, although the film was frequently torn apart in this country by the same critics who oohed and ahed over the *Star Wars* films. One example: early in the film, a Guild Navigator arrives in the Emperor's throne room in something that vaguely evokes a steam engine arriving in Grand Central Station in the 1940s. The navigator him(?)self looks ever so much like a monstrous, drugged-out vulva floating in clouds of brownish vapor. Lynch also came up with some novel casting, nowhere more so than in assigning the part of the villainous Feyd to a remarkably slim and trim Sting, made up to look ever so much like the punk rocker he never (fortunately) has quite become. And, making his film debut as Paul Atreides, Kyle MacLachlan, in his early twenties at the time, is the perfect character for the Montana-born Lynch, a squeaky-clean, golly-gee-whiz good guy right out of the '50s who makes you want to laugh while taking him completely seriously. And how can one forget obese arch-villain Baron Vladimir Harkonen (Kenneth McMillan), who with the help of some mysterious device is able to move his considerable bulk through the air, who suffers in relative silence while a doctor sucks out what looks like a case of super-acne, and who takes out his proclivity for homoerotic anthrophagia on pretty young blond men?

Given all of the above, and much, much more, it stands to reason that Lynch, even for what was supposed to be a commercial spectacular, would not go the usual route for *Dune*'s musical score. Indeed, a quick glance at Lynch's career reveals that, for all of his training in the visual arts, his vision extends equally into the domain of sound, and you'll notice that the director often takes credit for sound design in his films' end titles. And so, Lynch turned not just to one but to two rock-and-roll artists, or, rather, to one band (Toto) and one individual artist (Brian Eno, who wrote *Dune*'s "Prophecy

Theme"). But, of course, in this postmodern mix what Lynch asked for from these rock musicians was not a pop music but rather a solid "classical" score, and that is precisely what Toto (David Paich, keyboards; the late Jeff Porcaro, drums and percussion; Steve Porcaro, keyboards; Mike Porcaro, electric bass, acoustic bass, and percussion; and Steve Lukather, guitars) came up with as of the minute-and-a-half demo they submitted to Lynch. Toto's score (Eno's contributions have been omitted) has just been reissued by P.E.G. Recordings (Vienna Symphony Orchestra, Marty Paich and Allyn Ferguson, cond.) on a CD that includes some 14 previously unreleased tracks, along with Toto's original demo. Now, I've seen *Dune* several times, including in its initial theatrical release (and, more recently, on laserdisc), and listened to the music-track LP at least once. Each time, as the film opens with Princess Irulan (Virginia Madsen) looking at the camera and telling us what we're about to see, I've been struck by the resemblance between the opening music in the strings, with its slow drones and its icy open intervals, and the first movement of Shostakovich's 11th Symphony. And then I've forgotten all about it until the next time. Well, finally, David Paich, in his program note for the P.E.G. recording, clears up the mystery: "David Lynch put a set of headphones on me with Shostakovich's eleventh playing. He said in a raised voice 'do you like that kinda music?' I replied 'I love it.' He then said 'do you know what I want musically?' I answered with a definite 'yes!'." Interestingly, Paich and Toto came up with a few fragments that might be dubbed "impressions of the first movement of Shostakovich's 11th Symphony," and this characteristic sound turns up throughout the film in diverse cues that otherwise bear little resemblance to the Shostakovich 11th. Somehow, it works.

In sharp contrast to the Shostakovich 11th strains, Toto's main theme for *Dune* has such an over-the-top sci-fi-film portentousness to it (one is reminded of the over-the-top horror-film portentousness of John Carpenter's theme for his *Halloween*), complete with cathedral organ and vocalizing chorus at points, that, again, one would be tempted to laugh, save that it is somehow perfectly in sync with the Saturday-matinee earnestness that Lynch somehow forces us to take with utmost seriousness. This theme, which is already totally in place as of the demo, save the demo's all-synthesizer scoring, likewise turns up throughout the film, sometimes underscoring heavy drama but at other times appearing as almost a lyrical reminiscence. At other points, such as "Robot Fight" and "Big Battle," Toto takes full advantage of Jeff Porcaro's gift at manipulating percussion timbres. Toward the end of the score one becomes more aware of the rock origins of Toto's music, particularly in cues such as "Dune (Desert Theme)" and "Take My Hand," written in what might be called a big-band-rock style that creates a sense of apotheosis similar to what one often finds in Tangerine Dream scores. On the other hand, Toto also quite effectively creates, for cues such as "Paul Takes the Water of Life" and "The Sleeper Has Awakened," vast, sustained soundscapes, with a touch of oriental percussion, that reach down into the narrative's more mystical areas. All in all it has to be said that Toto's score beautifully sets up Lynch's film, but that, as the action gets going, it becomes less and less necessary, at least as Lynch uses (and doesn't use) it, as musical backing per se, and is perhaps best heard apart from the film as an aural evoker of feelings experienced and imaginary places visited.

Well, almost no sooner did the latest "Golden Age Classics" release, **From the Terrace**, arrive from Film Score Monthly than a cable TV channel obliged by screening it, and in its proper CinemaScope aspect ratio to boot. And so, armed with the very recent memory of this cinematically sanitized version, directed by Mark Robson, of John O'Hara's massive and apparently very steamy novel, I embark upon the following review of Elmer Bernstein's rather intriguing score for it. The first thing to be said is that this is one of those movies that reminds us that, not all that long ago, the United States had its own aristocracy—not just a class of wealth, but a class in which people with scads of servants and chauffeurs actually did things such as dressing (to the nines) for meals. The aristocracy in question in *From the Terrace* is that of post–World War II Philadelphia, where a young man named Alfred Eaton (Paul Newman), returning from the war, has to find a niche for himself in the face of both his antagonistic, industrialist father (Leon Ames), who is bitter over the death of his first son, and an alcoholic mother (Myrna Loy), who is also cheating on his father. The situation is so bad that even the family chauffeur (Malcolm Atterbury, who can also be seen as the laconic farmer in a brief encounter at the cornfield with Cary Grant in Hitchcock's *North by Northwest*) quits in disgust. Given this situation, it is not surprising that young Alfred ends up marrying in his class, but to an oversexed ash-blonde (Joanne Woodward) with whom he cannot form an intimate relationship. And here is the first area in which Bernstein's score intrigues: although the titles open with a big, romantic theme, complete with rhapsodic piano solo and a bridge, the music, as it turns out, has nothing to do with the Newman/Woodward love affair and marriage, and it takes a good half of the picture before we find out where that love music really belongs.

For Newman and Woodward, Bernstein instead concocted a very intense, very moody, almost Expressionistic waltz that, from the very outset, colors the relationship with decidedly psychotic hues, nowhere more strongly than in the strange, nighttime scene ("In the Bushes") where the couple necks outside the house of her parents. "In the Bushes" also features a brief transformation of the waltz by the solo piano, flute, and violin in a manner that looks forward to Bernstein's masterful score for *To Kill a Mockingbird* (1962). Motifs from this waltz turn up, often slowed down in quite dark and gloomy settings, in most of the cues where Woodward is involved. Indeed, much of Bernstein's score has a morose, brooding quality to it that more often than not seems to probe more deeply than the film, which is by and large a strangely uninvolving soap opera, ever does. The early "Homecoming" cue, for instance, stresses the family discord not only with a very dirge-like opening, but also with a bitonal clarinet solo echoed much later in the film, in the "Rejection" cue, by a solo saxophone, which subtly suggests a parallel between Newman's wife and his mother, who rather strangely vanishes from the movie after our first encounters with her. In two cues, "Morte, Morte" and "Les Adieux," Bernstein plunges momentarily into an almost Mahlerian melancholy. We also hear foreshadowings here and there of another Bernstein masterpiece from the same era, *Summer and Smoke* (1961).

But, of course, Newman must meet the love of his life. Having saved the grandchild (and, symbolically, that part of himself that got shunted aside by his father when his older brother died) of a major New York stockbroker (English actor Felix Aylmer, who plays Polonius in Olivier's *Hamlet*), Newman gets offered a job by that stockbroker, whose demands further alienate him from Woodward. On one of his frequent out-of-town business trips, Newman meets the dark, very natural, very quiet, but also apparently very sexual daughter, Natalie Benzinger, of a potential client (a Pennsylvania coal-mining tycoon played by Ted De Corsia), at which point Bernstein's romantic theme, which has lain in hiding for well over an hour, reemerges, at first rather quietly and wistfully in the winds and strings. Natalie is played by the then 23-year-old Ina Balin (née Rosenberg), whose career never took off the way people expected it to (quite possibly because she couldn't act), but who in 1973 helped evacuate hundreds of Vietnamese orphans (she adopted three of them in 1976). Her efforts are documented in a 1980 TV film, in which Balin plays herself, entitled *The Children of An Lac*. At any rate, Bernstein's theme, which like so many romantic themes opens with a big, upward intervallic leap (this one a major ninth), follows the vagaries of the very tender (but also very sexual) relationship between Newman and Balin, asserting itself most strongly as a rhapsody for piano and orchestra in "Awakening," but also (in the same cue) dying down to an achingly nostalgic violin solo. As with the Newman/Woodward music (which, as Newman and Woodward move further and further apart, eventually becomes simply Woodward's theme), fragments from the romantic theme turn up in most cues involving Balin, sometimes quite masterfully disguised. I would also note that there is just a hint, in this theme, of Bernard Herrmann's love music for *North by Northwest* from the same studio (MGM) the previous year, whose screenwriter, Ernest Lehman, also scripted *From the Terrace*. This CD features an excellent essay on the film by Nick Redman, and an equally probing look at Bernstein, complete with a cue-by-cue description of the action and the music, by Lukas Kendall and frequent *Film Score Monthly* contributor Jeff Bond. The elements used in recording the score do not seem to have been in the best of shape, the sound has a strong studio-based tubbiness to it, and the orchestral playing is at times less than smooth. But none of this matters much in light of the importance of the music, which represents Elmer Bernstein at the peak of his considerable talents, although I have to say I haven't noticed a whole lot of valleys in the still-active career of one of Hollywood's most gifted composers.

OK. Just for starters let me give you a list of the instruments that make up the ensemble that performs Thomas Newman's score for **Erin Brockovich** (Sony): Fender Rhodes, Wurlitzer (John Beasley); Teisco electric guitar, 12-string acoustic guitar (George Doering); tongue drum, tonga drum, tuned gongs, whacker tubes (Michael Fisher); high sustains, jagged guitars, extended mouthpiece (Rick Cox); phonograph, mid/low sustains (George Budd); bloogle (Steve Tavaglione); six-string bass guitar (Bill Bernstein); piano (Thomas Newman). Do I know what half these instruments are? No way. A bloogle? You've got to be kidding. And only in the age of rap can a phonograph become a percussion instrument. What I do know is that in all probability only such a concatenation of offbeat and funky timbres could produce the kind of offbeat and funky music that has by now become such a Thomas Newman trademark that my stepdaughter, a very musically sensitive individual but one not normally "into" film music, immediately recognized the score as coming from the composer of *American Beauty* when the family started watching *Erin Brockovich* on DVD. What sounds like violins and several other instruments make their way into the mix as well, but I suspect that these have electronic origins, particularly since no orchestra or conductor is listed in the CD insert. It's difficult to say why Newman's distinct instrumentals work so well in such a wide variety of different films. One reason might be that the composer somehow, in a style that has elements of blues, funk, rock, Minimalism, and many other things, including his own patented brand of chattering percussion and bent sostenutos, defines a facet of the American collective unconscious as it has evolved at this point in time. In certain instances, such as Gillian Armstrong's 1997 *Oscar and Lucinda*, one has the impression that Newman's music is there more to tell the audience members where they are than where the film is. For a film such as *Erin Brockovich*, on the other hand, the assertively different music seems to go hand in glove both with the film's eponymous character, played by Julia Roberts in a performance that will probably win her an Oscar, and, particularly at those moments when the music dies down to a cosmic hush, sometimes with a wistful piano, of sustained, open-interval string(-timbre) chords, with the tragedy in which the character, as a legal researcher, gets involved.

That tragedy is based on the by-now cinematically familiar, and in this and many other instances true, story of a whole community of Americans poisoned by chemicals—in this case a virulent form of chromium that the particular corporation, a California gas and electric company, has actually told the inhabitants of the community is good for them—that corporate and political greed have allowed to seep into the groundwater. Into this mess wanders a single mother whose apparel pushes her beauty-pageant figure into everybody's face, and whose mouth goes slightly too public with the kind of "foul" language that most Americans (and in particular the idiotic movie-rating system) claim not to be "appropriate" but that most of them, from the new "aristocracy" all the way down to the working classes, constantly use in an only slightly more private way. The filmic action, both with respects to the character herself and with respects to the lawsuit she almost single-handedly mounts, is a classically manipulative nail-biter put together with such superb pacing and visual flair by director Stephen Soderbergh, who also works a genuinely touching and often funny performance out of Albert Finney as Brockovich's lawyer boss (Ed Masry), that you beg for more . . . manipulation, that is. For *Erin Brockovich* I'll forgive Soderbergh his 1989 *sex, lies, and videotape*, which, since it opened, has occupied a place of honor on my 10-worst-films-that-everybody-else-loved list. And with his *Traffic*, which was released at the end of 2000, Soderbergh and company may need a semi to cart away all their Oscars this year. One particularly effective moment in *Erin Brockovich* comes when Soderbergh consistently uses a very low camera angle to shoot the tall, blond, extremely attractive waitress who serves Erin Brockovich and her children in a diner early in the film. As it turns out, that actress is the real Erin Brockovich (now Brockovich-Ellis), and Soderbergh's camera angle lets at least your unconscious know that you're looking at a truly imposing person. That impression, conscious or unconscious, is confirmed when you watch the DVD special feature that includes Brockovich-Ellis herself describing the events, and nearly breaking down as she tells of the cancers and other ailments suffered by Masry's clients, for whom he, with Brockovich's help, won a $333 million class-action suit against PSE&G. One would also like to think that Brockovich-Ellis slipped screenwriter Susannah Grant at least some of the character's lines, many of them so brassily audacious that you burst out laughing. At any rate, Newman's score for *Erin Brockovich* turns up throughout the film mostly in short cues, many of which sound like moody accompaniment figures for themes lurking just out of sight, and most of which seem to set both an internal tone for the viewers and an external tone for the settings and characters. Once in a while a cue ventures into a kind of New-Agey dreaminess, as in "Pro Bono" (1'10"), with resonant mallet instruments playing haunting figures over a sustained, electronic haze that sounds as if it had wandered over from a Michael Mann film. At the other end, many of the cues have a jaunty, dance-like quality. The CD is presented in the HDCD mode; as with other HDCD CDs that I've heard, this one features amazingly resonant bass and wonderful clarity in defining the separate instruments. Also included with Newman's *Erin Brockovich* score are two previously recorded songs by Cheryl Crow, "Redemption Day" and "Everyday Is a Winding Road." While I must admit that they seem totally appropriate to the film, it is the kind of music that always seems to be coming over the speaker system at my gym at much too loud a volume, making me want to finish my workouts as fast as I can (not that I need the music for an excuse).

One film that has stayed in my soul ever since I first saw it in the theater is Mark Rydell's **The Fox**, this in spite of the fact that, by the end, it has totally betrayed the D. H. Lawrence short novel on which it is based. In the US in the '60s, those who liked to imagine that sexual liberation was upon us latched onto certain "forbidden" texts, smirkingly flaunting the reading of works such as Lawrence's *Lady Chatterley's Lover* all over the place. Trouble is, most people didn't have a clue as to what Lawrence, whom they saw as the high priest of free love, is really about. In Lawrence's story, two women in their late twenties, known by their surnames, March and Banford, try to make a go of running a poultry farm (I'm presuming near Islington in England) on their own. Lawrence describes March as follows: "[S]he looked almost like some graceful, loose-balanced young man," while Banford, "though nervous and delicate, was a warm, generous soul." Various things, most particularly a fox that keeps killing the chickens, conspire against them, but they stay on. The arrival of a young man (fox number two), known mostly as "the youth," who ends up proposing to March, undoes March and Banford's idyll. But, ultimately, nobody gets what he or she wants. The youth, almost at the second March becomes "his" woman, no longer desires her: "He did not want to make love to her. He shrank from any such performance, almost with fear. She was a woman, and vulnerable, accessible to him finally, and he held back from that which was ahead, almost with dread." March, having given up her strength and freedom, sees herself at the end like "the seaweeds . . . never looking forth from the water until they died, only then washing, corpses, upon the surface." And Banford . . . well, you'll have to read the story and/or see the film. Now, director Rydell and his crew, in making a film based on *The Fox*, had several things going for them. First of all, they upped the ante on March and Banford by setting the farm in snowbound fields somewhere in Canada. Yet, through the lens of William A. Fraker's camera, never has cold looked more beautiful than it does in this film. Further, Rydell got two truly outstanding actresses, the late Sandy Dennis and British-born Anne Heywood, to play the lead roles. Dennis manages to communicate, through the hysteria that was somewhat her trademarked style, the warmth and generosity Lawrence describes in the character, while Heywood, although perhaps a bit too beautiful for the role, likewise brings the appropriate strength and bemused detachment to the role. Out of all this Rydell and company, strongly including composer Lalo Schifrin, create a feeling that perhaps might best be described as "exquisite loneliness."

But, of course, Hollywood being Hollywood, and the '60s being the '60s, the film creates a lesbian relationship between the two women, also strongly suggested by the poster art, that is nowhere to be found in Lawrence; there is also a stunningly photographed scene, also nowhere to be found in Lawrence, in which Heywood, standing nude in the dark in front of the bathroom mirrors, masturbates. And, of course, when "the youth" (Keir Dullea, whose utter coldness is perfect for the role) arrives, he "rescues" the woman in March by giving her that great gift from on high, sex with a male (here again, however, I have to say that the long sequence in which the film cross-cuts between Heywood and Dullea's lovemaking in a shed and Banford's frantic search for her lost companion has an overwhelmingly sad intensity to it that I have rarely seen in any film). And thus does the highly complex sexual subtext of this and other Lawrence writings get simplistically boiled down to the portrait, common to Hollywood cinema and porno films alike, of the male as the great giver of salvation via orgasm. Only in the nude wrestling scene between the late Oliver Reed and Alan Bates in Ken Russell's *Women in Love* from the next year has a filmmaker captured something of that equal exchange of energy that seems to define a major part of Lawrence's sexual vision. Still, *The Fox* works exceptionally well within the limited parameters of Hollywood filmmaking, and another reason for this is the utterly captivating score by Lalo Schifrin, who has rerecorded it for his own label (Aleph; Sinfonia of London Orchestra). I would guess that the first thing Schifrin realized when he went to compose the score for *The Fox* was that the usual symphonic film score would totally mismatch the open-spaced coldness and isolation that the film communicates as of its opening shots. And so Schifrin came up with a relative film-music rarity, a chamber score, in this case for string quartet, flute, clarinet, oboe/English horn, bassoon, piano, harp, electric harpsichord, and percussion, with other instruments (horns, for one, I think) making rare appearances. Further, a composer who rarely gets evoked in film scores, Maurice Ravel, makes furtive appearances in several cues, most notably "Lonely Road," where Schifrin actually sneaks in a Ravel motif or two. Some pretty solid dissonances, often starting in the lower registers of the piano, also turn up briefly here and there in this otherwise fairly lyrical score.

But, as those familiar with the film and its music cannot help but be aware, the thing that stands out above all else in *The Fox* is Schifrin's haunting theme, generally given to a solo wind (initially a flute), and also presented as a pop tune, not heard in the film, written to the characteristic bossa nova beat Schifrin used in many of his film scores. Entitled "That Night," with lyrics by Norman Gimbel, the song was actually recorded some 20 times before the film was even released. Sung by an unidentified (why?) female vocalist on the Aleph CD, "That Night" gets a better performance (an appropriately breathy Sally Stevens) and a better arrangement (a solo flute often doubles the vocalist, for instance) on the original Warner Bros. music-track recording, one of the few LPs remaining on my shelves. Moving in total sync with the film, Schifrin's theme (which also has a bridge) mirrors the loneliness, sadness, and, ultimately, tragedy, but also the warmth of the relationship of the two women, not just to each other but to their isolated but beautiful surroundings. The Aleph CD contains cues not heard on the original LP, although a lot of them are not heard in the film either, which never strays as far afield from the original material as several of the Aleph cues do. Strangely, Aleph does not include "Ellen's Image" (the masturbation scene), one of the subtlest and most strangely moving cues in the score; the LP also offers a fairly raunchy song, "Roll It Over," by Oscar Brand, as sung by Heywood in the film. And where "Dead Leaf" is a Latin-flavored interpretation of the main theme on the original LP, it is a totally different, longer (and quite lovely) version of the main theme on the remake. To be honest, I rather prefer the "original soundtrack" to this remake, not only because of cues such as "Ellen's Image" but also because the more understated interpretations of the diverse cues are more in keeping with the tone of the film.

May/June

Even before Thomas Harris' novel *Hannibal* was brought out toward the middle of 1999, my guess was that, finally, Harris was going to give his readers the prequel to his novel *The Red Dragon*, which was the source for the first Hannibal Lecter movie, Michael Mann's 1986 *Manhunter*, which, in my opinion, remains overall the best of the Lecter films. At last, I thought, we're going to see the good doctor in action before he was first apprehended. Instead, *Hannibal* turned out to be a sequel to the second Lecter novel (and film), *The Silence of the Lambs*, which in many ways simply replays the drama of *The Red Dragon*, with Lecter sitting in a maximum-security cell and helping an FBI agent (Jody Foster) track down a serial killer (Ted Levine) before he strikes again. In *Manhunter* the mere presence of Lecter (Scottish actor Brian Cox, cold as ice and scathingly ironic) helps the former FBI agent (William Peterson) who captured him regain the mindset he needs to hunt another serial killer (Tom Noonan, in a brilliant performance). Initially disappointed, I quickly discovered, as I read *Hannibal*, that Harris, having returned Lecter to freedom at the end of *Silence*, was ready to head off in new directions. Those new directions ultimately produce one of the most cynically subversive stories ever written. For starters, Harris puts Lecter squarely where he belongs, namely in the seat of European high culture, Florence, where the former psychiatrist, speaking perfect Italian, curates a museum of fine manuscripts, plays Bach's *Goldberg Variations* on the clavichord in his apartment, drinks fine wine, and, um, dines on fine food (never mind that he has had to off the previous curator). In other words, the perfect incarnation of the upper class, European intellectual.

Secondly, Harris gets us rooting for Lecter by creating one of the vilest and, thanks to Lecter, physically repulsive characters in literature, one Mason Verger, a super-wealthy, born-again, child- (and sister-) abusing hog farmer from a family of hog farmers who is out to exact a gruesome vengeance on Lecter, who, playing avenging angel, had persuaded Verger, high on Angel Dust, speed, and LSD, to let his dogs eat off his face, and then had broken his neck with a noose Verger had just used for a round of autoerotic asphyxia. Thirdly, Harris also gets us rooting against just about the entire legal establishment, whether the FBI, which, with the help of Starling's superior Paul Krendler, has methodically destroyed Starling's career, or a hapless Florentine police inspector, a loser from a noble family of losers who is out to get things back on track by helping Verger set up, with the help of some less-than-noble Sardinians, the live devouring of Lecter by wild boars. Finally, and most significantly (skip to the next paragraph if you haven't read the novel and plan on doing so), Harris ultimately brings about what he faintly promised in *The Silence of the Lambs*: the union of Lecter and Starling, both of whom manage to heal each other's damaged psyche, and both of whom, a "handsome couple," end up leading the aristocratic life in Buenos Aires, attending the opera, sleeping until noon, dancing at lunch, occasionally visiting each other's "memory palace," and having sex, "a splendid structure they add to every day." How can we not love them? They have reached the capitalist/aristocratic goal aspired to but almost never attained by almost every member of modern Western culture. And if getting there means devouring members of a human species that has descended one rung on the food chain, including the brains of one's superior as he sits and watches, well, then, so be it. As I said: subversive.

Now, from the moment Dino De Laurentiis Productions started to put together the film version of **Hannibal**, the project was surrounded with controversy. Screenwriter Ted Tally and director Jonathan Demme, who worked together on *The Silence of the Lambs*, turned down *Hannibal*, and it was not long thereafter that actress Foster followed suit. All, apparently, were scandalized by and indignant over the subversiveness of Harris' novel, particularly the conclusion, which is ironic, since those final scenes, except for the sautéed brains, are nowhere to be found in the film, which Ridley Scott ended up directing, with a screenplay from no less a figure than David Mamet, who was later replaced (to what extent?) by Stephen Zaillian, whose credits include *Schindler's List* and the incredibly poignant *Awakenings*. None of those losses turned out to be particularly significant. Anthony Hopkins opted to stay on board as the good doctor, forever exuding an ironically detached awareness of his complete mastery over himself and others (including, as it turns out, animals). If ever an actor has owned a role, it is Hopkins as Hannibal Lecter (another example that immediately comes to mind, interestingly enough, is Anthony Perkins as Norman Bates). But Julianne Moore plays Agent Starling, world-weary and straight-faced from start to finish, as if she had just walked off the set of *The Silence of the Lambs*, even while working without the strong character development brought out in *Silence* and reexamined in the novel *Hannibal*. And veteran Italian actor Gian-Carlo Giannini seems a particularly inspired choice as the Florentine police inspector who makes the worse-than-fatal mistake of crossing Lecter. Director Scott, his dreadful *Gladiator* to the contrary notwithstanding, has almost always been a master at creating visual mood, which he does to perfection in *Hannibal*'s Florence sequences, suggesting the Old World elegance that suits Lecter to a T, but also creating just enough of a sense of the ominous to make us wary of what lies beneath this elegance—historically, socially, psychologically . . . .

Where *Hannibal* fails, not surprisingly, is in some of its omissions and, ultimately, the lack of courage on the part of all involved (or perhaps almost all; see below) to follow through on the novel's ultimate subversiveness. Averting its gaze, for instance, from the character's truly loathsome peculiarities, the film asks us to hate Mason Verger (Gary Oldman, sort of) strictly on the basis of a particularly bad job of makeup and prosthetics. The film also eliminates the particularly important character of Verger's lesbian sister, Margo, also excising a poignant flashback to Lecter's distant past that invites the reader to understand, if not appreciate, his lifestyle. I also found myself grateful for having read the novel, because I'm not sure I would have come terribly close to understanding key points in the action if hadn't, so thoroughly do Scott and company skim over them. Obviously, there is a tremendous amount of material from a 500-page novel that cannot even be suggested in a 130-minute movie. *Hannibal*, like so many films these days, needed more time to unfold. Even with a longer running time, however, by copping out on the novel's brilliant and in many ways devastating conclusion *Hannibal* ultimately relegates the Lecter/Starling relationship to the ethics of pure evil versus pure good of which so many Americans seem enamored. Even the poster art portrays Lecter as a pretty scary bogeyman, which is hardly how he comes across in the book and, to a lesser degree, the movie. It is, in fact, principally due to Hopkins' brilliant performance that we even begin to perceive that Hannibal Lecter, [who has become something of a folk hero], is the cannibal we all want to be. . . .

Ah, but could somebody (director Scott? composer Hans Zimmer?) have decided to tell us in music what the film does not dare tell us? Could it be that one of the generally least interesting composers writing for the movies today has come up with one of the cinema's most, yes, subversive scores? I remembered the music for *Hannibal* as being fairly morose, in a string-heavy kind of way, and atmospheric. But as I began listening to the "original motion picture soundtrack" on a Decca CD (Lyndhurst Orchestra, Gavin Greenaway, cond.) and allowed myself to be bathed in the incredibly full sound (with sometimes plaster-cracking bass), I started to become aware of a pattern taking place. While many of the cues initially come across as something close to an elegy for string orchestra (with added sounds, many of them electronic, but also including a vocalizing boys' chorus part performed by a group called Libra), they often acquire such an intensity that one begins to have the impression of listening to the concluding instrumental strains of a tragic opera. But this, in spite of the movie's setting, is not Italian opera but rather Wagner filtered on up through the hyper-affectivity of Mahler and the morbidity of the Schoenberg of *Verklärte Nacht*. And then, lo and behold, the penultimate cue ("To Every Captive Soul"), performed in extremely full and resonant sound by a string orchestra, moves so close to *Tristan und Isolde* that you can almost see the drama unfolding before your eyes. You can certainly feel it—deeply. At the very least the music floods our emotions, making us ache for what feels like the tragedy of Lecter's unfulfilled longing for Starling, who ultimately, in the movie, stands as the Achilles' heel of the otherwise perfect, Nitzschean *Übermensch* (or perhaps Machiavellian prince, a figure referred to in Harris' novel) that is Hannibal Lecter. Keep in mind, however, that in *Tristan* the overwhelming passion is shared equally by both characters. Within that light the music seems to invite us to follow its two main characters where the movie refuses to go, ultimately putting the concept of the *Liebestod*—the love death—into a whole new perspective.

But there's more. Through the use of the vocalizing boys' chorus and other voices as well (probably sampled), and by creating a very solemn musical backdrop to accompany them, Zimmer's music constantly suggests the presence of the Church, not as the enemy of the devil (Lecter, if you buy the film's PR) but rather as a major element of the Renaissance ethics and aesthetics that define in large part the former psychiatrist's new life. The film in fact concludes on this tone, with a lovely, quasi-sacred aria for soprano, tenor, and chorus, "Vida Cor Meum," composed by Patrick Cassidy and based on words from Dante's *La vita nuova*, playing behind the end titles (stick around to the last second, however, since the CD, like the film, provides a little twist to send you home even more wiped out). All in all, then, while the music on more than one occasion complements the mildly ominous hues of Ridley Scott's visuals, it constantly moves toward resolving those impressions not in the direction of the horror/suspense film but rather toward a spiritual transcendence that feels like an ongoing series of bittersweet but ultimately tragic conclusions. In certain ways Zimmer's music turns *Hannibal* into something resembling one of the highest art forms spawned by the Renaissance, grand opera (I really need to see the film a second time, however, to confirm this impression). Sir Anthony Hopkins speaks lines from the film in several of the cues on the CD, although the music tends to drown him out. The CD also offers the Aria da capo from Bach's *Goldberg Variations* as played and hummed by Glenn Gould, although I don't think that's the version heard in the film when Lecter sits at what should have been a clavichord to plunge himself into one of the great glories of the past. A grating "Gourmet Valse Tartare" written by Klaus Badelt, who simply tears the aristocratic *Blue Danube Waltz* to shreds, does not seem to belong with the rest of the score, and, frankly, I don't remember it being in the film. On the whole, however, Hans Zimmer, no doubt with major coaching from the musically sophisticated Scott, has produced a score that on more than one occasion seems to detach itself and float free of the film the producers wanted you to see. Quite amazing.

July/August

In writing about James Horner's score for **Enemy at the Gates** (Sony; London Voices) in Vol. 6, no. 3, of *Film Score Monthly* (the same issue in which a letter-writer felt it necessary to put in a disclaimer for praising a score—*Mary Reilly*—that I had also praised), the reviewer suggests that some viewer/listeners may find one of the score's principal motifs "all too similar to the main theme from *Schindler's List*." All too similar? There are moments—many of them—when the motif is downright identical in its first eight notes and its rhythmic configuration; even when Horner plays around with it a bit, it is so close that even those who don't pay attention to film music are bound to be distracted, particularly since it plays a substantial role in a theme (a love theme, I believe) that dominates the later cues, by which point it's too late to forget the model. The same reviewer notes that "this same theme makes a guest appearance toward the end of *Apollo 13*." Well, that just proves that Horner has been ripping off John Williams for six years rather than just recently (*Apollo 13* is from 1995, *Schindler's List* from 1993, in case you're interested), and, for the life of me, I just cannot understand why so many people react so casually to this massively annoying proclivity. Along the way Horner also flirts with moments from Prokofiev's *Alexander Nevsky* (both the motif for the German invaders and the song of mourning after the battle) and, in "The Tractor Factory," from the first theme (after the introduction) of the first movement of Shostakovich's Fifth Symphony (Horner has used this one before as well, if I remember correctly). He dips even more substantially into Shostakovich (the first movement of the 11th Symphony) at the outset of "Danilov's Confession." Again I ask: What is the point? Horner, a composer with a major amount of classical training, obviously has the skills to come up with his own musical ideas. Those ideas may not be on a level with those of the composers whose work he borrows; but Horner's often conspicuously used borrowings are not only degrading, they consistently draw the informed listener's attention away from whatever qualities his own music may have. The interesting thing in the score for *Enemy at the Gates* is that it, like several other Horner scores I have heard of late, starts off quite promisingly, in this case with a quiet passage in the high strings that sets a cold and desolate mood probably appropriate to the film's narrative, based on a true story of a Russian sniper (Jude Law) and his German adversary (Ed Harris) in and around the battle of Stalingrad in World War II. It feels as if the composer handily engages his creative juices at the outset of a given score and then suddenly loses confidence. I can also imagine some of Horner's more militaristic cues stirring the blood at particularly dramatic moments in the film. But there is no way I would pay today's ticket prices to see a film directed by Jean-Jacques Annaud and scored by James Horner (as good an example as any for why I'm losing interest in the game).

In a course I taught this past fall on European cinema, the one film I showed that got what appeared to be a unanimously enthusiastic reception from all the 30-plus students was *Antonia's Line* (1995), directed by the Dutch-born (in 1948) Marleen Gorris. Those of you who haven't seen this hauntingly warm, quietly understated, visually stunning portrayal of an old woman's last day on Earth and her flashbacks to the two generations of women that preceded her should rush out and either rent, if possible (try Facets in Chicago), or purchase the DVD. I was not particularly enamored with Gorris' ensuing film (she made three before *Antonia's Line*, none of which I have seen), *Mrs. Dalloway*, a much less than successful Virginia Woolf adaptation. But from where I sit she has definitely returned to form in **The Luzhin Defence**, in which John Turturro plays Alexander Ivanovich Luzhin, writer Vladimir Nabokov's single-minded and tortured chess genius, and Emily Watson the young Russian aristocrat named Natalia with whom he improbably falls in love (and she with him), sometime between the two world wars, at an Italian lakeside resort where he is about to play in a tournament for the world championship. Flimsy material for a film, one might think; and, in fact, I noticed that quite a number of the people who were in line to see *The Luzhin Defence* seemed to be chess fans. I have to think that they were probably quite disappointed, as the film gives little idea of what the game of chess is all about and even less of an idea of what it's like to play in a tournament, or so I would imagine, since I've never been to one (but I have played a reasonable amount of chess in my life). In compensation, however, Gorris and her crew probe with soul-shattering depth, mostly via flashbacks, into the child- and early adulthood events, many of them revolving around various forms of abandonment, that formed the chess-player's obsessive-compulsive psychology. Gorris, here with the help of director of photography Bernard Lutic, also has a genius for setting up shots that both take the breath away and that, in an indefinable way, tie in to the narrative themes she is developing. Note, for instance, the first moment of contact between Turturro and Watson, with the latter a splash of red emerging, on the right, from the gray and the former descending from the middle of the screen while, on the left, a perfectly even row of massive and gorgeous trees watches over the action. The film's ending, while totally hokey, is one of the most satisfying I have experienced in a long time.

This is the first score (Silva) I have heard from Alexandre Desplat, who has worked almost exclusively in French film and television over the last 10 years. Critic A. O. Scott, reviewing The *Luzhin Defence* in the April 20 issue of *The New York Times*, felt that Gorris uses "Desplat's lush score" in "sometimes heavy-handed" ways, "overemphasizing moments that should be treated with the concentrated quiet of a chess match." While I know what he means, I had quite the opposite reaction. One of the strengths of Gorris' filmmaking, it seems to me, is that she does not rely strictly on the narrative to tell the story but rather gives striking substance to the (in this case elusive) story through her use of visuals and, in the case of *The Luzhin Defence*, much more so than in her previous two films, music. Let's start with what is called the "Love Theme." There are, perhaps, in the history of film music maybe a half-dozen scores—Georges Delerue's *Contempt* and Akira Senju's *The Mystery of Rampo* come immediately to mind—that feature an elegiac, minor-mode theme that, very much in the manner of Barber's Adagio for Strings, announces unspeakable sadness, even tragedy, from its opening chord forward. I now add to that category Desplat's Love Theme for *The Luzhin Defence*, a string-heavy (which appears to be de rigueur for this type of theme) poem that seems to be ever reaching upward without ever giving the viewer/listener a moment of resolution even within the various minor modes. One could attribute this to the fact that we have two Slavic souls coming together, although there is almost nothing Slavic about the theme. But I suspect, from my reaction to the music's effect in the movie, that Gorris had deeper things in mind. Most love themes attempt to express the joy and overwhelming passion that come with the initial stages of romance. Desplat's theme, on the other hand, seems to contain all of the psychological baggage that Alexander Ivanovich Luzhin brings with him, and from which, as the music surely tells us, he will never find release. And since the film indistinctly defines whatever psychological baggage Natalia brings with her, this profoundly heartrending music, heard as of that first encounter described above (I love the way this cue ultimately dissolves away into accompaniment figures that still outline the theme), seems to tell us more about what attracts Natalia in Alexander than what attracts him in her.

There is, of course, more to Desplat's score than the love theme, most particularly a mildly jaunty (probably an Allegretto) but moody theme divided between the strings, solo piano, and celesta that also never leaves the minor mode and that, in the diverse forms it takes throughout the score, seems to evoke the filmic present via its various past tenses. Some of the cues get quite heavily serious, in particular "The Dark Side of Chess," which, with its low-string ostinatos and occasional hits from a prepared piano, could easily accompany action in a dark alley somewhere in a suspense thriller, or "Leaving Childhood." The music for Luzhin's mentor/betrayer, Valentinov (Stuart Wilson), also gets pretty heavy. At other moments Desplat briefly and broodingly explores more dreamlike areas, always with an intriguing palette of assorted timbres. Desplat's original music also includes a '20s pastiche foxtrot for violin, bass, and piano, while the surreal scene in which elegantly dressed aristocrats waltz about a life-sized chessboard at the Italian estate (where, apparently, director Luchino Visconti grew up) on Lake Como are accompanied by the Waltz No. 2 from Shostakovich's Second Jazz Suite, which is particularly well recorded, and which is performed (twice on this CD) by the Prague Philharmonic (the score itself features the London Symphony conducted by the composer). Just why the producers felt they had to highlight this piece on the CD cover mystifies me. The music is so anodyne that I had to remind myself that Shostakovich composed it.

Those used to the wallpaper music, filled with every musico-dramatic cliché possible, for TV documentaries, which have proliferated in huge quantities these days thanks to cable-TV channels devoted to everything from history to animals, are due for an aural reawakening almost from the opening instants of Alex North's score for **Africa** (Prometheus; Symphony Orchestra Graunke, Alex North and Henry Brant, cond.). To be sure, the quiet but highly dissonant sustained chords in the upper strings, interrupted here and there by brief percussion figures, that open the first cue suggest the possibility of an extended mood piece. But as the music gathers momentum and skips, without the slightest hint of tonality, from timbre to timbre (including piano and harpsichord) and from fragmented chordal motif to fragmented chordal motif with only a soupçon of continuity, one begins to ask questions: can these often strident, ultramodern-to-avant-garde strains really have turned up in an American TV documentary (narrated by Gregory Peck) from 1967? It's difficult to say without access (all but impossible, it would seem) to the film. What the first four cues on this limited-edition (2,000 copies) recording offer is not the somewhat more anodyne, particularly in moments such as the rather cloying playfulness of "The Joyful Days," Suite for the 200-minute film dealing with various aspects of the African continent but rather a "Symphony for a New Continent" inspired not by *Africa*, which, amazingly, North never saw, but by Africa itself. North recorded the music in Munich and then shipped the tapes off to New York, where the score was laid in on *Africa*'s music track without one second of supervision from the composer. The otherwise informative program notes for this CD do nothing to set things straight on this issue, and I had to turn to reliable sources (John Waxman and the composer's widow, Anna) for the information you have just read. At any rate, the middle two movements of the symphony relent a bit, concentrating more often than not on quieter interactions between various timbres, and occasionally generating a rather dark lyricism characteristic of the composer. But the last movement often sounds like the work of someone exploring the outer limits suggested in the styles of composers such as Bartók and Hindemith, with the tension building in seemingly endless spurts forward, and with North forever breaking up quasi-melodic lines in the unison strings with frenetic punctuation from dissonant chords in the lower brass. One can hear something of the same compositional style in the Suite from *Africa*, but mitigated, and one can certainly recognize the composer of *Spartacus* in certain moments of "The Joyful Days." This CD also offers two newly discovered cues not contained on the original ABC LP (long a collector's item), a "long version" of the "Main Title Theme," and a cue entitled "Progress." As it turns out, that Main Title Theme was mistaken, at the time Jerry Goldsmith and Varèse Sarabande were putting together the materials for the CD of North's unused score for *2001: A Space Odyssey*, for a cue from the latter film. The recorded sound is fairly pinched and somewhat shrill for the Symphony, somewhat richer and fuller for the Suite, probably because of the smaller orchestral forces needed for the score itself.

Speaking of CinemaScope, and speaking of Africa, in Franz Waxman's **Untamed** (Film Score Monthly) we have one more widescreen vehicle from Hollywood's early battles with the new medium of television, in this case with a pretty virulent dose of racism thrown in for bad measure. Directed in 1955 by Henry King, who made his first film in 1915, and who made something of a specialty of this kind of work, *Untamed* is a 19th-century drama dealing with the Irish who, in order to escape the potato famine, move to South Africa. Starring Tyrone Power, Susan Hayward, Richard Egan, John Justin, Rita Moreno, and Agnes Moorehead—among many others—*Untamed* manages to throw two love triangles and a mess of heavy action, including a Zulu attack brilliantly accompanied in the score by nothing but native percussion instruments and other sounds, into its under-two-hour running time. And here we have Franz Waxman going hundreds of miles beyond the call of duty in coming up with a masterful score for a film solidly unworthy of his musical gifts. In cue after cue in this score Waxman mobilizes his middle-of-the-road-modern style to create music whose dramatic intensity sometimes feels as if it will never let up. This is particularly true of a cue such as "Lightning," a near-rape scene that starts at a frenzied level with toccata-like scurryings in the strings (one of the composer's trademarks), only to become even more potent and ominous as the music slows down into steadily insistent, highly dissonant figures. And where the music could run out of steam, as the would-be rapist lies beneath a tree struck by lightning, it instead simply shifts into a quieter but equally powerful mood of gloom and pain. I particularly like the way Waxman's trek music, for a cue such as "Vorwärts," manages to blend march and dirge, signaling ominous things to come without in the slightest way sounding obvious. And at several moments in this score I was once again struck, as I have been in other Waxman scores, by certain somewhat Expressionistic combinations of texture, harmony, and rhythm that occasionally move the music in slightly Russian directions—a bit of Stravinsky here ("The Accident"), a bit of Shostakovich there. Waxman's lyrical moods range from the heavily passionate (note the almost screaming yet also hymn-like climax in the huge swell that takes place in "After the Dance") to the more than slightly morbid, as in the elegiac "Goodnight," which features a chilling cello solo. Of all the Waxman recordings out there, this one may do more justice to the composer than just about any other I can think of. For starters, it is impossible to imagine anyone other than Waxman conducting this music with what appears to be involvement that is so total as to be almost manic. One wonders, in fact, what the composer might have produced if he had devoted some of his time to conducting the "classics." And he is blessed with recorded sound that reproduces the music's often-complex textures with incredible richness and fullness. And the lack of artificial reverberation here gives the orchestral playing something close to a concert-hall sound. Essential Waxman, essential film music. And be sure to let the CD run its course after the final cue.

And. . . . *That's all folks.*

~

Film Index

~

Name Index

~

About the Author

Royal S. Brown is internationally known as a scholar and critic. He has published two books, *Focus on Godard* and *Overtones and Undertones: Reading Film Music*, as well as numerous articles on film and film music. He is a regular contributor to *Cineaste* magazine and, as a public scholar, has also written for such magazines as *High Fidelity*, *Fanfare*, of which he was Music Editor for several years, *The Perfect Vision*, and *The Absolute Sound*. A Full Professor at Queens College in the City University of New York, Dr. Brown is former Director of the Film Studies Program at Queens College, and served three years as Deputy Executive Officer of the Ph.D. Program in French at the City University's Graduate Center in Manhattan, where he also teaches in the Film and Music programs. He is currently Chair of the Department of European Languages and Literatures at Queens College. He also teaches film and musical aesthetics part time at the New School in Manhattan. Scholarly articles in several different languages by Professor Brown have appeared in journals and anthologies throughout the world, and he has given invited talks and seminars in such venues as Vienna, Seville, Melbourne, London, and Rio de Janeiro.

A French scholar as well, Professor Brown has published in such journals as the *Nouvelle Revue Française*. In 1989, Professor Brown curated the first complete retrospective of the films of Alain Robbe-Grillet. The subject of numerous radio interviews, Professor Brown has also appeared in two film documentaries, the Oscar-nominated *Music for the Movies: Bernard Herrmann*, and the German television documentary on David Raksin, *Bilder, die Mann hören kann*. Original photographs taken by Professor Brown have appeared in various publications. Over the last several years Professor Brown has made a number of radio appearances on such programs as National Public Radio's *Performance Today*. Professor Brown's most recent articles include the 20-page "Sound Music in the Films of Alain Robbe-Grillet," in the anthology *Cinesonic: The World of Sound in Film*, ed. Philip Brophy (Melbourne: AFTRS, 1999); "Ein neue musikalische Form schaffen. Bernard Herrmann und der

Hollywood-Filmscore." Trans. Petra Metelko. *Film und Musik,* ed. Regina Schlagnitweit and Gottfried Schlemmer (Vienna: Synema, 2001), pp. 85–98; and "Music and/as Cine-Narrative," in A *Companion to Narrative Theory* (Oxford, UK: Blackwell, 2005), pp. 451–65. He is currently at work on a book entitled *Images of Images: Myth, Lacan and Narrative Cinema.*